LONGMAN LINGUISTICS LIBRARY

GENERAL LINGUISTICS
Fourth Edition

LONGMAN LINGUISTICS LIBRARY

General Linguistics

An Introductory Survey

R. H. Robins

FOURTH EDITION

LONGMAN
LONDON AND NEW YORK

Longman Group UK Limited,
Longman House, Burnt Mill, Harlow,
Essex CM20 2JE, England
and Associated Companies throughout the world.

Published in the United States of America
by Longman Inc., New York

First published 1964
Second edition 1971
Third edition 1980
Fourth edition 1989
Second impression 1991

British Library Cataloguing in Publication Data
Robins, R. H. (Robert Henry), *1921–*
General linguistics: an introductory survey.
– 4th ed. – (Longman linguistics library).
1. Linguistics
I. Title
410

ISBN 0-582-29144-5

Library of Congress Cataloging in Publication Data
Robins, R. H. (Robert Henry)
General linguistics.
(Longman linguistics library)
Bibliography: p.
Includes index.
1. Linguistics.   I. Title.   II. Series.
P121.R6   1989   410   88-5619
ISBN 0-582-29144-5

Set in Linotron 202 10/11pt Times
Produced by Longman Singapore Publishers (Pte) Ltd.
Printed in Singapore

Contents

8 Linguistic comparison

9 Wider perspectives

Preface to first edition

An apology is perhaps desirable for the appearance of a book purporting to survey the whole range of general linguistic studies. In a period of increasing specialization, experts in several branches of linguistics are likely to find that, in their opinion, their own speciality is treated scantily, superficially, and with distortion in emphasis and selection. Indeed, it has been said that it is now no longer proper or practicable for an introduction to general linguistics to be attempted by one author, as his own competence in the different branches now recognized must be very unequal.

If this were true, it would be a great pity. The various approaches to language accepted as falling within linguistics are so accepted by virtue of some unifying theme or contribution to an integrated body of knowledge. Students are surely entitled to read, and teachers should be able to write, textbooks which take into account recent developments in the subject, as far as they may be made available to beginners, and attempt to show these in relation to its continuing course and progress as part of a set of studies sharing in common more than a mere title.

My intention in writing this book has been to produce an introduction to linguistics as an academic subject, that will be comprehensible and useful to the student entering on the study of linguistics at a university in work for a first degree or a post-graduate degree or diploma, and at the same time will serve to present the subject in outline to the intelligent general reader as one that is both important and interesting in its own right.

Where controversy still surrounds aspects of the subject encountered in the early stages of a student's acquaintance with it, I have not tried to hide this or to suggest that there is one road to salvation alone worthy of serious attention. Nothing is more pathetic than the dogmatic rejection of all approaches but one to language (or anything else) by a person who has not troubled himself even to consider the arguments in favour of others.

The writer of an introductory textbook has a further consideration to bear in mind. No branch of a living and developing subject stands still. In linguistics, outlooks, theories, and procedures are constantly being revised, and new methods appearing. Such changes, in so far as they represent or promise progress, are to be welcomed, but they inevitably alter in some degree the state of the subject during the unavoidable lapse of time between the writing of the book and its publication; and further changes must be expected in the future. Some experienced readers and teachers may well feel, as a result, that certain matters are given greater emphasis than they now merit as the expense of newer and more significant topics and viewpoints.

In a book such as this, there is little or nothing original, except perhaps the choice of topics and their arrangement; nor should there be. I shall be well satisfied if, after reading it, people are both enabled and encouraged to go further into the subject, undertake further reading, and perhaps to specialize in one branch of linguistics or another, after achieving an adequate understanding and picture of the subject as a whole.

In writing an introductory account of linguistics, one is made very conscious of the debt owed to one's predecessors and contemporaries. Anyone engaged in linguistics in Great Britain lies greatly in debt to the late Professors J. R. Firth and Daniel Jones, who between them did more than any others to establish the subject in this country and to determine the course of its development. To Professor Firth, my own teacher during the eight years between my joining him at the School of Oriental and African Studies in the University of London and his retirement from the Chair of General Linguistics in that university, I owe the main directions of my work in the study of language, both in teaching and research. Equally, no one engaged in general linguistics anywhere in the world can forget or treat lightly the enormous debt owed to American scholarship in this field. Without such international figures as Sapir and Bloomfield it is doubtful if linguistics would have made anything like the progress it has made, or achieved the academic recognition it enjoys the world over. Any serious student of the subject must become quickly aware of the great part American scholars in linguistics have played and are now playing in all its branches. On the continent of Europe, de Saussure, Trubetzkoy, Meillet, and

Hjelmslev, to mention only four names, have been responsible for contributions to linguistic theory and method that are now indispensable components of present-day linguistic scholarship. I hope that in the form this book has taken I have discharged in some measure my debt to my predecessors and contemporaries. If I have failed, the fault is mine, not theirs.

More specifically, I am indeed grateful to successive classes of students whom I have taught in the past fifteen years. Much of what I have written here has arisen in the preparation, delivery, and revision of lecture notes and tutorial material. Some points were first brought clearly to my attention by the work of students themselves. To Professor C. E. Bazell, Professor of General Linguistics in the University of London, and to my other colleagues in the university, past and present, I owe the stimulus of constant discussion, argument, and collaboration. Professor N. C. Scott, Professor F. R. Palmer, and Dr, now Professor, J. Lyons were kind enough to read through a draft of this book. Each made many helpful and important suggestions, not least in trying to save me from a number of inclarities, inaccuracies, and downright absurdities. I hope I have made proper use of their comments; where I have not, and for all errors and imperfections remaining, I am, of course, wholly responsible. To all those who, wittingly or unwittingly, have helped and encouraged me in the production of this book, I offer my sincere thanks.

University of London RHR
1964

Preface to second edition

That a new edition of a textbook should be in demand some six years after its first publication is, naturally enough, gratifying to the author. But it is no less apparent that, in a subject developing as rapidly and vigorously as linguistics is today, more radical alterations are required than the mere correction of errors and the clarification of points hitherto left in obscurity, if the book is to continue in usefulness.

As regards unresolved controversies and competing views on the theoretical understanding and the analysis of language, on which readers were warned in the preface to the first edition, the passing of years has not diminished this characteristic of current linguistics, although older disputes now arouse less heat as the newer ones attract more attention.

I have made an attempt in the sections at the end of Chapter 7 to indicate the main lines on which linguistic theory and linguistic practice seem to be moving in Europe and America today. No one should regard these sections as substitutes for the further reading indicated in the relevant notes, if one wants to gain a real understanding of current developments; but I hope that what I have written will serve as an entry and a guide to the main contemporary 'growth points' in the subject.

On the other hand I have left the account of phonemic phonology and descriptive grammar of the 'Bloomfieldian' period much as it was, because, although these have been under attack from a number of directions, a good deal of what is taken for granted in the way of technical terminology and linguistic concepts was brought into being by linguists working in this tradition (itself by no means dead), and the rigour that was displayed by much of the best in this tradition can serve as an inspiration and an example to those who may, nonetheless, prefer alternative approaches. Moreover, all those scholars who are responsible for valuable progress in contemporary developments were themselves first masters of 'Bloomfieldian' linguistics and started from a full understanding of what was aimed at and achieved in this stage of linguistics. I remain convinced that the careful study of the linguistics of the 1940s and 1950s is still the proper foundation for scholarly comprehension of the subject today.

Several reviewers of earlier printings of this book were good enough to make detailed and helpful suggestions for improvements, and I have tried to take these into account and make use of them. Once again it is one of the pleasures of academic life to record the help unstintingly given by colleagues whom I have consulted, drawing on their specialist knowledge and on their experience in using this book, along with others, in tutorial work with students. In this respect I am particularly grateful to Dr Theodora Bynon, Professor M. A. K. Halliday, Dr N. V. Smith, and Mrs Natalie Waterson. The deficiencies that will no doubt become apparent are fewer and less glaring, thanks to their co-operation, and the reader as well as the author will be indebted to them.

University of London   **RHR**
1970

Preface to third edition

In preparing the third edition I have revised the content of this
book to a considerable extent in the endeavour to bring it up to

In preparing the third edition I have revised the content of this
book to a considerable extent in the endeavour to bring it up to
date as regards current developments in linguistic theory and
practice, so far as these can be made readily available to beginners. In making these revisions I have again benefited from the
helpful advice from my colleagues, and particularly from Dr
D. C. Bennett, Dr Theodora Bynon, Dr R. J. Hayward, Dr
N. V. Smith and Mrs Natalie Waterson, as well as from students
and correspondents, who have drawn my attention to various
omissions and infelicities in previous editions.

Although I have carried out some considerable reordering and
reworking in the presentation of the elements of linguistics as I
understand them, the basic balance of the book remains much
as it was. That is to say, 'classical' phonemic phonology and
'structuralist' grammar of the Bloomfieldian era are still
explained to the reader in some details as the proper groundwork
on which to build an appreciation and understanding of contemporary theories and methods. Some readers may consider that
too much space is given to 'structuralist' linguistics and that an
introductory textbook is no longer the place for these topics. For
such readers there are several excellent textbooks available, but
in my opinion one can best evaluate the merits and the objectives
of linguistic work today if one is familiar with the theoretical
background within which many of the linguists who are now most
influential themselves grew up, and if one has a firm grasp on the
basic concepts with which any linguistic description and analysis
must be concerned.

I have also tried to maintain a broad coverage of the different
topics involved in any comprehensive account of general linguis-

tics as an academic subject. For further details in these topics the reader must consult the specialist literature, to some of which attention is drawn in the bibliographies and notes that follow each chapter. But I consider it quite essential for the student of linguistics to acquire as soon as possible an awareness of just how extensive the study of human language must be and how many different paths of enquiry it opens before him, paths that he should at least recognize, even though he may not follow them all through, if he is to comprehend properly the richness of this field of knowledge upon which he is entering.

University of London   RHR
1979

Preface to fourth edition

In preparing this edition of my *General Linguistics* I have endeav-
oured to maintain the structure and the purpose of earlier
editions while taking proper notice of recent and current developments in linguistics that have come to prominence since the
third edition.

I remain in the conviction that readers of an introduction to
a subject as rich and as rewarding as general linguistics, whether
they be university students or interested members of the lay
public, need and deserve a survey of the subject as a whole in
its various branches and aspects, in so far as these can be made
reasonably accessible in a single textbook. Perhaps this may now
be a vain hope. If this is the case, I am sorry, since linguistics
is, for all its diversity, a basic unity as the quest for an understanding of the structure, the history, and the working of human
language.

Teachers are usually research workers in their own speciali-
zations, and naturally they are anxious to lead their students and
their classes to the 'frontiers of knowledge' where they themselves are engaged. They are right in such an objective; exciting
research leads to exciting teaching, and the best of our students
should be acquainted early in their courses with the 'growth
points' of their subject. But there is a danger here; one can only
tackle with understanding current advances and specialties
against a firm command of basic principles, concepts, and
methods. Linguistics is not a science that 'destroys its past' (even
if any science can be said to do this), and much of its subject
matter has been well set out in books and articles published
earlier in this century that have now achieved something of the
status of classics in the discipline. While I hope I have drawn

attention in the chapter bibliographies to important current and contemporary literature for further reading by advanced students and intending specialists, I have not hesitated to retain references to earlier writings where these appear to me to present basic information accurately, adequately, and accessibly.

An attractive television advertisement for a brand of beer claims that it 'refreshes the parts that other beers cannot reach'. I would like to express the reverse hope that this book reaches those parts that are sometimes neglected or passed over too briefly by some other introductory textbooks. More seriously, I am wholly in sympathy with the thoughts of a reviewer of a recent such textbook (*Language* 58 (1982), 896): 'It is easy for linguists of different theoretical persuasions to overlook the extent of their common ground . . . . . . To teach a 'professionalist' introductory course without first ensuring that some of the thickets of misconception are cleared away is like teaching a course on immunology to a population that does not yet believe in the germ theory of disease'.

In planning and preparing this edition, as with previous editions, I am very conscious of the help that my colleagues have given me, whether in seminars when I was trying out my ideas, in casual conversations, or in direct consultations. In particular I must thank Dr Geoffrey Horrocks for reading drafts of chapters 5, 6, and 7 and making many helpful suggestions, as well as saving me from errors in areas about which he knows far more than I do. Dr Katrina Hayward was no less generous in reading a draft of chapter 8 and giving me the benefit of her expert knowledge in this field. To Professor Theodora Bynon, my successor as Head of the Department of Phonetics and Linguistics, I owe much for her constant encouragement to me to continue my academic work in the Department, and for her patience in responding to my repeated questions about what might be acceptable German, often at times when she was at her busiest as Head of Department. To all these friends and colleagues I offer my sincere thanks; this book is less imperfect for their help. Where obduracy, inattention, or incomprehension may have led me to neglect their proffered advice, *sit venia soli mihi*.

School of Oriental and African Studies,   R. H. Robins
University of London
1988

System of reference

Bibliographies

The chapters are followed by bibliographical lists of books and articles relevant to the topics discussed in them. These are numbered serially, and referred to in the chapter notes by author's surname and number; numbers following the serial number refer to pages in the work concerned. Thus '34, 11' means 'page 11 of number 34'.

The bibliographies to each chapter are independent of each other, relevant works being listed in more than one, where necessary. To avoid excessive overlapping the bibliographies of Chapters 5 and 6 are combined into one, appearing at the end of Chapter 5. After Chapter 1 a general bibliography of elementary and introductory works on linguistics is given, with some brief comments.

None of the bibliographies is intended to be anything like exhaustive; they are designed simply to serve as a guide for further reading on the various aspects of general linguistics.

Notes

In the notes to each chapter reference is made to books and articles which carry further the discussion of points made in the preceding chapter, set out alternative views, provide additional information justifying statements already made (particularly on languages not widely studied), or appear in some other way to be relevant.

In this edition the notes are numbered serially through each chapter, and superscript number appear in the text; but the intention is that the beginner and general reader should be able to get a picture of the subject as a whole without the need to look at the notes at all. They are directed more towards the student who knows something of the subject already and wants to check any data to which reference has been made or to follow up in more detail questions arising from what he has read.

Transcriptions and abbreviations

Linguistic material cited in this book in the examples is generally represented as follows:

English words and sentences are written in the normal orthography, followed by a reading transcription where necessary.

Words and sentences from most other languages that have a roman orthography are cited in this, followed, from Chapter 3 (Phonetics) onwards, by a reading transcription.

Languages without a recognized orthography and a few that have one but are little known, together with languages written in orthographies other than roman, are cited in reading transcriptions alone. The only exception to this is that Ancient (Classical) Greek words and sentences are given in the Greek script followed by the reading transcription.

Reading transcriptions are enclosed in slant lines / . . . /.

The reading transcription for English is the same as the one used by D. Jones in his *Outline of English Phonetics* and his *English Pronouncing Dictionary* (London, 1948). In other living languages the transcriptions are broad transcriptions, on phonemic lines. They are not necessarily strictly phonemic transcriptions; in some of the languages cited, an agreed phonemic analysis covering all the relevant features has still to be achieved, particularly in such features as stress. Sometimes deviations in the direction of narrower transcription are made if it is felt that a reader without a knowledge of the language will be helped to realize something of the sound of the words more readily thereby (thus in the German examples the glottal stop [ʔ] occurring initially in words like *arm* /ʔarm/ poor, and medially in some compound words, though not usually reckoned a separate phoneme, is transcribed). The terms *broad transcription* and *narrow transcription* are explained in 4.2.

The transcription of Ancient Greek is a transliteration, since in dealing with a dead language the phonetic information required as the basis of an adequate transcription is not ordinarily available; this transliteration follows the method set out by A. Martinet, 'A project of transliteration of Classical Greek', *Word* 9 (1953), 152–61, except that υ is transcribed with /y/ not /u/. The transcription of Latin is the same as the traditional spelling except that all long vowels are marked as long, and this is done with the length sign:, not the macron⁻. It is to be noted that Latin /c/ = [k] throughout. The transcription of modern German is based on W. Victor's *Deutsches Aussprachewörterbuch*, Leipzig, 1912.

It is hoped that these conventions will assist the reader unfamiliar with any of the languages from which examples are taken, without inconveniencing or annoying those already enjoying some acquaintance with them.

Transcriptions narrower than the reading transcriptions are printed, where necessary, between square brackets [. . .].

Abbreviations

BSOAS	*Bulletin of the School of Oriental and African Studies*
IJAL	*International Journal of American Linguistics*
JAOS	*Journal of the American Oriental Society*
Lang	*Language*
Sociol rev	*Sociological Review*
TCLC	*Travaux du cercle linguistique de Copenhague*
TCLP	*Travaux du cercle linguistique de Prague*
TPS	*Transactions of the Philological Society*

Chapter 1

General linguistics: the scope of the subject

1.1 General linguistics as the study of language

1.1.1 Language and languages

General linguistics may be defined as the science of language. As with other branches of knowledge and scientific study, such a definition involves the subject in certain relations with other disciplines and sciences outside itself, and in subdivision into different branches of the subject comprised within it. At the outset something must be said under both these headings, but it should be made clear that in these, as in several other important topics which must be examined in an introductory account, the opinions of scholars differ in considerable respects.

It must be realized that a subject like general linguistics, in common with most other subjects of systematic study, is not static. Viewpoints, including some of quite fundamental importance, may change or receive different degrees of emphasis in the course of years. No book can honestly pretend to deal with the subject in a way that will both be accepted in all respects by every recognized scholar in the field and remain unaltered for all time. In this book, some account is taken of major unresolved controversies, and the reader must be prepared for others to arise.

In the first place it is desirable to consider the difference between general linguistics as the science or scientific study of language and the study of individual languages. This latter study is, indeed, more familiar to the majority of people, and has played a major part in all stages of education in many parts of the world for some time; the study of linguistics, on the other hand, is, at least in its present form, a relative newcomer in the field of scholarship, though in the present century and particularly in the past three decades it has shown marked growth in the numbers of its students and teachers in the universities of Great Britain, continental Europe, the United States, the USSR, and several of the newly developing countries of the rest of the world.

General linguistics is concerned with human language as a universal and recognizable part of human behaviour and of the human faculties, perhaps one of the most essential to human life as we know it, and one of the most far-reaching of human capabilities in relation to the whole span of mankind's achievements. In so far as all languages share some features in common, whether in pronunciations, grammatical organization, or expressive power, one may speak of human language as an abstract set of characteristics, perhaps reflecting part of the biologically inherited structure of the human mind or brain. This is often referred to under such headings as universal grammar, linguistic universals, and universals of language. The extent to which such universal features are to be recognized or assumed as underlying all the known languages of the world is in part a matter of debate (7.2.3–4 pp 289, 292–4). Human language in this sense is certainly the province of the linguist, but it must be repeated that the only evidence we have for its recognition and study comes from the individual actual languages of the world and from their speakers and writers, past and present. There are at least three thousand different languages in the world, leaving aside dialect divisions within languages (2.2), many of them still uncounted and unstudied. The general linguist, in the sense of the specialist or the student concerned with general linguistics, is not as such involved with any one or more of them to a greater extent than with any others.[1] As an impracticable ideal he would know something about every language; that is, of course, impossible, and in practice most linguists concentrate on a limited number of languages including their own native languages, the number of languages studied, and the depth of knowledge acquired of each, varying by personal factors from one linguist to another. Thus it has been pointed out that the linguist as here defined and as understood in the context of general linguistics must be distinguished from the sense of the word *linguist* as often used by the public, to refer to someone who necessarily has a practical knowledge and command of a number of foreign languages.[2] It is, of course, desirable that the linguist should know quite a lot about some languages, and the more languages (especially those representing types different from his own and from each other) with which he has some acquaintance, the better he is equipped for his subject.

Language in all its forms and manifestations, that is all the languages of the world and all the different uses to which in the various circumstances of mankind they are put, constitutes the field of the linguist. He seeks a scientific understanding of the place of language in human life, and of the ways in which it is organized to fulfil the needs it serves and the functions it performs. Several of the subjects he has within his purview and several of the questions to which he seeks answers correspond to long-established divisions of the study of foreign languages and of the institutionalized study of one's own language. Pronunciation (phonetics) and grammar are familiar enough, and some study of meaning and of the way in which meanings are discoverable and statable is presupposed in the compilation and use of any dictionary or vocabulary book. It is, in fact, partly as a result both of the search for improvements in the techniques of such indispensable aids to the study of foreign languages, and of questions arising on the theoretical basis of their production, that people have been led to the investigation of the properties and characteristics of language as such. Part of the justification of general linguistics lies in its undertaking the examination of the theory lying behind the practice of the language teacher and the language learner. The practical teaching of languages will, for obvious reasons, be largely confined to languages possessing a world-renowned literature or serving considerable numbers of speakers either as a first (native) language or as an acquired second language for the purposes of trade, education, etc (such as English in large areas of the British Commonwealth and elsewhere, Spanish and Portuguese in Central and South America, Russian over much of the Asiatic area of the Soviet Union, and Latin in mediæval Europe). But it is an article of faith for the linguist that any language, no matter what the level of civilization reached by its speakers, how many speakers make use of it, or what area of the world they occupy, is a valuable and worthy object of study, able to teach him something more about language in general and the theoretical and practical considerations involved in the study of language.

It is well to reflect on the great diversity of the languages of the world. Some of the ways in which different languages may be compared are discussed in Chapter 8; here one may notice that language, and linguistics, the science of language, embrace equally living languages, that is languages still used today as means of communication, and dead languages, that is languages like Ancient Greek or Old English (Anglo-Saxon) now no more spoken but known from written records (manuscripts, printed texts, or inscriptions). Among the living languages the linguist finds his material both in the languages of worldwide use and with long literary traditions as the vehicles of civilization, and languages devoid of writing, unknown outside their own community, except to the linguist, and (as is the position of many North and South American and native Australian tongues) spoken perhaps by less than a hundred speakers and so in peril of extinction before the spread of some extensively used language.

1.1.2 Descriptive, historical, and comparative linguistics

General linguistics includes a number of related subjects involved in the study of language as understood in the preceding paragraphs, and each may be considered from the point of view both of linguistic theory and of its actual operations or procedures. The most important and immediate subdivisions of the subject are **descriptive linguistics**, **historical linguistics**, and **comparative linguistics**.

Descriptive linguistics, as its title suggests, is concerned with the description and analysis of the ways in which a language operates and is used by a given set of speakers at a given time. This time may be the present, and in the case of languages as yet unwritten or only recently given written form it will inevitably be the present, as there is no other way of knowing any earlier stages of them, though there are methods by which certain facts about such earlier stages may be inferred (8.1). The time may equally well be the past, where adequate written records are available, as in the case of the so-called dead languages like Hittite and (except in a few special circumstances) Latin, and in the case of earlier stages of languages now spoken in their current forms (*eg* Old French and Old English). What is more important is that the descriptive study of a language, and of any part of a language, present or past, is concerned with that language at the period involved and not, as a descriptive study, with what may have preceded it or may follow it. However, the many variant forms of pronunciation, grammar, and lexical content that the descriptive linguist records and describes in a language at a given time may mark the sources of subsequent historical changes ultimately having far-reaching effects (*p* 339).

Descriptive linguistics depends all the time on the minute and careful observation and recording of the ways in which each language is constructed and used, in phonetics, grammar, and the expression of meanings. It has been a weakness of many earlier and some modern grammars of less known languages rather unimaginatively to try to portray them in terms taken directly from existing grammars of familiar and prestigious languages such as English and Latin.

Descriptive linguistics is often regarded as the major part of general linguistics. Be that as it may, it is certainly the fundamental aspect of the study of language, as it underlies and is presupposed (or ought to be presupposed) by the other two subdivisions, historical linguistics and comparative linguistics.

Historical linguistics is the study of the developments in languages in the course of time, of the ways in which languages change from period to period, and of the causes and results of such changes, both outside the languages and within them. This sort of study, whether undertaken in general terms or concentrated on a particular language area (*eg* English from Old English to the present day), must properly be based on at least partial descriptions of two or more stages of the continuous language series being treated.

The terms *synchronic* and *diachronic* are in general use to distinguish respectively linguistic statements describing a stage of a language as a self-contained means of communication, at a given time, during which it is arbitrarily assumed that no changes are taking place, and statements relating to the changes that take place in languages during the passage of years.[3]

Historical linguistics might from one point of view be regarded as a special case of comparative linguistics, the third subdivision of general linguistics. In **comparative linguistics** one is concerned with comparing from one or more points of view (and the possibilities of this are very wide) two or more different languages, and, more generally, with the theory and techniques applicable to such comparisons. In historical linguistics the comparison is limited to languages which may be regarded as successive stages of the speech of a continuing speech community differing from one period to another as the result of the cumulative effects of gradual changes, for the most part imperceptible within a single generation.

As will be seen in more detail in Chapter 8, comparative linguistics is principally divided into comparison made with a view to inferring historical relationships among particular languages, and comparison based on resemblances of features between different languages without any historical considerations being involved.

In Europe and America historical linguistics and historically orientated comparative linguistics played a dominant role in linguistic studies during the nineteenth century, for reasons of academic history (8.1.1), rather antedating general linguistics in recognition as university subjects. These studies are familiar under the title of 'comparative philology' in English, and in some universities what are in fact general linguistic studies were until recently carried on and administered under this name.

1.1.3 The term 'philology'

In connection with the study of language the term *philology* is in frequent use. In some ways this is unfortunate, as the word and its equivalents in some European languages (French *philologie*, German *Philologie*) are understood and used in rather different senses.[4]

In British usage philology is generally equivalent to comparative philology, an older and still quite common term for what linguists technically refer to as comparative and historical linguistics (8.1.1). In German, however, *Philologie* refers more to the scholarly study of literary texts, especially those of the ancient Greco-Roman world, and more generally to the study of culture and civilization through literary documents, comparative philology in the British sense being designated *Vergleichende Sprachwissenschaft*. This meaning of *Philologie* is matched by similar uses of comparable words in other European languages, and in general with the use of *philology* in American learned circles. It may be held that in this usage the word is a convenient term to employ with reference to the links between linguistics considered as a science and the aesthetic and humanistic study of literature, and to the field wherein the historian of different aspects of a culture draws on the findings of the linguist in the decipherment of texts and inscriptions and in establishment of reliable versions of manuscripts and other documents as materials that provide him with part of his evidence. The relations of linguistics with philology in this last sense are very close and allow of considerable overlapping.

1.2 Linguistics as a science

1.2.1 Implications of the term 'science'

The term *science* has been used in the definition of general linguistics. It may be understood in two ways. In the widest terms it refers to the fact that the study of language in general and of languages in particular, as described in outline above, is considered worthy of scholarly attention and that a systematic body of facts and theory is built up around it. In more specific and particular terms it indicates the attitude taken by the linguist today towards his subject, and in this perhaps it marks a definite characteristic of twentieth-century linguistics.

In saying that linguistics is a science in the stricter sense, one is saying that it deals with a specific body of material, namely spoken and written language, and that it proceeds by operations that can be publicly communicated and described, and justified by reference to statable principles and to a theory capable of formulation. Its purpose in this proceeding is the analysis of the material and the making of general statements that summarize, and as far as possible relate to rules and regularities, the infinite variety of phenomena (utterances in speech or writing) that fall within its scope. In its operations and statements it is guided by three canons of science:

[i] Exhaustiveness, the adequate treatment of all the relevant material;

[ii] Consistency, the absence of contradiction between different parts of the total statement; and, within the limits imposed by the two preceding principles,

[iii] Economy, whereby, other things being equal, a shorter statement or analysis employing fewer terms is to be preferred to one that is longer or more involved. This is sometimes referred to as the 'capturing of generalizations'.

One can make the position of linguistics within the sciences more precise. It is an empirically based science, in that its subject-matter is observable with the senses, speech as heard, the movements of the vocal organs as seen directly or with the aid of instruments (3.1, 3.2), the sensations of speaking as perceived by speakers, and writing as seen and read. No linguist would disown empiricism in linguistics, but there is today lively discussion on the degree of empiricism that should be embodied in a linguistic theory (cp 7.1). Linguistics is also one of the social sciences, in that the phenomena forming its subject-matter are part of the behaviour of men and women in society, in interaction with their fellows. This last statement is not invalidated by the existence of purely secondary uses of language by persons alone and out of earshot of others, in monologue ('talking to oneself'), ejaculations of joy, terror, or annoyance, addressing animals, and the like; the essence of language and the vast majority of its uses involve two or more persons in social intercourse.

Linguistic science and the scientific study of language occupy a very special place among the sciences, in that the linguist is simultaneously the observer of language and of languages and the producer and evaluator of at least one language, his own mother tongue. This means that the linguist is free to adopt either the position of the 'external' observer of data, supplied by himself or by others in speech or writing, or the position of an 'internal' analyst of what is involved in being a speaker–hearer, in 'knowing a language'.

From the 'externalist' point of view the linguist treats his material as any other scientist does, observing, classifying, seeking underlying regularities, constructing hypotheses to be tested against further data in order to validate descriptions already made. This has been the basis of the grammars of foreign languages with which we are familiar, even though in many cases the writers have not explicitly stated their position. Linguistics in this sense is on a par with other sciences, such as physics, botany, or chemistry, where the scientist is necessarily viewing his material from the outside. All the phenomena with which he is dealing are potentially accessible to any and every other observer on the same basis as they are to him.

From the 'internalist' viewpoint the scientist is observing himself and asking what is involved, not just in what he says and writes, but in his brain, whereby he can produce and understand a limitless number of sentences of his own language. It is sensible to ask what is meant by 'He speaks Japanese, or English, or Swahili' when the person is not in fact speaking any of these languages at a particular time. In this interpretation 'A linguistic description of a natural language [*ie* somebody's mother tongue] is an attempt to reveal the nature of a fluent speaker's mastery of that language.'[5] The linguist as speaker–hearer of the language he is studying or the language which he knows well has access, not only to material that he can produce for himself without waiting until it turns up in other people's utterances, but also to essentially personal reactions and judgments on such matters as acceptability, what is well formed or correct (in contradistinction to mistakes, slips of the tongue, or the efforts of a non-native speaker), elegance, clarity and ambiguity, equivalence in meaning, implications and presuppositions (1.4.3), and so on. Such data are of course equally available to other speakers of the language, but in each person's case they are private phenomena not directly or publicly observable like the linguistic data referred to in the preceding paragraph.

To a limited extent linguists share their double orientation with the other sciences of human kind, such as general psychology, but in linguistics it is probably carried further than in any other descriptive science.

Linguists have tended to favour one standpoint over the other at different times, or even at the same time among contemporaries. In this century the contrast has been most markedly associated with the followers of Bloomfield, insisting on a strictly 'external' viewpoint, and the followers of Chomsky, concerned above all with the nature of linguistic knowledge, 'competence' in a language such as one's own, and treating linguistics as a branch of cognitive psychology.[6] Both groups claim that they have the interests of linguistics as a science at heart; and wherever one's personal preferences or specific abilities may lie, it is in the interest of linguistic studies as a whole that language should be studied, investigated, and analysed from both viewpoints. This subject will be considered further in Chapter 7.

There is one inference that might be made from the assertion that linguistics is a science, and it must be disclaimed at once. This is that because linguistics is a science, it is necessarily not one of the humanities or a humane discipline, and that in consequence linguistics is in some way hostile to the study of literature and the linguistic study of language inhibits its literary enjoyment and the pleasures that come of literary appreciation. The relations of linguistic studies and literary studies will be examined more closely in a subsequent chapter (9.5); but is should be made clear at once that nothing in linguistic science is such as to interfere with the analysis and appreciation of literary values in what is read or written. Indeed the reverse may be true, and if a linguist finds himself insensitive to the music of poetry, the appeal of oratory, or the flow of an unfolding story, he has only himself, and not his subject, to blame.

In the present educational situation disquiet has been expressed about the gulf that has widened between what are loosely called the arts and sciences, with the implied suggestion that scholars, and indeed the educated public in general, must either be 'literate', somewhat despising the sciences as pedestrian and illiberal, or, as it has been termed, 'numerate', considering the humanities and what are traditionally regarded as the mainstays of a liberal education to be largely subjective, irrelevant, and marred by imprecision. In any much needed rapprochement between scientific studies and what are called humane studies, linguistics, along with some of the other disciplines devoted to the ways of mankind, may have an important part to play. Indeed among all branches of knowledge linguistics is in a special position. Science, like all other publicly shared knowledge, demands the use of language to talk about its particular subject, and is a refinement and elaboration of our general habit of talking about the world in which we live. Linguistics differs from other studies in that it both uses language and has language as its subject-matter. For this reason among others linguistics may well come to occupy a key place in the studies embodied in higher education.

1.2.2 Practical applications

From what has been said about linguistics as a science, it should be clear that it is self-justifying as an academic subject. Language and the means whereby the forms of language and the working of language may be analysed and described are themselves regarded as proper subjects of academic study, without any further consequences being involved. Nevertheless, certain consequential and important by-products do result from linguistic work. One may consider a few examples. The greater one's understanding of language in general, the better one may expect to be able to set about the task of teaching foreign languages, both in their general aspects and with an eye to the many specialized needs for the knowledge of second languages in limited ranges of activities that the modern world seems increasingly to require. This covers both the actual techniques of teaching and the production of textbooks; textbooks differ from pure descriptions of languages in that their aim is to impart particular skills in speaking and understanding and in reading and writing (or in both), in a given language on the part of speakers of some other language. Such books are normative rather than simply descriptive; they set a standard, by some means or other, of what is correct and serve to impart a knowledge of it and foster familiarity with it.

Linguistic studies are already being applied to the practical problems of automatic or machine translation and the exploitation of statistical techniques connected with the use of language. The communications engineer is helped by some knowledge of the basic composition of the language signals whose transmission and reception are his responsibility. An understanding of the power language can exert among people and of different ways in which this power may be exploited and directed has proved to be a potent weapon in the hands of those who with the aid of what have come to be called 'mass media' are engaged in moulding opinions, disseminating views, and exercising influence on their fellows, whether politically, commercially, or socially; the fact that such activities may often be regarded as undesirable and even disastrous is, of course, to be recognized; by-products are not necessarily always beneficial. In another sphere of activity linguistic knowledge is a powerful aid in the remedial treatments known as speech therapy, for patients whose speech mechanisms, through injury or defect, are damaged or imperfect. The applications of linguistics to other activities serving particular purposes in the world are collectively known as **applied linguistics** and are considered further in 9.4.

It is important to recognize the by-products that may come from linguistic studies; but linguists themselves need not engage in applied linguistics. Their subject is of sufficient interest and significance in the world to maintain itself in its own right, just as is botany without reference to horticulture, and as is entomology without reference to the control of insect-borne disease or crop pests. The linguist is justified in his work in so far as he is successful in making human beings more aware of one essential aspect of their humanity, and, in the words of a contemporary, in 'presenting the fundamental insights about language to which every well educated person should be exposed'.[7]

1.3 The range of general linguistics

1.3.1 Levels of analysis

Language is immensely complicated. How complicated one discovers in the process of learning a foreign language; and the ability of all normal persons to acquire structural mastery and the basic vocabulary of their own language in childhood is one of the many wonders of human kind.[8] The obvious complexity of language makes it unworkable for the linguist to try and describe it all at once. Language itself, speaking and writing, is a unitary activity; people speak and write, and understand what is spoken and written in their own language, without necessarily being aware of such things as grammar and pronunciation, but merely reacting unfavourably to the mistakes of a foreigner without being able to specify in what respects he has transgressed one or more recognized standards.

The linguist, in order the better to make scientific statements about language and languages, concentrates at any one time on different though interrelated aspects of his subject-matter, by attending to different types of features and by applying different types of criteria (asking himself different sorts of questions). These different and partial approaches have been called **levels of analysis** and the statements made about them **levels of linguistic statement**. Such relatively familiar terms as *phonetics* and *grammar* refer to two such levels. By extension the term **level of language** is used to designate those aspects of a language on which at any time the linguist is focusing his attention.

Just as the limits and comprehension of an academic subject may vary between one scholar or group of scholars and another, so do the different levels that it is considered profitable to recognize. Even those who agree on the overall range of topics proper to the linguist's purview may disagree on the number of levels with which to operate and the criteria to be applied to them. In an introduction such as this, no more than a general survey can be given.

One must recognize at the outset and as the basis of any division of linguistic analysis (or of language) into levels the two aspects, form and meaning. Speech is purposeful, and form and meaning are related at least in part as means and end. An understanding of language in human life requires both an understanding of the formal composition of utterances and of their relations with the rest of the world outside language.

1.3.2 Language and communication

Many definitions of the word *language* have been attempted and they are to be found in dictionaries and in some textbooks. One definition, first set down in 1942, has enjoyed a wide currency: 'A language is a system of arbitrary vocal symbols by means of which a social group cooperates'.[9] This definition covers much that is important, but in a sense all definitions are, by themselves, inadequate, since, if they are to be more than trivial and uninformative, they must presuppose, as does the one just quoted, some general theory of language and of linguistic analysis.

More useful at this point in an elementary book on linguistics will be some notice of certain salient facts that must be taken into account in any seriously intended theory of language.

Language is, so far as we know now, species-specific to man. Every normal human being has acquired one language, his mother tongue, by late childhood, the basic lexicon, grammar, and pronunciation within the first ten years of life, apparently without effort and without the requirement of systematic instruction, in contrast to the actual teaching or conscious self-teaching necessarily involved in the attainment of literacy and the mastery of foreign languages at school. Much that passes among conscientious parents as 'teaching a child to speak' really amounts to the deliberate widening of his vocabulary along with his knowledge of the world.

The skills involved in speaking, being an acquisition taken for granted and largely unnoticed in the process, excite no comment and evoke no admiration; their absence in pathologically defective persons arouses sympathy. We praise people for particular and relatively rare abilities that depend on speech, for having a fine singing voice, for being a stirring preacher, an inspiring orator, or a good story-teller, and for being able to recite wih clarity a patter-song of the type written by W. S. Gilbert, an unnatural exercise that taxes the powers of most otherwise fluent speakers of a language. But all these accomplishments represent additional abilities over and above the mastery of one's own first language.

Conversely, no other members of the animal kingdom have been shown to possess anything like a human language. Of course animals communicate, and socially organized animals cooperate by means of vocal and other forms of communication. Much study has rightly been devoted to animal communication. Interestingly, the animal communication system in some respects nearest to human language (though a very long way off!) is the so-called language of bees, whereby bees that have been foraging are able, by certain formalized movements often called 'dancing', to indicate to other bees still in the hive the direction, distance, and richness of a source of nectar, so that these others can make straight to it. This system shares with human language the ability to impart detailed information about matters not directly accessible to the senses of those receiving it; but we notice at once that the medium employed, the 'substance', as it is sometimes called, has nothing in common with the spoken medium in which all human language is primarily expressed.[10]

Naturally studies in animal communication have centred on our nearest kin among the mammals, the primates, and specific investigations have been made, for example, into the calls of gibbons in their natural habitat.[11] But the area best known and most exciting to the general public in this type of research has been the attempts to teach chimpanzees to communicate with humans by human methods. Of these chimpanzees, Washoe and Sarah, the subjects of prolonged training and study in America, are the most famous. Some references to the accessible literature on them are given in the notes.[12] Here it must suffice to point out that attempts to teach chimpanzees actually to speak have largely failed; the signs used are in the main visual, involving gestures and facial movements. With this medium, intercourse involving information, questions, and requests, together with responses directly linked to them, and the rudiments of syntactic structures, has made astonishing progress, far beyond the scope of the language of bees, for example. But, and this is an important reservation, bee language developed entirely within natural communities of bees; chimpanzees have learned their language only after prolonged association with human beings who have devoted themselves to teaching them and studying them.

Such studies tell us much about the latent and inherent potentialities of chimpanzees, but they do not affect the unique species-specificity of language in mankind.

Human language, unlike every other communication system known in the animal kingdom, is unrestricted in scope and infinite in extent. Against the severe restrictions placed on the topics about which bees and even trained chimpanzees can communicate, human beings can, in any language, talk about all the furniture of earth and heaven known to them and about all human experience. Languages are adaptable and modifiable according to the changing needs and conditions of speakers; this is immediately seen in the easy adaptation of the vocabulary of English and of other languages to the scientific and industrial developments, and the concomitant changes in people's lives, that took place in Europe and North America in the eighteenth, nineteenth, and twentieth centuries.

The immense power and range of language have been perceived in all societies, and the realization of them was, no doubt, partly responsible for the magical associations felt among some peoples to belong to certain words relating to things and events vital to their lives or fearful in their effects. Traces of such a magical outlook on language are to be seen today in some familiar attitudes (2.2.1).

For all this flexibility and power, human languages have developed through the millennia in which mankind has existed on earth as a separate species through the medium of speech. The earliest known writing systems do not date back more than about 4,000–5,000 years, a minute distance in the time-scale of human existence. The elementary physiology of speech will be treated in Chapter 3; here it need only be pointed out that all human language and everything in human life that depends on language rests ultimately on the distinguishable noises that humans are able to make out of the passage of air through the throat, nose, and mouth.

Human infants inherit a biologically determined ability to acquire and use a language, and this inheritance may account for the universal features found in all known languages and assumed in the rest; but we do not inherit any particular language. A child learns the language of those with whom he is brought up in infancy and early childhood, whether they be, as is usually the case, his actual parents or others. There is no biological preconditioning to acquire English rather than Malay or Italian rather than Swahili.[13]

Human progress is greatly hastened by the use of language in cultural transmission (one of its functions); the knowledge and experience acquired by one person can be passed on to another in language, so that in part he starts where the other leaves off. Most teaching, after all, depends in great part on the use of language, written and spoken. In this connection the importance of the invention of printing can hardly be exaggerated. At the present time the achievements of anyone in any part of the world can be made available (by translation if necessary) to anyone else able to read and capable of understanding what is involved. From these uses of language, spoken and written , the most developed animal communication system, though given the courtesy title of language, is worlds away.

One topic connected with the study of language that has always exercised a strong fascination over the general public is the question of the origin of language. There has been a good deal of speculation on this, usually taking the form of trying to infer out of what sort of communicative noise-making fully fledged languages in all their complexities gradually developed. Imitative exclamations in response to animal noises, onomatopoeia and more general sound mimicry of phenomena, exclamations of strong emotion, and calls for help have all been adduced. Linguists, however, tend to leave this sort of theorizing alone, not because of any lack of intrinsic interest, but because it lies far beyond the reaches of legitimate scientific inference, since we can have no direct knowledge of any language before the invention of writing. In relation to the origin of language, every known language is very recent.

Two frequently used analogies for attempted inference on the origin of language are the acquisition of speech by children and the structures and characteristics of so-called 'primitive' languages. Both are invalid for this purpose. Children acquire their native language in an environment in which language is already established and in constant and obvious use all around them for the satisfaction of needs, some manifestly shared by themselves. Their situation is entirely different from that of mankind as a whole in the circumstances assumed to obtain while language itself was taking shape.

The second argument, based on the alleged nature of 'primitive' languages, rests on a common, though deplorable, misconception of these languages. Linguistically, there are no primitive languages. There are languages of peoples whose cultures as described by anthropologists may be called primitive, *ie* involving a low level of competence in the exploitation of natural resources and the like. *Primitive*, however, is not a proper qualification of *language*. Investigations of the languages of the world do not bear out the assumption that structurally the languages of people at different levels of cultural development are inherently different. Their vocabularies, of course, at any time reflect fairly closely the state of the material and more abstract culture of the speakers; but languages are capable of infinite adjustment to the circumstances of cultural development, and their phonetic and grammatical organization may remain constant during such changes. It is a palpable fact of informed observation in the linguistic study of the languages of culturally primitive peoples that phonetically and grammatically their languages are no less (and no more) systematic and orderly than the languages of Western Europe and of the major world civilizations. Nor are the processes of change, that affect all parts of languages, any less active or any slower in operation in these languages than in others; indeed, the converse may be the case, as it has been held that the establishment of writing systems and standards of correctness tend, if anything, to retard linguistic changes in certain situations. Every language has aeons of changes, irretrievably lost to knowledge, lying behind it. To argue from the language of primitive people to the nature of a primitive stage in the evolution of language is valueless.

Attempts at gathering useful and reliable information on the origin of language from the inspection of existing languages, and the falsely grounded search for the 'oldest' language among them, efforts which go back to antiquity, have rather discredited the whole question among linguists. The foundation rule excluding papers on the origin of language from meetings of the *Société Linguistique de Paris* is well known. But though the quest for man's original language (formerly called *lingua Adamica*) and for the reconstruction of the ways in which actual lexical and grammatical forms emerged from hominids' prelinguistic noises are seen not to be accessible to scientific study, some linguists and anthropologists have recently looked at the subject from a rather different point of view. They have been considering not what the earliest manifestations of language were like, but how speaking hominids, *homo loquens* as they have termed the species, would be immeasurably advantaged in the struggle for survival by the possession and use of such a faculty.

Apart from its unconstrained range in communication, setting it apart from all other known types of animal communication, already referred to, speech requires little expenditure of energy; it is independent of light and darkness and of mutual visibility, requiring only that those involved remain within earshot; it does not interfere with locomotion, food gathering, tool using, fighting, and other manual activities, as do gesturing and pointing. It can generally be combined with eating and drinking; the discouraging of children today from talking with their mouths full of food is more a matter of aesthetics and good manners than avoidance of the occasional choking fits that may arise. In the co-operative warning of sources of danger, their description and the concerting of means to avoid or counteract them, in collaborative efforts in finding, gathering, and storing food, locating shelter and so on, the development of language must be counted as by far the most important evolutionary development in the human species. And once man's survival and preeminence had been assured through language, it was language that made possible our living in larger stable and more viable communities, followed ultimately by the emergence of language-based intellectual, moral, and legal systems of rational thought, literature, song, and drama, such as are the glories of civilized life.[14]

Languages fall into the class of symbol systems, symbols being a special class of signs. The science of sign and symbol systems, sometimes called semiotics, lies outside the range of an outline introduction to general linguistics, but a brief clarification of the terms is desirable.[15] Signs in general are events or things that in some way direct attention to, or are indicative of, other events or things. They may be related naturally or causally, as when shivering is taken as a sign of fever, or as when earthquakes are, or were, said to be signs of the subterranean writhing of the imprisoned god Loki; or they may be related conventionally and so used, and they are then called symbols, as, for example, the 'conventional signs' for churches, railways, etc on maps, road signs, and the colours of traffic lights.

Among symbol systems language occupies a special place, for at least two reasons. Firstly, it is almost wholly based on pure or arbitrary convention; whereas signs on maps and the like tend to represent in a stylized way the things to which they refer, the words of a language relate to items of experience or to bits of the world in this way only in the proportionately very small part of vocabulary called onomatopoeic. The connection between the sounds of words like *cuckoo*, *hoopoe*, and such imitative words as *dingdong*, *bowwow*, *rattattat*, etc and the creatures making such noises or the noises themselves is obvious; and in a wider set of forms in languages a more general association of sound and type of thing or event is discoverable, as in many English words ending in *-ump*, such as *thump*, *clump*, *stump*, *dump*, which tend to have associations of heaviness, thickness, and dullness. It has been found experimentally that made-up words, like *maluma* and *oomboolu*, and *takete* and *kikeriki*, are almost always treated alike by persons who hear them for the first time and are asked to assign them to one or the other or a pair of diagrams, one round in shape and the other spiky; the first pair are felt appropriate to the former shape, and the second pair to the latter.[16] More abstractly, there does seem to be an association in parts of the vocabulary of many languages between close front vowels, as in *wee* (/wiː/3.3.3), and nearness and smallness, and of open back vowels, as in *far* (/fɑː/), with distance. Consider, for example, the popularity of the recent neologism *mini*, and such contrasts as *this* (here) and *that* (there), Hungarian *ez* and *az*, French *ici*, here, and *là*, there, and the re-creation of *teeny* after the first vowel in *tiny* had lost its close front quality to become the present-day diphthong (/taini/), as part of the Great Vowel Shift (8.1.2).

The onomatopoeic and 'sound-symbolic', or phonaesthetic, part of language is of great significance, but its extent in any vocabulary is quite small, and despite attempts by some to see the origin of language in such imitative cries, it must be realized that the vastly greater part of the vocabulary of all languages is purely arbitrary in its associations. Were this not so, vocabularies would be much more similar the world over than they are, just as the conventional picture signs of several historically unrelated pictographic systems show obvious resemblances.

It is this arbitrariness of greater part of language that gives it its almost limitless flexibility; unlike most other symbol systems language is double-structured.[17] At the level of phonology artic-ulated speech sounds are organized into distinctive units, such as phonemes, and these are grouped into syllables (4.3.1; 4.3.4). In turn, these units and syllables are used as the spoken manifes-tation of words and of words concatenated in sentences. It is at this second level of structuring that meaningful items of language and interpretable sentences come into being. The distinction between these two levels is discussed further in 5.1.1.

Secondly, what is conveyed by all other symbol systems can be explained in language, and these other systems can be inter-preted in language, but the reverse is not the case. The instruc-tions given by road and railway signals can be expressed in words, the propositions of logic can be translated into ordinary language, though with loss of brevity and precision, those of classical Aristotelian logic fairly directly, those of modern symbolic logic more indirectly. But in languages we deal with whole areas of human life and engage in modes of communi-cation with which logical systems as such have no concern.

These considerations apply in the use of the word *language* in reference to such human activities as instrumental music or dancing. Certainly these are social and communicative activities, and they can both express and impart various emotional attitudes and in some cases they can mimetically convey the general impression of a situation, as, for example, the country scenes embodied in the successive movements of Beethoven's *Pastoral Symphony*. But such communication is not language, nor even surrogate language. These are different sorts of communicative art, to some extent conveying, like gestures, but often with intense aesthetic force, emotions and impressions comparable to those expressed in explicit detail by speech and writing. When, therefore, critics write of the 'grammar' (basic principles) of some non-verbal art or science, or of 'the immense tragedy of the first movement of Brahms's first symphony' (Sir Donald Tovey), we must remember that such words are being used metaphorically and understand them as such, however profound an artistic judgment may lie behind them.

1.3.3 Phonetics, phonology, grammar, semantics

That part of linguistics that deals with the material of speech itself is called **phonetics**. Chapter 3 is devoted to this, and here it need only be said that it is immediately concerned with the organs of speech and the movements of articulation, and, more widely, with the physics of sound transmission and the physiology of hearing, and ultimately with the neurological process involved in both speaking and hearing. The subsidiary and less extensive study of written language in its different forms is sometimes called graphics or graphonomy, or on the model of *phonetics*, graphetics; but as this material is less complex, and writing is a secondary manifestation of language compared with speaking (3.1.1), this has not been accorded such an important place in linguistic studies.[18]

Within the scope of meaning are involved the relations between utterances, written and spoken, and the world at large. Meaning is an attribute not only of language but of all sign and symbol systems, and the study of meaning is called **semantics**, which, therefore, embraces a wider range than language alone. However, since language incorporates by far the most extensive symbol system in man's use as well as the central one, much of semantics and of semantic theory is concerned with language and languages.

In order to fulfil their symbolizing and communicative functions, languages must organize the available noises that can be produced by the vocal organs into recurrent bits and pieces arranged in recurrent patterns. This formal patterning and arrangement in languages is studied at the levels of phonology and grammar. These two levels of linguistics are the subjects of separate chapters (4, 5 and 6); here it need only be said that **phonology** is concerned with the patterns and organization of languages in terms of the phonetic features and categories involved, and **grammar** is concerned with the patterns and arrangements of units established and organized on criteria other than those referable to phonetic features alone. It is for this reason that in the case of languages studied only in their written forms, such as Ancient Greek or Latin, a full grammatical statement and analysis of the written language, based on orthographic text, is possible, but any phonological analysis of such languages must necessarily be uncertain and incomplete, since it can be made only from such phonetic descriptions of the languages as can be deduced from the orthography itself or gathered from the contemporary accounts of ancient scholars and commentators. Further discussion of the relation between these two levels may be deferred until Chapter 5.

Both phonetics and semantics involve linguists with the findings and the researches of other sciences. In the case of phonetics the other sciences that are relevant are restricted in number; physiology is immediately involved as far as it concerns the structure and movements of the vocal organs, and in any specialized study of phonetics the physics of sound wave transmission, the physiology of the hearing process, and the neurology of the processes of both hearing and speaking are brought into relevance. In semantics, however, since the meanings of utterances may relate to the whole world of the actual and potential experience of the speakers, the appeal to sciences and disciplines outside linguistics, as well as to the whole range of unscientific acceptance called common sense, is, in theory, unlimited. But in view of the essentially social nature of language, the sciences principally concerned with persons in society, such as social anthropology, are especially involved. In both cases it must be pointed out that the statements made, the categories established, and the terms employed are still primarily linguistic in relevance, even though they must necessarily rely on the findings of other sciences. They are linguistic in that they are made specifically with linguistic ends in view, that is the study and analysis of language and languages, and they are not necessarily the sort of statements, categories, or terms, that the specialists in these other sciences would want to make. For example, an important distinction is made in phonetics between the front and the back of the tongue (3.2.2); physiologically and with reference to other activities, such as gustation and swallowing, this distinction may not be of fundamental importance.[19]

1.4 Semantics

1.4.1 Philosophical and linguistic interest in meaning

As has already been said, the study of meaning, **semantics**, brings in symbol using and symbol systems outside language; but the central place of language in human symbol systems makes language very much its primary concern. The problems arising from the study and analysis of meaning have been recognized and have received attention during the whole of man's intellectual history. Much of the work involved has been undertaken by philosophers, especially logicians (to whom linguistics in the West owed much of its original impulse, 9.6). The study of logic is closely connected with the study of language, however the relations between the two may be interpreted by successive generations of philosophers, since language is the vehicle of philosophical discourse and even the specially devised systems of modern symbolic logic are derived from and refer to particular types of sentence in natural languages. The logician is, however, primarily concerned with the inferential uses of language, the formal means by which statements or propositions may be reached or inferred as valid conclusions from preceding statements or propositions acting as premises. Much of Aristotelian logic is devoted to the different types of syllogisms, as sets of premises followed by conclusions are called, that may be used in valid chains of reasoning.

The concern of the linguist for the uses of language is much wider. Formalized logical inference and philosophical discourse in general are an important part of people's use of language in several civilizations; but they are by no means the only, or indeed anything like the most frequent, uses. The linguist's concern is with language in all its uses and manifestations as part of the processes of daily living and social interaction by members of groups, as well as in the specialized applications that form the provinces of philosophers and literary critics, and the approach to meaning on the part of the linguist must be based on this much wider range of language use and types of utterance.

Semantics can be recognized as a level of linguistic description and as a component of linguistics, but it is a much less tidily circumscribed field of study than are phonetics, phonology, and grammar, unless its range is so restricted as to exclude a great deal of what the plain man and the common reader would wish to include under the heading of *meaning*, with which semantics is concerned.

What one is really trying to do in semantics, or in making statements about meaning, is to explicate, to make explicit, the ways in which words, and sentences of various grammatical constructions, are used and understood by native or fluent speakers of a language. Sentences consist of words, but of words in specific grammatical relations within constructions, and words are used in speech (and in writing) as components of sentences. This applies equally to the so-called one-word sentences, in which a single word comprises a complete sentence (6.3.1). Nonetheless semantics can be considered from the point of view of word meaning and from that of sentence, or structural, meaning.

1.4.2 Word meaning

Word meanings are what are sought and what should be provided in comprehensive dictionaries of a language. For much of the history of semantic studies, and still to a considerable extent today, the investigation of word meaning has been based on the relationships of reference and denotation. Certainly meaning includes the relations between utterances and parts of utterances (*eg* words) and the world outside; and reference and denotation are among such relations. But for the purposes of linguistics it is desirable to deal with meaning by a more comprehensive treatment.

Sentences have meaning, are meaningful; and a child learns the meaning of many words by hearing them in other people's uttered sentences and practising such utterances himself subject to the correction of others and the test of being understood by those to whom he is talking. The process goes on all our lives, and we learn new words and extend and increase our knowledge of the words we already know, as we hear and see them in fresh utterances and used slightly differently from the ways which we are accustomed to. The meaning of a word, therefore, may be considered as the way it is used and understood as a part of different sentences; what the dictionary does is to try and summarize for each word the way or ways it is used in the sort of sentences in which it is found in the language.

The grammatical structure and certain phonological features such as intonation may themselves give an indication of part of its meaning (3.5.3, 3.5.4, 4.3.6, 6.6.3), as we can easily see when we consider the part played in English and in many other languages by word form, word order, and intonation in the indication of questioning, commanding, and making statements. Though familiar in literate languages and apparently universal in all languages, word divisions are not immediately audible in connected speech, and the formal features that determine words as separable units, and the recognition of such features, intuitively by the speaker and objectively by the linguist, must be examined further within grammatical analysis (5.3).

The potential sentences of any language that may be uttered and understood by a speaker of it are infinite in number, but they are formed from the total stock of words known to the speaker at any time. A speaker's word stock is always variable, but it may be regarded as fixed at any given point in time. Words, therefore, are, in general, convenient units about which to state meanings, and no harm is done provided it is borne in mind that words have meanings by virtue of their employment in sentences, most of which contain more than one word, and that the meaning of a sentence is not to be thought of as a sort of summation of the meanings of its component words taken individually. With many words particular meanings or uses are only found when they are used in conjunction with other words, and these are often scarcely deducible from their other uses apart from such combinations (one need only think of such phrases as *cold war, black market, wildcat strike* (unofficial strike, particularly in American English), *white noise* (in acoustic engineering); this topic is further discussed under 'Collocation', 2.4.2).

Reference and denotation are clearly a part of the meaning of many words in all languages. The many problems arising about the nature of these relations have been the subject of much philosophical discussion. Here it suffices to point out that by the use in sentences of certain words one is able to pick out from the environment and from the general knowledge of speaker and hearer particular items, features, processes, and qualities, draw attention to them, give or elicit further information about them, make them the objects of action or speculation, and, most importantly, recall them from past experience and anticipate them in the future provided only that the words used have had such associations in the previous experience of speaker and hearer. These are the words whose meanings may, in part, be learned and taught by pointing. But the relationship between the word and that to which it may be said to refer is not a simple one. Proper names (*John, Mary*, etc) refer to individuals as single individuals, however many there may be so referred to; *boy, girl*, etc refer to an indefinitely large class of individuals by virtue of being grouped together in some respect; in the same way, *climb, fly, swim,* and *walk* refer to four different types of bodily movement in space. In the strict terminology of logic *denotation* is sometimes used in a specific and technical sense, but in general usage the term is more loosely made equivalent to *reference.*

It is often said that the meaning of a word is the idea it conveys or arouses in the mind of speaker or hearer. This is associated with a general definition of language as 'the communication of ideas by speech' or the like. Such accounts of the meaning of words and the working of languages are objectionable. *Idea* as a technical term is notoriously hard to pin down with anything like precision. It is often taken as equivalent to *mental picture* or image, for which drawings are sometimes made in books dealing with linguistic meaning. Mental pictures are no doubt perfectly genuine components of our private experience, but as such they seem of little relevance to linguistics. Firstly, it would appear that they are not aroused by anything like all the words in a language, even of those for which a referential meaning is fairly easily statable in isolation; secondly, even in the most favourable cases, the idea as a mental picture does not help explain one's ability to use a word correctly and understand it. Any picture is necessarily particular; as Berkeley pointed out, *triangle* refers to all of the mutually exclusive sorts of triangles (isosceles, scalene, right-angled, etc), but any picture, mental or otherwise, of a triangle must be of one triangle only.[20] Even if we did recognize what a word referred to by having a mental picture in our mind, we should have to be able to justify the classing together of what is actually observed and the mental picture by some further piece of knowledge. It is best to regard knowledge of the meaning or meanings of a word as part of a speaker's competence, an ability to use the word in ways other people will understand and to understand it when uttered by other people; this knowledge includes knowing the range of items, processes, and the like to which words that do have referents of one sort of another may be said, often indeterminately, to refer.

The use of words in utterances to focus attention on particular bits and features of the world involves a segmentation and an organization of our experienced environment. Verbalization is not a mere passive labelling of discrete items and objects; the process of classification implicit in the use of what are often called common nouns (*boy, girl, tree, house,* etc) has already been noticed. Moreover, the very permanence of names and designations presupposes that we recognize continuing identities in the stream of successively observed phenomena. Recognizing

John today as the John of yesterday and this table today as the same as this table yesterday is more than just perceiving what is before one's eyes; it is imposing some order on such perceptions. Other words with more abstract meanings involve a much more far-reaching organization of the world of immediate experience; words like *motion, gravity, inertia, energy*, and *equilibrium* do not refer to things in the way words like *table* and *chair* do, nor do even more abstract words like *cause* and *effect* (still less do they call up definite pictures in the mind), but they have distinctive and important meanings, and their use is a mark of the high degree of order and systematization imposed by us on the world we live in. In the same way the use of words like *right* and *wrong, duty, crime* (and many others subsumed under them: *property, theft, punishment, reform*, etc), and of comparable words in other types of society, presupposes a social nexus of expected ways of behaviour enforced by precedent and the sanctions of disapproval and legal penalties.

Quite apart from the examples just above, many words used quite ordinarily in everyday life, whose meanings are in no sense part of a specifically scientific or philosophical vocabulary, bear much more abstract and complex relations to our world of things, actions, and processes than words like *chair, stone, sun, kick*, and *run*. The difficulties, intricacies, and delicacies of much semantic analysis are concealed from the beginner when, as is too often the case, such words are exclusively chosen as examples in elementary semantics, just because of their rather obvious directness of reference, at least in many of their uses. One may, in this context, reflect on what is involved in the semantic analysis of such ordinary words as *succeed* (*success*), *prepare* (*preparation*), *loyal*(*ty*), and *persuade* (*persuasion*).

Some of these ways in which human life are experiences are ordered in our languages appear to be universally recognized in the use of words in all languages, and must therefore be regarded as the general property of mankind (for example, the recognition of objects occupying space and persisting through time). In other matters languages differ in the way they most readily tend to organize parts of the speakers' experience. Relatively trivial instances of such differences are the obvious non-correspondences of the colour words in different languages (2.4.3); more significant are the difficulties involved in trying to translate words relating to moral, religious, legal, and political matters between the languages of communities having different social systems in these respects. Such difficulties arise from the differences in peoples' ways of life, and are made prominent by the work of anthropologists in examining societies far removed historically from the Greco-Roman and Hebraic inheritance characterizing Western Europe and those countries most influenced by it. We do not all inhabit exactly the same world, and differences in the significant items of vocabulary in languages bring this out clearly.[21]

Not only does reference cover a very wide divergence of relationship between words and the bits and pieces of the world, but many words in all languages can scarcely be said to refer to anything by themselves, for which, consequently, pointing is useless as a means of explaining their use. This does not mean that such words are meaningless, which is nonsensical, as they have quite definite uses in languages; words like English *if*, *when*, *of*, *all*, *none*, *the* are frequent and essential components of sentences. But as it has been seen that it is the utterance and the sentences in it that are the primary meaningful stretches, the meanings of the component words must be taken as the contribution they make to the meaning of the sentences in which they appear. The fact that the contribution of some words is partly that of reference does not make reference the same as the whole of meaning; and it is not to be assumed that the meaning of a word when it constitutes a one-word sentence is the same as its meaning when it forms part of a larger sentence. There are also quite complex systems of reference involved in the uses of pronouns (*I*, *you*, *he*, *himself*, etc). Some of these are mentioned again in 7.2.3–4.

The ease with which a statable meaning can be assigned to a word in isolation varies very considerably, and in part it depends on the degree to which the word is likely to occur in normal discourse as a single (one-word) sentence; and even in the case of such a favoured word one has no right in advance of the analysis to assume that there will always be found a common 'core' of meaning underlying all the various uses the word has in the sentences in which it may occur. With words scarcely ever occurring in isolation, like those cited in the preceding paragraph, it is almost impossible to describe their meaning adequately in any other way than by saying how they are typically used as part of longer sentences and how those sentences are used. The question whether a word may be semantically described in isolation is more a matter of degree than of a simple answer yes or no.

Preoccupation with reference and denotation has troubled semantic theory, by putting an excessive importance on that part of word meaning which can be stated easily in isolation and treated either as a two-term relation between the word and the referent or thing meant (or between word-image and concept, *significant* and *signifié*), or as a three-term relation between word, speaker or hearer, and referent. The meanings of sentences and their parts are better treated in linguistics in terms of how they function than exclusively in terms of what they refer to. The different types of reference indicated above are then included as part of the function performed, the job done, by certain words in the sentences in which they are used, and the dictionary entry of a word simply summarizes the function or functions, referential or other, of the word in the sort of sentences in which it typically occurs.[22]

In addition to reference, excessive emphasis on historical considerations colours popular discussion on language, especially on word meanings, as when it is urged that the 'real' meaning of a word is to be found in its etymology or earlier form and use in the language. Thus it is claimed that the 'true' meaning of *holiday* is 'holy-day' or day set apart for religious reasons, and that *awful* and *awfully* are wrongly used like *considerable, very* (*there was an awful crowd there, awfully nice of you to come*), since its 'real' meaning is 'awe-inspiring'.

If it is accepted that statements of word meanings in descriptive linguistics are simply summaries of the ways words are used in sentences by speakers at a particular time, it is clear that historically antecedent meanings are outside the scope of such statements. Without specialized study speakers are ignorant of the history of their language; yet they use it to communicate with each other and they understand each other. Certainly the meaning of any word is causally the product of continuous changes in its antecedent meanings or uses, and in many cases it is the collective product of generations of cultural history. Dictionaries often deal with this sort of information if it is available, but in so doing they are passing beyond the bounds of synchronic statement to the separate linguistic realm of historical explanation.

1.4.3 Sentence meaning

The semantic component carried by phonological and grammatical structures (sentence meaning or structural meaning) is readily illustrated, though a great deal of detailed investigation is required for its full explication in any language. Different intonations may signal excitement, irritation, anger, friendliness, social distance, and many other feelings and personal relations, as well as the more formalized differences between statement and question (3.5.4). The grammatical categories of declarative (indicative), interrogative, and imperative have a partial correlation with the semantic categories of statement, enquiry, and command (request, prohibition, etc), though with the reservations noticed in 6.6.3.

While the lexical content is the same, we all know that the word order of *John loves Mary* marks a different sentence from that of *Mary loves John*, indicated in a language like Latin by word form:/Johannes Mariam amat/and/Maria Johannem amat/, the word order, though the most frequent in Latin sentences of this type, being largely a matter of style, topicalization, and emphasis. In English questions expecting an answer *Yes* or *No* can be distinguished by different word orders: *Mary is going to Church this morning*; *is Mary going to Church this morning?* In modern Greek, and in some English sentences (3.5.4) intonation alone marks the difference.

More subtly, much attention is paid today to the semantic implications or presuppositions of certain constructions. In English *John regretted* (or *didn't regret) that his son had failed his examination* implies ordinarily that his son had failed. *John was sure that his son had failed* carries no such implication.[23] The rather famous sentences involving *the King of France: the King of France is*, or *is not, bald; the King of France opened the Exhibition yesterday*, etc are puzzling just because the use of the definite article *the* implies that there is a King of France, so that *the King of France is bald* is not straightforwardly false in the way that the sentence *the Queen of England is bald* is.[24] It may well be that the philosophical problems of the alleged certainty of 'knowledge' as against 'mere belief' derive from the presupposition that the sincere use of *know*, and of equivalent words in other languages, unlike such words as *believe, expect, think, suppose*, etc, involve the speaker's reliability in regard to what he says he knows. One can readily say and readily accept *I think/believe/am pretty certain that he is coming today, but he may not come*, but not †*I know he is coming today, but he may not come* (see further 9.2; † here and elsewhere marks a sentence that is in some way deviant and unacceptable).

1.4.4 Extralinguistic context

Clearly the understanding of word and sentence meanings involves intralinguistic and extralingusitic factors. Certain semantic functions are learned and understood apart from any specific extralinguistic context, for example, the implications of *regret* mentioned just above, the fact that all crimson roses are red flowers and that all red things are coloured, but not vice versa (*hyponymy* is the technical term). Words like *mare* and *ewe* designate female animals, words like *stallion* and *ram* designate male animals, and words like *horse* and *sheep* animals of either sex. But fully to know how to use and understand any of these words one must have seen the animal or a picture of it, or have read or been told a certain amount about it. To know when a request, *please close the window*, a politer request, *would you mind (very much) closing the window*, or a brusque order, *close that window!*, would be appropriate requires a considerable knowledge of personal relations, social conventions, etc; in part these can be taught, but in general they are acquired in daily life, or in the course of learning a second language. Similar knowledge is required fully to control such uses of language as are involved in sarcasm, irony, flippancy, rhetorical questions, etc.

In addition to what has been said so far, it must be remembered that most sentences, especially in spoken discourse, are not uttered 'out of the blue'. They are normally heard and interpreted in relation to an accepted set of background knowledge and assumptions, presumed to be shared by all or most of those involved, together with more specific and relevant knowledge relating directly to the utterance. This latter may and usually does include earlier utterances in a conversation or a discourse. As a brief example, in *I think it's going to snow tonight, although we're well into late April; bother this weather, I've just bedded out the dahlias* at least two relevant assumptions are involved: *although we're well into late April* assumes that by this time of year snow is usually unlikely, and the second half of the conversation assumes the shared knowledge that dahlias are injured by cold conditions.

A humorous writer can achieve his effect by the deliberate introduction of irrelevant information into the context of a conversation, defying generally accepted mutually shared knowledge and assumptions. In Lewis Carroll's *Alice in Wonderland*, famous for this sort of humour, the March Hare, reproved for having lubricated his watch with butter, replies '"It was the *best* butter"; "Yes, but some crumbs must have got in as well", the Hatter grumbled, "You shouldn't have put it in with the bread knife".' The oddness arises from our knowledge that butter is not a lubricant for clockwork. Replace *butter* by *oil* and *breadknife* by *dirty brush*, and the conversation becomes sensible and not in the least amusing.

Writing intended to be long lasting, historical records, laws, literature, and so on sets out much of its context within its own text. Conversely emergency calls in situations outside normal contexts are necessarily short and sharp, relying on the hearers' immediate grasp of what is wrong and what must be done: *Fire!*, *stop thief!*, *man overboard!*, etc. On the other side, legal and legally binding documents of all sorts are notorious for their intended explicit coverage of every detail of the matter involved so as to leave no loophole for subsequent misinterpretation, evasion, or successful challenge. Part of Shylock's downfall was clearly due to his failure to tie down his bargain for a pound of flesh in sufficient detail.

Linguists differ on which aspects of meaning they are most concerned with; some would relegate much of extralinguistic function to **pragmatics** as distinct from semantics. Those who regard the extralinguistic factors as very much the province of semantics try to identify the relevant factors in terms of context of situation, social setting, personal and group roles, etc. Work along these lines has been an especial interest of those concerned with anthropological linguistics, such as Malinowski and Firth, and sociolinguistics (9.1).[25] It is being actively pursued today under the heading of 'Relevance theory'.

Language serves a great variety of purposes, and utterances perform a very wide range of functions. Within any one language notable differences of use, in part employing differences of vocabulary and composition but mainly drawing on a common grammatical and lexical stock, must be recognized. To mention only a few uses of language, one can distinguish poetry of all kinds, rhetoric, narrative and historical records, ritual and ceremonial utterances, the forms of legal, political, commercial, and administrative operations, the professional intercourse of technical, learned, and academic persons, as well as all the general functions of talking and writing in the maintenance of all daily life of every individual in co-operation with his family and other members of the community, including the sort of idle chatter ('phatic communion') and modes of greeting and leave-taking engaged in where silence would be taken for discourtesy.[26]

Language thus embraces very much more than the formal discourse of philosophy and the works of written literature, just as mastery of a foreign language in anything like completeness involves the command of its uses in all manner of different environments and different circumstances. Native speakers, as the result of experience gained from early childhood in the process of acculturation, know how to behave in speaking in the various roles they come to fulfil in their lives. To describe this the linguist tries to pick out the essential features of the situations that are characteristic of these different roles and to state them in sets of related categories as contexts of situation. In doing this he is trying to formalize and systematize, to set down, succinctly and explicitly, the vital information about the working and the use of languages that native speakers, for the most part unconsciously, discursively, and gradually, acquire throughout their lives in a community.

Treated in terms of contexts of situation, the meaning of an utterance includes both those aspects that can be described as the reference or denotation of individual words, and those that must be stated as belonging to the sentence, or even a series of sentences. Differences of personal status, family and social relations, degrees of intimacy, relative ages, and other such factors, irrelevant to the consideration of sentences as the expression of logical propositions are all handled under the appropriate headings of a context of situation.

Meaning in language is therefore not a single relation or a single sort of relation, but involves a set of multiple and various relations holding between the utterance and its parts and the relevant features and components of the environment, both cultural and physical, and forming part of the more extensive system of interpersonal relations involved in the existence of human societies.[27]

1.4.5 Translation

Experience has shown that some sort of translation between two languages is always possible, but it is usually difficult, and in no sense is it an automatic conversion process except in specifically restricted contexts (eg weather reports, air traffic control messages, etc). This accounts for the very slow progress being made in mechanical translation.

Questions of translation are very closely connected with semantic analysis and the contextual theory of meaning. The details of this part of language study cannot be covered in an elementary introduction, but the existence of bilingual speakers and the possibility of learning foreign languages and of forming utterances in one language serving nearly if not exactly the same purposes as corresponding utterances in another (ie of translating) are universally obvious facts that must be taken into consideration. Indeed, Malinowski was led to the framing of his theory of context of situation in working on the translation into English of key words and sentences found in the accounts given him of their way of life by some of the Trobriand islanders, a people inhabiting a small group of islands to the east of New

Guinea, a people whose whole culture, to which he devoted a great deal of study, was entirely removed from that of the European culture of his readers.

The term *culture* is widely used in a number of different ways, and it will be useful to make explicit its use in this book, a use fairly general in present-day linguistic writing. The term is taken from the technical vocabulary of anthropology, wherein it embraces the entire way of life of members of a community in so far as it is conditioned by that membership. It is manifest that on such a conception of culture language is a part thereof, and indeed one of the most important parts, uniquely related to the whole by its symbolic status.[28]

The need for contextual explanations of meaning was made clear in working on languages whose speakers were culturally remote from Europe; but context of situation is just as pertinent to the explanation of linguistic meaning in any language, though obviously the relevant factors and components of such contexts will differ according to the cultural differences between peoples. The need is less noticeable in dealing with familiar languages, just because the common inherited culture surrounding the use of one's own language and, though to a lesser extent, the use of other languages within the same cultural area, is taken for granted and so not made explicit. Translation, in Malinowski's words, implies 'the unification of cultural context'. This is apparent when one considers the sort of words in other languages that are relatively easy to translate into English and the sort that are not. Word translation, or the finding of lexical equivalents, is easiest with the words of languages within the unified culture area of west Europe or of parts of the world that have come under European influence, or with words in other languages which are such as to have a referential meaning more or less uniform in all cultures, for example the names of many physical objects and natural parts of the world's surface, widely distributed objects and natural parts of the world's surface, widely distributed botanical and zoological species, and the like, although any of these words may for one reason or another have special uses and therefore special meanings peculiar to the culture of a particular linguistic community (for example, *sheep* and *lamb* among practising Christians).

Wherever a cultural unity is lacking, the translation of words having reference to particular features or having particular uses in a limited field is more difficult to achieve by means of single lexical equivalents, and requires at best circumlocutions and often more lengthy explanations themselves in part recreating the relevant contexts of situation. One may instance the words peculiar to the ceremonies of particular religious communities, and in recent years the misunderstandings of such words, however translated, as *freedom, democracy, equality*, across the cultural frontier between communist and capitalist Europe; on either side such words are used in contexts different in certain important respects from each other. Translation and mutual understanding across such frontiers are not impossible; but much hard work is required in making clear just what factors are relevant and assumed to be relevant by speakers on each side, in the use and understanding of key words of this sort. Good translators are doing such work all the time, with varying degrees of success. Description by means of contexts of situation is an attempt to make explicit what is involved. The existence in several languages of words formally resembling English *democracy* and ultimately derived from Ancient Greek δημοκρατία/deːmokratía/ is in itself of little assistance.

Further difficulties of translation arise when all the complex functions of words in extralinguistic reference and in sentence composition, as well as the sentences themselves in their contexts of situation, must be considered and sometimes weighed against one another in the choice of the means of translation. In its familiar form, the choice may have to be between the literal and the literary, in cases where the nearest translation equivalents of individual words taken in isolation are stylistically unattractive or misrepresent some other aspect of the original when they are put together in sentences. This sort of difficulty arises especially in the translation of works of literature, of some kinds more than of others, in which features at other linguistic levels, such as the grammatical form of sentences and the phonetic form of words, are stylistically exploited as parts of the literary form of the whole piece. At the opposite end of the scale to the contextually restricted types of message referred to at the beginning of this section, in the case of certain types of poetry the production of a translation that fulfils anything like all the functions of the original may approach the impossible. The ability to achieve as excellent a translation as may be, balancing all the components at all levels against one another in constructing a version as near in all respects to the original as is possible, requires a delicate and sensitive appreciation of all aspects of language; though its. principles can be referred to linguistic science, its achievement is more in the nature of an art, in which individual and personal feeling for the artistic possibilities of the two languages is of the highest importance.

General bibliography

A considerable number of books have been written in the present century to give an introduction to general linguistics and the coverage of the subject as the authors see it. It must constantly be borne in mind in reading more widely in this field that no two books on linguistics agree in all respects with each other. Scholars have differed sharply not only on what range of studies should properly be comprised within linguistics, but also on points of linguistic theory and methods of analysis and description, some being of quite basic importance. One's reading should not be confined to the latest publications, important and exciting as they are. In the present century a number of the books listed below have achieved something like the status of classic texts in the subject, and should be read as such, even though on certain factual and methodological points they are now somewhat dated. The works by de Saussure, Sapir, Vendryes, Jespersen, Bloomfield, and Trubetzkoy (see the bibliography for Chapter 4) clearly belong here. Linguistics is a science, and it has its practical applications (1.2.2), but it is not a purely practical science that 'destroys its own past'. Those entering on the study of linguistics as part of a liberal education should read as widely as they can on it. Some of the books published in the earlier years of this century are recognized as being of lasting value; of course, enlightening books on language written in earlier centuries are also to be recommended, but they are not included in this general bibliography (reference to some of them will be found in the concluding section of this book (9.6). No attempt is made here to provide a complete bibliograhy of the subject. A number of the general books mentioned below contain bibliographies of varying extents; at the times of publication those in Bloomfield's *Language* and Vendryes's *Le language* were very comprehensive. Since 1949 an annual bibliography of linguistic publications, covering the years from 1939 onward, has been published: *Bibliographie linguistique*, Utrecht and Brussels.

Scholarship should know no frontiers, and facilities for exchanging theoretical viewpoints and methodological strategies have never been greater than in this age. It is, nevertheless, convenient to list some important general books under three geographical heads.

Continental European

F. DE SAUSSURE, *Cours de linguistique générale*, fourth edition, Paris, 1949. This is the posthumous compilation of de Saussure's teaching course on linguistics, based on his notes and those of his pupils. De Saussure in many ways marks the beginning of linguistics as an independent academic subject in its present form, and many of the distinctions and topics now almost universally recognized as essential to it were first made explicit by him. The book is not hard to read, though the circumstances of its publication involve occasional lack of clarity on certain points. There is an English translation by R. Harris, London, 1983.

De Saussure's thinking on language has exercised an important influence on the whole of twentieth-century linguistics. Perhaps the attempt to carry his teaching to its logical conclusion is to be seen in the 'glossematic' theory of Hjelmslev and his followers, mostly in Denmark. This theory is set out in L. Hjelmslev, *Prolegomena to a theory of language*, trans F. J. Whitfield, Baltimore, 1953. This book is full of interest and is well worth mastering, but partly because of the many special technical terms involved and its concise presentation this theory has not made a large impact outside Denmark. It will not be further treated in this book.

J. VENDRYES, *Le langage*, Paris, 1921, also translated, P. Radin, London, 1925.

O. JESPERSEN, *Language*, London, 1922. Though rather old-fashioned in some respects by now, this book is well worth reading. Jespersen was a Danish scholar, but this, like a number of his other books, was written in English and published in England.

W. PORZIG, *Das Wunder der Sprache* (second edition), Berne, 1957.

A. MARTINET, *Eléments de linguistique générale*, Paris, 1960 (English translation, *Elements of general linguistics*, London, 1964).

Martinet introduces some terminology and points of theory of his own, also seen in his less elementary *A functional view of language*, Oxford, 1962, and the chapter on the evolution of languages (historical linguistics) presents in simplified form the approach set out in his *Economie des changements phonétiques* (in Chapter 8, bibliography).

K.-D. BUNTING, *Einführung in die Linguistik*, Frankfurt a.M., 1971.

R. BARTSCH and T. VENNEMANN, *Grundzüge der Sprachtheorie*, Tübingen, 1983.

A clear and concise presentation of the subject may be found in Italian in G. C. Lepschy, *La linguistica strutturale*, Turin, 1966. (English version, *A survey of structural linguistics*, London, 1970.)

American

Modern American linguistics can now be seen as divided by the publication of Chomsky's *Syntactic structures* in 1957 into two periods, the earlier period sometimes called structuralist or, after its leading figure, Bloomfieldian, and the subsequent, transformational-generative period inaugurated by Chomsky and named after the distinctive orientation of his linguistic theory. Other developments in this period must also be recognized, including some theories derived from Chomsky's teaching, but now recognizably separate; the more important are mentioned in 7.3, 7.4, below. American textbooks fall into two comparable classes, with some overlap, depending on the date of composition and the standpoint of the author. As representative of the first period one may notice the following:

E. SAPIR, *Language*, New York, 1921.

L. BLOOMFIELD, *Language*, London, 1935.

These two books of the same title by American scholars are probably two of the most important books in the development of American linguistics, and their influence has been felt over the whole world of linguistic scholarship. Of the two, Bloomfield's book is the larger and perhaps the more important, though the style of Sapir makes his *Language* one of the most brilliant and readable books on the subject ever to be published. Bloomfield's *Language*, first published in America in 1933, defined and circumscribed the subject and at once established itself as a textbook that has not yet been superseded. For a generation most United States linguists considered themselves in some sense Bloomfield's disciples, whether they actually studied under him or not, and a great deal of American work has taken the form of working out questions raised and methods suggested in Bloomfield's *Language*. The two writers are very different in outlook and complement one another. Sapir's interests were wide-ranging, and though his linguistic scholarship was unchallenged he was always probing the boundaries of linguistic studies and the contribution they could give to and receive from other fields, such as anthropology, psychology, and literary criticism, subjects in which he himself was qualified. Bloomfield deliberately concentrated on the theory and techniques of linguistics as a circumscribed and defined science. Many of the generally used technical terms in linguistics today were introduced into the subject by Bloomfield in this book *Language*.

Sapir and Bloomfield have been contrasted more than once, as centrifugal and centripetal by S. Newman (*IJAL* 17 (1951), 180–6), and as genius and classic by M. Joos (*Readings in linguistics*, Washington, 1957, 31). American linguistic scholarship is indeed fortunate to have had two such men during its formative years.

Sapir's work can be seen in greater detail in his *Selected writings* (ed D. G. Mandelbaum, Berkeley, 1949), and more recently in W. Cowan, M. K. Foster, and K. Koerner (eds), *New perspectives in culture and personality*, Amsterdam, 1986. Bloomfield's attitude to language studies is further illustrated in 'A set of postulates for the science of language', *Lang* 2 (1926), 153–64 and 'Linguistic aspects of science', *International encyclopædia of unified science*, 1 (Chicago, 1939), part 4. Many of Bloomfield's most important articles and reviews have been collected and republished by C. F. Hockett in *A Leonard Bloomfield anthology*, Bloomington, 1970.

C. F. HOCKETT, *A course in modern linguistics*, New York, 1958.

R. A. HALL, *Linguistics and your language*, New York, 1960.

H. A. GLEASON, *An introduction to descriptive linguistics*, second edition, New York, 1961.

A. A. Hill's *Introduction to linguistic structures*, New York, 1958, is, in fact, largely a linguistic analysis, on Hill's lines, of English, concentrating on phonology and grammar; it also contains brief appendices on Latin and Eskimo.

A rather different type of book is seen in Z. S. Harris's *Methods in structural linguistics*, Chicago, 1951, which concentrates on phonology and grammar, working out procedures and methods in great detail and with great rigour of theory, exemplified from a number of languages. It is scarcely an elementary book, and it presupposes a knowledge of Bloomfieldian linguistics, developing certain aspects of it to their logical conclusion.

The course of development of the first period of American linguistics from the twenties of this century is partly set out in a collection of important articles and monographs arranged in chronological order, *Readings in linguistics*, ed M. Joos, New York, 1958.

Among introductions to linguistics cast in a basically transformational-generative mould one may recommend:

R. W. LANGACKER, *Language and its structure*, New York, 1968.

V. A. FROMKIN and R. RODMAN, *An introduction to language*, New York, 1974.

A. AKAMAJIAN, R. A. DEMERS, and R. M. HARNISH, *An introduction to language and communication*, Cambridge, Mass., 1984.

Many other introductory books on transformational-generative grammar, some of which are listed in the bibliography to Chapter 7, are just that. The books listed above are introductions to the subject of linguistics as a whole, though oriented towards transformational-generative theory.

The following books cover both periods of American linguistics:

F. P. DINNEEN, *An introduction to general linguistics*, New York, 1967.

D. BOLINGER, *Aspects of language*, New York, 1968.

G. YULE, *The study of language: an introduction*, Cambridge, 1985, brief (220 pages in all) but very comprehensive.

British

J. R. FIRTH, *Speech*, London, 1930, brief and provocative.

J. R. FIRTH, *The tongues of men*, London, 1937, a popular book, with relatively little detail.

L. R. PALMER, *Descriptive and comparative linguistics: a critical introduction*, London, 1972.

J. F. WALLWORK, *Language and linguistics*, London, 1969.

J. LYONS, *Introduction to theoretical linguistics*, Cambridge, 1968, was a very significant contribution to linguistic publication in this country. It incorporated a fuller and deeper treatment of semantics than is found in most linguistic textbooks, and it was one of the first to treat grammar predominantly from a transformational-generative point of view. It is, perhaps, except for the most able and energetic students, a second-year rather than a first-year book.

Three good first introductions to the study of language, very clearly written, elementary, and easy to read are D. Crystal, *What is linguistics?* London, 1985, J. Aitchison, *General linguistics*, London, 1972, and R. A. Hudson, *Invitation to linguistics*, Oxford, 1984.

A rather more advanced encyclopaedic work in four volumes, containing many essays on different aspects of linguistics today, is to be found in F. J. Newmeyer (ed.), *Linguistics: the Cambridge survey*, Cambridge, 1988.

A glance through the linguistics periodicals shelves of a college or university library will give an idea of the now very expensive scope of this branch of academic literature. For a comprehensive cumulative list see the annual *Bibliographie linguistique*, referred to on *p* 34 above.

Bibliography for Chapter 1

1 J. AITCHISON, *The articulate mammal: an introduction to psycholinguistics*, London, 1976.

2 W. P. ALSTON, *Philosophy of language*, Englewood Cliffs, 1964.

3 R. BARTHES, *Eléments de sémiologie*, Paris, 1964.

4 B. BLOCH and G. L. TRAGER, *Outline of linguistic analysis*, Baltimore, 1942.

5 L. BLOOMFIELD, *Language*, London, 1935.

6 G. M. BOLLING, 'Linguistics and philology', *Lang* 5 (1929), 27–32.

7 R. CARNAP, *Introduction to semantics*, Cambridge, Mass, 1948.

8 C. R. CARPENTER, *A field study in Siam of the behaviour and social relations of the gibbon*, Comparative psychology monographs 16 (1940), Part 5.

9 J. B. CARROLL, *The study of language*, Cambridge, Mass, 1953.

10 J. C. CATFORD, *A linguistic theory of translation*, London, 1965.

11 N. CHOMSKY, *Language and mind*, New York, 1972.

12 C. J. FILLMORE and D. T. LANDENDOEN (eds), *Studies in linguistic semantics*, New York, 1971.

13 J. R. FIRTH, *Speech*, London, 1930.

14 'Personality and language in society', *Sociol rev* 42 (1950), 37–52.

15 'Synopsis of linguistic theory, 1930–55', *Studies in linguistic analysis*, special publication of the Philological Society, Oxford, 1957, 1–32.

16 'Ethnographic analysis and language with reference to Malinowski's views', *Man and culture*, edited by R. W. Firth, London, 1957, 93–118.

17 K. VON FRISCH, *Bees, their vision, chemical senses and language*, Ithaca, 1950.

18 A. L. GARDINER, *Theory of speech and language*, Oxford, 1932.

19 H. P. GRICE, 'Logic and conversation', *Syntax and semantics* 3 (1975), 41–58.

20 S. R. HARNAD (ed), *Origin and evolution of language and speech*, New York, 1975.

21 S. I. HAYAKAWA, *Language in thought and action*, London, 1952.

22 C. F. HOCKETT, *A manual of phonology*, Indiana University publications in anthropology and linguistics 11, 1955.

23 *A course in modern linguistics*, New York, 1958.

24 D. HYMES, 'Models of the interaction of language and social life', J. J. GUMPERZ and D. HYMES (eds), *Directions in sociolinguistics*, New York, 1972, 35–71.

25 *On communicative competence*, Philadelphia, 1971.

26 O. JESPERSEN, *Language*, London, 1922.

27 F. KAINZ, *Die 'Sprache' der Tiere*, Stuttgart, 1961.

28 R. M. KEMPSON, *Presupposition and the delimitation of semantics*, Cambridge, 1975.

29 *Semantic theory*, Cambridge, 1977.

30 P. KIPARSKY and C. KIPARSKY, 'Fact', M. BIERWISCH and K. HEIDOLPH (eds), *Progress in linguistics*, The Hague, 1970, 143–73.

31 W. KOHLER, *Gestalt psychology*, New York, 1947.

32 A. L KROEBER, 'Sign and symbol in bee communications', *Proc National Academy of Sciences* 38 (1952), 753–7.

33 R. W. LANGACKER, *Language and its structure*, New York, 1968.

34 G. N. LEECH, *Principles of pragmatics*, London, 1983.

35 E. H. LENNEBERG, *Biological foundations of language*, New York, 1967.

36 P. LIEBERMAN, *On the origins of language*, New York, 1975.

37 J. LYONS, *Semantics*, Cambridge, 1977.

38 B. MALINOWSKI, *Coral gardens and their magic*, London, 1935.

39 A. MEILLET and M. COHEN, *Les langues du monde*, Paris, 1952.

40 T. F. MITCHELL, 'The language of buying and selling in Cyrenaica', *Hespéris* 1957, 31–71, reprinted in T. F. Mitchell, *Principles of Firthian Linguistics*, London, 1975, 167–200.

41 C. MORRIS, *Signs, language, and behaviour*, New York, 1946.

42 P. NEWMARK, *Approaches to translation*, Oxford, 1981.

43 E. A. NIDA, *Toward a science of translating*, Leiden, 1964.

44 C. K. OGDEN and I. A. RICHARDS, *The meaning of meaning, eighth edition*, London, 1946.

45 F. R. PALMER, *Semantics*, Cambridge, 1976.

46 J. P. POSTGATE, *Translation and translations*, London, 1922.

47 E. PULGRAM, 'Phoneme and grapheme: a parallel', *Word* 7 (1951), 15–70.

48 R. H. ROBINS, 'A problem in the statement of meanings', *Lingua* 3 (1952), 121–37.

49 'John Rupert Firth', *Lang* 37 (1961), 191–200.

50 E. SAPIR, 'The status of linguistics as a science', *Lang* 5 (1929), 207–14.

51 F DE SAUSSURE, *Cours de linguistique générale, fourth edition*, Paris, 1949.

52 T. H. SAVORY, *The art of translation*, London, 1957.

53 W. SCHMIDT, *Die Sprachfamilien und Sprachenkreise der Erde*, Heidelberg, 1926.

54 N. C. SCOTT, 'Obituary, John Rupert Firth', *BSOAS* 24 (1961), 413–18.

55 T. A. SEBEOK, *Perspectives in zoosemiotics*, The Hague, 1972.

56 'Semiotics: a survey of the state of the art', T. A. SEBEOK (ed), *Current trends in linguistics*, Volume 12, 1974, 211–64.

57 N. V. SMITH (ed) *Mutual knowledge*, London, 1982.

58 D. SPERBER and D. WILSON, *Relevance: communication and cognition*, Oxford, 1986.

59 G. L. TRAGER, 'The field of linguistics', *Studies in linguistics*, occasional paper 1 (1950).

60 S. ULLMANN, *The principles of semantics*, second edition, Glasgow and Oxford, 1957.

61 *Semantics*, Oxford, 1962

62 R. A. WALDRON, *Sense and sense development*, London, 1967.

63 J. F. WALLWORK, *Language and linguistics: an introduction to the study of language*, London, 1969.

64 L. WITTGENSTEIN, *Philosophical investigations*, trans G. E. M. Anscombe, Oxford, 1953.

Notes to Chapter 1

1 On the languages of the world, Meillet and Cohen, 39, give brief accounts of all languages so far as information is available. See also Schmidt, 53, and E. Kieckers, *Die Sprachstämme der Erde*, Heidelberg, 1931; M. Ruhlen, *A guide to the world's languages*, London, 1987.

2 On the linguist as opposed to the polyglot, Bloch and Trager, 4, 8.

3 *Synchronic* and *diachronic*, like a number of other basic terminological distinctions in linguistics, are Saussurean in origin (51, 114–43). De Saussure gave us the term *état de langue* to refer to a stage of a language at a particular period; thus Chaucerian, Johnsonian, and contemporary English are each different *états de la langue anglaise*.

4 On the different uses of the world *philology*, Carroll, 9, 3, 65–6; Bolling, 6.

5 J. J. Katz and P. M. Postal, *An integrated theory of linguistic descriptions*, Cambridge, Mass, 1964, 1.

6 Chomsky 11, 1.

7 Langacker 33, v.

8 Further discussed in 9.3, with references.

9 Bloch and Trager, 4, 5.

10 On bee dancing, von Frisch, 17; Kroeber, 32; Aitchison, 1, 39.

11 On gibbons, Carpenter, 8. In general, Kainz, 27; Sebeok, 55.

12 Excellent summary in non-technical language in Aitchison, 1, Chapter 2; *cp* also R. A. and B. T. Gardner, 'Teaching sign language to a chimpanzee', *Science* 165 (1969), 664–72; D. Premack, 'A functional analysis of language', *Journal of experimental analysis of behavior* 14 (1970), 107–25; G. Mounin, 'Language, communication, chimpanzees, *Current anthropology* 17 (1976), 1–8.

13 Biological inheritance, Lenneberg, 35.

14 On the question of the origin of language, Hockett, 23, Chapter 64, and in *The scientific American*, September, 1960; Harnad, 20; Lieberman, 36.

15 On semiotics, Barthes, 3; Sebeok, 56. There is a journal, *Semiotica*, specifically devoted to semiotics.

16 On sound symbolism and onomatopoeia, Jespersen, 26, Chapter 20; Firth, 13, Chapter 6; Köhler, 31, 224–5.

17 *Cp* A. Martinet, 'La double articulation linguistique', *TCLC* 5 (1949), 127–52.

18 On graphonomy, Hockett, 23, Chapter 62. On the analogy of *phonemics* (4.3.1) a branch of linguistics called graphemics has been suggested (Pulgram, 47).

19 On a narrow interpretation of *linguistics*, Trager, 59; Hockett, 22, 14.

20 George Berkeley, *A treatise concerning the principles of human knowledge*, 1710, Introduction, §13. On the technical distinction between reference and denotation, Lyons, 37, 176.

21 On different cultural worlds, Sapir, 50.

22 On 'thing meant', Gardiner, 18, 15; *significant* and *signifié*, de Saussure, 51, 99; triadic relationship of meaning, Odgen and Richards, 44, Chapter 1. On meaning as function, Bazell, *Word* 10 (1954), 132; *cp* Wittgenstein, 64, 126 etc. Bloomfield developed a rigorous theory of meaning in behaviourist or mechanist terms (5, Chapters 2 and 9). These topics are discussed from a number of viewpoints by Ullmann, 60; *cp* 61. More recent treatments may be found in Kempson, 29, Chapter 2, Lyons, 37, Chapter 7, and Palmer, 45, 19–30.

23 On presupposition generally, Kempson, 28; see also Fillmore, 'Verbs of judging: an exercise in semantic description', Fillmore and Langendoen, 12, 273–89; Kiparsky and Kiparsky, 30.

24 Logicians and specialists in semantics are in dispute about the technicalities involved in interpreting sentences like the *King of France is bald* said with reference to the present day. Broadly two views are taken: either, in the case that there is no King of France, *ie* that *there is a King of France* is false, then *the King of France is bald* is simply false (that is, *the King of France is bald* entails the truth of *there is a King of France*); or, alternatively, if there is no King of France, then the truth (or the falsity) of both *the King of France is bald* and of *the King of France is not bald* does not arise, both sentences being neither true or false but uninterpretable in a normal context (the utterance of any statement about the King of France presupposes the existence, at the time referred to, of such a person.)

Faced with such an apparently odd sentence the ordinary listener, as opposed to the logician in his professional capacity, would try to interpret it in a normal manner, perhaps by assuming that *the King of France* was a currently well-known nickname of a prominent politician, popular entertainer, sportsman, or even a notorious and successful criminal gang leader.

For a full discussion and further references, see Kempson 29, Chapter 9; also Lyons, 37, 182–3, 600–2.

25 Hyponymy, Lyons, 37, 291–5; semantics and pragmatics, Morris, 41; Kempson, 28, Chapters 7–9; more generally, Alston, 2. On context of situation, Malinowski, Supplement 1 in Ogden and Richards, 44, and 38, Volume 2, Chapter 1; Firth, 14 and 15, 7–11.

Firth's general theory of language and linguistic analysis is set out in Firth, 15 and 16. A complete bibliography of his publications is to be found at the end of his obituaries, by Scott, 54, and by Robins, 49.

Those who take a restrictive view of semantics and draw a line, however difficult in practice to make precise, between linguistic meaning and language use, between semantics and pragmatics, would assign most of the material studied in Firth's and Malinowski's context of situation theories to pragmatics, and much else. Kempson, for example, writes (29, 192): 'Within the domain of pragmatics, according to the position adopted in this book, fall topics such as metaphor, stylistics, rhetorical devices in general, and all the phenomena relating to what we might call thematic structure – the way in which a speaker presents his utterance.'

On this view studies of language use, such as are undertaken in 'speech act theory' and in the investigation of the conventions of conversation (see 9.2, and Grice, 19), would fall within pragmatics (Kempson, 29, Chapters 4 and 5). This is no way affects the relative importance assigned to such studies, any more than does the Firthian virtual inclusion of all pragmatic topics within his contextual semantics. It is a question of the manner in which the highly complex subject of human language is divided and assigned to the different branches of linguistics.

For the most recent investigations into this rich and fascinating aspect of our use and understanding of language the reader should study Smith, 57, and Sperber and Wilson, 58.

Those who remember reading, or having read to them, *Alice in Wonderland* and *Alice through the looking glass* in childhood should reread them and notice how much of their particular brand of humour arises from the deliberate neglect or perversion of normal 'maxims of conversation' (*cp* Grice, 19, 45).

26 *Phatic communion* was used by Malinowski, in Ogden and Richards, 44, 315, as a technical term to denote this type of socially necessary 'idle chatter'; *cp* Hayakawa, 21, 72: 'The prevention of silence is itself an important function of speech.' The successful handling of the various types of language appropriate to different situations has been called 'communicative competence' (Hymes, 25). See also Hymes, 24; Lyons, 37, 573–91; R. Bauman and J. Sherzer (eds), *Explorations in the ethnography of speaking*, London, 1974.

27 On semantics generally, two elementary books are especially to be recommended, Waldron, 62, and Palmer, 45. In the more technical range, Kempson, 29, is an excellent textbook on semantics, with particular reference to logic; semantics is here treated, in the author's words, 'as a bridge discipline between linguistics and philosophy (29, ix). Lyons, 37, is a most comprehensive exposition of all aspects of semantics in a wide-ranging application of the term.

Leech, 34, provides an excellent introduction to pragmatics, with some discussion (5–7) of the different conceptions of the relations between pragmatics and semantics in the study of linguistic meaning. See also S. C. Levinson, *Pragmatics*, Cambridge, 1983.

28 On translation, Malinowski, 38, volume 2, 14; Postgate, 46; Savory, 52; *IJAL* 20 (1954), part 4, translation issue; Catford, 10; Nida, 43, which contains a very full bibliography; Newmark, 42.

Chapter 2

Theoretical and methodological considerations

2.1 Abstractions

2.1.1 The status of linguistic abstractions

Linguistic analysis proceeds in the manner of other sciences by making abstractions, at different levels (1.3.1), of elements having the status of constants and of categories and rules expressing the relations between the elements, to which the continuous flux of the phenomena comprising its subject-matter can be referred, and by means of which the phenomena may be explained and accounted for. At any level the abstractions can be of different degrees of generality. Thus at the grammatical level, in relation to English, the words *foot* (abstracted from utterances containing certain sound sequences), *noun*, and *word* are progressively higher degrees of abstraction, that is, they subsume successively more material under themselves. Phonetically, *the consonant* /b/, *plosive consonant*, and *consonant* show a similar gradation in degree (for the phonetic terms here used as examples, see 3.3).

Some abstractions may be indirectly rather than directly or immediately referable to the spoken (or written) forms; and one abstract element may, in fact, have a number of different sets of forms corresponding to it. Thus at the grammatical level the element 'plural' as a component in English plural nouns may be variously represented in speech by the forms /-s/ in /kæts/ (*cats*), /-z/ in /dɔgz/ (*dogs*), /-iz/ in /'hɔːsiz/ (*horses*), /-ən/ in /'ɔksən/ (*oxen*), the relationship between /mæn/ (*man*) and /men/ (*men*), however it may be analysed, and in other ways (see Further 5.4.2). Similar statements can be made, for example, for the Latin and German cases and for many other grammatical categories. The indirectness and complexity of this relationship between abstraction and actual form is particularly apparent in some parts of transformational-generative analysis (7.2.3).

The status of the abstractions employed in the description and analysis of linguistic form has been the subject of considerable debate. It has been variously maintained:

[i] That the constants abstracted in an analysis, if the analysis is correct, are in some way inherent in the actual material of the language under analysis;

[ii] That the linguist's abstractions are also abstracted, albeit unconsciously, by native speakers of the language as the product of certain innate mental structures (1.2.1; 7.2.4) and as the result of their having learned the language in childhood, and are part of the content of the speakers' minds or brains;

[iii] That the linguist's abstractions have no other status than as part of his scientific terminology, and are justified by their utility in stating regularities and making predictions about the forms of utterances, but have no express relevance to the speakers' mental or cerebral states or equipment, though certain correspondences between the two are not ruled out and are *prima facie* quite probable.

These three viewpoints follow somewhat along the classical philosophical lines of realism, conceptualism, and nominalism respectively. In so far as their differences fall within the field of philosophy or of general scientific theory, they need not be the direct concern of the linguist. But there are certain implications for linguistics in each view, which should therefore be mentioned.[1]

The first view implies as a consequence that languages have an organization independent of any analyst, and that the analysis consists in discovering the inherent patterns of that organization, so that one's statements are correct or incorrect according as they correspond or do not correspond to the pre-existing organization of the language, even though it may never be actually possible to declare for certain that any particular analysis or analytic statement is the correct one.

The implication of the second view is that the linguist's analysis of a language as he observes it corresponds in some way to the linguistic working of the speaker's mind or brain, and that the language should be described in terms such as could be related to the production of speech by a speaker and its comprehension by a hearer.

This attitude was expressed rather strongly by de Saussure in his well-known antithesis between *langue* and *parole*; the terms have now passed into general usage in linguistics. *Langue* is the lexical, grammatical, and phonological constitution of a language, and was considered by de Saussure to be implanted in the native speaker's mind (or brain) in childhood as the collective product of the speech community envisaged as a supra-individual entity in its own right. In speaking his language the speaker could only operate or perform within this *langue*; what he actually uttered was *parole*, and the only individual control he could exercise was when to speak and about what to speak. Lexical, grammatical, and phonological rules were laid down in the *langue* he had acquired and was speaking, and they prescribed the limits within which the individual might make his choices. There are some difficulties arising from the full implications of this interpretation of linguistic abstractions. A comparable, but not identical, distinction is drawn by Chomsky between **competence**, what a speaker intuitively knows about his language, and **performance**, what he does when he actually uses his language.[2]

All three of the standpoints mentioned above possess a degree of validity in relation to the work of the linguist, and probably most linguists, whether they expressly intend it or not, maintain some part of each, tending to give preference in scientific attitude to one of them. On any view the description and its elements are justified by their explanatory power and validated by their application to further material, *ie* by their ability to predict by extrapolation from a necessarily limited body of material the forms and functions of a much larger and in living languages necessarily unlimited body of similar material. As might be expected linguists looking at language primarily from the 'internalist' point of view tend to take up position (ii), above, and those who lay most emphasis on methodology and on language as wholly to be viewed from 'outside' prefer either (i) or (iii) (*cp* 1.2.1).

Those features and parts of utterances which are in one way or another referred to each abstraction may be said to serve as its **exponents**.[3] Thus from the English utterance *take care*, the phonetic consonant and vowel segments, the phonological consonantal and vocalic elements, the grammatical elements verb and noun related as imperative verb and object noun, and the lexical items *take* and *care* are all abstracted at their appropriate level, and are severally represented by exponents in the actual or assumed utterance.

In the illustration given above the exponency of all the levels of analysis was sought in the actual utterance; but it is usually convenient to employ the elements of one level to serve as exponents of the analysis at another. This is done, for example, when lexical items and grammatical elements are indicated and identified by means of a phonological transcription (4.2), and when phonological elements have their exponents stated as phonetic segments and features, themselves abstractions at the phonetic level from the actual utterance.

2.1.2 Structural linguistics: syntagmatic and paradigmatic relations

It is a commonplace today to say that linguistics is **structural**, and that languages, as analysed by linguists, are treated **structurally**. This is a statement about the elements (constants) set up by abstraction in the description and analysis of languages. These are considered and treated as being related to one another by their very nature and so forming interrelated systems rather than mere aggregates of individuals. A metaphor may clarify this distinction. The members of an orchestra are all related to each other by their specific roles as orchestral players therein, both within smaller groups and in the whole orchestra (*eg* member of the woodwind section, first fiddle among the strings, and so on). Each performs his function by virtue of his place in relation to the others, and players cannot be added to or taken away from an orchestra without altering its essential musical quality and potentialities. On the other hand the audience at a concert is more like a simple aggregate; ten more members or five fewer, be they men or women and wherever they may choose to sit, make no difference to the whole audience in its capacity as an audience.

At each level the formal constituents of the analysis, the elements abstracted, are established and defined as parts thereof by their relations with other constituents at the same level. Some linguists go so far as to say that the actual 'content' or exponential features assigned to an abstracted element are of little account, or of none, in determining and defining it. This is not necessary; the actual material of utterance in a language is the ultimate basis of any analysis or description, and reference to phonetic features in phonological analysis and to phonological (or phonetic) shapes in grammar is perfectly compatible with the prime consideration being given to the interrelations within the level in determining the status of analytic elements.[4]

Essentially the relations between linguistic elements are of two

kinds of dimensions, usually designated syntagmatic and paradigmatic. **Syntagmatic** relations are those holding between elements
forming serial structures, or 'strings' as they are sometimes
called, at a given level, referable to, though the course not identical with, the temporal flow of utterance or linear stretches of
writing. To take again the previous example: the word sequence
take and *care*, the transcription /'teik/'kɛə/, the more abstract
phonological representation CVVC CVV (C = consonantal
element, V = vocalic element), and the grammatical arrangement verb + noun are all, at different levels, structures of
syntagmatically related components. By reason of their referability to the actual material of the spoken (or written) utterance,
syntagmatic relations may be considered the primary dimension.
Paradigmatic relations are those holding between comparable
elements at particular places in structures, *eg*

    initial consonant *take* /teik/
                  m   /m/
                  b   /b/
    postverbal noun *take care*
                      pains
                      thought
                      counsel

and more generally between the comparable elements of structures in classes (*eg* consonants, verbs), or in the language as a
whole (*eg* phonemes (phonological elements), word classes ('part
of speech')).[5]

Structure and *system*, and their derivatives, are often used
almost interchangeably, but it is useful to employ *structure*, as
in the preceding paragraph, specifically with reference to groupings of syntagmatically related elements, and *system* with reference to classes of paradigmatically related elements.[6]

Relations may be manifold between linguistic elements, and so
structures may be divided into substructures, and systems may
comprise various subsystems. In particular, the paradigmatic
dimension, at both the phonological and the grammatical levels,
covers many different types of contrast, according to the different
criteria employed.

The use of relational criteria in the analysis of the forms of
languages is apparent in practically all modern descriptions. The
status of a particular case as a grammatical category applicable
to certain word endings in a language like Latin is stated syntagmatically in terms of the different syntactic structures (constructions) in which it may be used in relation to other grammatical

constituents (verbs, prepositions, etc), and paradigmatically in terms of the numbers of different cases formally marked in the language; it is not stated in terms of a common semantic meaning ascribable to all words exhibiting the particular case (often leading to a fruitless search; see further 6.6.2). The status of a phonological element (*eg* a particular consonant) is not established solely by reference to its exponents (phonetic segments or fractions of utterance), but syntagmatically in terms of its possible places in relation to other phonological elements in phonological structures, and paradigmatically in terms of the different elements with which it contrasts in the different places of its occurrence.

The illustrative statement of the preceding paragraphs are necessarily anticipatory; the terms employed and the processes of analysis involved at the different levels will be dealt with in subsequent chapters.

2.2 Dialect, idiolect, style

2.2.1 Dialects as subdivisions of languages

Among the abstractions that are made in linguistics, one of the most important has so far been assumed without receiving any examination. This is the term *language*, in the sense of *the English language, the French language*, etc. It is an empirically obvious fact that no two individuals have identical speech. One is seldom unable to recognize the voice of one acquaintance as distinct from that of another and from that of a stranger. Nevertheless in everyday affairs one readily speaks of *the English language*, etc without confusion or misunderstanding, and the linguist in making statements about a given language at any level of analysis does the same. In each case one is deliberately ignoring certain differences between the speech habits of separate individuals. The linguist, who must recognize explicitly what he is doing, bases his abstractions, generalizations, and descriptive statements on features and characteristics that can be ascribed to all speakers recognized for his purposes as speakers of the language concerned. Science must proceed in this way, seeking to compass the manifold diversity of phenomena by statements applying to what can be said to be common to them. In the case of languages one can proceed in two ways, either making one's statements general enough, admitting permissive variation of structures and systems in one's description and a wide range of actual exponents, so that the inherent diversity of different speakers is allowed for, or, more usually, selecting certain speakers only and restricting one's statement to them alone as fictitiously representing the language as a whole.

In practice, except with languages spoken by a few people in a compact area, the second procedure is normal. Traditionally and customarily, the speech of educated persons in the capital city of a country is selected as representing 'the language'. Grammars of English and French and books on English or French pronunciation, unless it is expressly stated otherwise, describe educated English as spoken in London and the south-east of the country and educated Parisian French. These are the types of English and French taught as foreign languages in schools, though as types of speech they may represent the speech habits of only a minority in each country.

Whatever the practical merits of this procedure, linguistic science and linguistic theory must be able to deal with the actual diversity of linguistic phenomena more precisely. Within the domain generally recognized as 'one language', many clearly observable differences of pronunciation; grammar, and vocabulary are not haphazardly mixed, but occupy different regions within the territory, shading continuously into one another in all directions. This sort of situation is apparent to anyone journeying by stages, for example, west from London to Cornwall or north from London to Edinburgh.

To cope with this state of affairs, the linguist distinguishes within all but the smallest language areas different dialects. **Dialect** is an abstraction of the same sort of language; but as it covers fewer people, it enables one to keep one's statements closer to the actual speech of the speakers; each abstracted element in the description of a dialect covers a less wide range of actually different phenomena. The number of dialects to be recognized within a language is clearly not fixed in advance; it depends on the fineness of the scale on which the linguist is working; the smaller each dialect is taken to be and therefore the greater the number of dialects distinguished, the more precise each description can be, as each generalization will cover a smaller range of divergence. In such circumstances dialects will fall into successively larger groups of dialects, the largest group being the language itself as a unity. The lower limit of dialect division comes down to the individual speaker, and for the limiting case of dialect the term *idiolect* (the speech habits of a single person) has been coined.

Even here, however, one has not reached the end of the possible subdivisions of linguistic phenomena. Each individual's speech habits vary according to the different situations he is in and the different roles he is playing at any time in society. One readily distinguishes the different types of speech used by the same person in intimate family circles, among strangers and with persons of different social positions, in official, professional, and learned discourse, and so on, though with intermediate border-lines between each; and in writing, the composition of a family letter is very different from that of a technical article. As an obvious example, in educated London English the word sequence *the author to whom I was referring* is considered natural and appropriate in a formal lecture, and the sequence *the author who I was referring to* is likewise felt appropriate to conversation. The latter might be found in a lecture, especially in an extempore one without a full script, but the former would appear strangely stilted in general conversation.

These differences within the linguistic range of a single person are often called **styles**. At the present state of linguistics, the style chosen in first investigating the speech of an individual as representing a particular dialect or language is conventionally that designated 'slow colloquial', the style appropriate to fairly formal discourse with strangers, other styles being described usually by reference to the description of this.[7]

The peculiar slangs and jargons of closely knit groups within a community, such as some schools and colleges, certain skilled trades, semi-secret societies, and the like, fall under the general heading of style; their use on appropriate occasions by the individuals concerned helps to give the 'insiders' an enhanced sense of group unity and to distinguish them from the 'outsiders', to whom such modes of discourse are unfamiliar and in part unknown.

A special case of style variation is seen in the working of linguistic taboo, the avoidance by speakers either of whole topics or of certain words in particular situations (*eg* the presence of strangers, members of the opposite sex, children, older persons, etc). As far as is known, this phenomenon is found in all communities, though the sorts of topics and the types of vocabu-lary thus interdicted and the situations in which the taboos operate vary considerably. In England such topics as excretion and sexual reproduction ('dirt', 'obscenity'), details of one's own professional activities ('talking shop'), personal success ('swank'), and the making and investing of money have all been found objectionable to varying degrees in certain types of situation and company. If certain types of bodily processes and some much feared or unpleasant diseases have to be mentioned, a different vocabulary is substituted in most circumstances, usually having reference to other less distressing activities or experiences (euphemism), and the vocabulary whose principal reference is to taboo topics is reserved for intimate and other special situations.[8] In relation to the death of close friends and members of one's family terms such as *passed away*, *left us*, and the like may be preferred in informal conversation as being less distressing. In other communities, one notices that among certain American-Indian tribes the mentioning of the names of persons recently known to have died is strictly avoided; and among some Australian aborigines a highly restricted form of language is the only one permitted in conversation with one's kinsfolk by marriage, with a much reduced vocabulary. A similar taboo often lies on the sort of vocabulary that may be used in ejaculations of anger, enthusiasm, and the like, in the hearing of strangers. Names of the deity and words with religious associations (doubtless relics of earlier magical attitudes towards language), as well as those labelled obscence, sometimes seem to relieve tense feelings merely by being uttered; but in most situations their use is disapproved of as 'swearing', and other expressions are substituted. Of course a native speaker's knowledge of such taboos and customary restrictions enables one, if one so wishes, deliberately to outrage other people's feelings or to cause embarrassment to one's hearers by indulging in objectionable, obscene, or blasphemous expressions. But one must know what is ordinarily expected in order to behave convincingly in such ways. For this reason is has been said not without truth that to be able to swear convincingly in a foreign language is one of the marks of its thorough mastery.

The study of style in literary criticism is a field wherein the linguist has his contribution to make. This is briefly discussed in 9.5, below.

2.2.2 Dialect mapping: isoglosses

The differences of personal styles and of dialects are the summations of large numbers of individual differences of speaking (and writing), discernible at all levels, in pronunciation, in grammar, and in the meanings of particular words. Examples from English are the trilled *r* of parts of Scotland, the separate second person singular pronoun forms of parts of the north of England, the use of local words not current in other regions, such as *nesh*, 'liable to damage or distress from cold' (parts of North and West England), and the use of words in senses not generally current, *eg: to starve*, 'to perish of cold' as well as 'of hunger' (parts of North England and the Midlands), *homely*, 'comfortably disposed' (British English), 'ugly, plain' (parts of the United States).

Considerable attention has always been paid to dialect differences within languages. Though their accurate and systematic description and differentiation are matters for the linguist, the division of most languages into dialects has always been a matter of general knowledge and acceptance. Among amateur scholars dialect observation has been a favourite linguistic topic, and the several dialect societies in existence bear witness of this. Antiquarianism (where modern conditions are tending to displace an earlier distinct dialect) and local pride are two main motivating causes. Some linguists specialize in dialect studies within one or more language areas, and *dialectology* is available as the title for this specialization.

Dialects are constituted at any degree of abstraction by their features at each level of analysis, both those they share with others and those peculiar to a particular dialect. So dialects have been defined as the sum of their characteristics, a statement equally applicable, of course, to whole languages.[9] In so far as these characteristics are locally distributed, they can be plotted on a map of the area concerned. This is done in 'dialect geography' by drawing lines as closely as the nature of the material allows demarcating areas exhibiting a particular feature and so dividing them off from areas exhibiting other features. These lines are called **isoglosses**, a term modelled on geographical terms like *isotherm* (a line marking areas of equal temperature) and *isobar* (a line marking areas of equal atmospheric pressure). In several countries (*eg* Britain, France, Germany, and the United States) semi-official dialect surveys have been, or are being, made, covering features at all levels.

As was said above, the dialect features plotted by isoglosses are not randomly scattered over an area, but tend roughly to coincide in distribution, so that a dialect map shows several isoglosses more or less following the same track, especially those relating to features of grammar and pronunciation, though it must be remembered that every time a speaker of one dialect moves or settles in another dialect area without changing his own speech, he infinitesimally blurs several isoglosses.

Examples of isoglosses on dialect maps are given in diagrams I and 2. Lines followed by several bundles of isoglosses are taken as dialect boundaries, the number required being partly dependent on the degree of fineness of scale in dialect division employed by the linguist; but sometimes a single isogloss, especially if it joins together several bundles in different localities

or if it lies along the mean of several roughly convergent
isoglosses is partly arbitrarily taken as a dialect boundary marker.
The so-called 'Benrath line' is an example of this, running
roughly east-north-east across Holland and Germany just north
of Benrath on the Rhine (to the south of Düsseldorf) and
keeping north of Berlin, to the limits of German-speaking territory, and often regarded as the dividing line between the group
of Low German dialects to the north and the group of High
German dialects to the south. The particular features

DIAGRAM I

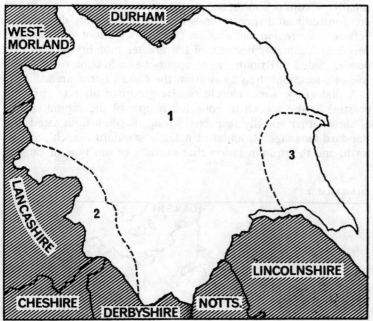

Representation of the definite article, *the*, in spoken dialects of Yorkshire,
England (based on the map of W. E. Jones, 'The definite article in living
Yorkshire dialect', *Leeds studies in English and kindred languages* 7–8 (1952),
81–91).

The lines (isoglosses) within the unshaded area of the map divide the county
of Yorkshire into three areas, according to their spoken representation of *the*:

1 A *t*-sound and/or a glottal stop (ʔ)* before consonants and vowels;
2 A *t*-sound and/or a glottal stop before consonants, a *th*-sound (θ) or *tth*-
  sound (tθ) before vowels;
3 No spoken representation.

*For the phonetic symbols, see chart on pp 88–9.

distinguished by this line are the pronunciations of the word spelled *machen* in German, with a 'k' sound as second consonant to the north and a 'ch' sound (as in Scots *loch*) to the south.[10]

2.2.3 Class dialects and 'standard languages'

So far geographically marked dialect differences have been considered, but in many language areas there are, besides these, manifest 'vertical' or social dialect divisions. The special status often accorded to educated speech of capital cities has already been mentioned, as in many areas differences in speech can be correlated with social or class differences. There is, however, usually a connection between the two dimensions of dialect division; educated speech tends to be less markedly different as between one region and another than the speech of less educated people, presumably because of the greater mobility of educated people, aided in Britain by the upper-class addiction to boarding school education often away from the child's home area.[11]

A dialect, or some closely similar group of dialects enjoying prestige as the speech of educated people of the capital city or of some other socially respected group, is often designated '**the standard language**', 'standard English', 'standard French', and so forth; and the pronunciation characteristic of this type of English

DIAGRAM 2

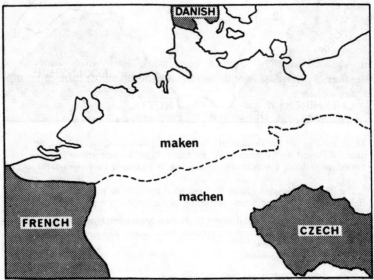

has been called 'received pronunciation' or 'RP'. The use and consequent spread of 'standard languages' outwards and downwards in the social scale, as it were, is often encouraged in modern states by their employment in official broadcasts, as the approved types of speech for school instruction, their recognition as the form of the language to be learned by foreigners, and in other similar ways. The term *capital city* may be more in the nature of a cultural focus or centre than just the political capital of a country; Parisian French sets the standard of educated speech in the French-speaking areas of Belgium and Switzerland as well as of France. With a language as widely spoken and taught as a second language as English is today more than one standard may came to be recognized, for example a variety of American English in the USA and in areas politically and culturally under its influence.

The term *standard language* must not mislead. Such forms of speech are descriptively dialects, just like any other dialect, to be described and delimited on just the same criteria as the less socially and officially favoured 'regional' dialects. It is a popular assumption on the part of those speaking standard dialects that other dialects, especially those spoken by groups lacking any social prestige or recognition, are both 'incorrect' and more or less formless, without a true grammar or precise means of discourse. Epithets such as 'ugly', 'slovenly', and the like are freely employed with reference to the pronunciation of such dialects (countered to some extent by accusations of 'affectedness' and 'putting on airs' made by some non-standard speakers of those speaking a standard dialect). Needless to say, the linguist faithful to the principles of objective scientific statements must abjure all such modes of expression and value judgments, aesthetic and quasi-moralistic, as outside his field, though he may take note of them as sociolinguistically relevant (9.1.2). The statement that certain utterances are 'incorrect' (*eg: we ain't done nothing*) is to the linguist equivalent to the statement that in a corresponding situation the speaker of the standard dialect would say something else (*we haven't done anything*). Reactions to other people's speech is valuable evidence of part of the social function of language within a community; but the linguist, whatever his private feelings on these and kindred matters, can, as a linguist, have no part in them. His task is to describe and analyse the phenomena of languages (and of the dialects within them) as he finds them, and his techniques and procedures are devised for this purpose. He has no concern with preferring one dialect over another, nor with prescribing how people should use their language. Description, not prescription, is his work, and it is work enough.

It may be worth insisting that any claims for some dialects being better organized than others do not bear examination. Of course the social situations in which they are predominantly used determine the sort of sentences produced and the vocabulary most frequently employed; but the phonetics, phonology, and grammar of non-standard dialects are as amenable to exact description as are those of standard dialects (one may compare the similarly prejudiced misapprehension about the so-called 'primitive' languages).[12]

2.2.4 Criteria for determining dialect status

At this point the question is properly raised about the reasons for describing some differences of speech habits as being dialects within a language and others as being different languages. In one usage, springing from the misguided attitude referred to in the preceding section, forms of speech without a writing system, or those held to be characteristic of uneducated persons, are regarded as 'dialects' and contrasted with the 'true language' of the literate and educated. By this usage, certain types of colloquial Arabic are contrasted, as 'the dialects', without further discrimination or qualification. Apart from this, several different and often conflicting criteria are commonly and tacitly admitted. *Dialect* is used for:

[i] Forms of speech that are different but mutually intelligible without special training;

[ii] The forms of speech current within a politically unified area; and

[iii] Forms of speech of speakers sharing a common writing system and set of written classics.

By [i], the various types of English spoken in the British Isles are regarded as dialects of English, whereas Welsh, Irish, and Scots Gaelic are different languages. By [ii], the various types of Low German spoken on either side of the Dutch-German frontier are sometimes described as dialects of Dutch and German respectively, without regard to their mutual similarities and intelligibility. In the same way Swedish, Norwegian, and Danish are usually termed different languages, despite their relative intercomprehensibility, and in particular that between standard Norwegian and Danish. By [iii], the different tongues spoken in China and among the Chinese outside China (Malaysia, Formosa, etc) are traditionally called dialects, although spoken

North Chinese (Mandarin) and spoken Cantonese (a South Chinese tongue) are mutually incomprehensible. These usages are somewhat reinforced by such factors as the existence and official use of standard Dutch and standard German over the whole of Holland and Germany, respectively, and by the quasi-official status of Mandarin Chinese.

Linguists tend to concentrate on the first criterion, mutual intelligibility, as relating to specifically linguistic facts, though from a sort of courtesy *dialect* is used in certain areas, such as Chinese, of what would strictly be regarded elsewhere as separate languages, themselves each subdivided into many dialects. Mutual intelligibility, however, is not an all-or-none matter, and admits of degrees from almost complete and unhindered comprehension to nearly total incomprehension without special training. In such situations the standard of intelligibility that is required to admit of dialect status must be decided by the linguist, unless reliance is placed on traditional or extralinguistic factors. Intelligibility need not be the same each way; speakers of dialect A may understand speakers of dialect B more readily than the other way round. Ways of quantifying fairly accurately relative intelligibility have been devised, by the use of texts in each of the types of speech under investigation divided into short stretches, each of which speakers of the other types of speech are asked to translate into their own tongue. In this way they can be awarded a graded or numerical mark against each stretch and their total summed up and compared. To some extent the degree of mutual intelligibility correlates with the number of major structural and lexical isoglosses dividing dialect from dialect, but this correlation need not be anything like uniform.[13]

A special situation obtains in some areas, in that there are successions of different dialects lying next to one another so that each is mutually intelligible with its near neighbours but those at either end are mutually unintelligible (*eg* a succession ABCDEFGH, in which ABCD, DEFG, and FGH are sufficiently intercomprehensible to rank as dialects, but not A and F, B and H, etc). Here the linguist must either recognize some mutually unintelligible tongues as comprised within one language, or, better, divide the area into several languages with the admission that some dialects of one may be also intelligible with some dialects of another that lie adjacent to them. Or he may fall back on extralinguistic, political, or geographical divisions. In a more complex form, such a situation is said to hold between the French of North France and the Italian of South Italy, with a chain of mutually intelligible dialects linking the more distant and mutually unintelligible types of speech (*eg* Parisian French and Roman Italian). Here, at least among educated people, speakers of dialects on the French side of the frontier are likely also to be able to use standard French, or something like it, as a common dialect, and those on the Italian side are similarly likely to be able to use standard Italian. This can be said to help justify linguistically the politically based division of the speech chain into French and Italian respectively.[14]

Such a situation does not exist across all frontiers. Between France and Germany there is an area of bilingualism, in which many speakers, with varying degrees of proficiency in each, use both French and German (each in many ways influenced by features of other), as occasion requires; but a chain of mutually intelligible dialects as such is not found. This same state of affairs is found in Britain, as between English and Welsh in several parts of Wales, though unilingual speakers of Welsh are now becoming increasingly rare and it may be expected that they will soon cease to exist. This does not, of course, mean that the Welsh language itself need face extinction.

2.2.5 Linguistic tendencies affecting dialectal divisions

Dialect divisions must be seen as the product of the universal tendency of speech habits to vary, at every level, in the course of transmission from one generation to another. This will be discussed further, in Chapter 8; here one may notice two factors in constant conflict, that govern the genesis and spread, and also the obliteration of dialect differences. One's speech habits are normally acquired in early childhood and are more or less fixed, in the absence of special circumstances or efforts, thereafter. It is during those years that one's circle of acquaintance is most limited, and consequently differences peculiar to one's parents are easily acquired along with the rest of one's mother tongue. But membership of an expanding circle, with the objective need to be able to communicate readily with all its members and the subjective need to integrate oneself therewith, tends towards the acquisition by all members of similar modes of speech and the lessening of purely personal differences. Among small isolated groups of persons, rarely moving beyond their own localities and having little external intercourse, regional differences of speech habits readily develop and become affectionately regarded as part of the personality of the members of the group. Conversely, in conditions favouring large-scale travel, regional mobility, urban-ization, and the like, local speech differences, especially where they are such as to hinder intercourse or where they have come to be associated with lack of education, low social prestige, or other unfavourable circumstances, are liable to be replaced with conscious effort on the part of speakers by a more widely recognized and socially advantageous type of speech. The ultimate product of this tendency is the spread of 'standard languages' over whole regions; but a frequent result, especially where a regional dialect has a fairly wide extent and where local feeling remains strong, is the acquisition by many speakers of two separate dialects, local and standard (or an approximation thereto), used according to the type of situation prevailing at the time, the local dialect being reserved for more intimate family occasions (as in many parts of North England). In these circumstances, speech in the local dialect acquires a special meaning or function in the situations in which it is used.[15]

It is noticeable that bundles of isoglosses tend to coincide with or to follow boundaries that either now hinder mutual intercourse or did so in earlier times, such as physical barriers, wide rivers, mountains ranges etc, or political frontiers. It may be surmised that the fairly extensive dialect differences in Germany and Italy are in part the result of the relatively late political unification of those territories.

The two constantly counteracting tendencies in dialect development were called *l'esprit de clocher* (parochialism) and *la force d'intercourse* (pressure of communication) by de Saussure. Clearly modern civilization greatly favours the latter, with the forces of urbanization and centralization everywhere rampant. One must assume that dialect differences were more numerous in earlier days, despite the smaller populations; it has been estimated that in medieval Europe a peasant could live and die without having enlarged his circle of acquaintance beyond 300. Today local dialects are generated and persist more easily in scattered rural communities than in urban ones, and in regions where from geographical or other causes movement is restricted. In most modern countries the dialect differences of town dwellers are less noticeable than those of rural people in corresponding parts of the country. Those engaged on dialect surveys in France noticed the spread of features from one urban centre to another along the main railway lines and roads, missing out more isolated intervening rural areas.[16]

While antiquarian interests sustain the study of rural dialects, sociologically inclined linguists have recently concerned themselves actively with the dialect situations within urban areas, particularly where there have converged speakers of different dialects and, indeed, of quite separate languages (as in New York City). In these circumstances dialect divisions are greatly delocalized and tend to be realigned in terms of social class and to be influenced by the drive towards social approbation or by the acceptance of a particular status. Labov has studied the present dialect situation in New York, and a study on the same lines has been made of the English city of Norwich.[17]

The recognition of dialect divisions in language areas, and a cognizance of the principles and methods of dialect study are an important part of general linguistics for a number of reasons. The linguist is enabled to make a more precise statement of the phenomena of the language or languages he is concerned with at any time. The reactions of speakers to each other's dialects often throw much light on the social working of language in communities and on its functions both as a unifier and as a diversifier of social groups. Moreover in the more minute and detailed scale possible in dealing with the relatively small areas of some dialects, one has, as it were, a small-scale picture of the linguistic situation of the world as a whole. The frontiers between totally distinct and mutually unintelligible languages are, in fact, very closely packed bundles of coinciding isoglosses. In the processes of dialect splitting and dialect merging, dialect contact and interaction, in the spreading of some features and the disappearance of others, the rise of prestige dialects and national 'standard languages', and so on, one is able to study closely and on a small scale the same types of occurrence which give rise on a much larger scale and over long eras of time to the distribution of languages over the globe and the material of linguistic history (8.1).

Dialect study is very relevant to historical linguistics; the splitting of a single language (eg spoken Latin) into several separate and mutually unintelligible languages (eg the Romance languages) begins in dialectal division within the original language while it is still effectively one language. In studying the minute, detailed, and individual features of dialectal variation, one is often studying at close quarters the sort of synchronic situation in which the phenomena of linguistic change, studies on a large scale in historical linguistics, have their origin.[18]

2.3 General and particular

The nature of linguistic abstractions has already been discussed, and it was pointed out that any level of analysis they may be of different degrees of generality, and that whatever abstractions the linguist make must ultimately be relatable to an infinite number of exponents in the utterances of a living language (2.1.1). But of the abstractions that form the language system set up by the linguist for the description and analysis of any language, or dialect, some are by their nature and purpose abstracted as general categories, and others are abstracted as particular items. The categories of **phonetics, phonology**, and **grammar** are general; the components of the **lexicon** of a language are particular. Abstractions like *plosive, bilabial, consonant, noun, genitive case*, etc apply repeatedly to parts of utterances that must be referred lexically to different words in a complete description. Traditionally the dictionary or lexicon of a language has been regarded as that part which requires particular and different statements for each item, and grammar, phonology, and phonetics as dealing with what can be brought under general rules, classes, and categories, embracing many individually different words. The same material is under examination all the time, but in the one case what is peculiar to particular items is the focus of attention, and in the other what can be abstracted as common to many such items or parts thereof. Hence in general usage the 'grammar' of a language often includes, in addition to grammatical categories and rules, details of its pronunciation, transcription, and orthography, topics often treated separately as different levels of analysis in the technical language of the linguist.

Bloomfield described the lexicon as an appendix of grammar and the list of basic irregularities.[19] This is because, as has been said, it deals with that part of the functioning of words that has not already been and cannot be treated under the general classes and categories of grammar (and phonology and phonetics). This does not imply that it is exclusively concerned with meanings in isolation or with reference. A good deal of the particular function of some words must be stated in terms of their relations with other words in the sentences of which they typically form a part. Nonetheless, the semantic function that can be stated of a word must be dealt with in the dictionary entry; it is probable that there are no two words that are exactly equivalent semantically in all the sentences in which they can occur. Each word's semantic function or meaning must be described separately. The meaning of a word, in so far as it can be stated of it as an individual lexical item and so encapsulated in a dictionary entry, may be called its lexical meaning; the term *lexis* has been used to refer to the lexical aspect of language and languages, and to the linguistic study of this aspect.

Dictionary-making presupposes grammar and phonology in a way that they do not presuppose it. The grammar and phonology of a language can be stated with the use of no more of its words than are required to exemplify the classes, categories, and structural rules involved; nor, provided they are sensible, does it matter much what sentences are used as examples and illustrations of grammatical constructions. But the dictionary entry dealing with each word must assign it to its grammatical class and any subclass (6.5), and must transcribe it, unambiguously represent its pronunciation, which is not necessarily done by its orthographic spelling (4.1), though in a dictionary of an unwritten language the transcription alone will necessarily constitute the word as entered in the dictionary. In particular, the grammatical class of a word cannot be inferred just by looking at it; its assignment to a class as a member thereof (or 'part of speech') is therefore part of the individual information to be given for each word. In most cases such a class assignment is all that the dictionary needs to do as far as the grammatical level is concerned; the rest of the grammatical information about it may be found in the appropriate parts of the grammatical description. But what are called 'irregular' forms, just because they are irregular (*ie* exceptional, individual), cannot be inferred from the class assignment and must be stated in the dictionary entries of the words concerned. An obvious example in English is the verb *go* with past tense from *went*, as against *walk, walked, tramp, tramped*, and countless others. Often, in fact, this same information is given twice in the description of languages, in the grammar as breaches of general rules, and in the dictionary as the peculiarities of individual words. This topic is treated in more detail in 6.5.

For the semantic information to be given in dictionary entries summaries are obviously required; no entry could possibly list every potential use in a sentence, and even in a dead language with a consequently restricted body of material it is not feasible to refer to every use except in a few rare words. The extent of the summary is necessarily governed by the size of the dictionary as a whole. The easiest and generally least helpful means is to give one or more synonyms, or near translation equivalents, in a dictionary of a foreign language, and no more. But more detailed definitions, together with citations exemplifying typical uses of the word in sentences, implicitly relating it to actual contexts, are very much more useful, and it is the practice of larger dictionaries (see, for example, the layout of entries in the full edition of the *Oxford English Dictionary* and in comparable dictionaries of other languages). In this way the individual meanings of words that are not fully statable in terms of direct reference to the external world may be more adequately described.

The techniques of successful dictionary-making lie rather outside the scope of an elementary introduction to linguistics, but one question that arises is relevant to general linguistic theory: how many separate meanings are to be recognized amid the often continuous ranges of potential uses of words? The question is partly one of convenience and ready accessibility of the information to be conveyed by the dictionary entry. Subdivisions are more easily presented and understood than overlong unsystematized accounts purporting to fall under a single head. But in part criteria can be given in the degree of relatedness of the different contexts of situation in which the word in question is used. In many words, their meaning ranges are related in recognized and similar ways; physical and abstract (metaphor: *summit of a mountain, summit meeting; depth of water; depth of despair*), or personal and non-personal (*Prince Edward; Cox's Orange is a prince among apples*). Further elaboration is easy to the native speakers of any language, and would be tedious here.[20] The different semantic usages of these kinds of words share contextual links and also share somewhat similar lexical company in sentences (*reach the summit, plumb the depths*, etc), which speakers intuitively understand and which can be explicitly stated. Generally metaphors seem to arise from the transference of the usage of a word or phrase from a direct designation of a physical object or action to a more abstract concept which shares some of its supposed or actual features. This is the case with the examples just given, but some transfers in the opposite direction are found. *Sloth* as an abstract noun is cited from a much earlier date in the *Oxford English Dictionary* than as a concrete noun referring to the allegedly slothful animal, *sloth*.

Different, though there may be borderline cases, are apparently unrelated meanings of single word forms, perhaps due to historical accidents or to associations now forgotten (*eg: case* (container), *case* (circumstances); *premises* (building), *premises* (of a syllogism); *mail* (post), *mail* (armour); *port* (wine), *port* (harbour); *post* (stick), *post* (mail), *post* (appointment), etc). Historical connections can in some cases be shown between meanings now very disparate; some dictionaries, like the *Oxford English Dictionary*, include historical facts such as the earlier

forms of the words and their presence in earlier stages of the
language or their entry from a foreign language as 'loans' (8.1.8);
but synchronically, such facts are strictly irrelevant to the listing
of the lexical components of a language at a given time and the
description and classifying of their meanings or uses by speakers
at the time, just as they are unavailable in dealing with the
dictionaries of hitherto unwritten languages.

The related question of word forms that occur in more than
one grammatical class (*eg* English *work* as noun and as verb) is
more easily dealt with, as the criteria for the assignment of words
to word classes (6.2) are in general clear-cut and lead to deter-
minate classifications. Multiple entry often is the simplest
solution. Here also one meets quite unconnected homophones
(words pronounced alike): *bear* (the animal), *bear* (endure);
pairs with some semantic connections; *stomach* (part of the
body), *stomach* (put up with); and pairs very close in semantic
function: *paint* (the material), *paint* (cover with paint, or depict
with paint).[21]

2.4 The structural treatment of lexical meaning

2.4.1 Lexical interrelations
Mention has already been made of the necessary diffuseness of
the analysis and description of meanings (1.4). Attempts have
been made to impose a formalism on semantics nearer to that
which is characteristic of grammar and phonology by restricting
its scope to observed and quantifiable data. The interpretation
of meaning of linguistics as equivalent to the distribution of the
items concerned (words, etc) in relation to other items in
sentences is an example of this. Such an approach to semantics
simply fails to 'save the phenomena' if *meaning* in linguistics is
to bear a proper relationship to the normal usage of the term.[22]

However, distributional semantics, while inadequate by itself,
does bring to notice the significant fact that part of the total
meaning of many words in all languages is to be determined by
their individual relations with other words, in both the basic
dimensions of linguistic analysis, syntagmatic and paradigmatic.
The syntagmatic relations between words as lexical items have
been studied under the title of *collocation*, and the paradigmatic
relations are considered in the theories of the *linguistic field*.

2.4.2 Collocation
By **collocation** is meant the habitual association of a word in a
language with other particular words in sentences. Collocation is

distinct from syntax in that one is concerned in collocation with each word as an individual lexical item in the company of other words as individual lexical items, and not, as in syntax, part of the grammatical level of analysis, with words as members of classes in relation to other words also as members of classes. Speakers become accustomed to the collocations of words and the mutual expectancies that hold between them in utterances irrespective of their grammatical relations as members of word classes or as 'parts of speech' (6.1, 6.2, 6.3). A rather obvious example is given by Firth, who made use of the term as part of the technical terminology of linguistics: *dark* collocates with *night*, and vice versa. 'One of the meanings of *night* is its collocability with *dark*, and of *dark*, of course, collocation with *night*.' This statement does not, of course, exclude word groups like *bright night, dark day*, but just because of the less usual concomitance of such pairs, they stand out as marked, more prominent in an utterance in which they occur than do *dark night* and *bright day*. Collocations such as these are manifestly related to the referential and situational meaning of the words concerned, but collocation and situational meaning are different parts of the total statement of the use of words. In some other cases collocations are habitual but less closely connected with extralinguistic reference. *White coffee, white wine, white race* all have a range of situational reference, but apart from the collocation of the particular second words in each pair the word *white* would not, in most utterances, be used with reference to the colours of the referents. Similar collocations in English involving colour words, but further removed from reference to actual colour surfaces, are *green with jealousy, red revolution, purple passage*. Some words in languages have, at least in certain styles, very limited uses almost wholly circumscribable in their collocations. The word *maiden*, for example, in modern spoken English, is scarcely ever used as a synonym for *girl*, but principally occurs in collocation with a limited set of other words such as *voyage, speech, over* (in cricket), *aunt, lady* (English speakers can readily supply the others).

Conversely, words like *the, a, if, when*, and so on, are hardly subject to any collocational restrictions, and are found in almost any lexical company in the language that the grammar permits. For such words collocation is not a relevant part of the statement of their use; but with others (the majority) it is possible to set up collocational ranges of words with which given words will be found associated in their various grammatical constructions. The conjunction of two or more words quite outside the range of collocation and unprepared by any explanation, is likely to be incomprehensible or downright nonsensical, although its grammatical composition may be unexceptionable. A now famous example of such a grammatical but nonsensical sentence is: *Colourless green ideas sleep furiously*.

Collocational ranges are unlike grammatical classes in that they are peculiar to each word, and almost certainly no two words in a language share exactly the same range and frequency occurrence within a range, whereas grammatical classes may each contain many different words as members. Moreover collocations are far more personally variable among speakers of a single dialect within a language than are grammatical classes; borderline cases there are in grammar, where speakers may differ, or be uncertain, as to whether a particular word form or word sequence is grammatically acceptable; but these are very few compared to the personal differences in collocational use and acceptance.

Sometimes different styles, types of utterance appropriate to specific types of situation are characterized by different collocations (consider the differences between *He's a proper rascal* and *that is a very proper observation*, and between *we've had a nice time today* and *we have a nice point to decide*).

In some uses of language precision for particular purposes is obtained by deliberately excluding certain collocations. Some philosophers (John Locke, for example) would hold that in the context of philosophical discourse *free* does not collocate with *will* ('it is as insignificant to ask whether man's will be free, as to ask whether his sleep be swift, or his virtue square').

It obviously does in everyday speech (*he did it of his own free will*, etc); but it is said that if this collocation is used and understood in the same way as *free* in other collocations, such as *free agent, free man*, and so on, one will be misled in argumentation. Philosophers have been much concerned in recent years over the dangers inherent in what they designate as 'systematically misleading expressions'.

The justification of these philosophical views and their further implications lie outside the sphere of the linguist's jurisdiction; but they are examples of the deliberate restriction of collocation in a particular context of situation.

Special cases of collocations are what are called idioms and clichés. *Idiom* is used to refer to habitual collocations of more than one word, that tend to be used together, with a semantic function not readily deducible from the other uses of the component words apart from each other (*eg* English *she went for him hammer and tongs, they ran off hell for leather*). Knowledge of such individual features of a language, acquired by long experience, but unnecessary for ordinary intercourse, usually comes at the end of one's learning of a foreign language; hence a complete or near-complete mastery of one is often said to be 'idiomatic'. Some idioms preserve in use words that have otherwise become obsolete (*eg* English *to and fro, waifs and strays, kith and kin*).

When a collocation has become almost universal in a particular style, the contribution of some of its words comes to be nugatory, and as a result it often appears irritating and inelegant to listeners or readers who do not relish (as some seem to) that mode of discourse (for example the house agent's *desirable residence* (residence), the stump-orator's *in this day and age* (now), the politician's *let me say just one thing* (listen to me); the reader will be painfully able to multiply the examples from his own experience).[23]

2.4.3 Semantic field theory

In the theory (or theories, as the basic conception has been developed in different ways) of the **linguistic field**, or the field theory of meaning, we are concerned to show that the lexical content of a language, its total vocabulary, or such of it as is available to a speaker at any time, is best treated not as a mere conglomeration or aggregation of independent items, and that word meanings cannot be understood or adequately described as if it were. The meaning of a word depends, not just on its reference, or on any other aspect of its meaning considered simply as the individual property of the word in isolation from all other words in the language. In part the meaning and use of most words are governed by the presence in the language or availability to a speaker of other words whose semantic functions are related in one or more ways to the same area of situational environment or culture.

It was observed above (1.4.2) that the use of many words presupposes the imposition of order and stability on the sequences of sensory experience, and that the employment of certain words rests on a high degree of such abstract ordering. It appears that certain features of this sort of ordering are universal, or at least very general, and this is the basis of the translatability of the utterances of one language into those of another; but other features are peculiar to particular cultural traditions of particular areas, with the consequence that the translation of words and sentences relating to such features requires more explanation and circumlocution. In no case is the lexical content of a language equivalent to a nomenclature, the labelling with separate words of independently existing entities.[24] Nomenclature is possible when linguistic labels are secondarily put to entities already distinguished as a class by the lexicon of a language, as in the cases of the naming of individual houses in a street, or streets in a town, or of rooms in a mansion. 'The world as we know it' is in part the product both of our culture and of the lexical system of our own language.[25]

In a language each word with a reference to the external world bears the meaning it does, functions as it does in sentences, in that it relates to a part of the world in some way differently from all other words. Every such word is, therefore, determined in its meaning by the presence of other words in the vocabulary of the language related to the same or to associated ranges of phenomena, and its meaning is liable to be further determined or altered both by the appearance of other words in a speaker's available vocabulary or by changes in the meanings of associated words.

By the nature of things as they are perceived by all men, and by the nature of certain specific aspects of different cultures, some words are more tightly bound in systems than others, and the semantic fields involved are more readily separated. Colour terms, which notoriously do not correspond from one language to another, are an obvious example of naturally delimited fields. Every language has a range of words that divide up the potentially almost unlimited range of colour differences in visible phenomena. It is probable that children learn the principle colour words fairly closely together in time (*eg* in English, *red, green, blue, yellow, white, black*; the fact that green is not a primary colour and that white and black are not colours in the sense that the others are is not relevant here). Certainly one only knows the meaning of *red* as a colour word (knows how to use it in sentences) when one knows also the colour words bordering on it in various directions (*pink, purple, orange, brown*, etc) and the principal words for colours comprised within the class designated by *red* (*eg: vermilion, scarlet, rose*).

Colour constitutes a naturally separate field of reference, or semantic field, for which every language may be expected to provide sets of lexical terms in which the meaning of each is determined by the co-presence of the others in a speaker's vocabulary. It is well known that languages do not correspond in their most used colour vocabulary. Welsh *gwyrdd, glas*, and *llwyd* roughly cover the same colour range as English *green, blue grey*, and *brown*, but do not have the same approximate boundaries.

The same surfaces designated *green*, *blue*, and *grey* in English might all be called *glas* in Welsh. Likewise in Japanese the adjective *aoi* refers to much of the range of colour distinguished in English by *blue* and *green*.[26]

Military ranks and ranks in any strictly hierarchical organization of people in relationships of seniority, command, and subordination are examples of a culturally produced field that is closely delimited and ordered. Part of the meaning of any military rank word (*major, captain, corporal*, etc) is the product of the whole system of such terms in the relevant part of the language and of exact place of each in relation to the others. These factors may be decisive in the translation of words referring to ranks in armed services and the like from one language to another.

In a very practical context of situation, the selection and grading of hotels, the word *good* has a very different meaning when used non-technically (in the field of *bad, indifferent*, etc) from when it is used, as it is by some travel agents, in a strictly limited system of comparative gradings as the lowest in the field of *first class, luxurious, superior, good*.

An amusing tale involving the wrong choice from lexical field is told of the pre-1914 German army. A raw recruit was unwise enough to enquire of his sergeant the time of the evening meal, using the verb *speisen*, to dine, with which at least two other verbs are associated, *essen*, to eat, and *fressen*, to feed (used primarily of animals). He received the reply: 'Die Offiziere speisen, ich esse, du frisst'.

Part of the power and flexibility of language lies in the ability of speakers to multiply their vocabulary in any given field in the interests of greater precision and clarity. It follows that the more words there are closely associated in meaning the more specific each one's meaning may be in the particular field (irrespective of its uses in other fields). As an organization becomes more complex and its members more numerous, new ranks and grades appropriately named may be devised, restricting the holders to an exact place in the hierarchy. Occupations whose operations involve much colour discrimination (paint manufacture, textile manufacture, etc) develop an extensive technical vocabulary, partly from existing colour words, partly by adding new and specialized meanings to words having reference to coloured things (*eg: magnolia, cream*), partly by adapting other words and phrases to give them a definite place in the technical field to colour terms (*summer blue, mistletoe green*, etc). Such technical vocabularies may sometimes employ numbers of words unknown to non-technical speakers of the language and devise meanings for others quite different from those they bear outside these specialized contexts.

The supreme example of this infinite flexibility is in the use of numerical terms with reference to measurable features of the world. Between any two adjacent number terms another may be added for greater precision; between *eleven* and *twelve* may be put *eleven and a half*, and between *eleven* and *eleven and a half* may be put *eleven and a quarter*, and so on indefinitely.

The choice of an appropriate level of degree of exactitude depends almost wholly on the context. When precise timing or precise temperature specification is required, as, for example, in railway timetabling and chemical experimentation, figures such as 15.59 hours or 87.6 degrees Celsius are appropriate; in giving the time of a dinner party or the outside temperature of a district, figures such as 7.30 and 15 degrees would be normal, further specification sounding deviantly pedantic. Where anything like exact figures would be not only irrelevant but actually unobtainable, the broadest of bands is used, as in dating the final ice age as enduring from (about) 75,000 to (about) 10,000 ago. In fact almost every utterance underspecifies the situation or state of affairs that it reports or to which it refers; to attempt anything like a total specification would lead to an intolerable prolixity, even if it were possible. The necessary and relevant information is taken in by the hearer or reader from what is said or written, together with what has been said or written before, with shared knowledge, and with what is relevant in the context itself. Failures (misunderstandings, etc) do, of course, occur; this is the necessary price of economy and therefore of overall efficiency of communication (*cp* 1.4.4).

It is apparent from the investigation of collocations and semantic field associations in their relations with the full description and analysis of the meanings of words, that syntagmatic and paradigmatic relations are nearly as important in dealing with the lexicon of a language as they are at the levels of grammar and phonology. Internal relations of elements within complex wholes are of the essence of language. 'Un système où tout se tient', one all-embracing system, was the characterization of language by the French linguist Meillet. This emphasizes one of the most fundamental features of language and of the treatment of language in modern linguistics. But it might be more appropriate to think not so much of one overall system, as of many interlocking and interdependent structure and systems at all levels, the functions of every linguistic element and abstraction being dependent on its relative places therein.[27]

Bibliography for Chapter 2

1 R. BARTSCH, *Norms of language*, London, 1987.
2 L. BLOOMFIELD, *Language*, London, 1935.
3 R. P. BOTHA, *The place of the dictionary in transformational generative theory*, The Hague, 1968.
4 G. L. BROOK, *English dialects*, London, 1963.
5 C. D. BUCK, *Introduction to the study of the Greek dialects*, Boston, 1928.
6 N. CHOMSKY, *Syntactic structures*, The Hague, 1957.
7 'Some methodological remarks on generative grammar', *Word* 17 (1961), 219–239.
8 *Aspects of the theory of syntax*, Cambridge, Mass, 1965.
9 E. DAUZAT, *La géographie linguistique, Paris*, 1922.
10 J. R. FIRTH, *Speech*, London, 1930.
11 'Personality and language in society', *Sociol rev* 42 (1950), 37–52.
12 'Modes of meaning', *Essays and studies*, 1951, 118–49.
13 'Synopsis of linguistic theory 1930–55', *Studies in linguistic analysis*, special publication of the Philological Society, Oxford, 1957, 1–32.
14 W. N. FRANCIS, *Dialectology*, London, 1983.
15 Z. S. HARRIS, *Methods in structural linguistics*, Chicago, 1951.
16 S. I. HAYAKAWA, *Language in thought and action*, London, 1952.
17 H. HICKERSON, and others, 'Testing procedures', *IJAL*, 18 (1952), 1–8.
18 J. HJELMSLEV, *Prolegomena to a theory of language*, trans F. J. Whitfield, Baltimore, 1953.
19 C. F HOCKETT, *A course in modern linguistics*, New York, 1958.
20 H. M. HOENIGSWALD, *Language change and linguistic reconstruction*, Chicago, 1960.
21 F. W. HOUSEHOLDER and S. SAPORTA (eds), 'Problems in lexicography', *IJAL* 28 (1962), No 2, Part 4.
22 I. IORDAN, *Introduction to Romance linguistics*, trans J. Orr, London, 1937 (revised by R. Posner, Oxford, 1970).
23 K. JABERG, *Sprachgeographie*, Aarau, 1908.
24 M. JOOS (ed), *Readings in linguistics*, Washington, 1957.
25 R. E. KELLER, *The German dialects*, Manchester, 1961.
26 W. LABOV, 'The social motivation for a sound change', *Word* 9 (1963), 273–309.
27 *The social stratification of English in New York City*, Washington, 1966.
28 A. LEHRER, *Semantic fields and lexical structure*, Amsterdam, 1974.
29 J. LYONS, *Semantics*, Cambridge, 1977.
30 R. I MCDAVID, 'The dialects of American English', Chapter 9 of W. N. Francis (ed), *The structure of American English*, New York, 1958.
31 A. MCINTOSH, *An introduction to a survey of the Scottish dialects*, Edinburgh, 1952.
32 A. MEILLET, *Aperçu d'une histoire de la langue grecque*, third edition, Paris, 1930.
33 *La méthode comparative en linguistique historique*, Oslo, 1925.

34 B. NEWTON, *The generative interpretation of dialect: a study of modern Greek phonology*, Cambridge, 1972.

35 E. A. NIDA, 'The analysis of meaning and dictionary-making', *IJAL* 24 (1958), 279–292.

36 S. OHMAN, 'Theories of the "linguistic field"', *Word* 9 (1953), 123–34.

37 H. ORTON. S. SANDERSON, J. WIDDOWSON, *The linguistic atlas of England*, London, 1978.

38 L. R. PALMER, *Descriptive and comparative linguistics: a critical introduction*, London, 1972.

39 P. PASSY, *Petite phonétique comparée*, third edition, Paris, 1922.

40 M. PLATNAUER, 'Greek colour-perception', *Classical quarterly* 15 (1921), 153–62.

41 E. SAPIR, 'The status of linguistics as a science', *Lang* 5 (1929), 207–14.

42 F. DE SAUSSURE, *Cours de linguistique générale*, fourth edition, Paris, 1949.

43 E. SIVERTSEN, *Cockney phonology*, Oslo, 1960.

44 N. C. W. SPENCE, 'Linguistic fields, conceptual systems, and the Weltbild', *TPS* 1961, 87–106.

45 D. SPERBER and D. WILSON, *Relevance: communication and cognition*, Oxford, 1986.

46 H. SWEET, *Collected papers*, Oxford, 1913.

47 P. TRUDGILL, *The social differentiation of English in Norwich*, Cambridge, 1974.

48 W. F. TWADDELL, *On defining the phoneme*, Language Monograph 16, 1935.

49 S. ULLMANN, *The principles of semantics*, second edition, Glasgow and Oxford, 1957.

50 C. F. VOEGELIN and Z. S HARRIS, 'Methods of determining intelligibility among dialects of natural languages', *Proc of the American Philosophical Society* 95 (1951), 322–9.

51 I. C. WARD, *The phonetics of English, Cambridge*, 1948.

52 J. C. WELLS, *Accents of English*, Cambridge, 1982.

53 J. WRIGHT, *A grammar of the dialect of Windhill in the West Riding of Yorkshire*, English Dialect Society, London, 1892.

54 *The English dialect grammar*, Oxford, 1905.

Notes to Chapter 2

1 For a general discussion on the status of linguistic abstractions see Twaddell, 48 (also in 24, 55–80, where see comments by Joos).

　　The realist and nominalist points of view were nicknamed 'God's truth' and 'hocus-pocus' respectively by F. Householder (*IJAL* 18 (1952), 260–8), and have since then been discussed under these titles. Firth took up a strongly non-realist 'hocus-pocus' line (11, 42). Chomsky and most transformational-generative linguists maintain the second position, requiring that the linguist's statements reflect in some degree the intuitions of the native speaker, and that the linguist's abstractions have some measure of psychological reality (see further 7.2). Recently a version of the realist view has been put forward and strongly defended by J. J. Katz, *Language and other abstract objects*, Oxford, 1981.

2 *Langue* and *parole*, de Saussure 42, 23–39. For the relations between the Saussurean *langue* and transformational-generative *competence*, see Chomsky, 8, 4.

3 On exponency and renewal of connection, Firth, 13, 15–17.

4 The unimportance of the actual phonetic exponents of phonological elements was maintained by de Saussure, among others (42, 166); *cp* Hjelmslev, 18, 50.

De Saussure is generally regarded as the main founder of the concept of structure in modern linguistics. In this he was in the company of other contemporaries in the early twentieth century, who were rethinking their disciplines on structural lines (M. Lane (ed), *Structuralism: a reader*, London, 1970; D. Robey (ed), *Structuralism: an introduction*, Oxford, 1973; J. Culler, *De Saussure* London, 1976).

5 The terms *syntagmatic* and *paradigmatic* go back to de Saussure (42, Part 2, Chapter 5), though he actually used the term *associative* (*associatif*) instead of *paradigmatic*. The latter term, whose use in this Saussurean distinction is now general, was first suggested by Hjelmslev (*Acts of the fourth international congress of linguists*, 1936, 140–51).

6 On the distinction of *structure* and *system*, Firth, 13, 17.

7 On 'slow colloquial' as the accepted basis of the linguistic analysis of spoken language, Passy, 39, 4.

8 In connection with linguistic taboos, it is amusing to notice that among some *soi-disant* 'progressive' circles of people who pride themselves on their freedom from the 'irrational' taboos of obscenity and blasphemy, by which others in their community feel bound, the serious discussion of moral issues in specifically moral terms arouses very similar reactions, discomfort, embarrassment, and contempt, unless they fall within the scope of some current fad. Taboo restrictions, though doubtless an irrational feature of linguistic behaviour are more pervasive than some like to think. On taboo restrictions in other communities A. L. Kroeber, *Handbook of the Indians of California*, Washington, 1925, 48; T. Sophen (ed), *Languages and their speakers*, Cambridge, Mass, 1979, 209–39; R. M. W. Dixon, *The languages of Australia*, Cambridge, 1980, 23–9.

9 On dialects as the sum of their characteristics, Palmer, 38, 276.

10 On the 'Benrath line', see further Bloomfield, 2, 343–4. It should be borne in mind that this map and Bloomfield's comments on it were based on the population of the area prior to the upheaval that followed the end of the war in 1945.

11 On the relative delocalization of standard dialects, Firth, 10, Chapter 8.

12 Many detailed descriptions of non-standard English dialects have been made, *eg* Wright 53 and 54, and recently Sivertsen, 43. A

comprehensive account of the phonetic differences between dialects of English over the whole English-speaking world may be found in Wells, 52.

On the relations between standard and non-standard dialects in English, see further I. C. Ward, 51, Chapter 1; A. C. Gimson, *An introduction to the pronunciation of English*, London, 1970, 83–9. On prestige dialects and languages in general, H. Kahane, 'A typology of the prestige language', *Lang* 62 (1986), 495–508.

One may observe that the non-standard dialectal use of *hisself* is more 'systematic' (*cp: myself, yourself*) than the standard use of *himself*.

A possible exception of the statement that every dialect is equally capable of precise description may be found in the special standards of 'correctness' laid down in some countries with reference to the speech approved for educated persons by such bodies as the French Academy, which attempts to prescribe the semantic and grammatical use of some words within strict limits; but these prescriptive rules are by no means always followed by speakers generally recognized as speakers of the standard dialect of the language. More generally on linguistic norms, Bartsch, 1.

13 On quantifying mutual intelligibility, Voegelin and Harris, 50; Hickerson and others, 17; E. H. Casad, *Dialect intelligibility testing*, Norman, Oklahoma, 1974.

14 On the French–Italian dialect chain, Hockett, 19, 324.

15 The significance of regional dialects as markers of social cohesion and local loyalty is well brought out in Labov's study (26) of the inhabitants of Martha's Vineyard, an island off the coast of Massachusetts. He found that, largely irrespective of age and income level, specifically local features predominated in the speech of those most attached emotionally to the island, as compared with those who felt no such local attachment.

16 On the terms *esprit de clocher* and *force d'intercourse*, de Saussure, 42, Part 4, Chapter 4; limited world of the mediaeval peasant, J. A. Williamson, *The evolution of England*, Oxford, 1931, 86; spread of urban features, Palmer, 38, Chapter 12.

17 New York, Labov, 27; Norwich, Trudgill, 47.

18 On the relevance of dialect study to comparative and historical linguistics, Meillet, 33, Chapters 5 and 6. On dialect study in general linguistics, Bloomfield, 2, Chapter 19; Hockett, 19, Chapters 38 and 39; Palmer 38, Chapter 12.

The course of dialect history is well illustrated in the Greek language. By the time at which written records are available, Ancient Greek was split into a number of major dialect divisions. North-west Greek, Doric, Attic-Ionic, Aeolic, and Arcadocyprian, themselves subdivided into smaller dialects. This dialect fragmentation was due to the different periods of the settlement of the classical Greek world by Greek speakers, and to the mountainous terrain and the numerous islands of the area. Classical Greek literature, other than the Homeric poems, was mostly written in Attic, the dialect of Athens, which spread during the Hellenistic and Roman periods over much of the rest of Greece and Asia Minor as the language of administration and general intercourse. In the course of this spead it suffered considerable changes; New Testament Greek is an example of this resultant κοινή, /koiné:/, as it came to be called (κοινή διάλεκτος /koinè: diálektos/ common dialect). Modern Greek dialects are for the most part the result of the Byzantine and post-Byzantine fragmentation of this κοινή, not survivors of other ancient dialects, which largely disappeared during these years. But Tsaconian, spoken today in part of the Morea (Pelopennese), is said to preserve features of the old Laconian dialect of Sparta. See further Meillet, 32, Buck 5. For a treatment, of modern Greek dialects on transformational-generative lines, see Newton, 34.

A considerable amount of specialist literature has been devoted to the study of dialects. A good short introduction to the study as a whole may be found in Francis, 14. The following books may also be noticed: Jaberg, 23; Dauzat, 9; McIntosh, 31; McDavid, 30; Keller, 25; Brook, 4; H. Orton *et al*, 37.

A special aspect of dialect study is known as *Wörter und Sachen* (words and things). This involves the detailed study in different dialects of the forms of words relating to material objects and processes of all kinds found in the dialect localities, and of the forms of the objects and processes themselves (plants, agricultural implements, etc), together with general ethnographical investigations of the areas. This study was instituted formally by R. Meringer and H. Schuchardt around the turn of the present century, largely centring on Romance dialectology.

In 1909 a journal *Wörter und Sachen* was started; it has now ceased publication, and the specific *Wörter und Sachen* studies, though still undertaken, have somewhat receded in attention with the development of modern structural linguistics, although these two aspects of linguistic study, as far as dialectology is concerned, would not appear to be antagonistic. See further Iordan, 22, 62–74; Y. Malkiel, review of J. G. H. de Carvalho, *Coisas e palavras* Lang 33 (1957), 54–76.

19 On the individual nature of dictionary information, as against the general information given in grammar and phonology, Bloomfield, 2, 274; *cp* Sweet, 46, 31.

On the methods and purposes of the dictionary-writer, *cp* Hayakawa, 16, 56: 'The way in which the dictionary-writer arrives at his definitions is merely the systematization of the way in which we all learn the meanings of words beginning at infancy and continuing for the rest of our lives.'

20 On metaphor, Bloomfield, 2, 149; Sperber and Wilson, 45, 231–7; on a possible source of some semantic changes, including the development of metaphors, J. M. Williams, 'Synaesthetic adjectives: a possible law of semantic change', *Lang* 52 (1976), 461–78.

21 On the theory and practice of lexicography (dictionary-making),

Nida, 35; Householder and Saporta, 21; R. W. Burchfield (ed), *Studies in lexicography*, Oxford, 1987.

The reader should consider just what information he would wish to find in a comprehensive dictionary entry for a particular word in a language in which he is interested, and how that information could best be set out. He should then turn to a recognized dictionary (*eg* the large *Oxford English Dictionary*), and see how far he is satisfied with what is there given.

22 On meaning as distribution, Harris, 15, 7, note 4; 'Distributional structure', *Word* 10 (1954), 146–62; Hoenigswald, 20, 16. Criticism in R. B. Lees, review of N. Chomsky, Syntactic Structures *Lang* 33 (1957), 394–5.

23 On collocation, Firth; 12; 13, 11–13. For a somewhat similar notion of 'attachment', C. E. Bazell, *Linguistic form*, Istanbul, 1953, 36–7. On collocational ranges, A. McIntosh, 'Patterns and ranges', *Lang* 37 (1961), 325–37.

Colourless green ideas sleep furiously appears in Chomsky, 6, 15.

In further examination of the deviance of unacceptable sentences it has been seen that the boundary between rule of grammar and lexical or collocational features is by no means clearcut. On this, within the context of transformational-generative theory, Chomsky, 7 and 8, 148–60.

John Locke, *Essay concerning human understanding*, ed A.S. Pringle-Pattison, Oxford, 1934, 140.

On 'systematically misleading expressions', A. Flew (ed), *Logic and language*, Oxford, 1951, 11–36.

On idiom, Hockett, 19, 171–3.

Further examination of lexical meaning, in an attempt to make explicit part of the knowledge a speaker has of the lexicon of his language, C. F. Fillmore, 'Lexical entries for verbs', *Foundations of language* 4 (1968), 373–93.

24 Language not a nomenclature, de Saussure, 42, 34, 97.

25 This is part of what has come to be known as the 'Whorf hypothesis' (Chapter 6, note 47, below; *cp* Sapir, 41).

26 Colour words in Welsh and English, Hjelmslev, 18, 33; *cp* Platnauer, 40; E. H. Lenneberg and J. M. Roberts, *The language of experience* supplement to *IJAL* 22 (1956), Part 2.

The germ of the field theory of meaning is to be found in de Saussure's 'associative relations' (42, 173–5). For a brief account and further references, see Ullmann, 49, 152–70; Öhman, 36; Spence, 44; Lyons, 29, 250–69; Lehrer, 28.

27 A. Meillet, *Linguistique historique et linguistique générale*, Paris. 1948, 16.

Chapter 3

Phonetics

3.1 Articulatory phonetics

3.1.1 The spoken foundation of language

Language makes contact with the world outside language on two sides, in the physical medium employed in communication from person to person, and in its interaction with the world at large.

The only universal medium of linguistic communication among all normal human beings (*ie* excluding the deaf and dumb, some congenital idiots, etc) is speech, and the scientific study of speech is known as **phonetics**.

We must assume a period of many thousands of years when speech was the exclusive manifestation of language, before the development of writing systems at the dawn of recorded history, perhaps some 5,000 years ago. In many communities today languages are spoken for which no system of writing has been devised, and whose speakers are illiterate (or, as it is optimistically put in the context of educational developments the world over, preliterate, with the consequential use of the term *preliterate language* to refer to the languages of such peoples). It may be observed (*cp: pp* 15–16) that, contrary to a widespread assumption, the languages of such totally illiterate communities do not differ in any significant way as regards their speech sounds from the languages of peoples long literate and well known as the foci of world civilizations.

Moreover, a moment's reflection shows that in literate communities speaking antedates writing in the acquisition of language by normal children and the output of spoken language, speech, far exceeds the output of written language, books, newspapers, letters, notices, private notes, and the like, on the part

of every member of the community. The same applies still more
to the other media of communication in language such as Morse
code signals, deaf and dumb symbols, and telegraphic codes,
which are all derivatives of written language.

Certainly a full understanding of language as a form of man's
activity requires an understanding of the basis and nature of
human speech.

3.1.2 Primacy of articulatory phonetics

The essence of speech is that one human being, by movements
beginning at his diaphragm and involving various parts of his
chest, throat, mouth, and nasal passages, creates disturbances in
the air around him, which within a limited distance from him
have a perceptible effect on the ear-drums and through them on
the brains of other people, and that the hearers can, if they
belong to the same language community, respond to these
disturbances, or noises, and find them meaningful.

Speech can therefore be studied in phonetics from three points
of view.

[i] It can be studied primarily as the activity of the speaker in
terms of the articulatory organs and processes involved; this
is called **articulatory phonetics**.

[ii] It can also be studied with the main attention focused on the
sound waves generated by speaking and their transmission
through the air.

[iii] The perception of these sound waves by the hearer's ears can
be given primary emphasis, both in terms of the physiology
of the ear and associated organs of hearing, and in terms of
the psychology of perception.

These two latter aspects, [ii] and [iii] above, are referred to as
acoustic phonetics and **auditory phonetics**,[1] respectively.

From the point of view of the study of language and as part
of general linguistics (which it is here considered to be), there
are good reasons for prime attention being paid to articulatory
phonetics. The principal parts of the body responsible for the
production and differentiation of speech sounds, the vocal organs
or organs of speech, are fairly easily accessible to visual observation, either directly or by means of various devices such as
laryngoscopes and X-ray photography. Several of them, such as
the lips, teeth, and tongue are familiar to everyone, and almost
all of them can be described as far as concerns the part they play
in speaking by the use of terms not difficult of comprehension
to the non-specialist. The processes of speech are in the speaker's

control to the extent that he can choose to speak or not to speak, and what to say in his language. Moreover, everyone has some kinaesthesis of the processes of speaking, that is to say, an awareness of some of the organs involved and of what they are doing (the widespread use of words like *tongue* in many languages both in the physiological and in the linguistic sense is an obvious illustration of this); and this kinaesthesis can be developed by attention, training, and practice to a considerable extent in most people and to a very marked extent in some.

With this development of the awareness of the processes involved in articulation come the increasing ability to recognize and discriminate different speech sounds not forming part of one's own language ('ear training'), and a practical control over the speech organ not merely as regards speaking one's own or a foreign language, but in the conscious control of particular organs as such in making particular movements productive of speech sounds of definite sorts. These latter skills are part of the equipment and qualification of the phonetician, or linguist who has developed this branch of the subject to a high degree of specialization.

None of the foregoing statements applies to anything like the same extent to the physical and auditory aspects of speech. One is not normally aware of sound waves as one is aware of the movements of the tongue, teeth, and lips; nor are their diffusion and impingement on the ear readily observable visually, without the use and specialized interpretation of appropriate machines. One has virtually no kinaesthesis of hearing (an awareness of the hearing process apart from the hearing of the noise itself); nor has one control of hearing in being able to start and stop as one can start and stop speaking; and the physiology and working of the ear-drum and the bones and membranes of the inner ear associated with it are inaccessible to the naked eye, and much less amenable to observation through the sort of apparatus whose operation and understanding are likely to be available to the general linguist. An array of elaborate, delicate, and expensive apparatus, in phonetics laboratories, is now available for the detailed investigation of the processes studied in articulatory, acoustic, and auditory phonetics. Their specialized use is known as **instrumental** or **experimental phonetics**.

Experimental phonetics falls, very broadly, into two divisions, complementary to each other. On one side, various instruments enable us to gain perceptual access to those parts of the vocal tract not amenable to direct visual or tactile perception. On the other side, machines of different sorts enable us to display the

sound waves of speech in visual forms; this latter is known as
sound spectrography (3.4).

Linguists can and should acquaint themselves with the work
and findings of specialists in acoustic phonetics, in the physics of
sound wave transmission, and in the physiology and psychology
of hearing; and it is proper that some linguists should specialize
in the aspects of these branches of knowledge that concern the
study of language; but for the non-specialist general linguist and
for the student entering on the study of the subject, attention
should first be concentrated on articulatory phonetics, wherein
speech can most readily and profitably be studied.

In the general study of phonetics it is very desirable that a
student, at the same time as he reads about the mechanisms and
processes of speech, should make a practical study of the
phonetics of his own language and of at least one other language.
A great deal of work has been done on the phonetics of English,
and for this and obvious practical reasons the phonetics of
English, whether as one's native language or as a foreign
language, is one of the most useful practical accompaniments of
theoretical phonetics.[2] What is written in this chapter is in no
sense a substitute for such practical study.

3.1.3 The physiological basis of speaking

Speech is in one sense a wonderful by-product of the physiologically necessary process of breathing out, ridding the lungs of
spent air, charged with carbon dioxide. When one considers the
totality of the part played by spoken language in human life, one
may wonder whether any other by-product of waste matter has
been evolved remotely comparable to speech. The great majority
of speech sounds are originally generated by the force of exper-
ation, breath expelled through the mouth or nose from the
lungs. Those initiatory processes other than pulmonic or lung
pressure, which play a restricted part in the languages in which
they are used at all, will be referred to later (*pp* 97–8). Just as
the main material of speech, expiratory breath, is itself part of
the biologically necessary process of breathing, so it may be said
that the organs of speech are themselves not organs or parts of
the body specifically devoted to speech production, but organs
that are used for this purpose among others. Of all the main
organs controlling articulation it would be hard to assert that this
is the exclusive funcion of any one of them, as is obvious from
a consideration of the other uses of the tongue, teeth, lips, and
throat. It has, however, been asserted that man's acquistion of
upright posture, and his adoption and subsequent abandonment

The organs of speech

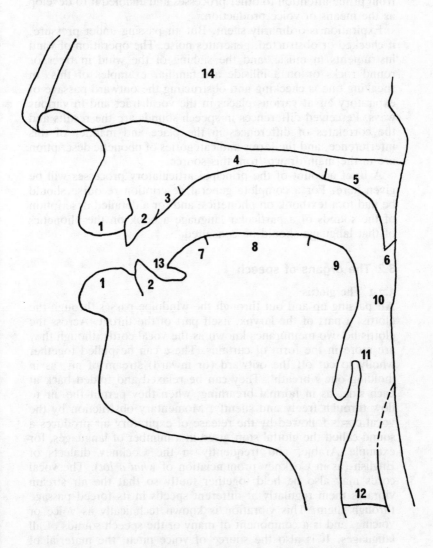

1 Lips	5 Soft palate (Velum)
2 Teeth	6 Uvula
3 Teeth-ridge	7 Blade of tongue
4 Hard palate	8 Front of tongue
	9 Back of tongue

10 Pharynx
11 Epiglottis
12 Position of vocal cords
13 Tip of tongue
14 Nasal cavity

of an arboreal habitat liberated part of the throat mechanism from prime attention to other processes and enabled it to develop as the means of voice production.[3]

Expiration is ordinarily silent. But air passing under pressure, if checked or obstructed, generates noise. The operation of wind instruments in music, and the sighing of the wind in trees or round rocks or on a hillside are familiar examples of this. In speaking one is checking and obstructing the outward passage of expiratory air at various places in the vocal tract and in various ways. Perceived differences in speech sounds are the results and the correlates of differences in the place and manner of this interference, and the terms and categories of phonetic description are in the main drawn from this source.

A brief account of the principal articulatory processes will be given here. For a complete general description recourse should be had to a textbook on phonetics, and for a detailed description of the sounds of a particular language a book on the phonetics of that language should be consulted.[4]

3.2 The organs of speech

3.2.1 The glottis

Air passing up and out through the windpipe passes through the glottis, a part of the larynx, itself part of the throat. Across the glottis lie two membranes known as the vocal cords, though they are more in the form of curtains. These can be pulled together wholly to cut off the outward (or inward) stream of air, as in 'holding one's breath'. They can be relaxed and folded back at each side, as in normal breathing, when they permit the air to flow through freely and silently. Momentary obstruction by the vocal cords followed by the release of expiratory air produces a sound called the glottal stop, used in a number of languages, for example Arabic, and frequently in the Cockney dialects of English (as in Cockney pronunciation of *what a lot*). The vocal cords may also be held together tautly so that the air stream vibrates them regularly at different speeds in its forced passage through them. This vibration is known technically as voice or voicing, and is a component of many of the speech sounds of all languages. It is also the source of voice pitch, the material of intonation (and of singing), and of the pitch phenomena of 'tone languages' (3.5.4). It may be felt externally by lightly touching the front of the larynx or 'Adam's apple' with the finger-tip while humming or saying *Ah*. Its absence is called voicelessness, and several pairs of similarly articulated sounds are distinguished in many languages as voiced and voiceless (*eg* the initial sounds on *van* and *fan*, and the *d*'s of *did* as against the *t*'s of *tit*).

Apart from voicing, the vocal cords may be held fairly close together, so as to interfere with the egressive air by making it push through a restricted aperture. This process plays some part in the type of speech called whispering (in which the glottal vibrations of voicing are not made). The audible passage of air through the glottis is also responsible for the production of *h*-like sounds (as in English *hand, behind*). This is largely caused by increased air pressure from the lungs (hence the *h*-like sounds in panting). In addition to the glottis the rest of the vocal tract is under pressure and so *h*-sounds take on much of the audible qualities of the following vowels, and in languages that permit final /-*h*/, of the preceding vowels.

3.2.2 The supraglottal organs of speech

Above the glottis and the vocal cords, obstruction can be caused principally between a part of the tongue and the upper teeth or part of the roof of the mouth, between the upper front teeth and the lower lip, or between the two lips. The main places involved are the back, front, and blade of the tongue (the extreme front of which is the tip), the uvula, soft palate (velum), hard palate, teeth ridge (alveolus), teeth, and lips.

These places illustrate part of the theory of phonetic categorization. Terms like *teeth, lips, hard palate, soft palate*, and *uvula* designate physiologically distinct parts of the mouth, recognized as such quite apart from any articulatory function they may have, and are terms used in any physiological description of the human body. The tongue, however, as a physiological organ, is a unity; as a structure the blade, front and back are not sharply distinguished (whereas the boundary between the hard (bony) palate and the soft (fleshy) palate may be easily felt with a finger or the tip of the tongue). These divisions in the tongue are imposed by phoneticians to facilitate the description and analysis of different articulations; the relative position of the part of the surface of the tongue in contact or proximity with the other part of the mouth involved in a particular articulatory obstruction is a necessary part of the accurate description of many speech sounds.

The tongue is an extremely mobile organ and is responsible for more varieties of articulation than any other. Broadly speaking five places on the roof or upper surface of the mouth are involved in articulation with some part of the surface of the tongue. Behind and below the soft palate the uvula, a small tab of flesh, hangs down; and in some languages, for example Arabic, but not English, sounds are articulated with closure between this and the extreme back of the tongue. The other positions of obstruction or closure involving the surface of the tongue are the soft palate or velar area (closure here with the back of the tongue produces the initial sounds of English *come* (voicelessness) and *go* (voiced), the hard palate (narrowing of the space between here and the front of the tongue produces the initial sound of English *yet* and *yeast*), the teeth ridge (alveolar ridge), just behind the upper front teeth and in front of the hard palate (closure here with the tip of the tongue produces the initial sounds of the English *tooth* and *den*), and the upper front teeth (partial obstruction between these and the tip of the tongue produces the initial sounds of English *thin* and *then*, and closure produces the French *t* and *d* sounds, which differ in articulation and acoustic effect, among other factors, by this slight difference of the place of closure with the tongue tip).

Apart from the tongue and the area of the roof of the mouth, obstruction or closure can be made between the upper teeth and the lower lip (where the English *f* and *v* sounds are produced, as in *five*), and between the two lips (the articulatory place of English *p* and *b* sounds, as in *pip, bib*).

3.2.3 Nasalization

Any articulation at any place in the mouth may be accompanied by **nasalization**. The soft palate can take up two positions in articulation; when raised it seals off the nasal cavity from the mouth (as in the diagram on *p* 81); when lowered the two cavities are united at the back (this is the position in normal breathing). The articulations just described were illustrated with sounds produced with the soft palate raised. When it it is lowered, part or all of the air passes out through the nose. This is called nasalization, nasality, or nasal articulation; and with nasalization all articulations produce a different sound from that of their non-nasalized counterparts (*ie* articulated with the soft palate raised and the nasal cavity sealed off). Nasalization is what distinguishes English *m* from *b* (*mad, bad*), *n* from *d* (*not, dot*), and the sound represented by *ng* at the end of a word from that represented by *g* (*bung, bug*). These may be designated nasal consonants. Nasal articulation requires a free passage of air through the nose; this is why persons suffering total obstruction of the nostrils with a bad cold cannot readily pronounce /m/, /n/, etc as distinguishably different sounds from /b/, /d/, etc.

3.3 Segmentation: vowel and consonant

3.3.1 Segmentation[5]

Speech sounds are, very broadly, classified in two dimensions, according to the place of articulation (lip, tongue tip, and teeth ridge, etc) and according to the manner of articulation (complete closure, partial closure, and other factors to be described later). It must be realized that speech is a continuous process, broken by pauses, and that in speaking the various movable organs involved are more or less continuously in motion. Speech sounds are not separate and discrete events or actions serially put together to form utterances in the way that the letters of the roman alphabet are serially put together to form printed words. One is, in a literate community, so used to thinking of speech as represented by spelling, which in a sense it is, that care must be taken to avoid considering speech as a kind of audible analogue to using a typewriter. Particularly tiresome is the habit of some older books on languages which refer to the constituents of spoken forms as 'letters'.

It is, however, possible, with the reservations just mentioned, to analyse the continuous process of speaking by reference to various events taking place in time but merging into one another. Many recognized speech sounds, indeed, cannot in the nature of things be articulated all by themselves, but only as part of an utterance including at least one other sound. Letters are discrete entities that can be put together to produce words; speech is a continuum which, for the purpose of description, may be segmented into speech sounds in order to analyse and symbolize the articulatory movements involved in its production. The speech sounds or segments that result from this analysis are abstractions of the nature referred to above (2.1.1).

3.3.2 Vowels and consonants: transcription

Traditionally and familiarly speech sounds are classified as **consonants** and **vowels**, though this division is not always as easy as it looks, and a clearcut definition of *vowel* and *consonant* valid for all languages is very hard to arrive at. Less appropriately letters of the alphabet are distinguished as consonants and vowels according to the type of speech sound most usually represented by them. The vowel–consonant distinction is a convenient point at which to begin in the description and classification of speech sounds, but it must be emphasized that there are several important types of sound and sound features in language that must be described in other terms (3.5).

Two definitions of *vowel* as a general phonetic category may be quoted, with *consonant* in each case being defined as a segmental speech sound other than a vowel: 'Vowels are modifications of the voice-sound that involve no closure, friction, or contact of the tongue or lips' (Bloomfield); 'A vowel is defined as a voiced sound in forming which the air issues in a continuous stream through the pharynx and mouth, there being no obstruction and no narrowing such as would cause audible friction' (Jones; the presence of voicing in the articulation of vowels is not, in fact, essential, as Jones admits with regard to whispered speech, qualifying his definition by reference to 'normal speech'; though not found as essential components of European languages, voiceless vowels do occur in the normal speech of some languages (*eg* Comanche), but they are admittedly rare).[6]

Essentially a distinction is being drawn between short stretches or segments (with the reservations made above) wherein the sound is formed by the shape of the supraglottal cavity as a whole (in addition, in most cases, to voicing from the vibration of the vocal cords) and those wherein in addition to this there is some audible obstruction at a particular point or points within the cavity. Since the difference lies along a scale rather than on either side of a sharp dividing line, and some categories of sound segments share both consonantal and vocalic characteristics, there will inevitably be marginal sound types hard to assign definitely to either category, and an element of arbitrary decision may be necessary in particular cases.

Segmentation and orthographic representation go closely together, and in fact the invention of an alphabet depended on some sort of early analysis of the utterances of particular languages into series of identifiable speech sounds. Different writing systems vary in the degree to which they faithfully represent the actual sound sequences of the words for which they stand. This is discussed elsewhere (4.1). Among languages written in a roman alphabet, English spelling comes quite a long way down in the scale of phonetic clarity (for example, *-ough* represents a different sound sequence in each of the following words: *cough, rough, dough*, and the following three words, all spelled differently, are exact rhymes: *whey, neigh, gay*).

For the purpose of accuracy in phonetic detail, phoneticians have developed systems of **transcription**, using symbols whose only purpose is to indicate on paper precisely the sounds or sound features into which an utterance has been analysed. Such transcriptions whose sole aim is accuracy of phonetic detail are called **narrow** transcriptions, to be distinguished from **broad**, sometimes called reading, transcriptions, which make use of fewer different symbols but rely on some further linguistic analysis; the differences between the two are further discussed in 4.2. While the complete representation of every discriminable sound difference is an unattainable ideal, transcriptions can be more or less narrow according to the amount of detail required. The International Phonetic Association has been responsible for a set of symbols for narrow transcriptions that are widely used in Great Britain, and a table wherein these symbols and modification marks expressing finer shades of phonetic detail has been brought together is known as the International Phonetic Alphabet (IPA); it is revised periodically in the light of progress in phonetic research, the latest edition (1989) being reproduced on *pp* 88–9. Other transcriptional systems are in use, but the differences are not of theoretical importance.

It was said above that, with few exceptions, speech sounds are produced by the audible interference with expiratory breath from the lungs; and in practice the resultant acoustic differences can be accounted for by reference to a limited number of articulatory factors or components. Other than the glottal stop itself (3.2.1), expiratory sounds are all either voiced or voiceless, with intermediate degrees of partial voicing according to whether and to what extent the vocal cords are vibrating during the articulation. This applies equally to h-sounds or aspirates; the glottal friction involved in their production does not preclude some vocal cord vibration characteristic of voicing. Voiced and voiceless *h*- sounds are symbolized [ɦ] and [h], respectively, in the IPA. Except in whispering, voiceless vowel sounds are rare, but their production presents no difficulties.

3.3.3 Vowels
Vowel sounds are differentiated principally by two factors, the position of the tongue in the mouth and the shape of the lips. The tongue may be kept low in the mouth, or raised in varying degrees in the front towards the hard palate or in the back towards the soft palate. These positions give what are called open, front close, and back close vowels, respectively, with as many intervening grades (front half open, etc) as may be required. Different degrees of openness and closeness also involve the extent of the opening between the upper and lower jaws. Open vowels may also be distinguished as front or back according to the part of the tongue that is highest, but the latitude of variation when the tongue is low in the mouth is more restricted. The tongue may also be raised centrally in the mouth,

THE INTERNATIONAL PHONETIC

CONSONANTS

	Bilabial	Labiodental	Dental	Alveolar	Postalveolar	Retroflex	Palatal	Velar
Plosive	p b			t d		ʈ ɖ	c ɟ	k g
Nasal	m	ɱ		n		ɳ	ɲ	ŋ
Trill	ʙ			r				
Tap or Flap				ɾ		ɽ		
Fricative	ɸ β	f v	θ ð	s z	ʃ ʒ	ʂ ʐ	ç ʝ	x ɣ
Lateral fricative				ɬ ɮ				
Approximant		ʋ		ɹ		ɻ	j	ɰ
Lateral approximant				l		ɭ	ʎ	ʟ
Ejective stop	p'			t'		ʈ'	c'	k'
Implosive	ƥ ɓ			ƭ ɗ			ƈ ʄ	ƙ ɠ

Where symbols appear in pairs, the one to the right represents a voiced consonant. Shaded areas deno

DIACRITICS

̥	Voiceless	n̥ d̥	̹	More rounded	ɔ̹	ʷ	Labialized	tʷ dʷ	~	Nasalized
̬	Voiced	s̬ t̬	̜	Less rounded	ɔ̜	ʲ	Palatalized	tʲ dʲ	ⁿ	Nasal release
ʰ	Aspirated	tʰ dʰ	̟	Advanced	u̟	ˠ	Velarized	tˠ dˠ	ˡ	Lateral release
̈	Breathy voiced	b̤ a̤	̠	Retracted	i̠	ˤ	Pharyngealized	tˤ dˤ	˺	No audib release
̰	Creaky voiced	b̰ a̰	̈	Centralized	ë	~	Velarized or pharyngealized	ɫ		
̼	Linguolabial	t̼ d̼	̽	Mid centralized	ě	̝	Raised	e̝ ɹ̝		
̪	Dental	t̪ d̪	̘	Advanced Tongue root	e̘		(ɹ̝ = voiced alveolar fricative)			
̺	Apical	t̺ d̺	̙	Retracted Tongue Root	e̙	̞	Lowered	e̞ β̞		
̻	Laminal	t̻ d̻	˞	Rhoticity	ɚ		(β̞ = voiced bilabial approximant)			
						̩	Syllabic	ɫ̩		Non-syllab

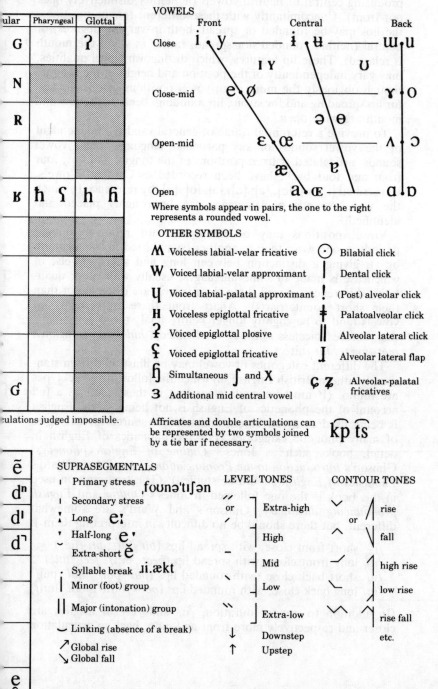

...PHABET (revised to 1989)

	ular	Pharyngeal	Glottal
G			ʔ	
N			
R			
	ʁ	ħ ʕ	ɦ ɦ
Ɠ			

...ulations judged impossible.

VOWELS

Front   Central   Back

Close   i•y ———— ɨ•ʉ ———— ɯ•u

I Y   U

Close-mid   e•ø ———— ɤ•o

ə θ

Open-mid   ɛ•œ ɜ•ɞ ʌ•ɔ

æ ɐ

Open   a•ɶ ———— ɑ•ɒ

Where symbols appear in pairs, the one to the right
represents a rounded vowel.

OTHER SYMBOLS

ʍ	Voiceless labial-velar fricative	⊙	Bilabial click
w	Voiced labial-velar approximant	ǀ	Dental click
ɥ	Voiced labial-palatal approximant	ǃ	(Post) alveolar click
ʜ	Voiceless epiglottal fricative	ǂ	Palatoalveolar click
ʡ	Voiced epiglottal plosive	ǁ	Alveolar lateral click
ʢ	Voiced epiglottal fricative	ɺ	Alveolar lateral flap
ɕ	Simultaneous ʃ and x	ɕ ʑ	Alveolar-palatal fricatives
ɧ	Additional mid central vowel		

Affricates and double articulations can
be represented by two symbols joined
by a tie bar if necessary.

k͡p t͡s

SUPRASEGMENTALS

ˈ	Primary stress	foʊnəˈtɪʃən
ˌ	Secondary stress	
ː	Long	eː
ˑ	Half-long	eˑ
˘	Extra-short	ĕ
.	Syllable break	ɹi.æk
ǀ	Minor (foot) group	
‖	Major (intonation) group	
‿	Linking (absence of a break)	
↗	Global rise	
↘	Global fall	

	LEVEL TONES		CONTOUR TONES
̋ or ́	Extra-high	̌ or ╱	rise
	High	̂	fall
	Mid	᷄	high rise
̀	Low	᷅	low rise
̏	Extra-low		rise fall
↓	Downstep		etc.
↑	Upstep		

ẽ
dⁿ
dˡ
d̚
e̝

producing central or neutral vowels (*ie* neither distinctively back nor front). Concomitantly with these different tongue positions, the lips may be rounded or spread, both in varying degrees, or neutral (neither rounded nor spread, rather as when the mouth is relaxed). These lip features, which distinguish vowel qualities, may vary independently of the position and height of the tongue, though obviously the more open vowel positions give less scope for lip spreading and for strong lip rounding, because the jaw and mouth are wide open.

To provide a referential frame of general validity, independent of the vowel sounds of any particular language, eight vowel sounds, articulated at fixed positions of the tongue and lips, four front and four back, have been recorded as Cardinal Vowels, transcribed [i], [e], [ɛ], [a], [ɑ], [ɔ], [o], [u], by reference to which the vowel sounds of languages can be roughly placed and identified.[7]

Vowel positions may be maintained for relatively longer periods in one word than in another (symbolized in transcription by ː), giving a distinction between **long** and **short** vowels, of which use is made in some languages, usually with other qualitative differences as well (long close vowels are often closer than their short counterparts). Apart from these differences, all vowels tend to be slightly longer before final voiced consonants than before voiceless ones: *eg mad* /mæd/, *hid* /hid/ as against *mat* /mæt/, *hit* /hit/.

The different categories of vowel may be illustrated from standard Southern British English, in which the following vowel types are found. (It must be made clear that in these sections a full account of the phonetics of English is not being given. English is being used as a convenient and familiar source for examples of many phonetic categories. For the phonetics of English in detail, books such as Jones's *Outline of English phonetics*, Gimson's *Introduction to the Pronunciation of English*, or Ward's *Phonetics of English* should be studied). (The transcription used in this book is the one followed in Jones's *Outline* and *English pronouncing dictionary*; Gimson's and Ward's are somewhat different, but there should be no difficulty in interpreting them.):

/i/   short front close, with spread lips (*bit* /bit/; *fin* /fin/)
/iː/ long front close, with spread lips(*beat* /biːt/; *feel* /fiːl/)
/u/   short back close, with rounded lips (*put* /put/; *pull* /pul/)
/uː/ long back close, with rounded lips (*boot* /buːt/; *fool* /fuːl/)

(In addition to greater duration, /iː/ and /uː/ in English are closer and respectively more front and more back in articulation than /i/ and /u/; indeed, the qualitative difference is often as noticeable as the length difference.)

/e/   short front half close, with spread lips (*met* /met/; *tell* /tel/)

/æ/   short front half open, with lips neutral (*man* /mæn/; *hat* /hæt/)

/ɑː/   long back open, with lips neutral (*calm* /kɑːm/; *hard* /hɑːd/)

/ɔ/   short back open, with rounded lips (*cot* /kɔt/; *on* /ɔn/)

/ɔː/   long back open, with rounded lips (*cord* /kɔːd/; *caught* /kɔːt/)

(In the last pair of English vowels, /ɔː/ is less open than /ɔ/.)

/ʌ/   short central half open, with lips neutral (*cut* /kʌt/; *hum* /hʌm/)

/ə/   short central half close, with lips neutral (*sofa* /'soufə/; *upon* /ə'pɔn/)*

/əː/   long central half close, with lips neutral (*herd* /həːd/; *earn* /əːn/)

It will have been noticed that the English front vowels are mostly accompanied by lip-spreading, and the back vowels by lip-rounding. These are certainly the most common combinations, but others are perfectly normal and quite frequently found. French and German have front vowels with lip-rounding, symbolized [y], [ø], and [œ], corresponding to [i], [e], and [ɛ] (*eg* French *tu* /ty/ you (singular); *deux* /dø/ two; *bœuf* /bœf/ ox); and a number of Far Eastern languages have back vowels with spread lips, symbolized [ɯ], and [ɤ] corresponding to [u] and [o].

Long vowels involve the maintaining of an articulatory position relatively constant, but temporally equivalent articulations may be made by moving from one vowel position to another through the intervening positions. These are called **diphthongs**, and English furnishes several examples of them:

/ei/   front half close to close with spread lips (*may* /mei/; *made* /meid/)

/ou/   back half close to close with rounded lips (*hole* /houl/; *go* /gou/)

---

*Customarily but illogically *half close* and *half open* are used distinctively in a system of four terms in English phonetic terminology, *half close* being closer than *half open*. More detailed and therefore more precise descriptions of the English vowels may be seen in the appropriate sections of Jones's *Outline* and Gimson's *Introduction*.

The special phonological status of short /ə/ in English, which necessitates its illustration in words containing more than one vowel, is referred to in 4.3.4.

corresponding with /ei/, fails to indicate the more central starting point of this diphthong, as pointed out by Jones, p. 99; for this reason Gimson transcribes it /əu/)

/ai/ central open with lips neutral to close front with spread lips (*lie* /lai/; *might* /mait/)

/au/ central open with lips neutral to close back with rounded lips (*cow* /kau/; *owl* /aul/)

/ɔi/ back open with rounded lips to front close with spread lips (*boy* /bɔi/; *coil* /kɔil/)

/iə/ front close with spread lips to central half close with lips neutral (*pier* /piə /; *fierce* /fiəs/)

/ɛə/ front half open with spread lips to central half close with lips neutral (*air* /ɛə/; *pared* /pɛəd/)

/uə/ back close with rounded lips to central half close with lips neutral (*poor* /puə/; *gourd* /guəd/)

These last three diphthongs are often called centring diphthongs, from the direction of their movement.

The passage from one vowel position to another may not be by the most direct route; where a detour, as it were, is made, a sequence sometimes called a triphthong results. Examples of these in English are:

/aiə/ central open with lips neutral via front close with spread lips to central half close with lips neutral (*tyre* /'taiə/; *hired* /'haiəd/)

/auə/ central open with lips neutral via back close with rounded lips to central half close with lips neutral (*tower* /' tauə/; *hours* /'auəz/)

/ɔiə/ back open with rounded lips via front close with spread lips to central half close with lips neutral (*coir* /'kɔiə/; *loyal* /'lɔiəl/)

In the articulation of these triphthongal sequences the movement towards the midway position is normally not as marked as in the corresponding diphthongs.

All vowel sounds may be characterized by **retroflexion**, the slight upward turning of the tongue tip toward the centre of the hard palate. Retroflex vowels such as [ɑ˞] and [ə˞] are common in American English and in most south-western dialects of British English in the pronunciation of words spelled with an *r* after a vowel letter (*hard, word*, etc). This retroflexion is one of the characteristics of what is loosely called in Britain 'an American accent'.

All types of vowel sounds may be uttered with **nasalization**, that is with the soft palate lowered and with the air passing partly through the nasal cavity and nostrils as well as through the mouth. Nasalized vowels, as such vowels are called, are not distinctive (4.3.1) in English as they are in some languages, for example, French, but they are often heard from certain speakers. People who use such vowels very noticeably or frequently are said to 'talk through their nose', which is a true though rather careless way of putting it. In French nasalized and non-nasalized vowels are found distinguished by this feature alone (*eg: son* /sɔ̃/, sound; *un* /œ̃/ one), though apparently in all such languages the number of distinctively nasalized vowels is smaller than that of the non-nasalized vowels. In whispered speech voiceless vowels can be nasalized in the same way as voiced vowels.

3.3.4 Consonants
As the vowel sounds in speech can be classified and described by reference to a limited number of articulatory factors, so the **consonant sounds** can be similarly treated, and broadly speaking these are the terms in which the IPA chart is set out. In consonants the two most important components are the place of articulation and the manner of articulation. The glottal stop (symbolized [ʔ]) and the voiced and voiceless aspirates (glottal fricatives) ([ɦ] and [h]) which are in a special class as being glotally articulated, have already been described. At the main supraglottal points of articulation already mentioned (3.2.2), obstruction may be total, producing what is called a **stop** and, when the obstruction is audibly released and the air passes out again, a **plosive**; or the air passage may be restricted in various ways, and for sounds so produced the general term *continuant* may be used. Each may be voiced or voiceless. Continuants wherein the air is forced through a narrow passage in the mouth, so as to cause definite local friction at that point, are called **fricatives**, and continuants may be divided into those articulated with local friction (fricatives) and those without it, the latter including most laterals, nasals, and the so-called semivowels.

Some of these articulations may be illustrated from standard English:

/g/ voiced velar plosive (*get* /get/ ; *gag* /gæg/)
/k/ voiceless velar plosive (*kick* /kik/; *neck* /nek/)
/d/ voiced alveolar plosive (*did* /did/; *hand* /hænd/)
/t/ voiceless alveolar plosive (*tot* /tɔt/; *hate* /heit/)
/b/ voiced bilabial plosive (*bet* /bet/; *bib* /bib/)
/p/ voiceless bilabial plosive (*peck* /pek/; *cup*/kʌp/)

/ð/   voiced dental fricative (*then* /ðen/; *wreathe* /riːð/)
/θ/   voiceless dental fricative (*thin* /θin/; *wreath* /riːθ/)
/v/   voiced labiodental fricative (*vote* /vout/; *thieve* /θiːv/)
/f/   voiced labiodental fricative (*fife* /faif/; *fifth* /fifθ/)

In English and other European languages final consonants involving total stoppage of the egressive air stream are generally released audibly, thus constituting plosives. In some South-east Asian languages, *eg* Thai (Siamese), such final consonants are not audibly released, and are therefore pure stops, not plosives. Such stop articulation of finals is acceptable in English, but it is less common than plosive release; it is, however, normal when another stop consonant follows immediately, as in *apt* /æpt/ and *cocktail* /ˈkɔkteil/. If necessary a symbol such as [pᵒ], [tᵒ], [kᵒ], etc, may be used to indicate unreleased stops.

Velar fricatives are not found in English, but the voiceless velar fricative [x] is the final consonant of the Scots *loch*. The voiced counterpart is symbolized [ɣ]. Both these sounds occur in Dutch.

Uvular plosives, voiced and voiceless, are found in some languages; the voiceless plosive is commoner, occurring, for example in Arabic. Voiced and voiceless palatal plosives, in which the front of the tongue makes closure with the hard palate ([ɟ] and [c], are found in Hungarian and in some other languages.

The distinction between voiced and voiceless consonants is a basic and important one in many languages, but the terms are sometimes used more in the way of labels than as complete designations. Other differentiating factors often accompany voicing and voicelessness, reinforcing their distinctiveness. In particular, voiced consonants are frequently articulated more laxly, *ie* with less breath force and muscular tension then the corresponding voiceless consonants, since, with the same force of expiration, the vibration of the vocal cords in voicing reduces the pressure of air above the glottis and so the force of the supraglottal articulation.

Various processes accompanying obstruction and release produce different types of sound at the articulatory places mentioned above. Closure may be released slowly, with friction resulting from partial obstruction (as in fricatives) audibly intervening before the free passage of air, producing **affricates** (plosive plus fricative). The initial and final consonant sounds of English *church* /tʃəːtʃ/, and *judge* /dʒʌdʒ/, are examples of palato-alveolar affricates.

Release of closure (with or without affrication) may be

followed by a small puff of air (**aspiration**). This is the case with the standard English voiceless plosives in initial position (narrowly symbolized [pʰ], [tʰ], [kʰ]), and distinguishes them from the French voiceless plosives and from those in some northern English dialects, which do not have this aspiration; these latter are called unaspirated voiceless plosives. Voiced plosives can be aspirated, with voiced aspiration intervening, though these are less common. Some languages of India have all four types ([t], [tʰ], [d], [dʰ], etc). In English whispered speech the aspiration of the voiceless plosives is one of the features maintaining the distinction between normally voiced and voiceless consonants (compare the whispered words *pack* and *bag*).

The lateral surface of the tongue instead of being more or less flat may be made slightly convex and cause stoppage in the centre of the roof of the mouth while allowing air to pass at the sides. Consonants so articulated are called **laterals**. Voiced laterals are found in English and French, at the alveolar and dental points of contact respectively, [l] and [l̪]. Voiceless fricative laterals are found in Welsh and some other languages, and a few languages use laterals with velar contact distinctively, but these are rare. Voiced laterals are seldom produced with enough friction to be classed as fricatives, though there are languages employing voiced lateral fricatives.

When the lateral surface of the tongue is made slightly concave, as opposed to convex, release of air is down the centre of the tongue with closure between the sides and the roof of the mouth. English /s/ and /z/, as in *size* /saiz/, are produced in this way (voiceless and voiced), respectively; and so is one pronunciation for English /r/, [ɹ], with the tongue tip a little further back in the mouth and the main part of the tongue kept low as in *red* /red/, *rule* /ruːl/.

There are a number of r-sounds in English, and the letter 'r' stands for a variety of different pronunciations. In standard English /r/ as a consonant only occurs before a vowel, where it is usually an alveolar fricative as described just above in the preceding paragraph; but a flapped or tapped /r/, [ɾ], when the tongue tips lightly and momentarily touches the alveolar ridge, is common between two vowels (as in *merry* /'meri/; *very* /'veri/). In parts of Northumberland a voiced uvular fricative (the 'Durham burr') is heard as a pronunciation of /r/. In standard English 'r' finally or before a consonant letter represents not a consonant at all but usually a long vowel or a centring diphthong (*farm* /faːm/; *near* /niə/). In Scotland /r/ is often pronounced as an alveolar trill, an articulation wherein the tongue tip vibrates

against the teeth ridge; in Scots English, /r/ occurs both pre-
vocalically and postvocalically (*cart*, standard /kaːt/, Scots /kart/).
In Parisian French, /r/ is often pronounced as a uvular trill, with
the uvula vibrating against the back of the tongue in a stream of
air [ʀ]. *r* sounds are generally voiced, but voiceless ones are found
sporadically in many languages and distinctively in some.

In the speech of most speakers of standard English, words
whose orthographic form ends in an -*r* have two pronunciations:
with a final /r/ when followed without any break or pause by a
word beginning with a vowel sound, the /r/ being thus intervocalic, and without the final /r/ in all other positions. Thus in
isolation *fear* is /fiə/ and *war* is /wɔː/, but the phrase *the fear
of war* would be /ðə 'fiər əv 'wɔː/. Many English speakers pronounce a 'linking *r*' where no orthographic *r* is present ((*the*)
idea of (it) /ai'diər əv/, *Hosanna in* (*the highest*) /hou'zænar
in/), but some find this objectionable.

When articulations similar to /s/ and /z/ are made with the
tongue slightly further back in the mouth, the consonants /ʃ/ and
/ʒ/ are produced, palato-alveolar fricatives as against alveolar
fricatives. These are exemplified in English *shine* /ʃain/ (compare
sign /sain/) and *measure* /'meʒə/. Voiceless and voiced affricates
are articulated in this position in English (/tʃ/ and /dʒ/, as in
church /tʃəːtʃ/ and judge /dʒʌdʒ/).

In addition to making contact at various places in the mouth
with its upper surface, the tongue may have its tip curved upward
in the mouth in varying degrees, as in retroflex vowel articulation. This retroflexion is found in a number of languages. Some
Indian languages have a series of markedly retroflex consonants,
[t], [tʰ], [ɖ], [ɖʰ], [ɭ], which are distinct from their dentally
articulated counterparts [t̪], [t̪ʰ], [d̪], [d̪ʰ], [l̪].

The different types of supraglottal consonant articulations can
have a nasal counterpart, when the air is released through the
nasal cavity and the nostrils with the soft palate lowered. In the
case of total mouth obstruction (the nasal counterparts of the
stop consonants) the air passes exclusively through the nose; with
other, partial, obstructions, it passes out through both mouth and
nose, as with the nasalized vowels. Nasal consonants with
complete mouth closure are common in almost all languages, and
may be exemplified by English /m/, /n/, and /ŋ/, the counterparts of /b/, /d/, and /g/ (*mob* /mɔb/; *bomb* /bɔm/; *nod* /nɔd/;
don /dɔn/; *gang* /gæŋ/). /ŋ/ is not found initially in English
words. All nasal consonants are continuants as the egress of air
is never completely cut off; they are commonly voiced, though
voiceless nasal consonants, as in English whispered speech, do

occur; and nasalized fricatives and laterals are found in some languages, but rather rarely.

A rather marginal category of articulation, usually classed with the consonants of a language, is designated **'semivowels'**. In English this category is exemplified in /j/ and /w/, both normally voiced, as in *yet* /jet/ and *wet* /wet/. They are formed in the same manner as the vowels /i/ and /u/, sometimes with a narrower passage between the tongue and the hard palate or between the lips, to cause some slight noise from the local obstruction. In assigning articulatory segments to the category of vowel or semivowel in a particular language, recourse is often made rather to phonological considerations of patterning in relation to other segments than to purely phonetic criteria in the strict sense (4.3.4).

Just as vowels can be long (*ie* longer than other vowels in the same position in an utterance and at the same speed of speaking), so consonants can be long, or geminate, when the closure or obstruction is held momentarily before release. This is found in English words such as *night-time* /'naittaim/ and *solely* /'soulli/; consonant gemination distinguishes the two Italian words *fato* /'fato/ fate, and *fatto* /'fatto/ fact.

Pulmonic or expiratory lung air was mentioned as the principal source of speech in all languages; but certain other initiatory processes are found and need brief treatment. Although a weird but intelligible sort of speech can be made while breathing in instead of breathing out (and may be used by some people when talking very quickly) no language is known to make regular use of this method. But three non-pulmonic types of consonant articulations are used in some languages: ejectives, implosives, and clicks, in this order of commonness of occurrence in languages.

In **ejective** consonants, which are found at all the previously mentioned places of articulation and with all types of obstruction and release, air pressure is created, not by expulsion from the lungs, but by contraction of the space between the closed vocal cords and closure or restriction at some supraglottal point in the mouth, and consequent compression of the air prior to release. Ejective consonants, which are sometimes also called glottalized consonants, are most commonly found with plosive or affricate release, and a series of this type at several places of articulation matching a series of pulmonic consonants is found in Georgian and in a number of languages of the Caucasus as well as elsewhere. The acoustic impression of these sounds on someone in whose language they do not occur is one of sharpness when the glottalic pressure is released. They are usually symbolized with an apostrophe after the letter sign ([p'], [t'], [k'], [tʃ'], etc). Plosives and affricates can also be certiculated with weaker simultaneous glottal closure, not really as ejectives. These are often called glottalized consonants, but this term is also used to cover all consonants articulated with glottal closure, including the ejectives.

Implosion is something of the reverse process, and is found in Swahili and several other African languages, and sporadically elsewhere.[8] Closure is made at one of the supraglottal places already referred to, and a partial vacuum is created by closing the glottis completely or bringing the vocal cords together to vibrate as in voiced articulation and then drawing the glottis downward. When the supraglottal closure is released air flows momentarily inward, giving a different sound from that produced by closure released outwards. Implosive consonants can be voiced or voiceless, but the voiced implosives are much the commoner. In Swahili, implosive and plosive (egressive) voice consonants are found.

Clicks are probably confined as regular components of utterances to certain languages of southern Africa, though sounds of the click type are found elsewhere, and in English the exclamation of distaste (usually spelt *tut-tut*) is in many speakers a sort of click, as is the 'clucking' sound used to urge horses on. Essentially, clicks consist of the creation of a suction between the tongue surface and the roof of the mouth by making closure at two places (bilabial, alveolar, palatal, etc, and velar) at the same time, drawing the centre of the tongue downward and then releasing the partial vacuum. The English click is generally alveolar, but some African languages have a series of such sounds as an integral part, with velar closure combined with closure at one of a number of other places distinctively.

3.4 Acoustic phonetics

For reasons given earlier it was said that articulatory phonetics was the proper object of the initial study of the speaking process in general linguistics. But as the term *sound wave* has been used, a brief account of the physical acoustics of speech may be useful.

Noise of whatever source or origin consists physically of displacements in the air involving rapid increases and decreases of pressure moving outwards from the source and gradually decreasing to vanishing point. Comparison with the waves caused by a stone dropped into a smooth surface of water is often made, though differences in pressures are not involved in liquids in such cases.

The properties that characterize sound waves are:

[i] The amplitude, or the distance from the highest and lowest pressures to the mean; this is the main physical counterpart of the perceived loudness of a sound, the greater the amplitude the louder the sound, other things being equal.

[ii] The frequency, or the number of oscillations between the high and the low points in pressure in a given time, say a second; this is the physical counterpart of pitch, the higher the frequency, the higher in scale the pitch. The ranges of frequencies audible to the human ear lie between 15–20 cycles (complete repetitions of a movement) per second at the lower end and 15,000–20,000 cycles per second at the upper.

[iii] Simplicity or complexity; a simple sound wave consists of oscillations like this:

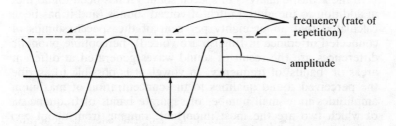

and is generated by a regular source of vibration such as a tuning fork; complex sound waves involve waves of different frequencies superimposed on one another to produce wave forms like:

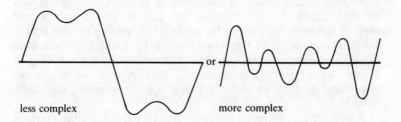

In speech, the vocal cords (when vibrating in voicing), the various places and processes of articulation, and the different shapes of the whole supraglottal cavity in the production of consonant and vowel sounds generate sound waves at different frequencies, which added together constitute the sound waves of speech. These are far more complex than those just illustrated. The supraglottally generated frequencies are often called inherent, in contrast to the glottal frequency which is variable according to the speed of the vibration of the vocal cords and produces the different pitches of voiced speech sounds irrespective of their own specific supraglottal frequencies. This glottal pitch is, of course, only a feature of voiced speech sounds, whereas the inherent frequencies, resulting from the configurations and movements of supraglottal articulation, characterize voiced and voiceless sounds equally. Glottal pitch differences may be illustrated by singing a scale on any sound sequence (*la la la*, etc), or on the conventional *do re mi* syllables. Differences of inherent pitch may be noticed by alternating between hissing and 'hushing' (saying *sh sh*), when the lower inherent note of 'hushing' is heard.

In the acoustic analysis of speech sounds it has been found that in addition to the glottal pitch of voiced sounds (and it has been calculated that about eighty per cent of the speech sounds of connected utterance in English are voiced), perceptible phonetic differences are the result of sound waves generated at different areas or 'bands' of frequency. In vowels it is possible to ascribe the perceived sound qualities to the concentration of maximum amplitudes in a small number of separate bands of frequencies, of which two are the most important, ranging from about 200 cycles per second to about 750 cycles per second and from about 700 cycles per second to about 3,000 cycles per second respectively. These are called **formants**, and the two most important ones are called formant one and formant two. Formant one is controlled articulatorily by the configuration of the vocal tract behind the highest part of the tongue, and formant two is controlled by the shape of the cavity in front of the highest part of the tongue. In this context the part of the tongue raised highest towards the roof of the mouth (depending on the articulatory classification of the vowel) serves to divide the vocal tract into two interconnected cavities, each with its own resonating or sound wave generating capacity. This is one of the most important factors in differentiating speech sounds, especially vowels.

Among the consonants some continuants are also characterized by a fairly clear formant structure, but in others there is a more random distribution of frequencies. In the case of voiceless consonants involving complete stoppage (stops and plosives) especially, experiments have shown that their distinctive qualities are most readily perceived at the points of transition between them and the preceding or following vowels, although they do have their own characteristic frequencies. This is why vowels and continuants are inherently more sonorous than stop consonants. In the even distribution of amplitude over the whole range of audible frequencies no distinctive qualities would be perceived, and we would have what in the technical jargon of acoustics is called 'white noise'.

In the artificial production of speech sounds by mechanical devices, or speech synthesis, as it is called, recognizable vowels and consonants can be produced by generating and combining sound waves at a limited number of different frequencies that have been found essential for each sound. Many other components are involved in the sound waves of actual speech, some of which are not fully understood yet, but the basic and essential nature of the sound waves in the air by which speech is transmitted is now clearly known.[9]

3.5 Plurisegmental features

3.5.1 The continuum of articulation
It was stressed earlier that speech is essentially a continuum of movements by the vocal organs and that the segmentation of it into successive consonants and vowels is an artificial process, though a practical and necessary one in the study and analysis of language. Inevitably the assignment of features to a particular place in the stream of utterance represented by a discrete symbol in the transcription is a distortion of the actual state of affairs, and it is often found in careful analysis and experimentation that the transitions from consonant articulation to the following vowel, and from vowel to the following consonant, are the most important clues to the hearer as to what speech sounds are being uttered.[10] The continuous temporal interpenetration and overlapping of articulation processes must be constantly kept in mind, and certain features of speech that are of great significance in all languages must be referred to sequences of at least one consonant and one vowel segment and often to longer stretches, sometimes from pause to pause, or even to a whole utterance.

The most important features that must be treated as plurisegmental, extending over stretches of various lengths, are stress, pitch, and general voice quality. But certain articulatory processes themselves, though assignable to individual consonant or vowel segments, are often best regarded in this light.

3.5.2 Glottal and supraglottal features

Lip-rounding has already been referred to as a feature of the articulation of some vowels. It is also a feature of certain consonants such as [w] and in some languages of a set of velar plosives with concomitant lip-rounding called labiovelars (symbolized [kʷ], [gʷ], etc). It is often appropriate to regard this lip-rounding as a phonetic feature of a sequence of such a consonant and the following vowel, as it may persist to some degree in the articulation of both segments and characterize them both acoustically, even if, as in English *queen* /kwiːn/, the lips move from a rounded to spread position as the vowel articulation takes place.

Glottalization is a feature that may characterize short stretches. Its production involves a series of irregular total or partial glottal closures like a succession of glottal stops, giving an effect of 'creakiness' to the sounds, as well as signal glottal closures briefly interrupting a vowel articulation or being concomitant with a consonantal obstruction. Ejective consonants are a special case of glottalization, where, in addition to closure, pressure on the air above the closed glottis replaces pulmonic pressure in the consonantal articulation. Such consonants are often followed by vowels in which glottal constriction persists. Non-ejective glottalized plosives, with concomitant glottal and supraglottal closure, are a feature of Cockney English, and, to a certain extent, of the English of some standard speakers; they are distinct from the Cockney use of simple glottal stops in the place of the /p/, /t/, and /k/ in the middle of some words as pronounced in standard English.[11] In some languages continuants may be glottalized, when during the supraglottal articulation the vocal cords are momentarily held together, producing a simultaneous glottal stop. Such sounds may be transcribed [m̰], [n̰], [w̰], [y̰], etc.

The spread of a feature over vowel and consonant segments is found with **retroflexion**, well exemplified in several languages of India, in which the acoustic effect of the upturn of the tip of the tongue is heard in the vowels adjacent to a retroflex consonant. Likewise is **palatalization**, the raising of the front of the tongue towards the hard palate, the position of the articulation of the palatal consonant themselves, may characterize the articulation of other consonants, as an additional feature, together with their adjacent vowels. The effect of this is that front vowels are more front in articulation than the corresponding vowels adjacent to non-palatalized consonants, and other vowels are somewhat fronted. What may be regarded as the opposite process to palatalization is known as **velarization**, in which the back of the tongue is raised, as during the articulation of the velar consonants themselves. A velarized or back /l/ is heard in English in final position (*eg: ill* /il/). In Arabic four velarized consonants contrast with the four non-velarized [s], [z], [t], and [d]; vowels adjacent to such velarized consonants are generally more back in articulatory position than the corresponding vowels in other positions.[12] The alternation of palatalized and non-palatalized (sometimes velarized) consonants, often called 'soft' and 'hard' respectively, together with concomitant differences in the quality of adjacent vowels, plays an important part in a number of languages, for example Russian and Irish.[13]

The acoustic analysis of the sound waves of speech is now a well-developed part of the work of phonetics laboratories, and the tracings or other translations into visual representation of the different components of the waves resulting from different articulatory processes show very clearly how the features mentioned above, and many others, extend over the boundaries (in so far as these are themselves sharply definable) of the successive consonants and vowels to which they are attributed. Indeed, there have just been given only some examples of a principle always to be kept prominently in mind in phonetic analysis.

3.5.3 Stress
Stress and **pitch** differ from the sort of features mentioned in the preceding section, in that they are not related to any particular process of supraglottal articulation. **Stress** is a generic term for the relatively greater force exerted in the articulation of part of an utterance. It is, therefore, an articulatory term, and it is to be distinguished from prominence, a more subjective term relating to the more noticeable acoustic impression conveyed by certain parts of a stretch of speech as against the rest. Stress is often associated with greater loudness, and it may be a component part of prominence, but other factors involved include the inherently greater prominence, or sonority, of certain speech sounds as compared with others (vowels are more prominent than consonants, voiced sounds more prominent than voiceless ones, etc), and the prominence of a pitch level higher or lower than neighbouring pitches (3.5.4).

Two fairly distinct types of stress, as defined above, may be seen in language. As a general and perhaps universal process, the whole or any part of an utterance may be stressed, that is to say uttered more loudly and with more forceful articulation for the purpose of emphasis, so as virtually to compel the hearer to take more notice of it than to the rest. This exploitation of the greater noticeability of strongly stressed utterance is one of the less arbitrary features of speaking as a symbolic activity (*pp* 17–18), comparable to the use of capital letters, boldface type, and the like for similar purposes in printing. Moreover, it admits of an infinite number of gradations in loudness correlatable with different degrees of emphasis in both the intention of the speaker and the effect on the hearer. Separable from this is the use of differences of stress in normal speech as an inherent part of the articulation process of particular languages, but not all languages.

Stress in this latter sense is often accompanied by differences in vowel qualities as between stressed and unstressed segmental sequences. Unlike stress for emphasis, its extent and function in languages differs considerably from one to another, and this aspect is a matter for phonological analysis (4.3.3). One may distinguish fairly readily languages in which stress placement occurs at fixed points between pauses, as in French wherein the final prepausal segments are somewhat stressed, those in which its place is determined in the main by word boundaries (*cp* 5.3.2), such as Hungarian (putting stress at the beginning of words) and Polish, Swahili, and several others (mainly stressing one place before the end of words), and languages like English, in which its position may vary from word to word. Stress falls on a different place in each of the following four words: *solitary* /'sɔlitəri/; *dependency* /di'pendənsi/; *apperception* /æpə'sepʃən/; *carabineer* /kærəbi'niə/. Some pairs of otherwise identical spoken words are distinguished in English by different stress placement (*eg: export* (noun) /'ekspɔːt/, *export* (verb) /eks'pɔːt/, *billow* /'bilou/, *below* /bi'lou/).

In longer English words there may be, and usually are, more than two different degrees of stress, or force of articulation, on different parts; in *apperception* there is more force on /æ/ than on /pə/ or /ʃən/. It is placement of the major or full stress that is discussed and marked here.

The statement of stress occurrence in isolated words, wherein one part must be regarded as bearing full stress, and the stress is therefore left unmarked in words having only one available position, must be distinguished from the statement of stress occurrence in the words of connected discourse. Here, according to the speed of utterance and some other factors, many words are uttered unstressed or with a lesser degree of stress. Thus the phrase quoted above in 3.3.4 would most naturally be stressed in connected speech: /ðə 'fiər əʌ 'wɔː/, and *after that they went away* would be /ɑːftə 'ðæt ðei went ə'wei/.[14]

Different distributions of stress in utterances can carry important differences in sentence meaning, with different presuppositions and implications (1.4.3), though the lexical content of the sentences remains the same. Such differences of stress will involve differences in the sequences of the pitches in intonations (4.3.6).

The sentence *then she insulted him* would normally be stressed *'then she in'sulted him*. But if we look at this as part of a longer sequence of utterance, an interesting distinction arises, dependent wholly on stress placement. In *John told Susie that she was at heart a republican; then 'she insulted 'him*, if *she* and *him* are stressed (as here), then the term *republican* must be understood, at least on Susie's part, as in some way insulting. This has nothing to do with lexical meanings. The substitution of *monarchist, anarchist, capitalist, communist*, etc makes no difference to this aspect of the sentence meaning. And if we replace it with a word lexically difficult to interpret as insulting, *eg flower-arranger*, then the hearer is forced to cast about for a special sense or a special context in which the word could be so used. But with normal stressing no such implication is found, and the whole utterance simply states that following John's action Susie insulted him: for example, *John proposed marriage to Susie (held the door open for Susie, bumped into Susie accidentally, etc); 'then she in'sulted him*. Of course, *insulted* could be replaced by other verbs, *eg praised, flattered, teased*, etc, with comparable results. The implicational differences depend wholly on the stress differentiations.

3.5.4 Pitch
Pitch is the acoustic result of the speed of the vibration of the vocal cords in the voiced parts of utterances. It follows that the term does not properly apply to voiceless sounds, nor to whispered speech. But the latter is a fairly infrequent variation from normal utterance, and in all languages voiced sounds outweigh voiceless ones in frequency and in numbers. The ratio in English speech has been calculated as eighty to twenty.[15]

Irrespective of the supraglottal components of individual consonants and vowels and features like those mentioned above (3.5.2), variations in the speed, or frequency as it is called, of the vocal cord vibrations produce sounds acoustically higher or lower. The faster the cords vibrate the greater the number of regular changes in pressure in the sound waves and the higher the pitch as heard.

Speech is nowhere said on a monotone, except for special purposes such as the intoning of parts of some church services. One is not normally very conscious of the rises and falls in one's own speech and that of persons of one's own immediate dialect, but unfamiliar sequences of pitch levels, in persons from other dialect areas for example, are immediately noticeable.

Pitch variation is found in all languages, but its function is very different from one type of language to another. Broadly, there are two ways in which languages make use of pitch variations in speech. In languages such as English, French, and German, and many others, regular sequences of different pitches characterize stretches of speech between pauses and are known collectively as **intonation**. Individual and personal variations are numerous, but there are general patterns of intonation characteristic of the utterances in each language and usually in different dialects within a language. These differences of intonation may correlate with different types of utterances. As an example from English one may compare the normal intonation of *Thursday at ten o'clock then*, as a statement of a fixed time for an appointment with that of the same sequence of words *Thursday at ten o'clock then?* as a request for confirmation of the time of the appointment.[16]

In some languages, widely scattered over the world, but perhaps most notably in China and parts of Africa and South-east Asia, pitch differences help to distinguish one word from another and may be the only differentiating feature between two or more words whose composition in terms of consonants and vowels is the same. Pitch is also used as the exponent (often the sole exponent) of grammatical differences in some languages (6.4.6). Pitch differences used in these ways are called **tones**, and these languages are called **tone languages**.[17] The different Chinese languages are the most widely spoken group of tone languages. Tones may be mainly on a single level of pitch (level tones), the relative height being what differentiates one such tone from another, or they may rise or fall, or rise and fall, or fall and rise (rising, falling, rising-falling, falling-rising tones, respectively), and be distinguished by the actual direction in which the pitch moves.

In certain tone languages, particular tones or distinctive pitches are regularly accompanied by other features of articulation, such as 'creakiness' (caused by glottal constriction) and breathiness.

The differences between the two uses of pitch features may be seen in the fact that in English, a non-tonal language, wherein pitch sequences (intonation) are the property of sentences and part of sentences, the lexical content of a sentence does not affect the pitch sequences, except that the substitution of longer or shorter words may spread the intonation over more or fewer sounds, and differently stressed words may alter the position of the high and low pitches; thus if one takes the simple question *are you feeling hungry?*, usually said on a sequence of pitches falling to a low on *hun-* and then rising, this pitch sequence is not altered by the replacement of *hungry* by *thirsty, sleepy, happy*, and so on. But in a tone language, in which the pitch levels or the rising and falling pitches are properties of the words as lexical items, the substitution of a different word in a sentence may change the pitch sequence, if the two words concerned are different in tonal compositions. In Northern (Mandarin) Chinese, the sequence /ta/, for example, may represent four different words according to the tone on which it is said: level tone, to raise; rising tone, to penetrate; falling-rising tone, to hit; falling tone, great.

These two types of language are not sharply exclusive of each other. Many tone languages have a well-defined set of intonations superimposed on the tones of the words in sentences, so that the tones of each word may be somewhat different in actual pitch, while remaining distinct from other tones, according to the intonation on which the whole sentence is uttered. And some European languages (*eg* Norwegian, Swedish, and Serbo-croat) are partially tonal, in that certain words have a pitch pattern inherently different from the patterns of other words. Occasionally these patterns may be the only differentiator of otherwise identical word forms (*eg* Norwegian *bønner* /'bønnər/ with the 'double', falling-rising tone, beans; *bønder* /'bønnər/, with the 'single', rising tone, farmers). These languages have their own intonation patterns, and the tonal distinctions just mentioned are generally maintained in the different intonation tunes as are the tonal distinctions in fully tonal languages.[18]

The different ways in which pitch differences are exploited intonationally and tonally in languages of all types will be dealt with further in 4.3.5 and 4.3.6. They fall within the purview of phonology, rather than of phonetics, which is concerned primarily with the physiological basis of pitch differentiation and the actual types of pitches that occur.

3.5.5 Voice quality

Voice quality is one of the most elusive aspects of utterance to analyse adequately. The words, and phrases like them, are in frequent use non-technically, and it is terms like these, rather than technical terms specifically invented for linguistics (even though linguists often differ in the exact way in which they define them), that are likely to cause trouble. In general parlance, the 'quality of a person's voice', like the 'tone of someone's speech', may cover almost any part of his utterance, such as the actual sense of what is said, the general impression made on the hearer, the choice of vocabulary, or dialectal features differentiating it from what the hearer is accustomed to or was expecting. All of these features are handled separately elsewhere in linguistic description, but there remains in utterance a residue of pronunciation features, not accounted for in the description of the segmental articulations and the plurisegmental features such as have been illustrated hitherto, but which are perceptible and may be significant, and are consequently part of the subject-matter of the phonetic level of linguistic analysis.

Voice quality in this sense refers to differences in what is heard, caused, like everything else heard in speech, by differences in some part or parts of the whole process of articulation reflected in differences somewhere in the resultant sound waves. It covers a multitude of rather different components, some of which are at present not fully understood as regards their articulatory basis. Some are nearly, if not quite, universal, as for instance, the greater loudness and force of articulation of an entire discourse, as against the greater relative loudness of a single utterance or part of an utterance referred to as emphatic stress; this correlates with, and communicates to the hearer, excitement, anger, or some other emotional involvement in what is being said.

At the opposite pole to this is quiet speech, which is not the same as whispering, though this by its very absence of voicing throughout is necessarily quiet and is employed for similar purposes and in similar situations. Quietly spoken, but normally articulated speech, carries connotations in both speaker and hearer of secrecy, confidentiality, intimacy, tenderness, and the like. It may be observed that both quietness and loudness of speech are, rather like onomatopoeia, directly suggestive, as features, of their functions, part of the total meaning of the utterances. As with stress for emphasis, both these features are infinitely variable in degree on a scale; there are as many degrees of forceful utterance as speaker and hearer can distinguish, whereas significant distinctions of consonant and vowel segments and of most other features, including stress as an inherent part of normal speech in some languages (3.5.3), are organized into contrasts of a fixed number of categories by each language according to its phonological system.

Apart from the use of pitch differences in intonation tunes, or as lexically distinctive tones in tone languages (accompanied in some languages by other articulatory features), persons vary both in the ranges of high and low pitch within which they speak, and in the relative height of their overall range. The speech of children is generally, for physiological reasons, higher than that of adults, and generally the speech of women is higher than that of men. Within these general limits each individual has his own normal pitch range. The deliberate use of a pitch range wider than one's usual one, or higher or lower than that normally used, correlates in various speech communities with various situations and intentions on the speaker's part (excitement, mockery, wheedling, and so on) and is understood in these lights by others of the same community.

Other aspects of voice quality are purely personal. It is highly unlikely that any two people are exactly alike in their speech (the articulations and the sound waves produced thereby), even if we had ways of determining what 'exactly alike' actually is. Everyone is aware that differences in voice quality are part of each person's total individuality, and different speakers can be distinguished behind closed doors, and the voices of acquaintances recognized even over such imperfect lines of transmission as telephones.

The totality of such features includes several different items. Some are probably physiological; different types of facial structures are likely to condition one's general speech production. These physiological differences do not affect the ability of any physically normal person to articulate all the speech sounds and maintain all the contrastive differences of any language. A baby born into a speech community will in the absence of interference acquire a perfect (*ie* native speaker's) mastery of the language, or dialect, of that community, whatever his physiological type. The belief that the actual physiology or race of certain peoples prevents them pronouncing certain sounds or enables them to pronounce others is nothing but a myth of ignorant ethnocentricity, on a par with travellers' tales of languages with no more than 600 words and no proper grammar. It is, incidentally, part of the task of general linguistics to dispel such harmful prejudices about other people's languages. Nonetheless the different configurations of the jaw, lips, nose, and other organs of speech in different physiological types do probably contribute something to the differences in the overall quality of people's voices that are universally recognized, though without effect on their use of language.

Some features may be cultural, acquired by speakers as part of the general behaviour patterns of their community, and so characterizing a dialect or even a whole language. Types of speech popularly categorized as 'harsh', 'precise', 'careful', and 'slurred', and referring to specific though as yet ill-defined aspects of the sound waves and their production, belong to this group. Thus it is said that French consonants are articulated more sharply, giving something of a staccato effect, than are English consonants.

It has already been said that little is known yet about the exact articulatory basis of all these subtle though highly significant differences between the speech habits of groups and of individuals falling under the general heading of voice quality. Clearly this side of phonetics cannot be pursued further in an elementary treatment of linguistics such as this; but it is important that these aspects of speech should be recognized as a proper (and perhaps urgent) object of phonetic study and research.[19]

3.6 Phonetics in linguistics

The account of speech sounds, their production, description, and analysis, given in this chapter has been intended as no more than a brief introduction to this part of the study of language in general linguistics. It can and should be supplemented by the further reading of books specifically devoted to phonetics, both general phonetics and the phonetics of particular languages. This should be further supplemented, if at all possible, by some practical acquaintance with and control over the recognition and production of different speech sounds by oneself (practical phonetics).

Speech is certainly the oldest form of language, and everywhere the most widespread form. The physiological conditions of its production and reception, and the physical means of its transmission, must in great part have determined the ways in which languages have developed and are organized as systems of human communication. These are sufficient reasons why an understanding of the principles of phonetics is a necessary basis for the study of other branches of linguistics, and for a reasonable comprehension of the working and significance of language the world over.

Bibliography for Chapter 3

1 D. ABERCROMBIE, *Elements of general phonetics*, Edinburgh, 1967.
2 J. M. AITCHISON, *The articulate mammal*, London, 1976.
3 L. E. ARMSTRONG, *The phonetics of French*, London, 1932.
4 J. BITHELL, *German pronunciation and phonology*, London, 1952.
5 L. BLOOMFIELD, *Language*, London, 1935.
6 D. BOLINGER (ed), *Intonation: selected readings*, Harmondsworth, 1972.
7 G. J. BORDEN and K. S. HARRIS, *Speech science primer: physiology, acoustics, and perception of speech*, Baltimore, 1980.
8 S. C. BOYANUS, *Russian pronunciation*, London, 1965.
9 D. CRYSTAL, *Prosodic systems and intonation in English*, Cambridge, 1969.
10 *The English tone of voice*, London, 1975.
11 D. CRYSTAL and R. QUIRK, *Systems of prosodic and paralinguistic features of English*, The Hague, 1964.
12 R. DANILOFF, G. SCHUCKERS, and L. FETH, *The physiology of speech and hearing: an introduction*, Englewood Cliffs, 1980.
13 F. B. DENES and E. N. PINSON, *The speech chain*, New York, 1973.
14 J. L. FLANAGAN, *Speech analysis, synthesis and perception*, Berlin, 1965.
15 D. B. FRY, *Homo loquens: man as a talking animal*, Cambridge, 1977.
16 A. C. GIMSON, *An introduction to the pronunciation of English*, London, 1970.
17 M. GRAMMONT, *Traité de phonétique*, Paris, 1950.
18 W. J. HARDCASTLE, *Physiology of speech production*, London, 1976.
19 R. S. HARRELL, *The phonology of colloquial Egyptian Arabic*, New York, 1957.
20 R. S. HEFFNER, *General phonetics*, Madison, 1952.
21 C. F. HOCKETT, *A manual of phonology*, Bloomington, 1955.
22 D. JONES, *Outline of English phonetics*, Cambridge, 1947.
23 *The phoneme*, Cambridge, 1950.
24 M. JOOS, *Acoustic phonetics*, Baltimore, 1948.
25 J. S. KENYON, *American pronunciation*, Ann Arbor, 1935.
26 R. KINGDON, *The groundwork of English intonation*, London, 1958.
27 P. LADEFOGED, *Elements of acoustic phonetics*, London, 1962.
28 *Preliminaries to linguistic phonetics*, Chicago, 1973.
29 E. H. LENNEBERG, *Biological foundations of language*, New York, 1967.
30 P. LIEBERMAN, *Speech physiology and acoustic phonetics*, New York, 1977.
31 H. MOL, *Fundamentals of phonetics I: the organ of hearing*, The Hague, 1963.
32 V. E. NEGUS, *The mechanism of the larynx*, London, 1929.
33 J. D. O'CONNOR, *Phonetics*, Harmondsworth, 1973.
34 J. D. O'CONNOR and G. F. ARNOLD, *Intonation of colloquial English*, London, 1978.

35 C. PAINTER, *An introduction to instrumental phonetics*, Baltimore, 1979.
36 M. PICKETT, *The sounds of speech communication*, Baltimore, 1980.
37 K. L. PIKE, *Phonetics*, Ann Arbor, 1943.
38 *The intonation of American English*, Ann Arbor, 1946.
39 *Tone languages*, Ann Arbor, 1948.
40 R. G. POPPERWELL, *The pronunciation of Norwegian*, Cambridge, 1963.
41 E. SAPIR, *Language*, New York, 1921.
42 M. SCHUBIGER, *English intonation: its form and function*, Tübingen, 1958.
43 S. SINGH and K. S. SINGH, *Phonetics: principles and practices*, Baltimore, 1982.
44 E. SIVERTSEN, *Cockney phonology*, Oslo, 1960.
45 R. H. STETSON, *The bases of phonology*, Oberlin, 1945.
46 *Motor phonetics*, Amsterdam, 1951.
47 I. C. WARD, *The phonetics of English*, Cambridge, 1948.
48 C. M. WISE, *Introduction to phonetics*, Englewood Cliffs, 1957.

Notes to Chapter 3

1 On auditory phonetics, Mol, 31; Daniloff *et al.*, 12. Denes and Pinson, 13, has a good chapter on the physiology of hearing.
2 On the phonetics of English (British standard English), Jones, 22; Ward, 47; Gimson, 16. The transcription in Jones's *English pronouncing dictionary* follows that of his *Outline*. On American English, Kenyon, 25.
3 No organs of speech as such, Sapir, 41, 7. Aitchison, 2, gives some evidence for their partial adaptation for the articulation of speech.
    On the development of the larynx as an organ of voice production, Negus, 32, appendix 1; Lenneberg, 29.
4 On general phonetics, Abercrombie, 1; Pike, 37; Heffner, 20; Grammont, 17; Fry, 15; Gimson, 16, 6–26; Ladefoged, 28; O'Connor, 33; Pickett, 36; Singh and Singh, 43; Wise, 48. With special reference to instrumental techniques, Stetson, 45 and 46.
    On French phonetics, Armstrong, 3.
    On German phonetics, Bithell, 4.
5 On segmentation, and some of the problems involved, Pike, 37, Chapters 3 and 7.
6 Bloomfield, 5, 102; Jones, 22, 23; *cp* Pike, 37, 78. Vocoid: 'a sound during which air leaves the mouth over the centre of the tongue and without friction in the mouth'. Contoid: 'any nonvocoid'. The use by Pike of *vocoid* and *contoid* as newly invented terms in general phonetics is in order to keep *vowel* and *consonant* for use exclusively as phonological terms with reference to particular languages (*cp Phonemics*, Ann Arbor, 1947, 253).
    On the voiceless vowels of Comanche, E. D. Canonge in *IJAL* 23 (1957), 63–7.
7 Cardinal vowels, Jones, 22, 28, 34; Gimson, 16, 36–9.

8 Swahili, E. G. Ashton, *Swahili grammar*, London, 1944.
9 There have been many publications on this aspect of phonetics. Joos, 24, is now an early classic on the subject. See also Hockett, 21; Ladefoged, 27; Flanagan 14; Lieberman, 30; Painter, 35.
10 On the perception of stop consonants in relation to adjacent vowels, C. D. Schatz, 'The role of context in the perception of stops', *Lang* 30 (1954), 47–56.
11 Glottalization in Georgian, Robins and N. Waterson, 'Notes on the phonology of the Georgian word' *BSOAS* 14 (1952), 55–72; on Cockney, Sivertsen, 44.
12 On retroflexion, Firth, 'A short outline of Tamil pronunciation', in A. H. Arden, *A progressive grammar of 'Common Tamil'*, Madras, 1934.
   On Arabic phonetics, Harrell, 19.
13 On Russian and Irish, Boyanus, 8; B. OCuiv, *The Irish of West Muskerry*, Dublin, 1944. In Russian four different words involving the sequence bilabial nasal, open unrounded vowel, and voiceless dental stop are distinguished according to whether palatalization affects neither consonant, both consonants, or one of the consonants, with concomitant differences of vowel quality (Jones, 23, 26).
14 On stress, Jones, 22, Chapter 29.
   On prominence and sonority, Jones, 22, §§101–2; Bloomfield, 5, 120–1.
15 Ratio of voiced to voiceless sounds in English, Jones, 22, 255.
16 On British English intonation, Jones, 22, Chapter 31; O'Connor and Arnold, 34; Kingdon, 26; Schubiger, 42; Gimson, 16, Chapter 10; Crystal, 9. On American English, Pike 38. On German intonation A. Fox, *German intonation: an outline*, Oxford, 1984. In general, Bolinger, 6, and *Intonation and its parts: melody in spoken English*, Stanford, 1986.
17 On tone languages, Pike, 39.
18 On intonation in tone languages, Pike, 39, 16–17, 85–6. On tone distinctions in Norwegian, A. Sommerfelt and I. Marm, *Teach yourself Norwegian*, London, 1943, 33–41. On Norwegian phonetics, Popperwell, 40.
19 It may be that further understanding of all the features involved will enable us ultimately to demonstrate and describe the individuality of each person's speech sounds.
   For a recent treatment of this topic, J. Laver, 'The concept of articulatory settings', *Historiographia linguistica* 6 (1978), 1–14.
   On what have been called paralinguistic features of speech, Crystal, 10; Crystal and Quirk, 11.
   It should be noted that in items 9 and 11 the terms *prosodic* and *prosody* are not used in the specific technical sense found in Chapter 4, in outlining prosodic phonology (4.4.3).

Chapter 4

Phonology

4.1 Speech and writing

The two media or substances used by natural languages as vehicles for communication are air disturbed by the movements of
articulation and marks made on a flat surface by chisel, writing
brush, pen, pencil, etc. These two modes of linguistic communication, speech and writing, virtually exhaust the field, as one
may, particularly in an elementary account, leave aside such
specialized and restricted systems as the gestural communications
of the deaf and dumb, and such other secondary systems as
semaphore, heliograph, and the like.

The familiar languages of Europe, but not all their dialects,
and the languages of the major areas of civilization in the world
are both written and spoken; that is to say a system of writing
and a system of speaking are recognizable and recognized as 'the
same language'. Many languages are spoken languages only, and
the spread of literacy does not necessarily bring them all within
its compass; spoken languages of relatively small communities,
living within a larger political or cultural group, are often
bypassed as the speakers are taught to be literate in a more
widely used language of the area as a 'second' language or one
acquired in the course of education and not in infancy (as is also
the case with many speakers of non-standard dialects of written
languages). This situation is found among the American Indians
of North America (literate in English), the American Indians of
Central and South America (becoming literate in Spanish or
Portuguese), many of the inhabitants of parts of Africa (literate
in English, Swahili, or some widely used language), and the
people of several other parts of the world.

Some languages are known at the present time only in their written forms, the so-called dead languages, though one can make estimates with varying degrees of confidence and exactitude as to their once spoken forms. Ancient Greek and Hittite are well-known examples of such languages. Latin is virtually a dead language, though in a specialized development it is used as a spoken medium, always a second language, in some services of the Roman Catholic Church and more widely within certain religious communities.

As in spoken languages, one recognizes various different styles, usually merging into one another through intermediate styles. Some written styles are virtually unintelligible if read aloud or if used as a spoken medium, for example the formal language of legal contracts and legislative enactments. But ordinarily the written words and sentences of a language represent in one way or another its spoken forms, and a spoken sentence in a literate language can be written down, and a written sentence can be read aloud. The relationship between these two forms of language is not uniform, and several different systems of representing speech by writing are found, with varying degrees of phonetic accuracy, that is the direct indication, without the reader necessarily knowing the word represented, of the sounds of the corresponding spoken form.

Chinese is the best-known example of a language wherein the written symbols are graphic representations of individual lexical and grammatical items as wholes. There are in consequence several thousand such individually different written symbols, or **characters**, as they are often called, often thought of as directly representing ideas and hence also called, ideograms, but more sensibly treated as the representation of spoken forms, in many cases words, but more strictly morphemes (5.4). Though the representation is directly of the word or of its grammatical components (morphemes) bypassing its phonetic composition, an indication is given in many Chinese characters of something of the sounds by a part of the character, called for this reason 'the phonetic'. The invariable nature of most Chinese words, whether containing one or more than one morpheme, makes such a writing system more usable than in a language with considerable word form variation (5.3.1, *p* 188).[1]

Most writing systems use written shapes to represent in some way the phonetic composition of spoken forms directly, thus avoiding the need for as many different written symbols as there are lexically different items in the language. These systems recognize the phonetic segments referred to in the preceding chapter as consonants and vowels, and represent them by written signs as they appear in the spoken forms, usually isolated spoken forms, forms spoken alone and not as parts of larger sentences (4.2, *p* 119).

Some orthographic or writing systems use a single written sign to indicate a consonant, and sometimes two consonants, followed by a vowel, with other special signs to mark consonants not followed by a vowel. Such systems are syllabic in their representation of spoken sounds, and they are called **syllabaries**; there is reason to regard them historically as intermediate between the character type of writing still used in Chinese and attested in parts of the Middle East and elsewhere, and the alphabetic systems widely used all over the world today. The main writing systems of several of the languages of India are syllabaries, as is the orthography of Javanese. The writing system of Sanskrit, the classical language of North India is of the syllabic type, though often referred to as the Sanskrit 'alphabet'. It differs from most writing systems in that it was, and is, the general practice to represent word forms as they appeared when uttered in sequence with one another in sentences, rather than as isolates. These sequential forms are known as 'sandhi forms' of words (5.3.3). The recently deciphered Mycenaean script (the earliest written records of Greek) is largely syllabic, with some character-like symbols as well.[2] The ancient Semitic writing system used by the Phoenicians and the Hebrews was of the syllabary type; modern Hebrew writing is a development of this, and so is the Arabic script as used in the Middle East today. But in these languages it is the consonant articulations of the spoken forms that are in the main indicated by the syllabary symbols, the different vowels being indicated by dots or other marks separate from the symbol itself and not always put in where the consonantal outline in its context is considered clear enough without them.

This sort of development of syllabary writing seems half way to the **alphabet** or letter systems of Europe and elsewhere, in which consonant and vowel articulations are separately marked by individual letters. Indeed, our alphabet (the Roman alphabet) and other alphabets, such as the Cyrillic, used for Russian and some other East European languages, are derived historically from the Greek alphabet (still used in Greece). This was an adaptation, subsequent to and separate from the Mycenaean syllabary, of the symbols of the Phoenician syllabary, to represent individually by separate symbols the consonants and vowels of the Greek language. Alphabetic writing, which has now spread all over the world, and is being developed either at the expense of syllabary writing, as in Java, or alongside it as a second system of writing, is just one of the many debts that civilization owes to the peculiar genius of Ancient Greece.

Not all orthographic systems are anything like pure examples of the above mentioned types. Mixed writing systems are found. To a very limited extent written English makes use of characters not unlike those of Chinese in principle, in employing the numeral signs 1, 2, 3, etc and the ampersand (&). More typical of such a mixture is written Japanese. The Japanese learned writing along with a good deal else from long cultural contact with the Chinese, and took over the Chinese system of characters; but, unlike Chinese, Japanese is a language with a high proportion of variable words, or groups of word forms sharing a common part or root, rather like English word series such as *walk, walks, walking, walked.* In dealing with this situation, Japanese writing today employs a set of characters substantially the same as those in use in Chinese (from which they were acquired) together with a syllabary script formed by the use of fragmentary parts of certain characters; broadly speaking invariable words and the root parts of variable words are represented by the character and the affixes are indicated by the signs of the syllabary (called *kana,* borrowed names). Similar developments took place in Ancient Egypt, parts of the Middle East, and Central America. The Korean script (*Hangul*), traditionally ascribed to the invention of King Seijong (1397–1450), represents the syllables of the language by the combination of separate signs for initial consonant, vowel, and final consonant into a square figure, looking superficially rather like a Chinese character, though essentially they are quite different.[3]

Alphabetic systems may vary considerably as regards the closeness they bear to the phonetic composition of the forms they represent, or, put another way, in the degree to which they mark the actual pronunciations. English is well known as a language wherein spelling and pronunciation may be far apart; the same sound sequences may be spelled in several different ways and the same series of letters may represent several different sound sequences (3.3.2). In so far as aphabetical spellings are ambiguous phonetically, and the pronunciation of the words must be known by knowledge of the spelt form of the word as a whole, the groups of letters function in part rather like a Chinese or other character. Other languages, for example Italian, have a far closer correspondence of spelling and pronunciation; French and some other languages stand in a peculiar position, in that the pronunciation is usually (not always) inferable from the spelling, but the spelling system employs a remarkably high proportion of 'silent letters' of differently spelt variants of the same sound sequences (*donne, donnes, donnent* /dɔn/; *à, a* /a/; *cas* /ka/, *chat* /ʃa/; *thé, nez, aller, quai, et*, all end in /e/, etc). Languages like English, wherein spelling and pronunciation frequently disagree, receive the constant attention of spelling reformers. The anomalies of English spelling, however, are not wholly a nuisance; orthographic *-s* as the sign of the plural in *dogs, cats*, and *horses*, though it indicates three different pronunciations /-z/, /-s/, and /-iz/ which a more 'accurate' spelling might represent differently with separate letters, does give a single sign for a single grammatical element, and this may be a definite advantage.

However, in the course of centuries, orthographies are bound to become out of line with pronunciation in some words, as spoken forms change (8.1.1) while spellings tend to be conservative especially since the invention of printing, though in Norway and Holland, for example, official spelling reforms have been made. English *fine, line*, and *mine* (for minerals), and some other words were once pronounced with a final sound sequence more like that of *machine*, having been taken from French (in which the /iː/ vowel has persisted, *fine* /fiːn/, *ligne* /liːɲ/, *mine* /miːn/); but in English at a later date the /-iːn/ changed to /-ain/ (part of the 'Great Vowel Shift' (8.1.2)), so that *-ine* now represented this pronunciation; but the change had come to an end by the time the French word *machine* was introduced. In the normal course of the development of a language the creation of such disharmonies between orthography and pronunciation is inevitable unless the spellings of words are constantly adjusted to pronunciation changes.

4.2 Narrow and broad transcription: phonetics and phonology

During the nineteenth century and after, when phonetics was rapidly advancing as the scientific study and accurate analysis of the speech sounds used in languages, the representational inadequacies of orthographies became more and more apparent and more and more a nuisance, not to be overcome by any tinkerings in the way of spelling reforms. In two respects all orthographies are deficient in representing the spoken sounds of utterances, though they are satisfactory for their purposes of recording spoken utterances and forms as wholes for ordinary purposes. Firstly, they are usually inadequate in marking the different forms words take in continuous discourse as compared with isolated utterance. To some extent English spellings like *'ll, 'd, 's* (*I'll do it, he'd be there, he's all right*) help to fill the gap, but the normal pronunciation of *the*, /ðə/ or /ði/ as against the isolate pronunciation /ðiː/, and the common variants of *for*, /fə/ as against isolate /fɔː/, and *to*, /tə/ and /tu/ as against isolate /tuː/, are hardly indicated at all, and, far worse, when they are written *fer* and *ter*, etc, this is done as a supposed mark of uneducated speech, whereas it is in fact a normal and indeed essential part of any dialect or style of English. Secondly, sound features such as stress and pitch, noticed in the preceding chapter, which are equally a part of uttered sentences and essential to correct pronunciation, are often entirely unrepresented.

The International Phonetic Alphabet (3.3.2) was devised and is progressively modified to provide a precise and universal means (*ie* one valid for all languages) of writing down the spoken forms of utterances as they are spoken without reference to their orthographic representation, grammatical status, or meaning. This is an essential part of phonetic analysis and of the phonetic study of the sounds of languages; but the increasingly accurate '**narrow**' transcriptions that are produced in this way led to the realization of their inherent inadequacy as a means of systematically and unambiguously representing the pronunciation of the spoken forms of a particular language for the purpose of reading. It is at once apparent that anything like a fully accurate narrow transcription is an unattainable though approachable ideal, since one cannot assume that any two utterances of 'the same sound', *ie* intended repetitions, are in fact precisely and demonstrably the same, and as between any two speakers they are often demonstrably not the same. Moreover, such a transcription is far too unwieldy to serve just as a regular representation of what is pronounced; what it is is a detailed symbolization of each successive sound segment and sound feature.

It was discovered that transcriptional systems of far fewer symbols and diacritical signs (signs of the type appearing at the bottom of the IPA chart) could be devised for each language separately, to serve the purpose of representing the pronounced forms. These are known as **broad** transcriptions, and there is clearly a minimal number of distinct symbols required for the unambiguous indication of the pronunciation, as opposed to the potentially infinite number needed to symbolize separately each difference of actual sound.[4] It must be clearly understood that the same graphic symbol may well have different phonetic values when written as part of a broad transcription (between / and /) and when used more narrowly between [and], or when appearing on the I.P.A chart (see *pp* 88–9, above). Two facts stand out as a result of distinguishing these two types of transcription. Firstly, many of the differences between sounds in a language may be shown to be conditioned by the phonetic environment of each sound, *ie*, the other sounds, or strictly speaking the articulations, near it in the uttered form, and therefore do not need separate symbolization in a transcription devised for the language in question. Secondly, this conditioning differs from language to language; and consequently, whereas a narrow transcription can be indifferently used of the material of any language, or indeed of a series of speech sounds made up for the purpose and belonging to no language, such as are used in phonetic training in pronunciation and recognition (ear training), a broad transcription must be separately worked out for each language, and often each dialect, under analysis.

The study of the phonetic composition of utterances in the light of these considerations led to a realization that different languages both make use of different selections from the articulatory possibilities of the human vocal tract, and may be shown to organize these selections differently in systems of contrasting sounds and combinatory possibilities in utterance. As a result, two separate ways of studying speech sounds are recognized in linguistics: phonetics, the study and analysis of the sounds of languages or of a particular language, in respect of their articulation, transmission, and perception; and phonology, the study and analysis of the exploitation of different ranges of speech sounds by languages and of the systems of contrasting sound features (phonological systems) found in them.

Phonetics and phonology are both concerned with the same subject-matter or aspect of language, speech sounds as the audible result of articulation, but they are concerned with them from different points of view. Phonetics is general (that is, concerned with speech sounds as such without reference to their function in a particular language), descriptive, and classificatory; phonology is particular (having a particular language or languages in view) and functional (concerned with the working or functioning of speech sounds in a language or languages). Phonology has in fact been called functional phonetics. General accounts of phonology and phonological theory, such as are to be given in outline in this chapter and are set out in detail in books devoted specifically to this part of linguistics, are general only in the sense that they deal with the functioning of speech sounds in the phonological systems of various languages, with the analysis of such systems, and with the phonological possibilities of languages; phonology always has in view a language as a communication system in its theory and procedures of analysis.[5]

It will be seen from this summary statement of the province of phonology that it goes considerably beyond the question of workable broad transcriptions; but such a transcription, as opposed to a narrow, purely phonetic, transcription, presupposes some phonological analysis, as does an adequate alphabet, even though it is implicit and unrealized; and it is a fact that while the phonological analysis of a language and the working out of a broad transcription for it are different, though related, matters, the development of phonological theory and of the procedures of phonological analysis has been largely conditioned by transcriptional requirements. This must be borne in mind in the understanding and evaluation of the approaches by different linguists to this part of their subject.

4.3 The phoneme theory

4.3.1 The phonemic principle, phonemics

The theory of phonology that evolved over the years as the result of the search for adequate and efficient broad transcriptions centred round the phoneme concept, and still today the majority of linguists base their phonological analysis and derive their principles of phonology from the theory of the phoneme. The theory has in the course of its evolution taken a number of rather different forms, and some of these have been carried to greater extremes by some scholars than by others. A great deal of ink has been spilled on controversies within and about the phoneme theory which it is neither necessary nor profitable to follow through in an elementary treatment of the subject. The essentials of the theory and of the analytic methods that are based on it can be presented relatively simply in outline. Anyone entering on the study of linguistics must be sure to master these essentials, in order to be able adequately to understand and evaluate the different varieties of phonological analysis now in use or under development.

In terms of the phoneme theory and by means of phonemic analysis languages can be shown to organize the selection they make of the available sound differences in human speech into a limited number of recurrent distinctive units. These are called **phonemes**, and it is found that their number in any language is relatively small, as compared with the great and potentially unlimited number of actually different sounds uttered by speakers. The numbers of phonemes in any language differ both from one language to another and according to the way in which the linguist analyses his material, but upper and lower limits of around fifty and fifteen have been calculated, the most frequent count being around thirty.[6] Moreover the same phonemic system is found to be valid for large numbers of speakers of the same language or dialect, despite their obvious differences of individual speech. Phonemic analysis and the theory behind it were first worked out in regard to the segmental consonant and vowel elements of languages, and the basic principles can well be illustrated in these terms.

4.3.2 Segmental phonemes

The linguistically essential property of a sound segment or feature in an utterance or in any fraction of an utterance is that it should be distinct or differentiable. De Saussure indeed, went so far as to say that the differences were all that mattered in languages, the means by which the differences were maintained being irrelevant.[7] To differ distinctively, two sounds must be able to occur in the same position and in the same environment as far as other distinctive sound units are concerned. Thus in English /p/ and /b/ can each occur in the environment /-æn/, in /pæn/ *pan*, and in /bæn/ *ban*. Where two phonetically different sounds are restricted to different environments in relation to other sounds, their differences are accounted for and cancelled out by their environment or distribution, and in these terms serve no distinctive purpose (this is not the same as saying that their differences are phonologically irrelevant). They need not, therefore, be represented by more than one symbol in a broad transcription, as the different sound involved will be clearly indicated in each case by the copresence of the other symbols, to anyone knowing the phonological system of the language on which the broad transcription is based.

The two notions of phonemic distinctiveness and phonetic difference may be illustrated from English. English /p/, /t/, and /k/, when pronounced in initial position are aspirated ([pʰ], [tʰ], [kʰ]), as in *ten* /ten/ ([tʰen]). But immediately following initial /s/ in a consonant cluster they are without aspiration, as in *steam* /stiːm/, [stiːm]. Such a difference is not necessarily noticed by a native speaker of standard English, but a little attention and phonetic training make these differences readily apparent. As aspirated [tʰ] and unaspirated [t] cannot replace one another in the same environment in English, they cannot contrast or distinguish one utterance from another. One therefore groups these two sounds, phonetically different as they are, into one phonologically distinctive unit, or phoneme, symbolized by /t/, whose phonetic implications are determined by its phonological environment in an utterance, as represented in terms of other phonemes established in the same way. The phoneme /t/, therefore, consists of several phonetically different sounds, or 'members' and may be regarded logically as a class. Likewise the phonemes /p/ and /k/ consist of different sounds similarly distributed in their environments (compare the [pʰ] and [p] of *pan* and *span* and the [kʰ] and [k] of *can* and *scan*). Sounds are grouped into a single class or phoneme if they can be shown to be phonetically similar (having something in common, articulatorily or auditorily distinctive) and in complementary distribution (not occurring in the same environment and so not distinctive). The condition of phonetic similarity keeps [t] and [tʰ], [p] and [pʰ] in the same phonemes respectively, as against the equally non-contrastive grouping of [t] and [pʰ], [p] and [tʰ].

The condition of complementary distribution is supplemented by that of free variation; where two phonetically different sounds may occur in the same environment but are always interchangeable therein in all utterances, they are equally non-distinctive, and are grouped into the same class or phoneme. As the pronunciation of either variant is indifferent a broad transcription need only represent the phoneme by one symbol. English utterance final /p/, /t/, and /k/ illustrate this; they may be exploded (audibly released) or released without sound. (*ie* outward air pressure has ceased during the maintenance of the closure). In utterance final position, either sort of stop consonant can occur without any distinction being made thereby. In some languages this is not the case; in Thai (Siamese) and Vietnamese, voiceless final stop consonants are never audibly released and there is no free variation of the English type in this position.

All the segmental sounds used in each language can be classed into a limited number of phonemes, and conversely the consonant and vowel phonemes exhaustively cover all the consonant and vowel sounds so occurring. All consonant and vowel contrasts between distinct forms in a language can be referred to one or other of its component phonemes. Thus English *man* /mæn/, containing three phonemes, may contrast at three points or places wherein a distinctively different sound unit may be substituted: *man, pan* (/pæn/); *man, men* (/men/); *man, mad* (/mæd/). In establishing the phonemes of a language 'minimal pairs', or pairs of words differing by one phoneme only like the above examples, are a convenience, if they can be found; but they are not essential to the analysis or to its justification. The essence of phonemic distinctiveness lies in phonetic differences between two or more sounds that are neither in free variation nor wholly determined by their environments. The phoneme has been defined as 'a class of phonetically similar sounds, contrasting and mutually exclusive with all similar classes in the language'. Looked at from a rather different point of view, the phoneme has often been defined as the minimal distinctive or contrastive phonological unit in a language.[8] Just because different phonemes are distinctive and the different sounds within the phoneme are by themselves non-distinctive, native speakers in acquiring their first language unconsciously learn to notice the former and ignore the latter. For this reason some linguists have spoken of the phoneme as a psychologically real element.[9]

Phonemic analysis consists in allotting all the indefinite number of sounds occurring in the utterances of a language to a definite and limited set of phonemes contrastive in at least some environments; and a phonemic transcription or broad transcription at its simplest consists in the use of one letter or symbol and one only for each phoneme. Manifestly, while there is a minimal number of symbols required for a broad transcription, transcriptions of different degrees of narrowness can be made employing more or fewer separate signs for actual phonetic differences among variant members of phonemes.

Members of phonemes are often called **phones** or **allophones**, and it is common practice to write phone symbols between square brackets and phoneme symbols or the symbols of a broad transcription between oblique brackets. Thus in English, [t] and [tʰ] are allophones of the /t/ phoneme. The use of oblique brackets in this book is explained on *pp* xxii–xxiii, Transcriptions and abbreviations.

Apart from the criterion of phonetic similarity, which is usually maintained in the phonemic analysis of languages, the ways in which sounds are distributed and contrast with one another may vary very considerably from one language to another. The degree of phonetic difference required to maintain a distinction is a matter for the language system and not merely the phonetic nature of the sounds themselves, provided there is some perceptible difference. [t] and [tʰ], non-contrastive in English, are contrastive, and so belong to different phonemes, in several varieties of Chinese and in a number of Indian languages: in north Chinese /tan/ and /tʰan/ are both found as distinct parts of utterances, alike in all other respects including the range of possible tones (3.5.4, 4.3.5), and in Hindi /t/ and /tʰ/ are in contrast in the distinctive pair /sat/ seven and /satʰ/ with.

Other examples of allophonic differences and phonemic groupings in English are:

[i] 'Clear' and 'dark' /l/ (respectively with the front of the tongue raised toward the hard palate and the back of the tongue raised toward the soft palate) in prevocalic and postvocalic position, as in *Lil* /lil/, or in *lip* /lip/ as contrasted with *pill* /pil/. This distinction is phonemic in some dialects or Polish, in which 'clear' and 'dark' /l/ can occur in the same phonological environment and so be contrastive.

[ii] Fricative and flapped /r/ are in free variation intervocalically in words like *very* /'veri/, *merry* /'meri/, and *marry* /'mæri/, in many varieties of standard English: an alveolar fricative [ɹ] or an alveolar flapped [r] may be uttered indifferently; the two sounds are treated as members of the same /r/ phoneme, freely variant in this environment.

[iii] Three slightly different qualities of the vowel /ə/ are heard in many speakers, a lower central vowel in utterance final position as in *china* /'tʃainə/, and *colour* /'kʌlə/, a higher and rather back vowel when the /ə/ in non-final position adjoins a /k/ or a /g/, in *again* /ə'gein/, and a vowel somewhat between the two in other environments, as in *along* /ə'lɔŋ/, *salad* /'sæləd/.[10]

In general, all English vowels are pronounced with slightly shorter duration before final voiceless consonants than before final voiced consonants, without obscuring the relatively greater length of the distinctively long vowels (*eg:* *hit* /hit/, *hid* /hid/, and *heat* /hiːt/, *heed* /hiːd/, *p* 127).

Many of the allophonic differences in the members of phonemes in languages may be accounted for by the fact that speech is a continuous process and that the segments that form the basis of the consonant and vowel phonemes are more or less artificially abstracted from the stream of speech. Necessarily the position of the organs in one segment will affect the articulation of the following segment, as will the movement towards the position of a subsequent segment; indeed, the conditioned variants juxtaposed to a segment frequently assist the recognition of its distinctive qualities, and while in phonemic analysis environmentally conditioned features are as such non-distinctive, they cannot be dismissed as phonologically irrelevant or neglected in language learning.

This conditioning of allophonic differences is clearly illustrated in English by the different varieties of the /k/ and /g/ phonemes found according to the nature of the following, or in final position the preceding, vowel. A slightly different position of contact between the back of the tongue and the soft palate may be observed for each different adjacent vowel phoneme, but three varieties illustrate this variation best: with /iː/ a very front contact point is used, as in *keep* /kiːp/ and *peak* /piːk/, with /ʌ/, as in *cup* /kʌp/, and *muck* /mʌk/, a middle contact point is used; with /uː/ a back contact point is used, as in *coop* /kuːp/, and *flook* /fluːk/. These differences can be made clear by preparing to say *keep* and from the point of closure uttering *coop*, or vice versa, when a noticeably unnatural pronunciation results.

It will have been observed that so far the terms *contrast* and *distinctive* have been used in the description of the phoneme and of phonemic analysis, and in the preceding chapter, without further comment. Many linguists are prepared to accept these term as primitives, *ie*, as requiring no further definition within linguistics; but others have sought to define the terms. Generally the distinctiveness or contrast between phonemes has been taken as their ability to differentiate one form from another; thus /p/ and /b/ are distinctive in English because words like *pan* /pæn/, and *ban* /bæn/, are different words with different meanings. The phrase *ability to differentiate* is important in this context, as some pairs of phonemes, generally distinguishing forms with different meanings, are in a few words used interchangeably; thus *difficult* may be pronounced with /i/ or /ə/ (/ˈdifikəlt/ or /ˈdifəkəlt/), and *economic* may be pronounced indifferently /iːkəˈnɔmik/ or /ekəˈnɔmik/; but /i/ and /ə/, and /iː/ and /ə/ are minimally distinctive elsewhere (*eg: city* /ˈsiti/, *sitter* /ˈsitə/; *eel* /iːl/, *ell* /el/). An alternative explanation of *distinctive* or *contrasting* has been made in terms of the 'pairs test', in which it is asserted that a native speaker can consistently tell apart members of pairs of utterances differing by one phoneme, but not when they differ solely by one of two allophones in free variation in a certain position. Both of these accounts of the terms, it will be seen, involve an appeal to a native speaker's competence (2.1.1), his necessary, though unconscious, awareness of how his language works, and what units are functionally distinctive in providing for a sufficient lexical stock. Considerable discussion on the theoretical basis and necessary presuppositions of phonemic analysis has taken place, but what has been said above may be sufficient in an introduction to the subject.[11]

4.3.3 Phonemic analysis of length and stress
The difference between long and short vowels has been mentioned in the preceding chapter (3.3.3). Not all languages make use of this sort of difference (often referred to as quantity)

as phonemically distinctive. It is, of course, always possible to vary the length of any articulatory segment, but in some languages this is a matter of style or even of random variation, and not part of the distinctive apparatus of the phonological system. The phonemic constitution of the distinctively long vowels of English has been subjected to different analyses, and it is instructive to compare some of these as an illustration of how different and equally valid analyses of the same material may produce different phonemic systems and different numbers of phonemes. This is simply an illustration of the general situation obtaining in the descriptive analysis of languages, namely that at any level the same body of data may be liable to a number of different analyses, depending on the criteria employed and on the relative weight given to them. Each analysis is justifiable in the terms in which it is worked out; though sometimes one will be preferable to the others, or preferable for certain purposes (*eg* highlighting particular features of a language), often there is little to choose between them, each having some advantages and some disadvantages as a means of explaining the phenomena involved.

One analysis of the British English long vowels simply treats and transcribes them as separative vowel phonemes, with the differences of relative length just one of the features distinguishing them from other vowels; this treatment may be reinforced by the use of special symbols and no length mark (*eg* /i/ = /iː/, /ɪ/ = /i/, /u/ = /uː/, /ʊ/ = /u/, /ɔ/ = /ɔː/, /ɒ/ = /ɔ/, /ɜ/ = /əː/, /ə/ = /ə/, /a/ = /ɑː/). Another treats the long vowels as sequences of two corresponding short vowels, with the differences of quality accounted for as allophonically conditioned by the environments of the two vowels concerned (the first vowel of each pair being part of the environment of the second, and vice versa /iː/ = /ii/, etc). A third treats length as having phonemic status itself as a length phoneme, symbolized by /ː/, so that /iː/ and /i/ both represent the /i/ phoneme, with and without length, respectively. Any of these analyses is legitimate, and they may be weighed against one another according to the results achieved. The first makes use of more phonemes and therefore of more transcriptional symbols than the second or third, and obscures a definite phonetic relationship between several pairs of vowels in English; but it does serve to emphasize that differences of quality, and not simply of relative duration, help to distinguish the long and short vowels of English; the second employs fewer phonemes, but perhaps obscures the qualitative differences between the members of long and short vowel pairs; the third is nearly as economical in phonemic inventory, marks the length correlation without suggesting that a long vowel is the equivalent of two short vowels, which phonetically it is not, and is, generally speaking, the system most used as a phonemic analysis of the British English vowels and as the basis for a broad (phonemic) transcription of the language.[12]

In English, as in some other languages, vowels and consonant articulations and vowel length are not the only phonetic differences employed to produce lexically distinct forms. Stress in the second sense referred to above (3.5.3), or relatively greater force of articulation on one part of a word form, is an essential part of the correct pronunciation of English words of more than two vowels or consonant-vowel sequences, and its position cannot be predicted or explained by reference to other phonetic factors. Distinctions of stress must therefore be included in the inventory of the English phonological system, and in a few word pairs, as was seen above, differences of stress placement alone may differentiate lexically distinct forms. Linguists have differed as to the number of distinctive degrees of stress required for the analysis of the potentially infinite number of actually different degrees of phonetic stressing. Jones and Gimson operate with one degree of stress (rarely with two) contrasting with the absence of stress (there can, of course, be no absence of all force in an audible sound; phonologically unstressed segments are uttered with varying amounts of phonetic stressing always contrastively less than those of stressed segments).

Most linguists regard the function of stress in languages like English as justifying phoneme status for the distinctive degrees recognized. Several American linguists have set up three degrees of stress as well as absence of stress as four phonemically distinctive elements, symbolized by /ˈ/, /ˆ/, /ˋ/, and /ˇ/ or by the absence of a mark, and illustrated in the compound word *elevator-operator* /élivèitərɔ́pərèitə/. The phonetic phenomena of stress are very similar between British and American English, and the difference in the number of distinctive degrees of stress largely depends on the theoretical basis of the analysis.

In addition to the phonemic degrees of stress found in some languages, all languages make use of extra-loud contrastive or emphatic stress, symbolized /ʺ/, on a particular word or part of a word, as in *that's mine* (*not yours*) /ðæts ʺmain/. This use of stress described in 3.5.3, is of a rather special nature in that it includes not only a contrast with normal unemphatic pronunciation, but also the possibility of an infinitely gradable scale of extra-loudness (within the limits of articulatory possibilities) correlated with a similarly gradable scale of emphasis or the like, meant and understood. For this reason some linguists do not recognize this as a phoneme in its own right. Much the same sort of effect can, of course, be achieved in languages making use of stress contrasts in normal diction, by putting full stress on a different word or different part of a word from that whereon it would otherwise fall (*eg: uncommon* /ˈnˈkɔmən/, but *uncommon* (*not common*) /ˈʌnkɔmən/).[13]

Phonemes of stress and length, when abstracted as phonemes in their own right, are often classed among what are called the suprasegmental phonemes, to distinguish them from the segmental consonant and vowel phonemes, as the suprasegmental phonemes do not relate to phonetic segments so much as to phonetic features concomitant with and characterizing a whole segment or succession of adjacent segments.

4.3.4 The syllable

Word is a term primarily of grammatical significance, though in many languages it may be phonologically delimited as well (5.3.2). The principal purely phonological term for a group of consonants and vowels with the status of a unit is *syllable*. This term, familiar enough in general usage, has not been employed as a technical term so far in the main text of this book. It is, in fact, used technically in at least two ways, as a phonetic unit and as a phonological unit. Phonetically the term *syllable* has frequently been used to refer to a sequence of speech sounds having a maximum or peak of inherent sonority (that is apart from factors such as stress and voice pitch) between two minima of sonority. Generally speaking, vowels are more sonorous than consonants, and continuant consonants than stop consonants (*cp: p* 101); to a large extent, though not wholly, sonority varies with the degree of openness of the vocal tract, and this has led some to delimit phonetic syllables by such features as the degrees of 'stricture' or obstruction of the air passage in articulation. In each case the results are similar.[14]

However, the term is more widely used in general linguistics as part of the phonological level of analysis, and the **syllable** is defined as a unit for each language separately. In this usage *syllable* refers to a number of different sequences of consonants and vowels, together with other features such as length and stress, or to single consonants or vowels, which in the language concerned are suitably considered as a unitary group for further analysis. The linguist decides by criteria that may include purely phonetic factors what sequences comprise the syllables of the language he is describing in the course of devising a full phonological analysis thereof; and it is normally found that there is a considerable correspondence between syllables established on purely phonetic criteria of stricture or sonority and those established for the purpose of further phonological description. It is frequently the case that the syllable may be defined phonologically as the unit that can bear a single degree of stress, as in English, or a single tone, as in many tone languages (3.5.4, 4.3.5). Words may be classified as monosyllabic, disyllabic, trisyllabic, etc, according to the number of syllables they contain. Phonetically it is often hard to decide to which syllable an intervocalic consonant belongs, as the minimum of sonority and the maximum of stricture may occur in the middle of its articulation, and such consonants may have to be described phonetically as ambisyllabic, belonging to both. But when a decision is taken phonologically to allot the consonant to a particular syllable, in general single intervocalic consonants within a word are assigned to the following vowel (V-CV, not VC-V). This is done principally on the distributional grounds that CV is in all languages a commoner sequence than VC, and indeed in some languages VC sequences are very much restricted and found only with certain consonants; moreover in a word stressed on a non-initial syllable, in stress-marked languages, the stressed articulation usually begins on the consonant in such sequences. There is, too, a tendency to seek a parallelism between the possible absolute initial consonant clusters of a language and those ascribed to its syllable initial positions. Thus English permits absolute (word or utterance) initial /tr/ and /kl/ (*tree* and *climb*), but not /lk/ or /dn/, which provides one reason, among others, for syllabifying sequences like *bulky* and *badness* as /'bʌl-ki/ and /'bæd-nis/.

In the case of intervocalic sequences of consonants the phonetic criteria of sonority and stricture may be referred to for a decision, but sometimes stress is observed to begin on an inherently less sonorous consonant and the syllable division is, accordingly, made before that consonant. Thus in English words like *astray* and *mistake*, the stress often begins on the /s/, and despite the sequence /st/ being fricative followed by stop, the syllable division is made /ə-'strei/ and /mi-'steik/. But in some words containing the element *mis-*, where the semantic union is less close, the stress onset is often on the second consonant, with different syllable division in consequence (*eg: mistime*, /mis-'taim/). Sometimes phonetic features characteristic of a final consonant may assign an intervocalic consonant to the preceding syllable, especially in fairly loosely compounded words like *book-end* /'buk-end/, and this is a common practice in English across word boundaries, as in the contrasting sequences such as *an aim* and *a name*, /ən'eim/ and /ə'neim/ (*cp* in this context the syllabification of *robe-room* /'roub-ruːm/, and *cobra*, /'kou-brə/). In this respect English is in marked contrast to French, wherein word final spoken consonants are generally syllabified with the initial vowels of words following without pause, irrespective of the boundaries (*liaison*). Some English words classed phonologically as monosyllables could by strictly phonetic criteria be regarded as disyllabic, as, for example, *strain* /strein/, but the stress always begins on the /s/.

In English and in the majority of languages phonological syllables (the term *syllable* will henceforth be used in this sense unless it is stated otherwise) consist of one or more consonants and a vowel. But a single vowel can constitute a syllable, as in *ah* /aː/, and a syllable division can be established between two vowels as in *seeing* /'siːiŋ/, where one observes a fall in sonority in the transition between the two vowels. Conversely a syllable may contain no vowel, as in the case in English with syllables ending in /n/, /m/, and /l/, in words like *cotton* /'kɔtn̩/, *bosom* /'buzm̩/, and *apple* /'æpl̩/. In such words it is not easy to find definitive criteria, either at the phonetic or the phonological level for locating the syllable division. Some words of more than two syllables contain syllables of this type, *eg: coddling* /'kɔdl̩-iŋ/, as contrasted with *codling* /'kɔd-liŋ/. In quick speech a syllable consisting of a single consonant may be found in utterances like *'s terrible*, *'s true*, /s'teribl/, /s'truː/, in which the longer duration of the [s] sound, the onset of stress, and the aspirated [tʰ] establish /t/ as initial consonant of the second syllable. In Japanese /ŋ/ occurring after a vowel, or in initial position, constitutes a separate syllable, as in /saŋ/, *three*; this is established on the grounds of its having its own pitch possibilities as well as on its greater relative duration than non-syllabic consonants.[15]

A phonological analysis, based on the identification of the phonemes to be set up in a language, must take into account not merely the paradigmatic dimension of contrast but also the syntagmatic dimension of the permitted phoneme sequences in the lexical forms of a language (*cp* 2.1.2). Phonologically the syllable is of prime importance as a unit within which the relative distributions or possibilities of sequential occurrence of phonemes and phonological features can be stated. Languages differ very much in the types of syllable structures they exhibit and the places these occupy in words. While CV is a universal structure, beyond that each language has its own rules. Some languages, like Arabic, do not allow any syllable not beginning with a consonant; others, like Fijian and Hawaiian, do not permit any syllable ending with a consonant. Italian allows no word final syllables ending in CC sequences, and not many ending in a single consonant compared to some other languages. English and German allow a good deal of consonantal clustering both initially and finally, exemplified in such words as *strengths* /streŋθs/ and *sprichst* /ʃpriçst/ you (singular) speak, both very difficult to pronounce for speakers of languages not permitting such clustering.[16] It seems to be a general observation that types of consonant clustering in syllable initial and syllable final position are often comparable, though several sequences may be found in one position that are not permitted in the other.

Languages thus differ both in the selection they make from the available articulations of the vocal apparatus and in the positional arrangements of syllabic groupings that they impose on them; and the principal difficulty in learning to pronounce foreign languages lies in the overcoming these two sorts of limitation ingrained into one in learning one's native language as a child. It has been said that the greatest obstacle to learning a language is speaking one already. The mastery of foreign sounds is one obvious difficulty, but learning to pronounce sounds found in one's own language in positions from which that language excludes them presents almost equal difficulty. English /ŋ/ is confined to intervocalic and postvocalic positions (*singer* /'siŋə/, *sing* /siŋ/). For an English speaker to pronounce and to recognize correctly words like Swahili /ŋgoma/ drum, and Sundanese /ŋaran/ name, requires training, attention, and effort, as does the pronunciation and recognition of syllable final [h], as in Malay /təŋah/ middle, a sound confined to initial and intervocalic position in English (*hand* /hænd/, *behind* /bi'haind/). These aspects of phonology are often referred to as phonotactics.

Considerations of syllable structure often help in deciding on the best analysis of sounds and sound groups that are phonetically ambiguous. There has been some discussion on whether English /tʃ/, as in *church* /tʃəːtʃ/, is one consonant phoneme, like /t/, or two as /tr/ and /ts/ are regarded. In favour of treating /tʃ/ as a sequence of /t/ and /ʃ/ are the economy in phoneme inventory, as /t/ and /ʃ/ are both required anyway as English phonemes, and the phonetic similarity of /tʃ/ and /ts/; but in favour of treating it as a single affricate phoneme, the usual practice, is its occurrence in syllable final position, unlike /tr/, and in syllable initial position, unlike /ts/, except in a few words of obvious foreign origin such as *tsetse* (*fly*) /'tsetsi/ (also often pronounced /'tetsi/. Similar considerations support the analysis in Yurok (a language of North California) of /kʷ/ as a single phoneme, but of /ky/ as a sequence of two phonemes.

So, too, considerations of syllable structure, in which the /w/ and /j/ of words like *wet* and *yet* (/wet/ and /jet/) occupy consonantal rather than vocalic places, are often decisive in classing them, as semivowels, among the consonants of language (*cp: p* 97).

English diphthongs have been variously analysed, as have the diphthongs of other languages. Some, like Jones and Gimson, have chosen to regard them as separate unitary phonemes, phonetically complex but otherwise like other vowel phonemes; others analyse them as sequences of two phonemes functioning in the syllable like a long vowel, and identifying the starting and ending points of each diphthong with one of the phonemes already set up elsewhere in the English phoneme system. Thus the first phonemes of English /ei/, /ou/, and /ɔi/ may be regarded as /e/ and /ɔ/, with a closer allophone of /ɔ/ being used before /u/ than before /i/ or before consonants; the initial phonemes of /ai/ and /au/ are identified with /a/, as allophones of the vowel phoneme otherwise found with length as /ɑː/. It must be remembered that the transcription in which these diphthongs are represented in this book follows the system of Jones (Transcriptions and abbreviations, *pp* xxii–xxiii) not the phonemic analysis just mentioned. The second phonemes of these diphthongs have been variously identified with the semivowel consonants /j/ and /w/ and with the vowels /i/ and /u/. There seems little to choose between the two, but the phonetic nature of the sounds themselves and the parallelism with the centring diphthongs /iə/, /ɛə/, and /uə/, where the matching of the second part with /ə/ in standard English seems obvious, may be held to argue in favour of analysing the second elements of all the English diphthongs as a vowel phoneme. English triphthongs are probably best analysed as disyllabic sequences of a diphthong followed by /ə/ (hence the stress marking in the examples on *p* 92 above).[17]

In many languages making use of stress as a distinctive feature in their phonological systems, the segmental composition of stressed and unstressed syllables differs in its range of possibilities. This can be illustrated from English, though some other languages carry the differences further. All English vowels and diphthongs, except short /ə/, can occur in stressed or unstressed syllables; but /ə/ and the consonant syllables with /l/, /m/, and /n/, can only occur in unstressed positions. The working of this distributional rule can be seen in some pairs of words such as: *convict* (noun) /'kɔnvikt/, (verb) /kən'vikt/; *permit* (noun) /'pəːmit/, (verb) /pə'mit/.

4.3.5 Tone phonemes

The phonetic feature of pitch variation was mentioned in the preceding chapter, where the traditional distinction between tonal and non-tonal languages was referred to (3.5.4). In phonology the tonal phenomena of tone languages were the first to be brought within the scope of the phoneme theory. This became necessary as soon as phonemic analysis was applied to such languages. In tone languages differences in pitch, or tone, as it is called, exhibit a limited set of contrastive distinctions, on one or more syllables of words, and these serve to differentiate one word from another just as segmental contrasts do, and may frequently constitute the only diffentiation in 'minimal pairs' (*eg* North Chinese /tanpau/ with level and falling-rising tones, to guarantee, with falling and rising tones, diluted; Mixteco (a language of Mexico) /ʒuku/ with two mid level tones, mountains, with mid level and low tones, brush). Tone differences may likewise mark grammatical distinctions in some languages; in Mixteco the distinction between the present and the future tenses of some verbs is maintained solely by different tone sequences in the syllables of the words (*cp* 6.4.6).

Tones as phonetic features present their own problems of apperception and description; as phonemes, however, the principle of their establishment is not different from that of segmental phonemes or phonemes of stress. As they may characterize more than a single segment, they are, like length and stress, often called suprasegmental phonemes. Sometimes the term *toneme* is used to refer to tone phonemes, but this is perhaps undesirable as it suggests that as phonemes they are in a class apart, which they are not, if phonemes are regarded as the units of distinctiveness of whatever sort into which linguistic forms may be analysed and by which they are distinguished by one another.

The potentially indefinite variations in the actual heights of pitches and in the types of pitches (level, falling, rising, falling-rising, rising-falling, etc) are analysed into a limited number of pitch or tone phonemes, each of which contrasts in at least some environments with at least one other such phoneme. The number varies from language to language, as do the types. In some tone languages, for example Yoruba, a language of West Africa, only level tone phonemes are found (phonetic falls and rises of pitch are analysed as successions of two different level tones each influenced allophonically by the other; thus $[/] = /\_^-/$, and $[\backslash] = /^-\_/$). Other languages require rises and falls and combinations of the two to be recognized among their distinctive tonal phonemes; thus North Chinese has four tone phonemes: (high) level, rising, falling-rising, and falling. Usually the domain of one tone, or the sequence of segments with which it is associated, is a single syllable, though in a few tone languages two distinct tones are found on the same syllable in sequence; for example in Mazateco, another language of Mexico, /ti/ with low followed by high tone, bowl, but with a single high tone, it burns. In speaking of the domain of a tone as a syllable it must be borne in mind that while this includes all its consonants and vowels, the actual manifestation of tones by vibrations of the vocal cords at different speeds is only possible in the voiced segments thereof.

Distinct differences of pitch in tone phonemes are wholly a matter of relative height. There are within the limits of the pitch possibilities of the human vocal cords no fixed points. In a system of two level tone phonemes, high and low, the high must be higher than the low in all positions where they can contrast, and a similar situation obtains with a three-term system of high, mid and low. In the speech of a single speaker at one time the tones must preserve their relative positions on the scale, but different people's voices vary in overall height, and clearly a child's low tone may be absolutely higher in pitch than the high tone of an adult speaking the same language.

In tone languages syllable structure must be stated jointly in terms of segmental and tonal phonemes, and sometimes length and stress are also involved as additional phonemic distinctions. The tones and segments are seldom, if ever, wholly independent of one another, and one finds that some tone phonemes are restricted to syllables of a certain segmental composition. Thus in Thai, syllables containing a long vowel and ending in a stop consonant are only found with two of the five tone phonemes set up for the language as a whole. In North Chinese certain unstressed syllables may be 'toneless' phonologically; that is to say the pitch on which they are said in connected discourse is wholly determined by the nature of the tone on the preceding syllable.[18]

Phonetic features other than relative pitch height and pitch movement and belonging phonetically more to the sphere of voice-quality are sometimes involved in maintaining tonal distinctions. In Vietnamese two of the six phonemically distinct tones are additionally characterized by 'creakiness' or glottalization (intermittent momentary closures and constriction of the glottis in addition to the vibrations of voicing).

The general category of tone languages conceals a number of different types. Such languages may be classified according to the number of distinct tones (*eg* North Chinese four, Thai five, Vietnamese six,[19] Cantonese six, and in some dialects more), and according to the nature of the tones (*eg* all level, or with falls and rises, or with additional features such as glottalization). But perhaps more significant linguistically are the different functions that tone distinctions play in tone languages. They are grouped together as a class of languages by the fact that, in them all, distinctive tones are phonological property of individual words as such. Lexical contrasts between words are the best known function of tones, but in addition tonal differences may in some languages mark grammatical categories, grammatical relationships, and syntactic groupings (6.4.6), just like the segmental or other suprasegmental phonemes of a language, from which considered simply as part of the distinctive signalling equipment of a language they are not essentially different.

It must also be noted that the distinction between tonal and non-tonal languages is not as absolute as is often thought. Chinese and Mazateco are tonal, English is non-tonal, but Norwegian and some other languages are tonal to a very limited extent (3.5.4)

4.3.6 Intonation
The phonological function of pitch differences in what are called tone languages has already been dealt with (4.3.5). Students of European languages are more familiar with the function of pitch sequences as intonations, that is the property of sentences or parts of sentences as such, and not of individual lexically different words. Isolated words are, of course, said with a regular pitch pattern, but this is, in other than tone languages, an intonation applied to a one-word sentence, and any differences of pitch between one word and another will be due either to a different sentence intonation or to differences consequential on the syllable structure and in some languages on the stress patterning of the word.

Intonation or intonation **tunes**, as they are called, are regular sequences of pitch differences coextensive with a whole sentence or with successive parts thereof, and constituting an essential feature of normal spoken utterances. As with distinctive tones in tone languages, it is the sequence of pitches of different relative heights that matters; the actual height of the pitches is determined in part by the age and sex of the speaker as well as any personal habits of speaking with a high- or a low-pitched voice.

The intonation tunes of a language may usually be associated in general, though not entirely, with particular contextual functions of speech and with various general semantic categories, such as emphasis, excitement, surprise, and the like. Intonational differences also correlate in part with different syntactic structures and functions. The two English tunes (Tune I and Tune II in Jones's terminology) associated respectively with statements and with questions expecting an answer *yes* or *no* have already been noticed (3.5.4); questions introduced by a specific interrogative word, like, *who have you come to see?*, are normally uttered with Tune I. These two are certainly not the only intonations recognizable in English, but they cover a good deal of ordinary speech. Similar differences of intonation with approximate semantic correlations can be discovered in other languages, including tone languages, in which the references of different pitches carry both tonal and intonational distinctions. Correspondences with semantic functions are seldom exact; too many as yet unknown factors are involved in the present state of our knowledge.

Single intonation tunes in sentences differ mainly as the result of differences in the length of the stretches of speech with which they occur, and, in languages with phonologically different stress patterns, according to the occurrence of the stressed syllables. The statement tune, Tune I, in English is in outline a rise to a relatively high falling pitch followed, unless it is final in the tune, by a sequence of lower pitches. In a longer sentence other high level pitches may precede the final fall; conversely in very short sentences the intonation may start as its highest point, and in monosyllabic utterances a single falling pitch will represent the entire intonation tune. If in one sentence a sequence of more than one such intonation tune occurs (as in very long sentences, or sentences slowly enunciated), the non-final tunes generally fall less at the end than does the final tune.

In English, as in several other stress languages, stressed syllables carry more intonational weight than unstressed syllables; and, indeed, much of the prominence accorded to stressed syllables results from the fact that these syllables stand out in intonation tunes. Generally speaking, in a falling or level sequence the stressed syllables are slightly higher in pitch than the unstressed or intermediately stressed, and the final falling pitch of Tune I occurs on the last stressed syllable, any following unstressed syllables uttered on a series of more or less low level pitches with a slight final fall. Where a 'change of direction' is involved, as when the highest point of Tune I is reached, or the lowest point in Tune II (a sequence of descending levels followed by a rise), the extreme point is always a fully stressed syllable. This may be easily noticed if the intonations are compared in the sentences *it was yesterday* and *it was today* said on Tune I, and in *was it yesterday?* and *was it today?* said on Tune II:

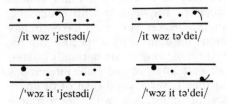

Intonation tunes may be modified and varied, often with the effect of emphasizing a particular word, by using an extra-high pitch standing above the rest of the sequence, or by a fall from high to low in the middle, as in such a sentence as *it's quite impossible to go any higher*:

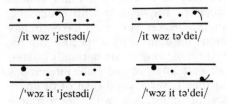

/its kwait im'pɔsible tə 'gou eni 'haiə/

Such a fall can only occur on a stressed syllable, which is often uttered with the additional force of emphatic stress.

A considerable amount of specialist study has been carried out on the descriptive analysis of the various classes of tunes that make up English intonation, both as regards the phonetic details of the pitch levels and pitch movements involved, and in their correlations with semantic functions and grammatical structures.

Many linguists have been content to use the phoneme concept for the phonological analysis of phonetic phenomena within accepted or established word boundaries (including the tones of tone languages), and to leave intonation outside its scope. But with the aim of bringing all phonological analysis within the scope of the phoneme theory much thought was given by some American linguists to the phonemic analysis of intonation tunes. Various systems were proposed, but the most generally accepted treatment, pioneered by Wells and Pike, analysed intonation tunes into sequences of distinctive pitch phonemes. In English four phonemes of relative pitch have been established in analyses.

The first two British English examples on *p* 138, above, could be transcribed in these terms:

/²it wəz ³'jestədi/   /²it wəz tə'³¹dei/²⁰

4.3.7 Distinctive features

Besides the theoretical and methodological work on the phoneme and a phonemic transcription that we have been following, the segmental phoneme itself has been subjected to further analysis. Considered simply as the basis and justification of a separate transcriptional sign in a broad transcription, the segmental phoneme is no more than one of the contrasting phonological units of a language, into which its spoken utterances may be analysed, and its linguistic essence lies in its being, at least in some phonological environments, contrastive, or distinct from every other phoneme in the language; the way in which this distinctiveness is maintained is of secondary importance.

However, phonology has always been concerned with wider linguistic considerations than the needs of an adequate transcription, although its development in terms of the phoneme theory has throughout been in large part determined by those needs. If the consonant and vowel phonemes are envisaged as the minimal distinctive units into which the sentence and word forms of a language may be analysed, their further analysis is revealing. This further analysis of the phoneme as a scientific concept rather than simply as a transcriptionally devised unit was first undertaken systematically by Trubetzkoy, the Russian linguist and leader of the Prague school of phonology between the two world wars, and is especially associated with his colleagues and those who have been most influenced by him.[21]

It is obvious on the most cursory examination that some phonemes are phonetically more closely related than others; thus English /p/ and /b/ are much more akin than are /p/ and /ŋ/. If the phonemes of a language are compared and their members phonetically analysed, it is found that they are distinct from one another by differing in certain specific features of articulation, and that these same features serve in many cases to distinguish a number of other pairs of phonemes. This has appeared already in the grouping together of /i/ and /e/, /u/ and /ɔ/ as front spread and back rounded vowels respectively. In the English phonemes /p/, /b/, and /m/, /t/, /d/, and /n/, and /k/, /g/, and /ŋ/, /p/ and /b/, /t/ and /d/, and /k/ and /g/ differ from each other in the same respects, as voiceless and voiced plosives at the same point of articulation (with the other features subsumed under these labels, 3.3.4); and both phonemes in each pair differ from the corresponding nasal in being oral stop consonants as against nasal continuant consonants. Looked at the other way, the triads /p/, /b/, and /m/, /t/, /d/, and /n/, /k/, /g/, and /ŋ/ all share the same three points of articulation, bilabial, alveolar, and velar, and the corresponding phonemes in each triad share the same three types of articulation, voiceless stop, voiced stop, and nasal continuant. The **oppositions**, as they are called, between the nine phonemes concerned in this may be represented in the diagrams.

/p/   /t/   /k/
/b/   /m/   /d/   /n/   /g/   /ŋ/

Features that distinguish phonemes in a language in this way are called **distinctive** or **pertinent features**, and their number is always less than that of the phonemes in the language. The contrast between the presence and absence of a feature, or between two distinctive features is called an **opposition**. It will be seen that some pairs of phonemes differ by only one such opposition, others by two, and others by more than two (thus in English, /p/ and /b/ are distinguished by one, /p/ and /d/ by two, and /p/ and /z/ by three).

Where two phonemes are distinguished by reference to a single distinctive feature, Trubetzkoy and the Prague school linguists made use of the concept of marked and unmarked members of such pairs. One member was regarded as possessing, *ie* marked by, the feature, the other as lacking it, *ie* unmarked by it. Thus English voiced and unvoiced consonants having all other features in common (/d/ and /t/, /z/ and /s/, /v/ and /f/, etc) were designated marked and unmarked respectively in regard to the feature of voicing.[22]

The nine separate phonemes of the three English triads are maintained as distinctive units by six features: plosion, voice, nasality, bilabiality, alveolarity, and velarity (orality and voicelessness being regarded as the absence of a feature, nasality and voice, respectively).

Vowel phonemes may be similarly analysed. A seven-vowel

/i//y/   /u/
/e//ø/   /o/
/a/

system can be analysed into the two binary oppositions, front and back, and rounded and spread, together with the three distinctive

degrees of openness; this latter is a feature wherein the contrast
is not between two features or between a feature and its absence,
but between different degrees of a feature; in the vowel system
just given, closeness could equally well have been taken as the
positive feature.

Two facts emerge from this sort of analysis:

[i] What appears to be phonetically the same sound in two
different languages may as a member of a phoneme enter
into different sets of oppositions. Thus in English /b/ as a
voiced bilabial plosive is opposed to /p/ and /m/ within the
triad of its closest phonological neighbours; in some
languages of India, for example Hindi, /b/ as a voiced
unaspirated bilabial plosive enters into a contrast system
with four other terms, /p/ voiceless unaspirated, /pʰ/ voiceless aspirated, /bʰ/ voiced aspirated, and /m/ nasal; and
other plosive consonants enter into corresponding systems.[23]
Part of this system can be shown diagrammatically.

/p/   /pʰ/
/b/   /bʰ/
/m/

[ii] Not all the oppositions of pertinent features between one
phoneme and another operate in a language in all phonological environments. It has already been seen that the
essence of the phoneme is contrast or distinctiveness, in at
least some environments. The phoneme system and the
phoneme inventory of a language (and so its broad transcription requirements) are established by reference to all
environments of maximal contrast; analysis of the phoneme
itself make clear the different contrasts obtaining in different
environments. In English, in initial position /p/ and /b/, /t/
and /d/ /k/ and /g/ all contrast; but after initial /s/ only
three plosive contrasts are possible, not six, at the three
points of articulation; there is no possibility of distinction
within the syllable between voice and voicelessness in the
sound segment occurring in such an environment (*eg: spill*
/spil/; *still* /stil/; *skill* /skil/). The sounds are spelled with
p, *t*, and *k*, and are usually assigned to the phonemes /p/,
/t/, and /k/ (as here); but their ranges of contrast in this
environment are more restricted than in absolute initial
position, where there is the additional contrast between the
voiced and voiceless plosive at each articulatory position.
After initial /s/ only plosivity, as contrasted with nasal

release (*spell* /spel/; *smell* /smel/), and place of articulation (*spill* /spil/; *still* /stil/; *skill* /skil/) are functional distinctions within the syllable. This restriction of the opposition occurring elsewhere in a language is called **neutralization**, and various examples of it are found in different languages. Neutralization of the distinction between two phonemes has just been noticed; in a language like Spanish with a five-vowel phoneme system

/i/   /u/

/e/   /o/

/a/

the distinction between the concomitant features front spread and back rounded is neutralized in the position of maximal openness with the single phoneme /a/. In German and Russian the contrast between voiced and voiceless plosives is neutralized in final position, only voiceless plosives occurring irrespective of the rest of the phonological environment. Thus while English has the contrast of *found* and *fount* (/faund/ and /faunt/), German has only /t/ in such a position; *Bund*, bundle, and *bunt*, mottled, are both pronounced /bunt/, though they are differentiated in other case forms, *Bundes* /'bundes/ and *buntes* /'buntes/.[24]

The examination of facts of this kind in phonology, though it may be irrelevant to mere transcriptional needs, leads to a fuller understanding of the different ways languages make use of their selected phonetic repertoire.

Distinctive feature analysis has developed since Trubetzkoy's time on somewhat different lines in alliance with the findings of acoustic phonetics (3.4). Distinctive feature phonology now plays a major part in phonological component of transformational-generative theory and transformational-generative descriptions of languages (4.4.4). The development of distinctive feature phonology in America owes much to the work done by a leading associate of Trubetzkoy, Jakobson, after his arrival in the United States during the Second World War. In the 1940s and 1950s this aspect of phonological theory developed in close alliance with the advances then being made in acoustic phonetics, and the articulatory basis of Trubetzkoy's distinctive features was largely replaced by sets of acoustically identified features. The features abstracted as distinctive components of phonemes were drawn not directly from articulatory processes (though articulation is the basis of all speech sounds and their component features), but from characteristic contrasting acoustic features in the sound waves resulting from these processes. Some of the distinctions are the same as Trubetzkoy's, such as oral and nasal, consonant and vowel; but some, such as grave and acute (velars and labials as against palatals and dentals), compact and diffuse (velars as against labials, open as against close vowels), strident and mellow (eg /s/ and /z/ as against /θ/ and /ð/), though referable to the different articulatory positions of the vocal organs, are primarily acoustic features, defined in acoustic terms, distinguished by the different sets of frequencies and differences in shape and structure displayed by the sound waves, in particular the place of the two major formants, along the scale of frequencies (3.4). As will have been noticed, their names have in some cases been chosen to reflect the general auditory impression that they give rise to. Until recently these acoustic distinctive features formed the basis of distinctive feature phonology, and this is still the case with many linguists who make use of them. But since 1968 there has been a return on the part of some transformational-generative linguists to an articulatory based set of features, more akin to those used by Trubetzkoy, though not identical with them. Whichever type of feature is adopted the claim is made that the consonantal and vocalic distinctions maintained in any language can be reduced to combinations of a minimal universal set of opposed binary features (eg vocalic, non-vocalic; consonantal, non-consonantal; nasal, oral; tense, non-tense) and that, strictly speaking, segments are just unitary marks or abbreviations for different combinations of specific distinctive features. These features are represented by the potentially limitless number of actual sounds produced by the human vocal organs and transmitted by sound waves through the air.[25]

The distinctive feature is perhaps the single most important theoretical concept in phonology during the present century, first proposed by Trubetzkoy and then magisterially developed by Jakobson and the various linguists and groups of linguists working with him. It has deepened our understanding of the ways in which languages operate as spoken means of communication, it has opened by new lines of thought and new and important connections between phonology and acoustic phonetics (3.4), and the concept itself has been extended to analysis at other levels, in semantics, morphology, and syntax.

Since the 1960s distinctive feature theory, in one or other of its forms, has been the accepted theory for the phonological component of a generative account of a language (4.4.4, *p* 161), and the theoretical basis of much recent acoustic and instrumental phonetic research. In morphology, as long ago as 1936 Jakobson proposed an analysis of the syntactic and semantic functions of the Russian case system in terms of combinations of grammatically distinctive features, and more recently nouns and verbs have been subclassified by reference to such binary contrasts as animate–inanimate, countable–non-countable, concrete–abstract, transitive–intransitive, animate object as against unspecified object (*eg frighten* as against *push*). Some linguists have pursued this line as far as suggesting that the whole of a word's lexical meaning could ultimately be stable in terms of sets of semantic and grammatical features, which should then form the content of an ideal dictionary entry. Thus, to take a well-known example, *bachelor*, in the sense of unmarried man, is analysed into the features 'human', 'male', 'adult', and 'never married'. It must, however, be regarded as at the least unproven and probably very doubtful whether this type of analysis can usefully be made coextensive with what we ordinarily understand as the meanings of most words in a language. We are certainly very far from achieving anything like complete analyses in these terms, useful though this method is for explicating a number of recurrent semantic attributes that characterize some fairly lightly knit lexical subclasses, for example kinship vocabularies (to which most efforts in this field have been directed so far).[26]

4.4 Further developments

4.4.1 'Classical phoneme theory'

The account so far given in 4.3 would be very generally agreed on as the basic outline of the phoneme theory, accepted by most linguists in the 1940s. Thereafter certain developments took place and are still taking place, all of which in varying degrees retain their adherents and their practitioners. From all these developments has emerged the current 'state of the art' in phonology, and they should be noticed in this light.

In the period 1940 to 1956, that is to say during the years immediately preceding the so-called 'Chomskyan revolution' (7.1.2), several very influential American linguists, basing their work on what they considered to have been the teaching of Bloomfield (who died in 1949) and under his inspiration, set out a programme of phonological analysis by which they thought that the scientific status of linguistics could be and should be greatly enhanced. This came to be known as the 'Classical phoneme theory' and, by special use of the term, as 'structuralist phonemics'. Later critical writers have referred to the theory as 'taxonomic', because some linguists at the time declared that the identification and classification (taxonomy) of linguistic entities were their first objectives, while some of their successors think that they should go further than these rather limited aims.[27]

As far as phonology was concerned they demanded that phonological analysis should be undertaken solely and exhaustively by the setting up of phonemes, building on the phoneme theory as already established, but with the additional requirement that all this analysis should be quite independent and separate from analysis at other levels, such as semantics, syntax, and morphology. Morphological and syntactic analysis, in fact, methodologically followed and theoretically presupposed a complete prior phonemic analysis. The counterpart of this independence was self-sufficiency: it was required that the phonemic system of a language and its representation in the phonemic transcription should be demonstrably derived exclusively from phonetic data in the utterances of the language. Conversely the phonemic transcription together with a phonetic description of all the allophones of the phonemes, segmental and suprasegmental, must provide all the information required for the realization of the pronounced sentences of the language, or for their representation in a narrow transcription. This requirement of two-way independence is often referred to today as the 'biuniqueness requirement'.

4.4.2 Juncture phonemes

This demand necessitated types of phoneme additional to those that have been introduced so far; a set of phonemes was required, to analyse the phonetic phenomena associated in some languages between word finals and word initials, some of the phonetic features of morphologically complex words, and with the final patterns of intonations before pauses.

The basic question was about the relation between the phonological and grammatical (syntactic and morphological) levels in the organization of the description of language structure. The phoneme theory so far set out in this book allowed references to some grammatical entities (*eg* words) and to the results of some grammatical analysis, not themselves based on phonetic phenomena and phonetic features as such, to form part of the context for phonemic analysis. And, of course, this included the use of spaces in a transcription where these were based on grammatical divisions between grammatically defined words (5.3.1).

In several well-known works on phonology in Britain and else-where, mostly concerned with languages having a long estab-lished writing system, terms such as *word, compound word, word group*, and the like have been used as part of the environment for assigning speech sounds to phonemes and determining distinc-tions of stress; that it to say, word final position and word initial position are used as part of the relevant data in phonemic analysis. In transcriptions based on such procedures, the spaces between words and the hyphens in some compound words as found in the orthography are themselves used as symbols and their significance is taken as part of the environment of the phonemes represented in the transcription, without their own status being questioned. In many languages, as in English, the boundaries of words and the junctions within compound words are often relevant to the assignment of sounds to phonemes; or, conversely, phonemes are often represented by different members or allophones in word initial and in word final positions. The distribution of English 'clear' and 'dark' /l/ is a case in point (4.3.2, *p* 125). But word boundaries as such and the boundaries between the components of compound words are not heard; they are not themselves part of the articulatory or the acoustic stream of speech, in the way that consonants and vowels, and features like stress and pitch are; nor, of course, are words in speech all separated by pauses, as words in print are in many writing systems separated by spaces. Word initial and word final are not, therefore, as such, phonetically observable positions like utter-ance initial and utterance final are (since silence is observable), though in isolated words they coincide.

Such considerations impressed themselves on those who were dealing with unwritten languages wherein no pre-existing ortho-graphic word boundaries thrust themselves on the analyst, but this theory and method of phonemic analysis has been developed and applied in working on the analysis of very well-known languages, and notably of English.

Linguists who admit in varying degrees what are sometimes called grammatical prerequisites in phonological analysis need not elaborate phonemic analysis further as regards grammatical inter- and intra-word divisions. But, theoretical objections apart, one of the chief difficulties is that in languages phonological and grammatical divisions usually neither consistently correspond nor consistently fail to correspond. In a case of consistent non-correspondence, perhaps approached in French, word spaces could simply be ignored in transcriptions as merely serving the purposes of ready comprehension and of no more phonological significance than the division of the text into successive lines. Pauses are, of course, phonologically relevant, but as periods of momentary or indefinite silence they are audible as breaks in speech, and the marks by which they are symbolized in transcriptions are clearly significant and based on actual phonetic observation.

Conversely, in a language, if there is one, in which a phonetic feature such as fixed place stress invariably marked every word boundary, a type to some extent represented in several languages (*eg* Hungarian word initial stress, Polish and Swahili stress on the penultimate syllable of words), the grammatical word could be shown to correspond exactly with a phonologically definable unit (the phonological or phonemic word), and the spaces marking word divisions would be no more than a symbolization of phonetically marked and phonologically relevant divisions in the audible material (though in the case of penultimate word stress the spaces would not occur at the same places as the features themselves).

Many languages exhibit partial correspondences between grammatical words and phonetically marked divisions. In English the phonetic marking of word divisions is often potential rather than actual; that is, the phonetic features that serve to mark them are such as may occur rather than such as invariably do occur. As an example most English words do not contain more than one full stress, but in connected speech many words are uttered without any syllable bearing a full stress, and a number of words (such as *the* and *a*) are very seldom stressed. Some orthographic and grammatical word divisions in English are not marked by phonetic division; words ending in -*r*, when pronounced with an /r/, link syllabically with the initial vowel of the following word (3.3.4, *p* 96), and some phrases like *not at all*, and with certain speakers *it is* and *at home* are regularly syllabified /nɔ-tə-'tɔːl/, /i-'tiz/, /ə-'toum/, thus reversing the more usual correlation of word and syllable division in the language. The rejection by an influential group of linguists of appeals to grammatically defined word boundaries engendered an acute analysis of the phonetic features that do, in fact, often coincide in varying degrees, depending on the language under examination, with grammatically significant divisions.

Such phonetic features are called **junctures**, and the phonemes based on them **juncture phonemes**.[28] They are often included among the suprasegmental phonemes. Between 1935 and 1957 a great deal of detailed controversy went on in regard to theoretical and practical questions about juncture phonemes. The main prin-

ciples can easily be illustrated. English pairs such as *an aim* and
a name, an ocean and *a notion, at ease* and *a tease* (*cp* 4.3.4) are
in many utterances audibly different, and exemplify differences
that are found in many environments across words boundaries
where no other minimal distinctions are involved. The phonetic
differences are not hard to state; they involve different phonetic
syllable division, with onset of stess and syllable initiality at the
consonant in the second member of each pair, with forcible
release and aspiration of the /t/ in *tease*, as against onset of stress
and syllable initiality on the vowel in the first member, with
weaker articulation of the syllable final consonant, somewhat
prolonged and 'drawled' in the case of /n/, and inaudibly or only
weakly released with little or no aspiration in the case of /t/. The
second members of each pair do not ordinarily differ audibly
from single words of the same segmental and stress composition
(*cp: attack, a tack* /ə'tæk/, and so no phoneme of juncture or
phonemic symbol is posited. In the first members of phoneme of
inter-word juncture, assumed as part of the phoneme inventory
of the language, is said to occur in the place between the
segments corresponding to the orthographic space, or order to
provide for the phonetic differences. It is often symbolized /+/
or /#/, but spaces could be used equally well in the transcription
if consistently and solely so used. In this method of analysis of
juncture phoneme /+/ would be set up to account for the syllable
division in examples such as those quoted above (4.3.4): *'s
terrible* /s + 'teribl/, *book-end* /'buk + end/. In the first example
/+/ would provide the environment for the greater duration of
/s/ and the initiality of /t/ (hence [tʰ]), as against its non-initiality
in such words as *steam* /stiːm/ (*cp: p* 122, above).

Two things must be noticed in connection with juncture
phonemes in this type of analysis: the features on the basis of
which the juncture phoneme is set up may in some cases not
occur in the part of the utterance corresponding to the place at
which the phoneme is located (this is so, for example, when
penultimate word stress is taken as the mark or exponent of
inter-word juncture); and these junctures are solely set up on the
basis of phonetic differences; they are not, as such, grammatical
symbols marking grammatical divisions, though in many
languages, such as English, their occurrences in a great many
cases parallel the inter-word spaces resulting from the separate
process of analysis at the grammatical level. Word sequences in
which a final /r/ is syllabified with the initial vowel of a following
word (3.3.4, *p* 96), and sequences like *a loan* /ə'loun/ and *a tack*
/ə'tæk/, show word divisions not marked by juncture, and the

pronunciation by some speakers of the name *Plato* /'pleitou/, with the first diphthong somewhat lengthened as if the word were '*play-toe*' has been adduced as an example of juncture occurring in the middle of a grammatical indivisible unit. The technicalities of juncture analysis gave rise to considerable discussion, some of which is referred to in note 28 at the end of the chapter. But detailed discussion of these questions attracts less attention than formerly and need not be pursued further here.

'Classical phoneme theory', in which the concept of the juncture phoneme played a major part, formed the basis of the phonological chapters of several once standard textbooks on linguistics, such as those by Gleason, Hill, and Hockett. It was expounded in detail by Trager and Smith and by Zellig Harris, as part of a general 'structuralist' theory of linguistic analysis and description.[29]

Of the currently active developing theories none would now wholly accept phonemic phonology in the form made definitive by Harris and his contemporaries. Nearest to what is now sometimes called 'classical phonemics' are the tegmemicists (7.4.2), whose central figure, Pike, however never accepted the separation of levels in all its rigour.[30]

Chomsky and the generative linguists take a diametrically opposed view to the 'classical phonemicists' on the relation between grammar and phonology, making phonological description dependent on a prior syntactic and morphological description, an attitude shared, within their different systems, by both the 'systemic grammarians' and the stratificationalists (7.4.3, 7.4.4).

Chomsky claims to have found a number of serious theoretical flaws and weaknesses in classical phonemic analysis, but his tribute to their work is well merited.[31] A great deal of the descriptive apparatus and terminology in use today has been taken from the work of these linguists, and it should be properly understood for this reason.

4.4.3 Prosodic phonology

Virtually all varieties of phonological theory currently maintained or under development may be seen as being built on the foundations of phonological analysis as outlined in the previous sections of this chapter. Several of them are also the result of reactions against what many linguists considered to be the too rigid and dogmatic positions taken up by adherents of the 'classical phoneme theory'.

At this point we may take notice of one of the earliest and

most radical of these reactions, prosodic phonology, centred on the ideas of Firth and developed by him and those working with him, mainly in London, in the years immediately following the end of the war in 1945. Prosodic phonology and the prosodic analysis of various languages aroused intense though limited interest up to 1960 and beyond. It can now be seen to have anticipated some of the principles and requirements of more recent theories.

Phonemic phonology, as has been seen, grew out of the need and search for adequate broad transcriptions; and while there has developed from it a complete theory and method of analysing and classifying phonological systems and the phonological struc- tures of languages, the requirements of a linear, readable, tran- scription to represent all the phonologically distinctive elements established in the analysis have always been kept to the fore. Phonological analysis and transcription have advanced together and mutually determined each other's progress.

Prosodic theory effectively decoupled phonological analysis from transcriptional requirements. A definitive formulation of this phonological theory, which is called **prosodic** phonology, has yet to be made, but a good deal of phonological description and discussion of phonological methods has been set in prosodic terms in Britain (and to a lesser extent elsewhere). Firth had worked on his ideas for a break with contemporary phonemic phonology for some time, but his proposals were first set out programmatically in 1948.[32]

Phonemic analysis concentrates on the paradigmatic relation of contrast in a given environment and on the serial treatment of the phonetic data; as far as possible all relevant phonetic features are assigned to phonemes occupying definite places in a linear succession of phonemes. This has been seen in the treat- ment of juncture phonemes and in the analysis of intonation into sequences of pitch phonemes; pitch and stress phonemes are distinguished from consonant and vowel phonemes as being suprasegmental, but relative to each other they are block-like units with definite segmental domains, usually syllables. And work has been done on the abstraction of phonemic 'long components' from successions of consonant and vowel phonemes all sharing a common feature, such as voicing or retroflexion. But in all such cases the analysis rests on a prior segmental phonemic one, and the groundwork and the bulk of phonemic analysis consist in assigning the relevant phonetic phenomena to a linear sequential series of phonemes, and setting up an inventory of such phonemes as the phonemic or phonological system of the language, wherein are contained all the phonetic distinctions employed by the language in communication. In this sense phonemic analysis is monosystemic.

As was seen, however, in the account given of the processes of articulation in the preceding chapter, speech is a continuous activity and any descriptive segmentation into successions of consonants and vowels involves some misrepresentation of the actual material being described. Manifestly some segmentation is necessary for any analysis, and total segmentation, or something near it, is a requisite for a broad transcription; but the study of the physiology of articulation, the neurological processes controlling it, and the behaviour of the sound waves thereby produced has emphasized still more strongly the interlocking and overlapping nature of the articulations and resultant phonetic features that are the object of phonological analysis.[33]

Prosodic analysis seeks to allow in some measure for this overlapping and partly simultaneous nature of speech, by abandoning a transcriptionally orientated and essentially unidimensional treatment of utterances and taking into account both the syntagmatic and paradigmatic dimensions in which features may be assigned to distinctive phonological elements relative to each other in ways not exclusively serial.

Broad transcription is essential to the study of a language, and phonemic analysis is a necessary procedure in the development of a broad transcription for it to be accurate, unambiguous, and usable; but phonological analysis and transcription are two different things, and there is no *a priori* reason to assume that the most useful theory of phonological analysis will be one embodying the same concepts and employing the same procedures as are needed for transcription.

Prosodic analysis is not as such concerned with transcription, but with providing a framework of categories for the analysis of the ways in which different sound features function in the utterances of languages. In fact *prosodic analysis*, as it is usually called, is a brief title for a method of phonological analysis that employs as fundamental concepts two types of elements, not reducible to a common type, **prosodies** and **phonematic units**. Phonological structures, in the terms of this theory, comprise phonematic units and prosodies. Phonematic units in this sense must be distinguished from phonemes or phonemic units; despite the unfortunate superficial similarity of the words they are of quite separate status; particular care is needed in reading the work of some writers who use *phonematic* as the adjective of *phoneme*, a use the must be kept quite distinct from its use in the phonology being outlined here.[34].

As is the case with phonemic analysis, different linguists employ somewhat different treatments within the broad limits of the theory they embrace, and interpret the theory in different ways; but a general account can be given in outline of prosodic analysis and the theory behind it, on lines that summarize the points of agreement between linguists working within it.

In the prosodic analysis of a language, phonological structures consist of phonematic units and prosodies, and the phonological system of the language comprises both sorts of element, subdivided into different types according to the structures of which they relate. The phonetic data found relevant are assigned to phonematic units and to prosodies irrespective of any graphic considerations that may arise in literate languages. The relationship of data to element is one of exponent to abstraction (2.1.1). Broadly speaking, those features that are most conveniently regarded as primarily involving linear or temporal succession are assigned to successive **phonematic units**. Phonematic units are divided into consonants and vowels, and occupy sequential positions within structures and their relative order is significant, corresponding to some extent to the temporal sequence of articulations and the production of audible sound features in the stream of speech; but it must be emphasized that in no case does speech consist of a succession of separate sound units produced by jerks of the vocal organs, and this must be kept in mind in interpreting any analysis or graphic representation of it.

Phonologically relevant features that for various reasons are found to be best assigned not to units but to stretches of speech actually or potentially larger than a single consonant or vowel unit are allotted to one or more **prosodies**, which by definition are elements capable of extension over or relevance to sequences of phonematic units of any length.

The consonant and vowel phonematic units bear some resemblance to the segmental phonemes of phonemic analysis, but they are not to be equated with them, and the basis of their establishment is different. Certain phonetic features that would constitute part of some segmental phonemes in the phonemic analysis of a language are likely to be allotted to one or more prosodies in prosodic analysis, leaving the phonematic unit as an abstraction representing fewer phonetic features than its nearest correspondent in phonemic analysis.

Prosodies are abstracted from whole sentences (sentence prosodies) and from parts thereof, but always with reference to a given structure; and the relevant phonetic data may be assigned to such different categories of prosody as sentence prosodies, sentence part prosodies, word prosodies, syllable prosodies, and syllable part prosodies. Where more than one phonematic unit or prosody is referable to a single structural position, these constitute a system. Systems are thus set up to state the structural possibilities of a language at the phonological level.

The order of working is generally 'downward', from the larger structure through the successively smaller structures to the units.

One of the illustrations of prosodic analysis may be seen in Henderson's treatment of Thai (Siamese), a tone language in which intonations are also relevant.[35]

The phonetic data have been analysed in terms of:

sentence prosodies: intonations
sentence part and syllable group prosodies: the relations of length, stress, and tone between successions of syllables
syllable prosodies: length, stress, and tone
syllable part prosodies (including syllable initial and syllable final prosodies): plosion, affrication, labialization, unreleased closure, etc
phonematic units: *k, t, p, n, m,* etc

Intonation sequences or tunes, as referrred to earlier, are clearly abstractable as sentence prosodies, phonological features characterizing or belonging to sentences as wholes; this does not exclude the possibility of long sentences being characterized by two or more successive intonations, each capable of constituting a sentence prosody, but, in the instance, being sentence part prosodies. The use of *prosody* to refer to intonational features is fairly general among linguists. The modifications to the lexical tones in Siamese and other tone languages under intonation tunes belong to the sentence prosody, and in such languages the actual pitch phenomena may be allotted to three separate types of prosody:

[i] Sentence prosodies of intonation;
[ii] Sentence part or syllable group prosodies, including word prosodies: modifications imposed on tones by their presence in closely linked tone groups; and
[iii] Syllable prosodies of the lexically distinctive tones available on any given syllabic sequence of consonants and vowels.

In Siamese, sentence part and syllable group prosodies, in which prosodies of word units must be included, involve the relations of length, stress, and tone between the component syllables (that is to say, the ways in which the features of these kinds ascribable to the syllables in isolation actually appear in the different groups of syllables within sentences). This same category of prosody involves other features in other languages, such as the non-release or weak release of stop consonants otherwise exploded (this feature is a syllable part prosody in Siamese), and covers much of the material treated under juncture phonemes in phonemic analysis; but the juncture phonemes concentrate emphasis on the breaks between stretches, where they are serially located in transcriptions, whereas the sentence part prosodies and word prosodies concentrate emphasis on the unity of the groups or stretches as prosodically marked whole structures.

The treatment of intonation as sentence prosodies, and of tone, stress, and length as syllable prosodies is not very unlike some phonemic treatments of such phenomena, and some features involved in syllable group prosodies and word prosodies are often similar to those assigned one way or another to juncture phonemes.

The prosodic analysis of the syllable, however, differs quite sharply from the phonemic analysis of the same sort of structure. The structure in question is the phonological, not the phonetic syllable, and it is a phonological structure defined in terms of phonematic units and prosodies. Certain syllable prosodies, such as length, stress, and tone, in languages where any or all of these are relevant categories, are comparable to the corresponding suprasegmental phonemes of a phonemic analysis; but phonemically length is usually assigned to the vowel phoneme and transcribed after it (as in one phonemicization of English, 4.3.3), whereas prosodic analysis treats it as a feature of the syllable as a single structure, not linearly related to any of the consonant and vowel units. Its exponents are vowel length and any other qualitative features present with it in the rest of the syllable, all features being taken as its exponents and not divided into distinctive (phonemic) features on one segment (the vowel) and non-distinctive (allophonic) features on other segments (consonants). This difference in treatment may be most marked in languages in which length phonemically ascribed to the vowel of a syllable is accompanied by other phonetic differences elsewhere.

In diagrammatic representations prosodies are usually marked with different typefaces or are set over the linear sequence of phonematic unit symbols, in order to make their separate status clear. Thus a long syllable phonemically representable /CV:C/ could be prosodically represented

L(ength)
CVC

Suprasegmental phonemes have been in practice restricted by linguists to the phenomena of length, stress, and pitch.[36] But features of any phonetic nature can be treated prosodically if their function in the structure to which they are assigned warrants it. As has been seen, all features overlap and interlock, but certain features involving a syllable or the sequence of phonematic units in a syllable are more obviously syllable features as such, or yield a more satisfactory structural analysis of the syllable if so treated. Features such as retroflexion and palatalization involving phonetic differences in the articulation of adjacent consonants and vowels within syllables (to which reference has already been made (3.5.2)) have been analysed as syllable prosodies in a number of languages. Phonemic analysis takes account of such concomitant variations, but is obliged in its own terms to allot the exponents to phonemic or distinctive status on one segment and allophonic or non-distinctive status on the other segments. In an account of Russian phonetics it has been said that in some positions the accompanying differences of vowel quality are more readily perceived than the differences in the consonantal articulation of the soft (palatalized) and hard (non-palatalized) consonants themselves; yet it is these that are treated as phonemically distinguished and the differences in vowel quality are given allophonic status.* In such cases a prosodic analysis that assigned palatalization as a syllable prosody to the syllable as a whole, with its exponents variously located in each segment, might be phonologically more suitable, if phonology were freed from the linear restraints of transcriptional requirements. The greater the weight borne in maintaining lexical and grammatical distinctions by plurisegmental features of this sort, the greater the gain may be in structural analysis by assigning them to appropriate prosodic abstractions.

Some other features in languages suggest similar prosodic analysis in relation to syllable structures. In some, but not all, languages nasal consonants are always followed by nasalized vowels within the same syllable, and nasalized vowels only appear after nasal consonants. This is substantially the position in Sundanese, a language of Java. In Georgian and Armenian it has been found that the glottalized or ejective consonants are

---

* It may be noted that the Cyrillic orthography (p 116) takes the opposite course, and in general marks the difference between palatalized and non-palatalized consonantal pronunciations, not by different consonant letters, but by the use of different vowel letters.

followed by glottalization or glottal constriction in the following vowels in the same syllable, a feature not found in vowels elsewhere in these languages. Such features may be treated as prosodies of the syllables concerned, abstracted from and manifested in the sequences of consonant and vowel (phonematic units), and not assigned phonologically to any one place as distinctive or significant as against any other place.

Prosodies of the type that have been discussed above may be abstracted from sequences of more than one syllable, usually within word boundaries. In Turkish and Hungarian, for example, the vowels may be classified into the categories of front and back, according to the part of the tongue that is highest in their articulation and the part of the roof of the mouth towards which it is raised, and into rounded and unrounded, according to the position of the lips. Words in these languages (other than those of foreign origin, 8.1.8) are largely characterized by what is called vowel harmony, whereby the vowels in polysyllabic words in Turkish, and similar words in Hungarian resulting from grammatical suffixation (5.4.3), are either all back or all front in type, and in certain word structures all rounded or all unrounded (thus Turkish:

ev /ev/ house, *evler* /evler/ houses, with front vowels
ayak /ajak/ foot, *ayaklar* /ajaklar/ feet, with back vowels
ev /ev/ house, *evim* /evim/ my house, with front unrounded vowels
göz /gœz/ eye, *gözüm* /gœzym/ my eye, with front rounded vowels
yol /jol/ way, *yolum* /jolum/ my way, with back rounded vowels
kiz /kɯz/ daughter, *kizim* /kɯzɯm/ my daughter, with back unrounded vowels

Hungarian:

tanulok /tɔnulok/ I learn, with back vowels
verek /vɛrɛk/ I hit, with front unrounded vowels
küldök /kyldøk/ I send, with front rounded vowels.)

In prosodic analysis these features that affect more than one syllable in word structures are abstracted from the whole word or from stated syllables of the word, as word or word part prosodies, separate from the sequence of phonematic units constituting the consonants and vowels of the structure. In such an analysis, the exponents of the prosodies are not only the vowel features concerned, but also any variations in the articulations of the consonants adjacent to them. Thus the Turkish word *yollar-imiz* /jollarɯmɯz/ our ways, is prosodically represented:

```
o——
w—————————
```
CaCCaCiCiC, or with the consonants distinguished,
```
o——
w———————
```
yollarımız

In this representation o and w mark the prosodies of lip-rounding and back articulation respectively, and the broken lines mark their structural extension. The phonematic vowel units, *a* and *ı*, indicate only the distinction between open and close, all other features ascribable to vowels as phonetic segments, or as phonemes in a phonemic analysis, being allotted to the relevant prosodies.

Just as languages differ and may be classified according to the types of syllable structures they exhibit as expressed in phonemic terms (4.3.4), so different languages lay themselves open to different prosodic statements of syllable structure.[37]

Prosodies of syllable parts fall into a rather different general category of prosody. Prosodies are abstracted from stretches and referred to structures for two main reasons. Firstly, as in the illustrations so far given, the relevant phonetic features serving as the exponents of the prosodies may themselves be articulated or realized over the whole stretch of speech corresponding to the structure to which the prosody is ascribed or at various points therein. Secondly a feature may phonetically be confined to a particular part of a structure (or, strictly, to a particular part of the corresponding stretch of speech), and even to a single segment therein, but because in the language its occurrence is restricted to a certain position in relation to the rest, it serves thereby as a signal of structural delimitation and so as a mark of structural unity. Prosodies fulfilling this type of function may be regarded as syntagmatically relevant to the structures they thus help to identify.[38]

In Siamese, aspiration, affrication, plosion, and a number of other features are confined to syllable initial position, and unex-ploded closure is confined to syllable final position (that is to say, syllable final stop consonants are not released audibly). In Siamese, or in any other language where this sort of statement is possible, the occurrence of one of them necessarily indicates a syllable initial or final boundary, and is thus syntagmatically significant beyond its immediate place as a phonetic segment, in addition to any contrastive function it may have in its particular environment.

Syntagmatic relevance of this kind is the basis for regarding certain features as belonging to syllable part prosodies, while others not so positionally restricted within the syllable are assigned to the sequence of phonematic units.

As will have been seen from the examples already given, prosodic analysis is represented in diagrams or phonological formulae rather than in transcriptions.[39]

Syllables are not the only structures that may be prosodically demarcated in this way. In languages with phonologically marked word divisions, the phonological features in question may be treated in prosodic analysis as demarcative word prosodies. Languages in which such word demarcative prosodies are usefully abstractable differ in the degree to which the units grammatically defined as words are marked by phonological features; but features, such as fixed place stress, or the English phonetic qualities associated in phonemic analysis with inter-word juncture (4.4.2), are syntagmatically significant, and justify prosodic treatment for just that reason.

Fixed place stress in words, whether on the initial, penultimate, or any other syllable, may be analysed as falling into two prosodic categories, with respect to different structures:

[i] By phonetic extension of the feature of forceful articulation it serves as the exponent of a syllable prosody, part of the phonological structure of a particular syllable; and

[ii] By virtue of its demarcative function in the word, it acts as an exponent of the prosody of word delimitation or of the syntagmatic unity of a succession of syllables having a particular grammatical status.

Prosodic analysis has been characterized as polysystemic in contrast to monosystemic phonemic analysis. It contrasts with phonemic analysis not only in the recognition of two basic phonological entities, prosody and phonematic unit, rather than one, but in other respects. Phonemic analysis is general throughout a language, and a sound segment assigned to a phoneme in one environment is generally held to belong to the same phoneme everywhere else. Phonemic systems are established without reliance on grammatical distinctions (eg between nouns and verbs or roots and affixes). They are, moreover, based on the structural places of maximal differentiation; the non-applicability of some contrasts in some environments is the basis of the theory of neutralization, already mentioned (4.3.7). Prosodic analysis admits the possibility, and often the desirability, of different grammatical elements being subjected to different phonological analyses, where a more satisfactory description can be shown to result thereby; and phonological analyses of the nominal words or the verbal words in particular languages have been separately undertaken. As was seen above, grammatical elements such as words, as well as purely phonological elements such as syllables, are open to treatment as structures from which prosodies may be abstracted.[40]

Moreover, prosodic phonology envisages the setting up of separate systems of contrastive phonematic units and prosodies at different places in phonological structures without necessarily identifying the units in one system with those in another (though in symbolization the same letters may sometimes be used). In a language that admits three nasal consonants in initial position in syllables and only two in syllable final position, as in some types of Chinese, there would be no need to identify any of the members of the initial system with any of those of the final system; and in the English case of plosive consonants after /s/ in initial position in the syllable, referred to above (4.3.7), prosodic phonology would not feel any requirement to identify the three consonantal phonematic units in this position with either the distinctively voiced three or the distinctively voiceless three that are found in absolute syllable initial position. The concept of neutralization need not, therefore, be invoked to deal with the non-comparability of some different systems that operate in different structural places.

In several respects, though within a different system and using different terminology, this aspect of prosodic phonology is much in agreement with some of the main principles of Chomskyan phonology (4.4.4). For both systems phonological analysis presupposes grammatical analysis (not the other way round) and serves to link grammar and lexicon to uttered speech and to narrow transcription. In the light of what has been said, an understanding of the theory and practice of phonemic analysis and some acquaintance with prosodic analysis are desirable for anyone seeking a comprehensive picture of phonological studies in linguistics today.[41]

4.4.4 Generative phonology
Where a general theory of linguistic analysis, or, looked at from another point of view, a general theory of language structure has been formed, the phonological component of this theory

embodies the major characteristics of the theory as a whole. This is the case, for example, with phonology in stratificational linguitics (7.4.4) and phonology in tagmemics (7.4.2). However, by far the most widely followed and actively researched types of phonology are those derived from the 'generative phonology' that became the standard form of the phonological component in transformational-generative descriptive analyses of languages (7.2.2, *p* 285). This simply reflects the dominant position taken up in the years 1960 to 1980 by Chomsky and his many followers, whatever other linguists may themselves have felt about this, and whatever have been the often quite sharp dissensions that arose between different Chomskyan schools and factions.

Following certain publications by Halle and others, distinctive feature phonology remodelled in the form of phonological rules became the standard method of stating and analysing the phonological forms in languages, coming after the statement of the syntactic and the lexical formations.[42]

Chomskyan linguistics regards phonology as the link between the surface syntactic structure and the phonetic representation of the sentence; a linguistic description includes a further component, the phonological component, a set of **phonological rules** converting the output of surface structure into a pronounceable and transcribable representation. Thus we have consistently with this rule-based model of linguistic description three components: P(hrase) S(tructure) rules, T(ransformation) rules and P(honological) rules. Orthographic rules could equally be stated to produce an orthographic sequence of written words (the orthography in the lowest lines of the examples so far given has been an abbreviation for these unstated rules). Lexical items are considered to have a certain basic phonological representation, which may be subject to modification in different environments to account for such different pronounced forms as /ˈteligrɑːf/, /teliˈɡræfik/, and /teˈleɡrəfi/. These representations are transcribable by serial symbols (/bɔi/, /wɒtʃ/, /geim/, /kæʃ/, etc, but they are mostly regarded as sets of distinctive features that constitute the segments (4.3.7). Grammatical elements are treated likewise, with special rules to indicate that 'past' is rewritten as /-d/, /-t/, or /-id/ according to the final segment of the verb stem in regular verbs, but as -∅ with verbs like *cut* and *put*, and that *see* + 'past' → /sɔː/, *go* + '*past*' → /went/, etc (the counterpart of the statements made in 5.4.2 and 6.5). Further phonological rules assign features such as stress placement and intonation to the strings of segments in the light of their surface grammatical structure.[43].

This last remark is important; these linguists take a quite opposite attitude to those (mostly American) linguists who in the 1940s and 1950s refused to regard any grammatical fact or statement as properly relevant to phonological (phonemic) analysis (4.4.1). In this respect they agree rather with Firthin prosodic phonologists in taking the grammatical classes and structures involved in a sentence as a legitimate, indeed, necessary, part of the context for phonological statement (*cp* 4.4.3). Phonological rules are framed so as to pass from surface structure to phonetic representation (narrow transcription) by the most economical path.

In recent years a separate area of study has been recognized, **generative phonology**. In general this is based on one or other version of distinctive feature analysis (4.3.7), and is devoted to the constructing of sets of phonological rules that will relate surface structures to phonetic representations as systematically and economically as possible.[44]

In 1968 the massive book by Chomsky and Halle, *The sound pattern of English*, expounded in detail their phonological theory and method, with prime reference to English, within the then current Chomskyan transformational-generative model; and this became and in a sense has remained a standard presentation of phonology within Chomskyan linguistics.[45] This may be briefly summarized and exemplified. The levels other than the phonological will be treated in more detail in a later chapter (7.2).

The sentences of English (or of any other language) are generated by the syntax and the lexicon in the form of what is often called a syntactic 'surface structure' of lexical items (words, word roots, and bound morphemes) with various grammatical specifications (noun, verb, plural formative, etc) in a syntactic structure. Taking the associated words *telegraph, telegraphy, telegraphic*, etc already mentioned, a basic primary form '+tele+græf+' is set up, the letters being 'understood as an informal abbreviation for a certain set of phonological categories (distinctive features)'.[46] Phonological rules, taking into account the grammatical class and structure of these items, assign stresses and modify the underlying lexical forms to produce actual isolate word forms like /ˈteləgræf/ (American = British /ˈteligrɑːf/), and after affixation /teləˈgræfik/ (/teliˈgræfik/), etc; and the syntactic structure of the sentence further modifies these forms to produce an actual sentence such as *we established telegraphic communication*, with its appropriate inter-word junctural features and stress modifications (for example a lower degree of stress on the adjective /teləˈgræfik/ than on the noun /kəmjuːniˈkeiʃən/), and the intonation of the sentence, although *The sound pattern of English* does not deal with this.[47]

In another set of examples single underlying lexical forms such as 'divi:n', 'sere:n', and 'profæ:n' give rise to the actual adjective and noun forms /di'vain/ /di'viniti/, /sə'ri:n/ /sə'reniti/, and /prə'fein/ /prə'fæniti/, through a series of vowel modifying and stress assigning rules (the transcriptions have been adapted to British pronunciation and to the usage of symbols elsewhere in this book).[48] These and many other underlying forms correspond more closely than the resultant forms with what is known of the earlier pronunciation of the adjectives before the 'Great vowel shift' (8.1.2), but this is not an essential point.

These and other underlying forms are notably 'abstract', that is to say the underlying form 'will be very different from the phonetic representations of its variants in particular contexts'.[49] This 'abstractness of phonological representations' has since become a subject of considerable controversy. The resultant developments have taken several forms, some of which must be noticed in a general introduction, though the reader must be referred to more specialist publications in order to achieve a mastery of the theoretical details and of the data brought into play.

4.4.5 Natural generative phonology

One question gave rise to debate almost at once. This was the 'abstractness' of phonology, the degree to which differences should be accepted between the phonological specification (and transcription) of underlying forms and their final representation as pronounced and narrowly transcribed phonological surface forms. In part this question comes within the more general one of choosing between strict economy of description and the re-alistic representation of the data. A few examples will illustrate this:[50] In order to make economical use of rules required elsewhere in English vocabulary, underlying forms 'rixt', 'mu:ntən', and 'mu:dlin' are set up for the words *right, mountain*, and *maudlin* (actual surface forms /rait/, /'mauntən/, and /'mɔ:dlin/; again, the transcriptions have been adjusted). The underlying forms proposed are phonetically rather remote from the actual pronounced forms, and in the case of *right* a consonant is introduced that is not found anywhere in present-day English, apart from some Scots dialects (as in the word *loch* and the dialectal pronunciation of *right* as /rixt/). Irrelevantly one might claim a historical justification by reference to the Germanic source of the word (*cp* German *recht*, /rext/, right), but even this

is not available for the long /u:/ vowels proposed for the other
two words.

In the light of this and much other criticism of what was judged
excessive and unnecessary abstractness, proposals have been
made in favour of what is now known as 'natural generative
phonology', of which there are already some relatively minor
variations. In this revision of the *Sound pattern of English* model
stress is laid on two basic requirements of a phonological
analysis: [i] underlying forms should neither be too far removed
from actual forms, nor should they incorporate segments or
segment sequences not found in actual surface forms of the
language under analysis; and [ii] any changes required to relate
underlying and surface forms should be phonetically plausible or
natural, that is, changes which, while not, of course, being
universal, can be seen to be in accord with the phonetic features
involved, for example homorganic nasal assimilation before non-
nasal consonants (/nb/ → /mb/, /nk/ → /ŋk/, etc). It is argued,
though not with everyone's agreement, that the more that underlying representations and phonological rules in a language can be
framed on phonetically 'natural' lines, the more readily we can
explain and understand the phonetic and phonological side of a
child's first language acquisition.[51]

4.4.6 Rule ordering

In *The sound pattern of English* it is insisted that the phonological
rules converting underlying forms to actual surface forms are
ordered; they are applied serially, each later rule operating on
the output of the preceding rule, as is the case with the syntactic
rules, and not vice versa. Chomsky and Halle proclaim: 'The
hypothesis that rules are ordered . . . seems to us one of the best-
supported assumptions of linguistic theory.'[52] As examples, the
two words *regal* and *regicide* go through the following sequences
of rule application (the transcriptions have been adjusted to
British English, but no difficulty should be experienced in
consulting the original text):

're:g + æl	're:g + i + ki:d	
	're:dʒ + i + si:d	g → ʤ, k → s before a front close vowel
	'redʒ + i + si:d	e: → e before the affix
're:yg − æl	'redʒ + i + si:yd	diphthongization of the long vowels
'ri:gəl	'redʒisaid	vowel changes

(The diphthongs written 'e:y' and 'i:y' are notional, not found in current English, nor perhaps in any stage of English; they are required to make a path for the application of the rules, and would be objected to by the proponents of natural generative phonology[53]).

Various problems and difficulties have been found or assumed in the strict application of rule ordering, and attempts are made to avoid or reduce them, restraining the range of the ordering among rules, either by rewriting some of them or by other means. Some have gone as far as denying all of what has been described as 'extrinsic' rule ordering, relying on the creation by each rule of the conditions activating other required rules. To take a fictitious example: suppose a language has the following two rules (among others), unordered and always 'in play': [i] intervocalic /s/ is voiced, and [ii] vowels preceding voiced consonants are lengthened. Rule 1 will always and 'intrinsically' trigger the application of rule 2, without any further ordering (though, of course, rule 2 will have many other conditions for automatic operation). It is not practicable to pursue this controversy here any further; some detailed discussions and exemplifications are to be found in publications devoted to theoretical questions in phonology.[54]

It must, of course, be remembered, particularly in cases where the progression from assumed underlying form to actual surface form bears some resemblance to what is known of the historical phonology of a language, as with the English pairs like 'divi:n' and /di'vain/, that the operation of sound changes in history is clearly ordered sequentially in time, unless the two changes occurred in the same period. But in synchronic descriptive linguistics the choice of rule ordering or of no rule ordering is in the last resort up to the linguist himself or herself to decide in analysing the language.

4.4.7 Autosegmental and metrical phonology
As we have seen, prosodic analysis was in great part a response to the fact that speech processes and the speech sounds resulting from them are in many cases not at all segmental in the way that discrete entities following one another, like, for example, the letters on a printed page, are segmental. All linguists have recognized this, and they have taken care in one way or another to make provision for it while they continue to assign at any rate the supraglottally articulated sounds of a language, the great majority of its consonants and vowels, to segmental phonological units, the phonemes. They have been encouraged in this, rightly, by the pretheoretical phonemic principles underlying alphabets

themselves and by the transcriptional convenience of phonemic analysis.

Two phonetic features have always proved especially recalcitrant to segmental treatment, namely stress and pitch, being very obviously characteristics observable as spread over sequences of segments, usually syllables or syllable groups, and only very arbitrarily assignable to a single segment, whatever may be decided about the position of the written stress or pitch mark. For this reason the term *suprasegmental phoneme* was devised for use by some linguists (4.3.3).

Generative phonology incorporated detailed rules for stress assignment, though in *The sound pattern of English*, at least, nothing was said about intonation. At about the same time, in the middle 1970s, proposals were made to develop within generative phonology a framework for dealing specifically and separately with these non-segmental or plurisegmental features; and these developments have attracted attention and encouraged further research.

Autosegmental phonology began as an outgrowth of generative phonology with the suggestion by Goldsmith that the tones of tone languages should be analysed, not as suprasegmental phonemes imposed as it were on a series of segmental ones, but as a separate 'upper' layer or tier of segments in their own right and mostly of longer extent than the consonant and vowel phonemes.[55] The actual phonetic domain of the tones in the word forms involved was indicated by stating the 'association' of the upper and the lower tiers.

An example from Shona, a Bantu language, may serve to clarify this system of analysis. There are words of more than one syllable all bearing a distinctively high tone, thus /mbúndúdzi/, worm; the prefix, also with a high tone, /né-/, with, requires that all high tones in the word to which it is prefixed be changed to low tones, irrespective of their number, while the prefix retains its high tone. The two tiers and their association are illustrated in the diagrams:

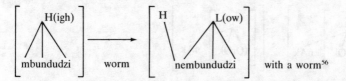

Metrical phonology has a similar motivation, but rather than tonal phenomena its main source was syllabic stress, which is indicated by a tree diagram notably similar to morphological or syntactic trees but quite separate and independent from them. The different degrees of stress in the long, and rather *recherché* botanical English word *hamamelidanthemum* are indicated in detail and accounted for like this:[57]

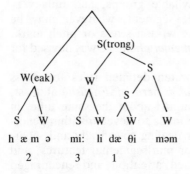

(the figures 1, 2, and 3 indicating primary, secondary, and tertiary stress, with minimal stress being left unmarked).

It is interesting to see that in both these phonological developments their range of application has been extended so that the 'upper tiers' can cover supraglottally articulated features where these are involved in structures such as vowel harmony. The two Hungarian nouns /torok/, throat, and /török/, Turk, which take different forms of the dative suffix, /-nak/ and /-nɛk/ respectively, are analysed in this way:

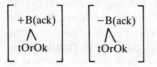

and with the vowel of the suffix determined by the vowel harmony of the nouns:

The capital letters in the transcriptions represent the other vowel qualities of half openness with lip rounding (O) and openness and concomitant lip-rounding with + back but not otherwise (the phonetic value of the two vowels in /-nAk/ being /ɔ/ and /ɛ/). This abstraction of harmony determined features, which could have been taken further, is remarkably similar to the abstraction of prosodic features from vowels under like circumstances in prosodic analysis, leaving the vowel segments with minimal feature specification (4.4.3).[58]

Some writers in this field have recourse to the terms *prosody* and *prosodic* in reference to these upper tiers. Others have gone further; Griffen, for example, calls for a 'non-segmental phonology', because 'speech is in reality nonsegmental'.[59] On this view the total or near-total phonological segmentation of the non-segmental phonetic reality is paying too high an analytic price for transcriptional convenience and traditional theory.

Bibliography for Chapter 4

1 S. R. ANDERSON, *The organization of phonology*, New York, 1974.

2 *Phonology in the twentieth century: theories of rules and theories of representations*, Chicago, 1985.

3 C. E. BAZELL, J. C. CATFORD, M. A. K. HALLIDAY, and R. H. ROBINS (eds), *In memory of J. R. Firth*, London, 1966.

4 J. T. BENDOR-SAMUEL, 'Some problems of segmentation in the phonological analysis of Tereno', *Word* 16 (1960), 348–55.

5 M. BIERWISCH, 'Regeln für die Intonation deutscher Sätze', *Studia grammatica* 7 (1966), 99–201.

6 B. BLOCH, 'A set of postulates for phonemic analysis', *Lang* 24 (1948), 3–46.

7 B. BLOCH and G. L. TRAGER, *Outline of linguistic analysis*, Baltimore, 1942.

8 L. BLOOMFIELD, *Language*, London, 1935

9 D. W. BOLINGER (ed), *Intonation: selected readings*, Harmondsworth, 1972.

10 A. BRAKEL, *Phonological markedness and distinctive features*, Bloomington, 1983.

11 J. CARNOCHAN, 'Vowel harmony in Igbo', *African language studies* I (1960), 155–63.

12 J. CHADWICK, *The decipherment of Linear B*, Cambridge, 1958.

13 Y. R. CHAO, *A grammar of spoken Chinese*, Berkeley, 1968.

14 N. CHOMSKY, *Current issues in linguistic theory*, Cambridge, Mass, 1964.

15 N. CHOMSKY and M. HALLE, *The sound pattern of English*, New York, 1968.

16 A. COHEN, *The phonemes of English*, The Hague, 1952.

17 H. N. COUSTENOBLE and L. E. ARMSTRONG, *Studies in French intonation*, Cambridge, 1934.

18 F. DELL, *Generative phonology*, trans C. Cullen, Cambridge, 1980.

19 D. DIRINGER, *The alphabet*, New York, 1968.

20 M. B. EMENEAU, *Studies in Vietnamese grammar*, Berkeley, 1951.

21 J. R. FIRTH, 'Sounds and prosodies', *TPS* 1948, 127–52.

22 E. FISCHER-JORGENSEN, *Trends in phonological theory*, Copenhagen, 1975.

23 I. J. GELB, *A study of writing*, Chicago, 1969

24 H. J. GIEGERICH, *Metrical phonology and phonological structure*, Cambridge, 1985.

25 A. C. GIMSON, *An introduction to the pronunciation of English*, London, 1970.

26 H. A. GLEASON, *An introduction to descriptive linguistics*, New York, 1961.

27 J. A. GOLDSMITH, *Autosegmental and metrical phonology*, Oxford, 1988.

28 'An overview of autosegmental phonology', *Linguistic analysis* 2 (1976), 23–68.

29 D. L. GOYVAERTS, *Aspects of post-SPE phonology*, Ghent, 1978.

30 M. HALLE, *The sound pattern of Russian*, The Hague, 1959.

31 'Phonology in a generative grammar', *Word* 18 (1962), 64–72.

32 M. A. K. HALLIDAY, *Intonation and grammar in British English*, The Hague, 1967.

33 Z. S. HARRIS, *Methods in structural linguistics*, Chicago, 1951.

34 P. HAWKINS, *Introducing phonology*, London, 1984.

35 E. J. A. HENDERSON, 'Prosodies in Siamese', *Asia Major*, new series I (1949), 189–215.

36 *Tiddim Chin*, London, 1965.

37 (ed), *The indispensable foundation: a selection from the writings of Henry Sweet*, London, 1971.

38 A. A. HILL, *Introduction to linguistic structures*, New York, 1958.

39 C. F. HOCKETT, *A manual of phonology*, Bloomington, 1955.

40 *A course in modern linguistics*, New York, 1958.

41 J. B. HOOPER, *An introduction to natural generative phonology*, New York, 1976.

42 H. VAN DER HULST and N. SMITH (eds), *The structure of phonological representations*, Dordrecht, 1982.

43 R. JAKOBSON, *Selected writings I: phonological studies*, The Hague, 1962.

44 R. JAKOBSON, G. FANT, and M. HALLE, *Preliminaries to speech analysis*, Cambridge, Mass, 1952.

45 R. JAKOBSON and M. HALLE, *Fundamentals of language*, The Hague, 1956.

46 W. JASSEM, *Intonation in conversational English*, Wroclaw, 1952.

47 D. JONES, *Outline of English phonetics*, Cambridge, 1947.

48 *The phoneme*, Cambridge, 1950.

49 M. JOOS, *Acoustic phonetics*, Baltimore, 1948.

50 M. KENSTOWICZ and C. KISSEBERTH, *Topics in phonological theory*, New York, 1977.

51 D. T. LANGENDOEN, *The London school of linguistics*, Cambridge, Mass, 1968.
52 W. R. LEE, *An English intonation reader*, London, 1960.
53 I. LEHISTE, *Suprasegmentals*, Cambridge, Mass, 1970.
54 N. LOVE, *Generative phonology*, Amsterdam, 1981
55 A. MARTINET, 'Un ou deux phonèmes', *Acta linguistica* I (1939), 94–103.
56 *Phonology as functional phonetics*, publication of the Philological Society 15, Oxford, 1949.
57 C. MOHRMANN, F. NORMAN, and A. SOMMERFELT, *Trends in modern linguistics*, Utrecht, 1963.
58 J. D. O'CONNOR and G. F. ARNOLD, *Intonation of colloquial English*, London, 1973.
59 F. R. PALMER (ed), *Prosodic analysis*, London, 1970.
60 K. L. PIKE, *Phonetics*, Ann Arbor, 1943.
61 *The intonation of American English*, Ann Arbor, 1946.
62 *Phonemics*, Ann Arbor, 1947.
63 'On the phonemic status of English diphthongs', *Lang* 23 (1947), 151–9.
64 'Grammatical prerequisites to phonemic analysis', *Word* 3 (1947), 155–72.
65 *Tone languages*, Ann Arbor, 1948.
66 'More on grammatical prerequisites', *Word* 8 (1952), 106–21.
67 P. VAN REENEN, *Phonetic feature definitions*, Dordrecht, 1982.
68 R. H. ROBINS, 'Aspects of prosodic analysis', *Proc University of Durham Philosophical Society*, series B (Arts) 1 (1957), 1–12.
69 'Distinctive feature theory', D. ARMSTRONG and C. H. VAN SCHOONEVELD (eds), *Roman Jakobson: echoes of his scholarship*, Lisse, 1977, 391–402.
70 G. SAMPSON, *Writing systems*, London, 1985.
71 F. DE SAUSSURE, *Cours de linguistique générale*, Paris, 1949.
72 S. A. SCHANE, *Generative phonology*, Englewood Cliffs, 1973.
73 A. H. SOMMERSTEIN, *Modern phonology*, London, 1977.
74 R. H. STETSON, *Motor phonetics*, Amsterdam, 1951.
75 *Studies in linguistic analysis*, special publication of the Philological Society, Oxford, 1957.
76 H. SWEET, *Handbook of phonetics*, Oxford, 1877.
77 G. L. TRAGER and B. BLOCH, 'The syllabic phonemes of English', *Lang* 17 (1941), 223–46.
78 G. L. TRAGER and H. L. SMITH, *Outline of English structure*, Norman, Oklahoma, 1951.
79 N. S. TRUBETZKOY, *Principles of phonology*, trans C. A. M. Baltaxe, Berkeley, 1969 (originally published in German, 'Grundzüge der Phonologie', *TCLP* 7, 1939).
80 W. F. TWADDELL, *On defining the phoneme*, Baltimore, 1935.
81 J. VACHEK, *The linguistic school of Prague*, Bloomington, 1966.
82 N. WATERSON, *Prosodic phonology: the theory and its application to language acquisition and speech processing*, Newcastle, 1987.

83 R. S. WELLS, 'The pitch phonemes of English', *Lang*, 21 (1945), 27–39.

There are several books that set out the main lines on which phonology has developed during the present century, and naturally they go into much more detail than is possible or desirable in an introduction to linguistics as a whole. One or more of them should certainly be studied by those who have mastered this chapter. Sommerstein's *Modern phonology* (73) is particularly to be recommended, but attention is drawn to the following as well (the data of publication, of course, will give some indication of the specific development covered): Anderson 1 and 2; Brakel, 10; Goyvaerts, 29; Hawkins, 34; Hockett, 39; van der Hulst and Smith, 42; Kenstowicz and Kisseberth, 50; Trubetzkoy, 79.

Notes to Chapter 4

1 On Chinese writing, B. Karlgren, *Sound and symbol in Chinese*, London, 1923.
2 On Mycenaean Greek, Chadwick, 12.
3 On the development of the Japanese writing system, E. B. Sansom, *Historical grammar of Japanese*, Oxford, 1928, Chapter 1.

   On Central American writing, D. H. Kelley, *Deciphering the Maya script*, Austin, 1976; J. E. S. Thompson, *Maya hieroglyphic writing: introduction*, Washington, 1950. On the relations between spoken language and alphabetic writing, W. Haas, *Phono-graphic translation*, Manchester, 1970. On the history of writing, including good coverage of Egyptian and Near Eastern writing, Diringer, 19 and Gelb, 23; more briefly Bloomfield, 8, Chapter 17; Hockett 40, Chapter 62. Sampson, 70, Chapter 7, deals with Korean writing.
4 The variant forms of some commonly used words in connected speech are called 'weak forms', the isolated forms being 'strong forms' (Jones, 47, Chapter 16; Gimson, 25, 262–6).

   On broad and narrow transcription, D. Abercrombie, *English phonetic texts*, London, 1964, 13–38.

   Early development of the theory of broad transcription, Sweet, 76, 100–8, 182–3. A selection of the more important writings of Sweet has been republished in Henderson, 37.
5 On the functional aspect of phonology, Martinet, 56. Many books on the sound systems of particular languages cover both phonetic and phonological descriptions, as do Jones, 47, and Gimson, 25.
6 Numbers of phonemes in languages, Hockett, 39, 139.
7 De Saussure 71, 166.
8 On definitions of the phoneme, *cp* Bloch and Trager, 7, 40; Gimson, 25, 44.
9 *Cp* E. Sapir, 'The psychological reality of phonemes', in D. G. Mandelbaum (ed), *Selected writings of Edward Sapir*, Berkeley, 1949, 46–60.
10 On the varieties of English /ə/, Jones, 47, §§355–61; Gimson, 25, 124.

11 Bloch, 6, made an attempt to define the phoneme very rigorously and without any semantic contrastiveness, avoiding even any appeal to the speaker's recognition of distinctiveness. This was challenged by others, and Bloch replied to their criticisms in 'Contrast' *Lang* 29 (1953), 59–61; but it seems doubtful whether this extreme position can be maintained.

12 A general discussion of the treatment of English short and long vowels in phonemic analysis and of other questions in English phonology is to be found in Cohen, 16; see too Gimson, 25, 96–7. American phonemic analyses have been rather different, partly because the phonetic phenomena are themselves different in American English. *Cp* Bloch and Trager, 7, Chapter 3; Trager and Bloch, 77; Trager and Smith, 78.

In contrast to the vowels, English geminated or 'long' consonants are usually analysed as sequences of two of the same consonant phonemes. Such occurrences within a word are always the result of grammatical composition or affixation (*eg night-time*/'naittaim/, *solely*/'soulli/).

13 *Cp* Jones on the analysis of English stress, 48, §§462, 468–9, with details in 47, Chapter 29; and Gimson, 25, 56, 222–35. American treatment of English stress, Trager and Smith, 78, 35–9; Gleason, 26, Chapter 4; Hockett, 40, Chapter 5.

14 On the syllable as a phonetic entity, Jones, 47, Chapter 12; Gimson 25, 51–3; Pike, 60, 116–17. Stetson, 74, 33, defines the phonetic syllable in terms of a stretch of sound produced with one chest pulse. Pike, 60, 119, distinguishes checked syllables, wherein a consonantal articulation stops or reduces the outward flow of air (as in *up* /ʌp/), and unchecked syllables, in which the outward air flow is checked at its source in the lungs (as in *too* /tuː/). See also D. Abercrombie, *Elements of general phonetics*, Edinburgh, 1967, 34–8. Sonority, Bloomfield, 8, 120.

15 On the syllable as a phonological unit, Trubetzkoy, 79, 170–81. On the nature of the Japanese syllabic nasal, on which there has been some discussion, B. Bloch, 'Studies in colloquial Japanese 4 (phonemics)', *Lang* 26 (1950), 86–125 (102); S. E. Martin, 'Morphophonemics of standard colloquial Japanese', *Lang* 28 (1952), part 3, section 2 (12); Jones, 48, 88.

16 On Fijian, N. C. Scott, 'A study in the phonetics of Fijian', *BSOAS* 12 (1947–8), 737–52; G. B. Milner, *Fijian Grammar*, Suva, 1957; Hawaiian, S. H. Elbert and S. A. Keala, *Conversational Hawaiian*, Honolulu, 1961.

17 These and similar topics are discussed in Martinet, 55; *cp* Pike, 62, 130. Yurok, R. H. Robins, *The Yurok language*, Berkeley, 1958, 4.

On the phonemic analysis of English diphthongs, Pike, 63. Jones, 48, §237, prefers to regard them as single phonetically complex phonemes, transcribed with digraphs (sequences of two symbols). American linguists generally phonemicize English dipthongs as sequences of a vowel phoneme and a consonant (semivowel) phoneme. This different treatment is partly due to the different nature of some of the sounds involved, as compared with British English (Bloch and Trager, 7, 51–2; Trager and Smith, 78, 15–20). General discussion in Cohen, 16, 89–107.

On triphthongs, Jones, 47, §§232–3.

18 The various problems involved in the phonological analysis of tone languages are treated exhaustively in Pike, 65.

Mixteco and Mazateco data in Pike, 65.

Tonal distinctions cannot be maintained in their normal way in whispered speech, though some compensatory distinctive features appear to be used in certain languages in whispering, in ways not yet fully understood (Pike, 65, 34–6).

On North Chinese tones, Chao, 13, 25–39.

19 On Vietnamese tones, M. B. Emeneau, *Studies in Vietnamese grammar*, Berkeley, 1951, 8; L. C. Thompson, *A Vietnamese grammar*, Seattle, 1965, 39–44.

20 On English intonation, see the references given in Chapter 3, note 16, and Jassem, 46; Lee, 52, Halliday, 32, sets out a somewhat different framework for the analysis of English intonation, integrated into the grammatical structure of sentences. On French intonation, Coustenoble and Armstrong, 17. On intonation in tone languages, Pike 65, 16–17, 85–6.

The phonemic analysis of intonation in terms of successions of pitch phonemes, Pike, 61, and Wells, 83. Note that Pike's numbers are in the opposite order to that now in general use in America, his 1 being highest and 4 lowest.

Descriptions of American English intonation on these lines may be found in Trager and Smith, 78; Hill, 38, Gleason, 26; and Hockett, 40.

21 The classical exposition of distinctive feature analysis is in Trubetzkoy, 79. For a similar analysis of vowel systems, Hockett, 39, 82–9. An account of the work of the Prague school may be found in Vachek, 81.

22 Marked and unmarked. Trubetzkoy, 79, 75; Vachek, 81, 55. The distinction has been used in analogous ways by other linguists, and it has been recently employed by Chomsky and Halle, 15, 400–35.

23 Hindi, T. G. Bailey, *Teach yourself Hindi*, London, 1950, xi–xli. A similar system obtained in Sanskrit, the classical language of India.

24 On neutralization, Trubetzkoy, 79, 77–83. The units that occur in such positions of neutralization (positions of less than maximal contrasts of distinctive features) are often designated *archiphonemes* (Trubetzkoy, *op cit* 79). Thus the /p/, /t/, and /k/ of English *spill*, *still*, and *skill*, and the final plosive consonants of German represent archiphonemes.

25 The details of acoustic distinctive feature analysis, which can only be summarily presented here, are to be found in Jakobson, Fant, and Halle, 44; Jakobson and Halle, 45; Jakobson, 43; Halle 30. For subsequent development in distinctive feature theory, see Chomsky and Halle, 15.

Distinctions on a scale of more than two contrasts, as for example with three degrees of vowel height, can be accommodated within the binary frame by different combinations of features and their absence. Thus we can analyse the scale as follows (+ standing for presence and − for absence):

	high	low	
close vowels	+	−	(high and not low)
mid vowels	−	−	(neither high nor low)

26 *Cp* Robins, 69; van Reenen, 67; R. Jakobson, 'Beitrag zur allgemeinen Kasuslehre', *TCLP* 6 (1936), 240–88; M. Bierwisch, 'Semantics', in J. Lyons (ed), *New horizons in linguistics*, Harmondsworth, 1973, 166–84 (criticism of this approach in D. Bolinger, 'The atomization of meaning', *Lang* 41 (1965), 555–73); on kinship terminology analysis, E. A. Hammel (ed), 'Formal semantic analysis', *American anthropologist* 67.5 (1965), part 2.

27 *Eg* C. F. Hockett, 'Linguistics is a classificatory science', *Lang* 18 (1942), 3. Chomsky's criticism of 'taxonomic phonemics' is seen in his *Syntactic structures*, The Hague, 1957, 75–95. It is, of course, just a part of the much wider divergence of expressed aims and objectives that separate the generative linguists from their predecessors (*cp* 7.1.2).

28 See Harris, 33, Chapter 8; Trager and Smith 78; see also Hockett, 39, 167–72.
   That phonetic analysis should be based on the word unit, however established, in isolation, is stated explicitly by Jones, in 48, §34, 668–9. This attitude is strongly attacked by Smith, *Lang* 28 (1952), 144–9.

29 See Gleason, 26; Hill, 38; Hockett, 40; Trager and Smith, 78; Harris, 33.

30 See Pike, 64 and 66.

31 Chomsky, 14, 75–95 (75): 'The development of taxonomic phonemics has led to standards of explicitness and precision that had been rarely attained in previous linguistic description.' On phonology in generative linguistics, Halle, 31.

32 Firth's programmatic article, 21. The best account of prosodic phonology is to be found in Palmer, 59.

33 On phonemic long components, Harris, 33, Chapter 10.
   The possible divergence of transcriptional requirements and the purposes of phonological analysis were stressed by Twaddell, 80.
   On neurological overlapping, Joos, 49,109–14.

34 The prominent place occupied by transcriptional considerations in any sort of phonemic analysis is seen in a comment by Harris on his own long component analysis, 'Simultaneous components in phonology', *Lang* 20 (1944), 184–205 (203): 'phonemics [*ie* prior to the abstraction of long components] is undoubtedly the more convenient stopping point in this development, because it fits alphabetical writing'.

In addition to the ambiguity of the term *phonematic*, one should note that some writers use *prosodic*, with reference to phonemes and features, as equivalent to *suprasegmental*. Care must always be exercised when what appears to be the same technical term is used in two quite distinct and separate senses in two different systems of analysis.

35 Siamese, Henderson, 35.

36 On the phonetic limitations on suprasegmental status, Pike, 62, 63. See also Lehiste, 53.

37 Reference may be made to the following publications in amplification of what has been said here about various languages:

Russian palatalization, Jones, 48, §183.

Sundanese, Robins in 75, 87–103

Georgian, Robins and N. Waterson, 'Notes on the phonetics of the Georgian word', *BSOAS* 14 (1952), 55–72.

Armenian, Allen, 'Notes on the phonetics of an Eastern Armenian speaker', *TPS* 1950, 180–206.

On Turkish, Waterson, 'Some aspects of the phonology of the nominal forms of the Turkish word', *BSOAS* 18 (1956), 578–91.

Waterson's prosodic treatment of Turkish is compared with a phonemic analysis of the same phonetic phenomena by Lyons. 'Phonemic and non-phonemic phonology: some typological reflections' *IJAL* 28 (1962), 127–33. It is to be noticed that the same phonemic status must be accorded to the different vowels in each syllable in this type of word structure, though the possible vowel contrasts in suffix syllables are much fewer than in initial syllables. The allocation of the relevant features to a word prosody brings this into prominence.

A further example of the prosodic treatment of vowel harmony may be seen in Carnochan, 11.

The feature of Sanskrit grammar traditionally known as cerebralization (*cerebral* being an old-fashioned term for retroflexion) is prosodically analysed in Allen, 'Some prosodic aspects of retroflexion and aspiration in Sanskrit', *BSOAS* 13 (1951), 939–46.

38 The theory of demarcative prosodies was partly foreshadowed by Trubetzkoy's 'boundary markers' (*Grenzsignale, signes oristiques*), 79, 273–97.

39 Further examples of formulaic diagrams of prosodic analysis in N. C. Scott, 'A phonological study of the Szechnanese monosyllable', *BSOAS* 18 (1956), 556–60.

40 Separate phonological analyses of different grammatical word classes, Palmer, 'The verb in Bilin', *BSOAS* 19 (1957)' 131–59.

In a study of part of the phonology of a language of South America, Bendor-Samuel, 4, treats the vowel segment transcribed /e/ as *o* with Y prosody in /'yeno/ you (singular) walked, and as *e* with zero prosody in the phonetically identical /'yeno/ his wife, because of the different contrast systems and phonological structures it enters into in in the two grammatical contexts. In this prosodic analysis, the three grammatical categories of first, second, and third person, in both nouns and verbs, can be shown to have as exponents the prosodies of nasalization (N), palatalization (Y), and zero prosody or the contrastive absence of N and Y. Each prosody in turn has a series of phonetic exponents identified in successive segments of the words concerned. Bendor-Samuel's article, though on a remote and little known language, provides a valuable example of phonemic and prosodic analyses placed side by side with reference to the same body of data.

41 Apart from Firth, 21, already mentioned, a general, though brief, account of prosodic phonology is available, Robins, 68. A short summary of prosodic phonology in the general context of British linguistics during the years 1930–60 is to be found in Mohrmann *et al.*, 57, 11–37. A bibliography of work illustrating the application of prosodic analysis to parts of the phonology of particular languages up to 1970 is to be found in Palmer, 59; see also Sommerstein, 73. It must not be expected that all the treatments of language material in prosodic terms necessarily agree in all respects in their application of the method; in a number of cases explicit disagreements appear (as they do in any other system of analysis).

3 and 75 contain a number of examples of prosodic analysis, though it cannot be said that all of them make easy reading.

An example of the application of prosodic analysis to the phonological description of an entire language may be seen in J. T. Bendor-Samuel, 'The verbal piece in Jebero', *Word* 17 (1961), supplement, Chapter 3, and in Henderson, 35.

Several of the articles already mentioned in these notes are reprinted in Palmer, 59. This book also contains an excellent introduction to this development in phonology. In a rather different context see also Waterson, 82.

A critical discussion of prosodic phonology from a transformational-generative point of view is to be found in Langendoen, 51; see also review by Robins, *Lang* 45 (1969), 109–16. For the application of prosodic phonology within a transformational-generative analysis, V. Fromkin, 'On system-structure phonology', *Lang* 41 (1965), 601–9.

42 Halle, 30 and 31; Chomsky, 14.

43 Chomsky and Halle, 15, Chapters 1 and 2; R. P. Stockwell, 'The place of intonation in a generative grammar of English', *Lang* 36 (1960), 360–7; Bierwisch, 5.

44 Schane, 72; Dell, 18.

45 Chomsky and Halle, 15.

46 *Op cit*, 12.

47 See Stockwell and Bierwisch references in note 43.

48 Chomsky and Halle, 15, 184.

49 *Op cit*, 44.

50 *Op cit*, 218–9, 233–4. Criticism in Sommerstein, 73, 211–13.

51 Hooper, 41; Sommerstein, 73, 220–37. Discussion in B. E. Dresher,

'Abstractness and explanation in phonology', N. Hornstein and D. Lightfoot (eds), *Explanation in linguistics*, London, 1981, 76–115.

52 Chomsky and Halle, 15, 342.

53 *Op cit*, 219–20.

54 *Op cit*, 340–50. Discussion in Sommerstein, 73, Chapter 7, and Goyvaerts, 29, 51–99.

55 Goldsmith, 27 and 28.

56 Van der Hulst and Smith, 42, 11.

57 *Op cit*, 32–4.

58 *Op cit*, 20–1.

59 There is a good summary of autosegmental and metrical phonology in van der Hulst and Smith, 42, 1–45, and further discussion and exemplification in other chapters in the book. See also Giegerich, 24; and M. Halle and J.-R. Vergnaud, 'Harmony processes', W. Klein and W. Levelt (eds), *Crossing the boundaries in linguistics*, Dordrecht, 1981, 1–22; R. M. Hogg and C. B. McCully, *Metrical phonology*, Cambridge, 1987.

For 'nonsegmental phonology', see T. D. Griffen, 'Towards a nonsegmental phonology', *Lingua* 40 (1976), 1–20; *Aspects of dynamic phonology*, Amsterdam, 1985.

For an application of these versions of phonological theory to morphological analysis and to the analysis of meanings see S. R. Anderson, 'Morphological theory', in F. J. Newmeyer (ed.), *Linguistics: the Cambridge survey*, Cambridge, 1988, 146–91 (especially 154–7 and 165–6), A. C. Woodbury, 'Meaningful phonological processes', *Lang.* 63 (1987), 685–740, and R. D. Hoberman, 'Emphasis harmony in Modern Aramaic', *Lang.* 64 (1988), 1–26.

Chapter 5

Grammar: grammatical elements

5.1 Preliminary questions

5.1.1 Uses of the term 'grammar'

Grammar has been a familiar part of the school teaching of languages for many centuries, and its very familiarity has given rise to some inconsistencies in the use of the word *grammar*. Some elementary books introducing a foreign language are entitled *German grammar, Elementary grammar of French*, etc and are designed to provide an outline account of the pronunciation, orthography, word formation, and sentence construction, as well as a basic vocabulary and some short texts. Since the establishment of linguistic science as a distinct discipline linguists have attempted to define and to delimit the term more rigorously, but even so their usage varies.

Until fairly recently, and still among many linguists, grammar, often divided into morphology and syntax (5.1.3), was distinguished from phonology, which in turn was related to it as a separate level in a specific relationship. On the nature of this relationship sharply opposed views have been taken (4.4). But Chomsky and the transformational-generative linguists have come to use *grammar* in a wider sense, specifically to include phonology (hence, in part, the title *Transformational-generative grammar* to designate this development in linguistics; *cp* 7.2.2, *p* 280). This usage is now shared very generally by several other 'schools' or groups of associated scholars in America and in the rest of the world. There is no occasion to argue which is 'the best' use of a term like *grammar*; what matters is to be clear to oneself (and to others!) how one is using it. In this book *grammar* is used in the narrower sense, *ie* excluding phonology, except when the doctrines of the transformational-generative linguists, or of others sharing their views on this question, are being explicity set out.

Grammar is concerned with the description and analysis of stretches of utterance or stretches of writing, and with the grouping and classification of their recurrent elements by virtue of the functional places they occupy and the relations they contract with one another. Grammar is thus organized on the two dimensions already referred to (2.1.2), syntagmatic and paradigmatic. It may be approached from the point of view of the grammatical analysis of the existing or recorded utterances, or from that of the generation of new utterances by grammatical rules framed for that purpose.[1]

It is an obvious fact, and this alone makes language capable of its infinite flexibility (1.3.2), that the unlimited possibility of different utterances in every language reveals in each a limited number of regular patterns composed of members of a limited number of classes of elements in various statable relations with one another. These elements and relations are expressible in phonological terms (as well as in orthographic terms, though the orthographic representation of spoken utterances does not normally indicate all their grammatically relevant features), but they cannot be reduced to phonological rules, that is rules primarily statable by reference to the phonetic categories involved.

A brief illustration from English will clarify the statement just made. Sequences such as *men live* and *man lives* are acceptable English sentences, as are *the man lives* and *the men live*; but †*man live* and †*men lives* are not, nor is †*men the live* († is a convenient mark used to indicate deliberately unacceptable word forms or sentence forms with reference to a given language). But nothing in the phonetic composition of the unacceptable sequences excludes them from the language; they can be written down orthographically, as they have just been written down here, transcribed in an English broad transcription, and easily pronounced by a native speaker of English, in the way that stretches impermissible in English phonology, either employing non-English sounds or sounds in positions from which English structures exclude them (*eg* initial /ŋ/), cannot. Moreover, the possible English sentences are patterns with an infinite range of component substitutions (since vocabulary can be, and is, constantly changing). In place of *man* in *the man lives* can be put *horse, dog, cat, woman*, etc, and in place of *lives* can be put *comes, eats, dies, perspires*, etc, and likewise in *the men live, horses, dogs, cats, women*, etc, and *come, eat, die, perspire*, etc,

provided always that there is adequate collocational compata-
bility between the individual items thus linked (2.4.2). The two
substitution lists just illustrated are not interchangeable and a
member of each first list requires a member of each second list
in the production of a three-word English sentence of the type
referred to. Phonetic composition and phonological structure
cannot decide these permitted and excluded word sequences; the
phonetic relations between *man* and *men* and between *horse* and
horses could scarcely be more dissimilar, but they are brought
together grammatically by their relations, which are typical of
those between thousands of other English words, with other
words in English sentences. It is this kind of relationship that
provides the material of grammar.

For this reason one can deal satisfactorily with the grammar of
a dead language surviving in written records, provided they
comprise an adequate and representative sample, but one cannot
do so for its phonology to the same extent, as the phonological
analysis can only be indirectly based on the phonetic interpretation of the writing system helped out by the remarks of ancient
writers on the pronunciation of the language. One can also
describe the grammar of the written form of a language (*eg* the
grammar of written English); this will partially correspond to the
grammar of the spoken language, but in view of the different
styles between the two forms of liguistic expression, the two
grammars will not be the same; in particular, stress and intonation, unrepresented in ordinary English writing, are not available
as marks of grammatical structures or categories in the written
language, as they are in transcription of spoken English.

5.1.2 Formal grammar
It is obvious that in grammatical description we are in some way
much more closely related to meanings, in the usual sense of that
word, than we are in phonological description. It would be absurd
to ask what the phonemes /p/, /t/, or /u/ mean in English, or to
try to link any phonological features, except some intonation
tunes, directly to identifiable semantic functions. But most words
do have a statable meaning, with the reservation made in 1.4.2,
above, and grammatical bits of words like the -*s* of *horses* and
the -*ed* of *wandered* have general associations with 'more than
one' and 'past time'. But these correlations seldom attain one
hundred per cent: *wheat* is singular and *oats* is plural in English
grammar, though there is no comparable distinction between their
usual meanings; and some obvious elements of grammatical word
structure (for example the -*ing* of *going* and *loving*), and the

-ceive of *receive* and *deceive*) have at best a very elusive meaning, even if it is sensible to attempt to analyse them semantically in isolation at all.

It is also an obvious fact that languages share a number of grammatical features in common: the terms *noun* and *verb* have been found applicable in some way to nearly all, if not to quite all, known languages, and this sort of grammatical similarity between languages has given rise since the seventeenth century to the study of universal grammar, part of the study of linguistic universals (8.2.5), a subject very much alive today. More practically, this has been the basis of traditional grammar, much of which, as will be seen, finds a proper place in contemporary linguistics. But it is also very clear that languages differ in what they present to the grammarian, and a set of categories and classes suited to one language is usually ill adapted to serve without modification in the description and analysis of another. Each language is self-contained as a system of communication; native speakers have no need to learn another language in order to conduct their affairs in their own and to make themselves understood as speakers of their own language and as members of their own speech community. Nor need they for these purposes know anything about the history of their own language, important as this is as part of a general education; speakers of unwritten languages are necessarily in this position, as are most speakers of written languages, in fact.

The historical development of the grammar of a language from one period to another is a very necessary part of the linguist's study, where the evidence is available. But this is a separate study from the description of the language at a given period, and indeed it requires at least some description of its grammar at two, or more, periods.

For centuries Latin was studied by all educated people in Western Europe, and the prestige of Latin literature and of the Latin language was enormous. This misled too many students of other languages, especially of the modern European languages, to most of which, of course, Latin is historically related (8.1.1), into applying without adequate reflection Latin categories to these languages even where they were plainly inappropriate. It is not very helpful in a grammar of English to call *to the man* a dative case, because (presumably) its Latin translation is /homini:/, dative case form of the noun /homo:/ man, while the structurally comparable *behind the man* is (rightly) called a prepositional phrase, because its Latin counterpart /po:ne hominem/ would also be so described.

For these reasons many linguists have concentrated on what is called formal grammar, based on observable forms abstracted from utterances actually produced or approved by native speakers, or writers, of the language under investigation. The semantic correlates of some grammatical classes and categories will be examined in 6.6.2. *Perspiration, death, woman, triangle*, and *virtue* are classed together grammatically in English by their similarity of formal relations and positional occurrence in sentences: each can occupy a place after *the* and before a collocationally compatible member of the class of words to which *comes, lives, eats*, etc belong, and each can begin a sentence of which the second or third word is *is* (*death is the end of life, a triangle is a three-sided plane figure*; the distinction between those words of the class that generally require *a* or *the* before them in sentences of this sort and those which do not is a matter of subclassing within the class). These statements are made on the basis of observation of how sentences appear and are put together in the language. Statements about a common type of meaning in all these and similar words, or about a common way in which their meanings are envisaged or conceived by speakers, must remain partly subjective, at least. In the process of establishing grammatical classifications one is concerned less with what there may be in common in the meanings of *cuts* in *this knife cuts the cake* and of *bisects in this line bisects the angle*, than with the fact that these words behave in sentences in the same way that the words like *comes, lives*, and *eats*, mentioned above, behave; and one groups them into the same general class accordingly.

5.1.3 The basic units of grammar

A question that must be faced at the outset in an account of grammatical theory and practice is that concerning the unit or units recognized as basic, in the way that in phonemic phonology phonemes are taken as basic (and in prosodic phonology phonematic units and prosodies are taken as basic).

In the European tradition grammar has been built on the word as the basic unit. But linguists have pointed out that within the grammatical structure of words smaller and, in fact, minimal grammatical units must be recognized. These are called morphemes (5.4).

It has indeed been a weakness of traditional grammar that it failed to recognize sufficiently the place of the morpheme in word structures, which restricted considerably its descriptive power and clarity. But words, as formal elements of a language, can be established and defined within its grammatical system; and when the sort of criteria on which their definition rests have been made clear (5.3.1), they can serve as a suitable basis, together with morphemes, for the description and analysis of languages at the grammatical level.

The retention of the word as a basic, though not the minimal, unit of grammatical description allows the retention of the traditional division of the grammar of most languages into **morphology**, the study of the grammatical structure of words, and **syntax**, the study of the grammatical structure of sentences as built up of words, though the relations between the two need careful consideration.

It should, however, also be noted that those linguists, especially transformational-generative linguists, who use the term *grammar* to include phonology, tend to use *syntax* to cover the relations between morphemes within words as well as the relations between words in constructions; for these linguists morphology is a part of syntax (7.2.2).

5.2 The sentence

Grammar is concerned, in the syntagmatic dimension, with the description and analysis of structures that may be abstracted from stretches of utterance. At the grammatical level, the structures are abstracted and analysed in terms of recurrent elements and patterns that are not explicable merely by reference to the phonetic categories involved. Traditionally the longest structure within which a full grammatical analysis is possible has been taken as the **sentence**.

Certain consequences follow from this. A sentence is by definition grammatically complete (the alleged 'incomplete' or 'elliptical' situationally tied sentences are discussed in 6.3.1); it may, therefore, be preceded and followed by indefinite pause or silence, together with those phonetic features associated in each language with prepausal position; it is usually marked in writing by final punctuation, full stop, question mark, exclamation mark, or semicolon, and in speech, by a characteristic intonation tune. Intonation tunes coextensive with a sentence often do, and in all cases may, close with a sentence final pattern of pitches. While in continuous discourse sentences may follow one another without pause or intervening silence, there is always potentiality of pause at sentence boundaries. Thus the sentence can be phonologically defined as a stretch of speech that may be uttered with a complete intonation tune, preceded and followed by silence. More briefly a sentence may be called a potentially complete

utterance. This congruence between the grammatical and phonological levels, though it is potential rather than always actual,
is an additional characteristic of the status of the sentence as a
structural unit. Notably in transformational-generative grammar
S(entence) is the only syntactic unit that may appear on the left
of an arrow ('rewrite as . . .') without having been introduced by
a prior rule on the right of an arrow (see further 7.2.2).

Some grammarians have gone further than this and have
declared that sentences express a complete predication, question,
or command and that each has a specific logical form. The
predicative sentence has been often equated with the proposition
of logic. But linguistics, and therefore grammar as part of linguistics, is not the same as logic, though both are in different ways
concerned with language and its use, and the same definitions will
not produce satisfactory structures for both studies alike. Propositions are defined, classified, and analysed by their logical form
and content, which are matters for logicians; sentences are
defined, classified, and analysed by their grammatical (and
secondarily by their phonological) structures, which are matters
for the linguist to determine. In all languages in which logical
enquiries have been systematically undertaken, there are certain
general, though not universal, correlations between sentence
types and proposition types; and in all languages there are similar
correlations between sentence forms and types of meaning or
situational function (command, enquiry, statement, and the like).
Linguists try to state them in any account of a language that
purports to be complete, and to allow for them in any theory of
language; and the relations between linguistic or grammatical
form and logical form are a very proper subject of interdisciplinary investigation.[2]

It has been said that the sentence is the largest structure wholly
describable in grammatical terms, or in Bloomfield's formulation
'an independent linguistic form not included by virtue of any
grammatical construction in any larger linguistic form'.[3] But this
does not exclude links of a grammatical kind between separate
sentences in some cases. Devices for cross-reference and
anaphora are examples. In English the pronouns *he, she, it*, and
they may refer to previously mentioned persons and things, and
the pronoun is selected by reference to the word for which it is
a substitute. *Man, boy*, and *king* are picked up by *he, mare,
woman*, and *ship*, and *stone, principle*, and *triangle* by *it; cousin*
may be followed by *he* or *she, baby* by *he, she*, or *it, dog* and
most words denoting domestic animals by *he* or *it*, and *committee*
and (governmental) *cabinet* by *it* or *they*. Similar relationships

between nouns and anaphoric pronouns are found in other languages.

Grammatical links of this sort are not the only connections between sentences in continuous discourse. Normal speech or writing does not consist of mere sequences of detached sentences; paragraphs are not just strings of sentences printed together. In recent years considerable progress has been made in formalizing the various relations, both grammatical and semantic, that characterize texts, that is, sequences of sentences related to one another in ways characteristic of stories, arguments, conversations, sets of instructions, etc, indeed all of the various uses to which language is put in actual situations. This study of inter-sentence links within texts is known as text grammar (see further 9.5), but it takes us beyond the bounds of grammar as strictly interpreted by most linguists.

Grammar thus operates between the **upper limit** of the **sentence** and the **lower limit** of the **morpheme** or minimal grammatical unit. Between these limits structures given such titles as clause, phrase, and word may be abstracted and formally delimited. Of these, in all languages the word appears as a particularly stable element, and serves as a basic grammatical unit in grammar as outlined in this book. The status of the word and the morpheme as formal units of grammatical structure and grammatical analysis will be considered in the following sections.

5.3 The word

5.3.1 Grammatical criteria of word status

The term *word* has been used hitherto in this book without comment on its linguistic status. To those brought up in the literate tradition of the West any such discussion may seem otiose. This is part of the legacy of western literacy, with words listed in dictionaries and distinguished unambiguously in writing by spaces, whereby their self-evident status in both spoken and written discourse comes to be taken for granted. Experience in the analysis of unwritten languages, and the need to devise theories and procedures of grammatical analysis that may be applicable to the language of any society, literate or illiterate, and irrespective of its cultural situation, have shown that words must be established as grammatical units for the language under investigation as part of grammatical analysis. They are essentially units of the language as a system rather than of speech, wherein they are not, save in quite exceptional circumstances, delimited by inter-word pauses as printed words are delimited in the roman alphabet by inter-word spaces. Malinowski went so far as to say words 'are in fact only linguistic figments, the products of an advanced linguistic analysis'; this is justifiable in so far as it stresses the need for the word, whether institutionalized by writing or not in a particular language, to be formally established, if it is to serve as a basic unit of formal grammar. But diverse experience goes to show that native speakers have an intuitive awareness of word-like entities in their own language, whether written or not, to a greater extent than they have of other grammatical elements and structures set up by the linguist. The use of orthographic spaces, or other marks as in some non-roman scripts, is evidence of this, and Sapir noticed how readily linguistically untrained speakers of unwritten languages could come to recognize stretches of utterance between which pauses could be made (as in dictation) but which were themselves in some way felt as indivisible. It is likely that words can be identified and delimited as grammatical units in all languages, and that this intuitive and ready awareness of such a unit is an implicit and largely unconscious response to a variety of formal criteria in the speaker's language, which the linguist in making his abstraction of word units must set out fully and systematically, and which linguistic theory must enable one to formalize and make explicit.[4]

When sentences of the same language are studied and compared, it is seen that certain stretches in them exhibit an internal stability peculiar to themselves. These stretches may appear at different places in sentences relative to each other (*the kitten saw the pigeons, the pigeons saw the kitten; two and five make seven, five and two make seven*), may be separated by other stretches (*the kitten I bought saw the pigeons*), and by momentary pauses (*the puppy, the kitten, and the children were all playing, when it started to rain*); but they do not permit internal rearrangement of their constituent parts, nor the insertion of comparable and virtually unlimited further stretches of utterance, and they may not in normal speech be interrupted by any pause. Moreover, many of these stable stretches may themselves stand alone to constitute a complete sentence in an appropriate context.

These unitary stretches represent what are called **words** in formal grammar; in written languages they usually (but not always or necessarily) correspond to the orthographic words, but they can be equally well established in unwritten languages, since they are based on the inspection and comparison of spoken utterances by the linguist.

Definitions of the word unit have not been lacking, but those relying on non-formal, extra-grammatical criteria such as 'possessing a single meaning' or 'conveying a single idea' are of little value. Bloomfield's classic definition of the word as the 'minimum free form'[5] of a language is really a special application of the criterion of stability. The word as a stretch of speech that admits momentary pause on either side may also appear between indefinite pauses as a minimal sentence. The sentence is a free linguistic form, and the word is its minimal version. The word, defined as a minimum free form, is an element corresponding to a stretch of speech that, with differences of intonation and in some languages of stressing, and sometimes differences of segmental composition, in a suitable context, may both appear recurrently and recognizably in longer sentences, and stand alone to constitute a sentence, but cannot be divided without remainder into such stretches. Thus in English *man* is a word, and so is *manly*, because though *man* can stand alone (*Who was made like the angels? Man*), *-ly* (/-li/) cannot (except as a citation of a grammatical form, and any element in a language can be cited in this way, virtually becoming a word in its own right in such a use).

Words, like many other analytic entities, are the products of several different though related criteria. Thus they comprise nuclear members of the category, to which all the criteria apply, more peripheral or marginal ones to which only some apply, and very marginal or doubtful cases in which the criteria may conflict and different conclusions may be reached by the different weighting of the conflicting criteria. Stability is the basic criterion, which splits into a number of separate features; of these minimum free form status is perhaps the most obvious. The actual probability of individual words in a language occurring in normal discourse as independent sentences accompanied by sentence final intonation and followed by indefinite pause is obviously variable, with proper names and a few exclamative words like *hello, goodbye,* and *bother!* being the commonest types so used; but most words can appear acceptably as one word sentences. A small number of very frequently occuring items are very implausibly regarded as constituting complete sentences, and some may be positively excluded from such a function. Here the criteria of positional mobility in the sentence and separability from what preceded and follows are invoked. English *a* and *the* hardly ever occur as complete sentences (and then as /ei/ and /ðiː/, instead of the normal /ə/ and /ðə/ or /ði/ of connected discourse); but in other respects they behave as independent words, being parallel in sentence structures to *this* and *that* (*the man is here, in this room; that man is here, in the room*), which obviously do occur as complete sentences, and being separable from the words following them (*a dog; a big dog; the big black shaggy dog*). In this respect it is clear that English *the* is quite different in grammatical status from the suffixed 'definite article' of the Scandinavian languages and Romanian which, however intertranslatable they may be with most uses of English *the*, are always attached to a preceding word to form part of it. Thus, Norwegian *hus* /huːs/ house, *huset* /'huːsə/ the house; Romanian *lup* /lup/ wolf, *lupul* /'lupul/ the wolf, *lupul mare* /'lupul 'mare/ the big wolf; Scandinavian languages do also have a separate definite article similar to English *the*, used with adjective noun groups: *det store hus* /də 'stoːrə 'huːs/ the big house.

More marginal as members of the class of the words are the French unemphatic pronouns, *je* /ʒə/ I, *tu* /ty/ you (singular), *il* /il/ he, etc; they are never found alone, as in this position the independent or emphatic pronouns are used instead, *moi* /mwa/, *toi* /twa/, *lui* /lɥi/, etc, and in sentences they always form part of a closely knit verbal group. Some can occur in the same place as a proper name, clearly a free form (*Jean commande* /ʒã kɔmãd/ *John orders, il commande* /il kɔmãd/ he orders), but others such as *y* /i/ cannot, but are only found in fixed positions relative to other similar forms in a verbal group, though separable from them by limited possibilities of insertion of other unemphatic pronouns and a few other elements, such as negatives *il l'y met* /i li mɛ/ he puts it there; *il ne l'y met pas* /il nə li mɛ pa/ he does not put it there). These unemphatic pronouns are generally regarded as words, but of strictly limited mobility in sentence structures. The fact that historically they are descended from free words (mostly pronouns) in Latin, though of significance in the history of the French language, is irrelevant to the statement of the grammatical status in the language today.[6]

Still more marginal in regard to word status in English *'s* (/s/, /z/, or /iz/), usually called the 'possessive suffix' or '-s genitive'; it is never free to occur alone, and it mostly consists of a single consonant (/iz/ occurs always and only after words ending in /s/, /z/, /ʃ/, /ʒ/, /tʃ/, and /dʒ/), and then it has no alternative longer form, as the 'weak forms' of English words do (*I'll go* /ail 'gou/, *I will go* /ai wil 'gou/, etc). Morever, it is very limited in its positional possibilities in sentences. But word groups do occur, in spoken rather than in written English, in which it belongs grammatically to a series of words rather than to the word to which phonologically it is attached (*cp* 6.3.4), such as *member of Parliament's salary*, and *the boy I saw yesterday's jacket*, and these make it unlike other English suffixes in its grammatical behaviour. It has been variously analysed as a suffix of unique behaviour and as a word of unique form; the balance of evidence is probably in favour of its treatment as a peculiar suffix, not as a word, but with elements as marginal as this, where the relevant criteria that normally reinforce one another are in conflict, more than one analysis can be justified.[7]

At the other end of the scale whole series of words, theoretically without an upper limit, may be used syntactically as single words in proper names, book titles, play titles, and the like: *William Ewart Gladstone, Anne of Green Gables, Three men in a boat, All's well that ends well.* We see that titles, whatever their internal structure, are always treated as singular nouns and picked up by *it*: '*Anne of Green Gables* is a pleasant little book; it gives a picture of Canadian rural life at the beginning of this century', but 'Anne of Green Gables was an amusing girl; she would have been more fun to meet than Rosa Luxemburg'; '*Three men in a boat* is a light-hearted tale; three men in a boat were rowing up the Thames and running into various mishaps'; '*All's well that ends well* is one of Shakepeare's comedies.'

Most languages contain both **variable** and **invariable** words. Variable words are those in which ordered and regular series of grammatically different word forms are found, wherein part remains relatively constant and the variations in the other parts are matched by similar variations in other words; in English *walk, walks, walking, walked, follow, follows, following, followed*, etc, and *cat, cats, car, cars, house, houses*, etc are variable words, and the ordered series of forms are called paradigms. Words appearing in only one form are invariable words, such as English *since, when, seldom.* Languages differ in the number and complexity of the paradigms of their variable words; German has more grammatical word form variation than English, and Latin and Sanskrit have more than German. Some languages, mostly in the Far East and parts of South-east Asia, of which classical Chinese is the best known example, contain virtually only invariable words, without grammatical paradigms.

5.3.2 Phonological markers of the word unit

It will have been seen that in setting out the criteria of grammatical word status recourse was not made to meanings, nor to questions of phonological features, other than the actual phonological shape representing the word in spoken utterance. As regards meaning, words are by definition mostly free forms, *ie* potential sentences, and as sentences are as such meaningful, words are generally speaking suitable units for the assignment of a meaning of some sort; and they are so used in dictionary making. But definitions of the individual word unit in terms of its having a simple meaning are often indeterminate and unreliable; particular words can be glossed in a dictionary with a greater or lesser degree of precision, depending on their various uses in sentences, but no observations can determine whether any meaning statable of a word is simple or complex. Pairs such as *lovelier* and *more lovely*, and *oculist* and *eye doctor* are formally one and two words respectively, though their lexical meanings are practically the same.

As regards phonological features, certain correlations can be found with grammatical word status in many languages, and in such languages this should be brought out clearly in the description. Languages differ considerably in the amount of such correlation exhibited between the phonological and grammatical levels. At one extreme French is often cited as a language wherein little information is given by phonological criteria on word divisions in connected discourse. In the feature of liaison in French, words ending phonetically with a consonant and followed without pause by a word beginning with a vowel syllabify the consonant and vowel across the word boundary (*eg: mes amis* /mɛzami/ my friends); English has the possibility of distinguishing between pairs such as *a name* and *an aim, a tease* and *at ease*, etc, by the sort of features referred to in the preceding chapter and treated as juncture phonemes or as word prosodies (4.4.2, 4.4.3). Some other languages show much more correlation; as noticed already (4.4.2), Hungarian stresses the initial syllable of most grammatical word units, while generally speaking Polish, Swahili, and Sundanese (spoken in Java), three totally unrelated languages widely separated from one another geographically, stress the penultimate syllable of words. Some languages restrict severely the consonants that can appear in word final position; Japanese only allows the syllabic nasal (4.3.4 *p* 131), and Ancient Greek has only the following word final consonants and consonant groups: /n/, /r/, /s/, /ks/, and /ps/ ; /k/ and /kʰ/ occur in two words only (ἐκ /ek/ out, and οὐκ /ouk/ not, before words beginning with a vowel, οὐχ /oukʰ/ before words beginning with /h/). As a consequence in such languages, other consonants give the negative information of word non-finality. Vowel harmony, or the restriction of the categories of vowels within words, whose working in such languages as Turkish and Hungarian has already been described (4.4.3), is a further example of grammatical and phonological correlation.

It must be remembered that phonological features of the types mentioned in the preceding paragraph, relevant as they are in the languages that exhibit them, are, of necessity, logically secondary considerations in the establishment of grammatical word units. They are seldom, if ever, entirely in agreement with the grammatical criteria over the whole of the vocabulary of a language, and where there is conflict between grammatical criteria of the types described in 5.3.1 and phonological features normally coinciding in delimiting the same stretch of speech, the grammatical criteria must be allowed to carry the day. Examples of this conflict are seen in some words of foreign origin in Swahili, stressed on syllables other than the penultimate, and words such as *a, az* /ɔ/, /ɔz/, the (definite article), in Hungarian, seldom stressed at all. A unit or a category must be established and defined by criteria from the same level of analysis as that at which it will subsequently be used. If the word is to be employed as a basic unit of grammatical description, both in morphology and syntax, grammatical criteria are the primary ones in its delimitation. It may be the case in some languages that usually congruent phonological features, such as fixed-place stress, are more obvious and so more immediately recognizable in analysis, but they remain secondary.

In cases where a language does exhibit any marked degree of phonological and grammatical correlations in its word forms, this is an added reason in a complete linguistic description of the language for treating the word as a basic unit of grammar, since one is then bringing into prominence a structure of which the grammatical and phonological description are maximally congruent and so giving a more coherent total analysis of the language.[8] This virtue in linguistic description, where the language permits it, may be called congruence of levels, and it is in many languages a characteristic of the word as a generic unit that it is the point below the sentence at which grammatical features and phonologically features are most convergent. (The syllable and the morpheme (5.4) are usually more exclusively phonological and grammatically characterized units, respectively.) It has already been seen that prosodic phonology treats phonological features that are characteristic of word structures as such, either demarcatively or by extension of their expenents over more than one place therein, under a particular category of word prosodies (4.4.3). For the phonological treatment of word boundaries see also 4.4.2.

5.3.3 Variant word forms

Languages differ not only in the phonological correlations they exhibit with grammatical word boundaries, but also in the degree to which words vary in form phonologically in sentences. In all languages, words differ in such features as intonation pitches and relative speed of articulation and stressing, according to whether they are uttered alone or as part of a larger sentence and according to their position and environment in the sentence. But other differences of word form in sentences vary from language to language. The existence in English of 'weak' and 'strong' forms of some words has already been mentioned, whereby a considerable number of commonly used words appear in one form when used in isolation or when stressed in a sentence, and in number of other forms, usually shorter, in connected discourse with normal stress patterning. Thus the sentence *I should have thought so* may appear as /ai'ʃud həv 'θɔːt sou/, with *should* stressed and emphasized, or, with normal stressing, as /ai ʃəd həv 'θɔːt sou/, and more quickly as /ai ʃədəv 'θɔːt sou/ or /aiʃtəf'θɔːtsou/. Such differences are to a limited extent marked in spelling, but never completely; this was one of the considerations that led to the devising of transcriptions to deal adequately with facts of speech like this.

In French several words have two forms, with and without a final consonant, according to whether they are followed without pause and in close grammatical relation by a word beginning with a vowel (again it must be emphasized that this is a statement about the phonological form of French words as spoken, not about their spelling). Thus *est*, is, in isolation and before consonants is pronounced /ɛ/, but before a vowel initial word /ɛt/ (*il est brave* /il ɛ braːv/ he is brave, but *il est aimable* /il ɛt ɛmabl/ he is agreeable; so, too, *bon* /bɔ̃/ good, but *bon air* /bɔn ɛːr/ good appearence). In Sanskrit word shapes are considerably affected by the shapes of adjacent words and the final consonants of many words differ in connected discourse according to whether the word is final in its group or sentence and according to the initial consonant of an immediately following word. These differences were represented in the Sanskrit spelling and are therefore known in some detail (*tat* /tat/ that; *taj jāyate* /tajjaːjate/ that is born; *tac chinatti* /tac chinatti/ he cuts that; *mahat* /mahat/ big; *mahad dhanuh* / mahad dhanuh/ big bow). The term used of this sort of word form variation by the ancient Indian grammarians was *sandhi* ('putting together'), and this has been generallized as a technical term in linguistic description for all such phenomena. The differences between the tones of words in tone

languages when conditioned by the tonal patterns of neighbouring words (4.3.5) have been called tone sandhi.[9]

A special case of word form variation is found in Celtic
languages (*eg* Irish, Welsh, and Gaelic), whereby some words
appear in a number of forms differing in their initial consonant
of its absence and dependent on the particular preceding
word or on the grammatical relation between them. Thus
Welsh:

tad /taːd/ father	*gardd* /garð/ garden
fy nhad /və/ or /ə nhaːd/	*fy ngardd* /və ŋarð/ my
my father	garden
ei dad /i daːd/ his father	*ei ardd* /i arð/ his garden
ei thad /i θaːd/ her father	*ei gardd* /i garð/ her garden
eu tad /i taːd/ their father	*eu gardd* /i garð/ their garden

It will be noticed that in some cases the distinction between 'his',
'her', and 'their' is shown by the differences in the initial segment
of the second word form. The traditional name for these Celtic
initial sandhi differences is *mutation*.[10]

Sandhi differences are not generally regarded as paradigms like
the paradigms of variable words referred to above (5.3.1),
because they are often determined by the phonological shape of
adjacent word forms, as in Sanskrit and French, and are not tied
to specific grammatical relationships or limited to specific
grammatical classes of words; they may affect words that are
grammatically variable or invariable.

5.4 The morpheme

5.4.1 The morpheme as the minimal grammatical unit

The word has been treated in this account of grammatical
analysis as a fundamental and unique grammatical unit; but it is
demonstrably not the minimal grammatical unit. The most casual
comparison of such word forms as *cats, dogs*, and *horses*, with
cat, dog, and *horse* reveals the divisibility of the former set into
two grammatically significant elements, *cat-, dog-, horse-*, and
-s (or, in phonological transcription, /-s/, /-z/, and /-iż/).

These elements are grammatically significant, not simply
because of a 'more than one' meaning attaching to most words
with such a plural formative, but because of the formal patterning
in English sentences *the cat eats*, and *the cats eat*, etc. It is further
apparent that below this, at the grammatical level, no further
analysis of these words into smaller units is possible; phonologically /kæt/, /dɔg/, and /hɔːs/ are further divisible into con-

sonant and vowel elements, but this division does not make for the abstraction of any grammatically relevant peices.

These minimal grammatical units are called **morphemes**. It is remarkable that adequate recognition of the morpheme as a grammatical unit, and consequently a proper treatment of morphological word structure was not achieved in Western scholarship until fairly recently, despite the preoccupation of grammarians throughout antiquity and the Middle Ages with the morphological aspect of grammar. Recognition of the status of the morpheme in linguistic analysis was one of the achievements of the ancient Indian linguists, of whom Pāṇini is the most famous, and this is one of the debts Western linguistic scholarship owes to Indian work, which became generally known in Europe during the course of the nineteenth century.

Morphemes are established and delimited in a language by comparing word forms with one another and noting the recurrent pieces that compose them, and every word is wholly analysable into one or more morphemes. Thus *-s* /-s/, is revealed by comparing *cap, caps, cat, cats, lock, locks*, etc, and *-ment* /mənt/, by comparing *establish, establishment, embarrass, embarrassment, atone, atonement*, etc. Morphemes may be represented by, or correspond to, any phonological feature or shape, and may be monosyllabic or polysyllabic. /-z/ in /dɔgz/ is a single consonant; /-li/ in *lovely* /'lʌvli/, shows a CV structure, /-i/ in *doggy* /'dɔgi/, is a single vowel; *tobacco* / tə'bækou/ contains three syllables. The syllabic (phonological) structure of a word and its morphemic (grammatical) structure do not necessarily correspond; in *loveliness*, syllabically and morphemically /'lʌv-li-nis/, they happen to coincide, but in *teller*, syllabically /'te-lə/, morphemically /'tel-ə/, they do not.

5.4.2 Morpheme variants (allomorphs)

It has already been seen that words may exhibit different shapes according to their position in spoken sentences; this much more characteristic of morphemes in almost all, if not in quite all, languages. But whereas variant word shapes in most languages (*ie* other than those in which rigid sandhi rules apply) are fairly freely variable and depend for the most part on style and speed of utterance, most variant morpheme shapes are strictly dependent on their enviroment within the word, like the variant allophones within a phoneme (4.3.1, 4.3.2). Thus the regular formatives of English noun plurals, /-s/, /-z/, and /iz/, are distributed according to the final vowel or consonant of the word base or singular form: words ending in a voiced consonant, other than /z/, /ʒ/, or /dʒ/, or in a vowel (which are all voiced in English), have /-z/ (*dogs* /dɔgz/, *cows* /kauz/, *hens* /henz/); those ending in a voiceless consonant, other than /s/, /ʃ/, or /tʃ/ have /-s/ (*cats* /kæts/, *tacks* /tæks/); those ending in /s/, /z/, /ʃ/, /ʒ/, /tʃ/, and /dʒ/ have /-iz/ (*horses* /'hɔːsiz/, *prizes* /'praiziz/, *rushes* /'rʌʃiz/, *churches* /'tʃəːtʃiz/, *judges* /'dʒʌdʒiz/).

In order to make the parallelism with phoneme and allophone more clear, some linguists reserve the term *morpheme* for the whole grammatically relevant class of shapes that are in complementary distribution of in free variation in a given environment, and call the different shapes themselves morphs or **allormorphs**. This, however, is not universal practice, and provided it is remembered that the word *morpheme* may be used by different writers both for the individual form and for the whole class, confusion need not arise.

The allomorphs or variant morpheme shapes /-s/, /-z/, and /-iz/ are phonologically predictable in their distribution relative to one another, but there are plenty of examples of allomorphs of a morpheme in complementary distribution but not predictable by any phonological criteria. The English plural *-en* /ən/, is a case in point; the pair of words *ox, oxen*, grammatically parallel to *dog, dogs*, establishes it as a member of the same morpheme (or morpheme class) as /-s/, /-z/, and /-iz/, but inspection of the singular form does not lead one to expect the form *oxen*, as inspection of the regular noun *box* leads one to expect *boxes*. Plurals like *oxen* have to be learned individually in learning English.

English noun plurals illustrate a number of the problems that arise in the morphemic analysis of word structures in different languages (it must be emphasized at this point that this and subsequent chapters do not set out to give an account of English grammar; English is simply used more than other languages to illustrate the theory and procedures of formal grammatical analysis and description). Beside the regular forms /-s/, /-z/, and /-iz/, and irregular /-ən/, other irregular plurals of nouns are found, such as *children, sheep, feet, men*. In the analysis of these word forms, the aim, as in all linguistic analysis and description, is to state the observed facts in as economical and consistent a manner as completeness permits. With *child, children* (/tʃaild/, /'tʃildrən/), two points are illustrated:

[i] The singular and plural forms of the word base itself differ (as also happens in the archaic plural of *brother, brethren*), and

[ii] A choice must be made between taking /-ən/ and /-rən/ as the plural allomorph. In favour of /-ən/ is the recognition of this form already in *oxen* /'ɔksən/, but in favour of /-rən/ is the consequent greater similarity of the singular and plural base forms /tʃaild/ and /'tʃild-/. The choice may be fairly evenly balanced, and either analysis is legitimate, though, clearly, in a description of English grammar one must be chosen.

Words like *sheep* in English must be regarded as having singular and plural forms with the same overt shape, since the same word shape appears in sentences like *the sheep is grazing* and *the sheep are grazing*. Such words are sometimes analysed as having a plural formative element like *cows, horses*, etc, but without overt shape; that is to say an analytic entity is introduced without exponents at other levels or in the material, written or spoken, in order to keep the words in question within the same grammatical structure pattern as the majority of comparable words. This procedure, which goes back to Pāṇini, involves the use of **zero** elements, the name given to analytic entities without actual or overt exponents; it is justified if the introduction of the zero element simplifies the resulting analysis by aligning the structures of more words together. If all English noun plurals are to be regarded analytically as involving a specific plural formative morpheme, this treatment of words like *sheep, aircraft, deer*, etc seems inevitable. Zero may be symbolized Ø, *sheep plural* being represented /ʃiːp/ +Ø.[11]

Pairs of words like *foot, feet* and *man, men* are more troublesome in morphemic analysis, but a study of the possible alternative treatments is instructive. It may be held that the plural-forming morpheme is represented in words like this not by a shape but by a process of changing /u/ to /iː/, /æ/ to /e/, etc added to the base or singular form, or that the plural morpheme is represented by /iː/, /e/, etc, the allomorph /f . . . t/, / m . . . n/, etc being used in conjunction with it, as /'tʃild-/ is used in conjunction with /-rən/. Neither of these solutions is very attractive, as a process is not really something that can be added to something else, and discontinuous roots like /f . . . t/ and infixed morphemes are not otherwise found as part of English morphology. Alternatively the plural formative can be said to have zero shape, as in the case of *sheep*, and that /fiːt/, /men/, etc are the alternant morpheme shapes or allomorphs used before the plural morpheme, here represented by zero. Yet another solution is to regard forms like *men* as single morphs representing two morphemes, because of their grammatical comparability with forms like *dogs*. In these cases the term *portmanteau morph* has been used to designate morphs cumulatively representing two morphemes.[12] This is perhaps the most acceptable analysis.

The analysis and classification of the different phonological shapes in which morphemes appear, or by which they are represented, both in individual languages and in languages in general, is often called **morphophonology** (or more briefly **morphonology**) or *morphophonemics*. The analysis of the different forms taken by the English noun plural morpheme, discussed in this section, is part of the morphophonological or morphophonemic analysis of English.

5.4.3 Bound and free morphemes: root and affix

Morphemes may be classified in more than one dimension (in this book the term *morpheme* will generally be used in referring to the actual form or representative shape, unless the specific use of *allomorph* is necessary for clarity). Firstly, morphemes are **bound** and **free**.

A free morpheme is one that may constitute a word (free form) by itself; a bound morphene is one that must appear with at least one other morpheme, bound or free, in a word. In English *cats, cat* is free, since *cat* is a word in its own right, and *-s* is bound, as it is not a word in its own right. Free morphemes therefore necessarily constitute monomorphemic words. It has been said of one or two languages, for example Vietnamese, that almost all the morphemes are free, that is to say that the word and morpheme almost coincide in exponency.[13] But such languages are a special case, and for the great majority the terms *word, free morpheme*, and *bound morpheme* are all required. Polymorphemic words may consist wholly of free morphemes, being accorded word status on the ground of uninterruptability and unitary behaviour in sentences (5.3.1); they are often called compound words, and English *penknife, aircraft*, and *housework* are examples.

Secondly, morphemes may be divided into **roots** and **affixes**, the root being that part of a word structure which is left when all the affixes have been removed. Root morphemes may be bound or free, and are potentially unlimited in number in a language, as additions to vocabulary are in the main made by the acquisition of new roots either taken from foreign languages ('loan words', 8.1.8) or created for the purpose (like a number of trade names for products and the like). Affixes are bound morphemes; they are limited in number, though their numbers vary from language to language, and they may be exhaustively listed. Some affixes serve to differentiate the paradigm forms of variable words, containing a common root; others recur in the formation of a large number of polymorphemic words together with a large number of different root morphemes. All words may be said to contain a root morpheme, and therefore monomorphemic words may be said to comprise a single root. Some words contain more than one root, and the number of affixes in words in addition to the root, or roots, varies considerably in different languages.

In the English paradigm *cat, cats*, the form *cat* /kæt/ is the root and *-s* /-s/ an affix; in *try, tries, trying, tried*, the root is *try* (*trie*) /trai/, and *-s* /-z/, *-ing* /-iŋ/, and *-d* /-d/ are affixes. In *loveliness, manliness, react, recover*, and *remove, love, man, act, cover*, and *move* are roots, and *-li-, -ness*, and *re-* are affixes. In these examples the roots exhibit only one form in terms of consonant and vowel structure; but variant forms, or allomorphs of roots may occur with different affixes. This is the case with the irregular plural form *children*, noticed above, and with a number of verbs, such as *sleep, slept* /sli:p/, /slep-/ + /-t/. Some verbs in many languages combine quite different forms as variants of their roots; compare English *go, went* /gou/, /wen-/ + /-t/, with *walk, walked* /wɔːk/, /wɔːk/ + /-t/, and French *aller* /al-/ + /-e/ to go, *irai* /i-/ + /-r-/ + /-e/ (I) will go, *vont* /v-/ + /-ɔ̃/ (they) go, with *donner* /dɔn-/ + /-e/ to give, *donnerai* /dɔn-/ + /-ər-/ + /-e/ (I) will give, *donnent* /dɔn-/ + Ø (they) give. Roots having totally different allomorphs are sometimes called suppletive.

Roots and affixes may be of any phonological structure and length, though affixes generally tend to be shorter than roots. The only relevant criterion for establishing a part or the whole of a word as a single root is the impossibility of dividing it further into constituent morphemes by matching its parts with the parts of other words in the language. The disyllabic English word *express* (noun or verb) may be compared with *press, impress*, and *expression*, etc, and its bimorphemic structure thereby established; but *bishop, turtle*, and *potato* admit no such division into further morphemes. Matching the *pot-* /pɔt-/ of *potato* with *pot* /pɔt/ would scarely help, because the remainder *-ato* /-'eitou/ cannot be similarly matched with recurrent elements of other words. The abstraction of morphemes such as *goose-* /guz-/ and *logan-* /'lougən-/ in *gooseberry* and *loganberry* is justified, by the occurence of *-berry* /-bəri/, with a number of other clearly defined morphemes, such as *black, straw, dew* (*blackberry*

/'blækbəri/, *strawberry* / 'strɔːbəri/, *dewberry* /'djuːbəri/), as
well as by itself as a complete word in the allomorphic form
/'beri/.

Cross-linguistic appeals to equivalents or to earlier forms in
other languages are interesting but wholly irrelevant to this sort
of question in synchronic analysis. The trimorphemic status of the
Ancient Greek word επίσκοπος /epí-skop-os/ overseer, guardian,
is irrelevent to the monomorphemic status of its derivatives in
several modern European languages, English *bishop*, French
évêque /evɛːk/, German *Bischof* /'biʃoːf/, Hungarian *püspök*
/pyʃpøk/, etc. This is just one illustration of the difference
between diachronic etymological studies and synchronic descriptive studies.

A particular relation holds between the root and the affixes in
languages subject to vowel harmony, a feature of word structure
characterizing Turkish, Hungarian, Finnish, and a number of
other languages (4.4.3). In such languages it is the vowel or
vowels of the root that determine the vowel qualities of the
suffixes. Examples of this have already been given in the section
just referred to in Hungarian and Turkish; in Finnish one may
compare *puu* /puː/ tree, partitive case form *puuta* /puːta/, and
pyy /pyː/ partridge, partitive case form *pyytä* pyːtæ/.[14]

The distinction between root and affix is not the same as that
between bound and free morpheme, except that affixes are
always bound within the word. Roots may be bound or free, and
the relative proportions of the two types vary between different
languages. In English the majority of root shapes are themselves
free forms, that is words in their own right. Bound roots are relatively few, but some are found, such as *-ceive*, *-tain*, and *-cur*,
in *receive, retain recur*, etc. These bound root morphemes are
established by comparing series of words such as *receive, recap-
ture, redeem, recover, recur, retain, deceive, detain, contain,
conceive*, and *concur*. A few English roots have bound and free
variants, such as *sleep* and *slep-* /sliːp/ and /slep-/, and *child* and
child- /tʃaild/ and /'ʃild-/ (or *childr-* /'tʃildr-/ with *-en* /-ən/, as
the plural affix morpheme instead of *-ren* /-rən/).

In some other languages root morphemes are very frequently
bound. In Latin the root morphemes of verbs are almost always
bound forms not having the same shape as any member of the
verb paradigms; thus the root of the Latin verb /amoː/ I love,
is /am-/, and this does not constitute by itself any complete word
form in the paradigm of /amoː/; similarly the root of the verb
/regoː/ I rule, appears in the variant forms, both bound, /reg-/
and /reːc-/, as in /regere/ to rule, and /reːctus/ ruled. Many

Latin noun roots are bound: /domin-/ in /dominus/, /dominum/, etc, master (the different forms represent different cases of the noun, 6.4.1), /puell-/ in /puella/, /puellam/, etc girl; but some are free: /consul/ represents both the nominative singular case form of the word /consul/ consul, and the root of the other case forms, /consulem/, etc.

In some languages roots are not only bound forms, but are often represented by sequences that would be impossible as complete word structures; Japanese and Swahili root forms often end in a consonant, although the words in these languages in almost all cases end in a vowel (or, in Japanese, in /-ŋ/ the syllabic nasal, 4.3.4, *p* 131). Thus Japanese /kas-/ to lend, appears as root in the verb forms /kasu/ lend, lends /kasi/ lending, /kase/ lend!, etc; Swahili /imb-/ to sing, appears in /waimba/ they sing, /hawaimbi/ they do not sing, /hawataimba/ they will not sing, etc, /wa-/, /ha-/, /ta-/, /-a/, and /-i/ being some of the numerous affixes used in the verbal forms of the language.

Affix is a useful general term for the recurrent formative morphemes of words other than roots, but affixes may be divided formally into three major positional classes according to the position they occupy in relation to the root morpheme: *prefix*, *infix*, and *suffix*. Prefixes and suffixes may be readily illustrated from English (indeed, examples of them have already appeared from a number of languages in this section); *re-, de-, con-, per-*, and *pre-*, as in *receive, remove, deceive, deranged, conceive, contain, perceive, perform, preconceive, preempt*, are all prefixes, and they always precede the root or other prefixes in English words; the plural formatives *-s* (/-s/, /-z/, /-iz/), *-en* (/-ən/), etc, are suffixes, and so are the verb paradigm affixes *-ing* (/-iŋ/), *-t* (/-t/), *-d*, *-ed* (/-t/, /-d/, /-id/), etc (*slept, walked, called, wanted*).[15] The regular forms of French and Latin verb paradigms involve suffixation, but German, Ancient Greek, and Sanskrit make use of prefixation in their verb paradigms as well (German *machen* /'maxen/ to make, to do, *gemacht* /ge'maxt/ made; Greek λύω /lýːoː/ I loose, ἔλυσα /élyːsa/ I loosed; Sanskrit *bhavāmi* /bhavaːmi/ I am, *abhavam* /abhavam/ I was).

Infixes are affixes that appear within the consonant and vowel sequences of root forms; they occupy fixed positions that are statable by reference to the consonants and vowels. Infixes are less commonly met with, and are not found in English apart from one mode of analysis of plurals like *feet, men* (5.4.2). Infixes are found in Cambodian, a language of South-east Asia (/deːk/ to sleep, /dɔmneːk/ sleep), in Sundanese (/gɤlis/ to be pretty, /gumɤlis/ to be vain), and in Yurok (/sepolah/ field, /segepolah/

fields /kemoʔl/ he steals, /kegemoʔl/ he is a thief).[16] Arabic is
particularly marked as a language by its large number of what
are traditionally called 'triliteral roots', roots represented by a
sequence of three consonants, from which different paradigm
forms of variable words are made by the addition of one or more
morphemes, represented discontinuously by prefixes, infixes, and
suffixes, to the roots. Thus /k-t-b/ to write: (spoken Egyptian
Arabic) /yiktib/ he writes, /tiktib/ she writes, /ʔaktib/ I write,
/katab/ he wrote, /katabit/ she wrote, /katabt/ I wrote. This
type of word formation is not confined to Arabic, but Arabic
provides a notable example of it in a fairly well-known group of
closely related languages and dialects.[17]

Polymorphemic words need not contain only one root
morpheme though they must contain at least one. Two or more
roots (*ie* morphemes able to constitute the roots of one-root
words) may co-occur in a single word, with or without affixes;
such words are often called compound words. They are exemplified in English by *aircraft* (root + root), *pickpocket* (root +
root), *broadcaster* (root + root + affix), etc. The unitary behaviour of such forms in sentences and their uninterruptability (*cp:
pp* 185–6) are the grounds for ascribing single word status to
them, although the component roots may all constitute free forms
as well. Compound words may include one or more bound roots,
as in *ethnobotony* (*ethno-botan-y*, root + root + affix), wherein
neither root morpheme is a free form. German is often said to
have a particular propensity for forming long compound words
containing several roots (*eg: Kriegsfreiwilliger* /ˈkriːksfraiviliger/
volunteer for active service (*Krieg-s-frei-will-ig-er*, root + affix
+ root + root + affix + affix), *Kriegverpflegungsamt*
/ˈkriːksfɛrpfleːguŋsʔamt/ commissariat department (*Krieg-s-ver-
pfleg-ung-s-amt*, root + affix + affix + root + affix + affix +
root)). Other languages, as the English translations of these two
examples show, tend to prefer word groups rather than
compound words of such length. Classical Latin writers are
said to have disapproved stylistically of an excess compound
words.

So far, the discussion has been concerned with word form
differences which can be readily described in terms of additions
bound forms to roots. However, there are some word form
differences that do not lend themselves readily to such an
analysis. English noun plurals involving vowel alternation, such
as *man, men, foot, feet*, have already been mentioned; and verb
paradigms that include such forms *as fight, fought* /fait/, /fɔːt/,
take, /teik/, *took*/tuk/, are of this type as well. In German

comparable forms are found, such as *finden* /'finden/ to find, *find* /fint/ find!, *fand* /fant/ (he) found, *essen* /'ʔesen/ to eat, *iss* /ʔis/ eat!, *ass* /ʔas/ (he) ate. In both languages these non-additive variations in word form are exceptional (though quite numerous), belonging mainly to classes of words that exhibit additive paradigm variations like *boy, boys, bake, baked, sagen* /'zaːgen/ to say, *sag* /zaːk/ say!, *sagte* /'zakte/ (he) said. But in some languages alternations in the consonant or vowel structure of root forms without any overt additions are regular parts of paradigm variations. In Sundanese two forms of verb roots are used both as grammatically different words and as bases for affixation, and in many verbs these are related by the alternation of non-nasal and nasal consonants at the same point of articulation (*eg* /batʃa/, /matʃa/ to read; /bere/, /mere/ to give; /tendʒo/, /nendʒo/ to see; /dibere/, be given, /pamere/, gift).

Some linguists have insisted that all such formations must be analysed in terms of the addition of morphemes, and in English the uses of zero morpheme shapes, infixes and allomorphs consisting of vowel changes, have already been noticed in such attempts (5.4.2). It is always possible to describe any difference between word forms as the result of the addition of something; but it may be urged that in many cases the apparent consistency of such a description is bought at too high a price in divergence from the actual forms of the language as spoken.

Alternatively, apparently non-additive variations may be explained directly in terms of processes, not processes as something 'added' to another form. On these lines, one form in the paradigm, either arbitrarily or because it is grammatically parallel to an unaffixed root elsewhere in the language, is taken as basic; *ie: take* is basic because it matches *bake* (past tense form *baked*); different forms of the paradigms are then described as the result of processes, vowel change, nasalization, etc applied to the root form. (*Process* in this use is a descriptive term; it has nothing to do with historical processes in time or with changes in the forms of the language through the years.)[18]

Process terminology can be generalized more easily than additive terminology, since affixation itself can be regarded quite reasonably as one process, among several others, to which the roots of many words are subject. It is then legitimate to regard *men* and *mice* as the forms resulting from the process of vowel change applied to the basic forms *man* and *mouse* (the change of written letters *s* to *c* in *mice* has no bearing on the final consonant in the spoken forms which is /s/ in both), and to say that *boys* and *rats* are the result of addition. This terminology also fits well into the word-formation rules of transformational-generative grammar (7.2.3), 4.4.4

A particular type of grammatical formation, whereby a part or the whole of a root form is repeated in the same word, is found in a number of languages to varying extents; this is known as **reduplication** and is describable either as a process or as an addition. Ancient Greek provides a well-known illustration of partial reduplication. The perfect tense forms of most types of verbs in Greek are formed, together with certain suffixes, by prefixing to the root a syllable comprising the initial consonant of the root followed by the vowel /e/; thus λύω /lýːoː/ I loose, λέλυκα /lélyka/ I have loosed; πιστεύω /pistéuoː/ I trust, πεπίστευκα /pepísteuka/ I have trusted (this is in no way a complete statement of the rules governing reduplication in Greek; the details are not relevant here). This type of formation is carried further in some languages. In Malay, Sundanese, and other Malayopolynesian languages, the reduplication of entire word forms is a regular means of forming noun plurals (it also serves other grammatical purposes); thus Malay /kapal/ ship, /kapalkapal/ ships; Sundanese /sirɣm/ ant, /sirɣmsirɣm/ ants.

The means principally exploited by languages to differentiate the paradigm forms of variable words, and the different modes of word formation in general, constitute one important factor in the classification of languages into various types (see 8.2.6). The use of tone (pitch) and stress differences in morphology is referred to in 6.4.6.

5.5 The semantic status of morphemes

Just because in grammar, as narrowly defined in this book (5.1.1), we are nearer to the semantic function of language than we are in phonology, several linguists have claimed that the morpheme should be regarded not only as the minimal grammatical unit but also as the minimal meaningful unit of language. This is obviously an attractive point of view. Certainly in the process of grammatical analysis the investigator breaks into the morphological structure of words by comparing forms and meanings along with membership of gramatical paradigms. Also, as we saw with most English noun plurals and verbal past tenses, it is both possible and highly informative to ascribe a meaning or one of several meanings to specific morphemes. Difficulties arise when having a specific meaning is made criterial for morphemic status. It seems hard to ascribe a separately definable meaning to English -ing or to the feminine suffix -e in French adjectives, (*lent, lente* slow, *vilain, vilaine* ugly, *écrit, écrite* written)* when it is borne in mind that every French noun is either masculine or feminine and requires an adjective constructed with it to 'agree' in gender, and that over the vocabulary as a whole little correlation can be found between grammatical gender and animate sex, or any other semantic feature (see further in 6.6.2).

Similar questions arise over any attempt at defining the meaning of -*ceive* and -*tain* in words like *receive, deceive, conceive,* and *apperceive,* and *retain, detain, contain,* and *appertain.* It has been suggested that these words should indeed not be regarded as polymorphemic, but this seems an uneconomical solution.[19]

Certainly the linguist should look for and analyse very carefully the semantic functions of the morphemes he abstracts from a language; and obviously in the actual conduct of his research, especially on little known languages studied in the field ('anthropological linguistics' 9.1.1), he will make use of any hypothesis, provisional semantic correlation, or indeed any 'hunch' that may help. But research practice and 'discovery procedures,[20] are not the same as descriptive theory, and on balance it seems that it would be better to recognize the morpheme as a formal constituent ultimately based on the systematic comparison of ordered series of word forms in the given language.

---

* The phonological shapes of both root and suffix morphemes of these words in spoken French vary considerably, but for present purposes the written representations will suffice.

Bibliography for Chapters 5 and 6

1 D. J. ALLERTON, *Essentials of grammatical theory*, London, 1979.
2 E. O. ASHTON, *Swahili grammar*, London, 1944.
3 C. E. BAZELL, *Linguistic form*, Istanbul, 1953.
4 'Meaning and the morpheme', *Word* 18 (1962), 132–42.
5 C. E. BAZELL, J. C. CATFORD M. A. K. HALLIDAY, and R. H. ROBINS (eds), *In memory of J. R. Firth*, London, 1966.
6 J. T. BENDOR-SAMUEL, 'The verbal piece in Jebero', *Word* 17 (1961), supplement.
7 B. BLOCH, 'English verb inflection', *Lang* 23 (1947), 399–418.
8 L. BLOOMFIELD, *Language*, London, 1935.
9 *Eastern Ojibwa*, Ann Arbor, 1958.
10 E. BOURCIEZ, *Eléments de linguistique romane*, fourth edition, Paris, 1946.
11 M. BRAUN, *Grundzüge der slavischen Sprachen*, Göttingen, 1947.
12 R. G. A. DE BRAY, *A guide to the Slavonic languages*, London, 1951.
13 E. K. BROWN and J. E. MILLER, *Syntax*, London, 1980.

14 J. L. BYBEE, *Morphology*, Amsterdam, 1985.

15 Y. R. CHAO, *A grammar of spoken Chinese*, Berkeley, 1968.

16 B. COMRIE, 'The ergative: variations on a theme', *Lingua* 32 (1973), 239–53.

17 W. D. ELCOCK, *The Romance languages*, London, 1960.

18 M. B. EMENEAU, *Studies in Vietnamese (Annamese) grammar*, Berkeley, 1951.

19 W. J. ENTWISTLE and W. A. MORISON, *Russian and the Slavonic languages*, London, 1949.

20 C. C. FRIES, *The structure of English*, New York, 1952.

21 H. A. GLEASON, *Introduction to descriptive linguistics*, second edition, New York, 1961.

22 W. HAAS, 'Zero in linguistic analysis', *Studies in linguistic analysis*, special publication of the Philological Society, Oxford, 1957, 33–53.

23 M. A. K. HALLIDAY, 'Notes on transitivity and theme in English', *Journal of linguistics* 3 (1967), 37–81, 199–244, 4 (1968), 179–216.

24 E. HAMP, 'Morphophonemes of the Keltic mutations', *Lang* 27 (1951), 230–47.

25 A. A. HILL, *Introduction to linguistic structures*, New York, 1958.

26 L. HJELMSLEV, *Les principes de grammaire générale*, Copenhagen, 1928.

27 *La catégorie des cas*, Aarhus, 1935.

28 'La structure morphologique', *Actes du 5me congrès international de linguistes* (1939), 66–93.

29 C. F. HOCKETT, 'Problems of morphemic analysis', *Lang* 23 (1947), 321–43.

30 'Two models of grammatical description', *Word* 10 (1954), 210–34.

31 *A course in modern linguistics*, New York, 1958.

32 H. HOIJER, 'The cultural implications of some Navaho linguistic categories', *Lang* 27 (1951), 111–20.

33 'The relation of language to culture', A. L. Kroeber (ed), *Anthropology today*, Chicago, 1953, 554–73.

34 (ed), *Language in culture*, Chicago, 1955.

35 G. C. HORROCKS, *Generative grammar*, London, 1987.

36 H. P. HOUGHTON, *An introduction to the Basque language*, Leyden, 1961.

37 J. M. JACOB, *Introduction to Cambodian*, London, 1968.

38 R. JAKOBSON, 'Beitrag zur allgemeinen Kasuslehre' *TCLP* 6 (1936), 240–88.

39 O. JESPERSEN, *The philosophy of grammar*, London, 1924.

40 M. JOOS, *The English verb: form and meanings*, Madison, 1964.

41 E. L. KEENAN and B. COMRIE, 'Noun phrase accessibility and universal grammar', *Linguistic inquiry* 8 (1977), 63–99.

42 J. LYONS (ed), *New horizons in linguistics*, Harmondsworth, 1970.

43 A. A. MACDONELL, *A Sanskrit grammar for beginners*, London, 1911.

44 P. H. MATTHEWS, *Morphology: an introduction to the theory of word structure*, Cambridge, 1974.

45 A. MEILLET, *Linguistique historique et linguistique générale* (I), Paris, 1948.

46 T. F. MITCHELL, *Introduction to colloquial Egyptian Arabic*, London, 1956.

47 J. MORRIS-JONES, *Elementary Welsh grammar*, Oxford, 1922.

48 E. A. NIDA, *Morphology*, second edition, Ann Arbor, 1948.

49 *Syntax*, Glendale, 1946.

50 *Synopsis of English syntax*, The Hague, 1966.

51 F. R. PALMER, *A linguistic study of the English verb*, London, 1965.

52 *Mood and modality*, Cambridge, 1986.

53 *Grammar*, Harmondsworth, 1984.

54 *The English verb*, London, 1987.

55 F. PLANK (ed.) *Ergativity*, London, 1979.

56 R. H. ROBINS, *The Yurok language*, Berkeley, 1958.

57 'Some considerations on the status of grammar in linguistics', *Archivum linguisticum* 11 (1959), 91–114.

58 'In defence of WP', *TPS* 1959, 116–44.

59 'Nominal and verbal derivation in Sundanese', *Lingua* 8 (1959), 337–69.

60 *A short history of linguistics*, second edition, London, 1979.

61 E. SAPIR, *Language*, New York, 1921.

62 E. SAPIR and M. SWADESH, *Nootka texts*, Philadelphia, 1939.

63 L. C. THOMPSON, *A Vietnamese grammar*, Seattle, 1965.

64 G. L. TRAGER and H. L. SMITH, *Outline of English Structure*, Studies in linguistics, occasional paper 3, Norman, Oklahoma, 1951.

65 H. VOGT, *Esquisse d'une grammaire du georgien moderne*, Oslo, 1936.

66 I. C. WARD, 'Tone in West African languages', *Proceedings of the third international congress of phonetic sciences*, 1938, 383–8.

67 R. S. WELLS, 'Immediate constituents', *Lang* 23 (1947), 81–117.

68 B. L. WHORF, *Four articles on metalinguistics*, Washington, 1950.

69 *Language, thought, and reality: selected writings of Benjamin Lee Whorf*, (ed) J. B. Carroll, New York, 1956.

70 R. O. WINSTEDT, *Malay grammar*, Oxford, 1927.

71 J. WRIGHT, *A grammar of the dialect of Windhill in the West Riding of Yorkshire*, English Dialect Society, London, 1892.

Grammatical analysis and description, the subject of Chapters 5 and 6, is covered in a number of general books. All the books referred to in the general bibliography appearing after Chapter 1 have chapters devoted to grammatical topics. Additionally attention may be drawn to the following: Hjelmslev, 26; Allerton, 1; Palmer, 53.

In the older European tradition, Jerpersen, 39, is an important contribution by an important writer.

It must be remembered that not all the questions raised in these books, and in other writings refered to in the notes, are answered in the same way. Somewhat different theories and different interpretations of theory apply in grammar as in the other levels of analysis. This does not mean that any one of the writers is 'right' and the others 'wrong' in some particular matter.

Notes to Chapter 5

1 See further 7.1.2 below.

2 Some of the relations between linguistics and logic are briefly noticed below, 9.2. On 'logical form' in transformational-generative grammar see 7.2.3, p 289.

3 Bloomfield, 8, 170.

4 B. MALINOWSKI, *Coral gardens and their magic*, London, 1935, volume 2, 11. Sapir, 61, 32–6. It may be noted that most languages have a word meaning 'word', but not usually a word for 'morpheme' before the development of formal linguistics in the speech community.

5 On the word as a minimum free form, Bloomfield, 8, 177–81. An earlier type of definition may be seen in Meillet, 45, 30: 'The association of a given meaning to a given group of sounds susceptible to a given grammatical use.' Further on the word as a grammatical unit, A. Reichling, *Het woord*, Nijmegen, 1935.

   On the use of the word as a basic grammatical unit, Robins, 58.

6 An exception to the statement about the unemphatic pronouns in French is found in the official formula *je soussigné certifie* /ʒə susiɲe sɛrtifi/ I the undersigned certify. This is a survival from an earlier stage in the language when these pronoun forms enjoyed greater freedom of position in sentences.

7 On 'weak forms', *cp* Chapter 4, note 4. English *-s* is also discussed by Bloomfield, 8, 178–9.

8 For a study of phonetic correlations with word boundaries as can be found in French, see W. Zwanenburg and others, 'La frontière du mot en françias,' *Studies in language* 1 (1977), 209–21, and references.

9 On sandhi in Sanskrit, MacDonell, 43, Chapter 2; W. S. Allen, *Sandhi*, The Hague, 1962.

   Tone-sandi, Pike, *Tone languages*, Ann Arbor, 1948.

10 Welsh mutations, Morris-Jones, 47, 35–7. Further study of this feature in Celtic languages in Hamp, 24.

11 Zero elements, elements posited in a structure at a particular place, but without overt shape or exponents at another level, are also used in phonology, Thus in the interests of structural regularity, syllables of phonetic composition [VC] could be analysed as /CVC/ the first C elements being a zero unit. On zero in linguistic analysis, Bloomfield, 8, 209. Haas, 22, suggests certain rules for the use of Zero elements. His proposals are not followed by everyone, but manifestly the excessive use of this device weakens one's total analysis and probably means that thorough re-analysis is required to eliminate some of the apparently irregular structures that occasion it.

12 Portmanteau morphs, Hockett, 29.

13 Vietnamese, Emeneau, 18, 2. A few bound morphemes of less than syllable length are recognized in Thompson, 63, 106.

14 Finnish, C. N. E. Eliot, *Finnish grammar*, Oxford, 1890; J. Atkinson, *Finnish grammar*, Helsinki, 1956; H. Fromm and M.

Sadeniemi, *Finnisches Elementarbuch*, Heidelberg, 1956. Grammatical features like vowel harmony are, of course, analysed differently in phonemically 'based phonology, prosodic phonology, and autosegmental phonology' (4.4.3; 4.4.7).

15 The rules of formation of the regular English past tense forms may be stated in a manner similar to those governing the formation of regular noun plurals: verb roots ending in a voiceless consonant other than /t/ suffix /-t/; those ending in voiced consonants other than /d/ and in vowels suffix /-d/; those ending in /t/ or /d/ suffix /-id/ (*hissed* /hist/; *fanned* /fænd/; *tried* /traid/; *carted* /'kaːtid/; *traded* /'treidid/).

The regular distribution of /-s/, /-z/, and /-iz/ in verb forms is the same as that of the regular allomorphs of the noun plural morpheme (*gets* /gets/; *holds* /houldz/; *goes* /gouz/; *twitches* /'twitʃiz/).

English verb forms are analysed in Bloch, 7; Palmer, 51 and 54.

16 Cambodian, Jacob, 37.

Sundanese, Robins, 59.

Yurok, Robins, 56.

17 Arabic, Mitchell, 46.

18 'Two models of grammatical description' involving respectively 'items and arrangements' and 'items and processes' are compared on somewhat similar lines by Hockett, 30.

19 Definitions of the morpheme involving its necessary possession of an individual meaning, Bloomfield, 8, 161; Hockett, 31, 123. Contrast Trager and Smith, 64, 53; Robins, 57; Bazell, 4.

A useful discussion on the relations between meaning and form in grammatical statement is to be found in Palmer 51, 6–9.

20 On the relation between research procedure and descriptive statement, N. Chomsky, review of J. H. Greenberg, *Essays in linguistics Word* 15 (1959), 202–18.

Chapter 6

Grammar: grammatical classes, structures, and categories

6.1 Syntactic relations

Sentences can be shown to be series of words (and printed sentences in roman orthography are obviously so), and grammar is concerned with the analysis of the structures and regular patterns of sentences. In taking the word as a basic grammatical unit one may say that the heart of grammar is that part which deals with the patterned interrelations of words in the sentences of a language, and with the means of analysing them and stating them systematically. This is the traditional province of syntax, and it may reasonably be claimed that syntax in this sense is the most important part of grammar. Languages vary in the amount of word form variation that is found in them. Latin, Ancient Greek, and Sanskrit have a good deal; so do Arabic and many American-Indian languages. English has much less, and languages with few or no paradigms of variable words, such as Chinese and some of the languages of South-east Asia, show hardly any. The unfortunately popular confusion of grammar with morphology alone leads to the absurd statements still heard such as 'English has less grammar than Latin', and that 'Chinese has no grammar'. If a language had no grammar, no systematic ordering of its words in sentences, it could never be learned by a native speaker or by a foreigner, nor could two people understand one another in it. Indeed, a language without grammar is a contradiction in terms.

What does emerge from a comparison of different types of language is that the relative weight borne by morphology and syntax in governing the forms and patterns of sentences may vary from language to language, and that the role of morphological word form variation in paradigms may be very much reduced or even non-existent, but the syntactic classification and ordering of words in sentences are essential components of the grammar of every language.

The fact that English sentences can be of the type *the men eat*, but not of the type †*men the eat* reveals one essential basis of syntax, namely that words, even when they are collocationally appropriate (2.4.2), cannot be put together in just any order; in addition to grammatical acceptability and intelligibility, the total meaning of a sentence may depend in part simply on word order, as in the English pair of sentences *the tigers killed the hunter* and *the hunter killed the tigers*.

Syntactic relations are fundamentally very simple ones, and fall into three classes, **positional** relations, relations of **co-occurrence**, and relations of **substitutability**. The first of these are overt relations, observable as the word order of sentences; the other two are covert, not revealed by the observation of sentences alone, but by the comparison of ordered series of sentences with one another.

By relations of **co-occurrence** one means that words of different sets of classes may permit, or require, the occurrence of a word of another set or class to form a sentence or a particular part of a sentence. Thus in English words of the class *man, horse*, etc may be followed by words of the class of *eat, live*, etc in short sentences, and usually are so followed, though it is a fallacy to say that all proper sentences must be of this type. Response sentences may often by of other types, and a good many of the one-word sentences of many languages are response sentences (*eg: Who are you? Travellers. Cp* 6.3.1).[1] Words of the class *man, horse*, etc may be preceded by words of the class *good, strong*, etc, and also by the words *the* and *a*. But *the* and *a* require the presence of a word of either the *man* class or the *good* class if they are to precede a member of the *eat, breathe, live* class. Here at once one sees that the positional order of elements is brought into play; *the* both presupposes *good*, etc or *horse*, etc (*the good are honoured, the horse eats*), and presupposes it in a fixed relative position. *The strong horse* is the only permitted order of these three words when they are all to precede *eats, works*, etc as a complete sentence or as the first part of one. Further examples of presupposition or obligatory co-occurrence are the relations uniting Latin words like /in/ and /ad/ to a following word of the class /dominum/ master, /urbem/ city, etc, or to an equivalent group of words: /ad dominum/ to the master, /in urbem/ into the city.

The third relation, **substitutability**, has already been mentioned in the illustration of classes or sets of words substitutable for each other grammatically in the same sentence structures; but additionally groups of more than one word, contiguous or discontiguous in a sentence, may be jointly substitutable grammatically for a single word of a particular set. In English the group *the man* is substitutable for *man*, but not for *the*, in *man lives, man wants little*, etc; and *strong man* is substitutable for *man* in *the man drank it all*, etc. In *yesterday he came, came* could be used in place of *yesterday . . . came*, but *yesterday* could not (*he came* is a sentence, but not †*yesterday he*).

The substitutability of word groups for single words according to certain statable principles in a language shows that sentences are not merely strings of words, but, except for the shortest sentences, they are hierarchically ordered in terms of interrelated groups. This is basic to the understanding by the hearer and the analysis by the linguist of longer sentences, and must be considered in more detail below.[2]

In transformational-generative theory transformations may be regarded as a separate and often complex class of substitutions. Further discussion of this is deferred until section 7.2.

6.2 Word classes

Words may be brought into **word classes** in a language by reference to the syntactic relations that they contract with one another in sentences, and sentences may be analysed grammatically in these terms. In languages like Vietnamese, wherein most or all of the words are invariable, the whole grammatical analysis must be carried out formally in this way.

However, in most languages, to a greater or lesser extent, many words are differentiated formally into sets of classes by paradigmatic variations in word forms. In English one finds classes of the type *horse, horses, maintain, maintains, maintaining, maintained*, and *hot, hotter, hottest*, as well as strictly limited classes of words, such as *I, me, we, us*, and *he, him, they, them*. Similar classes with more complex paradigms are found in German and Latin, among other languages (paradigms of hundreds of different word forms built on a single root morpheme are common in quite a large number of languages).[3]

Generally speaking paradigmatically differentiated classes coincide in membership with classes of words syntactically differentiated by the types of relationship illustrated in the preceding section. The centrality of syntax in grammar, even in languages having a high degree of morphological complexity in its word form paradigms is shown by two facts.

[i] Where there is a conflict between syntactic and morphological classification, syntax is almost always accorded precedence. English *pretty, hot,* and *big* are paradigmatically alike (*prettier, prettiest,* etc); *beautiful, temperate,* and *sizable* are invariable (the adverb formative *-ly,* as in *beautifully,* etc, is not considered here as part of the paradigm of *beautiful,* any more than *lover* is considered part of the paradigm of *love;* these two different sorts of word formations will be considered in 6.4.5). But both sets of words are treated as members of one class, usually called adjectives, because syntactically their relations with nouns (words like *horse, house,* etc) and words of other classes in sentences are the same; *pretty tree* and *beautiful tree, big house* and *sizable house,* and *hotter climate* and *more termperate climate,* are all examples of the same English construction or syntactic grouping of words whereby adjective + noun or adverb + adjective + noun forms groups subsitutable for single nouns in all or most places in sentence structures. Thus one can say in English *this is a tree, this is a pretty tree, this is a beautiful tree, this is a prettier tree,* and *this is a more beautiful tree,* and likewise *this is the prettiest tree, this is the tree,* and *this is the most beautiful tree.* Within some of these sentences the groups *more beautiful* and *most beautiful* illustrate another relation of substitutability, between adverb + adjective groups and single adjectives.

Within the noun and verb classes in English it is their identity of syntactic relations with other words in sentences that leads one to group the morphologically diverse pairs *man, men,* with *horse, horses,* and *sing, sang, sung,* with *chant, chanted (he sang the song and chanted the psalm; the song was sung and the psalm was chanted).* Recognition of these morphological differences is made as a subclassification within the larger, syntactically based, word class: variable and invariable adjectives, 'strong' and 'weak' verbs (traditional terms for English and German verbs forming different tenses with vowel alterations and suffixation respectively).

[ii] Among the invariable words of a language different word classes must often be set up or recognized, where their syntactic behaviour shows regular differences. Thus among English invariables some words (*eg: at, with, from*) precede nouns to form groups syntactically substitutable for adverbs,

words like *quickly, then, often*, etc; thus *he came with speed, he came quickly; we will discuss it at supper, we will discuss it then; he comes from London, he comes often*. These words are usually called prepositions, and are distinguished as such by this syntactic function. It is not their only function; sentences 'ending with a preposition', though frowned on by pedants, are very common; *where have you come from?* is commoner than *from where have you come?*, and *what are you driving at?* and *what are you up to?* have no alternative forms at all.

Other invariable words in English precede word groups that could otherwise constitute complete sentences, and produce groups syntactically substitutable for a single adverb: *he will have it if he sees it, he will have it then; he came home because he felt ill, he came home quickly*. The words are called conjunctions.

In the substitutions of words by which word classes are formally established, there is no need for the pairs of sentences to have the same or similar meanings; some of the pairs above are very much alike in meaning, others are not. The important thing is that the word group can occur in most or all the formal environments or structural places in which single words of a given class can occur.

In the grammatical analysis of languages words are assigned to **word classes** on the formal basis of **syntactic behaviour**, supplemented and reinforced by differences of **morphological paradigms**, so that every word in a language is a member of a word class. Word class analysis has long been familiar in Europe under the title *parts of speech*, and for many centuries grammarians have operated with nine word classes or parts of speech: noun, verb, pronoun, adjective, adverb, preposition, conjunction, article, and interjection. Difficulties have arisen with such a scheme because the various classes were not always clearly defined in formal terms; though for the most part they could be justified formally in Latin and Ancient Greek, in which languages they were first worked out, several of them were rather hazily defined in terms of types of meaning or philosophical abstractions (verbs being said to stand for actions or for being acted on, and nouns for things or persons). Because such extralinguistic criteria were taken as the basis of this word classing (though it could originally have been quite well grounded on formal criteria), these word classes were applied to the material of other languages without regard for their suitability in terms of the actual morphological paradigms and syntactic relations found therein, and it was assumed that their alleged meaning content guaranteed their presence in any language worthy of the name.[4]

In formal grammar, the number and nature of the word classes of a language must be worked out as the analysis proceeds, not assumed in advance, nor settled by reference to the grammatical class of the nearest translation equivalent of a word in English, Latin, or some other language. Traditional terms are useful as labels for formal classes, where they seem appropriate through some observed similarity of grammatical function with word classes already so named in other languages. The labelling of word classes by such names as *noun* and *verb* may be justified by a similarity of the meanings of some of its members of the classes called nouns and verbs in another language. Thus by the fact that persons and static objects are generally referred to by words of one particular formal class in a given language (whatever semantic functions other members of that class may fulfil), the label *noun* is applied to all the words formally assigned to that class. But when such labels, or any others, are given to word classes, it must be remembered that they add nothing to the formal grammatical description of the classes, or to their definitions, or to the assignment of words to them. The definition of a class, and its membership, arise from the criteria used to establish it in the first place.

In some languages, for example Chinese, prepositions do not stand out as a distinct class, and the nearest translation equivalents of several English prepositions, in so far as they may be found, exhibit the characteristics of the general class of verbs. In Japanese and some other languages the translation equivalents of many English adjectives also belong, as a subclass, to the class of verbs. This is often mis-expressed by saying that 'Japanese adjectives contain the verb "to be"'; thus /uma wa hajai/ the horse is–quick, /uma wa hajakatta/ the horse was–quick.

The most general word class distinction in languages seems to be that between the classes designated nominal and verbal. Even in Nootka, a language of the North-west Pacific coast of America, wherein it is said that all root morphemes may be indifferently nominal or verbal, the distinction appears in some of the affixes that form words of different grammatical functions, noun-like and verb-like respectively.[5] The noun–verb distinction would seem to be the absolutely irreducible minimum of universal grammar on any interpretation of this concept.

As many classes are set up as words of different formal behaviour are found. This means that some words in many languages, especially words in frequent use, have to be classified under more than one head. The English classes noun, verb, and adjective are required respectively for words like *death, pursue,* and *malicious,* each of which belongs to one class only. Words like *work* belong both to the noun and verb classes (*he works well, his work is good, their works are good*); such words may be treated as separate entries in a dictionary; since the grammatical distinctions between two word classes are just as clear between the two uses of the word form *work* as they are between two word forms only functioning as noun and verb respectively. Words like *mature* belong to the verb and the adjective classes (*the scheme is maturing, this is a mature garden*). Words like *choice* belong to the adjective and noun classes (*choicest flowers, you may take your choice*). The English classes of preposition, adverb, and conjunction are required for words like *at, with,* and *from, soon, seldom,* and *prettily,* and *if, when,* and *because,* respectively, each group having its own syntactic functions in the language. But words like *before* and *after* belong to all three classes: preposition in *he came before tea* (cp: *he came at tea-time*), adverb in *he had come before* (cp: *he had come often*), and conjunction in *he came before we expected him* (cp: *he came when we expected him*).

The English word *round* belongs to five classes: noun in *one round is enough,* verb in *you round the bend too quickly,* adjective in *a round tower,* adverb in *he came round,* and prepositions in *he wandered around the town.* Naturally, languages with less morphological word form variation admit of multiple-class membership more readily than languages wherein several of the distinct word classes are characterized by separate morphological paradigms.[6]

Word classes may be **open** or **closed** in membership; all languages have open classes, and most have some closed ones as well. An open class is one whose membership is in principle unlimited, varying from time to time and between one speaker and another. Most loan words (words taken in from foreign languages, 8.1.8) and newly created words go into open classes. Closed classes contain a fixed and usually small number of member words, which are the same for all the speakers of the language, or the dialect, and which do not lose or add members without a structural alteration in the grammar of the language as a whole. In English, nouns, adjectives, adverbs, and verbs are open classes; pronouns, prepositions, and conjunctions are closed classes, although prepositional phrases (word groups substitutable for prepositions, like *in the neighbourhood of,* grammatically substitutable for prepositions, like *in the neighbourhood of*, grammatical substitutable for *near* or *at*) are open. In some languages the nearest equivalents of the English pronouns are members of an open class, and treated as a subclass of the nouns; Malay, in which the forms of personal address and reference are quite numerous and vary according to the degree of intimacy and the relative status of speakers, is such a language.

6.3 Immediate constituents

6.3.1 General principles: basic syntactic structures

Among the fundamental relations between words in sentences constituting the material of grammar, the relation of group substitutability has been mentioned as the basis for the understanding and analysis of the longer sentences in languages.

Although the term *string* is often used technically to refer to sequences of words, sentences are not merely strings of words in an acceptable order and 'making sense'; they are structured into successive components, consisting of groups of words, contiguous or discontiguous, and of single words. These groups and single words are called **constituents**, and when they are considered as part of the successive unravelling of a sentence, they are known as its **immediate constituents**. Immediate constituent analysis is basic to syntax, and it formalizes part of the means whereby native speakers form and understand longer sentences. It can be shown that each of the longer sentences of a language (and these are in the majority) is structured in the same way as one of a relatively small number of irreducibly short sentences, called **basic sentence types**. The ways in which the longer sentences are built up from, and conversely analysed into, short basic sentence patterns may be called expansions. The characteristic of language help to account for one of the most important, and on the face of it astonishing, facts about language, that one can immediately understand sentences that one has never heard or read before in own's own language, provided only that the words in it are already familiar or may be interpreted from the rest of the sentence in its context. This ability implies the mastery of the basic patterns of sentence structures and of the regular means by which these patterns are expanded.

Examples from English will illustrate and clarify these terms and procedures. Sentences like *John spoke, run!, do you see?, where is it?* may be taken, on this scheme of analysis, as examples of basic sentence structures, in terms of which almost all longer sentences in English can be structurally analysed. In *John*

saw Mary, John was admired, and *does Jennifer like cheese?*, *saw
Mary*, *was admired* and *like cheese* (each being verb and noun
respectively in class membership) appear in a position in which
a single verb could appear (*John spoke, does Jennifer cook?*). The
constituents can be discontinuous; in *tomorrow we leave,
tomorrow . . . leave* replaces a single verb, *eg: leave, go*, etc, in
sentences like *we leave*.

In many English sentences, though not in all, the longer
constituents tend to have their component words in a continuous
sequence, though we have just seen examples of discontinuous
sequences belonging to a single constituent. In some languages,
especially where morphology makes clear the relevant syntactic
linkages, such discontinuous constituents may be far commoner.
In a line of Latin verse (Vergil, *Eclogue* 4.4), by no means an
unusual one, only one of the consitutents has its component
words in juxtaposition:

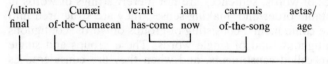

/ultima   Cumæi   ve:nit   iam   carminis   aetas/
final   of-the-Cumaean has-come now   of-the-song   age

The English translation, 'The final age of (foretold by) the
Cumaean (prophetess's) song has now come', and the syntactic
constituency of the sentence would be unchanged and unambiguous no matter in what order the six words were arranged. The
differences would be largely matters of emphasis, foregrounding,
and literary style, and some arrangements might be ruled out
stylistically as unacceptably clumsy.

In longer sentences like *old father Thames keeps rolling along*,
one sees successive immediate constituents. The same could be
seen in the Latin example, but for the sake of simplicity this has
not been marked in the diagram. For *father Thames* (noun +
noun) could be substituted *father* (noun) alone, and for *old father
Thames* could be substituted a single noun, *water, John*, etc, or
an article + noun group like *the river* (itself an expansion of a
single noun constituent); for *keeps rolling along*, could be substituted *keeps rolling*, and for *keeps rolling* could be substituted
flows, runs, etc (single verbs). The immediate constituent structure of the sentence can be set out like this:

Old father Thames keeps rolling along,

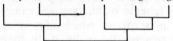

each lower bracket uniting a successive pair of immediate constituents.

The patterns common to large numbers of the sentences of a language may be called its **favourite sentence types**; and a basic syntactic structure is the simplest form of any favourite sentence type, from which innumerable longer sentences can be built up by a series of expansions at various structural places.

Sentences are, however, found in all languages, that do not conform to and are not reducible to one of the basic syntactic structures. Some such sentences may be frequent in utterances, but as types they underlie very few expanded structures or longer sentences. Sentences of this sort may be referred to as **non-favourite**, or **minority pattern**, sentences. They fall into two main classes:

[i] Those that are not referable to a longer sentence syntactically, are independent of a previous sentence, and may initiate a discourse or conversation. Sentences of this sort are often exclamatory: *John! hello! bother! drat! gracious!* Some are expandable in certain directions: *poor old John! hello there! drat that noise! good gracious me!* Others may be gnomic, such as *the more the merrier, easy come easy go.* Sentences of this latter type are lexically restricted in most cases, and little or no variation of their particular word content is normally permitted in them; in consequence they are hardly at all productive.[7]

[ii] Sentences that are referable to longer sentences containing the same word or sequence of words. These are often non-initial in a discourse, and constitute responses to a previous utterance, particularly a question: (*where do you live?*) *in Ashford*, (*what's that stuff?*) *porridge*. But they need not be. Sentences like *here!, hands up! all right, fifteen all* (in tennis scoring), *twenty pence a pound, jolly well done* can all be said (or written) and understood irrespective of previous utterance, in an appropriate situation.

What distinguishes them all from those of the first class is that each may be replaced in the situation by a longer and more explicit sentence (of a favourite type) serving the same purpose, and of which they may form a part: *we live in Ashford, that stuff is porridge, the score is fifteen all, these cost (or the price is) twenty pence a pound, that was jolly well done*. A natural way of making clear the meaning of a non-favourite sentence of the second class to a child or foreign speaker who had not understood it would be to use such a longer, more explicit, sentence in its place. It is for this reason that such short sentences are often called 'incomplete' or 'elliptical', and explained grammatically in terms of other elements being 'understood'. Sentences like this, though referable to sentences of a basic syntactic structure, cannot, as they stand, be said to represent one.

Non-favourite sentences of class [i] have no such referability to a longer sentence in which they may be incorporated. Their meaning must be explained directly by reference to the situation, or indirectly by a paraphrase.

The so-called 'one-word sentences' of languages mostly belong to one of these two classes.

It will have been noticed that the favourite sentences so far cited all include a verb form, and a large number of sentences in all languages are expansions of a noun + verb structure, either as a basic structure, as in English or German, or as a first expansion of a single-verb sentence as in Latin, where verb forms such as /veːniː/ I came, and /viːdiː/ I saw, constitute complete sentences.

In some languages a favourite, productive, sentence type ('equational') is found beside those containing a verb, namely a noun + noun or a noun + adjective structure, with no verb required to complete it. Such sentence types are found in Sundanese, Malay, and Yurok: /manehna pradʒurit/ he is a soldier; /buroŋ itu sakit/ that bird is sick; /wok nelet/ this is my sister. Tense and aspectual meanings, where these are not apparent from the context, and negation are indicated by separate words, often the same words that would be used in sentences in which a verb is present: Malay /hari sudah malam/ the daylight is already fading (lit. the day is already night), /buah ini tidak baik/ this fruit is not good; Yurok /kic peg.ɪk ku ʔnɹmɹm/ my son is already grown up (lit. already a-man (the) my-son). In Russian and Hungarian the situation is rather different; where present time is involved there is no overt verb form, but with other time references are involved a verb form is found: Russian /on moi drug/ he is my friend, /on bɯl moi drug/ he was my friend.

The principal criterion for the grouping of words into constituents is the possibility of syntactic substitution of a single word for the whole group while preserving the rest of the sentence structure intact. It must be remembered that one is concerned here with words as members of word classes, not as individual lexical items; the examples already given must in all cases be interpreted in this light.

6.3.2 Endocentric and exocentric: subordinate and coordinate

Words cohere into groups or constructions of two main types, **endocentric** and **exocentric** constructions; the distinguishing criterion is whether the group in question is syntactically equivalent or approaching equivalence to one or more of its component words or successively smaller constituents, or not. The former type are endocentric, the latter exocentric.

Exocentric construction types are fewer in number than endocentric types in languages, and exocentric constructions are fewer in number in most sentences; but the basic irreducible sentence patterns, if of more than one word, are necessarily exocentric, or they would not be irreducible. In the examples of English so far given in this section, most of the consituents have been endocentric except for the basic sentence structures themselves. Other typical English exocentric constructions are preposition followed by noun or noun group, *towards London, from the country*, etc, and conjunction followed by clause group, *if we had the money, because it is no good*, etc. These groups of words function in the same way as single adverbs, but not in the same way as any of their component words or groups, and are therefore not substitutable with any of their components.

Apparently corresponding sentences may be syntactically different in these respects in different languages. The English basic sentence type represented by *John walked, I ran*, etc is exocentric, because neither a single noun, nor a single verb has the same syntactic possibilities as the group noun + verb; but in Italian, *Giovanni camminava* /dʒo'vanni kammi'nava/ John was walking, and *io correva* /'io kor'reva/ I was running, are non-basic endocentric constructions since single verb forms, *camminava, correva*, etc, can stand alone as complete sentences and are syntactically similar to those consisting of noun or pronoun followed by a verb. One might make a typological distinction between languages like French, English, and German, wherein a favourite sentence type is minimally represented by an exocentric noun or pronoun plus verb group, and those like Latin, Italian, and Spanish, in which the favourite sentence type could be taken as a single verb form. Some transformational-generative grammarians regard such sentences as incorporating an 'underlying' pronoun, omitted or dropped in the sentence as uttered. They refer to these languages as '*pro*(noun) *drop*(ping)' languages.[8]

English sentences consisting of a single verb or an expansion thereof, and equivalent to an exocentric favourite type do occur, but only contextually bound as response sentences (6.3.1) in the special situation of immediate reply to a question: *What did he do all day? Walked; Where have you been? Climbing over Scafell.*

Imperative sentences of a single verb, *run!* etc, which are basic in their type as being irreducible and self-sufficient, are different grammatically in employing different forms of the verb paradigm and in having different possibilities of expansion.

Endocentric groups are either **subordinative** or **coordinative** according to whether they are syntactically comparable to only one word or smaller component group within them, or to more than one. Thus *men and women* (noun conjunction noun) is coordinative, since it could be replaced by either *men* or *women*, and *men* and *women* are coordinate; but *clever boys* (adjective noun) is subordinative, since it could be replaced by *boys*, but not in all syntactic relations by *clever*. The schematic subdivision of constructions can therefore be represented:

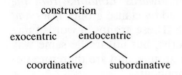

The word or group sharing the syntactic functions of the whole of a subordinative construction is called the **head**, and the other components are **subordinate**. Thus in English adjective noun groups, the noun is head and the adjective subordinate. In adverb adjective groups the adjective is head and the adverb subordinate, since in general the group is equivalent to a single adjective but not to a single adverb; in *reasonably clever boys, boys* is head and *reasonably clever* is subordinate, and within this latter group *clever* is head and *reasonably* is subordinate.

The following two fairly long sentences illustrate all the distinctions just mentioned, and provide examples of analysis into successive immediate constituents (the vertical line with a semicircle in the first diagram indicates a discontinuous constituent).[9]

Subordination has been mentioned in this section already. But it has a much wider role to play in every language in the structure of all but the shortest and simplest sentences. Groups of words in syntactic structures comparable to independent sentences may be joined to each other and to more elementary structures, often called main clauses in this context, as distinguished from subordinate clauses, by various devices. Broadly this means making a sentence-like structure substitute for a noun or an adjective or an adverb in relation to some part of a main clause; and this is the principal way in which basic sentence patterns are expanded.

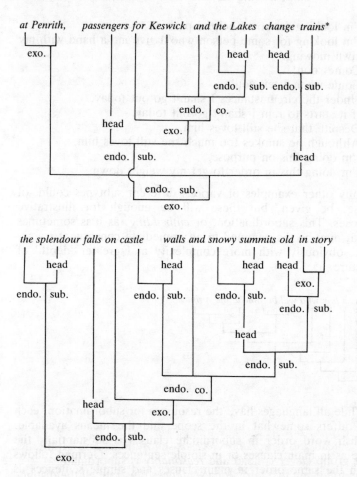

Examples from English will make this everyday process clear:

1. He reported an accident.
2. He reported that several cars were involved in an accident.
3. He reported how a careless driver had caused the accident.
4. He asked a question.
5. He asked who had caused the accident.
6. John is a fleet-footed boy.
7. John is a boy who will become a fine sprinter.
8. John, who is the best sprinter in the school, will run for the university.

---

* It is to be regretted that this sentence, which was true when first printed, is true no longer. The attractive railway line that linked Penrith with Keswick has been closed.

9. I'm looking for some helpful person.
10. I'm looking for some person who'll give me a hand with my lawn mowing.
11. Come soon!
12. Come when I tell you!
13. Under the circumstances I shan't go out today.
14. If it starts to rain I shan't go out today.
15. Despite that she still loves him.
16. Although he smokes too much she still loves him.
17. I'm doing this on purpose.
18. I'm doing this in order to get my weight down.

Many other examples of various different subtypes could, of course, be given, but these will be enough for illustrative purposes. This subordination, or *embedding*, as it is sometimes called, may be diagrammed in an immediate constituent framework, obviously with more complexity and greater 'depth' of structure.

John is a boy who will become a fine sprinter

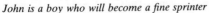
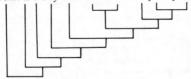

While all languages have the resources for subordination, each one differs somewhat in the scope and the means available. English word order in subordinate clauses is substantially the same as in main clauses or in simple sentences; German follows much the same order in main clauses and simple sentences as English, but in subordinate clauses the verb is put in final position: *Der Personenzug nach Spietz hat Verspätung* /deːr pɛr'zoːnentsuːk nax 'ʃpiːtz hat fɛr'ʃpɛːtuŋ/ the slow train to Spietz is running late (has delay), *er sagt, dass der Personenzug nach Spietz Verspatung hat* /ɛr 'zaːkt das deːr pɛr'zoːnentsuːk nax 'ʃpiːts fɛr'ʃpɛːtuŋ hat/ he says that the slow train to Spietz is running late.

In relative clauses, like 7, 8, and 10, above, many languages employ a specific set of pronouns (relative pronouns) at the head of their clauses, like English *who, which*, and *that* (in certain cases these may be omitted in English: *the man*(*who*(m)) *I saw that*) *yesterday*). Most European language follow this pattern.

In English we can have relative clauses like the following:

1. The man who sold me an umbrella.
2. The man to whom I sold an umbrella.
3. The man who I poked with my umbrella.
4. The man (from whom) I bought an umbrella.

But some languages restrict this 'accessibility' for relative clause formation, even down to a single syntactic relation. Tagalog, a Philippine language, and Malagasy, could only make a direct translation of sentence 1 in the list above, and there are other languages that lie between these two ranges.[10]

In a more fundamental difference several languages do not have anything like relative pronouns, but use forms of their verbs (attributives) to subordinate a clause to a noun. Japanese, for example, has sentences like /watakusi ga hito o mita/, I saw the man, and /watakusi no mita hito/, the man whom I saw. This is more clearly brought out in classical Japanese, where different verb forms are used: /ware ga hito o mitari/ and /ware no mitaru hito/. Turkish is similar in this respect:

kardeşimin	gönderdiği	mektub, the letter which my brother sent
/kardeʃimin	gœnderdiji	mektub/
of-my-brother	he-sent	letter
benim	geldiğim	gün, the day (when) I came
/benim	geldijim	gyn/
of-me	I-came	day.

Yurok likewise uses attributive forms of the verb in place of relative pronouns: /wahpew ʔohkʷin nɹmɹm/, my married son (literally, his-wife there-is my-son).

Complex sentences may also arise through coordination, as most coordinate conjunctions can join sentences as well as simple words and phrases, *eg: he likes apples and pears; he grows apples and he plans to grow pears; he grows apples but he doesn't grow pears*. Such sentences involve less structural complication and do not require further examination here.

Immediate constituent analysis and the diagrams illustrating it are the source of the trees of the transformational-generative linguists (7.2.2), though there are some differences:

[i] (trivial). Immediate consituent lines are generally drawn below the words involved (as here), while transformational-generative trees are drawn above them (a nearer analogy than trees, which generally grow and branch upwards, would

be bunches of mistletoe, which usually hand down and bifur-
cate from a single initial node).

[ii] The junction points of trees are labelled, by reference to the
class equivalent of the constituent.

[iii] The branches of trees must not cross each other and discon-
tinous constituents under a single head are not allowed;
various devices are designed to overcome the problems
presented by this restriction (7.2.2; *pp* 284–5, 7.5).

The example given on *p* 216 would look like this

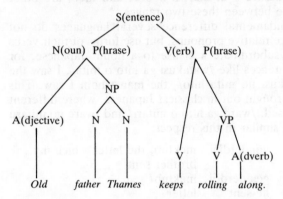

The two verbs *keeps* and *rolling* are, of course, different both in
their syntax and morphology, but this is left out of account here.
Subordinations (embeddings) are treated in the same way in
more complex trees. All this is discussed in greater detail in
7.2.2.

6.3.3 Word order and syntactic structure

Word order, the overt grammatical relations referred to above
(6.1), is important not so much for itself as for its serving, in
varying degrees from one language to another, as the mark or
exponent of syntactic relationships within constructions. Sometimes word classes may be in part defined by positional criteria
relative to other words, as in the case with prepositions, but even
so the syntactic relevance of their positions lies in their obligatory
occupancy of it when forming part of a particular syntactic
structure.

Languages vary according to the weight put on word order as
a mark of syntactic construction and immediate constituency.
English makes more use of it in this way than did Latin of the

classical period. Languages also vary in the relative order used to mark specific syntactic relations. With a few exceptions for individual words and word groups (*princess royal, court martial*), English reguarly puts a adjectives before the nouns to which they are subordinated in endocentric constructions, as does German; in consequence of this, in English noun + noun groups, such as *government control, university teacher*, and the two groups from the examples given above, (*old*) *father Thames* and *castle walls*, it is the final noun that is regarded as the head of the construction, by virtue of its occupying the position of the head in adjective + noun constructions (coordinate noun + noun groups are distinguished by a coordinating conjunction between at least one of the nouns: *men, women, and children*). French adopts the opposite word order for the most part with noun + adjective endocentric groups, though some of the commonest adjectives regularly precede their head nouns, and a few precede or follow with different meanings *homme brave* (/ɔm braːv/ brave man; (*brave homme* /braːv ɔm/ good (type of) man). In French noun + noun groups it is the first noun that is regarded as the head of the construction: *l'affaire Dreyfus* /lafɛːr drɛfys/ the Dreyfus affair.[11]

Some languages go further than this in making word order a general mark of syntactic subordination. Japanese, for example, regularly adopts the order of subordinate before head; so that adjectives precede nouns in endocentric constructions; adverbs precede verbs, and nouns and pronouns precede verbs when forming part of their expansion, and subordinate word groups all precede the heads to which they are subordinated (*eg* /watakusi no mita hito/ the man whom I saw (literally '(the) I-saw man').

One notices also the special syntactic function of certain words in some languages in closing endocentric constructions; thus in English adjective + noun groups are in theory indefinitely extensible by the addition of adjectives (*black dog, big black dog, great big black dog*, etc), but the words *a, the, this, that, my, your, his, their*, and some others exclude further expansion of these constructions by preceding subordinate words. Only *all* and *both* can be endocentrically preposed to constructions closed in this way (*both my big black dogs*, etc); constructions like *each of my big dogs, two of my big dogs*, etc are of a different syntactic form, though very similar in meaning, with *each* and *two* as heads and following groups introduced by *of* subordinate to them, as with *each of them*, which is syntactically comparable with *each* (*each of them was guilty, each was guilty*).

6.3.4 Cross-cutting of immediate constituents and word boundaries

In most cases, with the majority of languages, it is found that a satisfactory immediate constituent analysis leads to single words as the ultimate constituents of the sentence structure, and this is part of the justification for operating with words as basic units of grammatical description and as the elements of syntax. However, sentences are found in which the most obvious immediate constituent analysis cuts across the word boundaries between bound morphemes within words. A well-known example is the English possessive *'s* suffix in sentences, already referred to (5.3.1), like the *Warden of New College's lodgings*, which would be analysed

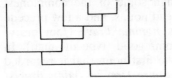

the Warden of New College's lodgings,

being equivalent to *the lodgings of the Warden of New College.*

A similar cross-cutting appears in Japanese; the bound form /-rasii/ (is) like, may be added to nouns (/kodomo/ child, /kodomo-rasii/ like a child) and to groups constituted by noun and postposition (postpositions being words similar grammatically to prepositions in English, but following, instead of preceding, the nouns with which they are syntactically linked). In /kodomo norasii/ like a child's (/kodomo no/ child's, of a child) the constituent analysis would be

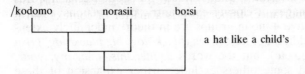

/kodomo norasii boːsi/

a hat like a child's

In Latin and Ancient Greek the forms generally known as enclitics sometimes involve cross-cutting. Though listed as words in dictionaries, forms like Latin /que/ (and) must be regarded formally as part of the word to which they are added; they can never occur initially in a sentence nor be separated by pause from the word they follow; and phonologically the word plus /que/ was treated as a single word for accentual purposes. A Latin sentence like /deː proːvinciaːque reveːnit/ and he came back from the province, would be structured

/de: pro:vincia:que reve:nit/

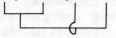

In a language in which cross-cutting of word boundaries by immediate constituent analysis was at all frequent in sentence structures, the word would be correspondingly less useful as a basic unit of grammar, and a description wholly in terms of morphemes, with less weight on the distinction of morphology and syntax within grammar, would be more appropriate. But it may be surmised that such languages are relatively few, and where this sort of cross-cutting is confined to a small part of the system and to few actual sentences, it scarcely justifies the abandonment of a framework of grammatical analysis eminently satisfactory in other respects.[12]

6.3.5 Comparison with traditional practice

It will be observed that the processes of immediate constituent analysis illustrated here, by which the longest and most complex sentences can be reduced by analysis to successive expansions of one of a few simple basic sentence structures, bear some resemblance to the traditional processes of 'parsing and analysis' of school grammars. But immediate constituent analysis is both more explicit in its methodology and more formal in its operations. In particular, the formal categories of *head* and *subordinate* must not be confused with the semantic categories of *important* and *less important*. The head is the head because it determines the syntactic class of the whole constituent. It is true that the head word of an endocentric construction is often the most important one therein in relation to the whole sentence, though it is not easy to lay down criteria for assessing this sort of relative importance. Importance is a matter of context and is usually governed by pragmatic considerations (1.4.4). In some sentences it would appear that the formally subordinate word is the most vital semantically, as in *infected persons must be isolated*, wherein the essential word *infected* is formally subordinate to the relatively less significant *persons*.[13]

6.4 Grammatical categories

6.4.1 Number, gender, case

Just as different names are given as useful labels to formally defined word classes, different names or labels are also given to the types of formal relationship between words and word groups such as have been outlined above. Terms of this sort such as *subordination, coordination, endocentric construction,* and *exocentric construction* have already been instanced and explained; and such classifications are often subdivided according to the word classes involved. Thus the relation between subordinate adjective and head (or superordinate) noun is often called qualification or modification, a semantically derived label taken from a frequent, though by no means universal, function of adjectives in such constructions. Again it must be stressed that these terms are no more than labels, and can add nothing to the formal grammatical status of the elements and relationships involved.

These labels and other similar ones referred to in previous sections are the **grammatical categories** of a language. The term is sometimes taken as including the word classes, but is sometimes distinguished from them, the exact range of its application being unimportant provided clarity and consistency are maintained in any grammatical description or exposition of theory. But *grammatical category* covers more than the groupings already discussed, and, indeed, it is most familiar in applications that have not yet been dealt with in this chapter.

This has been deliberate; attention has been concentrated upon syntactic inter-word relations both in dealing with word classification and the structural analysis of sentences. These sorts of relationship, which virtually comprise the whole of the formal grammar of some languages (6.1), are the heart of all grammar and its indispensable condition.

Nevertheless, in the majority of languages, and to varying degrees, just as paradigm differences in word forms parallel and supplement syntactic differences in the establishment of word classes, so syntactic relationships between members of word classes are accompanied by specific morphological forms in some or all of the variable words involved. Such syntactic requirements are the basis of the splitting up of the total set of forms of variable words into several different categories (exemplified by the traditional categories of number, gender, tense, person, case, etc). Some examples will make this clear. Leaving aside the possessive suffix -'s, English nouns exhibit two grammatically different forms, which vary together with variation between verb forms consisting of root and root plus /-s/, /-z/, and /-iz/ (*man eats, men eat*) in the basic exocentric noun + verb sentence pattern. These two forms of nouns and the verb forms required with each are labelled *singular* and *plural*, and together form in English the category of **number**. In French the nearest corresponding category applies to nouns and verbs much as in English, except that there is more extensive variation in the verb forms; but in addition adjectives and the article *le* /lə/ the (singular) and *les* /le/ (plural), show variations in number according to the number of the noun with which they are syntactically associated. English adjectives appear in the same form whatever the number of the associated noun, but in French one finds *le cheval royal* /lə ʃəval rwajal/ the royal horse, *les chevaux royaux* /le ʃəvo rwajo/ the royal horses (in French these differences in word form are more marked orthographically than in speech, as they are in general maintained by the final letters of the spelled words, which often have no corresponding differences in pronunciation (thus *le parc royal* /lə park rwajal/ the royal park, *les parcs royaux* /le park rwajo/ the royal parks)). In English only one pair of adjectival words varies in number in this way, *this* and *that, these* and *those* (*this man, that man, these men, those men*).

Distinctions in grammatical number between singular and plural are the commonest representation of this type of category, but some languages formally distinguish three numbers, called singular, dual, and plural (the dual forms being used with reference to two items). Ancient Greek, Sanskrit, and Old Slavic all have three formally distinct numbers; a few have four, singular, dual, trial or 'paucal' (when three or a small is referred to), and plural. Fijian is one such language, in which four numbers find formal expression in the pronouns.[14]

The word forms of the article and the adjectives of English and those of French illustrate another difference in grammatical categories between the two languages. The English noun form variations are covered by the one category of number. French adjectives and the article require another category, with much less semantic correlation, usually called gender, to account for the forms exhibited by these words in sentences. English adjectives and the English word *the* do not vary according to the grammatical subdivision of the nouns with which they are syntactically associated (the occurrence of the forms /ðə/ and /ði/, /ðə 'mæn, ði 'ɔks/, is controlled entirely by whether the following word begins, as pronounced, with a consonant or a vowel).

In French, as in a number of other languages, nouns are divided into two classes according to the forms of the article and adjectives that are required with them; these two divisions of the category of **gender** are called masculine and feminine. Thus one finds *beau cadeau* /bo kado/ fine gift, *le cadeau est beau* /lə kado ɛ bo/ the gift is fine but *belle robe* /bɛl rɔb/ fine dress, *la robe est belle* /la rɔb ɛ bɛl/ the dress is fine.

Gender in English is a category with more restricted overt

exponency or marking. Nouns may be divided into three main gender subclasses according to whether they require *himself,* *herself,* or *itself* in sentences like *the boy hurt himself, the girl hurt herself,* and *the snake hurt itself.* Membership of these gender classes also governs the lexical relationship of anaphora or back reference which may hold across sentence boundaries. *Boy, girl,* and *snake* are referred to by *he, she,* and *it,* respectively (5.2). The choice of pronominal forms in back reference is governed by the gender of the noun originally used in other languages in which the category appears. In French the preverbal unemphatic pronoun referring to *cadeau* is *il* /il/; referring to *robe* it is *elle* /ɛl/. It may be noted that in English gender distinctions only apply with the singular number category, all plural nouns forms requiring *themselves* in the sentence type quoted above (*the boys* (or *girls* or *snakes*) *hurt themselves*), and being referred to by *they.*

A few identical word forms are lexically distinguished in French by the gender to which they belong: *le poêle* /lə pwɑːl/ the stove, *la poêle* /la pwɑːl/ the frying pan, *le pendule* /lə pãdyl/ the pendulum, *la pendule* /la pãdyl/ the clock.

German is more complex in the categories required to account for all the differences between the word forms of the article, adjectives, and nouns in sentences. Number (singular and plural) operates much as in French, except that adjectives following verbs like *sein* /zain/ to be, show no variation in form (6.4.2); this also applies to adjectives that follow their head nouns, in poetic diction: *Röslein rot* /røslain roːt/ little red rose. Gender is similar, but three subclasses of noun are involved, called masculine, feminine, and neuter, and, as in English, no gender differences are found with the plural number category. In addition to these a category called **case** is required, whereby specific syntactic relations between nouns (and nominal groups) and other sentence constituents demand specific forms of the words involved. In English and French, nouns and adjectives do not vary in form according to their syntactic relation with a verb or other words in sentences. In German one finds the forms of some words in the exocentric noun + verb construction different from those in an endocentric verb + noun one: *ein guter Mann liebt Gott* /ʔain 'guːten 'man 'liːpt 'gɔt/ a good man loves God, *eine gute Frau liebt Gott* /ʔaine 'guːte 'frau 'liːpt 'gɔt/ a good woman loves God, but *Gott liebt einen guten Mann* /'gɔt 'liːpt ʔainen 'guːten 'man/ God loves a good man, *Gott liebt eine gute Frau* /'gɔt 'liːpt ʔaine 'guːte 'frau/ God loves a good woman. In a subordinating noun + noun construction one finds *die Liebe eines guten Mannes* /diː ˈliːbe ʔaines ˈguːten ˈmanes/ the love of a good man, and with a preposition such as *mit* /mit/ with, *mit einer guten Frau* /mit ʔainer ˈguːten frau/ with a good woman.

The category of case, involving different forms of nouns, pronouns, adjective, and some other classes of words, is prominent in the grammar of Latin, with six different cases, Ancient Greek, with five, and Sanskrit, with eight, among many languages exhibiting this category. Some languages carry it to great lengths; Finnish, for example, has as many as fifteen formally different cases in nouns, each with its own syntactic function.

English and French may be said to exhibit case distinctions in their personal pronouns: English *I hate him* but *he hates me*, french *je le déteste* /ʒə lə detɛst/, *il me déteste* /il mə detɛst/. French also has a dative form of the personal pronoun, corresponding to *à* followed by a noun or noun phrase: *je le lui donne* /ʒə lə lyi dɔn/ (*je le donne à Pierre* /ʒə lə dɔn a pjɛːr/) I give it to him (to Peter).

German adjectives involve yet another formal difference; the forms of the adjective in certain genders and case differ according to whether the adjective is preceded by the definite article (or some other words) or not. This category is sometimes called **determination**: thus *der arme Mann ist hier* /deːr ʔarme ˈman ʔist ˈhiːr/ the poor man is here, but *ein armer Mann ist hier* /ʔain ʔarmer ˈman ʔist ˈhier/ a poor man is here.

6.4.2 Concord and government

The control over the forms of variable words exercised by certain syntactic groupings may be divided into two main types: concord (or agreement) and government (or rection). **Concord** may be defined as the requirement that the forms of two or more words of specific word classes that stand in specific syntactic relationship with one another shall also be characterized by the same paradigmatically marked category (or categories).

English nouns and verbs in sentences of the type *man eats* and *men eat* exhibit concord of number, in that both noun and verb in this construction must be either singular or plural. In the examples given in the preceding section, French noun + adjective constructions showed concord of gender and number, and similar constructions in German showed concord of gender, number and case. French and German genders are generally not indicated in the form of the noun, except for such pairs as *tigre* /tigr/ tiger, *tigresse* /tigres/ tigress and *Verfasser* /fɛrfaser/ author, *verfasserin* /fɛrfaserin/ authoress. But every noun in these and many other languages is specifically of one particular gender. Some languages of Africa have a highly developed concord system, whereby nouns, verbs, and adjectives show category correspondences within sentences, marked by prefixes. In the Swahili sentence /mti ule umekufa/ that tree is dead (tree that-one it-is-dead), the prefix /u-/ in the second and third words shows concord with the noun /mti/, whose concord category is itself indicated by the prefix /m-/.[15]

Concord of category between pronoun and verb is seen in English in what is usually called person, as well as in number; *I, you, we*, and *they* are followed by *eat; he she*, and *it* (like all singular nouns and nominal groups) are followed by *eats*; and with one verb, *to be, I, you*, and *he, she, it* are distinguished by threefold verbal concord: *I am, you are, he is*. In many other languages the category of person as a concord category between pronoun and verb forms is more extensive in its manifestation. The pronouns requiring different forms of verbs with which they are related are referred to as first person, second person, and third person. In some languages there is concord between pronouns and nouns, marked by affixes in the noun forms (often loosely called 'possessives'); Hungarian has pronominal suffixes: *az én házam* or *házam* /ɔz eːn haːzɔm/ or /haːzɔm/ my house, *a te házad* or *házad* /ɔ tɛ haːzɔd/ or /haːzɔd/ your (singular) house, (*a*) ház / (ɔ) haːz/ (the) house (*én* I, *te* you (singular)).

Though concord may often be expressed by phonologically similar forms in different words, as in Latin /bona feːmina/ good woman (feminine), /bonus hortus/ good garden (masculine), this is only contingent; the primary fact is that corresponding forms are required in words syntactically related in particular ways; Latin /bonus hortus/ (masculine), /bona humus/ good ground (feminine), and /bonus nauta/ good sailor (masculine), are all marked by concord of gender in the same syntactic relationship, though the word forms are different. As was seen in English, it is the concord with verb forms that united the word forms *boys* and *men, boy* and *man*, respectively, as grammatically equivalent.

In the endocentric constructions in which concord of categories is involved, the category of the head word normally determines the category of subordinate words in concord with it. In the examples of noun and adjective groups given above, the gender, number and case of the noun determined those of the adjectives and articles. Nouns belong to a specific gender in those languages where the category is relevant; adjectives have forms for all genders, the form used depending on the gender of the noun; the case in which the noun appears depends on its syntactic relations with other parts of the sentence.

It can be seen that the concord patterns of different languages are not necessarily the same, even when the syntactic constructions involved and the sentence translations appear to correspond. French and German make more use of concord than does English; Latin and Greek make more use of it than French and German. Sometimes corresponding constructions in different languages show a quite different concord requirement; in several languages adjectives and nouns are related in sentences in two principal types of constructions, endocentric or 'modifying', and exocentric, or 'predicative' (in English, *good man* and *the man is good*, respectively). In French (as in Spanish and Italian) adjective and noun in both types of construction 'agree', are in concord, in number and gender (*le château est beau* /lə ʃato ɛ bo/ the castle is beautiful, *beau château* /bo ʃato/ beautiful castle (masculine), *la fille est belle* /la fiːj ɛ bɛl/ the girl is beautiful, *belle fille* /bɛl fiːj/ beautiful girl (feminine)). In German the endocentric construction alone shows concord of number and gender (*guter Mann* /'guːter 'man/ good man (masculine), *gute Frau* /guːte 'frau/ good woman (feminine), but *der Mann ist gut* /deːr 'man ʔist 'guːt/ the man is good, *die Frau ist gut* /diː 'frau ʔist 'guːt/ the woman is good, *die Frauen sind gut* /diː 'frauen zint 'guːt/ the women are good (plural)). In Hungarian the concord pattern is the reverse of that in German. Adjectives in endocentric constructions are invariable as regards number (gender is not an applicable category in this language) *a szép könyv* /ɔ seːp køɲv/ (singular) the beautiful book, *a szép könyvek* /ɔ seːp køɲvɛk/ (plural) the beautiful books, but *a könyv szép* /ɔ køɲv seːp/ the book is beautiful (equational construction, 6.3.1), *p* 218), *a könyvek szépek* /ɔ køɲvɛk seːpɛk/ the books are beautiful. In English no concord between adjective and noun (except with *this, that, these those*) is found in either type of construction.

The other type of syntactic control over word form, **government** or rection, may be defined as the requirement that one word of a particular class in a given syntactic construction with another word of a particular class shall exhibit a specific category. Common examples are prepositions, which in languages like German and Latin require the noun associated with them to be in a specific case form. Latin /ad/ to, requires or governs an accusative case (/ad montem/ to the mountain); /deː/ down, from, requires or governs an ablative case (the case names are of ancient origin and traditional in use): /deː monte/ from the mountain. In a more general sense words, like prepositions, that regularly presuppose the presence of another word of a particular class in a specific relation with them in sentences are said to govern the whole word; the two uses are combined when it is said that a particular preposition governs a noun in the accusative case.

Prepositions may govern different cases, and sometimes the same preposition governs more than one case, either indifferently or with a difference of meaning. In Latin, /ad/ and /deː/ govern, respectively, only accusative and ablative cases; /in/ governs the accusative case to mean 'into', /in urbem/ into the city, and the ablative case of mean '(placed) in', /in urbe/ in the city. In German von /fɔn/ of, governs the dative case, von dem Manne /fɔn deːm 'mane/ of the man statt /ʃtat/ instead of, governs the genitive, statt des Mannes /ʃtat dɛs 'manes/ instead of the man; gegen /'geːgen/ against, governs the accusative, gegen den Mann /'geːgen deːn 'man/ against the man; längs /lɛŋs/ along, governs the dative and genitive indifferently, längs dem Flusse /lɛŋs deːm 'fluse/, or längs des Flusses /lɛŋs dɛs 'fluses/ along the river; an /ʔan/ governs the dative to mean 'at' or 'in', an der Türe /ʔan deːr 'tyːre/ at the door, and the accusative to mean 'to', an die Türe /ʔan diː 'tyːre/ to the door.

In English, government, as the term has been used here, applies only to pronouns among the variable words. Prepositions and verbs govern particular (case) forms of the paradigms of pronouns according to their syntactic relation with them: to me, to us, I helped him, he helped me, we came, save us!, etc.

Languages with case differentiation in nouns and other words often distinguish two cases of the noun as employed in the two commonest constructions with the verb of a sentence, as exemplified in Latin /fiːlius patrem amat/ (nominative accusative) the son loves the father, and /fiːlium pater amat/ (accusative nominative) the father loves the son. In Latin these are two types of endocentric construction (cp /pater viːvit/ the father lives, /viːvit/ he lives), the one applicable to almost all verbs, the other, with the accusative, applicable to some only, though a large number. In Icelandic the exocentric and endocentric noun and verb constructions are marked by different case forms; faðirinn elskar soninn /faðirinn elskar soninn/ the father loves the son (nominative accusative), sonurinn elskar föðurinn /sonyrinn elskar føðyrinn/ the son loves the father (nominative accusative).[16] The exocentric status of the nominative verb construction is due to the fact that in Icelandic, as in English and German, noun (or pronoun) and verb constitute a minimal basic sentence type (*eg: hann rennur* /hann rennyr/ he runs, *cp* 6.3.2). In both languages, these two uses of the noun in relation to a verb are often called subject and object respectively.

A different type of government is found in Hungarian; a noun in the accusative case in construction with a verb requires a different form of the verb according to whether it is preceded or not by the article. Thus one finds *látok* /laːtok/ I see, embert látok /ɛmbɛrt laːtok/ I see a man, *látom az embert* /laːtom ɔz ɛmbɛrt/ I see the man. These distinctions in verb form, which are separate from the other formal categories such as person and number, are usually called subjective and objective respectively.

This general use of *govern* and *government* must be distinguished from the more specialist use of the terms in some developments of transformational-generative grammar (7.2.4).

6.4.3 Subject and object

The terms *subject* and *object* have been variously applied in different languages, with equal validity. In English and German the term *subject* may be applied to the noun, or equivalent word or word group, found in the minimal basic exocentric sentence type represented in English by *John works*. In Latin the same term may be defined by reference to the concord of person and number that is found between one noun (or pronoun or corresponding word group) in the nominative case and the verb, and not between the verb and any other noun; word order is irrelevant. One may instance sentences like /pater fiːlium amat/ the father loves the son, /patrem fiːlius amat/ the son loves the father, /pater fiːlioːs amat/ the father loves the sons, and /patreːs fiːlius amat/ the son loves the fathers, in which /pater/ and /fiːlius/ are throughout seen to stand in the relationship labelled subject to the verb by their being in the nominative case and in concord of number with the verb /amat/, irrespective of the order of the words in each sentence.

When subject has been satisfactorily defined in a language, *predicate* may be used to refer to the rest of the sentence apart from the subject; this is often useful, as a fundamental division into two immediate constituents frequently divides the subject part and the predicate part of a sentence.

Similar criteria to those used in Latin may also be applied to the identification of the subject element in sentences in German, and to a lesser extent in French and English; but in these languages word order is a relevant factor as well, and in English the concord between the noun and verb is much less in evidence. *John saw Mary* and *Mary saw John* are distinguished as different sentences, with different words as subject by word order alone, a situation that could not occur in Latin.[17]

Object may be partly defined in some languages by reference to the case of a noun in the sentence, and partly by reference to word order in languages like English. In the Latin sentences quoted above, /fiːlium/, /patrem/, and /fiːlioːs/ are so identified as object nouns; /patreːs/ as a word form is ambiguous, since it represents both accusative and nominative cases; it is identifiable as object in the sentence quoted by its absence of concord with the singular verb; in the two English sentences in the preceding paragraph, *Mary* and *John*, occupying postverbal position would be objects in the first and second, respectively. In immediate constituent terms the major division is found to fall between the subject noun (or pronoun) and the verb + object noun (or pronoun): *eg*

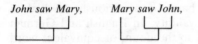

and likewise in other languages. Subject and object are, however, often most satisfactorily defined by reference to transformational correspondence in pairs of lexically equivalent sentences, active and passive respectively (7.2.2, *p* 282); /pater fiːlium amat/, /fiːlius aː patre amaːtur/ the son is loved by the father, and in English *John saw Mary, Mary was seen by John*. This also makes it possible to distinguish the relationship between the verb and following noun phrase in sentences like *he died last week* and Latin /viːxit septuaːginta anoːs/ he lived seventy years, where no passive transformation is possible, from that between verbs and object nouns.

It must not be assumed that subjects and predicates will be formally identifiable in all sentences of a language. In most sentences of the imperatival type, represented in English by *run! catch him!* etc, no such subject noun or pronoun is present.

The correspondence, in many sentence structures, of what is formally identifiable as a grammatical subject of the sentence with the logical subject of a proposition, and with a psychological subject, or principal topic, is not surprising, but it is not necessary, nor it is invariable.

It will have been noticed that in the familiar languages of Europe, such as English, French, German, and Latin, the same features of position, case form, etc, characterize the subject noun or pronoun of both transitive and intransitive verbs: eg: *he followed her*, and *he ran; she followed him* and *she ran*; and we can have *he ran and followed her*. This is a very general state of affairs, and so far in this book all the examples have been drawn from languages of this type; but it is by no means universal. In some languages, for example in Basque, in Georgian, and in Hindi (with certain verbal tenses only), and in the native languages of Australia, the subject of an intransitive verb often corresponds grammatically to the object of a transitive verb. Thus in Basque, /gizona etorri da/ (man-the come he) the man has come, and /mutilak gizona jo du/ (boy-the man-the hit him-he) the boy hit the man; the noun /gizona/ man is in the same case in both sentences (absolute or nominative), and the noun /mutilak/ boy is in the ergative case, as it is called. The term *ergative* ('effective') is used in analysing sentences in which the agent or 'effector' (as here *the boy*) is not in the general subject case.

An example from Dyirbal, an Australian language, will make this type of construction clear:

/balan guda   buɲan/

the dog   went downhill

/balan guda   baŋgul jaraŋgu   buran/

the dog   the man   saw

The latter sentence means 'the man saw the dog'; the words designating 'the dog' are in the same case in both sentences, and the word designating 'the man' are in a separate, ergative, case. If we coordinate the two sentences to form /balan guda buɲan baŋgul jaraŋgu buran/, omitting the second instance of the words meaning 'the dog', the whole new sentence translates 'the dog went downhill and (the man) saw the dog'.

Constructions of this type are called ergative as distinct from nominative–accusative constructions, and languages in which they play a conspicuous part are called ergative languages. Recently this kind of construction has attracted considerable attention, and traces of it have been identified by some linguists in other languages, as in English sentences like *these apples bake well* (*cp the cook baked the apples*).[18]

6.4.4 Morphology in relation to syntax
The preceding sections have shown some of the ways in which languages may employ morphological differences in the paradigms of variable words to mark and distinguish syntactic

relationships. The extent of this use, as well as the different forms it takes, varies from language to language. Languages wherein morphological word form variation of this sort is almost or wholly non-existent have already been mentioned, the various Chinese languages, especially Classical Chinese, and Vietnamese being among them. Among other languages, English uses relatively little morphological word form variation, German uses more, and Latin, Ancient Greek, and Sanskrit considerably more; and some American-Indian languages and some of the languages spoken in the Caucasus, such as Georgian, are morphologically very complex. This does not mean that such languages are more complicated grammatically as entire systems of communication, or even that they are harder to learn or describe; it simply means that more of the essential grammatical distinctions of the language are maintained wholly or partly by the means of exponents in the morphological structure of words, instead of, or in addition to, word class membership, word order, stress and intonation grouping, and other devices.[19] As it appears that children acquire spoken command of the first language at about the same rate all over the world, it would seem that all languages are of about an equal complexity over their whole structure; but there is clearly a 'trade-off' between complexity in different parts of the grammars of languages.

To some extent greater reliance on overt morphological forms as markers of syntactic relations may be matched by less use of word order, the overt relation between words (6.1), for these purposes. This is not universal; some languages combine morphological complexity with a fairly rigid order of words in sentences of different syntactic types. But in general one may say that Chinese and English lay more weight on word order than does Ancient Greek, and as between Latin and one of its descendants, modern French (8.1.1), one notes the change from complex morphology and fairly free word order to simpler morphology (especially in noun forms) and syntactically determined word orders. As a result of the Latin situation, word order was available in that language as a mark of exponent of categories at other levels than the grammatical (emphasis, contrast, etc), and was freely so used in classical literature of stylistic effects by the great masters of the language, both in prose and poetry.

One may compare the possibilities in this field of choice with reference to different languages. Most, if not all, languages have the means of focusing attention on a particular word or phrase for stylistic or other communicative reasons. Japanese has the

particle /wa/, placed after the first word or phrase, and a number
of languages of the Philippines make an extensive use of particles
and verb morphology to mark the semantic focus of different
constituents of a sentence.[20]

English can place a word or a phrase not otherwise likely to
occur there in inital position for the sake of prominence by a
number of devices. The choice of a passive construction (6.6.3)
brings the object into initial position; or a more complex sentence
may be formed through one or more transformations (cp 7.2.2).
Classical Latin, with its very free word order as far as syntactic
structure is concerned can achieve a like effect without any other
change but word order. The poet Vergil has a line (*Aeneid* 2.3)
/infandum, reːgiːna, jubeːs renovaːre doloːrem/; in the most
plain prose order this would be

/reːgiːna,	doloːrem	infandum	renovaːre	jubeːs/
Queen,	grief	unspeakable	to renew	you order,

Queen, you order (me) to renew an unspeakable sorrow. To
emphasize the unspeakable depth of grief Vergil merely needs
to reorder the sentence, the syntactic relations remaining the
same and being indicated by the forms of the words themselves.
English with its simpler morphology must make a more complicated syntactic change, bringing about the new sentence *unspeakable is the grief, Queen, that you order me to renew*.

German has more marking of subject and object by morphological means (case inflections) than English and may, therefore,
prepose an object noun or noun phrase where English would
have to use a passive sentence. German, in fact, uses passive
constructions less than English does. Lions are not normally
found in public lavatories, and the oddity of such an occurrence
was reported thus: *einen jungen Löwen fand die Mainzer
Polizei am Donnerstag im Toilettenraum einer alten Konserven-
fabrik im Stadtteil Finthen* /ˀainen ˈjuŋgen ˈløːven fant diː ˈmain-
tser poliˈtsai ˀam ˈdɔnerstaːk ˀim toaˈlɛtenraum ˀainer ˈˀalten
kɔnˈsɛrvenfabriːk ˀim ˈʃtattail ˈfinten/, the Mainz police found a
young lion on Thursday in the lavatory of an old food canning
factory in the Finthen area. A word for word translation in
English, with *a young lion* at the head of the sentence would
convey just the opposite sense to the German sentence; although
the normal word order in German main clauses is
subject–verb–object, as in English, the change or order in this
German sentence preserves the original meaning because the
noun phrase *einen jungen Löwen* is marked as being in the accusative (object) case morphologically. English, not having such

means at its disposal, would have to register the same surprise by reworking the sentence into a passive one, *a young lion was found by the Mainz police . . .*[21]

6.4.5 Inflection and derivation

Morphological differences in word forms are grammatically relevant and are classified under various headings and categories by virtue of the different syntactic functions they enable words to fulfil in sentences and the different syntactic relations they help to mark. These differences, both additive ones, resulting from affixation of some sort, and those involving processes like vowel and consonant alternations and the like, may be divided into two main types, with some marginal members between the two. These two types are known as **inflection** and **derivation**, and the investigation of the differences between them, both in general theory and in the descriptive analysis of paticular languages, reveals some of the ways in which languages work. The morphologically marked categories referred to in this chapter so far have all been inflectional ones, and this type, though not necessarily more numerous than the categories of derivational formations, is more central to the grammatical system of a language and to the marking of syntactic relations within sentences.

Broadly speaking **inflectional** formations or alternations (5.4.2) are those which uniquely determine and restrict the grammatical functioning of the resultant word form, whereas **derivational** formations produce a form substantially the same for grammatical purposes as a root form or as a simpler or more basic underlying form (this purely synchronic use of *derivation* must be sharply distinguished from the use of the same word in historical linguistics, 8.1.1; note also that transformational-generative linguists use *derive* and *derivation* somewhat differently (7.2.2, p 282)).

Some examples will make clear the distinction between these two types of morphological formation. English noun plural formatives, of whatever morphological nature, produce words that cannot occur in certain positions or environments in sentences in which the singular (root or basic form, 5.4.3) can occur; conversely these plural forms can occur in positions and environments from which singular forms are excluded. Thus (*the*) *horses* may occur before *eat, sleep, are working*, etc, in a simple sentence, but not (the) *horse*, and this latter may appear before *eats, sleeps, is working*, etc, where (*the*) *horses* would not be found. These formations, therefore, and the category of number in English nouns (and likewise in that part of the English verb paradigms where it is formally marked) are inflectional. The very small number of unpaired noun forms in English that are only used as grammatical plurals, such as *cattle* (*the cattle are grazing*), and for which no singular paradigm member is found, are not sufficient to affect the descriptive status of English noun plurals as a whole.

The grammatical cases of languages like Latin, German, and Sanskrit, to mention only a few, are inflectional formations. Each case has its own syntactic function, or range of syntactic functions, and though some overlapping or sharing of functions between two or more cases is found, the total syntactic range of use of each case is different from those of all the other cases in the language. Similar considerations place gender in adjectives and person in verbs among the inflections in the languages surveyed in preceding sections of this chapter.

Of necessity, inflectional formations, since they are syntactically restrictive, fall into those categories that serve to mark the distinguish different syntactic constructions and the different types of immediate constituent in sentences.

Derivational formations, by definition, do not directly involve the word in syntactic relations with other consituents of sentences in the way that inflectional formations do. Their grammatical relevance lies principally in the word class that results from their use; members of word classes that result from derivation have the same grammatical status, inflectional paradigms, and syntactic functions as do underived or simple members of the class. Such formations are, for this reason, best classified according to the class or classes of underlying form (which may itself be a root, or an already derived form) to which they may be applied, and the class or classes of the resultant words. As a first binary division one may distinguish **class-maintaining** derivations, which produce a derived form of the same class as the underlying form, and **class-changing** derivations, which produce a derived form of another class. Some derivational affixes or derivational processes may produce several different derivational formations on different underlying forms.

Both these types may be illustrated from English. *-hood* is a class-maintaining derivational suffix, in that it may be added to certain nouns (*nation, man*, etc), so producing words which are syntactically and for further morphological formations equivalent to simple, underived nouns: *nationhood, manhood*, etc.[22] The word *manhoods* (as in Shakespeare's 'hold their manhoods cheap') may be analysed:

man   –   *hood*   –   *s*
root   derivational suffix inflectional suffix

-er, in words like *runner, lover*, etc, is a class-changing derivational suffix, since added to verbs it produces a form which
syntactically and for further morphological formations is equivalent to a simple, underived noun. *Runner* and *lover* inflect for
plural number (*runners, lovers*) and function syntactically just as
nouns like *boy* and *girl* do.

The suffix appearing in the written forms *-ly* and *-li*-shows at
least three different derivational functions with different underlying words: class-changing in forming adverbs from adjectives
(*quick, quickly*), class-changing in forming adjectives from nouns
(*man, manly*), and class-maintaining in deriving adjectives from
simple adjectives (*good, goodly, kind, kindly; kindly* is a member
of two derived classes, adjective and adverb: *a kindly act, she
acted kindly; -ly* derived adjectives do not admit subsequent
adverb derivation with *-ly*, there being no words like †*kindlily*).

Several derivational formations may occur together in a single
word, and though there are practical limits to the length of words
in a language, it is impossible to determine in advance the exact
limits of tolerance to word length of this type. In part it is a
matter of style, context, and personal predilection; technical
writing readily tolerates complex word forms like *redehumidifi-
cation*, which in non-technical English might be rendered into
several words, such as 'removing dampness over again'.

English *manliness* shows two successive class-changing derivations; one use of *-ly* (*-li-*) produces adjectives from nouns
(*friendly, leisurely*, etc), and *-ness* produces nouns from adjectives. Thus *manliness* may be represented

man – *li* – *ness*
noun→adjective→noun

Modernization illustrates a different pair of class-changing
derivations:

modern – *iz* – *ation*
adjective→verb→noun

English prefixes are all derivational, and examples are found
of their use both as class-maintaining and as class-changing
derivations:

form, noun and verb, *reform*, noun and verb,
determine, verb, *predetermine*, verb,

new, adjective, *renew*, verb,
prison, noun, *imprison*, verb[23]

Cambodian provides examples of derivational infixes:

/deːk/, verb, to sleep, /dɔmneːk/, noun, sleep
/saɣm/, verb, to be wet, /sɔmnaɣm/, humidity

The distinctions between the two different types of derivation and between derivation and inflection are matters to be decided by reference to the formal classes of the forms involved in the language. It may happen that a derivational formation in one language and an inflectional one in another have very similar meanings or semantic correlations; but this is of no concern to the establishment of their grammatical status. In English the category of number has been seen to be inflectional; in Japanese the formation of words, mainly pronominal ones, referring to more than one entity (/kore/ this /korera/ these, /sore/ that, /sorera/ those) leaves the resultant words syntactically equivalent to unaffixed forms, there being no category of number in Japanese verbs, so that these formations must be classed as derivational.

As with other classifications, especially binary ones, marginal cases arise. Some formations in a language produce words that are syntactically equivalent to simpler or underlying forms in all but a few positional environments. Thus in English and Latin the comparative and superlative forms of adjectives (*hotter, hottest*, /calidior/, /calidissimus/) behave like the corresponding positive forms (*hot day, hotter day, it is hot today*, etc), except that they can each occur in a particular type of construction from which the others are excluded: *it is hotter today than yesterday, this is the hottest day of all*; /haec aqua calidior est quam illa/ this water is hoter than that, /fac aquam quam calidissimam/ make the water as hot as you can! Whether the category of grading in adjectives in these and similar languages should be regarded as derivational or inflectional depends on the relative weight given to the sameness of most of the uses of the words concerned against the differences of a few particular uses.

Inflections are much more regular and general in their forms and occurrences than derivations. Almost all nouns in English have singular and plural forms, and verbs almost all distinguish a paradigm of syntactically different forms like *try, tries, trying, tried*, and in almost all cases speakers of a single dialect, and often of a number of dialects agree on the forms of these paradigms. But the possibility of using particular derivational affixes or other formations varies with the lexically different members of one class, and may well vary from person to person; in English one finds *boyhood, girlhood, nationhood*, etc, but not †*animalhood* or †*planthood* (though, of course, it is always possible that such words could be formed and used by someone and then catch on; it is noticeable how the derivational suffix -*wise*, as in *likewise, otherwise*, has in a certain style of speech spread to several nouns, as in *prestigewise, profitwise*); in devising a noun from *comical*, one might hesitate between *comicality* and *comicalness*, with one person perferring the one and another the other while in other respects speaking the same sort of English.[24]

As a general rule, where inflections and derivations involving affixes appear in the same word, the inflections appear on the rim of the word rather than inside it, *ie* as initial prefix or final suffix.[25] This is shown in English words like *runners* and *nationalizing*, where the final suffix in each word, -*s* and -*ing*, is inflectional and the others derivational. But this is not invariably the case; and is not part of the definition of inflection as against derivation; in Welsh the derivational -*os* and -*ach* follow the inflectional plural suffixes in *merchetos* /merxetɔs/ little girls:

merch –   *et* –   *os*
(girl   plural   diminutive)

and *dynionach* /dənjɔnɑx/ puny men:

dyn –   *ion* –   *ach*
(man   plural   diminutive)

The term *stem* is often specifically to refer to that part of an inflected word less its inflections; stems may therefore be the same in form as roots, or they may consist of root morphemes together with one or more derivational affixes.

6.4.6 Grammatical functions of stress and pitch features
So far in this chapter grammatical word formations have been exemplified in the main by the affixation and the application of processes of alternation to the consonant and vowel content of words. This has been done for convenience of explanation and with the needs of persons coming newly to the subject in mind. Also these are the word form variations wherein orthographic spellings most accurately represent differences in the spoken words. But segmental consonant and vowel elements do not exhaust the phonologically relevant features of which speech in any language is made up; and stress and pitch are just as fit to serve as the markers or exponents of grammatical categories,

both inflectional and derivational, and of syntactic relations as
are segmentally represented morphemes, morphological alternations of vowels and consonants, and the order of words in a
sentence. Grammatically, it makes no difference how a category
or relationship is marked, any more than the phonological differences between the affixation of /-iz/ to /hɔːs/ in *horses* and the
vowel change of /æ/ to /e/ in *men* affected the grammatical function
of the forms as plural nouns.

In a strictly logical presentation, as opposed to the convenience
of exposition, it would be desirable not to treat the phenomena
of stress and pitch, when they serve as grammatical markers, in
a separate section as is being done here, but to use them as illustrations along with others all through. It must be emphasized that
there is nothing strange about these features, nor about what are
called the tone languages, which make use of pitch features in
ways unlike the practice of most European languages. It is indeed
unfortunate that such linguistic phenomena tend to be regarded
as something rather esoteric; this is due, no doubt, in part to the
facts that the use of pitch differences as lexical tones on individual words plays only a small part in some European languages
and none at all in most, that pitch differences have seldom been
adequately represented in orthographies, and that the ability to
perceive and differentiate the pitch phenomena of utterances in
foreign languages requires training and a particular ability sometimes developed later than other phonetic sophistication.

Stress features, as well as being an essential part of utterances,
may be shown to play a specific part in some grammatical
processes in English. English pairs of noun and verb
distinguished by different stress placements, sometimes together
with vowel differences consequential on the non-occurrence of
short /ə/ in stressed syllables, have been noticed already (*export*
/ˈekspɔːt/ and eksˈpɔːt/, *convict* /ˈkɔnvikt/ and /kənˈvikt/, 3.5.3,
4.3.4). In such word pairs it is possible to take the verb form as
basic and to treat the stress shift backwards as one of the means
whereby nouns are derived from verbs in English, along with
suffixes like *-ment* (*establishment*), *-tion* (*imagination*), etc.
Though historically the relative antiquity of the noun or the verb
may vary in different word pairs, synchronically it is a matter of
choice which class is treated as basic for grammatical description
of the working of this (or any other) formative process.

In English endocentric nominal groups, forms that are orthographically identical, but semantically different and in transformational terms (7.2.2, *pp* 283–4) differently generated, are often
distinguished by different placement of the full stress. *French*

teacher, for example, when equivalent to *a teacher who is French*, falls into the pattern with the final (head) noun fully stressed, as in *big book, good teacher, government control, French cooking*, etc, in normal speech when contrast stress or emphatic stress is not present; when the phrase is equivalent to *a teacher of French*, and is a transform of (*someone*) *teaches French*, it falls into the pattern in which the first (subordinate) word is fully stressed, as in *sheep farmer, Latin lesson*, etc.

Intonation in English may distinguish the immediate constituent structure of otherwise identical spoken sequences. *Tell me what you are doing on Sunday*, when *on Sunday* is immediately subordinate to *are doing* (*tell me your Sunday activities*), would ordinarily be uttered with a single Tune I, the final fall occurring on *Sunday* (4.3.6). If *on Sunday* is immediately subordinate to *tell me* (*tell me on Sunday what you are doing*), this may be marked by a falling sequence on *doing*, followed by a higher pitch on *on* before the final fall.

Among tone languages, that is to say languages wherein pitch differences are a property of individual words as lexical items, and not simply part of sentence intonation, as in English, tonal phenomena may serve, alone or with other features, as exponents of grammatical relations and categories. For example, it is reported that in Mixteco, a language of Mexico, the form /kaʔanna/ with the tone sequence mid low high exhibits the category of future tense ('I shall talk'), but the sequence high low high that of present tense ('I talk'). In Igbo, a language of West Africa, the three words, /ofɛ de ɔkə/ with a tone sequence high high low mid mid constitute a complete sentence 'the soup is hot', but with the sequence high high mid mid mid form an endocentric nominal group 'hot soup'.[26]

We have seen (4.3.3, 4.3.5) that pitch and stress differences must be marked in a phonological transcription, when they are distinctive in a language. English stress is a case in point, and in some morphemes the allomorphs differ in their stressing as well as in their segments: *eg* /ˈliːgl/ as the free form *legal* and in *illegal* /iˈliːgl/, but liːˈgæl-/ in *legality* /liːˈgæliti/.

6.4.7 Morpheme and category

It should be clear from the preceding sections that **grammatical category** and **morpheme** are quite different concepts. The relations between them vary according to the type of language; and these relations are one basis for the typological classification of languages (8.2.6). The morphemic composition of words is decided by comparing them with other partially similar words;

the number of grammatical categories involved in a word is decided by the number of separate derivational formations and syntactic relations that are or may be marked in sentences by its morphological form. A single morpheme may mark several such categories at once, or each category may be marked by a separate morpheme. One may compare the Latin inflectional suffix /-oːs/ in /libroːs/ books, wherein the categories labelled *plural number* and *accusative (object) case* are both marked by the morphologically indivisible /-oːs/, with the comparable Hungarian word *könyveket* /køɲvɛkɛt/ books, wherein -ek- and -et serially mark plural number and accusative case (*cp: könyvet* /køɲvɛt/ accusative singular, and *könyvek*/ køɲvɛk/ nominative plural (the nominative case in this language lacking an overt morphemic mark)).

In the Ancient Greek adjective form ἀνδρεῖος /andreîos/ brave, one may recognize a morpheme /-os/ by which three grammatical categories are indicated: masculine gender, by concord with masculine nouns, nominative case, by syntactic relationship with the main verb of the sentence, and singular number by concord with a noun and with the verb also marked by singular number. This is sometimes called the **cumulation** of categories, and may be contrasted with the serial representation illustrated in the Hungarian word above and with a Turkish word like *odalarimdan* /odalaɯmdan/ from my rooms, in which each morpheme marks a separate category:

oda –lar– im –   dan
noun plural first person ablative case

Languages in which this one–one morpheme and category correspondence predominates are called agglutinative languages, and the serial juxtaposition of morphemes is called agglutination.

The opposite process to cumulation is the **discontinuous** representation of a single category by two disjoined morphemes. This is seen in German words like *gebrochen* /ge'broxen/ broken, in which the category of past participle (traditional term) is marked by the prefix *ge-* together with the suffix *-en*, morpheme shapes able to serve independently as exponents of categories in other parts of the German grammatical system.

6.5 Subclasses, irregularities, and economy

As has been seen, grammar is concerned with the discovery, analysis, and statement of the regular patterns found in the word forms and the sentence structures of languages. It is these regularities that enable the linguist to class sentences together as examples of various syntactic structures and as being made up of various constructions, and to group words together in word classes whose members behave alike syntactically, and, if variable words, reveal similar paradigms of grammatically different forms. But the term *word class* is not as simple as may be at first suggested by the inevitable omission of detail in the preceding outline account of the ways in which words are classified grammatically. In most languages **subclasses** appear within several of the classes by the application of narrower criteria. Some such subclasses have already been mentioned above in other contexts.

The distinction between what are called **transitive** and **intransitive** verbs, made in the grammatical description of many languages, essentially depends on a syntactic distinction between those verbs that may construct with a second noun (*ie* other than the subject noun) under certain conditions, such as the noun exhibiting a particular case form or standing in a particular position in the sentence, or the whole sentence admitting the possibility of transformation into a passive (7.2.2, *p* 282; *cp* 6.6.3), and those verbs which may not so construct. Hitherto the distinction has, like other grammatical distinctions, been expressed in quasi-semantic terms, but in fact it has always rested on a difference of syntactic possibilities between two subclasses of verbs. The weakness of semantic definitions is well illustrated here: *hit*, in *I hit you* is syntactically a transitive verb, and is often chosen as an example because the action referred to may plausibly be said to 'pass across' via my first from me to you: but *hear* in *I hear you* is involved in exactly the same syntactic relations with the two pronouns, and is regarded as a transitive verb, though in this case, the 'action', if any actions is in fact referred to, is the other way round; and who does what, and to whom in the situation referred to by the syntactically similar verb in *I love you?*

In several languages, of which Malay and Japanese are examples, the translation equivalents of many adjectives in European languages are best regarded formally as a subclass of intransitive verbs (but compare English (*be*) *red*, adjective, and *glow*, intransitive verb, and the English adjective (*be*) *silent* with the Latin intransitive verb /taceːre/, and the German *schweigen* 'ʃvaigen/, with the same meaning).

Within the English noun class an important distinction must be recognized between what may be labelled countable (or bounded) nouns and mass (uncountable or unbounded) nouns, though there is considerable over-lapping since many nouns belong to both subclasses. This formal distinction is most clearly marked syntactically: countable nouns may only be preceded by /səm/, *some* unstressed, when in the plural form, which mass nouns may be preceded by /səm/ in their singular form as well. One may contrast *some flour* (mass) and *some flowers* (countable); the use of *some* in its stressed form /'sʌm 'flauə/ (*ie* an extraordinary flower) is quite separate, though orthographic representation fails to mark the distinction between them.

Wheat and *oats*, though denoting very similar 'things' in the world, belong grammatically to the mass and countable subclasses of noun respectively. Apart from the criterion chosen as the principal defining one, a number of other distinctions are observable in the use of these two subclasses of nouns. Mass nouns need not be preceded by *a* or *the* when standing otherwise alone in the singular at the beginning of a sentence (*flour makes bread, but a flower produces seeds*). When singular mass nouns are preceded by *a* or *the* or plural mass nouns are preceded by a number word, they usually have the specific meaning 'species, or sort, of the substance or thing', and longer sentences with such words actually present are more usual in such contexts (*this district produces two* (*sorts of*) *metal*(*s*), *iron and copper; a* (*species of*) *wheat has been developed that ripens early*). As is often the case with major grammatical divisions, a difference of generic or class meaning may roughly be correlated with the formal distinction; mass nouns tend to refer to unbounded continua, shapeless substances, extents, and the like (*water, time thought* (= *thinking*), *soup, sand, wheat, metal, silver*; hence the label), and countable nouns tend to be used of spatially or temporally discrete or formed objects and the like (*flower, bridge, house, idea, thought* (= *idea*), *season, boy*). But these semantic correlations, though of great significance in a total description of a language, cannot satisfactorily be used as criteria in the first place. Class meanings are not always easily identifiable, and do not always agree with the formally distinguishing features: *oats, pebbles, beans*, and *peas* are plural countable nouns; *wheat, shingle, millet*, and *rice* are mass nouns.

Among the invariable words of a language, subclassification, like the original classification, is carried out in syntactic terms. A distinction has already been noticed among the prepositions of several languages (6.4.2) according to the case of the noun or pronoun that each governs. In Vietnamese four subclasses of particles have been set up, according to their positional occurrence in sentences: initial particle, medial particle, final particle, and polytopic particle (unrestricted in place).[27]

English adjectives may be positionally subclassified according to the relative order, or most frequent relative order, in which they occur in groups before nouns. *Big black dog* is more likely than *black big dog*, and *little old lady* than *old little lady*. This is not to say that a series of prenominal adjectives is always fixed in its relative order of words in English, but many English adjectives do occupy specific positions relative to each other, and still more have a preferred, though not invariable position, and this can be used as a criterion of subclassification.

Morphological differences account for a good deal of subclassing of the variable words in a language. English adjectives divide, with some marginal members of both subclasses, into variable adjectives, having forms ending in *-er* and *-est* (*prettier, prettiest*), and those forming semantically and grammatically comparable groups with *more* and *most* (*more beautiful, most beautiful*). Morphological differences among the paradigms of syntactically equivalent forms are the basis of the separate conjugations and declensions of verbs and nouns in Latin, Ancient Greek, and Sanskrit, and of the distinction between the 'weak' and 'strong' verbs of English and German, these latter being further divisible according to the type of vowel alternation involved (*eg: sing, sang, sung; ring, rang, rung; take, took, taken; shake, shook, shaken*).

When, however, all these subclassifications have been made, it is almost always found that certain words cannot be accounted for wholly by assignment to any group, but must be described individually. These are the 'irregular' words. Ideally, perhaps, it might be supposed that the whole of a language should be such as to be brought within the compass of rules and classes, as far as the grammatical level is concerned; but for some reason or another no such language has ever been found, and within them all some words appear that exhibit forms outside the regular patterns, and some words differ syntactically in particular ways from the majority of members of the class to which they have been assigned.

Traditional grammar paid a great deal of attention to **morphological irregularities** and listed those words that displayed anomalous paradigms (irregular verb, irregular noun plurals, etc), but **syntactic irregularities** are just as noticeable, and should be described equally carefully. In both cases their establishment is the same, logically subsequent to the description of the regular forms. Irregularities may lie in the morphological alternations or affixations serving as exponents of a particular category (as in the English noun plurals *oxen, children, feet*) or in the use of more than one root in the same (suppletive) paradigm (as in *good, better, best*, or *go, went, gone*).

Another morphological irregularity appears in the absence of certain paradigmatic forms, for which comparable forms are found in other paradigms of the same class. The English noun *cattle*, established as plural by sentences like *the cattle are sick*, has no corresponding singular form, and the singular nouns *plenty* and *neglect* have no plural forms; the Latin verb /quatio:/ I shake, has no past tense form corresponding to /concussi:/ the past tense form of /concutio:/ I shake violently. Such words are called **defective** in respect of the paradigm forms not represented. This has nothing to do with lexical meanings. A single horned domestic animal and successive conditions of plenty or acts of neglect are all possible concepts, and so is the process of shaking referred to in the past. *Gluts, negligences*, and /concussi:/ all exist as words: it just happens that certain paradigms are formally incomplete.

Syntactically irregular words are those which behave differently from the majority of the words belonging to the class, or subclass, to which they are most readily assigned. The English words *afraid, asleep*, and some others behave in many respects as adjectives (*he is afraid, he is asleep, he is happy, he is afraid of losing his money, he is fearful of losing his money*). But they cannot occur in prenominal position; one finds *the child is afraid* and *a child afraid of water cannot learn to swim*, but not †*an afraid child*, nor †*an asleep child*, though *a fearful child, a timid child*, and *a sleepy child* are found. The adjective *mere*, on the other hand, can only occur prenominally; *mere folly*, but not †*this folly is mere*.[28] A few English words, best regarded as nouns, are of very limited syntactic distribution, being found only in a small number of constructions and with limited collocation therein; such are *sake* and *stead*, as in *for the sake of, for my sake, for this sake, for the king's sake, in his stead, in my stead, stand him in good stead*, etc (notice that *instead* has come to be written as one word, *instead of me*, etc, and that this type of phrase has largely replaced *in my stead*, etc in spoken English).

Obviously the fewer irregularities there are the simpler in that respect will be the grammatical description of language, and it clearly behoves an investigator to bring as much as he can of the morphology and syntax under general rules that will adequately account for them, without neglecting or rejecting any word form or sentence form that constitutes a genuine part of the material of the language. Sometimes a choice between alternative methods of statement will have to be made. Is a subclass of

English verbs ending in *-ind* /-aind/ to be set up, with a past tense form ending in *-ound* /-aund/ as part of the regular paradigm of that subclass (*bind, find, grind, wind* /waind/)? In this case *mind, minded* and *blind, blinded* will be irregular within the subclasses. Or are the strong verbs of this group simply to be set among the irregular verbs, leaving *mind* and *blind*, and any others like it (*rind* as a verb may be accepted by some speakers), simply as regular verbs without further comment? The former treatment adds one subclass to the verbal system, but within it the anomalous forms are fewer; the latter reduces the amount of subdivision among the whole word class, but leaves a larger number of verbs to be just listed as irregular.

It might reasonably be expected that, as languages develop, irregularities would gradually be eliminated in the interests of minimal effort in learning and in communication. This process does occur. Newly created and borrowed words (8.1.8) in a language nearly all follow the regular of most frequent patterns of the words in the class to which they are assigned in use. The comparison of Ancient Greek with Modern Greek shows that there were more subclasses and irregularities in the paradigms in antiquity than there are today; and several English strong verbs (minority type) have been replaced by a corresponding weak (majority type) form (*helped* has replaced *holp* and *holpen*, and *snowed* has replaced *snew*). This is the process known in historical linguistics as analogy or analogical formation (8.1.9).

On the other hand, a reverse process sometimes appears in the development of languages, though this is less easily accounted for. The suppletive verbs meaning 'to go' in most of the Romance languages (*eg* French *aller* /ale/ to go, *vais* /vɛ/ (I) go, *irai* /ire/ (I) shall go; Italian *andare* /an'dare/ to go, *va* /va/ (he) goes, *andiamo* /andi'amo/ (we) go) have developed from four separate Latin verbs, each of which showed a complete paradigm: /ambula:re/ to walk, /i:re/ to go /va:dere/ to go, /adna:re/ to approach (by swimming),[29] all except /i:re/ being, in fact, regularly inflected verbs.

The only wholly 'regular' language are the artificial ones like Esperanto, created as worldwide second languages. If somehow a speech community came to use Esperanto as its first language one wonders how long it would be before irregularities began to appear.

The discussion on the analytic treatment of apparently irregular forms focuses attention on one of the primary objectives of linguistic science (or indeed of any other science). This has already been referred to in 1.2.1, above, and is necessarily a constant concern of the linguist, whether he conceives his task as primarily the search for the most efficient means of describing and classifying the elements and structure of a language as he has observed and recorded it, or whether he is trying to make explicit the nature of a speaker's implicit and inherent knowledge or competence in regard to his own language (*cp*, below, 7.2.4).

Where more than one descriptive statement can be brought under a single statement a greater economy and efficiency is achieved. Part of German grammar will illustrate this. In main clauses and single-clause sentences, where no special emphasis or topicalization is required, German word order is much like word order in English. Thus *wir gehen morgen in ein Konzert* /viːr 'geːen 'mɔrgen ʔin ʔain kɔn'tsɛrt/ we are going tomorrow to a concert. But we may emphasize that it is tomorrow that we are going, and not the day after: *morgen gehen wir in ein Konzert*; or we may emphasize that is is to a concert that we are going, not to the theatre: *in ein Konzert gehen wir morgen*. And we find sentences lik *auf dieser Welt war mir das Glück nicht hold* /auf 'diːzer 'velt vaːr miːr das 'glyk niçt 'hɔlt/ on this earth fortune was not kind to me, but in the German the order of words is 'on this earth was to-me (the) fortune not kind'.

We can make separate statements that when an adverb comes first in the sentence then the subject must follow the verb, and that a similar shift in word order is required when a prepositional phrase comes first. But while all such statements of rules are probably helpful in teaching German to foreign language learners, a much more economical formulation is achieved by the statement that in German declarative main clauses the verb always occupies the place of the second major constituent, whatever syntactic role is taken by the initial constituent. This also covers German sentences in which the object noun or noun phrase comes first (6.4.4, *p* 239).

6.6 Grammatical semantics

6.6.1 Semantic correlations

The purpose behind the grammatical array of words, morphemes, constructions, and the rules associated with them is the provision of means adequate to express all the sorts of meanings required in human life and in the use of a language. This requirement can be put another way: the formal apparatus of grammar makes it possible for speakers to exploit the limited articulatory mechanisms of the vocal tract so as to be able to respond to the virtually infinite demands of human situations (*cp* 3.1.3).

The association of grammatical rules, forms, and structures with areas of meaning, or semantic functions, over and above the lexical meanings of individual words, has been mentioned already in this book (1.4.3), and it has been a subject of systematic study for many centuries by those interested in language and in the teaching of languages. Traditional grammar was well aware of the need for the semantic description of the uses to which grammatical elements and categories were put; and with the thorough knowledge that long continued study of the classical languages produced, its practitioners were able to make detailed, accurate, and subtle analysis of this sort.

It is, clearly, possible and legitimate to approach the semantic functions of grammatical forms and structures from two starting points. One can ask how various semantic categories (time, number, personal reference, interrogation, command, statement, negation, etc) are formally expressed in a language, or one can state the various formal arrangements of elements that the grammar of a language allows and then analyse their semantic functions. Half a century ago Jespersen thus distinguished the two methods of grammatical description.[30] It is fair to say that we are as yet very far from describing all that there is to describe about any language by any method.

All languages have some semantic functions to perform that would appear to be essential in human communication and in human social life, and the study of these is part of the study of linguistic universals. But not all functions are assigned to the same part of the grammar. To take a case in point already noticed, the distinctions of number (singular and plural) and sometimes distinctions of time reference (past, present, and future) are, generally speaking, indicated by some part of the morphological structure of words in European languages; but in some South-east Asian languages they are indicated lexically by individual words of various classes, that may or may not be present, depending on the requirements of the context.[31]

These two directions of grammatical enquiry are not, however, just reverse equivalents of each other. The actual forms recorded, whether from speech or from writing, are 'there' to be observed, described, and classified; their meanings, particularly when a degree of subtlety is sought (as it should be), are much more elusive and may have to be abstracted from the comparison of many utterances in many slightly different contexts and situations, or by the examination of many separate texts in the case of dead languages. Moreover, in working with naive and illiterate informants (native speakers), as in much anthropological linguistics (9.1.1), it is far easier to elicit the forms and the sentences of a language than to get an explicit and reliable semantic and pragmatic account of the specific uses of particular words, morphological formations, and syntactic structures.

In this chapter we will look at the semantic functions of some of the commoner grammatical categories in different languages. But it must be stressed that the categories chosen for discussion can only be a small sample of those to be found in the formal analysis of languages, and that the semantic investigation of each one chosen can and should be carried much further, both in depth and in subtlety, than is practicable or desirable in an introductory textbook.

6.6.2 Meanings of grammatical categories

Affixes and other markers of grammatical categories vary greatly in the degree to which their presence in a word correlates with a definite semantic function ascribable to the word as a whole. Where there is any sort of correlation, even though a very partial one, a semantic label attached to the affix and the category marked by it may be useful; and categories such as number, divided into singular (dual) and plural, and tense (past, present, future, etc) have been so used in the preceding two chapters, and are well known in grammatical writings; there is no point in rejecting them, provided it is realized that they are labels rather than definitions, picking out one, perhaps principal, meaning or functions of the forms concerned, but in no way exhausting their semantic analysis and description.

Semantic correlations of formally established categories may vary from tolerable closeness to extreme indeterminacy. Between the category of **number** and the actual singularity and plurality in what is referred to there is a fairly close correlation in most languages in which number may be used to label a formal category of grammar. It may be observed that within the category there is a tendency for the dual (specific word forms associated with two objects, persons, or the like) to be merged with the plural, the dual forms cease to be used and in situations in which they would have been used the corresponding plural forms come to be used instead. The gradual replacement of dual by plural forms was already beginning in Ancient Greek, and only singular and plural numbers are formally distinguished in Modern Greek, as also in all but two of the modern Slavic languages.[32] Dual is therefore a lexical, not a grammatical category in most European languages today; two persons or things can be so designated, and duality can be referred to, but doing so does not involve the sentence in any concord patterns other than would be involved for reference to three, or four, or any number greater than one.

One cannot assume that the semantic correlations of similarly labelled categories in grammar will be the same from language to language. Some sort of translation similarity over at least part of their uses must be the basis for matching the categories, and the morphemes marking them, of one language with those of another, and the justification for the use of the same label for them both. It is for reasons of translation that one matches the English noun suffixes /-s/, /-z/, /-iz/ (and the other less common variants) with the /-ər/ suffix, and any variant of it, in Norwegian, with the /-i/ suffix and any variants in Italian, with /-k/, /-ɔk/, /-ok/, /-ɛk/, and /-øk/ of Hungarian, and with the /-lar/ and /-ler/ of Turkish. The semantic function of number in English and in many European languages is, with minor exceptions, very much the same; that is to say, in similar situations, the same sort of factors in the actual environment governs the use of nouns, and other words in concord with them, in one form rather than the other. But the category of number in Hungarian and Turkish, and several other languages in different parts of the world correlates with a somewhat different semantic distinction, between definite and indefinite number, so that the same form of the noun and of the verb in concord with it that is used for referring to one entity is also used when a specific numeral word accompanies the noun; thus in Hungarian *könyv van* /køɲv v;ɔn/ there is a book, *könyvek vannak* /køɲvɛk vɔnnɔk/ there are books, but *két könyv van* /keːt køɲv vɔn/ there are two books.

The grammatical category of number, though a very widespread one among languages, is in no way universal. Presumably, every language is able to refer to plurality as opposed to singularity, but there is no more need for this to involve a specific grammatical formation in words of concordial relations in sentences than there is for duality to be referred to in this way. The Chinese can distinguish more than one from one as easily as any one else, but plural in Chinese is a lexical category; in addition to the numeral words themselves, words whose translation equivalent in isolation would be 'several' are employed in endocentric constructions with nouns when it is necessary to specify more than a single item, and this lexical addition to the sentence has no grammatical effect on any other part of it.[33]

One and more than one are reasonably clear concepts and languages like English correlate singular and plural noun forms with them fairly closely. But collections can be viewed either way, and a field of rolling grain is one or a myriad according to one's point of view, and it is no part of the linguist's task to decide between the two. But one definitely assigns the nouns *wheat, barley*, and *corn* to the singular number, and *oats* to the plural, by observing the concord required with a following present tense verb: *wheat grows well here, oats grow well here.*

Some other formal categories are less closely correlatable with extralinguistic categories and features in contexts of situation. The category of **gender** in languages such as French, Italian, and German bears some relation to actual sex differences, in that in denoting male and female animate beings, masculine and feminine nouns are generally used. But in French, in which only two genders are formally distinguished, masculine and feminine, inanimate beings and abstractions must be referred to by nouns of one of the two genders, with the same concord requirements with the rest of the sentence, and in these nouns and the words in concord with them the semantic reference of the specific gender is non-existent. The position in languages like German, Ancient Greek, and Russian, in which three genders are formally distinguished, masculine, feminine, and neuter, is not essentially different, as inanimates and abstractions are referred to by nouns of all three gender classes. Moreover, in all these languages what are called 'anamalous' genders are found, when animates whose sex is known are referred to by nouns of a non-corresponding gender. In French *bête* /bɛːt/ beast, simpleton, is feminine in gender whatever the sex of the animal or person referred to, and *sentinelle* /sātinɛl/ guard, sentry, is also feminine, though its reference is most often to a male being. *Souris* /suri/ mouse, is always feminine in gender, and specifically to indicate a male or female mouse one must add an adjective, *souris mâle* /suri mɑːl/ male mouse, *souris femelle* /suri fəmɛl/ female mouse. In German a number of nouns are neuter in gender that refer to persons: *Mädchen* /mɛːtçen/ girl, *Fraülein* /'frɔylain/ young lady, etc. Likewise, Ancient Greek, τέκνον /téknon/ and βρέφος /brépʰos/, both meaning 'child', are neuter in gender, irrespective of the sex of the child referred to.[34]

In English, gender is really only applicable to the anaphoric pronominal links between nouns and *he, she, it*, etc and the reflexive pronouns *himself, herself*, etc (5.2). We have already noticed certain anomalies in these: ships and sometimes cars, bicycles, and the like, and the names of countries (*England, France, Germany*, etc) are anaphorically picked up by *she*. One may notice that whereas *baby* may be referred to by *it*, where the sex is unknown, the word *cousin*, in which the sex distinction is equally unmarked (contrast *brother* and *sister*, and French

cousin /kuzẽ/ male cousin, *cousine* /kuzin/ female cousin), may
never be referred to in this way.

A slightly different formal distinction with a similar partial
semantic correlation is seen in some languages in the categories
of **animate** and **inanimate**, nouns belonging to one of the two
category classes and requiring correspondingly different concord
forms or grammatical arrangements in sentences. Here too
anomalies are noticeable. Ojibwa, one of the Algonkian
languages of North America, exhibits this category distinction,
and one sees such nouns as /aːkim/ snow-shoe, /ekkikk/ kettle,
and /essap/ net, with manifestly inanimate referents, belonging
formally to the animate gender.[35]

Case in nouns and pronouns and tense in verbs are two formal
categories to which a great deal of attention has been paid in the
search for ways of stating and systematizing the semantic ranges
applicable to the different members of each. Their formal status
as grammatical categories is not in doubt. In many, but by no
means all, languages, including several familiar Europeans ones,
and the classical languages, Greek, Latin, and Sanskrit, nouns
and pronouns (and adjectives in concord with them) exhibit
regular paradigms of morphologically different forms in different
syntactic relations with other words.

Since classical antiquity, the different cases have been labelled
by reference to some semantic characteristics, and these labels
are still with us in the traditional terms: *nominative, vocative,
accusative, genitive, dative*, and *ablative*. In most of them, these
names refer quite well to one of the semantic functions of the
case forms designated by them. As an example, the ablative case
(Latin /ablaːtus/ carried away) is used when motion away from
is indicated (/ab urbe discessit/ he departed from the city), but
this by no means exhausts the sorts of situation in which constructions requiring the ablative case are used. In German the dative
case is used when giving is involved (*er gab mir ein buch* /ʔeːr
'gaːp mir ʔain 'buːx/ he gave me (dative) a book), but it is also
used after the preposition *aus* (*aus der Mode* /ʔaus der 'moːde/
out of fashion, aus der Stadt /ʔaus deːr 'ʃtat/ out of the town).
In Greek and Latin the dative case is also used when giving is
involved (hence its name); but in Greek prepositions meaning
'out of', 'away from', etc construct with (govern) the genitive
case. In Latin, unlike Greek and German, the dative case is not
used with any prepositions.

From antiquity also attempts have been repeatedly made to
identify a common component of semantic function, underlying
and observable in all the various uses to which each different case

form is used in all the constructions in which it is found. An elementary book, such as this, cannot go into the details of this work, but the following facts stand out: important light is shed by investigations of this sort of the means of expression and semantic distinctions available to languages that give them their wonderful flexibility; many of the different uses of a single case form can be shown to rest on a common feature distinguishing the meaning correlation of the case from that of other cases; but it has yet to be shown indisputably that all the semantic functions of a single case form are reasonably to be linked to a common element of meaning or relation with the situation in which the forms are used; and the formal identification of the cases in different languages depends, not on semantic investigations of this sort, but upon morphological differences in word forms correlating with different syntactic constructions. Finally it must be remembered that a case in one language cannot be identified in its semantic range with a similarly labelled case in another. Similarity of some of its semantic functions must be the basis for the use of a common label, but one can go no further than that, and it is obvious that between languages in which there are different numbers of formally distinct cases, correspondences are bound to be very inexact and to involve much overlapping of function.[36]

The fact that many languages are without a formal category resembling the cases of German and Latin does not mean that they are less (or more) efficient as the means of communication about the world at large and the world of the speaker's culture; it merely means that they operate in different ways and by different means. In this lies part of the interest of linguistic studies.

The category of **tense** in verb forms is familiar in European languages. The semantic ranges covered by the different forms are mainly on two axes, time relations and what are usually called aspectual differences of completion, incompletion, continuation, and momentariness. In Latin and Ancient Greek the different tense forms combine semantic differentiations of the two axes together; one may contrast the Latin imperfect and perfect, and the Greek imperfect, perfect, and aorist. In Russian the aspectual differences of imperfective and perfective are prominently marked by differences in verb forms separately from the marking of formal differences correlated with time differences; in languages like this the former sets of differences are usually called aspects or aspectual forms, and the latter tenses.[37]

In English and German only two one-word tense forms are

found in the verbal paradigms (other differences in the single-word forms being referable to the categories of person and number): *write, wrote, begin, began, describe, described, schreibt* /ʃraipt/ (he) writes, *schrieb* /ʃriːp/ (he) wrote, *sagt* /zaːkt/ (he) says, *sagte* /'zaːkte/ (he) said. Compound verbal expressions, consisting of a member of the verb paradigm and one or more of what are often called auxiliaries, are very common in these languages, and fulful some of the semantic functions of the single-word tense forms of other languages (*will write, was writing, should have been writing*, etc). The forms of several of these auxiliaries resemble the forms of the verbs, *be, have,* and *will* in English, and *werden* /'veːrden/ to become, and *haben* /'haːben/ to have, to which they are etymologically connected; but it is a mistake to identify the auxiliaries with these independent verbs descriptively, as their syntax is quite different.

Though tense is a familiar category of the verb in European languages, there is no universal necessity for it, or for any category semantically associated with time distinctions, in the morphological structure of the verb forms in a language. Malay and Yurok are two languages in which no formal category of tense can be abstracted from the morphological paradigms of the verbs. Time and aspect relations, when not already clear from the situation, are indicated by adverbs and particles forming part of the immediate endocentric expansion of the verbs. Similar functions are performed in Chinese, where word paradigms in the ordinary sense are not found, by various members of the word class of particle.[38]

While time and aspect form the main semantic area of tense meaning, they do not exhaust it. Unfulfilled conditions in English are indicated by past tense forms in reference to the present state of affairs and by doubly past (pluperfect) forms in reference to the past: *if he was alive now, he would not permit this; if he had been alive then, he would not have permitted this.*[39] Other languages, such as French, German, Latin, and Ancient Greek, also used past tenses, in some cases combined with other grammatical differences (mood), for unfulfilled conditions.

A rather wide semantic field associated with verbs in most if not in all languages has been identified as **modality**, to some extent covering the meanings carried by the verbal moods in traditional grammar, but extending beyond them. Modality is used to cover such structural meanings as

factual statement: *the conservatives won the election*;
possibility: *the conservatives may* (or *can*) *win the election*;

probability: *the conversatives probably will win the election*;
necessity: *on their present showing in the opinion polls the conservatives must win the election*;
obligation: *you ought to vote for the liberals*;
command: *vote liberal and vote early!*;
questioning: *did you vote liberal?*

It will be seen that formally most of these semantic distinctions are indicated in English by auxiliary verbs or by adverbs within the verbal group. But this is not the case with all languages. A recent study gives examples of possibility and probability being marked by the morphology of the verb; obligation in Latin may be indicated by a subjunctive verb form (/quid agerem/ what was I to do?). In classical Japanese an inflection of the verb expresses obligation (/guntai wa teki o koːgeki subesi/ the army must attack the enemy). In some languages a specific form of the verb distinguishes declarative and interrogative sentences.[40]

Two formal categories exhibited by verbs in a number of languages, though not in the more familiar European languages, are **negation** and **causativity**. Of course every language expresses negation and causation. Latin and Yurok express **negation** in the simplest way grammatically, by the mere addition of a negative word: Latin /pluit/ it is raining, /noːn pluit/ it is not raining. Yurok /tenpeweʔɬ/ and /nimi tenpeweʔɬ/, same meanings. English is more complicated; the negative counterparts of affirmative sentences usually differ by more than the addiction of a single word: *it rained, it did not rain; he knows it, he does not know it*. This is also true of French: *donnez-le-moi* /dɔne-lə-mwa/ give it to me!, *ne me le donnez pas* /nə mə lə dɔne pɑ/ do not give it to me! But some languages incorporate a negative bound morpheme in the verb forms themselves.[41] Japanese is one such language: /mieru/ to be visisble, /mienai/ to be invisible; Swahili is another: /atasoma/ he will read, /hatasoma/ he will not read; /alisoma/ he read, /hakusoma/ he did not read.

Causation is a familiar semantic concept; in English a variety of verbs may be used to express it, notably *make* (colloquially *get*): *make it clean, get it clean*. A few derivational formations also have a causative function: *blacken* (*make black*), *whiten* (*make white*), and there is a number of transitive verbs related causually to intransitive verbs but without any morphological connections; *kill* and *cause to die* are in many contexts almost equivalent.

Japanese and Hungarian, however, to mention only two such languages, have the possibility of regularly forming **causative** verb stems from non-causative verbs by suffixation, and this formation is in principle available to every verb. Thus Japanese /taberu/ to eat, /tabesareru/ to make (someone) eat; Hungarian *olvasni* /olvɔʃni/ to read, *olvastatni* /olvɔʃtɔtni/ to cause to read. However these languages can also form periphrastic causative phrases, as can English, and there are in some cases subtle differences in meaning between the derived and the periphrastic causatives.[42]

In many languages pronominal words are organized into a system of three terms, or **persons**, as they are called, referring to the speaker (first person), the person addressed (second person), and the person referred to but not addressed (third person); different forms for each person category are often found, distinguished as singular and plural in the category of number, with a semantic correlation similar to that seen with number in nouns. In many European languages the category of person, like that of number, is a grammatical one, requiring concord with the forms of the verb with which it stands in specific relations. This is not universal; in Japanese, for example, verb forms do not vary according to the person category of the pronoun, and the category of person in such a language may be regarded as a lexical, rather than as a grammatical one.

In several European languages some uses of pronouns reveal a divergence between the number and person as formally marked categories and the actual number and relationship of those involved. Standard English has only one form of the second person pronoun, *you* irrespective of number, and one concord form of verbs associated with it (*you are a fool, you are all fools*). Some dialects in English, in the north of England and elsewhere have separate forms for singular and plural second person pronouns, with different forms of verbs in concord with them. These pronominal forms are etymologically connected with the forms *thou* and *thee*, familiar in this use in Biblical English, *eg* /'ðaː 'aːt/ you (singular) are, /ða 'noəz vari 'wiːl/ you (singular) know very well. These specifically singular forms with singular concord in the verbs are, however, only used in situations of familiarity and intimacy: in other circumstances only one form, corresponding to the plural in intimate use, is used, as in standard English. A similar situation is found in French, where in normal discourse, *vous* /vu/ functions indifferently in addressing one or several persons; among close friends, members of the family, and the like, *vous* is used as a plural and the specifically singular form is *tu* /ty/. There is a French verb *tutoyer* /tytwaje/ made up from two of the forms of the singular second person pronoun, *tu* and *toi*, meaning 'to speak familiarly to'.

In Italian and German formally distinct second person pronouns with second person concord forms of verbs are confined to familiar discourse. In other situations forms otherwise used in reference to third persons, with third person verbal concord are used; in Italian the usual pronominal forms are *lei* /'lɛi/, otherwise used for 'she', and *loro* /'loro/, otherwise used for 'they'. In German *Sie* /ziː/ otherwise used as third person plural pronoun, is used for both numbers as a second person form, with plural concord in the verb (in writing the second person use of *Sie* is distinguished by an initial capital letter); *sind sie fertig?* /zint' ziː 'fɛrtiç/ are they ready?. *sind Sie fertig?* are you (singular or plural) ready?; familiarly *bist du fertig?* /bist duː fɛrtiç/ singular, *seid ihr fertig?* /zait ʔiːr fɛrtiç/ plural.

The precise limits of familiarity within which the familiar second person forms are used naturally vary from language to language and from community to community, with individual differences of use between persons within communities; they are also subject to change along with changes in social conditions.[43] The formal distinction maintained by the languages is clear enough, and the detailed semantic examination of the contrasting forms involves setting up contexts of situation for each language and each community, with the relevant factors brought into relation with the forms of utterance (*cp* 1.4.4).

A different anomaly in relation to number in pronouns is seen in what is often called the 'editorial *we*'. It occurs in fewer utterances than the forms mentioned above, but its use is a widespread convention in European and other languages. It consists in the use of what in other contexts is the first person pronoun referring to more than one person, by a writer when he is referring to himself. Somewhat similar is the use of the 'royal *we*'; in strictly ceremonial circumstances reigning sovereigns in some countries (of which Great Britain is one) use what are otherwise first person plural pronouns in reference to themselves in their official or constitutional capacity.[44]

Relations of deference and social gradation are part of the relevant context determining the use of specific forms of pronouns within the personal categories in some languages. Different words correlating with differences in relative social status between speakers are used in a number of languages; Malay (in which pronominal words are a less clearly delimited word class than in many other languages), Japanese, Tamil, and some other languages of southern India are examples.

While a formal distinction of three persons is the commonest type of pronominal system, systems of four persons are found in some languages of North America. Four distinctions are made

in the category of person in pronominal forms and in the forms
of verbs and nouns syntactically related. The semantic reference
of the fourth person is to a person or object distinct from one
already referred to by a third person form. This further distinction is called **obviation**, and the fourth person forms distinguished
in this sort of language are called obviative. Thus in Ojibwa,
/nuwaːpemaː aw enini/ I-see that man (third person);
/uwaːpemaːn eniw eninuwan/ he-sees that man (obviative).
English has an obviative pronominal reference in *him, her* and
them in simple sentences; (*s*)*he saw her/him* can only refer to
someone seeing someone else (contrast (*s*)*he saw herself/himself*).

Some languages show a formal distinction in pronominal forms
between inclusive and exclusive plurals. Thus Ojibwa /niːnuwi/
we (he and I), /kiːnuwi/ we (you, he, and I), Fijian /keimami/
we (they and I), /da/ we (you, plural, and I). The personal
inflections of verbs may include similar differentiation of inclusion and exclusion.

Of course English and any other language can make explicit
the inclusive or exclusive use of plural pronominal forms, but this
must be done by circumlocution (*he and I, but not you*, etc), and
is not part of the semantic correlation of an obligatory formal
grammatical category. A language can express anything required
of it; they differ in the sort of situational features compulsorily
brought to notice by the grammatical system.

6.6.3 Class meanings and structural meanings

Beside the semantic correlations of formal grammatical categories, one finds similar correlations with different word classes
and with sentence structures and syntactic constructions. Such
correlations are familiar because traditional grammar often
sought to define word classes, or 'parts of speech', in semantic
terms.

Nouns are used to refer to discrete things, persons, and
abstractions; and verbs are used to refer to processes and activities. From this arises the possibility of matching many of the
nouns and verbs of one language with those of other languages
(6.2). But the semantic correlations are never complete, and in
the nature of things cannot be always clearcut in their applications. In assigning words to word classes, the linguist need not
worry whether dying, being silent (*cp* German *schweigen*
/'ʃvaigen/, Latin /taceːre/ to be silent), and bisecting, in geom-
etry, are actions or processes, nor with whether they are
'conceived' as such by native speakers, or whether brightness,
sunsets, electrons, and geometrical points are things. The formal

status of the words concerned is not in doubt and is not settled by considerations like these. Their place, in so far as the linguist can deal with them, is in subsequent analysis of the various semantic uses to which members of different word classes are put.

In the same way the linguist distinguishes sentence forms or structures (declarative or indicative *John is going home*, interrogative *are you going home?*, imperative *go home!*, etc) from the situational functions of utterances, such as giving information, eliciting information, and inducing or preventing action by others. Each of the three sentences structures exemplified above from English and represented by formal differences in many languages, correlates regularly with one of the situational functions just mentioned; but it is not hard to show that any sentence form can fulfil any function. Interrogative word order, with a particular intonation in sentences like *am I tired!* and 'rhetorical questions' like *is it not better to suffer in silence?* serve to make emphatic statements to the effect that one is tired and that it is better to suffer in silence. *I want to know the time* is in most contexts a means of eliciting information, like *what is the time?*, rather than a statement of one's feelings. *You will go home now* may be as much a command as a formally imperatival sentence *go home!* and in instruction manuals and the like, sentences like *to disconnect the water supply turn the main tap clockwise*, though formally imperatival, are more in the nature of informative statements (the borders between these situational functions are bound to be hazy, and the simplified illustrations given here scarcely begin to exemplify the numerous and diverse types of language functions in human society).

Endocentric adjective + noun and noun + noun constructions often do indicate some modification of the semantic reference of the noun, by further specification; *red flower* has a narrower range of application than *flower* does. But *a probable event* does not denote a particular sort of the event in the way that *a dangerous event* or *a nocturnal event* does, and the sorts of specification indicated in the latter two examples are not the same. In default of contextual specification *London trains* may equally well refer to trains going to London, trains coming from London, or trains running within London. *The Ems telegram* is understood only as the famous telegram sent by Bismarck in 1870 just because of its historical importance as a *casus belli*. Apart from this general knowledge the phrase could refer to any telegram sent to, from, or about Ems. Adverbs may qualify the verbs with which they are constructed in various ways, as adjectives do with nouns. A percipient writer may exploit these variations. In a delicious riposte in Oscar Wilde's *The importance of being Earnest* (near the end of Act II) Jack reproves Algernon for 'calmly eating muffins when we are in this horrible trouble'; Algernon replies 'Well, I can't eat muffins in an agitated manner. The butter would probably get on my cuffs. One should always eat muffins quite calmly. It is the only way to eat them.' In Jack's eyes Algernon was acting in a deplorably calm manner, under the circumstances, in eating muffins at all, while Algernon was explaining the manner in which muffins should be eaten. Knowing a language means knowing all the formal structures available for sentence formation and the different semantic functions to which they may, in various situations and with various lexical collocations (2.4.2), be applied.

The traditional association of syntactic subject (6.4.3) with logical subject is well known, and witnesses to the close connections maintained between grammatical analysis and logical analysis in the history of linguistic studies. Certainly the noun or noun phrase constituting the syntactic subject is frequently the same as the one that would be the subject of an Aristotelian subject-predicate proposition, in sentences directly translatable into such propositions. In a different context the syntactic subject often designates the actor or agent, where such a term is appropriate, as in *John kicked the ball* hence Bloomfield's adoption of the term 'actor-action' sentence.[45] It is less appropriate in sentences like *John saw the rainbow* or *John outlived his wife*, and, of course, passive constructions serve just the purpose of detaching the actor or agent from the subject position: *the ball was kicked by John*.

The distinction between active and passive is usually fairly clearcut in formal terms, except in predominantly ergative languages: *John hit Bob, Bob was hit by John*; Latin /Johannes Robertum pulsaːvit/, Robertus aː Johanne pulsaːtus est; French *Jean a frappé Robert* /ʒã a frape rɔbɛːr/, *Robert a été frappé par Jean* /rɔbɛːr a ete frape par ʒã/. But to say that they are equivalent in meaning is grossly inadequate.

In the narrowest truth-conditional semantic terms this may be the case.[46] Under whatever conditions or in whatever circumstances *Papageno kissed Papagena* is true, or false, then *Papagena was kissed by Papageno* is necessarily true, or false, respectively. But there are many factors semantically and pragmatically involved in choosing which way to report this event. In the first, the active, sentence we are being told what Papageno did; in the second, the passive, sentence we are being told what happened to Papagena. The active sentence *Grant defeated Lee in the spring of 1865* is *prima facie* more likely to be part of an account of General Grant's life and career, while *Lee was defeated by Grant in the spring of 1865* is more likely to be part of a biography of General Lee. In the grammar of English, as in many other languages, a passive need not have the agent (subject in the active sentence) expressed: *Lee was defeated in the spring of 1865* but not †*defeated Lee in the spring of 1865*. This makes passive sentences appropriate in cases where agent is either unimportant or unknown in relation to the event or the state of affairs being reported: for example, *during its long history the city of Troy was totally destroyed on several occasions*; *though the artist is not known, this picture was obviously painted during the seventeenth century*.

6.6.4 Methodological implications

The grammarian is concerned to give the most exhaustive and economical account of the sentence structures and word structures of a language that he can, and to relate the classes and categories involved to semantic classes and categories. Any system of analysis will involve hard cases and borderline examples. In trying to resolve these problems the ultimate decision turns on the balancing of one set of observational statements against another; and these statements are the ground on which that decision can be defended, or challenged.

The linguist should not stop short at the formal analysis of the grammar of a language, but should seek out the sort of meanings associated with the classes, categories, and structures that he has set up to describe it. He should discover the extent to which form classes and meaning classes are closely or loosely correlated in different parts of the systems, and note the sorts of semantic distinctions that are emphasized in this way by association with the obligatory features of word forms and constructions in the language. Grammatically emphasized ranges of meanings may in part be responsible for the different ways in which human beings envisage, categorize, and think about the world of their experience. Such linguistic or metalinguistic speculations are very far from advanced; they must depend on the detailed analyses of the grammatical systems of a large number of languages being carried out; and if they are to escape from circular and uninformative argumentation, they must start from rigorously conducted observation and formal analysis in the first place.[47]

Notes to Chapter 6

1 On response sentences as opposed to free or opening sentences *cp* Fries, 20, Chapter 3.
2 Further on substitution in syntax, Bazell, 3, 64–7.
3 Further on morphology, Matthews, 44, J. L. Bybee, 14. Invariability of word form is more characteristic of Classical than of Modern Chinese, which has developed some bound morphemes, though it scarcely exhibits morphological paradigms. On Chinese grammar, Chao, 15, 194; on Chinese see further J. Norman, *Chinese*, Cambridge, 1988.
4 On the development of the traditional system of word classes, Robins, 60, Chapters 2 and 3. The major differences between the system established in antiquity and that of traditional grammar were: 1. The adjective was treated as a subclass of nouns (*cp* the expression *noun substantive* and *noun adjective*); 2. The participle was regarded as a word class in its own right and not as part of the verbal paradigm; 3. The Greek article had no counterpart in Latin.
5 Nootka, Sapir and Swadesh, 62.
6 It would also be possible to set up additional and separate word classes of words like *work*, combining the morphological and syntactic characteristics of both nouns and verbs, but in view of the numbers of other such combinations (noun and adjective, verb and adjective, etc) that would, in consistency, have to be set up likewise, this procedure would not in general serve a useful purpose.
7 The Latin example on *p* 216 is also discussed in a similar context in P. H. Matthews, *Syntax*, Cambridge, 1981, 225–6.

    On some types of minority pattern sentences see A. Wierzbicka, 'Boys will be boys', *Lang* 63 (1987), 95–114.
8 Endocentric and exocentric constructions, Bloomfield, 8, 194–6. For a detailed examination of immediate constituent analysis, with examples from a number of languages, Wells, 67, 87–117. See also Gleason, 21, Chapter 10. 'Pro drop' languages. Horrocks 35, 143–4.
9 The serious student should not be content with merely following the immediate constituent analysis set out in the diagrams. He should examine the criteria by which each part is justified and construct similar diagrams of other sentences for himself. If he has any command of other languages, he should translate these or other English sentences into one or more of them, and compare the immediate constituent structuring, which need not be at all the same. A liking for taking the mechanisms of languages to pieces in this sort of way is what distinguishes the linguist from those who are content just to speak and understand languages.

    Hockett, 31, 185, 195–6, treats the verb + noun constructions of English *saw Mary, visit Bill, reads books*, etc, as exocentric, on the ground that the total construction does not resemble either the noun or the verb in its ranges ·of syntactic occurrence. This seems a doubtful decision; *reads books* can be matched with *reads* in *he reads at home, he reads books at home, he reads a lot, he reads books a lot, on holiday he just reads, on holiday he just reads books*, etc; *cp: he likes reading* and *he likes reading books*. Presumably the argument in favour of exocentricity turns on the impossibility in most cases of this sort of construction of adding a further noun in the way that further adjectives can be added to endocentric adjective noun constructions like *old man* (*nice old man*, etc). But this also applies to many types of construction reckoned as endocentric, such as those beginning with *the* or *a*, to which further articles cannot be added.

The decision rests, as so often, on the weighing of criteria against one another. For the student of linguistics, understanding the argument is more important than the particular decision reached, though, of course, in the description of a language a decision must be made one way or the other and justified on the evidence.

Immediate constituents are generally found to be binary in structure (consisting of two parts), though some coordinate constituents may contain more than two divisions immediately below them in size, as in the examples on *p* 221. This point is discussed further by Wells, 67.

A valuable treatment of English syntax on the basis of immediate constituent analysis may be found in Nida, 50.

10 Keenan and Comrie, 41.

11 See further on the ordering of French nouns and adjectives, L. R. Waugh, 'The semantics and paradigmatics of word order', *Lang* 52 (1976), 82–107.

12 Japanese example from Wells, 67; further examples and discussion in Robins, 57.

Word accent in Ancient Greek was one of pitch, by which one syllable in the word was higher and so more prominent than the others. The nature of the Latin accent is not certainly known, but both stress and pitch features may have been involved. On Greek and Latin pronunciation generally, W. S. Allen, *Vox Graeca*, Cambridge, 1968; *Vox Latina*, Cambridge, 1965; *Accent and rhythm: prosodic features of Greek and Latin*, Cambridge, 1973.

The 'enclitics' referred to by Bloomfield, 8, 187, include 'weak forms' like English /-z/ in *John's ready*; but these are in all cases variant word forms, besides which non-enclitic forms are always available without alteration of the grammatical form of the sentence (*John is ready*).

Pike, 'A problem in morphology–syntax division', *Acta linguistica* 5 (1945–9), 125–38, mentions a language in which phonological and grammatical criteria seem to conflict in the matter of word delimitation; comment, Robins, 58, 142–3.

Bloomfield, 8, 221–2, carries immediate constituent analysis within word boundaries.

13 The confusion of syntactic constituency and semantic importance mars Jespersen's earlier adumbration of this type of analysis, in 39, 96–7.

14 Old Slavic, de Bray, 12, 1–24.

Fijian, G B Miluer, *Fijian Grammar*, Suva, 1972; A. J. Schütz, *The Fijian language*, Honololu, 1985.

15 Swahili, Ashton, 2, 10–11.

16 Icelandic, S. Einarsson, *Icelandic*, Baltimore, 1949.

17 Where syntactically governed differences in word forms are available in English, as with the pronouns, word order may be freer. Hill, 25, 261, cites the contrasting sentences *two loves have I* and *two loves have me*, in which subject and object are distinguished by the pronominal forms alone; but neither sentence is really typical of normal spoken English.

18 Comrie, 16; Plank, 55. Further, Dixon, 'Ergativity', *Lang* 55 (1979), 55–138. For a description of the Australian languages, with observations on ergative constructions therein, see, for example, R. M. W. Dixon, *The languages of Australia*, Cambridge, 1980.

19 Further on the relations between pronominal complexity and anaphora rules, J. Heath, 'Some functional relationships in grammar', *Lang* 51 (1975), 89–104.

20 P. Schachter and F. E. T. Otanes, *Tagalog reference grammar*, Berkeley, 1972, Chapter 2.

21 Those who doubt the authenticity of this sentence may care to consult *Der Trierischer Volksfreund*, 29 August, 1987.

22 There is a change in subclassification here within the noun class (6.5); *man* is animate and its anaphoric pronoun is *he*, but *manhood* is abstract and its anaphoric pronoun is *it*.

23 An example of the derivational processes of a language formally analysed on the lines described here may be seen in Robins, 59.

24 Notice that grammarians themselves hesitate between *grammaticalness* and *grammaticality* as the noun corresponding to *grammatical*.

25 Rim position of inflection, Bazell, 3, 69–70.

26 The examples of these pages do not, of course, exhaust the function of stress differences in such word groups.

Mixteco examples from Pike, *Tone languages*, Ann Arbor, 1948, 23.

Igbo examples, Ward, 66, 385.

Further similar examples, Pike, *op cit*, 22–4.

27 Vietnamese word classes, P. J. Honey, 'Word classes in Vietnamese', *BSOAS*, 18 (1956), 534–44.

28 English *mere* is also irregular morphologically: *merest* is found (*the merest stupidity*), but not †*merer*, in current English.

On irregularities see further, R. Hetzron, 'Where the grammar fails', *Lang* 51 (1975), 859–72.

29 The original colloquial Latin verb from which Italian *andare* and the forms having the same root have descended is still a matter of dispute, and an alternative origin in an assumed verb /ambita:re/ to walk around, has been suggested. The origin of *aller* in /ambula:re/ has also been called in question, though no better alternative has found acceptance. These etymological questions do not affect the topic discussed in this section.

For the two possible sources of *andare*, see Bourciez, 10, §209, and W. D. Elcock, 17, 127.

30 Jespersen, 39, Chapters 2–3.

31 Vietnamese, Thompson, 63, 180, 209–10.

32 Among the Slavic languages, the dual survives in Slovenian (spoken in North-west Yugoslavia) and in Lusatian (spoken on the upper reaches of the river Spree in East Germany); see de Bray, 12.

33 A sort of pluralizing suffix /-mən/ is suffixed to some North Chinese words, notably the pronominal forms, /wo³/ I, /ni³/ you (singular), and /ta¹/ he, she (/wo³mən/ we /ni³mən/ you (plural), /ta¹mən/ they), and few others (/rən²mən/ men; /ʃyə²ʃəŋ¹mən/ students). This has no effect on the word forms of the rest of the sentence. The superscript numerals refer to the different tones of Chinese syllables (3.5.4, 4.3.5); ¹indicates a high level tone, ²a rising tone, ³a falling and rising or a low rising tone, and 4 (not exemplified here) a falling tone; /mən/ is an example of a syllable called 'toneless'; its actual pitch is determined by the tone of the preceding syllable.

The distinction between grammatical and lexical categories in languages is discussed by Hjelmslev, 28.

34 In the weaker relations of back reference across sentence boundaries (*cp* 6.4.1), 'anomalous' neuter nouns referring to animates are often taken up with the pronoun whose gender correlates with the sex of the being referred to, particularly in informal speech. Thus German *Mädchen* may be taken up by *sie* as well as by *es*, and French *sentinelle* by *il* as well as by *elle*.

35 Ojibwa, Bloomfield, 9.

36 The term *accusative case* is probably the result of an ancient mistranslation of the Greek αἰτιατικὴ πτῶσις /aitia:tikè: ptô:sis/ meaning 'causal case', as being the case in which the objects of transitive verbs are put, many of them referring to things or persons whereon are directed the actions denoted by verbs. But the verb αἰτιάομαι /aitiáomai/ meant 'I accuse' as well as 'I allege as a cause', and from this the translation of the related αἰτιατική (πτωσις) into the Latin /(ca:sus) accu:sa:ti:vus/ arose.

The search for common or basic meanings of the cases in Latin, Russian, and other languages has been taken as far as it can be in such works as Hjelmslev, 27, and Jakobson, 38.

37 On aspect as a grammatical category in Russian, Braun, 11, 95–125; Entwistle and Morison, 19, 106–9. On the English verbal categories, Joos, 40; Palmer, 51 and 54.

38 Malay, Winstedt, 70; Yurok, Robins, 56

39 Joos, 40, 121, calls English past tense forms 'remote', *ie* one stage away from actuality.

40 See further Palmer, 52; *Folia Linguistica* 21.1 (1987), special volume on 'modality'.

41 Very marginally, Latin provides two lexical examples of negative incorporation: /nequeo:/ etc, I etc cannot, and most members of the paradigm of /no:lo:/ etc, I etc do not want.

42 In English *cause to die* and *kill* are not equivalent in all contexts; one

could not replace *cause to die* by *kill* in a sentence like *he caused his victim to die last Sunday by administering a slow acting poison some days previously.* See further J. A. Fodor, 'Three reasons for not deriving "kill" from "cause to die", *Linguistic inquiry* 1 (1970), 429–38; M. Shibatani (ed), 'The grammar of causative constructions', *Syntax and semantics* 6 (1976).

43 Wright, 71, 144, 178–80.

There is also the French verb *vouvoyer* /vuvwaje/ to use *vous* in addressing one person; *cp* German *duzen* /'duːtsen/ to use *du*, and *siezen* /'ziːtsen/ to use *Sie*, in addressing a second person. Further, R. Brown and A. Gilman, 'Pronouns of power and solidarity', T. A. Sebeok (ed), *Style in language*, New York, 1960, 253–276.

44 Singular and plural number are distinguished in English in the pronominal forms *yourself* (singular) and *yourselves* (plural): *you saw it yourself* and *you saw it yourselves*; *you'll hurt yourself* and *you'll hurt yourselves*; so, too, the 'editorial *we*' is sometimes followed by *ourself* instead of *ourselves*.

The category of person in verbs, with concord with what is generally called the subject, is familiar in European languages, but bipersonal verb forms, with two separate and distinctive personal categories are quite common (*eg* Swahili /nilimwona/ I saw him, /aliniona/ he saw me, /mlituona/ you (plural) saw us, /tuliwaona/ we saw you (plural); Yurok /koʔmoyotʃekʼ/ I hear you (singular), /koʔmoyotʃʼoʔ/ I hear you (plural), koʔmoyosekʼ /I hear him, /koʔmoyopaʔ/ you (singular and plural) hear me). Bipersonal verb forms are found in Basque (Houghton, 36), Georgian (Vogt, 65), and in a number of American-Indian languages, among others. An isolated bipersonal form appears in Hungarian verbs, involving the first and second person singular persons only, *látlak* /laːtlɔk/ I see you, *szeretlek* (sɛrɛtlɛk/ I love you, etc (roots *lát-* and *szeret-*)). Bipersonal verb forms with distinction of inclusive and exclusive plurals are exemplified in Ojibwa and in Jebero, a language of Peru (Bendor-Samuel, 6).

45 Bloomfield, 8, 172.

46 *Cp* R. M. Kempson, *Semantic theory*, Cambridge, 1977, Chapter 3. On passives see further M. Shibatani, 'Passives and related constructions' *Lang* 61 (1985), 821–48, where it is pointed out that ergative sentences can also be passivized (836).

47 Speculation on the lines suggested in the final paragraphs of this section forms a main part of the Whorf hypothesis whose main principle is that the way in which one thinks is in part conditioned by the way one's language structure enables one most easily to think, and that in consequence different languages induce different ways of envisaging the world of experience. Considerations of this sort, in protest against the naive view that all of mankind live in 'the same world', full of 'the same things', to which each language merely attaches different labels, are at least as old as Sapir in linguistcs, but were forcefully put forward later by B. L. Whorf, who contrasted the

world view of the Hopi (an American-Indian people), for which he held their language partly responsible, with that of 'standard average European', conditioned by centuries of Aristotelian logic, itself cradled in the language structures of Ancient Greek and Latin.

Whorf's case has sometimes been overstated to the effect that one can only think on the lines laid down by the structure of one's language, and has in consequence not escaped criticism; but he was asserting no more than that certain ways of thinking about the world are made easier than others by the sentence structures of particular languages and the sorts of semantic functions most associated with its obligatory grammatical categories and word classes.

See further; Whorf, 68; 69; Hoijer, 32; 33; 34.

Anyone who reads German should consult H. Gipper, *Gibt es ein sprachliches Relativitätsprinzip? Untersuchungen zur Sapir-Whorf-Hypothese*, Frankfurt a.M., 1972. Gipper has himself carried out field research into the Hopi language, and he has corrected a number of Whorf's statements. Whorf's ideas are also discussed in the course of J. A. Fishman et al., *The rise and fall of the ethnic revival: perspectives on language and ethnicity*, Berlin, 1985.

Chapter 7

Current linguistic theory

7.1 Theory formation

7.1.1 Linguistic theory and linguistic practice

The term *theory* is of widespread and frequent use in any science. Like many words also in regular use in everyday language, it has a number of senses. Conversationally it may almost be equivalent to *hypothesis* or *supposition*, as in a sentence like *my theory is that the burglar got in through the scullery window at about 3 o'clock*. Scientific discourse, which would distinguish theory and hypothesis, would restrict the term *theory* to the basic principles, concepts, and goals of a particular science. A scientific theory delimits and defines the phenomena that are relevant to it and the concepts that it employs in systematic description and analysis. Newtonian physics, for example, make descriptive and explanatory use of such basic theoretical concepts as mass, gravity, and inertia to account for the observed and the inferred movements of bodies in the solar system, the fact that objects fall to the ground when unsupported, and the fact that moving objects continue moving in a straight line until checked or diverted by some other force. That most people find sunrise and sunset beautiful and that particular movements of balls in games like cricket, tennis, and football are approved while others are ruled out of the game are irrelevant to physics, although, of course, the rising and the setting of the sun and the physical constraints on moving things like balls are part of the phenomena of physics (and we all know that 'physically' it is the earth that is moving in relation to the sun in what we continue to call the sun's rising and setting).

Theory is also distinguished from practice. Factors excluded from relevance in a theory may nonetheless influence the actual facts that the scientist observes and studies. A theoretical engineer could say that a certain machine was designed theoretical to produce an output of ten horsepower, but when such 'practical' factors as the energy consumed in turning the machine itself and the losses due to the unavoidable friction between the moving parts were taken into account, the actual power output would be around nine horsepower. Of course, this could be countered by propounding a different theory that would incorporate such factors as friction, duly measured, into the relevant material from which the abstractions were made in describing the working of the machine and in estimating its power output.

Linguistics as the science of language operates in a similar way. We have already examined technical terms like *phoneme, syllable, word, morpheme, grammatical category*, and *sentence*, designating abstractions made from the limitless mass of spoken and written utterances of the languages of the world. Correspondingly the grammatical description of a language can be considered as a theoretical account of that language. But linguists differ, as do many other scientists, about what is or is not relevant. Some have argued, as strict empiricists (*cp* 1.2.1) that only publicly observable phenomena, specifically speech as heard and recorded and written records, are scientifically valid and therefore relevant data for linguistics, and that statements based on inevitably private and personal phenomena (though they may be 'real' enough for the percipients) such as intuitions, judgments, feelings, and the like, are to be excluded from linguistics as a scientific discipline. Others sharply disagree, but some of them would exclude another set of things from the domain of scientific theory.

Grammatical rules as such do not constrain the syntactic complexity or the length of sentences or even, in some languages, the morphological complexity and length of words. In *Alice in Wonderland* the dormouse tells Alice that the three sisters who lived in the treacle well learned to draw 'everything that begins with an M, such as mousetraps, and the moon, and memory, and muchness', and but for Alice's interruption this list of coordinated nouns could have gone on indefinitely. English-speaking children are familiar with the long and complex set of embedded relative clauses that make up *The house that Jack built*:

This is the farmer sowing his corn,
That kept the cock that crowed in the morn,
That waked the priest all shaven and shorn,

That married the man all tattered and torn,
That kissed the maiden all forlorn,
That milked the cow with the crumpled horn,
That tossed the dog,
That chased the cat,
That worried that rat,
That ate the malt,
That lay in the house that Jack built.

It ends with *that Jack built*, but we could easily go on with 'to live in, until he died, because he liked it . . .', and so on indefinitely; and we notice that this is children's literature, not technical writing of adults for adults. In English the words *antidisestablishmentarianism* and *antidisestablishmentarian* (being opposed to the separation of the Church of England from the country's constitution) are often said to be 'the longest words in the language', but we can readily create a longer one in such a sentence as *his politics seem to be very antidisestablishmentarianistically orientated*.

In practice excessive length and the grammatical complexities of words and sentences are constrained by such factors as the short-term memory of speaker and listener; this is why written sentences can be longer and more convoluted, as we can always 'go back' in reading them. One also avoids boring one's hearer into inattention or incomprehension, giving an impression of pomposity, frivolousness and so on, unless this is deliberate in a particular context; and we are all constrained by the physiological need to rest and to sleep. Such factors, though universal and ineluctable, can be ruled out of consideration in a grammatical theory as relating to performance and not to competence understood as the knowledge a speaker has of the grammar of his language, on the assumption that this is what grammatical and, more generally, linguistic theory is concerned with. The view was expressed some years ago by Chomsky and has been repeated on several occasions since then:

> Linguistic theory is concerned primarily with an ideal speaker–listener, in a completely homogeneous speech-community, who knows his language perfectly and is unaffected by such grammatically irrelevant conditions as memory limitations, distractions, shifts of attention and interest, and errors (random or characteristic) in applying his knowledge of the language in actual performance.

More challengingly he has declared that language (as opposed to grammar) 'is a derivative and perhaps not very interesting concept'.[1] Others disagree and include many of the factors relevant to performance within those relevant to linguistic theory. The term *communicative competence* has been used to cover such a wider range of relevance in linguistic theory.[2]

Theories emerge usually as the products of especially acute minds reflecting on what has been done and what might be done in a particular scientific field; Newton and Einstein in physics, and Darwin in biology, are examples. A good deal of work in linguistics, as in other sciences, is 'pretheoretical' in the sense that people try out ways of describing and analysing phenomena, and when it seems that results are showing or that results could be achieved by considering systematically what has been going on, certain of the people involved get around to an explicit formulation of principles. A well-known instance of this in historical linguistics was the declaration of principles by the Neogrammarians in the last quarter of the nineteenth century (8.1.7).[3]

7.1.2 Rival theories

Among formulated linguistic theories one major division lies between what we have called the 'externalist' and 'internalist' views on the investigation of language and languages (1.2.1). Textbooks setting out such different and opposed views are plentiful and have already been noticed (Chapter 1, general bibliography). Clearly the proponents and supporters of a particular theory think that it is, at least for many purposes, the best one with which to operate and to develop. But it is no part of an elementary introduction to claim any such exclusive rightness or correctness for any one theory. An introduction to British politics is not the same as a party election manifesto or the political views of the leader of one party. In linguistics one must try to show the newcomer, without smothering him or her with too much detail, something of the range of theoretical and practical stances that have been and are being taken by linguists whose scholarly merits and achievements are beyond question.

It may have been noticed that in several places in Chapters 5 and 6 there has been some emphasis placed on observational accuracy in recording and analysing linguistic forms together with some warning about the less tangible data of semantics and the description of meanings. For various reasons, which need not be investigated here,[4] linguistics, especially in the United States, where the subject was already well established, concentrated during the middle years of this century on an 'externalist' approach to language and laid much stress in this on spelling out, as part of theory, the procedures to be followed in gathering, identifying, and classifying linguistic data. Textbooks setting out this theoretical position are familiar.[5]

Some went to extraordinary lengths to make linguistics a wholly empirical science and therefore, in their view, a legitimate science. As meanings are less directly observable than linguistic forms attempts were made, probably in vain, to exclude even difference in meaning in defining phonemes and phonemic contrast, and to remove all considerations of grammatical as well as of semantic factors in working out a phonemic analysis of a language and the accompanying phonemic transcription.[6] One English-speaking writer of a grammar of English, precisely to avoid any subjectivity of judgments by a native speaker not subject to public verification, deliberately confined his corpus of material in English to a lengthy body of recorded conversations, so putting himself on a level 'scientifically' with a field worker investigating an unwritten language for the first time (9.1.1). By contrast one adherent to the opposed 'internalist' view has declared that only a native speaker who is himself linguistically trained is capable of writing a truly adequate grammar of his own language, because of the unique subjective insights into it that he possesses.[7]

The extremes of empiricist linguistics have probably been abandoned by most linguists today. But an observationally orientated 'externalist' attitude to the science is maintained, especially in studies of unwritten languages. Such work is often referred to today as 'structuralist', but the term is in this being used in a much more narrow sense than in *structural linguistics*, which in one way or another characterizes almost all linguistic work since de Saussure (*cp* 2.1.2). The work of these structuralists has been rightly praised by their opponents for the amount of facts and reliable information about languages that they have amassed, the methodological precision and clarity that they have achieved, and the scientific rigour and discipline that they have enforced on linguistic research. It is through their writings that technical terms which all linguists use and which many take for granted have been subjected to critical examination and scientific definition.[8]

Words drawn into technical vocabulary from everyday usage like *syllable, word*, and *sentence*, new creations like *phoneme* and *morpheme*, and traditional terms like *case, tense*, and *aspect* were all exposed to strict formal analysis and operational definition (*ie* they were partly defined by reference to the steps taken to identify them). This was a special contribution from American-Indian languages studies, which were strongly represented, as they are still are, by linguists holding to the 'externalist' position.

Such languages, having no prior scholarship, traditional grammar, or established writing system, for the most part, forced the researchers to ask and then to answer such basic questions as 'Where shall I write spaces between words, and why? Do I want to set up a class of adjectives or adverbs, and if so on what criteria?' Such questions are no less applicable in reference to language long studied and literate, for our understanding and critique of existing orthographic practices and grammatical traditions, and they have given linguists of all theoretical persuasions a deeper understanding of their material and of their tasks.

However, since the middle 1950s, and ironically just at the time when we saw textbooks setting out structuralist linguistics as a fully established theory and prescription for the study of language, several theories began to emerge posing definite challenges to the structuralist position. The name most prominently associated with this movement has been and remains that of Chomsky. Since 1957 he has initiated and carried through a revolution in theoretical linguistics, in the ways in which languages are researched, and in the purposes to which linguistics itself should be directed.

Chomsky is not alone in this period. Other theoretical innovations have been proposed. Some have arisen directly out of Chomsky's theorizing; others have come from efforts at developing different ways of understanding and analysing languages. An introduction cannot hope to mention, let alone describe, all of these, but an attempt should be made to give some understanding of the most significant of these developments in linguistic theory and associated linguistic practice.

It is probably impossible to say what all these theories have positively in common, as they differ widely in their basic concepts and analytic frameworks. But negatively they are all agreed that structuralist linguistics did not go far enough, and that, for all its merits and its contributions to our science and to our understanding of language, through its own self-imposed limits on what was admissible as linguistic data and what procedures were scientifically legitimate, it deliberately neglected much that both did and ought to interest scholars seriously concerned with language studies. Of course such criticisms applied most strongly to the more extreme interpretations of the empiricist constraints on linguistic science. All the innovators felt that too much had been sacrificed in the interest of scientific rigour, perhaps itself misunderstood, in particular through the relegation of semantics and pragmatics to the sidelines, the refusal to invoke the evidence of native speakers', necessarily private, feelings, intuitions, and judgments, the apparent limitation of science itself to description and classification, 'taxonomy', and the specification of methodology at the expense of seeking a deeper understanding of language itself and an insight into how and why languages are constructed and operate in the way they do. Naturally most, though by no means all, linguists who take such a stance place themselves on the 'internalist' standpoint in relation to language as an object of scientific investigation.

7.2 Transformational-generative linguistics (TG)

7.2.1 General considerations
To begin with Chomsky and the developments for which he has been directly or indirectly responsible, one must first realize that during the past thirty years he and his disciples and associates have not been propagating and refining a single variety of linguistic theory or a single set of descriptive and analytical principles. A full account of all this work over the past three decades could only be set out in a historical survey, which would be out of place here.[9] But an attempt will be made to outline the really major developments of Chomskyan theory in sequence, as they have led up to the present-day 'state of the art'.

7.2.2 Early formulation: Syntactic structures
In 1957 Chomsky's *Syntactic structures* was first published, effectively introducing what was immediately called *transformational* or *transformational-generative grammar*. It must be noted at once that in Chomsky's usage, followed by almost all those influenced by him, *grammar* covers the traditional levels of syntax, morphology, and phonology (all of formal descriptive linguistics, in fact, except the lexicon), and that *syntax* includes both inter-word and intra-word grammatical relations; morphology was treated along with the rest of syntax, in this wider sense of the term. Whether the fact that much initial and continuing work on transformational-generative grammar was done on English, a language with a notoriously restricted morphology, was at all influential in this can only be surmised.

In the first stage, represented by *Syntactic structures*, the grammar of a language was set out in the form of rules, a very traditional notion. Rules are prior to elements and structures, as they give rise to them, beginning with the rule dividing (or rewriting) S(entence) into N(ominal) P(hrase) and V(erbal) P(hrase), each subsequent element being further rewritable by later rules. S is the only element that appears as the input to a rule without having appeared in a prior output (5.2).

The first set of rules are P(hrase) S(tructure) rules. In **phrase**

structure the assumed largest syntactic unit, the S(entence) is progressively expanded by the application of rules into 'strings' (structures) of smaller units, terminating with a combination of lexical items and grammatical elements. This part of the theory is in many respects like the earlier immediate constituent analysis already described (6.3), except that at this stage this lines must not cross or converge, so that discontinuous constituents (*pp* 216, 221) are ruled out. Phrase structure may be illustrated with the following example, omitting much detail:

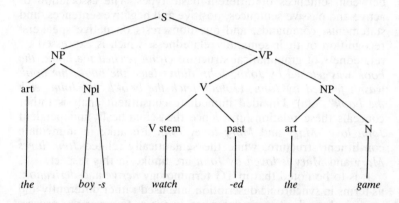

These diagrams are called labelled trees, because each successive representation of S consists of structural elements with a grammatical designation (NP, etc).

The description itself is framed in terms of sequentially applied rules, often called 'rewrite rules' because they may be read in the form 'Rewrite X as Y + Z' or (or 'X → Y + Z', + being here a concatenation symbol). Thus in the example given above the following rules are involved, some being applied more than once:

S → N(oun)P(hrase) + V(erb)P(hrase)
VP → V(erb) + NP
NP → art(icle) + N(oun)s(ingular) or N(oun)pl(ural)
V → V(erb) stem + past.

Other rules ('lexical insertion rules') supply the actual lexical and grammatical forms in the bottom line.

But at least in all the simplest sentences phrase structure rules are said to be inadequate for a full structural exposition, and therefore incapable of explicating the open-ended creativity of a natural language. This is the gravamen of the charge that TG linguists make against earlier 'Bloomfieldian' work centred on immediate constituent analysis.[10] Upon the output of the phrase structure rules **transformation** rules are applied to give the final output of the syntactic component of the description. These transformation rules (from which the *transformational* of *transformational-generative* is taken) involve, not the division of the sentence or its parts into smaller parts, but, as the name implies, the alteration or rearrangement of a structure in various ways.

Transformation as a relatively unformalized operation is well known in much traditional European grammatical paedagogy, and it reflects parts of speakers' intuitive awareness of relations between sentences of different basic types. The association of active and passive sentences, positive and negative sentences, and statements, commands, and questions rests on native speakers' recognition of their semantic relatedness, which is expressed by relatedness of grammatical structure (*John fetched the book, the book was fetched by John, John didn't fetch the book, the book wasn't fetched by John*, (*John,*) *fetch the book!*, *did John fetch the book?*, etc). Unaided immediate constituent analysis rather conceals these relationships, since the semantically independent *John loves Mary* and *Mary loves John* are alike in immediate constituent structure, while the semantically related *John loves Mary* and *Mary is loved by John* are unlike in this respect.

It is to be noted that in TG terminology *derive* and *derivation*, as terms in synchronic description, are used rather differently and more inclusively than as described in 6.4.5, to cover the process or the result of applying any grammatical rule.

Transformation rules may involve changes in the order of elements, additions, and deletions, all of which may be seen by comparing the active *John fetched the book* with the corresponding passive *the book was fetched by John* and the alternative passive *the book was fetched* (†*fetched the book* is, of course, not an independently grammatical sentence in English).

The sentence whose tree was set out above can be transformed into its passive counterpart by a set of formalized rules of word order change and morpheme insertion, producing a tree like this:[11]

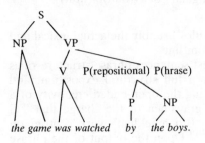

The 'elliptical', non-initial, context-bound sentence type referred to in 6.3.1 can also be explained as derived by means of one or more transformations involving the deletion of elements present in phrase structure strings or in one of the intervening transformed strings. Formal relations such as concord of grammatical categories and government (6.4.2) may also be handled by transformational rules.[12]

Those who have studied Latin grammmar at school will readily see how the rules given for converting direct speech to indirect speech are a relatively unformalized set of transformation rules (/Caesar eː castriːs proficiscitur/, Caesar sets out from the camp; /dixit Caesarem eː castriːs proficisciː/, he said that Caesar was setting out from the camp. The nominative case in the direct speech sentence is 'put into' the accusative case, and the indicative verb 'into' the corresponding infinitive form). In fact transformational-generative linguistics is more sharply differentiated from the descriptive linguistics immediately preceding it than it is from much traditional European paedagogic grammar, which was always ready to make use of any didactically profitable device that came to hand. This point was made in European reviews of *Syntactic structures*, and Chomsky has himself laid great stress on the continuities that may be established between seventeenth-, eighteenth-, and nineteenth-century grammatical work and TG linguistics.[13]

Examples can be given that show how sentences which are intuitively felt to be of different types and which have different structural meanings, but which yield the same formal analysis in terms of immediate constituents, can be shown to be structurally different in terms of their different transformational analyses (*ie* the sequence of rules by which they were derived). Thus *Port Stanley had been recaptured by the British expeditionary force* and *Port Stanley had been recaptured by June 1982* provide an identical analysis simply in terms of immediate constituents, or phrase structure rules unaided:

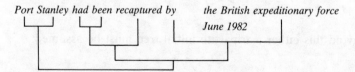

Port Stanley had been recaptured by   the British expeditionary force
June 1982

(leaving aside the internal immediate constituency of *the British expeditionary force*). But they are distinguished transformationally in that the first sentence is a straightforward passive counterpart of *the British expeditionary force had recaptured Port*

Stanley whereas the second is the passive counterpart of *something* or *someone had recaptured Port Stanley by June* 1982 with a subsequently ordered transformational deletion of the original subject.

Traditional grammar made use of implicit and informally stated transformational relations in explaining the potential ambiguity of certain constructions. Latin grammar distinguished between subjective and objective genitives by reference to the relations that would hold between the nouns and verbs of corresponding original sentences: 'Thus *amor patris*, the love of a father, may mean either "the love felt by a father" (where *patris* is a subjective genitive, *cf pater amat*, a father loves), or "the love felt for a father" (where *patris* is an objective genitive, *cf amō patrem*, I love father)'.[14]

Transformational rules reorder the words in a sentence, producing new trees. In this way one may avoid the discontinuous immediate constituents and crossing tree branches to which transformational grammar objects (6.3.2). In a language like Welsh, where the normal word order in a simple sentence is verb-subject NP-object NP (VSO), one problem arises at once. The immediate constituents of a sentence like *gwelodd y dynion y ci* /gweloð ə dənjon ə ki/, the men saw the dog, would be: *gwelodd y dynion y ci*

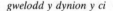

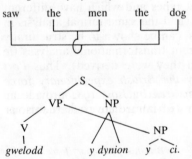

To avoid this either a tripartite initial tree must be assumed:

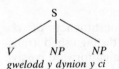

or a specific verb-fronting rule must be assumed for all such sentences,[15] though the meaning of the sentence is exactly the same as that of its English translation.

A third set of rules, P(honological) rules, converts the output of the two sets of syntactic rules (the bottom line of the trees) into the symbols of a transcription, or into an actual utterance. The phonological component of a transformational-generative grammar has been described in 4.4.4, above.

While structuralist linguists had not forsworn all recourse to rules of grammar, they gave much more prominence to elements and structures, which are more directly abstracted from what is observed. The Chomskyan primacy accorded to rules is consistent with their more 'internalist' attitude an their emphasis on linguistic creativity. Rules are part of the speaker's competence, in some sense held in his mind or brain. Ideally a grammatical description of a language should comprise rules that will generate every possible, grammatically acceptable, sentence and no grammatically unacceptable ones (the 'all and only' requirement), acceptability being a criterion drawn from the intuitive judgment of the native speaker.

Rules generate sentences; hence the second part of *transformational-generative grammar*. *Generate* is not used in any sense of 'producing' in its literal meaning, but more in the way that mathematicians use the term (and much transformational-generative terminology is taken from matematical usage). Rules generate sentences by giving them a structural description and by assigning them a place among the valid word sequences of the language, rather as x^2 generates or accounts for the special factorial property of the infinite but not continuous series of square numbers 1, 4, 9, 16, 25, and so on.

Of course sentences can be very much longer and more complex than the ones we have looked at so far. Coordination and subordination or embedding (6.3.2) are covered by various transformational rules allowing for the indefinitely continued coordinations, and the 'nested' subordinations, such as we have seen in *The house that Jack built*. This indefinite extensibility in syntax is known as *recursion* or the continued repetition of the same rule to the output of a prior rule. In recursion S(entence) can be introduced as part of the output of a rule thus bringing its own tree within a larger, matrix, tree of the main clause of a complex sentence, and, of course, this process can be continued indefinitely. From *I saw the man* and *the man took the cash* we can construct according to statable rules *I saw the man who took the cash*, and a further embedding could take place to form *I saw*

the man who took the cash that John had left at the bank.
This type of embedding involves both phrase structure and
transformational rules. In phrase structure it is represented by
the incorporation of S(entence) at a point within the structure of
a tree, the sentence structure within which the embedding takes
place being called the matrix sentence.

In the earlier example the matrix tree might take the form:

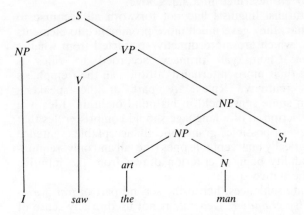

This latter S(entence) would itself contain an embedded S:

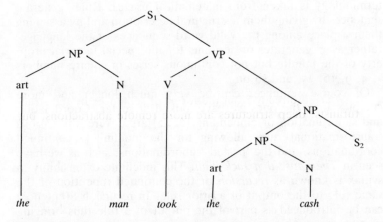

This last, most deeply embedded S₂ would represent the phrase
structure of *John had left the cash at the bank.*

The fully worked out tree for *The house that Jack built* would
extend over several pages. Indirect speech constructions are

further examples of embedding transformational structures, as are sentences like *his running quickly down the street aroused people's suspicions.*

Such, in the broadest of outlines was the theory of transformational-generative grammar in its first years, from 1957 to the early 1960s.

7.2.3 Later developments: Aspects **and after**

By 1965, when *Aspects of the theory of syntax* was published, a number of important changes were being brought about in the theory.

[i] In order to make the rules system (ideally) complete, semantics had been brought back into the descriptive linguist's central focus of attention. This was part of the response to the challenging definition of the description of a language as 'an attempt to reveal the nature of a fluent speaker's mastery of that language', published in 1964 (1.2.1). In Chomsky's formulation the semantic component of a linguistic description took the form of a set of interpretative rules operating on the syntax of sentences rather like the phonological rules.

[ii] The earliest transformational rules operated between sentence structures on the same level, and transformational relations had, indeed, been proposed as an additional component of structuralist grammar by a well-known structuralist, Harris, Chomsky's graduate teacher. But the gradual realization of the complexity of transformational rules and the problems arising from superficially ambiguous sentences such as we have been considering led to the distinction of the levels of **deep structure** and **surface structure**. Surface structures are much more like the structures abstracted directly from the forms of sentences by the structuralists; deep structures are more remote abstractions, but their recognition gave a much richer system for the analysis and explanation of the interrelations of syntax and semantics in the sentences of natural languages. The deep structure of the sentence analysed above might appear like this: *I saw the man (the man took the cash (the shopkeeper had left the cash at the bank)).* There would be two different deep structures for the sentences examined on *pp* 283-4, above. Deep structures are the output of phrase structure rules and lexical rules; transformations operate on these and give rise to the surface structures, which in turn form the input to the phonological rules. Recently, in later developments of the theory

deep structure and *surface structure* have been replaced by
D-structure and *S-structure*, to avoid any suggestion of
profundity on the one part or of superficiality on the other.[16]

[iii] The distribution of syntactic elements was progressively
changed, enriching the phrase structure base or deep structure, at the expense of the transformational rules; transformations were now controlled by the deep structure, and for
a time it was argued that transformations in themselves had
no effect on the expressed meanings of sentences. Categories
like negation, passive, question, and imperative, as well as
subordinate and coordinate relationships, had been formally
introduced as part of the transformational rules. These were
now incorporated in the base component responsible for
deep structure and lexicon, together with the subcategorization of nouns and verbs into such subclasses as mass and
count nouns, transitive and intransitive verbs, etc.

These elements of deep structure can be quite abstract and
remote in shape from spoken or written forms, and any
direct correspondence or similarity with actual utterance
forms is only attained at the level of surface structure,
whether in word shape or word order. As an example, question or interrogative can be marked in deep structure by an
abstract element written as Q, which is realized in English
via a number of transformations, themselves, triggered by
the presence of Q, in a specific word order (*did the boys
watch the game?*) or an interrogative word positioned at the
head of the sentence or clause (*who watched the game?*,
what did the boys watch?). Negative sentences may likewise
be marked in deep structure by *Neg(ative)*, which acts as a
trigger for various transformational changes, the addition of
a word such as *nicht* /niçt/ not, in German (*er geht* /eːr geːt/
he goes; *er geht nicht* /eːr geːt niçt/ he does not go), word
order and word form change in English (as in the translations of the German examples), and word form change in
Japanese (/dekimasu/ it is possible; /dekimasen/ it is not
possible).

All this encouraged the view that the meaning, the semantic
interpretation, of sentences could be assigned to their deep structures, and their phonological interpretation, through the P rules,
to their surface structure. Transformations themselves were in
this version of the theory semantically irrelevant, but simply
served to produce surface structures that, via the phonological
rules or the orthographic rules, can be phonetically or graphically

interpreted, *ie* pronounced or written down. Conversely, according to this view, the hearer, by his knowledge of the language, deduces from a surface structure the underlying deep structure, to which he supplies a semantic interpretation, *ie* understands what he has heard. It was also argued by some that deep structures may be much more alike as between different languages than their surface structures; the syntactic features of deep structure, and at least some of the semantic features of the sort mentioned above, were considered to be universals of human language as such. The investigation of universal grammar, to which TG linguists devote much attention, has generally been based on a notion of deep or more abstract structure, since, as they see it, the apparently obvious grammatical diversity of languages are primarily a phenomenon of their different surface structures. Correspondingly, more attention is paid to the possibility that certain very basic characteristics of grammatical structure may be universal and therefore probably innate in human beings.

This attractively but deceptively simple scheme can be set out diagrammatically like this:[17]

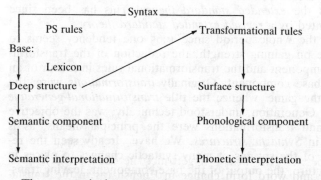

The semantic interpretation of deep structure included what came later to be called Logical Form (LF), covering such matters as the semantic interpretation of subjects and objects, actives and passives, reflexive sentences (*she washed herself*), and the 'understood' subject in sentences like *Judith wants (Judith) to go to Athens*, effectively 'those aspects of semantic representation which are strictly determined by grammar',[18] as against wholly lexically determined differences, like the difference between *they chose the white roses* and *they chose the red roses*.

This version of the theory was called, and still is called, the *standard theory*,[19] thus tempting providence to upset it. A principal difficulty soon made itself felt in the very complex nature of semantic interpretation, with added problems when aspects of meaning involved in pragmatics were brought in (*cp* 1.4.4). One radical solution was attempted in generative semantics (as againsts Chomsky's interpretative semantics), which was never espoused by Chomsky. In this version semantics not syntax was placed at the head of the generative apparatus.[20] But even greater complications led to the abandonment of such a solution.

Not that such ultimately unsuccessful efforts should be dismissed. The problems that they brought to light stimulated further enquiry and have given us insights into the relations between syntax and semantics, which have been incorporated into subsequent work. The 'scope' of quantifiers (*many, all*, etc) and negatives is a case in point. It may, for example, be affected by a passive transformation: *many arrows did not hit the target* and *the target was not hit by many arrows* are not exactly equivalent in meaning; one can say 'Many arrows did not hit the target, but many (other arrows) did hit it', but scarcely †'The target was not hit by many arrows, but it was hit by many (other arrows)'. Standard theory was later modified to allow for a surface structure contribution to semantic interpretation, to be known as the *extended standard theory*. This has been since supplemented by a *revised extended standard theory*.[21]

During the whole period since 1965 one tendency seems to have gone on gaining strength, the reduction of the transformational component and the transformational rules in favour of an enriched base component. Originally *transformations* were 'the name of the game' whence the title *transformational-generative grammar*. Generation, understood technically, was the objective or end, and transformations were the principal means, as is apparent in *Syntactic structures*. We have already seen the reallocation of the springs of many syntactic changes to places in deep structure, the output of the base component, leaving transformations as mere automatic responses to prior triggers. But additionally much derivational morphology, originally analysed transformationally, has been put back into the lexicon, again enriching the base at the expense of the transformations.

The motivation of this latter is understandable. Taking out examples from English (but, as always, those who speak or know well other languages should think this through in them), all English verbs can form a verbal noun (traditionally called a gerund) by suffixing -*ing: arriving, departing, reading*, etc), constructing with adverbs and sharing most of the syntactic functions of their associated verbs: *his selfishness was shown by his departing instantly from the disaster area; he keeps up with affairs by regularly reading all the latest periodicals.* Such informations can be readily dealt with through transformations. At first derivative nouns from verbal bases were treated in the same way (*arrival, departure,* etc), but this presents problems. Gerunds in *-ing* construct with adverbs, like the verbs, but verbal nouns derived in other ways construct with adjectives (*his immediate departure, his imminent arrival*). While all verbs can form an *-ing* gerund, it is hard to draw up rules for the morphology of other verbal nouns: *arrive* forms *arrival, depart* forms *departure,* there is no abstract noun formed form *read,* the noun corresponding to *despise* is *contempt,* and *ignorance* is sharply different semantically from *ignore,* whereas *pursuance* and *remittance* are closely akin in meaning to their associated verbs. One sympathizes with an English politician who declared that he would treat a remark by an opponent in the House of Commons 'with complete ignoral', but this bit of linguistic creativity did not catch on. For reasons like this, information about such derivational properties came to be assigned to the basic words themselves as individual items in the lexicon, along with subcategorizations, to be inserted as ready-made formations from the resources of the base component.

Things have now gone even further in this direction, more and more constraining the operation of transformations. In a fairly recent formulation by Chomsky transformations have been reduced to a single rule 'move α' (*alpha,* which includes some NPs and certain other phrases), and the rule simply says, in effect, 'Move the permitted constituent in the only way permitted by the lexicon and more generally by a number of purportedly universal constraints on what sort of movements can take place in any language.' One such is the coordinate structure constraint (CSC), whose effect in English can be seen in these sentences: *I met Jane* $^{and}_{with}$ *her sister at the opera last night* are virtually equivalent in meaning. We can perfectly well ask the question *Who did you see Jane with at the opera last night?*, with *her sister* being a prepositional phrase. But we cannot say: †*Who did you see Jane and at the opera last night?*, because *Jane and her sister* is a coordinate NP, and it is not permissible to move a part of such a coordinate out of its place in the phrase.[22]

Movements may leave 'traces', constraining other movements and affecting the semantic interpretation of the resultant sentences. Traces may have phonetic consequences, perhaps marked in the orthography. In English most sentences containing *I am, he is,* and other pronoun–verb sequences can appear in a colloquial abbreviated form *I'm*, *he's*, etc; but in a sentence like *he's a better general editor than I am now*, where *a general editor* has been removed and is 'understood' after *I am*, the forms as spelled, and pronounced /ai æm/ or /ai əm/, cannot be further reduced.[23]

A recent development of theory, diverging from the Chomskyan tradition, though derived from it, generalized phrase structure grammar, had dispensed with transformations altogether (7.3.2).

7.2.4 Government and binding
One of the most recent versions of Chomskyan generative grammar has come to be known as *government and binding theory* (GB for short to its afficionados). It takes its title from the two most prominent and important components from a total of seven that are considered to make up the basic grammar of all actual, and possible languages, as encapsulated in the human brain.

In this development we see the result of a gradual shift in the dominant interest of the linguists concerned. Transformational-generative grammar was from its first beginnings, as we have seen, primarily directed at the understanding of grammar and of language *in toto* as a set of rules acquired in infancy and then in some way present in the speaker's brain or mind. At first this led to a number of detailed analyses of parts of English grammar and of the grammars of other languages, and to some full-scale grammars, representing and exemplifying the state of the theory at the time and in the author's evaluation of it. More recently interest has turned much more towards the investigation of universal grammar, the set of properties that all languages possess, and by virtue of which children come into the world with a faculty, a language acquisition device, itself constituted by universal grammar, whereby they are able apparently without effort of any special degree of intelligence to acquire their first language largely from the stimulus of the mostly random snatches of speech spoken to them or in their earshot.[24] At the same time there has been a shift of interest to include syntactic relations other than those controlling relative positioning of elements, within the generative grammatican's purview. Attention has been focused on categories taken from traditional, and later formal, grammar, such as case, government, and agreement (concord, 6.4.1, 6.4.2), though often more abstractly interpreted.

All this amounts to a study by the linguist of part of the mind through the evidence of language, and it is wholly consonant with the 'internalist' stance of the Chomskyans on the status of linguistics as a science. Strict empiricists seek to account for first language learning simply through imitation, which certainly does seem a difficult hypothesis to accept as it stands.

Clearly the more constrained the brain or mind is at birth in respect of language, in other words the more we can accept a detailed biologically inherited structure of universal grammar, the easier it is to understand the ability of the infant to sort out and 'slot in' his random data of the language going on around him into the structures and the rules already 'there' and latent, waiting only to be activated by appropriate stimuli in the form of utterances. This is why so much effort is devoted to the working out in detail of a precise and articulated system of universal grammar.

As Bloomfield insisted, anything like a literal 'universal' grammar based on induction from a multitude of evidence cannot be fully confirmed until we know a great deal more about many more languages, ancient and modern, than we do at present or are likely to in the near future. The Chomskyans allow for this by substituting hypothesis and deduction for strict induction. It is fair, they argue, on sufficient evidence from some languages to make a hypothesis that all languages share a common feature or a common structural constraint or a set of rules, unless and until contrary evidence turns up that cannot be accounted for within the assumed universals.[25] They are prepared to weaken somewhat the application of universal grammar to each individual language by recognizing a 'core' grammar, based on universal grammar, a basic set of very widespread constraints, some few bits of which to a very limited extent may not be present in particular languages, for particular historical or other circumstances.

As an example of this, sentences of a certain type are ungrammatical in the judgment of speakers of English and of most other languages as far as is known at present. We cannot have a sentence like this: †*who do you believe the theory was the author of the Odyssey?* Of course, we know what it would mean, and there are no problems with *who do you believe was the author of the Odyssey?*, nor with *you believe the author of the Odyssey was who?* (in a surprised response to, say, the suggestion that the author was Homer's granddaughter). But though most known languages exclude sentences like the one excluded by English, it appears that such a sentence is acceptable in modern Greek:

pion   pistepses   ti   fimi   oti   proi ɣaje/
who   did-you-believe the story that (s)he promoted?

Must we sacrifice this part of universal grammar because of the Greek evidence, or can we wait and see to what extent other languages may appear in a similar state, or look for reasons for the special case of modern Greek?[26]

The components of universal core grammar, of which government and binding are two, are collectively responsible for the syntactic structures that appear in the grammars of languages and for their semantic interpretation, including the logical form of sentences. The whole of government and binding theory must be studied in detail within the specialist literature.[27] A great deal of interrelated terminology and several interlocking concepts are involved, in some cases differing markedly from previous transformational-generative usage, and the theory cannot be briefly summarized, nor can individual components, the so-called 'modules', be set out in detail without a full presentation of the whole theory. But it may be practicable and useful to give an idea of the main function of the two modules **government** and **binding**.

The term **government** is an extension of the traditional use of the word in grammar (6.4.2). Governing words assign cases to nouns, noun phrases, and pronouns, with which they stand in specific syntactic relations; by case assigning they determine the semantic role in the sentence that the case-assigned words play and on which the interpretation of the sentence depends. These cases are abstract thematic functions such as agent, experiencer, location, beneficiary, and so on. Though the term is taken from the traditional use of the word *case*, here it is much more abstract and may not have overt morphological exponents. In English we can recognize three different case forms in several pronouns, *I, me, my, they, them, their*, etc, but not in nouns, though their abstract case-assigned sentential functions are just the same. In languages like Finnish and Latin the relations between morphological case form marking and abstract case assignment is more complex.

Abstract cases, or 'thematic roles', are not in an exact one–one relationship with positionally or in morphologically marked cases, but where these are found they too are assigned by the operation of the rules of government. It is through the working of government in assigning thematic roles that we can interpret sentences like *I saw him, he saw me, I gave him the book; the book was given him by his headmaster, he was given a book (by his headmaster)*, sentences like *please write me a letter*, which can mean 'Write a letter to me', or 'Write one on my behalf' (if I have injured my hand, etc), and more complex sentences such as *I resent his denigration of his own country* or *he resents his denigration by his fellow countrymen.*[28]

No-one worries much about the use of pronouns in their own language or about the ways in which they refer to other nouns or to things or persons that form part of the context of the utterances. Linguists worry professionally about such things and they try to explain them, and this can be extremely complicated when set out in all its detail, which differs from language to language. We can readily distinguish between *he saw him*, when someone must have seen someone else, and *he saw himself* (reflexive), when only one person is involved. But in *he asked him to come and see him* the second *him* cannot refer to the person asked but only to the person asking (*he*), unless the context makes it clear that the second *him* refers to a third person. We can have sentences like *they love each other*, but not like [†]*each other love them* or [†]*each other are loved by them*. The sentence *they consider each other to be dedicated professionals* is all right, but not [†]*they consider that each other are dedicated professionals*, though if the latter sentence were permissible it would mean just the same. All this and much more is the field researched and set out by the binding module.

Consider the following paragraph:

> The librarian, Dr Bibliophilus, sent a sharply worded letter to Professor Hoarder asking him to return to him the books that he had borrowed six months ago, and not to keep them for himself so long. Professor Hoarder pledged himself to return them to him, saying that he would bring them back to him himself, and he asked him to excuse him for his having held on to them for so long, but he had taken on so much work for himself that he sometimes forgot to do what he knew he ought to do. Thereafter he and Dr Bibliophilus found themselves on the best of terms with each other.

There are fourteen instances of *he* and *him* as well as several occurrences of other pronominal words, *himself, his, them, themselves* and *each other*. Yet this paragraph is perfectly normal and presents no problems in comprehension or interpretation to anyone with a knowledge of English. It is moreover unambigous, interpretable in one sense only, except in very special contextual circumstances and with some abnormal stressing and intonation. Nobody teaches a child about this sort of thing, and the child would not understand such teaching until he already intuitively and unconsciously knew it already and could use it. An intuitive understanding of pronominal relations, binding and anaphora, like this in one's first language is a prerequisite for the fully conscious teaching and learning of the comparable but different realizations of the same sorts of relationships in other languages.

The objectives of the linguistic research involved in government and binding theory are far from fulfilment, and many revisions of the theory are no doubt still to come, as Chomsky and everyone else concerned with it agree. But in their quest, which we cannot but admire, they are seeking nothing less than an exact and detailed picture of our capability for acquiring and using the grammatical organization of our language, a capability built into our brain and activated by experience. Chomsky has written of a linguistic 'mental organ' comparable to such physiological organs as the liver, heart, and kidneys, with its own highly specialized and evolutionarily developed functions, though he does not attempt to place it in any physiological location in the brain.[29]

This accounts for the emphasis on universal grammar and the eagerness with which it is pursued, not as an 'optional extra' after a great deal of descriptive work has been done on many languages some time in the future, but here and now to be established, at least provisionally, by hypothetico-deductive procedures from relatively few or even just one language, and (this is the point) accepted until conclusively disproved, even at the cost of leaving aside apparent counterexamples on the periphery to be explained in some other way or attributed to some historical or other situation.[30]

Since the whole of a speaker's linguistic competence is to be made explicit, and what might be otherwise attributed to 'commonsense' must be got into the rules as far as the language is concerned, linguists engaged on this kind of research are as much interested in what cannot be said in a language, that is what would be rejected as ungrammatical by native speakers, as in what is and can be said. The informant, who may, of course, himself be a linguist researching his own language, must be accepted and trusted as far more than a source of data, and the language must be analysed on the basis of far more than a large and assumed fair sample of recorded speech or written records, such as was the material of the structuralists, who, as we have seen, had their reasons, in the interests of science as they saw it, for precisely such restrictions of their data.

For these reasons Hockett, by no means a supporter of this development in linguistic theory, has characterized Chomskyan linguistics as a whole as embodying the 'exact accountability hypothesis': everything that the native speaker has in his head the linguist must endeavour to get down on paper.[31] This is a sublime ideal, even if it ultimately proves unattainable. Despite the massive work in various languages that has been done and is being done within this theory, much more remains, and if the view expressed by one linguist (7.1.2, *p* 278) is to be accepted, then languages without trained linguists among their speakers may never be properly analysed. (This must not be allowed to stop research into these languages, particularly those likely to be extinct within a generation, while there are still speakers available.) Proposals for rules and constraints in universal grammar continue to be found to require revision and restatement in the light of new data, and the data on which research itself is based must contain a measure of subjectivity. But this research, even when it brings negative results, extends our knowledge and our understanding of language and of languages. Hitching one's wagon to a star may prove ultimately impracticable, but the attempt to do it may spur us, like Tennyson's Ulysses, 'to strive, to seek, to find, and not to yield'.

7.3 Other current theories

7.3.1 General context

It was pointed out earlier in this chapter (7.1.2) that while Chomsky and his direct followers are the best-known, the most numerous, and probably the most important of researchers and teachers in theoretical linguistics today, they do not in any way stand alone. We must now try to fill out the current scene in linguistics. In this we may treat the most prominent of recent and current 'schools' more briefly than was done in setting out Chomsky's work and its consequences. This is not because any of them is to be regarded as inferior or less interesting than Chomskyan work. Who can say at the present time what will be seen in the retrospective light of history in the twenty-first century as the most significant of our present preoccupations? We may deal more briefly with those working outside the main Chomskyan field simply because there are fewer of them in each group and at the time of writing less has been done by them as judged by their output of theoretical writing and particular language studies.

Firstly it must be made clear that descriptive accounts of languages continue to be published in forms very reminiscent of the 'structuralist' grammars of the 1940s and 1950s. This is particularly the case in presenting the facts about languages newly discovered or being systematically analysed for the first time. Dixon's *Grammar of Yidiɲ* is a good example of this.[32] In one chapter certainly he discusses the language in generative terms in relation to its 'deep syntax', but the bulk of the book contains a straightforward synchronic description of this native language of Australia. While expositions of 'structuralism' in the extremist terms characteristic of the decade immediately following Bloomfield's death are no longer being written, it must be clearly understood that some significant theoretical writings on syntax have been published relatively recently owing little or nothing to Chomskyan theory, nor indeed to any single specific theory.[33]

It was said earlier (7.1.2) that what unites all those propounding and developing post-'structuralist' theories is a negative reaction to the 'structuralists' themselves, charging them with having neglected important and indeed essential aspects of linguistics through the self-imposed constraints of their own total commitment to an empiricist science of language as they came to see it. But those linguists working on lines deliberately differing from the Chomskyan tradition (as it has now become) may be divided into various sets, though obviously all those who have worked on theoretical questions since around 1960, when transformational-generative grammar was clearly established in the forefront of public attention, have been in some sense also responding to the challenge that Chomsky and his associates had effectively thrown down.

Some may be regarded as diverging from some important parts of Chomskyan theory while maintaining other essential elements and sharing its major objectives. Other theorists have distanced themselves more widely from Chomskyan linguistics.

7.3.2 Generalized phrase structure grammar (GPSG)

Perhaps the most prominent among the first set is the theoretical work of a group of linguists which is known as *generalized phrase structure grammar*, a title largely derived from its principal features. Arising from some earlier discussions, the theory was set out in some detail in 1985 by four of its proponents, together with a full bibliography. It is also discussed by Horrocks and compared with government and binding theory in respect of various descriptive and analytical questions.[34] In its main objective it is in entire agreement with Chomskyan generative grammar in 'investigating natural language through the construction of fully explicit descriptions of particular languages.[35] It does this through the formulation of precise rules specifying the tree structures of grammatically acceptable sentences. Its main differences lie, methodologically, in abandoning as unnecessary all recourse to transformation and therefore also the distinction between deep and surface structures (or their successors in GB theory), and, intentionally, in disclaiming any attempt at probing the psychology of grammar. These linguists do not seek in their theory to identify through grammatical structure something of the structure of any 'mental organ' responsible for language acquisition and language use in the brain or mind. They do, however, claim that their theory is fully compatible with the 'learnability' of natural languages (that is, their acquisition as first languages without prior teaching); and from the experience of some of those working in the theory who have also been engaged in work with computers (9.4.2) it is said that this presentation of language structure is highly compatible with the requirements of computer programming languages.[36]

The absence of transformational rule is compensated for by a richer base component. Syntactic categories are specified for features, syntactic and semantic, determining their availability and use in specific structures. For example, verbs in English must be subcategorized (at least) into the following classes:

intransitive (*thrive*)
transitive (*devour*)
transitive without requiring an overt object (*eat*; we can say *he ate his dinner ravenously* or *he ate ravenously*, but we cannot say †*he devoured ravenously*)
ditransitive (*give (John a book)*)
transitive and clause embedding (*persuade (Parliament to repeal the Corn Laws)*)
and others.

The rules are of two kinds, generating a single level of structure, marked with a single labelled tree: immediate dominance rules (corresponding to Chomsky's rewrite rules to some extent), controlled by the feature subcategorization of the items involved, and rules of linear precedence, prescribing a grammatically acceptable word order to the product of the immediate dominance rules. Thus the English sentence *he gave his mother a birthday present* would be the product of immediate dominance rules

$S \rightarrow NP, VP$
$VP \rightarrow V, NP_1, NP_2$ (where V is subcategorized into the ditransitive verbs)

and the linear precedence rules

NP <VP

V <NP$_1$ < NP$_2$, < indicating linear precedence

(Immediate dominance rules do not themselves specify any particular linear order.) Where the clause structure permits some variation in word order, this can be indicated in the rule formulation.[37]

But more is needed to cover the ground assigned to transformations, especially in earlier versions of transformational-generative grammar. This is provided by what are called *metarules*, one such being the metarule prescribing that, subject to individual lexical exceptions, every transitive VP has a corresponding passive form, and that whatever lexical restraints there may be in an active sentence they are the same in the passive. Exceptions like *resemble* are presumably entered in the lexical specifications of the items concerned (*he resembles his father*, but not †*his father is resembled by him*). Other metarules are listed in *Generalized phrase structure grammar*.[38] These metarules are not just transformations under another name. They are part of the base generating component responsible for the whole of the single linearly ordered and syntactically structured strings that provide for the phonetic and orthographic realization of all the sentences of a language.

The trees representing these syntactic structures are more complex, when fully set out, than the corresponding trees of TG grammar, since they carry more information. A feature *AGR*(eement) is introduced to control the morphological representation of concord of number, gender, and person in cases like English *he runs, they run*; French *le garçon* /lə garsɔ/ the boy, *la fille*. /a fij/ the girl; Latin /(ego) curroː/ (tuː) curris/ you (singular) run. This feature also effects the relations of coreferentiality discussed above (7.2.3).[39]

In one respect, namely in its abandoning of transformations altogether, this theory might be said to have carried a long continued tendency in Chomskyan theory to its logical conclusion. But this theory, like all others, will have to be judged on its own merits by reference to its application to natural languages. In addition to the books by Gazdar and others and by Horrocks, already mentioned, there have been a number of studies on other languages than English, and most notably one on Japanese.[40]

7.3.3 Relational and functional grammar

Several groups of linguists have reacted against the restrictions deliberately imposed in most Chomskyan linguistics on the range of what is relevant to the linguist's, specifically the grammarian's, attention. Such a reaction may involve varying degrees of rejection of the general 'package' of transformational-generative grammar. One rather widely shared reaction has been against what is seen as the excessive formalism found both in 'structuralist' and Chomskyan linguistics. A particular topic at issue here is the familiar and often pretheoretical notion of subject and its correlate, object (*cp* 6.4.3).

Chomsky himself has used these terms freely, but he has been quite explicit on their prior definition by reference to the syntactic relations between S, NP, and VP in the most basic of the phrase structure trees. In the tree (slightly adapted from Chomsky)

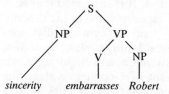

their relative positions on the tree define *sincerity* as subject and *Robert* as object (the so-called 'configurational' definition of these categories).[41]

What is now proposed by some linguists working within a basically Chomskyan frame and by others more generally rejecting this is that these essentially relational and functional concepts should be embodied in linguistic theory as primitives, that is to say accepted as universal concepts in language analysis without prior definition or formal establishment. Other such terms, with obvious semantic reference to the world outside language (*goal, location, beneficiary*, etc) may be included in the primitives that these linguists wish to bring in as basic components of their theory, or, where they are not themselves treated as primitives, they may be directly assigned to other primitives. Not surprisingly, therefore, such theories are designated by the titles *relational* or *functional grammar*.

There are, naturally, several varieties of these theories in current development; in particular the term *functional* is used in considerably different ways, some simply accepting grammatically functional categories like subject and object as primitives, while others include a range of features of the general context that are considered relevant to the formation of a theory of grammar.

Relational grammar as proposed by Perlmutter and Postal,

takes such syntactic concepts as subject, direct object, and indirect object as cross-linguistic primitives, relations discoverable in all languages, however they may be represented in each particular language. They retain transformations, but these are stated not in terms of positional relations between entities but of syntactic relations between relational categories. Transformational movements as such are, therefore, not needed. The distinction between active and passive, for example, involves turning subjects into agentive phrases and promoting direct objects (and sometimes indirect objects) to subject status (*she was kissed, she was given a kiss*). These changes may be marked by a specific word order, as in English, or by the morphological form of the words themselves, as in Latin. Statements of actual word order only come into play after the transformations of the relational categories have been affected. It is suggested that such a relational approach to syntax is of especial value in the description of languages with markedly free, *ie* syntactically non-significant, word order, such as classical Latin, modern Georgian, and modern Greek.[42] Readers with strenuous and enquiring minds should carefully read Harris's account of Georgian syntax. She sets out the theory of relational grammar and applies it to a grammatical description of Georgian, justifiably claiming that several of the notoriously 'difficult' aspects of the language, such as the use of different case forms with different tenses of verbs, can be more simply described in relational terms.

Much more within the Chomskyan fold is the theory going by the title *lexical-functional grammar* (LFG). This arose from certain problems that were seen in the evolution of the standard theory of transformational-generative grammar by some linguists who had been working within it.[43]

Whereas generalized phrase structure grammar espouses the links between grammatical theory and computer programming, regarding the search for psychological correlates as probably irrelevant and anyway impracticable at the present time, lexical-functional grammar considers the 'psychological reality' of its proposed structure of grammars to be highly important. Rejecting Chomsky's extreme idealization of the speaker–listener's competence, lexical-functional grammar aims at including the actual performance of actual speakers in the scope of what is relevant to the investigation of competence and its theoretical formulation, and it would claim that its purposes are consistent with the actual findings of experiments relating to the mental processing and interpretation of utterances.[44]

In lexical-functional grammar also syntactic concepts such as subject, object, and patient are taken as universals and as theoretical primitives. While maintaining its status as part of generative grammar, lexical-functional grammar, like generalized phrase structure grammar, dispenses with transformations. This is likewise compensated by an enriched lexicon and base component, in which, once again, syntactic and semantic features play a large part. Two parallel structures are set up, constituent structures and functional structures. Constituent structures are more or less equivalent to the rewriting rules of the earlier TG grammars, but concomitantly and in addition to them is a functional structure for the same sentence, which makes possible its semantic interpretation. Taking the example given by Horrocks,[45] we have a familiar looking constituent structure, except that its categories are functionally labelled:

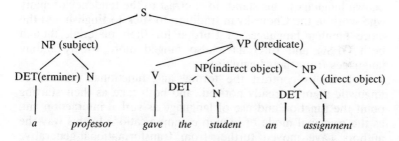

Here constituents and ultimately words are labelled and ordered on a tree. Beside this a functional structure sets out the relationship between the semantic roles that are assigned to the NPs associated with *gave* and the grammatical functions assigned to the constituents in the constituent structure, so that *a professor* is designated subject, and agent, *gave* (*give* plus *past*) is predicate, and lexically specified as constructing with a goal, and a patient, identified as the indirect and the direct object, *the student* and *an assignment*, respectively, both objects and the subject being further specified as singular in number. It will be noticed that these two structures are not at all the same as the S(urface) and D(eep) structures of government and binding theory; though they serve the same overall purpose, the way in which the relationships between the two are expressed is quite different: lexical-functional grammar does not employ structure-changing transformations for this purpose but relies on grammatical functions used in both constituent structures and functional structures to link syntactic categories with their semantic functions. Horrocks summarizes the theory drawing comparisons with both Chomsky's government and binding theory and with generalized phrase structure grammar.[46]

Two other versions of functional grammar are set out in Dik's *Functional grammar* and in Foley and Van Valin's *Functional syntax and universal grammar*. These versions of the theory show a much wider rejection of several tenets of the transformational-generative tradition, neither claiming to be a generative grammar. They do not present their theory in the same way, but they are in rather general agreement on the nature and the objectives of synchronic linguistic studies, and for the purposes of this introduction we may consider them together. Both illustrate their theory with examples from English, but they include exemplification and discussion drawn from a wide range of languages from different parts of the world. Foley and Van Valin's book is especially strong in its representation of lesser-known languages; this stands in contrast to the tendency of many who work in the Chomskyan tradition to stick to English and the more familiar languages of Europe for their material, though both GPSG and LFG have also ranged more widely among languages from their beginnings.

Both books contrast the formal and functional versions of linguistic theory already noticed, and both take as their starting point the function and use of language as verbal interaction and as the principal mode of human communication. In this way the authors have moved further from transformational-generative conception of language than have the adherents of lexical-functional grammar. For this reason Foley and Van Valin insist that their version of universal grammar is different from the Chomskyan and wider ranging.[47] They totally reject Chomsky's relegation of language as a derivative, imprecise, and perhaps not very interesting subject in favour of his abstract idealized grammar unsullied by the world of speech situations (*cp* 7.1.2, *pp* 276–7). In consequence the explanatory adequacy that they seek lies not in the mental organization of the individual's brain, but in the wider contextual and pragmatic circumstances and requirements in which speakers have always and will always use the language they have acquired.[48]

We are at once involved with pragmatics as well as with semantics, and with pragmatics on a much wider scale than in lexical-functional grammar. In Dik's version of the theory pragmatic factors as well as syntactic factors are part of the scheme of grammatical rules for sentence formation, and as in other versions of functional grammar basic syntactic concepts may be semantically defined, as beneficiary, manner, purpose, etc. More specifically, Dik identifies three levels of linguistic functions, each specifying part of the total meaningful structure of the sentence:

semantic functions: agent, goal, recipient, etc
syntactic functions: subject, object
pragmatic functions: theme and tail, topic and focus.

This takes us beyond the limit of the single sentence into the range of text linguistics (9.5), where the structure of one sentence may be determined by its place in a larger paragraph of narrative or a conversation in Dik's example (*Is there anything really spectacular in Paris?*) *As for Paris, the Eiffel Tower if really spectacular.* Here *Paris* is the theme; it 'sets the scene, specifies the domain . . .' in which the assertion about the Eiffel Tower is made. As well as the syntactic subject, *the Eiffel Tower* is the topic, that about which a statement is to be made; it is also the focus, that element in the sentence to which prime attention is being drawn.[49]

In this system some transformations are still found, but with a very much reduced part to play. A set of syntactic rules has responsibility for 'the linearisation of functional structures', the conversion of an interrelated set of elements with syntactic, semantic, and pragmatic functions into an ordered sequence, a string, of words. We notice the reversal of the Chomskyan role of word order as the *definiens* of syntactic relational terms, so that its role is now simply the linear display of these prior relational concepts, upon which syntax itself is built.[50]

7.3.4 Dependency grammars

So far, in examining various theories of grammar, structuralist, generative, and functional, we have found one analytic assumption shared by them all, namely that syntactic relations hold between constitutents, not individual words as such. Of course, if such an analysis is carried through to its completion we end up with single-word constituents and constituents consisting of only one bound morpheme or a grammatical category represented by one. But these are just limiting cases. The basic building blocks of syntactic structures are constituents, most of which consist of more than one word, which is why they are labelled in phrasal terms, *N(noun) P(rase)*, *V(erb) P(hrase)*, *P(repositional) P(hrase)*, etc.

There is, however, an alternative view of syntax, in which the basic unit is the word, and the syntactic structure of sentences is formally set out as relations between single words, except that in some versions of the theory coordinate structures (*John and*

Mary, etc) are treated as single constituents, the equivalent of single words. The relations holding between words in this theory are known as dependency relations, and writers have entitled the theory *dependency grammar*.[51] In its general outlines this theory has a long history; it constituted the basis of mediaeval scholastic syntax, and in some respects it is comparable with the syntax of the ancient Indian grammarians (9.6, *pp* 427 – 8). A version of it was published in French in 1959, undeservedly attracting little attention at the time in the continuing dominance of structuralism and the excitement of new-born transformational-generative grammar.[52]

Dependency grammar can perhaps best be grasped in outline through Hudson's *Word grammar*, in which a version of the theory is clearly and concisely presented. Essentially words are linked to other words in a sentence, contiguously or discontiguously, by relations of dependency. Non-head words stand in a relation of dependency to head words, which in turn may themselves be dependent on yet other words as their heads (it is to be noted that *head* in this use is not the same as *head* in immediate constituent analysis (6.3), though there may be co-incidences). For sentences containing a verb, *ie* most full sentences (6.3.1), the prime head word is the verb, and this is the only word not depending on another word. A system like this certainly suits 'pro drop' languages (6.3.2) very nicely. It is illustrated simply by Hudson:

she has brown eyes.

More complex sentences, which would have correspondingly more complex trees, turns out like this

John seems to like Mary[53].

Dependency structures of this sort cover the descriptive ground of immediate constituent analysis or phrase structure trees, but, of course, not in the same way. For one thing, these dependencies are between word and word (hence Hudson's title *Word grammar*); secondly, as the sentence immediately above shows, each sentences has only one, basically surface, representation, and the particular syntactic and semantic properties of verbs like *seem* have to be explicated elsewhere. Equally, having a single structural representation means that the problem of crossing branches, which is of concern for transformational-generative grammarians, may be avoided by permitting, where necessary, the crossing of dependency lines. This will not always be required; the Welsh sentence already discussed (7.2.2) would be represented like this in a dependency grammar:

gwelodd y dynion y ci
saw the men the dog

the men saw the dog

The order of dependency between article and noun is a matter still under discussion; the dependencies are marked here as they are in Hudson's book, but whichever way they are drawn, the point at issue remains unaffected

(*y dynion* or *y dynion*).[54]

However, in more complicated sentences, and especially in languages with a syntactically free word order, there would certainly have to be some crossed lines. Hudson admits this and discusses it, together with a general comparison of dependency and immediate constituency marking, but one does get the impression that he, like the early transformational grammarians, basing their work on English and some similarly structured languages, overestimates the extent to which 'word order tends to respect the integrity of the units defined by dependency structure'.[55]

Of course, dependency marking no more exhausts syntactic analysis than does constituency marking or the drawing of trees. The differences, syntactic and semantic, between the constructions involved must be described and analysed separately and linked with their corresponding dependency chains.[56] Dependency grammar has a respectable antiquity and promises a fair challenge to some other versions of current theories. We must look for further clarification of certain problems, and for detailed applications to languages of a variety of structural types.

7.4 Earlier post-'structuralist' theories

7.4.1 General context

The next three theories to be looked at are different from those considered in the preceding sections, in that they developed more or less contemporaneously with Chomskyan transformational-generative theory, and they were at the same time reacting in their different ways to the alleged deficiencies of 'Bloomfieldian' 'structuralism', only subsequently being examined side by side with Chomskyan theory in the stages of its own development.[57]

Each of these theories has acquired by now a quite considerable body of expository and critical literature, though nothing like to the extent that has occurred with Chomskyan linguistic theory.

We shall be taking notice of three theories in this set: tagmemics, systemic grammar, and stratificational linguistics.

7.4.2 Tagmemics

In some respects tagmemic theory remains fairly close to 'Bloomfieldian' linguistics, operating in phonology with a version of the accepted phoneme concept. Tagmemics is especially associated with Pike and those working with him and under his inspiration. In consequence much tagmemic work has been done by scholars attached to or working in collaboration with the Summer Institute of Linguistics, whose members are active and well known in descriptive linguistics and in missionary activity over much of the world. Their interests are strongly represented in Central and South American languages, and though their descriptive work is primarily directed towards Bible translation and the service of evangelism, their coverage of different languages, some spoken by quite small communities, is now very extensive. Notably, tagmemicists are one of the relatively two comtemporary 'schools' to set a high value on the specification of discovery procedures within linguistic theory.

Tagmemic theory developed from a more comprehensive theory of language within human behaviour put out by Pike in the years 1954–1960. Since its first appearance its terminology has been altered somewhat, and attention has been concentrated on grammar. A number of general accounts have been published, together with a wealth of tagmemic analyses of individual languages. Some references to these are given in the notes.

The central analytical and descriptive concept is the tagmeme. Note that current use of the term *tagmeme* differs in many respects from the now obsolete use made of the word in Bloomfield's *Language*. A tagmeme is a place in a structure (syntactic or morphological) together with the formal class of elements occupying that place (often referred to in the literature as a 'slot' with its 'filler'): 'The correlation of a grammatical function or slot with a class of mutually substitutable items occurring in that slot'.[58] Tagmemes unite such traditional concepts as subject, predicate, object, complement, locative, temporal, beneficiary, agent, etc with class concepts such as noun, verb, pronoun, adjective, adverbs, etc. As an example in the sentence *he loves Jill* we have three word tagmemes: subject filled by pronoun, predicate filled by transitive verb, and object filled by (proper) noun (in tagmemic analysis *predicate* does not include the object noun). Such statements can be formulaically abbreviated by means of symbols representing the function or functional place ('slot') followed by a colon, followed in turn by a symbol representing the class of 'filler': + S:pn + P:tv + O:n. More generally, the possibility in English of a noun or pronoun in subject or object place can be indicated: + S:n/pn + P:tv + O:n/pn.

While the tagmemes just illustrated are central to the system, structures above the word in size, and word structures themselves, are dealt with similarly in terms of tagmemes. Different sizes of unit, and of tagmeme, are referred to as levels (notice that *level*, here relating to relative size and inclusion, is used in a different sense from that given in 1.3.1). There are set up sentence level tagmemes, clause level tagmemes, phrase level tagmemes, and word level tagmemes; in so far as an analysis was facilitated thereby tagmemes at other additional levels could be brought into play. In other respects a tagmemic analysis involves a greater linear extension and less depth of structure.

In the above example a sentence comprises a base 'filled' by an independent clause and an intonation 'filled' by a sentence final, falling tune. Sent = + B:InCl + I:int. fall.

The clause consists of the three tagmemes mentioned above: InCl = + S:pn + P:tv + O:n. Recent studies have shown how the theory may be extended beyond the sentence to embrace text structures (9.5).[59]

In word structure (morphology) morphemically complex words may be represented in tagmemic formulae. In the example given above, *loves* may be accounted for by the statement: tv = + vnuc:tvs ± p:3s, *ie* a transitive verb consists of a nucleus 'filled' by a transitive verb stem which may or may not be followed by a personal suffix 'filled' by third person singular (other formulae would be needed to account for past tense verbs).

The + and ± signs are important in tagmemic formulae; in a generalized formula + precedes obligatory component tagmemes and ± precedes optional component tagmemes. Three-word English sentences whose verb can occur with or without a following object noun, like the verbs *eat, breathe*, and *fight (eg: John eats (meat))* can be represented in the formula + S:n + P:tv ± O:n, that is to say a noun subject is followed by a transitive verb predicate, and this may or may not be followed by a noun object. In a 'pro drop' language the optionality of an overt subject can be indicated by '± S:n/p.n.' Further elaboration and refinement make possible the representation of such structural relations as concord and government; more complicated tagmemic formulae are required for the word structures of more highly agglutinating and fusional languages.

One major difference may have already been noticed between immediate constituent analysis and tagmemic analysis of sentence structures. The binary cut between the nominal word or group (subject) and the verbal group comprising the rest of the sentence is a characteristic of immediate constituent analysis, as is seen in the examples in 6.3, and, in general, immediate constituent analysis proceeds with successive binary divisions. To some extent phrase structure trees in TG grammar follow binary divisions, and the initial phrase structure rule is almost invariably binary, S → NP + VP.

Tagmemic syntax involves tagmemes occupying sequential and equipollent places in structures; the example already given (*he loves Jill*) contains three tagmemes. Longer sentences can contain several more. There is therefore less depth, but each linear construction may be more complex. Tagmemic sequences are also referred to as strings, and the following example has been given to illustrate the structure of a longish sentence in tagmemic terms: *the slow lumbering covered wagon pulled the pioneer's family across the prairie just yesterday* is analysed into five tagmemes. (*the slow lumbering covered wagon /pulled/ the pioneer's family /across the prairie/ just yesterday*). Subject 'filled' by noun phrase, *the slow lumbering covered wagon*, Predicate 'filled' by transitive verb, *pulled*, Object 'filled' by noun phrase, *the pioneer's family*, Location 'filled' by adverbial phrase, *across the prairie*, and Temporal 'filled' by adverbial phrase, *just yesterday*.[60] These phrases would, or course, be further analysed at lower tagmemic levels.

Apart from this divergence from earlier accepted immediate constituent analytic method, tagmemics shares a number of features with 'Bloomfieldian' linguistics. On the lines of *phoneme* and *allophone*, and *morpheme* and *allomorph*, associations of place and class ('slot' and 'filler') that differ in some respect without grammatical distinctiveness or difference in structural meaning being attributable to them are designated tagmas or allotagmas of a single tagmeme. Thus the two tagmas T(emporal):adv(erb) occupying different but non-distinctive places in the English sentence or clause structures *John will go to town tomorrow* and *tomorrow John will go to town* would be assigned to a single tagmeme T:adv. The relatively free word order of written Latin would involve a good many different allotagmas representing a single tagmeme.[61] Of course, English adverbs whose position marks a separate meaning would be differently represented (*John was playing cricket happily; happily, John was playing cricket*).

As will have been seen, structural ('slot') titles may be those of traditional and formal grammar, like Subject and Object, or they may be more directly semantically derived, where an identifiable structural meaning can in general be assigned to a formally identified place in structure.

Recursions and subordinations are mostly handled by assigning a clause or phrase as the filler of a tagmeme within clause or phrase structure. Thus *he left before I came* would be InCl = + S:pn + P:i(n-transitive)v(erb) + T:T(emporal)C(lause); and this last tagmeme would be subjected to its own analysis into clause level tagmemes: TC = + S:pn + p:iv.

The bringing together into one unit, the tagmeme, of a grammatical function (with a structural meaning) and a formal class seems especially valuable in the analysis of languages where a variety of grammatical functions can be fulfilled by a variety of formally different elements (as, for example, in English nouns and pronouns can function both as subjects and as objects). In a Mexican language, Oaxaca Chontal, the predicate can, in certain sentence sructures, be filled by a nominal or by a verbal element, and conversely the personal affixes may function as goal (object), recipient, or subject[62]. On the other hand, where there is, or to the extent that there is, a one-to-one correspondence of function ('slot') and 'filler' (class), the two-term tagmemic formula may involve a redundancy.

Summarily, one of the fundamental aims of tagmemic theory, to continue the 'structuralist tradition and to be innovative, has been stated by Longacre: 'Tagmemics is a reaffirmation of function in a structuralist context.'[63]

7.4.3 M.A.K. Halliday: systemic grammar

National boundaries are of relatively little significance, and ideally should be of none, in the development and propagation of scientific theories and methodologies. But clearly the first effects of new development will be felt in the immediate circle of a scholar's colleagues and pupils. Transformational-generative theory started in America but has now spread its influence to almost all centres of linguistics in the world. Tagmemics, likewise American in origin, had found adherents in Europe and elsewhere, though, except among linguistis specializing in Central and South American languages, to a lesser extent.

In Great Britain the work of Firth and the theory of the context of situation associated with him has already been mentioned (1.4.4). Since Firth's death in 1960 work on these lives has continued, along with work on other lines;[64] but a body of linguistic theory in several respects stemming from Firth's teaching has been developed by Halliday. It represents, in fact, an attempt to do what Firth never did, namely to work out an explicit theory of language and of linguistic description on the basis of Firth's teaching and his published writings. For this reason it was first known as *'Neo-Firthian linguistics'*. It is, of course, an unanswerable question to what extent Halliday's theory has actually developed what Firth would have worked out for himself or would acknowledge as his own, and how far Halliday has projected his own thinking on to Firth. But Halliday's acknowledgment of his debt to Firth and to Firth's influence is made clear in the long article wherein he first expounded the outline of his theory, 'Categories of the theory of grammar' (1961), which was completed just before Firth died. It was followed by a more discursive presentation of the theory in *The linguistic sciences and language teaching* (1964).[65] More specialized papers by Halliday and by others have been published subsequently, together with descriptive treatments of languages on the lines laid down in the theory. Some references to these are to be found in the notes following this chapter. Needless to say, the theory has changed somewhat in the course of its development.

The general conception of language assumed in the theory contrasts linguistic form with substance (phonic or graphic representation) on one side and with situations (in relation to which linguistic form has meaning) on the other. Central in linguistic form are grammar and lexis (lexis being the vocabulary of a language, consisting of its individual lexical items (2.3)). Grammar and lexis are related to their phonic representation through phonology (*ie* the distinctive sound units and sound features of the language), and to their graphic representation through orthography (the alphabet and spelling rules of the language). On the other side the semantic functions, or meanings, of grammatical and lexical elements are stated in terms of contexts of situation abstracted by the linguist as descriptive and analytical frames within which to summarize the multiple relationships between linguistic forms and the world of human experience wherein they are meaningfully used (*cp* 1.4.4.). This general conception of language may be set out schematically in the following diagram:[66]

Substance phonic substance graphic substance	phonology orthography	Form grammar lexis	context	Situation extralinguistic features

Phonology serves to link grammar and lexis to their phonic representation (the term *phonetics* is used in this system to cover both the description of the phonic representations themselves and the phonological elements and structures). This envisages the place of phonology very much as Firth envisaged it (4.4.3), and, allowing for a different overall theory of language, as the transformational-generative linguists envisage it. But it may be noted that no one type of unit is expecially favoured, such as phoneme, prosody, or distinctive feature; the minimal unit is the phoneme, with larger units such as syllable, foot, and tone-group, ranged above it along the scale of rank (see below).

Within this theoretical framework important work has been done relating the intonation of English sentences to their grammatical structures and to the various semantic and pragmatic distinctions manifested in part by intonation, such as the distribution of different degrees of emphasis and contrast, and the differentiation of what is newly introduced into a conversation from what has already been mentioned.[67] In lexis considerable attention is devoted to collocational relations in the analysis of lexical meanings.

The fundamental 'categories' of Halliday's linguistic description, introduced and explained in 'Categories of the theory of grammar', are four in number: unit, structure, class, and system; additionally these categories are related to each other and to the phonic substance along three scales: rank, delicacy, and exponence. The prominence of the two terms, *scale* and *category*, also led to the use of 'scale and category linguistics' by some commentators to refer to this development.

Units in grammar are such entities as sentences, clauses, phrases, words, and morphemes. They belong to the same level (used in the sense of 1.3.1), and are related to each other in terms of size or inclusion: sentences include, or are made up of, clauses; clauses are made up of phrases (or groups); phrases are made up of words; and words are made up of morphemes. Likewise at the phonological level, tone-groups are made up of feet, feet of syllables, and syllables of phonemes.

The interrelations of units in size or inclusion are referred to the scale of rank, and in moving within one level (grammatical or phonological) up or down in size in a description one is moving up or down the rank-scale. Thus, broadly, Halliday's rank corresponds to tagmemic level.

Along the rank-scale, units, except the smallest at each level, exhibit structures, that is to say an ordered internal composition of units next below on the rank-scale within the level; sentence structures consist of clauses, clause structures of phrases or groups, and so on. It is a tenet of systemic grammar, criticized by some, that structures must always be regarded as comprising the units next below in rank. If a clause contains only one word, it must be analysed, for the sake of theoretical consistency, as a clause containing one phrase (or group) containing one word. As an extreme example, given by Halliday, the one-word response sentence *Yes* would be fully described as '(an exponent of) one sentence which is one clause which is one group which is one word which is one morpheme'. Tagmemics, on the other hand, does not impose such a requirement, and clauses can be described directly as composed of word tagmemes.[68]

Part of the recursive possibilities of linguistic structures are treated in terms of what is called rank-shift: a unit is shifted in rank when it occupies a structural place, not in the structure of the unit next above, but in the structure of a unit at the same rank-size as itself or below it.[69] Adverbial phrases can occur as part of other adverbial phrases (*by the pear tree in our garden*), and English (and other) relative clause constructions shift sentences to the status of modifiers in nominal group structures (*I admitted (him) to my house; the man whom I admitted to my house was in fact an escaped convict*).

In conformity with what has been said, units other than the highest in rank (the largest or most inclusive) at each level are grouped into classes according to the functions they can fulfil in the structure of units next above them. Thus in English clause structure nominal groups or phrases form a class in that they can (in general) function in the positions of subject and complement; and nouns form a class because they constitute the head, with or without a modifier, of noun groups.

Each class is either a closed class, to which new members cannot readily be added, like the class of English prepositions, or an open class, whose membership is freely extensible, like the English nouns or verbs. Classes consist of the units that comprise their membership; in the case of word classes the members are words.

Any classification may be made with wider or narrower criteria, involving more or less detail. In general terms *human beings* is a wider-ranging and less discriminating classification than *women*; likewise *women* is more inclusive than *English women*, and so on. By continually narrowing the criteria for acceptance classes may be reduced in membership to the point of diminishing returns in utility or to unitary membership of each classified individual in its own particular class. This much is common property of any classificatory system in linguistics or in any other science (*cp* 6.5). From an original suggestion of McIntosh, Halliday refers the progressive narrowing of class criteria, to take account of more and more detail, to the scale of delicacy, one of the basic terms in the theory.[70] Thus within the class of nouns in a language like Latin or German, masculine, feminine, and neuter nouns are classes abstracted at a higher degree of delicacy (by the application of finer criteria). Correspondingly the groups *the two able craftsmen* and *these two ablest craftsmen*, though both of the same basic structure deictic+numerative+epithet+head, can be more delicately distinguished according to the class differences of the deictic and epithet elements in the two examples.

Along the scale of delicacy the subclasses of a class are said to form systems, and when the practicable limits of subclassifying have been reached in lexis, the individual lexical forms themselves constitute the terms of systems. In logical terminology, class inclusion relations give way finally to class membership relations.

In phonology the classes of bilabial plosives and velar plosives are more delicate than the classes of plosives, bilabial consonants, and velar consonants; and a narrow transcription is more delicate than a broad (phonemic) transcription. This much is well within accepted phonemic theory; more discrimination may be needed in dealing with intonation tunes in some languages, English for example, to decide at what point further delicacy in setting up more and more separate (sub)classes of tune, based on ever finer criteria of pitch level and pitch movement, ceases to give useful returns in correlation with detectable semantic distinctions.

It is up to the linguist working on any language to determine, in the light of the material with which he is faced and the type of description he is undertaking, just how far along the scale of delicacy in grammar, lexis, and phonology it is practicable and profitable to go, before referring directly to the actual exponents.

The scale of exponence relates form to substance, that is, the abstractions of grammar, lexis, and phonology to the actual phonic (or graphic) data, the exponents (2.1.1). Any descriptive move nearer the data is a move along the exponence scale. Thus in passing from predicate as an element of clause structure to verb group one is passing nearer to the data, and in passing from verb to *enjoy* as a lexical member of the subclass of transitive verbs one comes nearer still to the data (the degree of abstraction is less); and the limit on the scale of exponence is reached when the verb *enjoy* is finally referred to an uttered sound sequence, or is narrowly transcribed as [enˈdʒɔi] (or written in an actual letter sequence 'enjoy').

Logically these three basic scales, rank, delicacy, and exponence, are independent in the theory, since they concern different sorts of relationships. In practice their lines may lie in part parallel to each other. *Transitive verb* is further along the scale of delicacy than *verb*, and *verb* is lower in rank than *predicate* since a predicate may comprise a whole verb group, so that *transitive verb* is at once more delicate, lower in rank, and nearer the data on the exponence scale. But this is contingent; it would always be possible to proceed directly from sentence to exponent, by simply transcribing *they enjoy their tea* narrowly, [ðei enˈdʒɔi ðɛə ˈtʰiː], without further description, at the absurd cost, of course, of abandoning any grammatical or phonological analysis. In a sense, as Halliday says, one tries to 'stay in grammar' as long as possible, only moving to exponents when forced to do so by having nothing useful to say further within an analysis in terms of the rest of the theory.

The descriptive apparatus just outlined has now been centred on the conception of grammar as involving a series of choices to be made from systems of classes along the scale of delicacy in the progressive development of a meaningful communication in a situational context. In the units of the various rank-sizes the options selected, as it were, are ultimately represented (find exponents) in the resulting utterances, and also directly make possible or, on the other hand, exclude, certain subsequent choices. The effect of this development in the theory is to place more descriptive weight on *system* as one of the four fundamental categories in linguistic analysis. This is the basis of the current title, *systemic grammar*.

As an example, an English sentence may be declarative, interrogative, or imperative in formal structure; also it may be independently positive or negative, and all six possibilities exist, from which a choice must be made. But the choice of interrogative admits, indeed requires, the further subsequent choice between *yes/no* interrogation (*is he coming?, isn't he coming?*) and *wh*-interrogation (*who is coming?, who isn't coming?, when is he coming?, why isn't he coming?*, etc). Either interrogative or declarative permit and require the choice of verbal tense, which is excluded by the imperative, because imperatives in English do not admit tense distinctions.*

These choices involve not only the selection within the options permitted of grammatical structures and of word ordering, but also of lexical items, intonations, and stress patterns, all to fit as far as possible the situation as the speaker perceives it and to bring about the effect that (s)he wishes on the hearer(s). In this respect systemic grammar is also a form of functional grammar, and this figures in the title of a recent book on the theory by Halliday, *An introduction to functional grammar*. Halliday's position as a linguist is on the whole on the 'externalist' side, observing how language is organized and how it is used in society by speakers and listeners. They exploit the paths open to them in framing what they say, be it a polite request, a brusque order, a brief minute, or a funeral oration, to maximize their intended effects; their relative success emerges as the listener interprets what (s)he hears and as the situation subsequently develops.

This is very much in the Firthian tradition (1.4.4). It is also very relevant to the situation of the language teacher and of the second (foreign) language learner. Native speakers have the full network at their command, and as in most aspects of the knowledge of one's native language this is largely unconscious; but they demonstrate their communicative competence (9.4.1) in the ways in which they are able to exploit this knowledge performatively for their own ends, social, personal, political, didactic, commercial, etc. The second language learner is building up his network; as he progresses his network becomes fuller, and more options are opened up and a greater delicacy of choice is at his disposal. Knowledge of vocabulary is an obvious illustration, but the equally important factors are involved, as in the choice of phrasing in greetings, requests for information, congratulations, expressions of sympathy, the expounding of lines of action and proposed plans, etc. 'I'm at a loss for words' states only a very temporary condition for a native speaker. Its relevance to the foreign speaker of a second language is all too familiar and all too embarrassing. Language teachers strive to build up their pupils' language networks as their teaching proceeds.

Halliday encapsulates the intention of his theory of language in the following question and answer: 'Why is language as it is? The nature of language is closely related to the demands that we

---

* This is not a universal fact of all languages, though it is widespread; Ancient Greek verbs formally distinguished present, aorist, and perfect imperatives, with various correlated semantic distinctions.

make on it, the functions it has to serve.' This last quotation shows the links that relate systemic grammar to the intentions of the writers on functional grammar discussed above (7.3.3). He justifies the title of his *Introduction to functional grammar* in that the book 'is designed to account for how the language is used', and he makes it clear throughout that 'the theory behind the present account is known as "systemic" theory'. This theory, which has been summarized in this section, and presented in detail in the writings of Halliday and others, to which reference has been made, has for long been oriented towards the explication of the functional aspects of linguistic structure.[72]

7.4.4 Stratificational linguistics

Stratificational linguistics, or *stratificational grammar* (using *grammar* in the wider sense, 5.1.1) is the accepted title of a theory of descriptive linguistics that has been developed since the 1960s. It owes its origins and main direction to Lamb in America, but it has attracted attention and support in other parts of the world. By now a considerable bibliography is available, including theoretical articles and introductory books by lamb and others. A number of linguists in America and elsewhere feel that stratificational theory provides a valid representation of the structure and operation of language and thereby makes possible useful descriptive analyses.[73]

Stratificational linguistics takes its title from the various 'strata', of which in terms of the theory languages are constituted. The strata very roughly correspond with the levels of linguistic analysis referred to in 1.3.1; their number has varied at different stages of Lamb's working out of the theory, but in the *Outline* six strata are set up.

There are two fundamental relations in stratificational linguistics: representation, or realization, and tactics. Realizational rules link the elements of adjacent strata, and, more generally, link meaning at one end of the language complex with sound (or writing), by which meaning is expressed. This relation is most readily illustrated between phonemics and phonetics, when it is said, for example, that in English /p/ is realized as an aspirated voiceless bilabial plosive in initial position (*p* 123, above) but as an unaspirated one after initial /s/; and it seems likely that the whole system has been modelled on an interpretation of the relationship between phonological and phonetic segments.[74]

Tactic rules apply within each stratum, specifying the permitted combinations of elements in it and their ordering for example the ways in which members of different word classes combine to form phrases, clauses, and sentences, and the ways in which phonemes combine in syllables to represent morphemes.

In the theory, linguistic communication involves passing from a meaning to be expressed (a situation to be described, a request to be made, a question to be asked, etc) through successive strata, involving representation by different sorts of units at each stratum, in combinations specified by the tactic rules, until the utterance itself is reached either as a physical event or as a representation by a sequence of phonetic features. Between these two end-points representation passes through the strata of lexemic (lexical), morphemic, and phonemic units.

Linearity is an order imposed on language by the fact that speaking and hearing take place in time; but at the highest level stratum the semantic relations between the components of what is to be expressed are free of such a requirement, and entities are conceived as related in more than one dimension, in terms of certain categories of relationship. An example of what is communicated by *the man caught the tiger* in English is shown thus:[75]

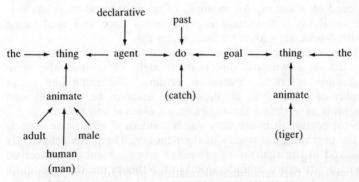

Of course if the system is to be fully worked out, much more numerous and more refined categories will be required, but inadequate development at this stage is not necessarily a flaw, more especially as considerable indeterminacy remains in semantics as yet in all systems and in all theories of language.

It is a commonplace that there is no universal one–one relationship between different levels in any language as regards the elements or units constituting each level: in English *see* + 'past' is expressed as /sɔː/; in Yurok /ʔ/ + n/ corresponds to (in stratificational terms is realized as) [ň] (glottalized [n]); conversely in Ancient Greek the past tense of many verbs is marked (realized) by prefix and a suffix παύω /paúː/, I stop, ἔπαυσα /épausa/,

I stopped. Stratificational grammar is well equipped to handle this type of phenomenon.

Language is envisaged as a network of relations linking meaning to spoken sound (or to writing). Two basic types of representation of realization are posited: AND relations and OR relations. Working downward between the strata, in AND relations a higher stratum element is realized as two or more elements at the stratum next below; in OR relations it is realized as one OR another element (including zero) at the stratum next below. AND or OR relations can each be ordered or unordered, and each stratum has its tactic pattern which specifies the particular combinations and sequences of elements permitted, in a language, at that stratum. As examples, phonemes are realized as simultaneous (unordered) combinations (ANDs) of phonetic features; English morphemes are realized as ordered sequences (ANDs) of phonemes; the lexical item 'man' is realized as /mæn/, with the phonemes in that order 'Good' is realized either as the morpheme (bet-/ OR as the morpheme /gud/ according to whether it precedes the suffix -er (/-ə/) or not. This last is an ordered OR relation. An example of an unordered OR relation is the possibility of the semantic components 'time' and 'goal' being realized lexically either by *until* or by *till*.[76]

These realization relationships can be 'read' (interpreted) in an upward or downward direction, though, of course, the term *realization* refers to downward 'reading'. Anything like a full display of an analysis on these lines involves very complicated diagrams as a glance through Lamb's *Outline* will show.

Stratificationalists are very much concerned with some aspects of the psychological reality of their theory. The paths collectively involved in the realization of speech from a mentally conceived semantic structure as understood in the theory are thought, quite possibly, to 'characterize language as it is represented in the brain'. Though they admit that much research remains to be done before anything can be asserted on these lines, some stratificationalists have argued that, to say the least, 'linguistic behaviour must have a close relationship to the brain in the real world, so the possibility of incorporating some properties compatible with neurophysiological notions of the brain into linguistic theory seems worthy of consideration'.[77]

7.5 Postscript

The various theories and versions of theories that we have surveyed briefly in this chapter are but a subset of what could have been selected for attention. In a subject as well populated with enthusiastic and able scholars as linguistics is at this time is both to be expected and to be welcomed. No-one thrives just by copying his colleagues or predecessors, and any idea of a 'one-party state' is as unattractive in science as it is in politics. 'Quot homines tot sententiae' (for everyone his own opinion) is as true of linguistics today as it was of mankind in Terence's time. It is hoped that in this chapter we have picked out those theoretical positions which are significant at the present time and will be significant for the future of linguistics; in most cases there has been no opportunity in an introductory book like this to do more than sketch in the main outlines of each theory, but attention is drawn in the bibliography and the notes at the end of this chapter for more detailed, critical, and wide-ranging treatment of them.

In the course of our survey one interesting and perhaps important question has presented itself on a number of occasions; whether it is possible (to put it no higher) that, at least in the present state of our theoretical sophistication and our empirical knowledge of languages, no single theory is to be categorically judged 'the best' for all scientific requirements or for all known languages, and therefore to be nearest to a representation of human language itself. This arises particularly over the treatment of word order and syntactic structure in the various ways in which this latter has been formally represented.

We have for long known a major difference on a rough and ready basis between languages having a fairly free word order (classical Latin being the best-known example) and languages where syntactic relations and syntactic constituency are in large part expressed through word order (English being a very well-known example of this class, cp 8.2.4). This matter has been noticed at various places in the preceding chapters, but it has come to the fore in this chapter at crucial points in the exposition of particular theories of syntax.

The prohibition of discontinuous constituents and crossed tree branches in transformational-generative grammar works relatively easily for English, where apparent counter-examples can be remedied by a transformational movement (6.3.2; 7.2.2). Latin on the other hand presents examples of many perfectly acceptable and 'normal' sentences in which this requirement can only be met by the *ad hoc* expedient of an all-powerful set of 'scrambling' transformations (*cp* note 15 of this chapter). Verb-subject-object languages like Welsh require more stages in the projection of quite simple basic sentence structures than are required for exactly equivalent sentences in subject-verb-object and subject-object-verb languages. In a different theory we saw that Hudson explicitly voiced what seems to be the view of many that dependency relations may be expected to hold for the most part between linearly adjacent units, as the norm in syntax (7.3.4).

This has led some linguists to assume that certain languages are syntactically 'flat'; that is to say that a verb phrase or a whole sentence consists of a series of several collateral branches (*eg* ⟨tree diagram⟩) rather than a lower set of nodes themselves dominating lower branches, as in most examples of trees in transformational-generative grammar ⟨tree diagram⟩ etc).

An Australian language, Walbiri, has been citied as an extreme case, but Japanese is also said to be 'flatter' or less 'configurational' than, for example, English, on the ground that the two NPs, subject and object, cannot readily be assigned separate places, the only firm requirement being that the verb must come at the end of the sentence or clause.[78].

As far as Japanese is concerned the facts are clear: the preferred and most normal word order is SOV, and, though they are not obligatory, the topic marking particle /wa/ or the subject particle /ga/ and the object particle /wo/ can be and usually are postposed to the nouns or NPs filling the subject and object roles, and they must be able to be 'understood' by native speakers in interpreting what they actually hear. This is to say that the grammatical functions of subject and object, like other phrasal components (*eg* dative with /ni/, etc) are as distinguishable as in a positionally marking language such as English; German, as we have seen (6.4.4), in many sentences shows both positional and morphological marks of subject and object, but just because of the morphological marking German allows more stylistic variation of word order in such cases than English.

The theoretical issue turns on the word ordering required or permitted in the S(urface) structures of different languages and the role played by linear order in the interpretation of sentences. Two features are declared to be characteristic of 'non-configurational' languages: [i] free or relatively free word order; and (as almost a necessary consequence) [ii] some discontinuous syntactic constituents.[79] But these questions, which are argued in detail in the article cited in notes 78 and 79 with reference to Walbiri and summarily in the case of Japanese, are just as important in Latin, ancient Greek, and modern Greek, which we have noticed earlier (6.4.4; 7.3.3, p 302).

The Japanese sentence /hito $\overset{wa}{ga}$ sakana wo tabeta/, the man ate the fish, is structurally marked by the presence or the availability of the particles /wa/ or /ga/ and /wo/, as is the Latin equivalent /homo: piscem e:dit/ by the case forms of /homo:/, man, nominative, and /piscem/, fish, accusative (object case). The same is true of the ancient Greek sentence ὁ ἄνθρωπος τὸν ἰχθῦν ἔφαγεν, /ho ánth ro:pos tòn ichtʰỹn épʰagen/, where the articles as well as the nouns are case marked.[80] The Greek and Latin subject, object, and verb can appear in any order with the same cognitive meaning (style, topicalization, etc being ignored here), whereas, of course, in English the order of words is crucial in determining what ate what.

What we have, then, is an assertion that S(urface) structure word order is more crucial than other grammatical characteristics in a major binary typological classification of languages, into 'configurational' and 'non-configurational' or 'flat' languages. If certain languages such as Welsh to some extent (7.2.2) and Latin and Greek, among others, to a very great extent exhibit discontinuous constituents or make little use of word order as a syntactic marker, and if these are designated as a special class of 'flat' languages, this certainly avoids the invocation of otherwise *ad hoc* rules like 'scrambling order' (note 15 of this chapter) or extra transformations, not otherwise required, to fit them into a frame developed for languages like English. But all this is a consequence of the insistence by transformational-generative linguists that tree branches shall not cross, a restraint not enforced by the structuralists' immediate constituent theory, and that subject and object shall be 'configurationally' (positionally) defined and only thus (6.3.1, p 216; 6.3.3, p 225).

Is this a long-term result of transformational-generative theory having been initially set out and greatly developed in English, a language wherein these conditions are fulfilled, or can fairly easily be made out so to do? In 1970 we read 'It is not absurd, I believe, to speculate that transformational generative grammar owes much in its development to the fact that English has been the major language studied, just as classical grammatical theory was influenced by the nature of Latin and Greek.'

In fact, at least for the present, may it not be prudent to allow for the possibility (to put it no higher) that some theories or some

versions of theories are better adapted for the explanation of
languages of particular structural types?[81] If this is the case, then
the assumption of a detailed psychological real universal
grammar may have to be treated with care, though in no way
abandoned, and it would seem that a crucial examination of
certain languages with this question at the centre of attention is
a research field needing urgent investigation. But we can hardly
take this inevitably controversial topic further in a general introductory book.

Bibliography for Chapter 7

1 A. AKMAJIAN and F. HENY, *An introduction to the principles of transformational syntax*, Cambridge, Mass, 1975.
2 D. J. ALLERTON, *Valency and the English verb*, London, 1982.
3 J. M. ANDERSON, *On case grammar: prolegomena to a theory of grammatical relations*, Cambridge, 1977.
4 M. ARONOFF, *Word formation in generative grammar*, Cambridge,
Mass, 1981
5 G. M. AWBERY, *The syntax of Welsh: a transformational study of the
passive*, Cambridge, 1976.
6 E. W. BACH, *Syntactic theory*, New York, 1974.
7 D. C. BENNETT, *Spatial and temporal uses of English prepositions: an
essay in stratificational semantics*, London, 1975.
8 M. BERRY, *An introduction to systemic grammar*, London, 1975.
9 M. BIERWISCH, *Grammatik des deutschen Verbs*, Berlin, 1963
10 R. M. BREND *A tagmemic analysis of Mexican Spanish clauses*, The
Hague, 1968.
11 (ed) *Advances in tagmemics*, Amsterdam, 1974.
12 R. M. BREND. and K. L. PIKE (eds) *Trends in tagmemics I and II*, The
Hague, 1976.
13 J. BRESNAN (ed), *The mental representation of grammatical relations*,
Cambridge, Mass, 1982.
14 E. K. BROWN and J. E. MILLER, *Syntax: generative grammar*, London,
1982.
15 M. K. BURT, *From deep to surface structure*, New York, 1971.
16 L. BURZIO, *Italian syntax: a government-binding approach*, Dordrecht,
1986.
17 N. CHOMSKY, *Syntactic structures*, The Hague, 1957.
18 *Current issues in linguistic theory*, The Hague, 1964.
19 *Aspects of the theory of syntax*, Cambridge, Mass, 1965.
20 *Topics in the theory of generative grammar*, The Hague, 1966.
21 *Language and mind*, New York, 1972.
22 *Reflections on language*, London, 1976.
23 *Essays on form and interpretation*, Amsterdam, 1977.
24 *Language and responsibility*, Hassocks, 1979.
25 'On binding', *Linguistic inquiry* 11 (1980), 1–46.

26 *Rules and representations*, Oxford, 1980.
27 *Some concepts and consequences of the theory of government and binding*, Cambridge, Mass, 1982.
28 *Lectures on government and binding*, Dordrecht, 1984.
29 N. CHOMSKY and M. HALLE, *The sound pattern of English*, New York, 1968.
30 V. J. COOK, *Chomsky's universal grammar*, Oxford, 1987.
31 W. A. COOK, *On tagmemes and transforms*, Washington, 1964.
32 *Introduction to tagmemic analysis*, Washington, 1969.
33 P. W. CULICOVER, *Syntax*, New York, 1982.
34 S. DIK, *Functional grammar*, Amsterdam, 1978.
35 W. O. DINGWALL, 'Transformational grammar: form and theory', *Lingua* 12 (1963), 233–75.
36 'Recent developments in transformational grammar', *Lingua* 16 (1966), 292–316.
37 B. ELSON and V. PICKETT, *An introduction to morphology and syntax*, Santa Ana, 1962.
38 W. A. FOLEY and R. D. VAN VALIN, *Functional syntax and universal grammar*, Cambridge, 1984.
39 R. FOWLER, *An introduction to transformational syntax*, London, 1971.
40 G. GAZDAR, E. KLEIN, G. PULLUM, and I. SAG, *Generalized phrase structure grammar*, Oxford, 1985.
41 J. T. GRINDER and S. H. ELGIN, *A guide to transformational grammar: history, theory, practice*, New York, 1973.
42 T. GUNJI, *Japanese phrase structure grammar*, Dordrecht, 1987.
43 M. A. K. HALLIDAY, 'Categories of the theory of grammar', *Word* 17 (1961), 241–92.
44 'Class in relation to the axes of chain and choice in language', *Linguistics* 2 (1963), 5–15.
45 'Notes on transitivity and theme in English', *Journal of linguistics* 3 (1967), 37–81, 199–244; 4 (1968), 179–216.
46 *Intonation and grammar in British English*, The Hague, 1967.
47 *An introduction to functional grammar*, London, 1985.
48 M. A. K. HALLIDAY, A. MCINTOSH, and P. D STREVENS, *The linguistic sciences and language teaching*, London, 1964.
49 A. C. HARRIS, *Georgian syntax: a study in relational grammar*, Cambridge, 1981.
50 G. C. HORROCKS, *Generative grammar*, London, 1987.
51 R. D. HUDDLESTON, 'Rank and depth', *Lang* 41 (1965), 574–86.
52 R. A. HUDSON, *Word grammar*, Oxford, 1984.
53 R. A. JACOBS and P. S. ROSENBAUM, *Grammar I and II*, Boston, 1967.
54 Y. KACHRU, *Introduction to Hindi syntax*, Urbana, 1966.
55 J. J. KATZ and P. M. POSTAL, *An integrated theory of linguistic descriptions*, Cambridge, Mass, 1964.
56 A. KOUTSOUDAS, *Writing transformational grammars*, New York, 1967.
57 S. M. LAMB, 'The sememic approach to structural semantics', *American anthropologist* 66.3, part 2 (1964), 57–78.

58 'On alternation, transformation, realization, and stratification', *Monograph series on languages and linguistics* 17, Washington, 1964, 105–22.

59 *Outline of stratificational grammar*, Washington, 1966.

60 R. W. LANGACKER, *Fundamentals of linguistic analysis*, New York, 1972.

61 R. B. LEES, *The grammar of English nominalizations*, Bloomington, 1960.

62 D. G. LOCKWOOD, *Introduction to stratificational linguistics*, New York, 1972.

63 R. E. LONGACRE, 'String constituent analysis', *Lang* 36 (1960), 63–88.

64 *Grammar discovery procedures: a field manual*, The Hague, 1964.

65 'Some fundamental insights of tagmemics', *Lang* 41 (1965), 65–76.

66 J. LYONS, *Introduction to theoretical linguistics*, Cambridge, 1968.

67 *Chomsky*, London, 1977.

68 A. MAKKAI and D. G. LOCKWOOD (eds), *Readings in stratificational linguistics*, Alabama, 1973.

69 E. MATTESON (ed), *Bolivian Indian grammar I and II*, Norman, 1967.

70 G. H. MATTHEWS, *Hidatsa syntax*, The Hague, 1965.

71 G. D. MORLEY, *An introduction to systemic grammar*, London, 1985.

72 D. M. PERLMUTTER (ed), *Studies in relational grammar*, Chicago, 1983.

73 V. PICKETT, 'The grammatical hierarchy of Isthmus Zapotek', *Lang* 36.1, part 2 (1960).

74 K. L. PIKE, *Language in relation to a unified theory of the structure of human behaviour*, Glendale, 1954–60.

75 *Linguistic concepts: an introduction to tagmemics*, Lincoln, 1982.

76 K. L. PIKE and E. G. PIKE, *Grammatical analysis*, Dallas, 1982.

77 *Text and tagmeme*, London, 1983.

78 P. M. POSTAL, 'Constituent structure', *IJAL* 30.1, part 3 (1964).

79 A. RADFORD, *Transformational syntax*, Cambridge, 1981.

80 D. A. REIBEL and S. A. SCHANE (ed), *Modern studies in English: readings in transformational grammar*, Englewood Cliffs, 1969.

81 H. VAN RIEMSDIJK and E. WILLIAMS, *Introduction to the theory of grammar*, Cambridge, Mass, 1986.

82 J. J. ROBINSON, 'Dependency structures and transformational rules', *Lang* 46 (1970), 259–85.

83 N. RUWET *Introduction à la grammaire générative*, Paris, 1967, trans N. S. H. Smith, *An introduction to generative grammar*, Amsterdam, 1973.

84 *Théorie syntaxique et syntaxe du français*, Paris, 1972, trans S. M. Robins, *Problems in French syntax: transformational-generative studies*, London, 1976.

85 P. SELLS, *Lectures on contemporary syntactic theories*, Chicago, 1985.

86 D. D. STEINBECK and L. A JAKOBOVITS (eds), *Semantics: an interdisciplinary reader in philosophy*, London, 1971.

87 R. P. STOCKWELL, P. SCHACHTER, and B. H. PARTEE, *The major syntactic structures of English*, New York, 1973.

88 L. TESNIERE, *Eléments de syntaxe structurale*, Paris, 1959.

89 V. WATERHOUSE, 'The grammatical structure of Oaxaca Chontal', *IJAL* 28.2, part 2 (1962).
90 *The history and development of tagmemics*, The Hague, 1974.
91 H. WISE, *A transformational grammar of spoken Egyptian Arabic*, Oxford, 1975.
92 D. S. WORTH, 'Transform analysis of Russian instrumental constructions', *Word* 14 (1958), 247–90.

Notes to Chapter 7

1 Chomsky, 19, 3; 26, 90.
2 D. Hymes, *On communicative competence*, Philadelphia, 1971 (abridged version in J. B. Pride and J. Holmes (eds)), *Sociolinguistics*, Hardmondsworth, 1971, 269–93.
3 *Cp* E. Heidbreder, *Seven psychologies*, New York, 1933, 368: 'Science, of course, is not above muddling through. Scientific practice often runs ahead of theory; it often proceeds unwittingly and unintentionally on assumptions that it discovers only after it has used them.'
4 These are briefly discussed in R. H. Robins, *A short history of linguistics*, London, 1979, Chapter 8.
5 One may instance the following: H. A. Gleason, *Introduciton to descriptive linguistics*, New York, 1961; Z. S. Harris, *Methods in structural linguistics*, Chicago, 1951; A. A. Hill, *Inroduction to linguistic structures*, New York, 1958; C.F. Hockett, *A course in modern linguistics*, New York, 1958. Linguists such as these intended by their books and by many of their articles to be expounding and developing the teaching of Bloomfield as set out in his great book, *Language*, (London, 1935). The period from the mid 1940s to the mid 1950s is consequently often referred to as 'Bloomfieldian'. But in some respects Bloomfield, who died in 1949, did not push his ideas as far as those whom he inspired went on to do.
6 *Cp* B. Bloch, 'A set of postulates for phonemic analysis', *Lang* 24 (1948), 3–46. On the procedural priority of phonemic analysis over morphological analysis in structuralist linguistics, Z. S. Harris, *Methods in structural linguistics*, Chicago, 1951, 6–7.
7 C. C. Fries, *The structure of English*, New York, 1952, 2–3; P. M. Postal, 'A note on "understood transitivity"', *IJAL* 32 (1966), 90–3.
8 *Cp* Chomsky's tribute to the structuralists in 18, 75–6.
9 On the history of transformational-generative grammar one may consult F. Newmeyer, *Linguistic theory in America*, New York, 1980, which despite its more general title is, in fact, almost entirely a history of TG theory up to 1980.
10 TG bibliography is now very extensive, and no attempt is made here to do more than list the most readily accessible works and those likely to be most useful for introductory study. These may be divided into three sets: (a) general theoretical works by Chomsky and others, (b) applications of the theory to particular languages, and (c) textbooks

setting out TG theory and methods. Works are listed in these three
sets; for reasons given in the chapter attention should be paid to the
date of first publication when studying any one of them.

(a) Chomsky, 17 (1957); 18 (1964), a general theoretical discussion, including replies to critics and the contrast between phonology in TG linguistics and earlier phonemic phonology; 19 (1965),
certain major revisions, with special attention to the subclassification
and further specification of major grammatical classes by reference
to syntactic features; it also contains a reapportioning of some grammatical categories between the phrase structure and transformation
components, with particular reference to the provision for embedding
transformations; 20 (1966). A summary of Chomsky's theory up to
1966 may be seen in his Appendix A, 'The formal nature of
language', in E. H. Lenneberg, *Biological foundations of language*,
New York, 1967, 397–442, Chomsky and Halle, 29 (1968), extensive
treatment of English phonology within the context of contemporary
TG theory; this book is likely to mark a definite stage in TG phonological theory for some years; Chomsky, 21 (1972); Chomsky, 22
(1976); Chomsky, 23 (1977). Chomsky, 24 (1979). Chomsky, 25
(1980). Chomsky, 26 (1980). Chomsky, 27 (1982). Chomsky, 28
(1984).

Katz and Postal, 55 (1964), incorporating a theory of linguistic
semantics within TG theory, and in some respects anticipating the
stage in Chomsky, 19.

Dingwall has written two useful articles reviewing the development
of TG theory and providing very full bibliographies of work published
at the time: 35 (1963) and 36 (1966).

Aronoff, 4 (1981). Lyons, 67 (1977), excellent brief introduction to
Chomsky's linguistic theory in the context of modern linguistics. The
revised edition deals usefully with developments since 1965.

(b) Worth, 92 (1958); Lees, 61 (1960); Bierwisch, 9 (1963);
Matthews, 70 (1965), an application of TG theory to an American-
Indian language; Kachru, 54 (1966); Reibel and Schane, 80 (1969);
Ruwet, 84 (1972); Stockwell, Schachter, and Partee, 87 (1973). Wise,
91 (1975). Awbery, 5 (1976). Burzio, 16 (1986).

(c) Koutsoudas, 56 (1967), draws attention to the framing of rules
to account for data given in the exercise material, followed by
solutions as well as by alternative rejected solutions with reasons
given for their rejection.

Jacobs and Rosenbaum, 53 (1967). These two short books (126
pages in all) provide an excellent introduction to mid-1960s transformational theory. They are very elementary and written very simply,
sometimes rather obviously verging on schoolroom style; but they
convey a remarkable amount of information, with examples drawn
wholly from English. Beginning students could be well advised to
read through these two little books at an early stage.

Ruwet, 83 (1967).

Lyons, 66 (1968), already noticed in the General Bibliography at
the end of Chapter 1, devotes the major part of its coverage to a

detailed exposition of TG theory as applied to grammar, surveying changes in the theory and introducing the reader to research and debate still in progress. See also the much shorter Lyons, 67.

Burt, 15 (1971); Langacker, 60 (1972), illustrative problems from several languages; Grinder and Elgin, 41 (1973); Bach, 6 (1974); Akmajian and Heny, 1 (1975), an excellent introduction to TG methods, with exercises. Fowler, 39 (1971). Radford, 79 (1981). Brown and Miller, 14 (1982). Culicover, 33 (1982). Riemsdijk and Williams, 81 (1986). Cook, 30 (1987). Horrocks, 50 (1987). The treatment of historical linguistics in TG terms is described in 8.1.10, below. Wide coverage in N. V. Smith and D. Wilson, *Modern Linguistics*, Harmondsworth, 1979.

For further reading by those who wish to pursue specialist interests, the bibliographic lists at the back of most of the books mentioned above should be consulted.

For a criticism of constituent structure analysis from a transformational point of view see Postal, 78.

11 Grinder and Elgin, 41, 138; Chomsky, 17, 41, 112 (with some details omitted).

12 For a transformational treatment of concord and government (in the traditional sense, Koutsoudas, 56, Chapters 4 and 5.

13 Cp W. Haas, review of *Syntactic structures, Archivum linguisticum* 10 (1958), 50–4; Chomsky, 18, Chapter 1.

14 B. H. Kennedy, *Revised Latin primer*, London, 1930, § 261.

15 Awbery, 5, 6. Rather different initial trees may be required for 'ergative languages' (6.4.3); see R. M. W. Dixon, *A grammar of Yidiɲ*, Cambridge, 1977, 384–406. In a language like classical Latin, in which word order is syntactically very free, special problems arise, to which one attempted solution is a final set of 'scrambling' rules providing for this stylistic variability of order (Horrocks, 50, 175).

16 Early use of *transformation*, Z. S. Harris, 'Co-occurance and transformation in linguistic structure', *Lang* 33 (1957), 283–340. An excellent early account of deep and surface structure is to be found in P. M. Postal, 'Underlying and superficial structure', in Reibel and Schane 80, 19–37. On the change to *D-structure* and *S-structure*, Riemsdijk and Williams, 81, 10.

17 *Cp* Horrocks, 50, 27. The orthographic representation corresponding to the phonetic interpretation is omitted (as often in TG literature).

18 Riemsdijk and Williams, 81, part III; Chomsky, 23, 5.

19 Chomsky, 'Deep structure, surface structure, and semantic interpretation', in Steinberg and Jakobovits, 86, 183–216.

20 See further Grinder and Elgin, 41, Chapter 10.

21 Revised extended standard theory, T. G. Bever, J. J. Katz, and D. T. Langendoen (eds), *An integrated theory of linguistic ability*, Hassocks, 1977, 5, 424. An excellent account of extended standard theory is given in Radford, 79.

22 *Cp* Chomsky, 26, 144–79; Riemsdijk and Williams, 81, Chapters 6 and 7.

23 *Cp* Riemsdijk and Williams, 81, Chapter 9.
24 On the language acquisition device, Chomsky, 'Principles and parameters in syntactic theory', in N. Hornstein and D. Lightfoot (eds), *Explanation in linguistics*, London, 1981, 32–75 (see *pp* 34–5).
25 On inductive universals, L. Bloomfield, *Language*, London, 1935, 20. Contrast Chomsky, 25, 2, cited in Radford, 79, 29. *Cp* 7.2.4, above.
26 This example comes from Horrocks, 50, 29. In fact a solution has been proposed, shifting the explanation of the clear surface difference between Greek and English from a possible exception to a basic feature of universal grammar to a difference in internal constituent structures in the two languages. This is an important step in our understanding of a particular part of modern Greek, but the fundamental question raised in this paragraph remains at issue (G. Horrocks and M. Stavrou, 'Bounding theory and Greek syntax: evidence for *wh*-movement in NP', *Journal of linguistics* 23 (1987), 79–108).
27 Much has been written and is being written on government and binding theory and on its application to particular languages. One may draw attention to Chomsky, 25, 27, and 28, which explore the theory very fully in relation to a number of European languages. Burzio, 16, gives a full discussion of the theory with reference to Italian. There is an exposition and critique of the theory in Horrocks, 50. All these books carry rich bibliographies for further reading. See also, Chomsky, *Barriers*, Cambridge, 1986 (barriers are types of syntactic structures imposing constraints on the operation of relations such as government).
28 A variant version of transformational-generative grammar, in which cases are introduced in the lexical specifications of verbs and in the branches of the phrase structure trees (marked K from German *Kasus*), has been worked out by Anderson, 3. See especially Chapter 1. The origin of 'deep', semantically specified, case in modern theory can be found in C. J. Fillmore, 'The case for case', in E. Bach and R. T. Harms (eds), *Universals in linguistic theory*, New York, 1968, 1–88.
29 *Cp* Chomsky, 24, 83, 97–8, 181; 26, 60, 241. *Cp* 22, 4: 'Language is a mirror of mind in a deep and significant sense.'
30 Chomsky, 28, 6–8; *cp* the modern Greek example on *p* 293, above.
31 C. F. Hockett, 'Sound change', *Lang* 41 (1965), 185–204 (quotation from *p* 196).
32 R. M. W. Dixon, *Grammar of Yidiɲ*, Cambridge, 1977; *cp* P. Austin, *A grammar of Diyari, South Australia*, Cambridge, 1981.
33 *Eg* P. H. Matthews, *Syntax*, Cambridge, 1961.
   F. W. Householder (ed), *Syntactic theory I: structuralist*, Harmondsworth, 1972, containing several essays first published well within the period of Chomsky's ascendancy.
   F. R. Palmer, *A linguistic study of the English verb*, London, 1965; *The English verb*, London, 1974; *Mood and modality*, Cambridge, 1986.

C. N. Li observes in his (ed) *Subject and topic*, New York, 1976, x–xi:

> It is noteworthy that none of the articles in this volume is concerned with the formal aspects of generative mechanisms. This represents a radical departure from the syntactic and semantic literature that was dominant in the 1960s . . . At this juncture . . ., it appears that one of the most productive developments of research lies in the collection of valuable facts from a diverse cross-section of languages.

34 Horrocks, 50, Chapter 3.
35 Gazdar *et al*, 40, 1.
36 Gazdar *et al*, 40, 65.
37 Horrocks, 50, 174–7.
38 Gazdar *et al*, 40, 249.
39 See Gazdar *et al*, 40, 111
40 Gunji, 42.
41 Chomsky, 19, 68–9; *cp* E. L. Keenan, 'Towards a universal definition of "subject"', in C. N. Li (ed), *Subject and topic* (note 33, above). This book contains various studies on the question, with reference to syntactic and semantic features.
42 Perlmutter, 72; Harris, 49; I. Philippaki-Warburton, 'Word order in Modern Greek', *TPS* 1985, 113–43.
43 R. M. Kaplan and J. Bresnan, 'Lexical-functional grammar: a formal system for grammatical representations', in Bresnan, 13; Horrocks, 50, Chapter 4.
44 *Eg* M. Ford, 'Sentence planning units: implications for the speaker's representation of meaningful relations underlying sentences', in Bresnan, 13, 797–827 *cp* Horrocks, 50, 226, 277.
45 50, 246–7.
46 50, Chapter 5; *cp* Sells, 85. For a recent application of L. F. G. see J. Bresnan and S. A. Mchombo, 'Topic, pronoun, and agreement in Chichewa', *Lang* 63 (1987), 741–82.
47 Dik, 34, 1–2, 6; Foley and van Valin, 38, 21–2.
48 Foley and van Valin, 38, 3–4, 13.
49 Dik, 34, 13, 17, 23, 141, 149–53.
50 Dik, 34, 20–2.
51 Hudson, 52, 76, Chapter 5 (on coordination); Allerton, 2; D. C. Hays, 'Dependency theory; a formalism and some observations', *Lang* 40 (1964), 511–25.
   Robinson, 82, comparing dependency grammar and transformational-generative grammar.
52 *Cp* M. A. Covington, *Syntactic theory in the high Middle Ages*, Cambridge, 1984, 48–51. The direction of the relationship was not the same in all cases, as the scholastic grammarians made the verb dependent on its subject and object. *Cp* R. H. Robins, *A short history of linguistics*, London, 1979, 82–3, 145–6. Tesnière, 88.
53 Hudson, 52, 77, 83. The arrows point from head to non-head.

54 Hudson, 52, 90–2.

55 Hudson, 52, 98 (general discussion 92–109).

56 This is dealt with in Hudson, 52, Chapter 4.

57 Halliday, for example, in his 1961 article sees the need to point out 'seven sins' in 'Bloomfieldian' linguistic method (43, 280).

58 See further Pike, 74; Elson and Pickett, 37; Cook, 31; Longacre, 63 and 65. Brend, 11; Waterhouse, 90; Brend and Pike, 12; Pike, 75, a very elementary account. Cook, 32 compares the two approaches to linguistic analysis. Longacre, 64 and Pike and Pike, 76 exemplify the continuing tagmemicist concern for dicovery procedures. Definition of *tagmeme*, Elson and Pickett, 37, 57. For tagmemic analysis applied to various languages see Pickett, 73; Waterhouse, 89; Matteson, 69; Brend, 10.

59 Intonation tagmemes, Elson and Pickett, 37, 122. On tagmemic textual analysis, Pike and Pike, 77.

60 Longacre, 63, 68–9.

61 Tagma, allotagma, and tagmeme, Elson and Pickett, 37, Chapter 20 Cook, 32, 19–20, 185–7.

62 Oaxaca Chontal, Waterhouse, 89, 27–30, 119.

63 Longacre, 65, 67.

64 Firth's own publications are conveniently collected in his *Papers in linguistics* 1934–1951, London, 1957 and F. R. Palmer (ed), *Selected papers of J. R. Firth* 1952–59, London, 1968, containing his later writings.

65 Halliday, 43; Halliday *et al.*, 48, chapter 2. Further reading, Halliday, 44; 45; Huddleston, 51; Berry, 8. Most recently Morley, 71; Halliday, 47. Illustrated from Yoruba, A. Bamgbose, *A grammar of Yoruba*, Cambridge, 1966.

66 Halliday, 43, 244; Halliday *et al*, 48, 18.

67 On intonation, Halliday, 46.

68 Halliday, 43, 253. Comparison with tagmemics, Elson and Pickett, 37, 85–6; Longacre, 65, 74.

69 Halliday, 44, 13; Halliday *et al*, 48, 27–9.

70 Halliday, 43, 242, 272–3; Halliday *et al*, 48, 30, 45, 56.

71 Halliday, 43, 263, 266–72.

72 Halliday, 'Language structure and language function' in J. Lyons (ed), *New horizons in linguistics*, Harmondsworth, 1970, 141–65 (quotation from p. 141); *An introduction to functional grammar*, London, 1985, x, xiii–xiv.

73 Stratificational theory was first outlined in two articles by Lamb, 57, and 58. Two textbooks are now available, Lamb, 59, and Lockwood, 62, Lockwood's being the easier of the two for first reading. The theory has been applied in detail to the semantic and syntactic analysis of English prepositions; see Bennett, 7, which also constitutes a clear and excellent introduction to the theory as a whole. There is a collection of articles in Makkai and Lockwood, 68.
   cp H. A. Gleason, *Linguistics and English grammar*, New York, 1965, vii, 214, 243. See also G. Sampson, *Stratificational Grammar*,

The Hague, 1970. R. Schreyer, *Stratifikationsgrammatik: eine Einführung*, Tübingen, 1980.

74 On connections between stratificational theory and Prague phonology see J. Vachek, *The linguistic school of Prague*, Bloomington, 1966, 81–2, 106, 115.

75 Diagram taken from Lamb, 57, 62.

76 Bennett, 7, 182–6.

77 Lockwood, 62, 282 (see *pp* 281–6 for discussion).

78 K. Hale, 'Warlpiri and the grammar of non-configurational languages', *Natural language and linguistic theory* 1 (1983), 1–43 (the spelling of this language name varies); Chomsky, 28, 127–35. Tagmemics, as we have seen, is strongly characterized by 'flat' structural representations, just because it loads much relevant syntactic information on to the tagmemes themselves (7.4.2).

79 Hale, *op cit*, 5. More generally on discontinuous structures, G. J. Huck and A. E. Ojeda (eds), *Discontinuous constituency (Syntax and semantics* 20), Orlando, 1987.

80 In modern Greek I. Philippaki-Warburton has pointed out that the English sentence *John kissed Maria* can be translated into the following six Greek sentences:

> *o Janis filise ti Maria*
> *filise o Janis ti Maria*
> *filise ti Maria o Janis*
> *ti Maria filise o Janis*
> *ti Maria o Janis filise*
> *o Janis ti Maria filise,*

with, of course, some stylistic and pragmatic differences ('Word order in Modern Greek', *TPS* 1985, 113–43).

81 K. V. Teeter, review of L. Bloomfield, *The Menomini language, Lang* 46 (1970), 524–33 (quotation from *p* 527); *cp* Horrocks, 50, 101, 266; Foley and van Valin, 38, 18–19; Harris, 49, 7.

Chapter 8

Linguistic comparison

8.1 Historically orientated comparison of languages (comparative and historical linguistics)

8.1.1 The material

Comparisons of one sort or another between different languages are as old as the study of languages. This is inevitable, since any acquaintance with or interest in one or more languages other than one's own provokes the comparison of various parts or aspects of these languages from some point of view. Often this has been naive and trivial, as when foreign languages were examined with a view to finding deficiencies and marks of inferiority when compared with a language enjoying high prestige like Ancient Greek, Latin, or Hebrew.

In general linguistics today **comparative** studies form an important part of the subject and of our understanding of the working and development of languages the world over. In particular, two types of linguistic comparison have come to be recognized, based on rather different principles and with different ends in view. It is desirable that the bases and methods of these two types should be clearly understood, as inconsistencies and confusions have not always been avoided, in a field in which, if satisfactory conclusions are to be reached, clarity of thought is essential.

One type of linguistic comparison, probably the one best known to the general public, is historically orientated comparison, which can strictly be designated **comparative and historical linguistics**, and is widely known as 'comparative philology' (cp 1.1.3). This branch of linguistic studies rather dominated the field during the nineteenth century in Europe, partly as a result of the stimulus derived form the discovery of Sanskrit, the ancient classical language of India, by Western scholars and the demonstration at the end of the eighteenth century of the indisputable historical connection of this language with Latin, Greek, and German.[1] In British universities chairs of comparative philology antedated by many years established posts in general linguistics. General linguistics, indeed, to some extent developed as comparative and historical studies aroused wider interests in the nature of languages and the means whereby they could be analysed.

The linguistic evidence, the facts on which comparative and historical studies are based, is in part very obvious. Word forms in languages are in the great majority of cases only conventionally linked with their referents or with their semantic functions; this has been expressed by speaking of the essentially arbitrary nature of linguistic forms.[2] Onomatopoeic forms, whose sound sequences suggest or vaguely imitate within the phonological system of the language noises characteristic of what the forms refer to, are well known linguistic phenomena (*cuckoo, dingdong, ting-a-ling-a-ling, cockadoodledoo,* German *Bimbam* /'bimbam/ noise of bells, *Kikeriki* /kikeri'ki/ noise of cocks crowing, etc), but their relative numbers in any vocabulary are extremely limited. Other semantic associations with certain word forms are found; several English words ending with *-ump* have connotations of thickness, bulk, heaviness, and the like (*clump, hump, dump, thump,* etc, *cp* 1.3.2). Such factors play some part in the determination of the word forms of all languages, so far as is known, but they leave untouched the greater part of their word stocks.

One is at once struck by the fact that among different languages greater or smaller numbers of words, in which onomatopoeia and sound symbolism are scarcely adduceable as relevant, and whose meanings are related or similar, exhibit manifest similarities of phonetic form (the limits of the application of the terms *related* and *similar* in this connection cannot be definitively circumscribed, but they are sufficiently clear in most cases, and borderline or doubtful examples can be left out of account as evidence).

Some samples from European languages will illustrate this:

MEANING	ENGLISH	GERMAN	FRENCH	ITALIAN	SPANISH
'hand'	*hand*	*Hand*	*main*	*mano*	*mano*
	/hænd/	/hant/	/mɛ̃/	/'mano/	/'mano/
'life'	*life*	*Leben*	*vie*	*vita*	*vida*
	/laif/	'le:ben/	/vi/	/'vita/	/'vida/

MEANING	ENGLISH	GERMAN	FRENCH	ITALIAN	SPANISH
'summer'	*summer*	*Sommer*	*été*	*estate*	*estio*
	/'sʌmə/	/'zɔmer/	/ete/	/e'state	/es'tio/
'give'	*give*	*geben*	*donner*	*donare*	*donar*
	/giv/	/'geːben/	/dɔne/	/do'nare/	/do'nar/

It will be seen from these examples that English and German constitute one group, and French, Italian, and Spanish another group, in which these word forms of similar meanings show obvious similarities with one another, but not between languages of the different groups.

One may now consider the following examples:

MEANING	ENGLISH	GERMAN	FRENCH	ITALIAN	SPANISH
'foot'	*foot* /fut/	*Fuss* /fuːs/	*pied* /pje/	*piede* /pi'ɛde/	*pie* /'pie/
'two'	*two* /tuː/	*zwei* /tsvai/	*deux* /dø/	*due* /'due/	*dos* /dos/
'three'	*three* /θriː/	*drei* /drai/	*trois* /trwa/	*tre* /tre/	*tres* /tres/
'me'	*me* /miː/	*mich* /miç/	*moi* /mwa/	*me* /me/	*me* /me/

In these word forms it is clear that, while the similarities within the two groups of languages mentioned above are closer, a general similarity in at least some part of each word unites all five languages into a larger group in terms of this evidence.

The immediately apparent basis for this sort of lexical comparison is similarity of word forms, but further examination reveals that similarity is only a special case of **systematic and regular correspondences** between component sound segments in semantically related words. Single pairs of similarly sounding words of the same sort of meaning are of no significance unsupported by others, and can be found between almost any two languages. The significance of Italian *piede* and English *foot* is not so much the similarity between /p/ and /f/, as the fact that the correspondence is matched by such further pairs as *padre* /'padre/ and *father, pesce* /'peʃʃe/ and *fish*, and that /d/ and /t/ correspond in *due* and *two, dieci* /di'ɛci/ ten and *ten*, and other pairs; and the same thing applies to all the other examples quoted. Examples of such correspondences become cumulatively weightier as their number multiplies.

When the series of words exhibiting correspondences of this sort between languages is set out and examined, it is found that they are far too numerous to be plausibly explained away as coincidental (as single unsupported examples could be), and that they are each confined to certain groups of languages. Languages can be grouped together on the evidence of these correspondences; some groups, such as the one that includes English and German, and the one that includes French, Italian, and Spanish, show a larger number of words related in this way, but include smaller numbers of languages, while other groups, such as one that includes in itself all the members of the two smaller groups just mentioned, and some more such groups, show fewer correspondences holding between word forms of the different included groups, but cover a much wider range of languages.

Since the particular correspondences and similarities by which languages may be grouped in this way are not universal as between all languages, nor reasonably regarded as coincidental, an explanation is required, and comparative and historical linguistics is an explanatory discipline. Some word-form similarities can be explained as the result of the word borrowing, the taking over of words from foreign languages into a language as the result of contacts with their speakers (8.1.8), though this explanation applies less readily to correspondences between sounds which are markedly different phonetically. While no type of meaning can be ruled out from representation by a borrowed word, and loan words, as they are called, cover all ranges of semantic functions, it is scarcely likely that a considerable number of words in several languages, covering meanings virtually essential to any language, should all be borrowed from a single source. The other, and the only plausible, explanation is that the different word forms related by one or more correspondences of phonetic composition are the result, after varying intervals of time, of the gradual divergence of the languages involved from an earlier linguistic situation in which their predecessors in time constituted something like a single language (itself, of course, like all languages, an abstraction and no doubt divided by isoglosses into regional dialects, 2.1.1, 2.2).

This is what is meant by saying that, historically, a language is **derived** from an earlier language, and that particular words in it are **derived** from particular earlier words.

It is important to understand just what is meant by this. Vendryes put it well: 'To say that French is derived from Latin is to say that French is the form taken by Latin in a certain geographical area over the course of time.'[3] This is to say that no conscious intention or decision to change one's language, nor indeed any noticeable process of change, formed part of any individual's personal experience; but the changes became gradually and cumulatively perceptible over the centuries. We may contrast this process with the quite separate one of a deliberate change in one's principal language of use, normally through a period of bilingualism, such as lead to the supersession of the earlier Celtic languages in Roman Gaul (France) by Latin, and which in this century has been part of the experience, and the choice, of many former speakers of Welsh and Irish who have become Anglophone.

This explanation, as well as accounting for the phenomena, describes a situation that one knows from other evidence to occur. The group of languages exemplified above with French, Italian, and Spanish, and actually comprising in addition Portuguese, Romanian, Catalan (spoken in part of Spain), Provençal (spoken in part of southern France), and some others, and commonly called the **Romance languages**, is especially illustrative in this connection, and it provides an excellent field in which to test and validate the theory and the practice of comparative-historical linguistics. It is known historically that the areas covered by these languages in Europe were for some centuries occupied by the Romans, beginning in the first century BC, and formed the most Romanized part of the Roman Empire (in much of the eastern half Greek was in use as the official language). In these areas spoken Latin, or Vulgar Latin, as it is often called to distinguish it from the literary language studied as 'Latin' then as now, soon became established as the language of the governors, the language of large-scale trading, the law, defence, administration, social advancement, and later of the Church, with the prestige of classical literary Latin, as the language of culture and education, behind it. So much did Latin displace the earlier languages of a great part of these provinces of the empire, that it survived the breakdown of it in the west and the inroads of barbarian invaders.

The gradual and continuous development of spoken Latin in these regions through successive stages into the present-day mutually unintelligible Romance languages can be traced in varying degrees of detail with the aid of inscriptions and old texts. Languages are constantly changing, though mostly imperceptibly at any time, except in the matter of vocabulary content, which can change very rapidly. Differences of pronunciation and grammar become noticeable when recorded forms of language of some centuries ago are examined and compared with examples of the language today, or, more generally, when the recorded forms of different stages of the language of a continuing speech community are compared and contrasted (*eg* the English of King Alfred's time (Old English), the English of Chaucer's time (Middle English), the English of Shakespeare's time, and the English of the present day).[4]

Where the social unity of a speech community is maintained, the general need for mutual intercourse prevent these changes from diverging too widely so as to produce mutually unintelligible forms of speech, and the changes, though they may be great, tend to be fairly uniform, with regional differences marking dialect areas rather than language divisions, and this must have been the situation during the years when the Roman Empire was more or less intact. Once the unity of speech communities is broken, and linguistic contacts between regions become few, nothing prevents the stream of changes from widening the differences between the types of speech in different areas, and in the course of time, producing separate languages. The relevance of synchronic dialect study to the diachronic study of historical linguistics has been noticed earlier (2.2.5).

Linguistic divergences resulting from geographical separation may be seen elsewhere. The Dutch of the early settlers in South Africa developed differently from the Dutch of Holland, and Afrikaans, as the development of Dutch in South Africa is called, is now reckoned a different language from Netherlands Dutch. Between the English of North America, Australia, and New Zealand, and between these and British English (and their various dialects) definite differences are observable in phonetics, grammar, and vocabulary; and the same is true of the Spanish of Central and South America and that of Spain, and between the Portuguese of Brazil and that of Portugal. But in all these the differences have not gone beyond the stage of dialectal differences, and contemporary conditions are almost certain to prevent them widening outside the limits of mutual intelligibility.

The fact of continuous, though gradual, change in languages at every level, phonetic, phonological, grammatical, and lexical, is indisputable; indeed, the assumption, for the purposes of description, of a stage of a language at which no change is recognized as occurring is strictly speaking in the nature of a fictional abstraction (1.1.2).

As a corollary of the successive stages of a language, through which its history and the history of later separate languages that arose from it can be traced, we may envisage a series of successive grammatical, phonological, and lexical systems, each representing part of the competence of speakers (2.1.1). It can be shown that no language is entirely homogeneous at any time, and that speakers control a number of dialectal and stylistic variations within their language; several of these variations or heterogeneities constitute the growth points for later historical changes and divergences.[5]

The causes of this continuous process of change are as yet not fully understood, but two sets of factors may be distinguished, external influences and internal processes. External causes of linguistic change are the contacts between the speakers of different languages, of the sort that occur when a foreign language is imposed on a people by conquest or by political or cultural domination, or when cultural and other factors produce a high degree of bilingualism between adjacent speech areas. Under such conditions speakers who acquire a second language in adulthood will inevitably bring into their use of it, phonetic, grammatical, and some lexical habits of their own first language. That is what is loosely known as 'speaking with an accent', and in the course of time such habits, passed on from generation to generation, becomes standardized and acceptable. In some cases, as in parts of Spanish-speaking South America, the effects of an originally spoken language on the form of Spanish now spoken by many speakers are still noticeable and have persisted long after that original tongue ceased to be spoken. Such linguistic phenomena are often called the effects of linguistic substrates or of substrate languages. External factors of one sort or another have been held responsible for many of the differences in languages that take place when an original language is diffused over wide areas displacing languages spoken there before, as happened with the spread of Latin over much of the western half of the Roman Empire and of English, Spanish, and Portuguese over large areas of the world in more modern times.

Much comparative and historical linguistic study has been directed to the results of sound changes in their effects on the languages concerned and on their historical implications. Recent research in the social motivation of sound changes (and of changes at other levels of language) pays attention also to these changes as they are taking place at the time and to the ways in which linguistic contacts and social influences actually operate.[6]

Under certain conditions, the prestige of a particular dialect or of particular speech habits characterizing a geographical group or a social class within a language area may cause or contribute to causing the spread of phonetic, grammatical, and lexical features over a large area. The spread in Great Britain, especially during the last two centuries, of varieties of English modelled on 'standard' English is in great part the result of such prestige.[7]

Internal causes of linguistic changes lie in the nature of the transmission of speech habits from one generation to another. Apart from all external influences, gradual changes appear to be inevitable, and in the processes some general tendencies are found repeatedly at work in various times and areas. It must be remembered that a language as such is wholly acquired by exposure to utterances in the language of those closest to the infant and young child, normally its biological parents. The general ability to acquire and to use a language is innate, biologically inherited (*cp* 1.3.2), and with it certain restrictions on the form that languages can take (*cp* 8.2.5), but the actual sounds grammatical forms syntactic constructions and lexical meanings are culturally transmitted, mostly in the child's early years. Herein lies the scope for small and gradual, but cumulative, changes at all levels.

Examples of changes at the phonetic level are the change of aspirated plosive into fricatives (as in Ancient Greek θέλω /tʰélo:/ I wish, Modern Greek θέλω /'θelo/), the voicing of intervocalic plosives (Latin /(via) straːta/ made-up road, Italian *strada* /'strada/ street), Latin /seːcuːrus/ untroubled, Spanish *seguro* /se'guro/ secure, and the changing of velar plosives before front vowels to affricates or alveolar fricatives (Latin /centum/ (Latin /c/ was a voiceless velar plosive), Italian *cento* /'tʃento/), French *cent* /sã/ hundred). Sometimes shifts in the whole mode of articulating certain classes of sounds, for example the change from unaspirated to aspirated plosives, take place in a certain area during a certain period. At another level, changes take place in grammar, for example in a gradual shift from a syntax relying on inflectional word forms to one relying on word order in the marking of structural relations.

A chain of internal changes may sometimes be seen to operate in the phonological and grammatical history of a language. The development in words of a strong stress on a non-final syllable may cause the articulation of the consonants and vowels of the final syllables to become gradually less distinct; this in turn renders these final syllables less effective as the carriers or exponents of grammatical categories and the indicators of syntactic relationships. These relationships as a consequence gradually come to be marked by other means, such as additional words in the sentence or a grammatically determined word order. Some inflections, such as the cases of nouns, are replaced by word groups or relative position in relation to other words in the sentence. Along with this process, the development of the new methods of marking grammatical relations renders inflectional differences in the final syllables of words less important and so more easily abandoned. Some such chain of causally connected changes may be seen at work in the gradual passage of spoken Latin to modern French.[8]

Various causal explanations of this sort of change over the course of generations have been put forward. The great diversity of the sorts of changes at all levels that have occurred in different areas and at different times rule out any simple or general explanation in terms of a single cause. Whatever the causes, continuous changes in the forms and systems of languages are a universal linguistic feature, and provide the material for the

historical study of sets of languages. Historical linguistics may in
a sense be said to be a special case of this sort of comparative
linguistics, in that one is comparing the forms exhibited by
temporally successive stages of the language of a continuing
speech community.[9]

8.1.2 The Great Vowel Shift in English

Apart from Grimm's Law the most familiar set of phonetic
changes known to English readers is referred to as the 'Great
Vowel Shift'. This is a term given to a series of far-reaching and
interrelated changes in vowel articulations that took place in
English principally during the fifteenth century, as part of the
passage from Middle English to early modern English and thence
to present-day English. It was the earlier long vowels that were
those most affected. Leaving aside many details, what happened
was a related raising of all the long vowels except for /iː/ and
/uː/, which could not be raised further. These were kept distinct
by diphthongization, first to /əi/ and /əu/ and then to /ai/ and
/au/. These changes may be diagrammed like this:

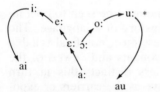

Later /eː/ from Middle English /ɛː/ fell together with /iː/ from
Middle English /eː/, /oː/ became /ou/ (/əu/, cp 3.3.3), and
/ɛː/ became /ei/.

This vowel shift is interesting from a number of points of view.
Much discussion has taken place on the extent to which the
individual changes influenced each other, which will not be
pursued here.[10] The changes most affected the emerging prestige
dialect of educated and Court circles in London and the south-
east of Britain, which became the pronunciation of standard
British English. Northern regional dialects were less affected
(cp some Scottish pronunciations of words like *house* and *mouse*
as /huːs/ and /muːs/). In many respects the impression immediately
given by standard English pronunciation is the final result of the
Great Vowel Shift.

---

* If a personal recollection is permitted in what is necessarily a rather dry textbook, one of
  my pleasantest memories is of an end-of-term party for which one student had decorated
  an iced cake with a full diagram of the Great Vowel Shift.

The same set of changes explains parts of the conservative nature of English spelling and its popular justification, as spellings preserve earlier pronunciations recorded before the changes had taken place. This tends always to happen with languages which have been literate for many centuries, but in which no systematic spelling reform has taken place (*cp* 4.1). *Bit* and *bite* were formerly distinguished by vowel length, being pronounced /bit/ and /biːt/ (much as modern English *bit* and *beet*, the latter formerly pronounced /beːt/). The same vowel letter *i* now represents the quite different phonemes /i/ and /ai/, but popular usage still refers to the vowel of *bite, white*, and similar words as 'long *i*'. The falling together of Middle English /eː/ and /ɛː/ to /iː/ accounts for the spellings *ee* ('long *e*') and *ea* both representing /iː/ today (as in *beet, beat, meet, meat, sweet, clean*, etc); and the changes /aː/ to /ɛː/ and then to /ei/ explain spellings like *name*, representing the modern English pronunciation /neim/, and so on ('long *a*').

8.1.3 Semantic changes

Part of the change that takes place in the history of all languages consists of change in the meanings or semantic functions of some of the words in their vocabularies, considered as the continuing lexical content of successive stages of the language. The study of **semantic change**, as it is called, though of less immediate concern in comparative linguistics, is very relevant to the historical study of languages.

The conditions of life of individuals in society, their artefacts, customs, forms of organization, and the like are constantly changing; and consequently the referents of many words in languages and the situations in which they are employed are equally liable to change in the course of time. New products often require new designations, and some words pass out of current vocabulary as the particular sorts of objects or ways of behaving to which they refer become obsolete. One need only think in English of the former specialized vocabulary, now largely vanished, relating to obsolete sports such as falconry, and of the vastly increased vocabulary relating to the mechanical sciences and technological developments that characterizes the language at the present time. For these reasons, as well as the more individual states of words as such, lexical and semantic changes in words are more rapid than are phonological and grammatical changes.

In the course of time many words, as they are used in

sentences, change in regard to the sorts of features in situations to which they refer, or in the ways in which they refer to them. These changes are very numerous and diverse, and it will not be necessary to do more than notice some of the most obvious. Some words come to be used and understood with somewhat different connotations (part of their total situational meaning) after a lapse of time. In part these changes may be correlated with social changes. One may revealingly compare the account given of the meaning of *enthusiasm* (generally unfavourable) in Dr Johnson's English dictionary, published in the eighteenth century, with that to be found in the *Oxford English Dictionary* today (generally favourable).

Some words have their contextual application reduced in scope. Thus *meat* is used to refer to butcher's meat, *ie* flesh food, though in the time of the translation of the Authorized Version of the Bible it meant food in general, as it still does in the fixed collocation *meat and drink*; this semantic survival may be compared with the survival, in certain collocations, of some older lexical forms not otherwise current in English today (2.4.2). Similarly *gobbet*, formerly used to mean 'piece' (of meat, bread, etc), is now almost exclusively used to refer to short passages in texts set for comment in examination papers. Middle English (c 1400) *dēor* /deːr/ beast, animal, has become *deer*, now denoting one species of animal. Some words change their principal reference; in parts of the western Roman Empire the Latin word /testa/ tile, also skull, came to be used with general reference to the head (whence French *tête* /tɛt/ and Italian *testa* /'tɛsta/ head). Some words widen the range of their application or meaning, when they come to be used in contexts in which they were previously not used or with reference to elements of the contexts with which they were previously not connected. Middle English *brid* /brid/ also spelled *bird* /bird/ meaning 'young bird', has become modern English *bird*, now used with reference to all birds irrespective of age. Proper names of persons noted in connection with some product or way of behaviour widen their meaning to cover the class thus designated; *Rolls* and *Royce*, the names of two motor manufacturers have produced the word *Rolls-Royce*, designating a set of cars. Some words increase their class membership in this process: *boycott* is both a noun and a verb, and is derived from the name of a Captain Boycott, an Irish land agent of the nineteenth century, subjected to the process. The English verb *pander* (*to*) is derived from the proper name *Pandar*(*us*), a character in Boccaccio, Chaucer, and Shakespeare, being a procurer or go-between. A very extensive type of semantic widening consists in metaphorical uses, wherein on the basis of some similarity in the meanings a word is used in different sorts of context and in reference to different sorts of features, usually of a more abstract nature, than was once the case. Metaphorical extension of meaning, already mentioned in 2.3, is too well known to require exemplification.

Sometimes changes in material culture directly cause some extensions of meaning. Thus in recent years *jet*, in addition to its meaning of 'forcibly ejected stream of liquid, gas, etc' and 'the nozzle through which it is ejected', has come to be used in reference to a jet propelled aircraft (*ie* one whose propulsion is derived from a jet of vapour of some kind). Similarly *nuclear*, in addition to 'central' now has the meaning 'referring to explosions involving the fragmentation of certain chemical atoms, and to armaments based thereon'.

We have already noticed the mutual determination of word meanings on the part of members of sets of words associated within specific semantic fields (2.4.3). Likewise the meanings of some words may be affected by changes in the composition and in the meanings of the associated field, over the language as a whole or in particular usages. To take a trivial example, if in the terminology of examination grading a mark of fair, good, or excellent was awarded to all candidates who passed, but after a certain date this grading was replaced by one of four items: fair, good, excellent, first class, it is obvious that, in this specialized field, the meanings of the three original terms, particularly that of *excellent*, will be somewhat lowered and contracted. The appearance in English after the Norman Conquest of the words of French origin (given in their modern orthographic form): *veal, beef, mutton,* and *pork,* caused a contraction in the semantic range of the English words corresponding to modern English *calf, ox, sheep,* and *pig* or *hog,* in that these were no longer employed in normal discourse to refer to the meat derived from these creatures, and their use in collocation with words like *flesh, meat,* etc became less widespread.[11]

8.1.4 The Indo-European family

The observed and attested facts of historical changes in many of the word forms in the Romance languages and some other groups both confirm the inferences that must be drawn to explain the systematic correspondences of phonetic composition in words of similar or related meanings in these languages, and give reason to assume similar developments as lying behind other groups of languages brought together by their exhibiting comparable sets of correspondences, but of whose earlier common descent nothing is directly known.

The languages represented earlier by examples from English and German are called Germanic languages, and to this group belong, besides English and German, Swedish, Danish, Norwegian, Icelandic, Dutch, and some other living languages, as well as the extinct Gothic language, which is preserved in Bible translations from the fourth century AD. In addition to Romance and Germanic, other languages are grouped on the same sort of evidence: into the Indo-Iranian languages, comprising Iranian (Persian) and Avestan (extinct), Hindi, Bengali, Marathi, and several other languages of northern India, together with Sanskrit which stands in a somewhat similar relation to them as Latin does to the Romance languages; into the Celtic languages, including Scots Gaelic, Irish, Welsh, and Breton (spoken in parts of Brittany); and into the Balto-Slavic languages, subdivided into the Baltic group, Lithuanian and Lettish, and the Slavic group, including Russian, Polish, Slovak, Serbo-Croat, Bulgarian, and some others, together with Old Slavic, an early written language now extinct apart from its use in some religious services. Latin, from which the Romance languages developed, was itself the principal member of the Italic group. The Anatolian group of languages comprised Hittite, its most important and best known member, and some others, spoken and written in wide areas of Asia Minor during the second millennium BC. This group is now wholly extinct.

All of these groups, and a number of other languages not immediately members of groups comparable to those given above, such as Greek (ancient and modern), Albanian, and Armenian, exhibit correspondences linking them all together, though less closely than within each constituent group. These more wide-ranging correspondences were illustrated above with the words for 'foot', 'two', 'three', and 'me'. On the basis of correspondences like these, and by the same arguments, all these languages are grouped into a larger family, usually called **Indo-European** (abbreviated to I-E), from the geographical distribution of most of its members. The term *Indogermanic*, and especially in German writings *Indogermanisch*, is also used with the same designation.[12]

I-E is the largest family into which the languages of most of Europe and some other areas can be grouped by the application of comparative methods with any degree of reliability. The relatively unitary state assumed to lie historically behind the family is in no general sense an 'original language', still less 'the original language'; it is merely as far back as one can at present go by comparative and historical inference. Whatever date may be ascribed to the relatively unitary state of I-E as a language in a speech community (at least as early as the third millennium BC),[13] aeons of linguistic history lie behind it. The peculiarity of I-E lies in the fact that it sets a limit on scholarly inference, not in anything special about the language or its speakers. In particular, language, a culturally acquired set of rules and habits, must not be confused with race, an inherited set of physical characteristics. The diffusion and dispersion of the I-E languages over most of Europe and North India was doubtless due to an early dispersion of population; but languages also spread by superimposition on existing communities, replacing their former languages, as in the case of the diffusion of Latin over much of the western part of the Roman Empire. The diffusion of a language over a wider area is not the same as, nor a necessary ground for inferring, the parallel diffusion of a racial type. At the present time the membership of a language in the I-E family has nothing to do with the membership of its speakers in any racial group.

8.1.5 Other language families
So far attention has been concentrated upon the I-E family. This is not by any means the only family of languages that may be set up by the methods of comparative and historical linguistics on the basis of systematic correspondences of word forms. Such linguistic studies developed mainly around the I-E family, and this family has had more attention devoted to it than any other. Rather as within the I-E family the Romance group of languages may be regarded as a specially privileged field for comparative and historical work, in that records of the 'parent language', colloquial Latin, are available, so the I-E family as a whole is a particularly favourable area for this sort of study, for a number of reasons. Among these are: [i] There is more detailed knowledge available of the continuous history of the I-E speech communities than is generally available with the other families; [ii] Three of the major classical languages of the world, Ancient Greek, Latin, and Sanskrit, are I-E languages, and they have been the objects of unbroken and minute scholarship from antiquity to the present day in the west or in India[14] [iii] There is a mass of inscriptional and manuscript records of successive stages in the development of many of the I-E languages; this enables the history of these languages to be documented, and the forms of dead languages to be brought into the material from which systematic correspondences are abstracted, and the more

material available there is, the more secure and informative are the correspondences taken from it.

The I-E family covers most of Europe and North India; and as a result of the European expansion by land and overseas in the modern world I-E languages predominate in North and South America (English, Spanish, and Portuguese), and in Australasia (English), while Russian, as the official language of the Soviet Union, is widely spoken over Asiatic Russia; and the I-E language family is represented all over the world today through the internationally current languages of trade, English, French, and Spanish.

Other language families have been set up on the same basis as I-E, systematic correspondences in the phonetic composition of words of similar or related meaning. In Europe much of the territory not covered by I-E languages is occupied by members of the Finno-Ugrian family, represented by Lappish, Finnish, Estonian, and Hungarian in Europe, and by a number of related languages in central and east Russia. The Altaic family includes Turkish, Tatar, Uzbeg, Mongolian and Tungus, and a number of other languages of Asiatic Russia stretching as far north as Siberia, and Korean and Japanese. Two non-I-E families that contain classical languages and a long tradition of literary culture are the Sino-Tibetan family, which includes the numerous Chinese languages and dialects, Tibetan, and some South-east Asian languages, and the Semitic family, represented by classical Arabic and the Arabic languages and dialects of the Middle East and North African coast, and by Ancient and Modern Hebrew and other related languages; in Europe this family is represented by Maltese, a language derived from Arabic as a result of medieval Arabic settlement on the island. This family is now included in the somewhat wider Afro-Asiatic family, containing several subfamilies of the northern half of the continent of Africa, including Ancient Egyptian.

Many of the languages of central and southern India belong to the Dravidian family (Tamil, Telegu, etc), and the Malayo-Polynesian (or Austronesian) family includes many of the languages spoken in the Malay peninsula, Indonesia, and the neighbouring islands (Malay, Sundanese, Javanese, Indonesian, etc); as the result of early migration, Malagasy, the language of Madagascar, also belongs to this family, as do the languages of the Pacific islands.

All these families contain languages which have for centuries been literate, and in them extant written records, inscriptions, and manuscripts, provide evidence of the forms of earlier stages of some of the member languages, as is the case on a larger scale with I-E. But some families have been established simply by reference to systematic correspondences in contemporary languages, as they are represented by languages spoken in parts of the world where before the coming of Europeans literacy was virtually unknown. Obviously the difficulties of operating in such areas are usually greater, and there is mostly a corresponding lack of reliable earlier history of the peoples, such as is available as supplementary information in I-E and other families with long literate member languages. Among these families, in Africa the Niger-Kordofanian family contains the best-known subfamily, the Bantu languages, including Swahili, a language widely used in much of East Africa, and many other sub-Saharan African languages. In North America, two families among several may be instanced, Athabascan and Algonkian, the former stretching with intermissions from north-western Canada to the southern states of the USA, the latter concentrated in the central and eastern plains area of Canada and the USA and in New England, but also represented by isolated languages in the western states, Blackfoot (Montana, and Alberta, Canada), and Wiyot and Yurok (California). The classification of the languages of South America is much less advanced.

The families mentioned above by no means exhaust those that can be and have been set up satisfactorily on comparative and historical lines. But the principles and methods are the same, and no very useful purpose would be served in an introductory survey by the listing of these families and their member languages. In principle, all languages could probably be assigned to a family together with other languages given adequate information; but in fact, and especially in the case of languages of which historical records do not survive, very many are not certainly known to be affiliated to any family, and are likely to remain thus isolated. In Europe the Basque language, spoken in a group of dialects on either side of the Franco-Spanish frontier in the eastern Pyrenees, is one such language, even though written records survive from some centuries ago. This language, which exhibits some grammatical features not otherwise found to any great extent in European languages, has been the object of extensive study (among others, Prince Louis Napoleon, cousin of the Emperor of France 1852–71, wrote on the grammar of Basque), and while tentative efforts have been made to include it in the Caucasian family (Georgian and others), despite its geographical remoteness, nothing can be said with any certainty about its historical connections.[15]

8.1.6 The representation of correspondences
A brief account has already been given of the sort of evidence
on which genetic relations between languages and the history and
development of language families is based. Of course not all the
words in any language can be related in the ways described to
words in other languages. Even in the smaller and more closely
knit groups with I-E, such as the Romance languages, there are
numbers of words appearing uniquely in each individual language
without certain cognates elsewhere; and the stock of words
represented in languages of more than one subgroup and so
regarded as of common origin within I-E is quite small; but the
words concerned (number words, names of some parts of the
body, kinship terms, etc) appear from their meanings to be the
sort of the words that any language is likely to need as part of
its central vocabulary. They are, therefore, credibly regarded as
derived from words in the common lexical stock of the unitary
'parent' language, rather than as words taken in by the separate
languages in the form of loan words (8.1.8) from other sources,
subsequent to their separation; and it is on these words of
common origin that the existence and linguistic history of the I-E
family is established.

As has been said, the significance of sound correspondences
between the words of different languages lies in their appearance
in series. A set of such correspondences that is well known is the
basis for what is generally called Grimm's Law, by which a
regular relationship can be stated between consonants of
particular articulatory types in the Germanic languages and in
languages of other branches of I- E.[16] These correspondences are
the result of sound changes that took place at an early stage in
the history of the Germanic subfamily, before the emergence of
the later separate languages. The full statement of all the correspondences in the different languages concerned would be a
lengthy procedure; the following pairs of words come under and
illustrate them:

Voiceless plosive and fricative (or continuant) in
Latin	/ped-/	foot	English	/fut/
	/tenuis/	thin		/θin/
	/cornu:/	horn		/hɔːn/

Voiced and voiceless plosive in:
Latin	/duo/	two	English	/tuː/
	/ed-/	to eat		/iːt/
	/ager/	field	acre	/'eikə/
	/ped-/	foot		/fut/

Voiced aspirated and voiced unaspirated plosives in:
Sanskrit /*bhar(āmi)* (to) bear   English /bɛə(r)/
     vidhavā /vidhavaː/ widow   /'widou/

The correspondences are between sound segments, not letters, though in dead languages the written letters may be only evidence for the existence, in the words concerned, of the sounds; and the attested correspondences of sound segments in the different languages in which they appear in the words may for convenience be summarily represented by a single symbol, usually prefixed by an asterisk, to distinguish it from the representation of an actual sound in a particular language, and referred to as a 'starred letter'. Thus **p* represents the series Sanskrit /p/ (*pitā* /pitaː/, father), Latin /p/ (/pater/), Ancient Greek /p/ (πατήρ /patéːr/), English /f/ (/'faːðə/), German /f/ (*Vater* /'faːter/), and so on in the other I-E languages; and in the same way **e* represents the series Sanskrit /a/ (*asti* /asti/ is), Ancient Greek /e/ (εστί/estí), Latin /e/ (/est/), etc.

When the same procedure is applied to several segments in the series of words compared in this way and showing regular correspondences of this sort, the series of related words may be jointly represented by a sequence of starred letters to give what is called a 'starred form', usually representing what appears to be common among the several languages concerned either to the root of the words, or, if any of them are variable words, to a similarly related series of bound affixial elements. Thus **septm* represents the sound correspondences in several words meaning 'seven', Sanskrit *sapta* /sapta/, Latin /septem/, Ancient Greek ἑπτά /heptá/, German *sieben* /'ziːben/, English /'sevən/, etc, and **nti* represents those in the third person plural forms of present tense paradigms of verbs in such words as Sanskrit *bharanti* /bharanti/ (they) carry, Greek φέρουσι /pʰérousi/ (Doric dialect φέροντι /pʰéronti/), Latin /ferunt/, and Gothic *bairand* /'bɛrand/.

It must be stressed that starred word forms can be set up from series of actual attested words because the sound correspondences found between them are paralleled by the same correspondences in the same languages in other word series. Not every vowel and consonant in each member of a series of related words can necessarily be brought into a set of correspondences; but where a number of segments in each of the words can be so related, the starred form is constructed to summarize these related segments.

* Only the roots of these words are historically related.

A single articulatory category of sound does not necessarily correspond to the same category of sound in another language, and one sound in one language may correspond to different sounds in different environments in another. Latin /qu/ is matched in Ancient Greek by /p/ before /a/ and /o/, and other consonants (/sequor/ ἕπομαι /hépomai/* (I) follow), and by /t/ before front vowels (/quis/ τίς /tís/ who?). Such multiple correspondences can be explained as the divergent changes undergone by phonetically different allophones of a single phoneme in an earlier stage in the history of the language family. This reinforces the point made above (8.1.1), that while similarities in the forms of words in different languages are the starting point in the establishment of historical relationships, it is upon regular correspondences that a fully documented language family rests, similarity of phonetic category being only a special and obvious case of correspondence.

The traditional view of the unitary language, with all the reservations about the phonetic implications of the starred forms set out in this chapter (*pp* 361-4), has been that there was a basic contrast in the plosive consonants between aspirated and unaspirated and between voiced and voiceless. Most historical linguists assumed a triadic system, represented for the denti-alveolar series by *d, *dh, and *t, the precise phonetic value of *dh being left indeterminate (some assumed a tetradic system *d, *dh, *t, and *th). But in the last decade two linguists of the Soviet Union, Gamkrelidze and Ivanov, have proposed a different triadic system with an ejective or glottalized set *t', *p', *k', a voiced set *d(h) etc, with allophonic aspiration, and a voiceless set *t(h) etc, with allophonic aspiration (the 'glottalic hypothesis').

If this hypothesis is accepted the historical processes underlying the correspondences in Grimm's Law will have to be revised, and so will much else in the early history of the Indo-European consonant changes. The phonemic distinction between glottalized and non-glottalized consonants is only found as a major phonological feature within the Indo-European family in Armenian, which borders on the non-Indo-European Causasian languages, in which such a contrast is much exploited. This will be an additional support, if the hypothesis is justified for the Indo-European homeland being located in the Caucasus area (8.1.11, *p* 366).[17]

8.1.7 The neogrammarian thesis

The maintenance of strict standards of regular correspondences between the component sounds of the words adduced as evidence of genetic relations between two or more languages is a key point in the scientific standing of historical linguistics. The need for this 'strict regularity hypothesis' was emphasized by a group of German scholars in the latter half of the nineteenth century. The name is a translation of *Junggrammatiker*, a nickname given to those who first insisted on this principle, as if they were a sort of political party, and from them what is called the **neogramma-rian** hypothesis or theory has, in a modified form, become part of the accepted theory of comparative and historical linguistics.[18]

As first formulated the hypothesis was that 'sound laws' were without exceptions; that is to say, within certain geographical limits and between certain dates a change of one sound in a language to another would affect in the same way all words containing the sound in the same phonetic environment of other sounds. It was soon seen that geographical and temporal limits in matters like this are hazy and indeterminate; one is dealing not with things, but with changes in rules and in habits, the ways people pronounce particular words. These changes cannot be expected to affect all words simultaneously, and on the borders between languages or dialects, some words may be subject to the change while others escape it or are affected by a different change.

The value of the hypothesis is not in the hypostatization of some sort of iron law operating blindly on languages in the course of time but as a working principle. As an ideal the linguist must not rest content with a series of sound correspondences between the words of two or more languages without being able to account for apparent exceptions, words which appear to contradict his statement of them. Broadly speaking four types of explanation may be called for:

[i] Words apparently belonging to a correspondence series are historically unrelated. Thus Latin /dieːs/ day, and the English word *day*, though similar in their initial consonants, and in their meanings, are not regarded as the result of divergence from a single word form, as the correspondences that regularly appear in such word pairs are Latin /d/ and English /t/ (/duo/ *two*; /ed-/ *eat;* /decem/ *ten*, etc, part of the more general correspondences system known as Grimm's Law (8.1.6, *p* 350)).

[ii] The rules by which the correspondences were stated were not drawn up strictly enough and must be modified by a number of subsidiary and more exact statements to account for all word series properly falling within their scope. For example the correspondence of voiceless plosive and frica-

tive does not apply when the sounds concerned follow a fricative in the word: Latin /tenuis/, English *thin* /θin/, but Latin /sta-/, English *stand*, Latin /est/, German *ist* /ʔist/. Another important modification to Grimm's Law is known as Verner's Law, from the name of the scholar who first worked it out; within the correspondences known under the general title of Grimm's Law some medial consonants show different correspondences according to the position of the accented (stressed) syllable of the word in the early period of I-E unity. This is most readily illustrated from Sanskrit and Gothic. We may compare Sanskrit /ˈbhraːtar-/, brother, with Gothic /ˈbroːθar/, and Sanskrit /piˈtar-/, father, with Gothic /ˈfadar/, with the Sanskrit accented syllables marked as they were pronounced in the earlier stages of the language. We see the different correspondences of the Germanic consonants with the Sanskrit /t/ (also seen in Latin /fraːter/ and /pater/). Later sound changes in Germanic languages such as English and German have obscured the earlier correspondences. The effect of differential stress placement on consonant articulation can be noticed in the English pair *exercise*, /ˈeksəsaiz/, and *exert* /egˈzəːt/.[19]

[iii] The apparently exceptional word is a loan word, that entered the language at a period subsequent to the operation of the sound change responsible for the particular form the correspondence takes.

[iv] The operation of the sound change in the particular word or words concerned has been prevented or reversed, or a different change has taken place, under the influence of analogy.

These last two factors are of great importance both in comparative and historical linguistics and in the history and development of every language, and must be considered in turn.

8.1.8 Loan words

Whenever there are culture contacts of any sort between the speakers of different languages, and this means virtually everywhere, speakers will make use of words from other languages to refer to things, processes, and the ways of behaviour, organization, or thinking, for which words or phrases were not available or convenient in their own language hitherto. Some of the foreign words so used by individual speakers pass into general currency in the language, being altered in pronunciation in the process in the direction of the sounds and phonological patterns of the language acquiring them. These are known, by a rather inappropriate metaphor, as **loan words** and their acquisition by a language is, equally inappropriately but traditionally, called 'borrowing'. They are most obviously exemplified in the words for foreign products; the words for coffee, tea, and tobacco, in English and in most European languages are all loans, from Arabic, Chinese, and an American-Indian language respectively, languages of the regions from which, or through which, these products were first imported into Europe.

Any prolonged cultural contact, especially with speakers of a language who enjoy political power or prestige in any sphere, leads to a considerable amount of borrowing of vocabulary from that language in the spheres concerned. One may instance the large influx of words of French origin into English after the Norman Conquest and the establishment of Norman rule in England, the borrowing of Greek words for terms in the sciences, arts, and philosophy into Latin as a result of Greek prestige in these fields in the ancient world, the similar borrowing of numbers of Sanskrit words into the non-I-E languages of India, and the later passage of a great deal of English vocabulary into all the languages of India during the period of English rule, especially in fields directly associated with it, such as government, railways, industrial development, etc. A noticeable linguistic result of the British development and popularization of organized sport in the nineteenth century and after is seen in the large number of sporting terms in European and other languages that are of British origin (eg French *le starter* /lə staː(r)tœːr/ the starter (of a race, etc), *le football* /lə futbɔl/ football, German *das Tennis* /das 'tɛnis/ tennis, Italian *lo sport* /lo spɔrt/ sport, etc). Apart from any other evidence, the strong representation of loan words form a single language in the vocabulary of one or more languages in an area is firm evidence of culture contacts of some sort.

Manifestly the term *loan* is only used sensibly in relation to a language assumed to be already in independent existence. One cannot regard the vocabulary of French that has been in continual use from Roman times, while the linguistic changes constituting the passage of Latin to French were taking place, as loan words from Latin, since French is simply the form taken by Latin in a certain part of Europe. Languages are in a continuous state of change, and loans must be considered as those words which were not in the vocabulary at one period and are in it at a subsequent one, without having been made up from the existing

lexical stock of the language or invented as entirely new creations, as, for example, certain names for products are (*kodak*,
etc). Loans are, in fact, entering a language all the time, but their
frequency and their sources are temporarily affected by political
or other factors leading to close cultural contacts of one sort or
another.

Loans entering a language after a sound change has ceased to
operate are not affected by it; conversely, loans entering before
or during its operation will be affected in the same way as any
other words containing the sound segments subject to the change.
Apparent exceptions to sound correspondences may be the
results of subsequent borrowing. Thus English *dental* does not
exhibit the /t/ /d/ correspondence with Latin /dent-/, tooth,
because it is a loan from Latin (*cp* French *dental* /dãtal/) subsequent to the period in which the sound changes involved in the
Grimm's Law correspondences were at work (the /d/ /t/ and
/t/ /θ/ correspondence is seen between Latin /dent-/ and English
tooth: cp Gothic *tunpus* /'tunθus/). French loan words with /iː/
that entered the English language soon after the Norman
conquest participated in the change of /iː/ to /ai/ mentioned
earlier (4.1); French *ligne* /liːɲ/ became *line* /lain/, just as Old
English *hwit* /hwiːt/ became *white* /wait/ but the later loan
machine /mə'ʃiːn/ still has the same type of vowel sound as in
French.

Normally loan words are assimilated to the phonetic sound
classes and the phonological patterns of the borrowing language,
the original consonants and vowels being replaced by consonants
and vowels as close to them as are available; thereafter, synchronically as opposed to historically, they are no longer recognizable
by their form as loans. However, in certain cases words continue
to be recognized and treated as foreign in origin, and attempts
are made to pronounce them as such. English *coupon* and *restau-
rant* when pronounced with the final analized vowel, and *rouge*
and *garage*, when pronounced with final /ʒ/, which does not
occur finally except in a few loans, are examples of this, and so
is the Italian *lo sport*; and the names of foreign persons and
places, unless so well known as to be almost international
linguistic property, are usually treated in this way also. This does
not mean that they are pronounced in the same way as they are
in the languages from which they have been taken (except by a
few specially gifted or trained persons), but it does mean that
they continue to be uttered with sounds or sequences of sounds
not found in the bulk of the vocabulary of the borrowing
language. There is a tendency for doublets of such words to

appear, assimilated and unassimilated, depending on the attitude or background of the speaker; /'restərənt/ is heard as well as /'restərɑ̄:/, and /'gæraːʤ or /'gæriʤ/ as well as /'gæraːʒ/.

Borrowed words are normally assimilated to the grammatical patterns of the borrowing language, along with its phonological patterns. German *Kindergarten* /'kindergarten/ as a loan word in English has the English plural *kindergartens* (the German plural form is *Kindergärten* /'kindergɛrten/). When the Russian noun *sputnik* /'sputnik/ satellite, came into English use after the first (Russian) space satellite was launced, its plural was at once *sputniks*, not *sputniki*, /'sputniki/, the Russian plural form. When the French culinary terms *purée*, pronounced as an English word /'pjuərei/, is used as a verb, it takes English inflections, *puréeing, puréed*, etc. But where a large number of words of one grammatical class are taken from a single source language, and especially if that language is itself an object of study, grammatical inflections may be borrowed as well. Thus we have in English Greek and Latin plurals like *phenomena* and *desiderata*, along with some doublets such as *cactuses/cacti* and *narcissuses/narcissi*.

In some cases a reanalysis of a complex loan word takes place as the result of the identification of a part of it with a quite different word in the borrowing language. The German proper name *Rothschild*, literally 'red-shield', is now pronounced /'rɔθstʃaild/ and hyphenated between two print lines as *Roths-child*, as if the second component was the English word *child*. After Greek speakers had come into contact with the Jewish people, the first half of the Hebrew name for their holy city Jerusalem, *Yerushalayim*, was identified with the Greek adjective ἱερός, /hierós/, sacred, and the regular Greek spelling became ἱεροσόλμα, /Hierosólyma/.

A special sort of loan word is found in many languages, loans taken directly from the vocabulary of dead languages that have attained the status of classics. Since the Renaissance all European languages have quarried in Latin and Greek for scientific, literary, artistic, philosophical, and learned vocabulary generally, freely producing from Latin and Greek morphemes words that have no necessary correspondent in Ancient Greek or Latin (*microorganism, reinvestment*, etc). This process took place in the Romance languages as well, themselves derived from Latin, as much as in other groups. Direct borrowing from a dead language is quite separate from the gradual change of one language over the course of time. Greek and Latin morphemes are often mixed in one word (*naturalism, monolingual*), though hitherto there has been some reluctance over the coining of neologisms with Latin or Greek morphemes and morphemes of other languages together in a single word. This process is, however, increasing, and is freely used in technological vocabulary (*speedometer, megaton*). Elsewhere, Sanskrit morphemes provide a similar source of loan neologisms in a number of Indian languages, and Chinese morphemes are formed into a number of polymorphemic Japanese words without counterparts in the stages of Chinese languages from which the component morphemes are taken.[20]

8.1.9 Analogy

The other factor that may account for divergences from the strict application of regular sound changes is **analogy**, a universal process in the history of languages.

It is only by virtue of regularities of word form and sentence structure that languages can operate at all as means of communication; nevertheless in all known languages a number of exceptions to the general patterns are found, the so-called irregular forms. Western antiquity was well aware of the two contrasting features of regularity and irregularity in the word forms of the languages they were interested in (Latin and Ancient Greek, in the main), and referred to them as analogy and anomaly respectively, different scholars stressing one or the other as a dominant feature.[21]

In so far as any universal trend can be properly discerned in the grammatical development of languages, it would seem that it lies in the direction of replacing irregular forms by more regular ones (although contrary instances are also found, 6.5). When the early history of mankind is considered, it may be surmised that, in the small speech communities that must have existed in sparsely populated areas without much wide intercourse or permanent contacts outside, irregularities would be far more tolerable than in a language serving ever wider spheres of communication. At the other extreme one finds the fewest irregularities in deliberately created artificial languages, like Esperanto, and in some of the trade jargons or Creole languages that arose out of the needs of intercourse between people of greatly different linguistic and cultural backgrounds (9.1.2).

In its widest sense analogy is at work in every utterance and understanding of a sentence not hitherto heard by either party, and in the similar use of forms of variable word paradigms that have not so far occurred with a particular root in the experience of a particular speaker.

The replacement of an irregular or suppletive form within a grammatical paradigm by a new form modelled on the forms of the majority of members of the class to which the word in question belongs is the work of analogical creation. Individual examples of this are repeatedly found in the speech of children and foreign speakers with incomplete command of a language; '*seed*' /siːd/ and '*hitted*' /'hitid/, as mistaken past tense forms of *see* and *hit*, are analogical creations. Often such forms are corrected by others and never pass beyond a stage in the acquisition of the language by individuals; but, for reasons not wholly understood, some such individual variations persist and are adopted by others in widening circles until they come to be accepted beside and ultimately to replace the older forms. The virtual supersession of *kine* by *cows* as the plural of *cow* is an example of successful analogical creation, and so are the more modern regular past tense forms *helped, climbed*, and *snowed*, for the earlier *holp, clomb*, and *snew*. A few contrary examples of analogy are found in which word forms belonging to regular, majority, patterns are remodelled on the analogy of minority patterns. *Rang* and *rung* as past tense and past participle forms of the verb *ring* are the result of analogy on such patterns as *sing, sang, sung*, as the earlier corresponding Old English verb *hringan* /'hriŋgan/ followed the regular past tense formation. But almost every newly created word that enters the vocabulary of a language, like loan words, if it is assigned to a class of variable words, follows by analogy the patterns of the majority of regular words in the class, for example *television* and *xerox* (*televisions, xeroxed*).

There is, however, in the very regularity of sound changes on which the neogrammarians insisted, a constant source of grammatical irregularities. Such changes working on every example of a sound in the same phonetic environment in the same way, irrespective of its place in a grammatical paradigm, may serve to produce paradigmatic irregularities. At a certain period in English the words *sword* and *swore* lost their /w/ sound before the back rounded vowel; *sword* is still pronounced /sɔːd/, but the current pronunciation of *swore* as /swɔː/ is the result of analogical reformation through association with the other members of the paradigm, *swear, swears, swearing*, in which the /w/ was not affected anyway. At an early stage in Ancient Greek intervocalic /s/ had ceased to be pronounced (*eg* (Homeric Greek) γένεος, /géneos/, race (genitive singular), *cp* Sanskrit /janasas/), but it was retained in past tense verb forms like ἔλυσα /élyːsa/ (I) loosed, under the analogic influence of forms like ἔπεμψα /épempsa/ (I) sent (root /pemp-/), in which it was not subject to loss, since it was not intervocalic. Latin intervocalic /s/ became /r/ (*cp* Latin /generis/, race (genitive singular)). So we have nominal case forms such as /hono:s/, honour (nominative), /hono:rem/ (accusative), /hono:ris/ (genitive), etc. Forms like /hono:s/, however, were already regarded as old-fashioned, as /honor/ and similar often nominative forms had begun to replace them through analogy with the rest of the paradigm of case forms.

The contrary and conflicting tendencies in the historical development of languages represented by phonetic change and analogy have been summarized by Sturtevant: 'Phonetic laws are regular but produce irregularities. Analogic creation is irregular but produces regularity.[22]

8.1.10 Sound change and generative grammar

We have seen (4.4.4) how generative grammarians frame their phonological descriptions of languages as series of P(honological) rules working on the surface syntactic structure of sentences and the underlying lexical forms of words to generate the actual phonetic forms of utterance. Just as synchronic grammars are grammars of rules, so linguistic change is treated as changes in one or more of the rules of a language or a dialetc of a language. Sound changes are changes in the operation of P-rules. Thus when the past tense of *snow* became *snowed* in place of the earlier *snew, snow* fell out of the set of words (the 'input') to which the vowel alteration rule applied. In phonological changes of the sort involved in Grimm's Law, these changes are listed as rules operating on certain sounds in certain phonological contexts, incorporated into the language in a certain period of time: 'By and large the familiar "sounds laws" are, in fact, rules added to the phonological component.' In addition to the incorporation of new rules, or the loss of existing rules, rules may be ordered differently, as between two dialects, to produce the different word forms that are observed.[23]

The description of these and other generative interpretations of sound changes is organized by the linguist so as to maximize the simplicity of the totality of rules in the language, in order to match what is held to be the child's intuitions as he builds up his grammar from the random material to which he is exposed in his early years. Ultimately it may be assumed that the underlying lexical forms of words, to which the rules are applied, are themselves restructured, so that some of the sound changing rules themselves may be dropped and the whole system thereby simplified. But it is notable that in their chapter on the evolution of the English vowels Chomsky and Halle operate a set of rules deriving present-day English forms from their Middle English counterparts, largely matching their descriptive sequence of rules that lead from underlying forms to actual pronounced forms.[24]

As with the synchronic rules of generative descriptive grammars, the formal notation of the rules expressing sound changes is best followed in the relevant specialist literature, but a simple example may be of help here as an illustration. Between early German and modern German final voiced stop consonants lost their voicing, so that today *Rat*, council, and *Rad*, wheel, are pronounced alike as /raːt/. We can say that at some time a devoicing rule was incorporated that affected word final stops:

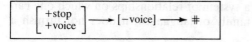

$$\begin{bmatrix} +\text{stop} \\ +\text{voice} \end{bmatrix} \longrightarrow [-\text{voice}] \longrightarrow \#$$

That is to say, a consonant segment that has the features stop and voice becomes voiceless in word final position. The orthography preserves the representation of the earlier form, and we continue to set up two underlying forms today, /raːt/ and /raːd/, and the devoicing rule, in order to account most simply for the genitive singulars *Rates*, /raːtes/, and *Rades*, /raːdes/, and other derivational and inflectional forms of these words.[25]

8.1.11 Historical inferences
After reviewing the processes that govern the changes taking place in languages in the course of centuries, one is now in a position to review the historical inferences that may legitimately be made in the light of the linguistic evidence. Since the systematic correspondences that form the basis of comparative and historical linguistics can only be explained on the assumption of a once closer relationship between the earlier stages of the languages that exhibit them, they may, in conjunction with what is known about the sources and dates of loan words, throw great light on the history of the languages and the linguistic communities concerned.[26]

It is important not to go beyond the legitimate historical deductions from the linguistic evidence. Languages are not peoples, they are simply the speech rules and the speech habits of peoples; and the history of languages is part of the material of the history of peoples, but no more. The evidence of the systematic correspondences of word forms must not be misinterpreted, as is often done in the case of the 'starred forms' that are set up to summarize them. Such misinterpretation is rather encouraged by the misleading title 'reconstruction' which is given to these forms and the general process by which they are established.

Basically 'starred forms' are abbreviations of the correspondences exhibited between phonetic components of series of words of similar or related meanings in different languages, that may be matched by like series of words in the languages. The fact that these forms can be set up within a group of languages indicates a historical relationship of divergence from a more closely related state between the languages, but the 'starred forms' themselves are simply formulae summarizing the attested correspondences. The great French philologist Meillet put the matter succinctly: 'Comparison provides a system of relationships on which one can base the history of a family of languages; it does not furnish a real language.[27]

The 'starred forms', or misdesignated 'reconstructions', give reasons for assuming the existence of an earlier relatively unitary stage of I-E (or any other family established in this way), the so-called Ursprache, or parent language; but they do not constitute it, or represent word forms in it or in any language. The evidence for the earlier existence of an Ursprache is not the same as bits of the Ursprache itself.

The letters of writing systems of actual languages, however inadequate they may be as phonological representations, can be referred to the sound units of the languages at a given time, and the words of actual languages may be represented in transcriptions as analysable into the units of phonological systems. But it cannot be assumed that all the letters of the 'starred forms' in I-E necessarily represent the actual sounds, or the actual phonemes, of the 'parent language' for whose existence at some time in the past they provide the evidence.

Certainly the choice of letter or symbols used in the representation of these forms is guided by the aim of indicating the earliest phonetic shapes that can be ascribed to members of the word series involved, on the basis of the forms actually attested. In the traditional view, in the Germanic languages earlier /b/, /d/, and /g/ changed under Grimm's Law to /p/, /t/, and /k/ (subsequently. to undergo further changes in some of the languages); one represents the initial consonantal element of the formula summarizing the correspondences of Latin /duo/, Ancient Greek δύο /dýo/, Sanskrit dvā /dwaː/, English two /tuː/, German zwei /tsvai/, etc, with a d, rather than with a t or some other letter. But these forms, in so far as they can be said to give any information about the early pronunciation of the words, simply reach back as far as is possible on the available evidence to what may reasonably be considered as the earliest pronounced forms we have any right to assume. Essentially they are formulae summarizing correspondences, but as these correspondences are historically significant, the letters in them, instead of being no more than arbitrary symbols, are chosen to indicate as much as can be inferred about the early history of the words concerned.[28]

The difference between 'starred forms' that summarize the evidence for I-E and the word forms of an actual once-existing I-E language may be made clearer by considering the position of these essentially different linguistic entities within the most controlled field of comparative and historical linguistics that we have, namely the Romance languages, in which we have copious correspondence series, historical knowledge of the communities, and actual material preserved from the earlier unitary language.

The formulae set up on the basis of corresponding word forms in present-day Romance languages do in many instances coincide with an actual word form in spoken Latin, in so far as its spelling may be used to infer its pronunciation, but in others this is not so. From the series Italian *capo* /'kapo/ head, Spanish *cabo* /'kabo/ end, French *chef* /ʃɛf/ chief, etc, one would not be led to set up the formula **caput*, as there is no evidence of a final /t/ in any of the cognate words of this series in the languages today; but written records make clear that the Latin word for head was /caput/. Apart from the local language of Sardinia, no present-day Romance language preserves the Latin /k/ before front vowels. Latin had words like /cervus/ stag, and /caelum/ (later /ceːlum/) sky, and it is known that in these and all other words /c/ was a velar plosive.[29] Sardinian still has a /k/ sound in the words /'kerbu/, /'kelu/; in the other Romance languages the sound has long since passed to an affricate or a fricative (Italian *cervo* /'tʃɛrvo/, *cielo* /'tʃɛlo/; Spanish *ciervo* /'θjervo/, *cielo* /'θjelo/; French *cerf* /sɛrf/, *ciel*, /sjɛl/). Alone among the existing Romance languages, only Sardinian happens to preserve the evidence for the pronunciation of a velar plosive in these words in Latin. This shows how wary one must be in attempting to reconstruct actual pronounced forms in parent languages, even in the relatively close-knit Romance languages, were it not for the external and fortuitous data that we have in our records of spoken Latin itself.[30]

With possibilities such as these of discrepancies between the actual forms of the earlier unitary languages and the formulae that arise from the existing evidence, one perceives the need to be very cautious indeed in assuming that the formulae set up for I-E as a whole, where the time gap is much longer, the linguistic divergences much greater, the attested forms of corresponding series of words much more varied, and the language itself irretrievably lost, represent any sort of actual word form in an actual, though no longer extant, language.

For the same sort of reasons, one must beware of interpreting the 'family tree' representation of linguistic families too literally. Leaving out many of the smaller languages, one can diagram the I-E family in this way:

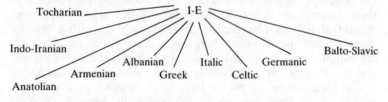

with all but Armenian, Albanian, and Greek followed by further major language branches:

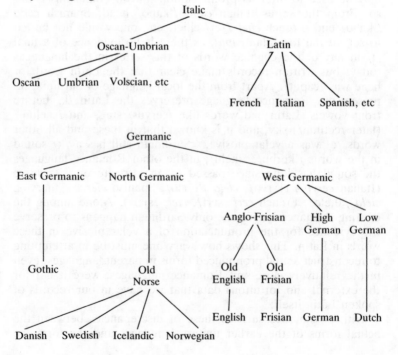

If dialectal differences within the modern languages are included, these appear at the bottom of the tree:

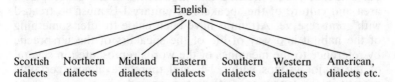

This suggests that the dialects are the most recent linguistic development, as of course some are, but the lack of easy communications between scattered and scanty groups of people in ancient and prehistoric times must have favoured greater dialectal variation, of which we shall never have any record. I-E itself, as the earliest stage of the I-E languages that we are able to infer (not literally to 'reconstruct'), though unitary as a language, must have been cut up by numerous dialect divisions, some of the differences between the major language groups within it being the results of a gradual widening of such divisions.[31] Many different languages of the I-E family developing in this way from dialects within it must have disappeared without trace, as Gothic in the East Germanic group might have done; we are just aware of some such vanished I-E languages, such as Phrygian, from external historical records, and a few inscriptions. Owing to the early development and spread of literacy among many different speech communities in Ancient Greece (Chapter 2, note 18) we know more about the dialect situation in Greece than in any other part of the Ancient World; but such knowledge is exceptional.

Languages do not live, beget children, and die, as people do, for whom the genealogical tree diagram was originally designed (though terms like *parent language* and *daughter* of *sister languages* suggest they they do). In particular, languages do not separate sharply, at a given time, as might be implied by the tree diagram; during periods of contact adjacent dialects may continue to influence each other to a considerable extent while in other respects the differences between them are widening.[32]

Though tree diagrams read downwards from the top do bear correspondences with the changes that have taken place in a development language family in the course of time, they should properly be read upwards as a diagram of how the linguist is able, on the evidence available to him, to set about grouping together different languages in historically connected sets of families.

The difference between the actual I-E attested and existing languages, and the 'starred forms' which are the summaries of our evidence for it, indicate that arguments on the geographical area and culture of the speakers of unitary I-E must be treated with great reserve. Attempts have been made to infer something of the habitat and way of life of the speakers of the Ursprache by reference to the meanings of the words represented in several of the major groups within I-E and therefore almost certainly present in the language in its unitary period.

Arguments for one area or another have turned on the likelihood of the words in several I-E languages for particular minerals, useful or cultivated plants, domesticated animals or those used as food, etc being derived from words forming part of the vocabulary of the inferred unitary language. This aspect of comparative and historical linguistics is sometimes given the title of **linguistic palaeontology**. It cannot claim more than probable conclusions. A common meaning for all attested members of a series of cognate words is no guarantee that an earlier common 'ancestor' form had the same meaning. Meanings are not labels carried around by words and remaining unchanged through time, but are simply what may be abstracted as common to the various uses of them in sentences uttered in situations as meaningful discourse (1.4). We have no sentences of a language whose existence is just inferred, and no way of hoping to get any. Moreover, one notices that some obviously related words have different referents in different languages; /faːgus/ in Latin means 'beech tree', φηγός/ pʰeːgós/ in Ancient Greek refers to a species of oak tree; where time differences are greater and culturally relevant factors in situations more divergent, more extensive semantic differences must be allowed for. But if the inherent limitations are recognized, some light may be shed on certain features of the possible way of life of the earliest speakers of I-E languages whose existence we may infer; and on this basis some scholars have argued that the unitary I-E language, or group of dialects, was spoken around 3000 BC by a people living in an area of South Asia north of the Black Sea and near the Caucasus mountains, with some use of domestic animals and with a patriarchal social order.[33]

The comparative and historical study of languages dominated the whole field of linguistics in Europe for nearly a century, and today it remains for many the most fascinating branch of the subject. This is partly due to the feeling that from linguistic evidence by linguistic inference we are enabled to pierce the veil of ignorance that shuts us off from so much of our own prehistory, and by similar methods to penetrate the prehistory of other peoples speaking languages of different families. It is necessary to proceed from the linguistic to the extralinguistic with great circumspection; but quite apart from such applications of this part of linguistic studies, the detailed investigations of the history of different languages, of the spread of languages over new territories and the replacement of one language by another among groups of people, of linguistic diversification in conditions of isolation and of linguistic unification in conditions of proximity and social intercourse, of the changes in word forms, of the acquisition of loan words, and of the operations of analogy, all serve to bring before our eyes that ways in which 'time and change' and changing conditions, internal and external, work out their effects on the languages of mankind.

8.2 Typological comparison

8.2.1 General principles

Historically orientated linguistic comparison, comparative and historical linguistics, or comparative philology, is probably the best known form of the comparative study of languages, and, indeed, of linguistic studies generally, to many people, both because of its traditional place in classical studies in European universities and because of the exciting prospects it offers of throwing light on some of the darker places in mankind's earlier history. It is, however, possible to compare languages, to study them systematically in relations to each other, simply by reference to any significant general features of form or structural organization that they share at any level of analysis. Such comparisons group languages together in that they jointly exhibit features of some sort in common, other than those features which are exhibited in common by all languages and so form part of the nature of language itself. Comparison of languages on this basis is usually distinguished from the comparison described in the preceding sections of this chapter by the title of **typological comparison**.

Typology is really an attempt to provide a formal and systematic way of answering every tiro's question about a language new to him: 'What is this language like?'

Comparative and historical linguistics, as was seen, bases its comparisons on the correspondences between the forms of individual words of similar or related meanings. Its material is individual lexical items in different languages. Typological comparison is based on general features of the systems and structures of languages, and thus forms part of the wider process of classification of any observed phenomena according to revealed similarities of form and structure. Its linguistic groups are set up irrespective of historical language families, and these may in part agree with them or they may cut across their boundaries.

The nature and function of human language imposes limits on the forms it may take. Every natural language is primarily a spoken medium of communication, and the forms of written languages, though not identical or to be equated with their spoken counterparts, are obviously controlled and are to be understood by reference to the essential spoken nature of language. These limitations may be seen on either side of language, where it is linked to the extralinguistic world. Phonetically, the physiology of the human vocal organs sets limits on the types of sounds that can be produced, and the physiology of the ear and the perceptual centres of the brain sets limits on the degree to which sounds used in continuous discourse may be acoustically similar and yet serve efficiently as phonologically distinctive units and features. Speech consists of serial events occurring in time, and the signalling devices in languages must, therefore, be such as can be manifested by means of a series of sounds and sound features, just as in writing they are manifested in linear successions of letters, syllable signs, or characters. Moreover, spoken communication must take account of the limits of short-term memory; otherwise the hearer will 'lose his or her way' in trying to follow what is being said. Spoken sentences must be adequately structured and these structures adequately signalled by means available to the speaker and accessible to the hearer. The hearer cannot 'go back', as the reader can, which is why, of course, sentences composed purely for silent reading may be both longer and more complicated than sentences intended to be spoken or to be read aloud.

On the other side, any language must be adequate for the communication needs of its speakers. The distinctive sound differences must be combinable in a sufficiently diverse number of separate word and morpheme forms to provide for an adequate word stock or lexicon; and these lexical resources of a language must be organized into a sufficiently flexible and productive grammatical system to produce sentences of the different types and patterns required for communication, readily understandable by other speakers of the same language. The double structuring of all languages in phonological and grammatical systems is the means whereby the physiologically limited possibilities of sound production and recognition can be made to serve the unlimited demands that languages have to meet in fulfilling the diverse and ever-changing needs of speech communities.[34]

Within these limits of speech production and speech requirements, languages differ in the ways in which they fulfil their purposes; and these differences may be observed at every level of language and linguistic analysis. This sort of comparison gives rise to typological classification, languages being assigned to typological classes. Languages are typologically classified according to the similarities of form they exhibit with other languages at any level or levels. This type of linguistic comparison is best explained by illustrations from the main levels in which similarities of formal constitution are exhibited. Some of the classifications so produced have already been noticed implicitly in earlier chapters in which the different features and categories were mentioned.

8.2.2 Phonetic typology

At the phonetic level it is an obvious fact, readily noticed by those acquainted with more than one language, that some groups of languages make use of similar ranges of sounds, while others differ more widely from them in the types of sound they employ. Often enough languages sharing a number of the major sound features of one's own language are regarded as easy to speak, and those differing more widely are felt to be hard to speak, since they require the learning of a greater number of different phonetic habits than do the former. The main articulatory positions, bilabial, dental or alveolar, and velar, and the main articulatory processes, voice and voicelessness, plosion and friction, oral and nasal release, and some other, are employed in all, or in almost all, languages, but within these limits very marked phonetic differences are found. This is part of the difficulty of learning to speak foreign languages and the reason why many people who do, do so 'with an accent'.

Standard English does not make any distinctive use of glottalized consonants. Cockney speakers often have glottalized stops intervocalically (*copper* /ˈkɔpˀə/, *ripper* /ˈripˀə/), and make frequent use of medial glottal stops in positions where speakers of standard English have /p/, /t/, or /k/ (*what bad luck* /ˈwɔʔ ˈbæd ˈlʌʔ/). But several languages in different parts of the world make regular and systematic use of glottalized consonants just as English does of voiced consonants. Languages may be grouped into classes on the basis of shared phonetic features or types of articulation that play an important part in their phonological systems while being only represented to a limited extent or altogether lacking in others.

Features like glottalization appear in languages spoken in several different parts of the world, and frequently cut right across linguistic families established by the methods of comparative and historical linguistics. It has been noticed that languages that occupy geographically contiguous areas, whether they are related or not in descent, often share common phonetic characteristics. Three instances may be cited. Ejective consonants, of limited or insignificant use in most European languages, are very prominent in the phonetics of several languages of the Caucasus area; among these are Georgian, Armenian, and Ossetic, languages spoken in contiguous regions, but belonging to different families, Armenian and Ossetic being I-E languages, and Georgian one of the members of the Caucasian family. In many languages of India, both the I-E languages descended from Sanskrit in the north and the genetically distinct Dravidian languages of the south, a series of retroflex consonants is found, articulated with the tongue tip curled back towards the roof of the mouth (3.3.4), and phonologically distinct from consonants articulated with dental closure or friction. This mode of articulation is also found in another language family, Munda, not related genetically to I-E or Dravidian, comprising some languages spoken in parts of central India. It is only sporadically represented in other I-E languages (*eg* in Scandinavia), except for the *r* sounds of some English dialects. Within Europe and the I-E family, the feature of distinctive front rounded vowels, familiar in French (*lune* /lyn/ moon, *peu* /pø/ little, *bœuf* /bœf/ beef), is found in neighbouring German, Dutch, Swedish, Norwegian, and Danish, all Germanic languages, but not in most dialects of English, nor in the Romance languages Italian, Spanish, or Portuguese. Facts such as these have been explained in part as the result of the spreading of phonetic habits across genetic family boundaries as a result of population movements and the effects of bilingualism. Similar regional resemblances in features of grammatical organization have also been found.[35]

8.2.3 Phonological typology

Perhaps of more significance are typological classifications based not primarily upon the presence in languages of particular phonetic features, but on the different ways in which the sounds and sound features of languages are organized into phonological systems and syllable structures. Such classifications have been made on a number of different dimensions.

The distinction between tone languages and the non-tonal languages, according to the functions assigned in them to differences of voice pitch, though not as clear-cut as is sometimes supposed, represents a major typological classification that has already been referred to (3.5.4). Within the tone languages a distinction may be made between those whose tones, phonologically considered, may be analysed in terms of different and contrasting levels (as in several tone languages of Africa) and those wherein rising and falling tones must be recognized as forming part of the tone system itself (as in the Chinese languages, 4.3.5). Further classifications may be made on the basis of the different numbers of tones involved and on the different uses to which they are put (cp 6.4.6).

One of the more noticeable differences between languages lies in the different types of syllable structures permitted (4.3.4). While syllables of the type CV are found in every known language, English and German are distinguished from many others by the degree of consonant clustering allowed in syllable initial and syllable final position, and Fijian and Hawaiian are languages notable for the simplicity of their syllable structures in terms of consonant and vowel elements occurring in the two positions and for their paucity of consonantal clusters. The possibilities of syllable structures in different languages may be arranged on a scale, with those languages that permit the greatest degree of syllabic complexity at one end, those with the least at the other. Languages then fall into relative places on the scale and may be grouped into classes on this basis accordingly; but as these classifying differences are on a more or less continuous scale, the number of different classes and the dividing lines between them have to be decided arbitrarily. On such a scale, some of the Caucasian languages would come near one end, with the greatest degree of syllabic complexity, English and German fairly up towards this end, and Japanese and some of the Oceanic languages at the other end with very simple syllable structures.

Syllabic structure classification relates to the syntagmatic dimension of phonology. Languages also differ in the paradigmatic dimension according to the composition of their phonological systems in terms of distinctive consonant and vowel elements, and may be grouped into classes accordingly. A scalar classification may be made according to the relative numbers of distinctive consonants and vowels. Languages have also been classified according to the interrelations of their consonant and vowel elements considered as distinct phonemes. This sort of classification was pioneered by Trubetzkoy. One may, for

example, distinguish languages with vowel systems organized in
two principal dimensions, open and close, and front and back,
with lip spreading accompanying front vowels and lip rounding
accompanying back vowels (Italian and Spanish), and languages
making independent use of the three dimensions, open and close,
front and back, and lip spreading and lip rounding (French,
German, Turkish). Consonant systems may similarly be classified
according to the number of articulatory places and processes
characterizing the greater part of each system. English plosive
and nasal consonants fall into a three-place and three-process
system, bilabial, alveolar, velar, and voiceless, voiced, nasal:

If the rectangle is extended, *eg* by including the affricates /tʃ/
and /dʒ/ in the alveolar column, it is no longer possible to fill
out all the places, as there are no bilabial or velar affricates in
English.

Ancient Greek had a three-place and four-process system,
bilabial, dental, velar, and unaspirated, voiced, nasal:

In terms of distinctive consonant units, or phonemes, the Greek
system has a gap in the velar column, as [ŋ] was a positional
variant of /n/ (an allophone of /n/), occurring before a velar
consonant (written with the γ letter in the Greek alphabet).

Sanskrit and some modern Indian languages have a system of
five contrasting processes: voiceless unaspirated and aspirated,
voiced unaspirated and aspirated, and nasal, /p/, /pʰ/, /b/, /bʰ/,
/m/, etc.[36]

8.2.4 Grammatical typology

At the grammatical level, languages may be classified according
to the predominant characteristics of their grammatical systems.
In one such dimension, Chinese and several languages of South-
east Asia stand at one extreme, in relying almost entirely on
word order and word class membership as the markers of
syntactic relationships and sentence structures, and are in
contrast with languages like Latin and Ancient Greek, wherein
word order is relatively free grammatically, and syntactic

relationships and sentence structures are mostly marked by the morphological categories of concord and government (6.4.2) exhibited by the word forms of different word classes. On this dimension, English, French, and German lie somewhere in the middle between the two extremes, with English further towards the Chinese end of the scale than the other two, and French further towards it than German.

Word order itself provides interesting typological criteria for classification. It has been found that two of the commonest preferred orders in simple sentences are subject–verb–object (SVO) and subject–object–verb (SOV), though other orders, VSO, for example, are found; modern English, French, and German are among examples of the former, SVO, and Japanese and Turkish of the latter, SOV, while Latin, despite its grammatically very free word order, showed a definite stylistic preference for an SOV order in sentences not specifically marked for emphasis.

Within the languages relying heavily on categories of concord and government (Latin, Ancient Greek, Sanskrit, Swahili, etc) further classifications may be made according to the types of categories involved (case, gender, number, tense, etc) and the relative weight placed upon each. Languages vary according to the relative weight of grammatical categories formally concentrated on words of different grammatical classes (6.2); but it appears to be a general feature of languages with morphologically marked grammatical categories that the verb classes carry more morphologically marked categories than the noun classes. Abaza, a Caucasian language, has been cited as an extreme case of a verb-centred language in which the verb form represents in itself a sort of small-scale model of the structure of the whole sentence, of which it forms the syntactic centre. For some linguists the division between ergative and non-ergative ('nominative-accusative') languages, with some languages lying between the two classes, is a typological distinction of high importance.

There may be observed a tendency for similar grammatical types to appear in geographically contiguous areas, comparable to the areas of phonetic similarity noticed in 8.2.2. The systematic study of the geographical spread of phonetic and grammatical features sometimes goes under the title of **areal linguistics**.[37]

8.2.5 Linguistic typology and linguistic universals

Clearly, features at any level are of major interest in typology if they characterize the language as a whole either by being themselves of major relevance throughout a level or by forming part of a set of such features. A phonological feature such as lexically distinctive tone or a grammatical feature such as ergativity are themselves features of pervasive importance. But, for example, the marking of yes/no questions by an enclitic particle, unless it could be shown to be typologically linked with other related features, would be of itself of limited interest in the typology of languages, however important it was in the individual description of that language. This quest for typological features of wide significance has been termed 'holistic typology'.[38]

Certainly basic word order, mentioned in the preceding section, is of considerable importance in itself, but it has become much more so since researches have shown a strong correlation, though a variable one, with other features. Languages with a basic SOV order mostly use postpositions to mark the syntactic and semantic relations marked in SVO languages by prepositions. Turkish and Japanese, for example, contrast here with English. Moreover, SOV languages generally put qualifying words and phrases before the words that they qualify, adverbs before verbs, and adjectives before nouns, again as in Turkish and Japanese. English and French, SVO languages, are less consistent in this respect; English adjectives precede their nouns as a general rule, though in French this is lexically variable (6.3.3), and in both languages the position of adverbs varies considerably, being dependent on a number of factors. The strict rule by which qualifiers precede the words that they qualify in Japanese and Turkish is matched by their lack of separate relative pronouns and postnominal relative clauses, such as characterize most European languages, and their prenominal embedding of clauses endocentrically attached to nouns by the use of specific verb forms and attributive verbal constructions (6.3.2, *p* 223).

Considerations of this sort, set out by Greenberg in 1961, [39] raise an important point. Typological classification is not an all or none question. As we have noticed before (3.5.4), the distinction between tonal and non-tonal languages is not absolute, and languages may share ergative and non-ergative syntactic structures. The associations and implications referred to in the preceding paragraph are tendencies, statistically evaluated, not strict rules, and in general languages should be classified typologically by their salient tendencies towards one sort of organization at each level rather than towards another, with some languages being 'purer', or more 'consistent' in their types than others, all this being no doubt partly the product of their historical circumstances (English, incidentally, is in several respects a rather mixed language typologically).[40]

This relative indeterminacy of typological classes has led to the formulation of hierarchical tendencies in regard to some features. As an example, some languages in Australia and elsewhere having both 'nominative-accusative' and ergative constructions, it can be shown that some nominals are more likely to occur as subjects in nominative constructions but that others are more likely to appear as ergatives in similar semantic relationships, and that the preferential ranking of nominal sets of words and phrases appears along the same hierarchy in quite unrelated languages. The first and second personal pronouns come at the top of the nominative ranking, while inanimate nouns and noun phrases come at the bottom and are the most likely to be represented as ergatives.[41] Essentially the more 'active' or 'agent-like' the referent of the nominal element is, the more appropriate it is for it to fall in with the subject in all sentence types.

We may note that in Latin and English, both nominative-accusative languages, classical Latin avoided making inanimate nouns the subjects of transitive verbs: /miːliteːs tempestaːte impediːti: sunt/, the soldiers were held up by bad weather, would be preferred to /tempestaːs miːliteːs impediit/, bad weather held up the soldiers. And in English the sentence *a rock damaged our car on the road* would imply that the rock was moving (falling or rolling) and so at the time quasi-animate; if it had been merely lying there, a passive sentence *our car was damaged by a rock on the road* would be more likely.

After relative neglect during the later nineteenth century, linguistic typology is now being actively researched in a number of European, Asian, and American universities, sometimes in institutes specifically devoted to its problems and its achievements.

Mention has already been made of linguistic universals in relation to typology. There is a twofold relationship here, depending on the conception of universals that is under consideration. In part this depends on the standpoint taken on the distinction between the 'internalist' and the 'externalist' approaches to the study of language as a human capability and activity (1.2.1). Many consider universals of language, linguistic universals, as a biologically inherited set of constraints characterizing the 'language organ' of the brain rather as the human liver, kidneys, etc or a fly's eyes are biologically determined to develop and perform the functions that they do perform, ultimately as the result of their evolutionary inheritance.[42] Comparable constraints on the phonetics of human speech are more readily understood, through an inspection of the physiological capabilities and limitations of the human vocal tract.[43]

Such a set of universals can, it is asserted, be inferred from the examination of a few or even of one language, as a working hypothesis to be tested, but to be accepted until falsified. These universals act as restraints on the ways and on the extent of language variations. This is the conception of universals broadly outlined in 7.2.4, above, but many linguists today aim at drawing the boundaries much more firmly and in greater precision.

On the other side, however, the sorts of clusters of features, or typological implications, being investigated by typologists following the proposals of Greenberg, also appeal to universals of language, as is clear from the titles of several books written on this aspect of typology.[44] These are inductive universals, not assumed as essential to the very existence of language, but arrived at from the analysis and comparison of many languages, in line with the 'externalist' approach to linguistic science. They are inductive rather than hypothetical, no less the objects of further testing and validation, but at no time are they considered to be more than statistical findings from existing data, taking the form of stating that if one feature predominates in a language then certain other features are more often than not found also in that language (some examples have already been given).

Ultimately these two attitudes may produce the same results; but as things are they view the variability of languages and the universals of language from different viewpoints: on the one hand, what we must assume in order to explain the way in which languages are acquired and used, and on the other hand, what associations and implications of features come to light in the typological analysis of many languages, not as absolutes or hypothetical necessities, but statistically always more than random co-occurrences.

8.2.6 Structural typology

In dealing with the typological classification of languages, the best-known procedure has so far been left unmentioned. This is the threefold division of languages into the **isolating** or 'analytic', **agglutinative**, and **fusional** or 'inflecting' types, and it is associated with Wilhelm von Humboldt, a German linguist of the late eighteenth and early nineteenth centuries, though others, in particular the brothers F. and A. W. Schlegel, had published work on these lines before him.[45] Just because it is concerned with a very central area of language organization and involves both phonological and grammatical structure, it may profitably be looked at in the light of what has been said in the preceding section. Von Humboldt put forward this tripartite division as a means of classifying languages as total systems of communication, but it is more strictly a classification of the word structures of languages and of the way in which phonological structures and grammatical structures are related in word forms. Features of isolation, agglutination, and fusion are usually to be found in most languages, though in different proportions, and as a mode of typological classification, like other typological classifications, the three types are best regarded as directions towards which languages approach with greater or lesser purity.

English is in fact a fairly mixed type of language in respect of the three types, and each can be illustrated from English. Invariable words, such as prepositions, conjunctions, and many adverbs, are isolating in type; they exhibit no formal paradigms, in many cases they are monomorphemic (*eg: since, from, as, when, seldom, now*), and their grammatical status and class membership are entirely determined by their syntactic relations with the rest of the sentences in which they occur, without formal mark of these appearing in their own word structure. Morphologically complex words, in which individual grammatical categories may be fairly easily assigned to morphemes strung together serially in the structure of the word, exemplify the process of agglutination; *illegalities* /i-liː'g-æ-iti-z/, *ungodlines*/ʌn-'gɔd-li-nis/, *unavoidably* /ʌn-ə'vɔid-əbl-i/, *and stabilizers* /'steibil-aiz-ə-z/, are examples from English of agglutinative word structures. Words in which several grammatical categories are marked by word forms in which it is difficult, if not impossible, to assign each category to a specific and serially identifiable morphemic section are instances of fusional word structure (the term *inflecting*, or *inflectional*, is the older and traditional name for the typological class here called fusional; but this latter term is preferable in view of the quite separate use of *inflection* as the designation of a type of morphological formation, 6.4.5). English noun plurals like *men, mice, geese*, and *women* are inflectional in structure as against the grammatically equivalent agglutinative forms like *cars, houses*, and *cats*. It may be noticed that the specifically inflectional structures of English words are in the minority subclasses and irregular forms of the word classes concerned. Regular morphological structures in English are usually agglutinative.

While pure exemplars of any of the three types of word form structure throughout a language are very rare among the languages of the world, some languages make use of one type of word formation to a predominant extent, and are consequently classified as isolating, agglutinative, or fusional languages.

Chinese and several of the languages of South-east Asia, Vietnamese being perhaps the purest example of the type, are classified as isolating. In them bound morphemes are rare, and words containing more than a single morpheme are not thereby grammatically different in other respects from monomorphemic words. Because the boundaries of syllables and morphemes in these languages largely coincide, though they belong to different levels of analysis, these languages are sometimes rather loosely referred to as 'monosyllabic'. Words in such languages are assigned to word classes on the basis of different syntactic functions, but they do not exhibit any marks of such functions or class membership in their forms or morphemic structures.

This typological classification of Chinese and some other languages is a separate one from that given in the previous section; the previous classification was based on the predominant syntactic characteristics of languages, while the present classification relates to characteristics of word structure; but the two characteristics of languages of the Chinese type are generally associated with each other, since a language devoid of morphological markers of syntactic relations must rely more on positional order for such purposes.

Turkish, Sundanese, and Japanese are among typically agglutinative languages of the world, with Turkish generally considered the purest example of such a language. But it must be insisted that languages of this type are only alike of necessity in respect of word structure. The grammars of Turkish, Sundanese, and Japanese are very different in other respects, and the grammatical categories carried by the morphologically complex words in them are in great part quite unlike each other's.

The classical languages, Latin, Ancient Greek, and Sanskrit, are the most obvious examples of fusional types. Latin /amo:/ (I) love, is morphologically divisible into two morphemes, root /am-/ and suffix /-o:/; but this suffix, though morphologically not further divisible, marks five separate categories, each syntactically relevant in different ways to other words in sentences in which the form may occur (and in varying degrees correlatable with separate semantic functions): singular number, first person, present tense, indicative mood, and active voice. Likewise the morphologically indivisible /-us/ of /magnus/ great, marks nominative case, masculine gender, and singular number. The monomorphemic /i:/ go!, cumulatively comprises five grammatical components, verb class root, singular number, second person, imperative mood, active voice.[46]

The last few paragraphs may be compared with section 6.4.7,

above, where the same sorts of features in languages were considered from a different point of view.

A fourth class of language or of word structure characteristic of some languages is sometimes introduced, under the title **polysynthetic** or **incorporating**. Eskimo and some American-Indian languages have been called incorporating or polysynthetic, as their word forms are said to be very long and morphologically complex, and to contain numerous bound morphemes the translations of which would be represented by separate words in more familiar languages. This fourth class of language types, however, is of little use in linguistic typology. Languages falling within it only differ from the agglutinative and fusional types by carrying these processes to extremes and uniting within single grammatical words what in most other languages one would find spread out among several words. This fourth type introduces no qualitatively new feature of word structure; it only multiplies the numbers of bound morphemes within its words. The muddled nature of this type is well illustrated by the amusingly circular definition in the *Shorter Oxford English Dictionary*: 'polysynthetic' characterized by combining several words of a sentence into one word.'[47]

Within the I-E family many different degrees of the fusional structural type are found, from highly fusional Latin, Ancient Greek, and Sanskrit, to languages like English in which features of isolation and agglutination are quite prominent. Examples have already been given of the diffusion across the boundaries of separate genetically based families, of certain general phonetic characteristics.

Typological and historical comparison, and classifications based on them, should be kept distinct; they serve different ends and employ different sorts of criteria differently orientated. In the I-E field this has generally been the practice, but in some less well documented language areas of the world a loose amalgam of quite disparate criteria has sometimes been used to bind together intended genetic families.

Considered as a means of classifying languages and further understanding their structure, typological criteria are a valuable aid in carrying this out objectively, and they reveal the several different ways in which, within the limitations imposed on it by its nature and purposes, language manifests itself in different speech communities. Within typological comparison, the 'Humboldtian' tripartite division, properly understood, may be said to be a more significant system of classification than some others, in as much as it involves at once two of the most central levels of linguistic structure and linguistic analysis, phonology and grammar. Among linguists of the present century, Sapir notably gave prominence to this sort of classification, and linguistic typology occupies a central position in his brilliant book *Language*, published in 1921. He here set out a more detailed scheme of classification, employing criteria in addition to those of the type used by von Humboldt, but working fundamentally on the same lines. This line of linguistic classification has been taken up again by Greenberg, and this too has become part of the wide interest now aroused by linguistic typology. Working in strictly formal terms throughout he takes a number of different but related features of phonological and grammatical word structuring (agglutination, fusion, prefixation, suffixation, etc), and quantitatively compares the parts they play in different languages. Languages are then classified into types on the basis of a combination of these quantified characteristics.[48]

8.2.7 Lexical typology

Besides comparisons of formal structuring in languages of the sort that have been discussed so far, languages differ in systematically describable ways in their lexical composition, and may be classified on this basis.

Every language must be or become adequate to the needs and environments of its speakers at any time, and vocabularies therefore vary from place to place and from time to time in their relative richness or poverty of lexical items in different semantic fields or ranges. There are several different words for distinct types and conditions of snow in Eskimo and Lapp, whereas English and many other European languages, to whose speakers snow is not an all-prevasive climatic and topographical feature, make do with one, further specifying its nature with additional words if necessary. Some Arabic dialects have been said to distinguish a large number of separate words for different types of camel, and for camels in different states of health and the like, and the use of a generic word for 'camel' without further specification is said to be rare. This has given rise to the absurd suggestion that such people are incapable of abstraction to the extent of visualizing a camel apart from one or more specific attributes.

Aside from the specialization of vocabulary in different semantic fields according to the cultural and environmental needs of different speakers, which is only to be expected, languages differ in their formation of parts of their vocabulary dealing with particular subjects. Kinship term systems, for example, are generally built around the lexical differentiation of three fundamental human family relations, filiation, consanguinity, and spouseship; but in languages of the type represented by English different words are used primarily to distinguish the sex of kin relations (the English words *spouse, sib*, and *parent* (in the singular) are rare), a process carried further in French and German (*cousin* /kuzɛ̃/ male cousin, *cousine* /kuzin/ female cousin; likewise *Vetter* /ˈfɛter/, *Base* /ˈbaːze/). Some other languages distinguish lexically between members of kin who are older or younger than the speaker or other point of reference, often with less lexical distinction of sex or degree of consanguinity. Thus in Malay /adeʔ/ is used for 'younger brother' or 'younger sister', /abaŋ/ for 'elder brother' or 'male cousin', /kakaʔ/ for 'elder sister' or 'female cousin', /bapa/ for 'father' or 'uncle', and /ˈəmaʔ/ for 'mother' or 'aunt'; this involves a lexical focusing of attention on a distinction not inherently marked in the principal kinship terms of English. Of course further distinctions can be made in any language, but different ones are central to these sections of the vocabularies in different languages. Other kinship term systems distinguish lexically relationships for which in English no single word is available (*eg* Latin /maːtertera/ maternal aunt, /aːmita/ paternal aunt; /avunculus/ maternal uncle, /patruus/ paternal uncle). A type of kinship terminology is found in some languages which provides separate words for such relations as brother and sister according to the sex of the speaker or other person taken as the point of reference (*eg* Yurok /nelet/ my sister (woman speaking), /neweyetʃ/ my sister (man speaking); /neleyʔ/ my brother (woman speaking), /nepaː/ my brother (man speaking).*

Lexical systems, whether of kinship terms or of any other semantic range, are not the same thing as systems of interpersonal relations, such as kinship systems forming a part of the social life of peoples, and differences between lexical systems do not necessarily imply differences of behaviour in the fields so designated, though some correlations are found, such as enforced respect for age differences together with lexical distinction of them in kinship terms.

Comparison of the lexical systems of languages is often undertaken as part of a more general comparative study of different social systems and different cultures. A more centrally linguistic classification of vocabulary types may be made by reference to the different preponderant characteristics of the words themselves. Ullmann has applied a number of criteria in this approach

---

* The Yurok roots /-let/, /-weyetʃ/, /-leyʔ/, and /-paː/ are all bound morphemes.

to lexical typology, in particular the extent to which languages employ specific as against generic words (already noticed in particular contexts above), and the relative frequency of what may be called motivated and unmotivated words. By the former, the specification of detail by lexically different words is contrasted with the normal use of words of more general meaning, further specification being supplied by other words in collocation or left inferable from the context (German *arbeiten* /'ʔarbaiten/ to work, *bearbeiten* /be'ʔarbaiten/ to produce by working, and *brechen* /'breçen/ to break, *zerbrechen* /tsɛr'breçen/ to shatter in pieces, are contrasted with the French words *travailler* /travaje/ to work, and *casser* /kase/ to break). By the latter, vocabularies are compared in the extent to which the morphemic structures of their words reveal any correlation with their specific meanings by association with other items of the vocabulary. Thus German *Handschuh* /'hantʃuː/ glove, *Faust-handschuh* /'fausthantʃuː/, mitten ('fist-hand-shoe'), and *Schlittschuh* /'ʃlitʃuː/ skate, are compared with the monomor-phemic French words *gant* /gã/, *mitaine* /mitɛn/, mitten, and *patin* /patɛ̃/; and *hineingehen* /hi'naingeːen/ to enter, and *hinausgehen* /hi'nausgeːen/ to go out, with *entrer* /ãtre/ and *sortir* /sɔrtiːr/. In a general lexical comparison of French, German, and English, based on these and some other similar criteria, French and German appear as relatively extreme oppo-sites, with English occupying a somewhat central position.[49]

8.2.8 Historical change and linguistic typology

It will have been observed that in section 8.1.1. most attention was paid to phonetic changes, leading to systematic and regular correspondences of sound units between semantically related words. This was because it is these correspondences, rising from cumulative phonetic changes, that provide the essential internal evidence for the genetic relations between languages and for their grouping into historical families. Hence the constant reference to 'sound laws', of which Grimm's Law is just one, but the most famous one.

Languages, however, change no less in their morphological, syntactic, and lexical organization, and for the same reasons. These changes are no less significant and they deserve equal attention and investigation. They result in typological changes; some of the most prominent features and sets of features that formerly characterized a language are gradually replaced over the centuries so that the language comes to be seen as belonging more to a typological class other than it, or the language from which it is derived, belonged to formerly. In this respect languages may also change their phonological type, in the phonological ordering of their distinctive segments, their phonemes (8.2.3).

Certainly in some cases a group of genetically related languages is found to continue sharing certain prominent typological characteristics that presumably also marked the parent language typologically. In many Bantu languages sets of prefixes indicating grammatical concord between words of different syntactic classes in sentences are a notable feature. A similar coincidence of typology and historical descent is reported for most of the languages of Australia.[50] But this is contingent; it is shared inherited lexical stock, not synchronic type, that is the basic evidence and proof of genetic classification.

Attempts at finding some order and correlation with extralinguistic developments in these matters have exercised scholars' minds. In particular it was felt that the dominant structural features of language must somehow be related to the level of civilization of its speakers. Notions of 'complexity' and 'simplicity' have played a prominent part in this sort of speculation; but it is hard to see how such attributes of languages can ever be objectively established. A 'complex' language may mean no more than one showing a considerable number of features unfamiliar in the linguistic experience and native language of the learner. All that one can say with certainty is that every normal person is able to master his own language in childhood and thereafter finds it 'easy' and 'natural' to use and understand, and that, when properly investigated, every language in the world is immensely complex in its organization. It has been found that every structural type of language can coexist with any level of civilization or cultural development. Only in the matter of actual vocabulary, as against phonetic composition, phonological systems, and grammatical systems, do languages directly reflect the cultural environment of their speakers. Sapir strikingly summarized this: 'When it comes to linguistic form, Plato walks with the Macedonian swineherd, and Confucius with the head-hunting savage of Assam.[51]

It need not be suggested that isolating, agglutinative, or fusional types of word structure are either more or less complex than each other when placed in the total context of the grammatical and phonological organization of the language. More is involved than the relations between the phonological and grammatical structure of words, central as this is as a means of typological classification. But there do seem to be signs of certain trends operating over long periods in one direction or another, though not necessarily irreversibly.

Changes in preferred word order have been observed in some languages and language families in the course of their history. One such change is from the predominant SOV order of Latin to the predominant SVO orders of the modern Romance languages; this probably began within popular (Vulgar) Latin during the period of unity. Changes in this sort have been detected in Chinese and in other languages over the centuries.

When Latin is compared with the present-day Romance languages, and Old English with Modern English, a general movement towards a more isolating type of stucture seems to emerge, with fewer morphologically marked grammatical categories and less extensive variations within those that there are, and more reliance on word order as an exponent of syntactic relations. One can instance the obvious differences between the morphologically distinct case forms of Latin and the prepositional phrases with invariant noun forms in the modern Romance languages, and their reliance on word order to distinguish subject and object. In the Romance languages, one can observe in Old French a language at a stage between the two types represented by Latin and by Modern French: two morphologically differentiated case forms are found in nouns, survivors of the Latin nominative and accusative respectively, with different syntactic functions, and the order of words in sentences, though less free grammatically than in Latin is freer than the word order of comparable sentences in modern French. A similar trend is apparent in other language groups in Europe, and it has been suggested that the present isolating form exhibited by the Chinese languages is the product of a gradual development away from fusional type of structure, small parts of which can be inferred from the study of existing word forms and those attested from earlier periods of the language.[52]

One must also notice, however, that despite the general overall trend towards more isolating types of structure in European languages, some of the Romance languages exhibit a partial tendency in the direction of agglutination within limited word classes and in particular categories. In place of the older and classical de-adjectival adverbs in Latin, like /lente:/, slowly, late Latin used the phrase adjective +/mente/, ablative case form of /mens/, mind, intention, *eg* /lenta: mente/, slowly. This phrase has become a single word in French, Spanish, and Italian, *lentement*. /lātmā/ *lentamente*, /lentamente/, and *lentamente* /lentamente/. The semantic weakening of /mente/ in this construction, still a full word but on the way to becoming an adverbial marker, was already to be found in classical Latin.[53] The French grouping together of unemphatic personal pronoun and verb forms has already been considered (5.3.1). Traditionally these structures are regarded as consisting of several separate words, and there are reasonable grounds for treating the pronominal forms as words, though rather marginal in word status in view of their limitations of positional occurrence in relation to each other and to the verb. If the relative solidarity and inflexibility of these pronoun + verb groups are emphasized, they could be compared to single loosely jointed word-like complexes but they incorporate a number of elements that are represented in other languages, and (historically) in Latin, from which the forms themselves are derived, by pronominal and other words positionally much freer in their occurrence in sentences. One may instance a sentence like *il ne m'y en a pas donné* /il nə mi ãn a pɑ dɔne/ he has not given me any of it there (literally 'he neg. to-me there of-it has neg. given'), in which the relative order of each of the word units is fixed, and which permits no further interpolation of other words between most of them.

Orthographic conventions of word spacing and hyphenation are not to be regarded as infallible guides to the establishment of word divisions in formal grammar, but one notes the practice in French of hyphenating unemphatic pronouns occurring in post-verbal position (*eg: donnez-le-moi* /dɔne-lə-mwa/ give it to me!), and in Italian of joining postverbal pronominal elements to the verb as bound forms (*eg: vogliamo andarcene* /voʎ'ʎamo an'dartʃene/ we want to go away, *cp: ce ne andiamo* /tʃe ne andi'amo/ we are going away).[54]

8.2.9 Summary

Unlike historically orientated comparison, which is directed towards the single goal of genetic relationship, and based on the systematic comparison of the forms of words of similar or related meanings, the typological comparison of languages, as it will have been seen, may be based upon numerous separate and different criteria; and languages will often form groups of different membership according to the criteria of classification selected. The examples of this sort of classification that have been given in the preceding sections are illustrative, and not in any way exhaustive. Enough has been said to show the ways in which the different languages of the world may be gathered into classes by sharing some features in common, other than those universal features necessarily shared by every language. The more far-reaching and deeply embedded in the structures and systems of the languages at various levels are the features that are made the basis of a classification, the more solid and significant will be the resulting typological grouping. But in every case, the study and working out of such classifications brings into prominence the various ways in which the human faculty of language may operate, in fulfilling the purposes of communication between speakers within the physiological limitations and the cultural and environmental requirements that are imposed on it, in Humboldt's words 'making infinite use of finite resources'.[55]

Bibliography for Chapter 8

1 J. M. Aitchison, *Language change: progress or decay?*, London, 1981.

2 W. S. ALLEN, *Phonetics in Ancient India*, London, 1953.

3 *Vox Latina*, Cambridge, 1965.

4 *Vox Graeca*, Cambridge, 1968.

5 *Accent and rhythm: prosodic features of Latin and Greek*, Cambridge, 1973.

6 J. M. ANDERSON, *Structural aspects of language change*, London, 1973.

7 R. ANTTILA, *An introduction to historical and comparative linguistics*, New York, 1972.

8 W. W. ARNDT, 'The performance of glottochronology in Germanic', *Lang* 35 (1959), 180–92.

9 C. E. BAZELL, 'Syntactic relations and linguistic typology', *Cahiers F. de Saussure* 8 (1949), 5–20.

10 *Linguistic typology*, London, 1958.

11 L. BLOOMFIELD, *Language*, London, 1935.

12 E. BOURCIEZ, *Eléments de linguistique romane*, fourth edition, Paris, 1946.

13 R. G. A. DE BRAY, *A guide to the Slavonic languages*, London, 1951.

14 M. BREAL, *Essai sur la sémantique*, fourth edition, Paris, 1908 (also available in an English translation by H. Cust, London, 1900).

15 C. D. BUCK, *Comparative grammar of Greek and Latin*, Chicago, 1933.

16 'Some questions of practice in the notation of reconstructed I-E forms', *Lang* 2 (1926), 99–107.

17 T. BURROW, *The Sanskrit language*, London, 1955.

18 T. BYNON, *Historical linguistics*, Cambridge, 1985.

19 A. CAMPBELL, *Old English grammar*, Oxford, 1959.

20 N. CHOMSKY and M. HALLE, *The sound pattern of English*, New York, 1968.

21 N. E. COLLINGE, *The laws of Indo-European*, Amsterdam, 1985.

22 B. COMRIE, *Language universals and linguistic typology*, Oxford, 1981.

23 (ed), *The world's major languages*, London, 1987.

24 A. DARMESTETER, *La vie des mots*, twelfth edition, Paris, 1918.

25 W. D. ELCOCK, *The Romance languages*, London, 1960.

26 M. B. EMENEAU, 'India as a linguistic area', *Lang* 32 (1956), 3–16.
27 W. J. ENTWISTLE and W. A. MORISON, *Russian and the Slavonic languages*, London, 1949.
28 L. FOULET, *Petite syntax de l'ancien français*, Paris, 1930.
29 H. A. GLEASON, *Introduction to descriptive linguistics*, second edition, New York, 1961.
30 J. H. GREENBERG, 'A quantitative approach to the morphological typology of language', R. F. Spencer (ed), *Method and perspective in anthropology*, Minneapolis, 1954, 192–220.
31 *Universals of language*, Cambridge, Mass, 1983.
32 *The languages of Africa*, The Hague, 1966.
33 M. R. HAAS, *The prehistory of languages*, The Hague, 1969.
34 M. HARRIS, *The evolution of French syntax: a comparative approach*, London, 1978.
35 A. G. HAUDRICOURT and A. G. JUILLAND, *Essai pour une histoire structurale du phonétisme français*, Paris, 1949.
36 E. HAUGEN, 'The analysis of linguistic borrowing', *Lang* 26 (1950), 210–31.
37 H. H. HOCK, *Principles of historical linguistics*, Berlin, 1986.
38 C. F. HOCKETT, *A manual of phonology*, Indiana University publications in anthropology and linguistics, 11, 1955.
39 *A course in modern linguistics*, New York, 1958.
40 H. M. HOENIGSWALD, *Language change and linguistic reconstruction*, Chicago, 1960.
41 H. P. HOUGHTON, *An introduction to the Basque language*, Leyden, 1961.
42 W. VON HUMBOLDT, *Über die Verschiedenheit des menschlichen Sprachbaues*, Berlin, 1836 (reprinted Darmstadt, 1949).
43 I. IORDAN, *Introduction to Romance linguistics*, trans J. Orr, Oxford, 1970.
44 K. R. JANKOWSKI, *The neogrammarians: a reevaluation of their place in the development of linguistic science*, The Hague, 1972.
45 B. KARLGREN, 'Le proto-chinois, langue flexionelle', *Journal asiatique* 15 (1920), 205–32.
46 R. D. KING, *Historical linguistics and generative grammar*, Englewood Cliffs, 1969.
47 W. LABOV, 'The social motivation of a sound change', *Word* 19 (1963), 273–309.
48 'The social setting of linguistic change', in T. A. Sebeok (ed), *Current trends in linguistics* 11, (1973), 195–251.
49 W. P. LEHMANN, *Historical linguistics*, New York, 1962.
50 W. P. LEHMANN and Y. MALKIEL (eds), *Directions for historical linguistics*, Austin, 1968.
51 H. LEWIS and H. PEDERSEN, *A concise comparative Celtic grammar*, Göttingen, 1937.
52 A. MARTINET, 'La double articulation linguistique', *TCLC* 5 (1949), 30–7.
53 'Structure, function, and sound change', *Word* 8 (1952), 1–32.

54 *Economie des changements phonétiques*, Berne, 1955.

55 A. MEILLET, *La méthode comparative en linguistique historique*, Oslo, 1925 (also in English, *The comparative method in historical linguistics*, Paris, 1967).

56 *Introduction à l'étude comparative des langues indo-européennes*, eighth edition, Paris, 1937.

57 *Les caractères généraux des langues germaniques*, seventh edition, Paris, 1949.

58 C. MEINHOF, *Grundzüge einer vergleichenden Grammatik der Bantusprachen*, Berlin, 1906.

59 S. OHMAN, 'Theories of the "linguistic field"', *Word* 9 (1953), 123–134.

60 C. OSGOOD (ed), *Linguistic structures of native America*, New York, 1946.

61 L. R. PALMER, *Descriptive and comparative linguistics: a critical introduction*, London, 1972.

62 H. PEDERSEN, *Linguistic science in the nineteenth century*, J. W. Spargo, Cambridge, Mass, 1931 (republished as *The discovery of language*, Bloomington, 1962).

63 R. PRIEBSCH and W. E. COLLINSON, *The German language*, London, 1934.

64 E. PULGRAM, 'Proto-Indo-European, reality and reconstruction', *Lang* 35 (1959), 421–6.

65 R. H. ROBINS, *A short history of linguistics*, London, 1979.

66 M. RUHLEN, *A guide to the world's languages* 1: *classification*, London, 1987.

67 E. SAPIR, *Language*, New York, 1921.

68 F. DE SAUSSURE, *Cours de linguistique générale*, fourth edition, Paris, 1949.

69 T. A. SEBEOK (ed), *Current trends in linguistics* 11: *Diachronic, areal, and typological linguistics*, The Hague, 1973.

70 H.-J. SEILER (ed), *Language universals*, Tübingen, 1978.

71 L. TESNIÈRE, *Eléments de syntaxe structurale*, Paris, 1959.

72 P. THIEME, *Die Heimat der indogermanischen Gemeinsprache*, Wiesbaden, 1954.

73 N. S. TRUBETZKOY, *Principles of phonology*, trans C. A. M. Baltaxe, Berkeley, 1969. (Originally published in German, Grundzüge der Phonologie, TCLP 7, 1939).

74 S. ULLMANN, 'Descriptive semantics and linguistic typology', *Word* 9 (1953), 225–40.

75 *The principles of semantics*, second edition, Glasgow and Oxford, 1951.

76 J. VENDRYES, *Le language*, Paris, 1921.

77 C. F. VOEGELIN, 'Models for cross-genetic comparisons', *Papers from the symposium on American-Indian languages*, Berkeley, 1954, 27–45.

78 A. WALDE and J. POKORNY, *Vergleichendes Wörterbuch der indogermanischen Sprachen*, Berlin and Leipzig, 1927–32.

79 U. WEINREICH, *Languages in contact*, Publications of the Linguistic Circle of New York 1, 1953.

80 J. WRIGHT and E. M. WRIGHT, *An elementary grammar of Middle English*, Oxford, 1928.

Almost all introductory books on general linguistics assign one or more chapters to comparative-historical linguistics, usually concentrating on Indo-European as being the most worked and the most accessible family. The relevant chapters in the following books may be recommended:

de Saussure, 68, part 3;

Vendryes, 76, 349–66;

Palmer, 61, Chapters 9–14.

Bloomfield, 11, Chapters 18–27, is particularly useful as it introduces material from other families into the exposition and exemplification of theory and practice. Buck, 15, provides a clear and simple account of the basic evidence and its interpretation, particularly helpful to those coming to Indo-European studies from a background of the classical languages. Similarly Meillet, 56.

Among the elementary books setting out the theory and practice of comparative-historical linguistics those by Aitchison, 1; Anderson, 6; Bynon, 18; and Hock, 37, are to be recommended. Bynon in particular explains the theory and methods of this branch of linguistics very fully, dealing successively with the neogrammarian, structuralist, and generative treatments of language change and its consequences.

Sebeok, 69, contains a number of valuable essays on aspects of the subject and studies on specific language groups and families.

Notes to Chapter 8

1 Sir William Jones enunciated the historical connection of Sanskrit with Latin, Ancient Greek, and German, in 1786 in a lecture which has since become famous (Pedersen, 62, 17–19).

2 On the arbitrary nature of words in relation to their semantic functions, de Saussure, 68, 100–2.

3 Vendryes, 76, 349.

4 On Old English and Middle English, Campbell, 19; Wright, 80.

5 U. Weinreich, W. Labov, and M. I. Herzog, 'Empirical foundations for a theory of language change', Lehmann and Malkiel, 50, 95–188.

6 On linguistic substrates, Weinreich, 79. Social motivation for linguistic change, Labov, 48. J. Milroy and L. Milroy, 'Linguistic change, social network and speaker innovation', *Journal of Linguistics* 21 (1985), 339–84.

7 *Cp* 2.2.3; A. C. Gimson, *An introduction to the pronunciation of English*, London, 1970, 83–9.

8 The loss of formal case marking in nouns in the later stages of spoken Latin can be shown to correlate with the growing preference for a subject-verb-object order in sentences (Harris, 34, Chapters 2–3)

A similar situation is reported at the present time in Puerto Rican

Spanish, where the loss of final /s/ has rendered the singular forms of several verb tenses homophonous and this has led to a corresponding greater use of the personal pronouns, which are not syntactically required in Spanish, to ensure disambiguation (J. G. Hochberg, 'Functional compensation for /s/ deletion in Puerto Rican Spanish', *Lang* 62 (1986), 609–21).

9 Among the causes adduced to account for phonetic changes have been climate, which has not been substantiated scientifically, and alleged 'ease of articulation' or 'economy of effort'. While this does clearly account for some changes, and in particular for the reduction or abbreviation of the forms of frequently used words ('allegro forms' like *howd'yedo*, and *hiya!* for *how are you?*, as well as the 'weak forms' of languages like English), it is clearly quite insufficient as a single cause; otherwise phonetic changes would be much more alike and universal in different languages than they are.

Many changes can be shown to be due to or facilitated by pressures that have arisen within the phonological systems of particular languages, or dialects, at certain periods; for example, to render four distinctive back rounded vowels. /ɒ/, /ɔ/, /o/, and /u/, more easily differentiated from one another, /u/, the closest, may gradually be fronted in articulation to /y/, to supplement its distinctive characteristics and to leave more room in the back for the others. On this aspect of linguistic change, see further Haudricourt and Juilland, 35; Martinet, 53 and 54.

10 See further O. Jespersen, *A modern English grammar*, London, 1933, chapter 8; Anderson, 6, 138–41; Bynon, 18, 82–3.

11 On semantic change, Bloomfield, 11, Chapter 24; Bréal, 14; Darmsteter, 24; Ullmann, 75. Changes in semantic fields, Ullmann, 75, Chapters 3 and 4; Ohman, 59; Hoenigswald, 40, 38–9.

12 Survey of the I-E family, Buck, 15, 3–4; Bynon, 18, 68–9.

Romance languages, Bourciez, 12; Iordan, 43; Elcock, 25; M. B. Harris and N. G. Vincent (ed.). *The Romance Languages*, London, 1987.

Germanic languages, Meillet, 57; Priebsch and Collinson, 63.

Indo-Iranian languages, Burrow, 17.

Celtic languages, Lewis and Pedersen, 51.

Balto-Slavic languages, Entwistle and Morison, 27; de Bray, 13.

The position of Hittite in relation to Indo-European was the subject of controversy for some time. On the view generally accepted today, that it belongs to the Anatolian subfamily, see J. Puhvel, 'Dialectal aspects of the Anatolian branch of Indo-European', in H. Birnbaum and J. Puhvel (eds), *Ancient Indo-European dialects*, Berkeley, 1966, 235–47.

13 Suggested dating of I-E, Buck, 15, 2; Bynon, 18, 280. For a summary of recent views, O. J. L. Szemerényi, 'Recent developments in Indo-European linguistics', *TPS* 1985, 171.

14 On the pronunciation of Ancient Greek, Latin, and Sanskrit, and the techniques by which the facts may be recovered, see Allen, 2; 3; and

4. A more advanced treatment of the non-segmental features of Greek and Latin as spoken languages may be found in Allen, 5.

15 General survey of languages and language families, Bloomfield, 11, Chapter 4; Chapter 18 contains examples of comparative and historical methods applied outside I-E; more recently Ruhlen, 66. On the Bantu family, Meinhof, 58; Greenberg, 32.

On Afro-Asiatic, Comrie, 23, 647–53.

The membership of the Altaic family has been and still is the subject of some controversy. At one time a larger family, Ural-Altaic, comprising the Finno-Ugrian and the Altaic languages, was set up, but this is now considered implausible. The inclusion of Japanese is relatively recent; see R. A. Miller, *Japanese and the other Altaic languages*, Chicago, 1971; for a general summary Ruhlen, 66, Chapter 4.

On American-Indian languages, Osgood, 60; Haas, 33.

Basque, Houghton, 41; R. Collins, *The Basques*, Oxford, 1986.

16 Grimm's Law, Bloomfield, 11, 347–51; Buck, 15, 120–1; Bynon, 18, 83–6.

17 More details on correspondences in Buck, 15, with special reference to Greek and Latin. See further Meillet, 56; O. J. L. Szemerényi, *Einführung in die vergleichende Sprachwissenschaft*, Darmstadt, 1970.

The important question raised by Gamkrelidze and Ivanov on the revision of our view of the probable phonological structure of the unitary I-E phonological system must be left for future research. It is set forth in T. V. Gamkrelidze and V. Ivanov, *Indo-European and the Indo-Europeans*, Moscow, 1986 (in Russian, but translations in Western European languages are in preparation). There is a summary in M. Mayrhofer, 'Sanskrit und die Sprachen Alteuropas', *Nachrichten der Akademie der Wissenschaften in Göttingen* 1: *Phil-hist Klasse* 5 (1983), 123–53, with full references to date. For two brief presentations in English, see P. J. Hopper, 'Areal typology and the early Indo-European consonant system', in E. C. Polomé (ed), *The Indo-Europeans in the fourth and third millennia*, Ann Arbor, 1982, 121–39; T. V. Gamkrelidze, 'Language typology and linguistic reconstruction', *Proc 12th International Congress of Linguists*, Innsbruck, 1978, 480–2.

18 Neogrammarians, Bloomfield, 11, 354–64; Pedersen, 62, 292–310; Iordan, 43, 15–24; Bynon, 18, Chapter 1; Jankowski, 44. The neogrammarian thesis was first set out definitively by Osthoff and Brugmann in 1878; an English translation is now available in W. P. Lehmann (ed), *A reader in nineteenth-century hitorical Indo-European linguistics*, Bloomington, 1967, 197–209.

19 Verner's Law, Bloomfield, 11, 357–9.

20 On loan words, Bloomfield, 11, Chapters 25–7 Bynon 18, 217–32. English loans in Romanian sporting terminology, I. Constantinescu in *Limba română* 6 (1972), 527–37.

The difference between loan words and inherited vocabulary is well illustrated by comparing the Norman French element in English vocabulary with the vocabulary inherited from Old English (before the Norman Conquest) and ultimately from the inferred common Germanic language. English at the present time contains a large body of words derived from Latin through Norman French, but it is counted a Germanic language in view of the earlier existence of the Germanic language, Old English, from which Modern English can be shown to have developed through Middle English by an unbroken series of gradual changes.

21 On analogy and anomaly, see further 9.6.

22 Quotation from E. H. Sturtevant, *Introduction to linguistic science*, Yale, 1947, 109.

23 Chomsky and Halle, 20, 249–50; Bynon, 18, Chapter 3.

24 Chomsky and Halle, 20, Chapter 6

25 On the treatment of historical linguistics within generative theory see Bynon, 18, Chapter 3; A. H. Sommerstein, *Modern phonology*, London, 1977, Chapter 10; Hock, 37, Chapter 11. King, 46, may be regarded as the pioneer work in this interpretation of historical linguistics. Collinge, 21, sets out forty-one sound change laws of Indo-European, including, of course, Grimm's Law and Verner's Law, analysed and discussed in these terms, with full bibliographies. He adds an appendix (*pp* 259–69) on the effect of the 'glottalic hypothesis' of Gamkrelidze and Ivanov on some of these (*cp* 8.1.7).

26 A fairly recent development in this branch of linguistics has been the attempt to quantify linguistic divergence from a common source and linguistic relationship based on it, and to calculate from the numbers of cognate (systematically related) words in them the period of time since the effective separation of two languages. This is known as lexicostatistics or glottochronology, and operates on the assumption that the rate of change that involves the replacement of one word by a different one (*ie* other than the word form resulting from gradual phonetic changes in the earlier word) in relation to the same range of semantic functions in the everyday basic vocabulary of languages is, in the absence of sudden cultural upheavals, relatively constant; around twenty per cent for every thousand years has been suggested. It is argued that on this basis one can infer the length of time two cognate languages have been separated and also determine the relative closeness of relationship between a number of cognate languages in one historical family.

At the present time a definitive statement of the effectiveness and reliability of glottochronology cannot be made. There have been trouble and disagreements about the sort of referential meanings that constitute a basic vocabulary likely to be common to languages spoken in different parts of the world and by speakers whose cultures are very different. Checks in the controlled fields of languages whose historical connections are known already, as in the I-E family have been made. It has been found that applied to the Romance languages within I-E the method gives a picture of the relative closeness of the relationships between the member languages that accords with what is known of their histories and geographical positions, though some adjustment is needed to bring the inferred dates in line with the historically known or probable times of separation; a similar picture of the relationships and chronologies of the Germanic languages has been obtained by glottochronological methods, which is claimed to agree well with recent historical and archaeological findings. These methods may be of considerable assistance in the investigation of language families where there are few historical records available. But theoretical as well as practical problems still remain to be overcome; see C. D. Chretien, 'The mathematical models of glottochronology', *Lang* 38 (1962), 11–37.

See further: Hockett, 39, Chapter 61; Gleason, 29, 450; Bynon, 18, 266–72. Applied to Romance, A. L. Kroeber, 'Romance history and glottochronology', *Lang* 34 (1958), 454–7; applied to Germanic, Arndt, 8.

27 Meillet, 55, 15.

28 On the nature of the formulae, Buck, 16.

29 On the phonetics of Latin, W. S. Allen, 3.

30 Latin /k/ in relation to Romance, Pedersen, 62, 268–9.
   See further, Pulgram, 64.

31 The fundamental division between the *centum* and *satem* languages in I-E is thought to reflect a dialectal split within the unitary period (Bloomfield, 11, 316).

32 The theory of common characteristics resulting from the spreading of linguistic features 'in waves' over adjacent dialects within a family is called the 'Wellentheorie' (Bloomfield, 11, 317–18; Pedersen, 62, 313–18).

33 Linguistic palaeontology, de Saussure, 68, 306–10; Bloomfield, 11, 319–20; Pedersen, 62, Chapter 8; Bynon, 18, Chapter 7; H. Krahe, *Sprache und Vorzeit*, Heidelberg, 1954.

South Asia, Buck, 15, 2. The geographical area has been the subject of much controversy. In 1954 P. Thieme, 72, argued in favour of northern Europe, in the region of the Vistula, Oder, and Elbe rivers.

Collaborative research by archaeologists has been directed at attempts to identify a possible culture and culture area of the unitary I-E speakers. The 'glottalic hypothesis' has an obvious bearing on this, associating the unitary language phonetically with the languages of the Caucasus. See further E. G. Polomé (ed), *The Indo-Europeans in the fourth and third millennia*, Ann Arbor, 1982, G. Cardona (ed), *Indo-European and the Indo-Europeans*, Philadelphia, 1970. Both these books contain various essays on what may be inferred about the unitary I-E language and different aspects of the life, habitat, and culture of its speakers.

In a recent study of the question of the homeland and dispersion of the I-E family C. Renfrew (*Archaeology and language: the puzzle of the Indo-European family*, London, 1957), taking into account recent archaeological findings, locates the homeland in Anatolia and associates the early diffusion with the slow spreading of expanding populations that resulted from the development of settled agriculture, and who took their techniques and their animal and vegetable products with them. The acceptance of this view would involve the assumption of a much longer time depth for the unitary language, perhaps as far back as 6000 B.C.

34 Double structuring of language, Martinet, 52.

35 These common features of adjacent languages are discussed under the title *affinités phonologiques*, by Jakobson in *Actes du quatrième congrès international de linguistes*, 1936, 48–58.

36 Phonological typologies, Trubetzkoy, 73, 90–227; Hockett, 38, Chapter 2; Voegelin, 77; I. Maddieson, *Patterns of sounds*, Cambridge, 1986.

  An example of phonological classification of some Scottish dialects, J. C. Catford, *TPS* 1957, 107–17.

37 W. S. Allen, 'Structure and system in Abaza', *TPS* 1956, 127–76 (see *pp* 138–9).

  On syntactic typology, Bazell, 9, L. Tesnière, 71, Chapter 14 (the whole book, which is very long is of considerable interest on questions of syntax); von Humboldt, 4, 114–26; W. P. Lehmann (ed), *Syntactic typology*, Hassocks, 1978. *Cp*. Bazell, 9. On areal affinities, Emeneau, 26; Weinreich, 79; K. Sandfeld, *Linguistique balkanique*, Paris, 1930.

  As an example of the areal diffusion of a feature over contiguous languages in consequence of prolonged contact and some bilingualism, it has been suggested that the obligatory subject pronouns of French, in this respect unlike Italian, Spanish, and Latin, is at least partly due to the influence of neighbouring Germanic language speakers (Bynon, 18, 248–50).

38 *Cp* P. Ramat, 'Is a holistic typology possible?', *Folia linguistica* 20 (1986), 3–14 (volume 20, parts 1 and 2, is a special issue devoted to typology).

39 Greenberg, 31.

40 *Cp* N. V. Smith, 'Consistency, markedness and language change: on the notion "consistent language"' *Journal of linguistics* 17 (1981), 39–54.

41 M. Silverstein, 'Hierarchy of features and ergativity', in R. M. W. Dixon (ed), *Grammatical categories in Australian languages*, New Jersey, 1976, 112–71.

42 N. Chomsky, *Language and responsibility*, Hassocks, 1979, 180–1; *Rules and representations*, Oxford, 1980, 33, 241: 'we may conceive of the mind as a system of "mental organs", the language facility being one'.

43 The analogy between the psychological aspect of universal grammar and the physiological aspect of universal phonetics was asserted in 1928 by L. Hjelmslev, *Principes de grammaire générale*, Copenhagen, 251.

44 Comrie, 22; Seiler, 70; J. H. Greenberg, C. A. Ferguson, and E. A. Moravcsik (eds), *Universals of human language*, Stanford, 1978.
45 Robins, 65, 176.
46 The morphological division /magn-us/ is partly arbitrary. The paradigm can also be analysed on the basis of a division /magnu-s/, with different root allomorphs (/magnu-/, /magna-/, /magno-/, etc), instead of the single form/magn-/. But the cumulation of several grammatical categories on a single affix is not affected. In a form like Latin /iː/ some of the cumulation could be avoided by the positing of zero morphemes serially representing certain of the grammatical categories, but this would not alter the general characterization of the language typologically.
47 'Polysynthetic' languages, *cp* Sapir, 67, 135–6.
    Eskimo, M. Swadesh, 'South Greenlandic (Eskimo)', in 60, 30–54.
    Typological similarity and genetic unity contrasted in Pedersen 62, 246–7.
48 Sapir's typology, 67, Chapter 6; Greenberg, 30.
49 Lexical typology, Ullmann, 74 (reference to Lapp, *p* 232).
50 *Cp* R. M. W. Dixon, *The languages of Australia*, Cambridge, 1980.
51 Sapir, 67, 234.
52 On word order in Latin and the Romance languages, Harris, 34, 18–20; in relation to various languages (including Chinese), C. N. Li (ed) *Word order and word order change*, Austin, 1975; J. M. Aitchison, 'The order of word order change'; *TPS* 1979, 43–65.
    On Old French, Foulet, 28.
    Chinese, Karlgren, 45.
53 Bourciez, 12, 113.
54 The conjoint pronominal forms of parts of the verbal paradigms of some of the Romance languages may be compared with the bipersonal verb forms referred to on *p* 272, above. Bipersonal verb paradigms in some languages may have started in this way from the gradual 'petrifaction' of once free pronominal elements. Some, at least, of the many suffixes in Hungarian and other Finno-Ugrian languages have developed from earlier independent words (P. Hajdu, *Finno-Ugrian languages and peoples*, trans G. F. Cushing, London, 1975, 96–8), M. Harris, 34, traces and interprets aspects of the syntactic changes undergone by colloquial Latin in its passage to modern French, with references to other Romance languages.
55 Humboldt, 42, 103. For a general survey of grammatical typology, see G. Mallinson and B. J. Blake, *Language typology*, Amsterdam, 1981.

Chapter 9

Wider perspectives

9.1 Linguistics, anthropology and sociology

9.1.1 Linguistics and anthropology

The bonds between the science of human language and other sciences devoted specifically to man are very obvious. In particular, linguistics, the study of language, and anthropology, the study of human culture as a whole, must be closely involved in each other's interests. In the practice of the two disciplines it may be claimed that some familiarity with the principles, and methods of each is a very desirable part of the equipment of a scholar in either.

It has already been said that languages are not mere collections of labels or nomenclatures attached to preexisting bits and pieces of the human world, but that each speech community lives in a somewhat different world from that of others, and that these differences are both realized in parts of their cultures and revealed and maintained in parts of their languages (1.4.2, 2.4.3). Apart from the fact that anthropological investigations into a culture remote from European influence may well require some command of the language of the community on the part of the investigator, many of the most significant details of a people's way of life are likely to be verbalized in certain key words belonging to different spheres (religion, ethics, kinship, social hierarchy, etc), for which one-word translation equivalents are not readily available, and are certainly unlikely to be known to a speaker merely because he happens to be partially bilingual. Indeed, part of the linguist's task is to translate and explain the uses of such words in the language.

Anthropological investigation involves observation as well as enquiry, and it is clearly possible to arrive at some description of a people's culture without learning anything of their language, but one may surmise that a description of a culture that had involved some acquaintance with the language or languages of that culture will be in certain important respects more penetrating and revealing, and that a description of a language by someone who has made use of some knowledge of the rest of the culture of its speakers will provide a more comprehensive account of the working of the language within the community as a symbolic communicative system. If the linguist wishes to deal at all in detail with semantics within his description, recourse to some cultural knowledge of the community may be a prerequisite if his statements of meaning, in important spheres of the vocabulary, are to rise above the superficially obvious and not to be confined to listing the nearest one-word translation renderings.

The specific study of the interdisciplinary links, both theoretical and practical, between anthropology and linguistics has been called **ethnolinguistics**.

The collaboration of the linguist and the anthropologist can be particularly close when the people whose language or culture is under investigation is remote from the well-trodden paths of European civilization and European influence. The reasons are obvious; in the case of such communities, knowledge on the part of the rest of the world is scanty, and in relation to the work to be done investigators are few. The more reliable and systematic information each can provide, the greater will be our total knowledge both of the languages and the cultures of mankind. In familiar and long-studied parts of the world, the cultural backgrounds involved in the analysis and statement of meanings are in part well known and so taken for granted, and have been the subject of diverse studies; conversely the languages of such communities, though no less intimately bound up with their way of life and culture, are more widely known and therefore less likely to be barriers to investigation, and serviceable accounts are available of them even if by modern linguistic standards some fall short of fully scientific descriptions.[1]

It is in dealing with distant and primitive cultures, and with largely unknown and hitherto unstudied languages that the anthropologist and linguist can come closest together. Where workers are inevitably few, and the languages and peoples are many, our knowledge may depend on the reports and analyses of one or, at best, of a small number of scholars. The task is the more urgent at the present time, as in many rapidly developing parts of the world, isolated languages and dialects, spoken in small communities only, are rapidly passing into obsolescence and oblivion before the spread of major world languages in the path of modern communications, technical advances, and industrial and commercial development. Such is the situation in parts of South-east Asia and of Africa, but perhaps above all in North and South America, which present among their indigenous (Indian) populations a bewildering and fascinating array of languages, of widely different genetic stocks and typological classification; some of these are still spoken by a hundred or even by less than a score of people, and they are likely to be lost without trace unless recorded in time and subjected to descriptive analyses at all levels.

Work among such languages, where there is a total absence of written records, and an almost total absence of prior scholarship, is known, appropriately, as **anthropological linguistics.**[2] The importance of linguistic studies to the language teacher engaged in teaching languages of international importance is obvious; but the linguist's field is all language and every language, and he hopes to learn more about language itself, and about the relations between languages and between language and life, and to make progress in the development of linguistic theory and linguistic techniques, from every individual language he studies. To anyone not made purblind by the demand that all scholarship should be directed at materially profitable objectives, the many languages in peril of unrecored extinction present a very special challenge.

Quite apart from the intrinsic value of the resultant descriptions, recorded texts, and dictionaries, the methods necessitated by the situation of most of these languages have a particular value to linguistic science itself. The absence of written records, and usually of an indigenous writing system, means that the linguist must obtain his material entirely through informants, in most cases by visiting the communities in their own territories, 'in the field'.

Since the primary material of language is spoken utterance, the **informant**, as he or she is called, is a familiar and necessary part of the study of any living language, whatever its position in the world. The informant is not a teacher, nor a linguist; he is simply a native speaker of the language willing to help the linguist in his work. Work with informants may take place in isolation, when the informant visits the linguist, or in the field, when the linguist visits the informant. In either case the informant speaks as naturally as he can be induced to in response to the linguist's elicitations. These may and do take the form of individual words as lexical items, and of ordered series of words for phonetic description and phonological analysis and for the discovery of paradigms and paradigm classes (of the types *gate, fate, Kate, late, spate, date; gate, gape, gave; gate, goat, gout; gate, gates; walk, walks, walking, walked*, etc), and of ordered series of sentences with controlled substitutions at various places for the discovery and analysis of syntactic structures and the formal patterns of sentences (*I see a dog, I see a cat, he sees a dog, he chases a cat*, etc). Finally, informants may tell whole tales, personal histories, accounts of particular activities, and the like, uninfluenced by the promptings of the linguist (inevitably coloured at the outset by his own language background). Only after such relatively lengthy stretches have been subjected to phonological and grammatical analysis, can the linguist be certain that his description is more or less a complete statement of the systems and structures required for the language he is dealing with.

Work of this sort with informants is a very general part of all investigations of living languages; but with languages having a writing system and a written literature, and a tradition of scholarship, it is at all stages supplemented by the material provided from these sources and the work of previous scholars.

Informant work in the informant's own community has certain manifest advantages over work with one in isolation at home. There are many personal variations in a language, and in any dialect of a language. An account may be deliberately, or inevitably, based on a single speaker acting as an informant, but the possibility of comparing one speaker's characteristics at every level with those of others of the same language or dialect results in a more representative statement. Language is rooted in social intercourse, not in isolated utterances to a foreigner.[3] Certain features, constructions, intonation patterns, and stylistic variations arise in conversation and in the use of language in its normal settings; these are liable to be missed away from the speech community to which the informant belongs. The analysis of semantic functions, or meanings, of words and locutions of prime significance within the culture of the speakers must be facilitated by one's presence in the actual environment from which contexts of situations may be abstracted.

It is, therefore, in **field study** on the speaker's home territory that linguistic work with informants can achieve the fullest success; and anthropological linguistics, working on languages with no orthographies and few if any previous published accounts, both reveals the possibilities of modern linguistic methods and puts them to their severest test. Whatever is to be discovered and set down about the language, its transcription, its phonological and grammatical systems and structures, and the meanings of its lexical items must here be the unaided product of the linguist's own resources. In a field situation, dealing with a language remote from the influences of European ways of thinking and European scholarship, the linguist is testing and refining his science in as pure an environment as its nature allows. The value of such a discipline to linguistics should need no stressing.[4]

In the field situation the linguist is of necessity concerned with all aspects of a language. Not the least of these are oral texts, continuous stretches of speech other than responses to the linguist's direct elicitations. The importance of texts in the analysis and description of spoken languages has already been mentioned in this section. But they have additional importance. Many texts, whatever their nature, are revealing of some part of the culture and traditions of the speakers. Traditional stories, songs, fables, myths, personal biographies, and group histories, ritual utterances, accounts of activities and processes of production within the culture (utensils, weapons, food, etc) are only some examples of the material that the linguist is in a unique position to be able to gather and analyse. Their significance may extend far beyond the confines of linguistics itself.

Many such traditional stories and the like exhibit aesthetic merits of their own; in communities at the preliterate stage, it is well known that oral literature often flourishes, and culturally determined forms of utterance are preserved from generation to generation in the long memories both of ordinary people and among those officially or unofficially recognized within the culture as preeminently qualified to preserve, transmit, and create such artistic uses of language.

Stories and accounts of activities may, of course, be gathered bilingually from informants with a knowledge of the linguist's language or of a mutually understood 'trade language'; they may also be gathered through interpreters. But there is a constant risk of loss in such transmissions. It requires a high degree of linguistic sophistication and a deep knowledge of both languages to render the culturally vital elements of one speech community into the language of another. The linguist may possess or acquire such skills: he cannot assume that his informant will have them. In earlier days, among the pioneers of modern linguistics, texts were recorded by dictation from informants, with inevitable limitations, delays, and possible distortions arising from the need to pause repeatedly. Present-day linguists are privileged; modern science has provided them with tape-recorders of great accuracy, many of which are constructed to work independently of mains electricity. With their aid the speech of communities whose language or particular dialect is soon to perish may be recorded and preserved for all time.

A recorded oral text needs a transcription and a translation, preferably accompanied by a description of the phonetics, phonology, and grammar of the language from which it is taken. Such accompaniments are the product of the trained linguist. The selection of representative and informative texts to provide something of a fair and balanced picture of the culture and way of life of the community requires knowledge of the theory and techniques of anthropology. In the realm of anthropological linguistics we see the needs and the achievements of collaboration between these two disciplines of the study of man.

9.1.2 Linguistics and sociology: sociolinguistics

Closely related to many of the aspects of anthropology is the range of studies known as sociology. The precise nature of the distinction between social anthropology and sociology is a matter of debate, in which the linguist is not involved; here it will be sufficient to cite the view that anthropologists tend to concentrate on cultures remote from those of familiar European industrialized communities, with particular references to the form and organization of different cultures, while sociology is mainly focused on the social groups of European and Europeanized communities, and concerned with their formation and interaction.[5]

The dialectal differences within a language involve, in many cases, not only regional variations, but class differentiations within and often transcending regional differences of speech (cp 2.2.3). The differences of social status and social gradations, observed by persons within a society and evoking responses from them, and systematically described by sociologists, involve far more behavioural aspects than just habits of speech. But these are vital, as the nervousness of some socially insecure persons' speech evinces, and the linguist is uniquely qualified to describe and classify formally the speech features concerned, at all levels of linguistic description. Imitation of a prestigious dialect in the supposed interests of socially approved 'correctness' has been adduced as one of the factors in linguistic change (8.1.1).

As Bernard Shaw's Professor Higgins demonstrated, the linguist in so far as he is a skilled phonetician can try to help people 'rise in the social scale' to the extent that the use of language is involved. It has also been said that his help has been sought by some young radicals suffering the misfortune of having been brought up speaking a standard dialect (2.2.3), to enable them to acquire a speech style thought to be more typical of less privileged people in their society. More practically than in either of these activities the linguist has much to contribute to our understanding and finding solutions for the problems of bilingual persons and groups in society, especially those or recent origin arising from large-scale immigration.

Recent movements of population in the form of immigration from less economically favoured areas to more favoured areas have highlighted what has always been a linguistic phenomenon in some parts of the world, bilingualism, the existence of people speaking and needing to speak and understand two languages in a community in which both languages (and sometimes others as well) are in regular use. Such bilingual or multilingual communities are an extreme form of the multidialectal communities found in many of the large cities of the world, wherein dialect differences reinforce the solidarity of groups, but also mark social class differences and aspirations among speakers of the same language. Studies of such dialectal phenomena within urban communities have been undertaken in recent years, both in relation to the motivations for language change and as part of the sociological research into the problems of contemporary city life.

In addition to class dialects, the jargons and slangs of various special groups in society, such as criminals, prisoners, seamen, regular servicemen, certain schools, semi-secret societies, etc, are valuable material for linguistic analysis if the linguist can get at them reliably. Slangs and jargons of this sort serve to integrate members of social subgroups and to foster group loyalty and 'togetherness', as well as keeping outsiders from finding out too much of what is going on. This is particularly the case with some thieves' argots. Slang words more widely used may pass into general vocabulary and their origin may then become unknown to many users. In London Cockney 'rhyming slang' a pair of words was often substituted for a single word, the second one rhyming with the original word (*eg trouble and strife*, wife; *rabbit and pork* talk; *bird lime* time (spent in gaol)); then the second, rhyming, word was dropped. Today many British English speakers, in no sense genuine speakers of Cockney, use *rabbit* (*on*) for *talk* (*too much*) and similar Cockney derivates in regular colloquial usage. Among some young people and in particular in university circles in the late nineteenth and earlier twentieth centuries it became fashionable to replace certain nouns by similar forms ending in *-er* or *-gger; nogger* (agnostic) was one such slang word, and, as a *tour de force*, the expression *wagger pagger bagger* (waste paper basket). Of these forms *soccer* and *rugger* have survived and passed into general use in place of their more formal counterparts *Association football* and *Rugby football*.

The relations between social class and language, especially in regard to vocabulary and syntax, have been an especial study of Bernstein. Labov's studies of dialectal variation among English speakers in New York City and in Martha's Vineyard and Trudgill's of the English city Norwich have been referred to already (2.2.5). Such studies are equally relevant here in relation to the sociological aspects of language and the use of language.[6]

Social changes and social and political conditions have always been a factor in the development and spread of some languages and of the decline in prestige and the disappearance of others. Such changes rightly claim attention today, both for theoretical and for practical reasons, and they are no less a part of the linguistic history of many countries in the world. One need only instance the spread of Latin over much of Western Europe, to become the present-day Romance languages (8.1.1), in the wake of the Roman Empire, and leading to the extinction of many of the previously spoken languages of these areas (not, of course, of the peoples themselves, who simply over the centuries learned and came to use Latin along with and then instead of their former languages). Similar situations led later to the spread of English, Spanish, and Portuguese over the continent of America, and of English in the British Empire and Commonwealth. In Central and South America, and in most parts of the British Commonwealth many of the indigenous languages survive as spoken and often as written media; but the condition of the Indian languages of North America under pressure from English is much more precarious. The conditions and the stages through which a language comes to lose ground and in the end to disappear in the face of a more dominant language have been studied and documented under the heading of 'language death'.[7]

Contacts between languages and their speakers on a continuing basis have several effects. Bilingualism and multilingualism, already mentioned, is one. This may take different forms. Sometimes two or more languages are used in fairly sharply differentiated situations, for example, one at home, and one for more formal contacts with others at work and in public. When these contacts involve higher social status, educational advance, political power, etc, the prestige attached to such a 'public' language is greatly enhanced, rather in the way that 'standard' dialects within a language enjoy a higher prestige (2.2.3). The term *diglossia* has been introduced to cover the relatively stable situation in which one language or one variety of a language enjoying high prestige coexists with others, each with specified functions in communication, as in parts of the Arabic-speaking world, German-speaking Switzerland, and elsewhere.[8] In other cases two or more languages may subsist side by side without much contextual or situational distinction, the choice being determined by the preferred language of the speakers concerned, as in the French–German bilingual areas of Alsace-Lorraine.

Prolonged linguistic contacts in a delimited area may have other effects than bilingualism. In particular, where ready communication in a restricted set of contexts is required, a simplified version of one of the languages involved often arises, modified phonetically, grammatically, and lexically in the direction of the other language. This has happened quite spontaneously in response to immediate needs in such situations as trading in local commodities, agricultural employment and work supervision, domestic employment, and so on. Such developments are known as **pidgins**, and there are many well-known and quite widely used examples.

Over the course of years, usually centuries, such pidgins may come to replace either or both of the original languages, or to take up a position of equality with them, with greatly enriched grammatical structures and more extensive vocabularies. They then become the first languages, or mother tongues, of many speakers, and are known as **creoles**, usually revealing something of their origin in two or more languages, *via* the stage of pidgins. One may mention such creoles as Jamaican, based mainly on English, and Haitian, based mainly on French.[9] Once creoles have become established as first, native, languages, they become much more complex in structure and rich in vocabulary than the pidgins from which they have sprung.

Work on topics of this sort is known as **sociolinguistics** or the sociology of language; a considerable literature, both theoretical and practical, has now grown up around it.[10]

9.2 Linguistics and philosophy

Philosophy and *philosophical* are often used non-technically in several ways. Sometimes 'a philosophy' is no more than a set of principles or guidelines for carrying on some activity or enterprise successfully ('the philosophy behind profitable retailing', and so on). 'Philosophical' may also designate someone who seems able to put up with life's minor and major setbacks with equanimity (*cp* the American humourist's remark that 'philosophy is just the discovery that weeds too make a nice lawn if you keep them trimmed').

More strictly speaking, however, philosophy has for many years embraced a body of systematic study of the basic concepts, epistemological, scientific, and ethical, by which we try to order our lives in this world and in society. In this sense linguistic and philosophical studies have for long been associated with one another. In Western Europe the earliest systematic grammatical analysis of Greek was undertaken by philosophers (9.6), and throughout the intellectual history of Europe connections have been apparent between philosophical and linguistic thinking. This is not surprising. All sciences and all organized knowledge depend on language for their preservation and dissemination. This is one reason for ascribing a central place to the study of language among the intellectual disciplines (1.2.1); but philosophy, not being an empirical science, claims no particular field of experience as its own, and concerns itself with the very general questions about human knowledge, perception, argumentation, and obligations, all matters dependent on language for their public communication and discussion.

Philosophic enquiries involve exact reasoning and a minute examination of the meanings of certain words, and of the relations between sentences in a chain of reasoning. The traditional Aristotelian syllogism was a first step in formalizing a substantial part of the processes of valid inference from one statement to another. Modern symbolic logic has carried this further and extended its scope.

Symbolic logic is closely akin to mathematics, and many scholars working in these fields regard themselves as operating within a single subject. The deduction of the concept of number from logical concepts by Bertrand Russell and A. N. Whitehead early in this century is well known.[11] Since mathematics is a strictly formal discipline, its very abstractness has aroused a great deal of interest among some linguists, especially in the analysis of grammar and of part of semantics on formal lines, that is, without reference to the actual content of the sentences involved. The sets of rules embodied in some generative grammars are a case in point, constructed to provide and explain an infinite number of well-formed sentences without formal limitation on their length (7.1.1). These can be set out in the manner of mathematical formulae, deliberately ignoring the obvious practical limitations on sentence length and discourse production imposed by the need for human beings to rest, to sleep, and ultimately to die, and by the limitations on the patience and receptivity of hearers. These all arise from the fact that human beings are finite creatures in a finite environment, but such finitudes are disregarded in such an analysis of linguistic competence, and are referred to linguistic performance for their own proper description and accounting. Rather similarly, the rules for squaring numbers, for working out *ad infinitum* the square roots of numbers not themselves squares (the product of a number multiplied by itself, 4, 9, 16, 25, etc), and the numerical value of the geometrical concept π, can theoretically be compassed by sets of rules and procedures protracted indefinitely, but human beings, including mathematicians, have to stop work at some point.

Formal semantics sets out the scope and function of such features as negation, quantification, and so on in terms of their logical implications. Thus we have sentences like *not all the arrows hit the target, but some did*, but not †*none of the arrows hit the target, but some did*, nor †*all the arrows hit the target, but some did not*. A public notice can read *any person who has been seen damaging the trees will be prosecuted, but we hope that no-one will be*, but not †*some person who has been seen damaging the trees will be prosecuted, but we hope that no-one will be*. The precise implicational properties of sentence structures like these can be spelled out in the special symbols of formal logic. Formal logic in its relations with linguistics is a highly interesting but specialist subject, and it will not be pursued further in this elementary introduction.[12]

In the case of some topics, the analysis of meaning, the relation of utterances to the world of experience, and the structural meaning of different sentence types (6.6.3), it would be hard and probably unprofitable to draw a sharp line delimiting the linguistic and the philosophic spheres of interest. In the present century the connections between these two disciplines have become closer. Philosophy has lost a number of its earlier fields of study to what are now recognized as separate subjects, for example, psychology, sociology, and political theory, and many philosophers have reacted against nineteenth-century and earlier efforts as 'system building', and have turned their attention more to a detailed investigation of the language used in philosophical discourse and to seeking the possible source of some philosophical questions in the misunderstanding and misuse of language. It is felt that a solution to many of them may be reached through a better realization of how both plain men and philosophers actually employ the resources of their natural languages.[13]

In their different ways G. E. Moore, L. Wittgenstein, and the logical positivists were all moving in this direction; they looked on many of the traditional problems of philosophy as the results of our misunderstanding and misinterpreting our normal everyday use of our language, and from attempts to construct metaphysical realities such as causation, universals as existents, ethical imperatives, etc out of the scientific, classificatory, and moralizing functions to which all languages in all cultures are in their various ways applied. But the linguistic involvement of philosophers increased with the more recent work of people like G. Ryle and J. L. Austin. Indeed one may see in some of Austin's writings the origin of a current special interest of linguists, the study of 'speech acts'. Beginning with a re-examination of the age-old question of the apparent infallibility of knowledge, as opposed to the fallibility of belief, Austin pointed out the social ritual of verbs like *know* and *promise*, whereby we do not just assert an opinion or an intention, but we pledge our honour and reliability on it. Hence we cannot say *I know he will get well, but he may not*, nor *I promise to visit you, but I may not*; but the verbs *believe* and *hope*, respectively, could be substituted in those sentences to yield wholly acceptable utterances.[14]

Austin and other 'ordinary language philosophers', such as J. R. Searle, have taken this further, in the analysis of what they have called 'illocutionary acts' or 'speech acts', utterances which, in an appropriate context, do something as well as saying something: the judge's *I sentence . . .*, the clergyman's *I baptize . . .*, the chairman's *I declare this meeting open* (or *closed*), etc. These kinds of performative uses, which are found in all languages, recall Malinowski's dictum that speech is 'a mode of action, not a countersign of thought'.[15] They belong to a field of prime concern to linguists investigating questions of language use.

Topics and fields of research that lie within an area shared by the traditional domains of philosophy and linguistics have come to be known by the title *philosophy of language*. A number of important books have been published on these aspects of linguistics in recent years.[16]

There is clearly common ground between the linguist and the philosopher, but they are not engaged in the same studies all the time. It is certainly desirable that each should know something of the other's interests and methods, if only to avoid naively misrepresenting his position.[17]

9.3 Linguistics and psychology

If psychology is concerned with the nature and working of the human mind and with the individual's mental phenomena, it is clearly a discipline related in a number of ways to linguistics. This is not affected by the various interpretations placed in words like *mind* and *mental* in relation to human life and behaviour. On any view of their subject, presumably, psychologists would assert that what have been called subjective events (experiences and activities essentially private to the individual and as such experienced only by him, popularly called feelings, thoughts, and the like) are an important part of their field of study. It is here that a principal link is found between such studies and the study of languages. Subjective events in human beings are, by definition, known only to him directly; but people's overt behaviour in publicly observable activities constitutes, deliberately or otherwise, evidence for such subjective personal events, and is confidently treated as such by other people, extrapolating from their own experience. A great part of this manifesting behaviour is speech utterance, or verbal activity. This is no less true because the relations between speech and these personal experiences are not simple or uniform. Straightforwardly one may seek to communicate one's feelings and thoughts to others; but one may also try to conceal them in a specialized use of lying (but it must be remembered that lying unilaterally presupposes truth telling; the liar's hope of successful deceptions rests on the credence given to speech as normally truthful). One's feelings and thoughts may unintentionally be revealed in what one says or the way one says it, without and even in spite of the set purpose of the speaker.

More generally, the continuing and developing set of features and dispositions, that one knows collectively as a person's individual personality, uniquely his and distinguishing him from others, are in part a reliable guide as regards his expected actions and reactions to external events and to other people. These are largely made known, deliberately or unwillingly, by a person's speech habits. The study of these at all levels, and in relation to the speaker's dialect situation, regional and social, must be counted an essential part of the study of human personality.

A more long-standing and traditional question within this field is that of the relation between language and thought, or speaking and thinking, and the extent to which the two can be separated and the extent to which language is necessary for thought. As with many questions worth examining, a short answer is not readily available. *Thought* and *thinking* are not simple terms, and such words, and their translations in other languages, are used in a variety of different contextual functions.

In one use *thought* and *thinking* are more or less similar in use to *care*. We speak of thoughtless actions, as, for example, stepping into a crowded motor road without looking ('He never thought of seeing if it was safe'). Many such spheres of application of words like *thought* involve trained and habitual responses to types of situation, failure in which is stigmatized as 'thoughtless', and which in the learning process are often accompanied by actual explicit thinking about the procedure to be adopted (as when children are taught how to cross busy roads). These words, however, are also used to refer to the conscious and deliberate process by which an individual handles some pieces of information up to the determination of some action, the solving of some problem, or the arrival at some satisfactory conclusion. Between this type of 'full dress' thinking and trained careful behaviour there are doubtless many intermediate stages. Explicit thinking has been identified by some as subvocal speech activities, involving the same cerebral and muscular actions but on a very small scale; and Bloomfield, espousing the then popular behaviourist psychology, wrote of 'talking to oneself or thinking'.[18] A great deal of thinking is just that, whether the unuttered sentences are fully rounded periods or disjointed note-like fragments, and in the privacy of one's own company such thinking may pass over the borders of silence into muttered or even fully articulated speech and back again as a train of argumentation proceeds. But one can operate similarly with imagined diagrams and pictures; no doubt the extent to which one can think in images differs from person to person. Most people can perform simple geometrical operations on imagined figures such as circles and triangles, though there is clearly an upper limit on the number of different lines that can be pictured at once. Such thinking may be interspersed with diagram drawing or figuring with the fingers. But 'thinking in words' is the commonest form of this explicit handling of information within oneself, and all thought is ultimately dependent on sentences for its communication to others or for its being set down on paper for subsequent personal use; if diagrams, actual or imagined, are used, their explanation and interpretation involves the use of language.

What should be borne in mind is that, in this type of situation, the thinking is not something apart from the language utterances in which it is expressed (uttered aloud or written down); as far as language is concerned in these private thinking processes, it is a form of monologue, or dialogue with oneself, usually silent but sometimes aloud.

In a more general sense, it is clear that the lexical composition of every language enshrines a vast collective way of forming, interpreting, and understanding the world in which the speakers live (1.4.2). Languages are the product of millennia of reflection and intuition handed from one generation to the next, and always developing, a process we must assume to have accompanied the earliest uses of language among mankind's most primitive ancestors. In particular places and periods of cultural advance, for example in the Greek-speaking world during the last eight centuries or so BC, one can see the language developing under the impact of the use forced on it by pioneers in various intellectual fields, wherein in many of the concepts taken for granted in European cultures today were first made explicit.

It is open to suggestion that the semantic correlations found in varying degrees with many of the formal categories and structures of the grammars of different languages (6.6) may have originated in various situational likenesses, real or assumed, but that these were variously blurred, diluted, or altered in subsequent periods by the extension of the categories and structures to formally associated words outside the original semantic spheres.[19]

Conversely, it is perfectly possible that the major formal patterns and classes in languages, by associating together different parts of the speaker's experience, have themselves taken a hand in the shaping of people's collective world pictures through the ages. The traffic between conceptualization and verbalization must be operating continuously in both directions.

We saw that work on the relations between language and society has been given the title *sociolinguistics*. In a similar way studies on the relations between language and the individual's behaviour and capabilities are known as **psycholinguistics**.[20] This is a field of considerable activity at the present time, more especially since several linguists see language as our best key to an understanding of the human mind in general.

Research is going on in regard to the relation of speaking to thinking (as discussed above), on speech perception, *ie* what is involved in perceiving speech sounds as speech, and on the connection between sentence structure and content and the individual's memory span (with what sorts of sentences and under what circumstances is verbal memory at its strongest?).[21] Research goes on in the search for knowledge of the ways in which language is 'processed'; how, in fact, are sentences interpreted by the brain, and how, or in what forms, are lexical items, including some very complex formations, stored in the brain? Some linguists are also concerned with what they call the 'psychological reality' of some linguistic concepts and abstractions: phonemes, syntactic structures, grammatical categories, etc. Such questions were raised half a century ago by Sapir, and they are of particular interest to those who espouse the view that the organization of language, as described by the linguist, should have some counterpart in the organization of the human being (*cp* 2.1.1).[22]

Some would go further, and attempts are being made, with promising results, physiologically to localize particular language functions and operations in particular areas of the cerebral cortex. Back in the nineteenth century the location of some parts of speech control in the left third frontal convolution gave rise to the term *Broca's centre*. It has been found that as part of adolescence speech production and reception are largely concentrated in the left hemisphere of the brain (in some persons, exceptionally, it is the right hemisphere). This process of 'lateralization', completed at puberty, has been linked with the remarkable ability of young children to acquire competence in (or to 'internalize') a language by random exposure, which is how we learn our first language, as compared with the conscious effort demanded later in life (1.3.2), when lateralization is complete.[23]

One of the most important aspects of psycholinguistic studies today is, in fact, **language acquisition**, in relation both to a child's first language and to subsequent 'second' languages. In view of the effortless and almost unconscious way in which a child acquires control over the essential structure of his or her language in early years, without specific teaching or active learning, specialists in this field of study prefer the time *first language acquisition* to *first language learning* with regard to a child's mother tongue. It must be emphasized that vocabulary extension, the early exposure to serious literature, and participation in informed conversation, which the children of careful conscientious parents enjoy, and which certainly do involve self-conscious learning, presuppose and can only be effective after the child has mastered, or 'internalized', without teaching or even realizing what has happened, the structure of basic short sentences, the syntax and semantics of interrogatives, the referential function of many nouns, the tense distinctions of verbs, and many other fundamental parts of his or her language. All of these are often difficult for the linguist to explain in a full descriptive analysis; but, whatever the reason may be, all normally endowed children gain control of these parts of their language, without, of course, being able to give an account of what they have gained, more or less irrespective of their future intellectual achievements or non-achievements in later life. A vital question, partly reflecting the conflict between rationalist and empiricist (in an extreme form, behaviourist) attitudes to the whole of linguistics, is the extent to which the grammatical, and perhaps also the semantic, structure of language is already 'innately' determined by the human brain and so constrains the form that grammars of individual languages can take, thus accounting for the linguistic universals that many linguists claim to be an important part of their subject. The physiological determination of phonetic universals by the structure of the human vocal tract is more obvious and accessible. Chomsky and TG linguists in general take a strong line in support of this innate linguistic structure; others rely more on general human learning abilities and the analogical extension of observed patterns to account for the astonishing ability, on any interpretation, that all normal children of every degree of intellectual achievement manifest in learning the complex structure of their mother tongue. Going beyond this very general question, detailed studies are now being done on the stages by which children progressively acquire a full control over the phonological and grammatical systems of their first languages. Language acquisition, especially of their first language by children, has now got an impressive literature and at least one specialist periodical.[24]

9.4 Linguistics and language teaching: linguistics and communications engineering

9.4.1 Linguistics and language teaching

The application of some of the results of general linguistic studies to the work of the language teacher and of the communications engineer were briefly noticed in an earlier chapter (1.2.2). At first sight these two subjects might seem strangely linked in a single section; but in relation to general linguistics, both essentially involve the application to specifically practical purposes of some of the findings of the study of language and the recognized subdivisions of this study; and, together with speech therapy, constitute a substantial part of **applied** linguistics.

The language teacher's aim in regard to a language is not the same as that of a descriptive linguist. The teacher is not simply concerned with its systematic and exhaustive description and analysis, but with facilitating the acquisition of a language other than their mother tongue by other people with the greatest ease and thoroughness. This both restricts the number of languages one is primarily concerned with, and determines the type of presentation one requires. Linguists describe and analyse many languages that will, for economic and practical reasons, never be taught to others, and may themselves be on the verge of extinction; indeed, this situation which renders a language utterly irrelevant to the teacher, may make it of especial interest to the general linguist (9.1). But it is to be hoped and believed that the techniques and methods of scientific linguistics, at every level of language analysis, will aid and improve the work of the language teacher. The teacher must present his material sometimes in a different order from that used in disinterested description, and has to vary his presentation according to the linguistic background of his pupils; there have to be somewhat differently constructed teaching grammars for students according to the principal typological differences of their own languages, since these to a large extent determine the chief difficulties in the path of learners and engender the sort of errors, in pronunciation and grammar, to which they are most prone. Considerations like this are extraneous to the work of the descriptive linguist as such; but his specialist knowledge should be a powerful aid in applied linguistics where these have to be taken into account.[25]

With studies of first language acquisition the linguist is in the main examining what happens anyway, in order to learn more about language and about the human being as a language learner and language user (though what he learns may be of great help in the treatment of children whose speaking abilities are in some way defective). But with the teaching and learning of second ('foreign') languages the linguist is very much concerned to offer whatever aid he can from his knowledge of language and of languages to facilitate and improve the necessary work both of teacher and pupil.

Linguistic science as one knows it today has been stimulated and nourished all the time by the work of language teachers. They, and others who for purely practical purposes have mastered foreign languages, have provided linguists with a great deal of their material, and the problems and difficulties they encountered stimulated linguistic research along fruitful lines. The science of language owes much to the work of people who would never have claimed for themselves the title of general linguists. But it may be asserted that the teacher who understands and can make use of the methods of scientific linguists will find the task of presenting a language to his pupils very much lightened and facilitated. In particular some part, at least, of the intuitive feeling for correctness in a language on which teachers have often relied as a fruit of their long experience will be replaced by an objective and publicly communicable knowledge of its elements and structures, which can by systematically imparted to others.

It is probable that the teaching of English as a foreign language and the study and development of methods and materials for the needs of different non- English-speaking countries and peoples in their learning of English form by far the greatest single 'application' of linguistics in the world today.

The English-speaking world, however, should not rest content with this. It is notorious that English is more widely taught and often better taught in non-English countries than are modern European languages in Great Britain and the United States. Perhaps the linguist should lend his influence to the encouragement of the teaching of foreign languages to all children in all schools, not primarily as an academic achievement and for literary purposes, though as a component of higher education the study of modern foreign literatures has the greatest value, but as a practical skill, part of one's preparation for living in the world today, and an aspect of communicative competence.[26]

9.4.2 Linguistics and communications engineering

The communications engineer is concerned with more than one type of process involving language material, the transmission of speech as such by wire and by radio waves, and the conversion of linguistic signals, written messages, into some other medium, via Morse code and the like, or directly into sequences of electric impulses, their transmission, and reconversion into written messages. The technical problems of the apparatus involved in all this are scarcely within the competence of the linguist as a linguist, though persons equipped with knowledge in these fields as well as in linguistics are of particular value in many of the aspects of this sort of work. But the linguist may be expected to contribute to the communications engineer's work in so far as the linguistic nature of the material to be transmitted is concerned. In the transmission of written messages, as long as the units serially transmitted are letters of a recognized alphabet, he has less of his own to offer, although information on the relative frequency of commonly occurrent letters, morphemes, and words in the likely message texts of a language may be of importance in planning the most economical use of channels of communication.

In any form of telephony something is lost in the process of transmission. In commercial telephones a great deal is lost, but the utility and efficiency of the instruments are virtually unaffected for the purpose they ordinarily serve. It is within the scope of the linguist's potential contribution to estimate the relative value of the different phonetic components in the sound waves that result from successive speech articulations; their localization into different bands of frequencies is part of this (cp 3.4). Controlled experimentation, including the production of artificial speech sounds by the generation of sound waves at the frequencies mainly responsible for the distinctive differences between the sounds of languages (speech synthesis) helps to reveal the limits of tolerable loss at the different frequencies under the conditions in which the apparatus is used, and as a result the extent to which costly technical improvements in fidelity would be justified economically.

The opposite process to speech synthesis is the mechanical analysis of speech. A number of instruments are now available of this type of work. One, usually known as the sound spectrograph, produces a permanent visual record of the succession of sound features in speech, in the form of different concentrations of energy at different frequencies. Another working in a similar fashion produces a transitory visual representation of the sound sequences, and was first devised as an aid to the deaf, being known for that purpose as 'visible speech'. The use of these processes in advanced phonetic research within linguistics itself is obvious, but their potential practical utility in various aspects of communications work is no less clear.[27]

An important and rapidly progressing branch of communications engineering lies in **computational linguistics**, the use of computers and computer techniques to further linguistic research and specific problem solving. Much of this exploits the capacity of computers to accept, retain, and process vast amounts of information, which might take several years for human research workers to carry out unaided, thus freeing them for the more vital interpretation of the results of the computer's calculations, sortings, and listings. Many traditional aspects of linguistic research, such as word frequency counts, lexical entries, syllable structure counts, the comparative study of syntactic constructions and lexical usages in authors' styles, the processing of some of the findings in experimental phonetics, and others are greatly facilitated and in some cases only made possible by the availability of computing apparatus.

On the other side, linguists have much to offer computer designers and programmers. The various special 'computer languages', *Fortran, SNOBAL, ALGOL,* etc are ultimately derived by a sort of translation from messages, instructions, and data expressed originally in natural languages and made acceptable to the computer machinery (this is part of programming).[28]

An extension of communications engineering in the field of linguistics lies in attempts to develop the techniques of translation by computers ('machine translation'). Apparatus has been designed into which can be fed the sentences, edited if necessary in various ways, of one language; the machine processes these lexically and grammatically, and produces translations of them in another language.

A great deal of effort and expense has been devoted to the practical and theoretical problems that lie in the path of mechanical translation. Quite possibly it will never be of significant use in literary translation and in fields where the infinite creativity of language, lexical and grammatical, is in play. But for stereotyped messages in restricted contexts it may be of great value. Considerable efforts are being currently devoted to this work in Great Britain, Europe, the United States, and the Soviet Union, but the human translator is not likely to be superseded.[29]

The whole of the field outlined in this section is compassed by the growing industrial development of information technology.

9.5 Linguistics and literature

Linguistic studies and literary studies are clearly connected in certain respects as intellectual disciplines. In the history of linguistics in Western Europe (9.6) literary criticism and literary scholarship, together with philosophical studies, constituted a main source of the systematic study of language.

There is a certain sense of rivalry and even at times of hostility expressed between literary pursuits and the study of language in linguistics today. This feeling, though one would think it wholly mistaken, may be attributed to the long dominance over linguistic work and the teaching and study of language exercised by almost exclusively literary considerations. This is mainly the result of the literary bias of education in Europe from the Renaissance onwards until the rise of natural science during recent years in educational esteem.

The effects of the literary domination of language studies are seen in the concentration of attention on written language and on the styles of well-known and highly respected authors. Grammatical rules and systems of grammar were drawn up on the basis of literary works and the types of sentence structures and word forms found therein. Within a language, the dialect of the literate and literary classes (usually also the socially dominant classes) was taken as representing a special standard of correctness, from which other dialects were uneducated deviations or debasements. This attitude, in fact, flies in the face of many palpable instances wherein at different linguistic levels non-standard dialects preserve older features once more widely present in a language and now lost in standard speech; grammatically, the separate second person singular forms of the pronoun and the corresponding inflected forms of verb paradigms, as preserved in some northern dialects, and phonologically, postvocalic /r/ as found in West Country and Scottish dialects, are examples from English.

A further effect of the same literary approach to language study was the relative neglect of phonetic studies, except by specialists, and of spoken utterance in general, except as part of the study of orthography; phonetics was treated in terms of 'the pronunciation of the letters', and not as the independent study of spoken language in its own right. The great prestige and educational preeminence of Latin and Ancient Greek, languages almost wholly studied in their written forms, reinforced these tendencies.

Such a situation can hardly be said to obtain today, and though old prejudices die hard, and old ways of thought linger on, it is most desirable that linguists, in the light of their contemporary understanding of their subject, should consider the links it may have with the work of students of literature.

Linguistics, as the scientific study of language, necessarily covers all aspects and uses of language, and all styles. Literature comprises a number of particular uses and styles, and forms an important and valuable part of the linguistic material in the study of a particular language and in the study of mankind's use of the faculty of language. Moreover, once the bias towards written language is overcome, it may be seen that literature, considered as utterances that are regarded for one reason or another as worthy in their own right of preservation and as aesthetically valuable, is a form of language use present, so far as is known, in all cultures, literate and preliterate. **Oral literature** is as much a distinct component of cultures as is **written literature**; and in the absence of writing, it may be preserved by memory from one generation to another, and in many such communities certain individuals are charged with its preservation and its transmission to other similarly charged persons as their successors. Narratives, myths, ritual utterances, poems, and songs are prominent parts of oral literature, and their possession in entirety by certain persons involves feats of memory prodigious by the standards of people in literate communities, wherein such capacities have been largely lost as being no longer needed (*cp* 9.1.1). Linguistics comprehends within its field much more than the literary uses of language. On the other hand, the evaluation, appreciation, and criticism of literature of all sorts covers much more than the relative excellence of the author's or the tradition's exploitation of the resources available in the language. Linguistics and literary scholarship do not operate on the whole of the same field, or in the same way; but within the subject-matter of each it is reasonable to see common ground and opportunities for profitable cooperation.

In all forms of literature, part of the aesthetic evaluation, whether of the author's skill or of the work itself, written or spoken, turns on the specific use made of the material employed, the phonetic, grammatical, and lexical constitution of the language (or a dialect thereof). The relative weight of this part of the literary merit of a composition differs according to the kind of work that is involved. To take a familiar field, in European literature poetry and oratorical prose are more dependent on the material of the language wherein they are composed than are prose narratives, histories, and textbooks; within poetry, what is called lyric poetry is much more dependent on the language itself than are epic and dramatic poetry. The degree to which the literary merit and character of any work depend on the material of the language, as against other extralinguistic factors, may be partly seen in the difficulties involved in its translation into another language (1.4.5). In all works of literature levels of language in addition to the semantic level are brought into play as aesthetically exploitable in their own right; but in certain types of poetry, known to be 'virtually untranslatable', the formal levels of language play a preponderant part in giving the work its literary form and literary excellence.

The literary artist, the orator, story-teller, dramatist, or poet, need not himself be a linguist or be explicitly concerned with the study of the structure of his own language. Art is the product of intuition; it is personal and not communicable by sets of rules to other people, though the techniques of different schools can be taught, and the inspiration of a master can in part be communicated. But any great artist's intuition works in and through the material in which he expresses himself, whether it be bronze or marble, paint, music, or a language. The nature of the material imposes its own limitations and conditions on the artist, and artistic genius consists in part in seizing on these inherent limitations and building in them and by means of them products that are recognized as of enduring merit. To take an obvious point from outside language: nothing could be more unlike materially than solid marble and fine-spun human hair. The genius of Praxiteles and other sculptors lay partly in their ability so to work on and with their marble that they could in their sculptures portray human hair, not literally, but convincingly in an aesthetically glorious whole statue. So to the orator and the poet the features of the language in which he works are not of his choice, nor did they arise to suit the literary artist. They evolved over the centuries primarily in everyday unrecorded and unremarkable uses. Such are the strong word stresses and the consonant clusters of English and German, the alternations of long and short vowels in Greek and Latin, their inflectional subtleties and their syntactically free word ordering, the rich vowel repertoire of French, the many open syllables of Japanese, the lexical tones and the syntactic conciseness of Chinese, and the complex consonantism of Arabic. Great poets and prose writers do not come to be so because they happen to speak a particular language, but because, without necessarily being explicitly conscious of what they are doing, they are able to exploit the phonological, grammatical, and lexical resources of their language in ways that hearers and readers find beautiful, convincing, and memorable. We judge an author by what he does with what he has, not by what he has. To do otherwise would be in Sapir's words 'tantamount to loving "Tristan und Isolde" because one is fond of the timbre of horns'.[30]

A familiar poem by the sometime English poet laureate John Masefield may be cited in exemplification of what has been said in the preceding paragraph. In the first and third stanzas of a short poetical sketch of different types of ship, Masefield contrasts the gracious passage of a ship propelled by oars in Middle East waters carrying articles of artistic and aesthetic charm with a British tramp steamer carrying a utilitarian cargo on the rough North Sea routes:

Quinquereme of Nineveh from distant Ophir
  Rowing home to haven in sunny Palestine,
With a cargo of ivory, and apes and peacocks,
  Sandalwood, cedarwood, and sweet white wine.

Dirty British coaster with a salt-caked smoke stack
  Butting through the Channel in the mad March days,
With a cargo of Tyne coal, road rail, pig-lead,
  Firewood, iron-ware, and cheap tin trays.

The phonetic compositon of the vocabulary in the two stanzas
is matched phonaesthetically or sound-symbolically to the two
types of ship and shipping activity portrayed. On the basis of a
standard British English reading of the poem we have in stanza
one 60.5% of consonants out of the total number of segmental
phonemes and 39.5% of vowels, and the precentage of stop
consonants in the totality of consonants in 30.5%. In stanza three
the proportions of consonants and vowels are much the same,
61% of consonants, 39% of vowels, but 46% of the consonants
are stops. The percentage contrasts are more strongly marked in
the first lines of the two stanzas: in stanza one, 61% of consonants, 39% of vowels, and 21% of the consonants are stops; in
stanza three, 66% of consonants, 34% of vowels, and 56.5% of
the consonants are stops. The smooth sequences of continuant
consonants and vowels, contrasting with the more harshly interrupting stops are attuned to the total impression that Masefield
aims at conveying.

This segmental contrast is reinforced by the syllabic organization of the two stanzas. English words, other than prepositions
and articles, generally bear a single major stress, on a syllable
determined by the lexicon. More monosyllabic words, therefore,
usually imply more stresses. Taking the hyphenated words as
disyllables, in stanza one out of a total of 28 words we find six
trisyllabic words, seven disyllabic words and five stressable
monosyllables. Out of a total of 31 words stanza three contains
no trisyllables, eleven disyllables, and ten stressable monosyllables, thus giving us on a normal reading double the number of
stressed monosyllables, sometimes following one another, accen-
tuating the jerky movement of the lines as they present the movement of the steamer 'butting through the Channel'. More delicate
analyses could be achieved by further counts of consonant types
and syllabic properties, but the figures given here should be
ample for the illustration of the point being made.

Masefield could accomplish the poetic affect that he wanted,
because English has syllables with consonants and consonant
clusters initially and finally, as well as more open syllables
comprising single vowels and single consonant–vowel sequences;
the language has also the potentiality of strong word stresses. It
should not be hard to translate this poem into German, which

in these features is similarly structured to English; but it would be much harder, and probably not possible, fully to preserve the phonaesthetic effect in a translation into Japanese, which does not permit such a degree of consonantal clustering (*cp* 8.2.3) and does not have a comparable word stress.

The linguist is not necessarily, or usually, an artist, any more than a literary artist is a linguist; but it is part of the linguist's task and competence, by the application of the specific methods of linguistics, to analyse the forms and patterns of languages, and so to make explicit some of the features in them that in varying degrees, according to the nature of the work, constitute the material which the author must use and exploit in expressing himself to his public.

In 5.2 the sentence was given as the largest linguistic structure wholly describable in grammatical terms, but it was pointed out that the sentences of any continuous passage or conversation, any text, bear various semantic and syntactic relations with each other.

The study of these relations, essentially of what distinguishes a text (in the widest sense) from a mere sequence of sentences, has been a province of the the rhetorician and the stylistician at all times; but linguists have taken it up, and have attempted to formalize the relations involved in the same sort of way that grammatical relations have been formalized. This study has been called **text grammar** or **text linguistics**, and this takes up some of the themes traditionally studied under the heading of *rhetoric*.

Halliday and Hasan have dealt with the analysis of texts in English under the title of *cohesion*, listing, among the cohesive factors involved, pronominal anaphora, deixis, verb substitution by *do* ("'They lived on treacle", said the dormouse, after thinking a minute or two. "They couldn't have done that, you know"'), the use of elliptical sentences (6.3.1) and of temporal, causal, and other conjunctions and adverbs.[31] Earlier Propp identified a number of recurrent patterns in narratives whereby folktales and other stories are enabled to hang together.[32] Further examples will be found in books listed in the bibliography.[33]

It is known that not all forms of literary composition flourish equally in al languages, even though the cultural conditions may in other respects be fairly similar. This is one cause of difficulty in translating literary works from one language into another. The correlation of such differences of literary styles in different languages with characteristics of the formal structures of the languages themselves suggests itself as a field to be worked jointly by literary critics and linguistic specialists, though, of course, such work alone will not exhaust the analysis and explanation of the differences of the literary styles peculiar to certain languages.

Certain such differences of style have long been recognized as partly due to linguistic differences. English poetry has been as a whole far less dependent on the use of rhyme than has French poetry, and in the classical periods of Greek and Latin literature rhyme in poetry was virtually unknown. These facts have been correlated with the differences between the stress based rhythms of English, in which stressed syllables contrast with unstressed syllables, and within these limits different degrees of stress operate, the quantitative rhythms of classical Greek and Latin, in which long syllables contrast with short, and the syllable unit rhythms of French, in which distinctions of stress and length are, by comparison with English and Latin, relatively slight.

The metres developed in Greek poetry were taken over by Latin poets of the classical age of Latin literature; but in doing so, those Latin authors recognized as the greatest masters of each style of poetry felt compelled to alter the rules of composition in some respects, despite the similar quantitative rhythms of the two languages. In particular, the elegiac couplet in the hands of Ovid, the greatest elegist of Latin literature, was subjected to very stringent rules governing the position of word boundaries in relation to the sequences of long and short syllables. The need for these, as against the more permissive patterns of Greek elegiac couplets, must reflect certain differences in the Latin language, considered as the material of poetry, compared with Greek, features of which the poet recognized as preeminent in his style became aware as vitally affecting his art. Such statements, valid as far as they go, have by now the crudity of the obvious. As linguistics progresses in the analysis of features like stress and length, and the many concomitant characteristics of utterance as yet not fully investigated or understood, in the comparison from different points of view of the syllable structures of languages and of their word structures, and in the statement of their grammatical and collocational patterns, linguists may expect to be able to penetrate more deeply and move more delicately in making explicit the many components of languages that great authors and generations of composers of oral literature have unconsciously seized on and moulded into works of literary art.

In research of this sort, the linguist in applying his own methods to a specific body of linguistic material may be able to deepen the appreciation of different literary styles, and of the artistic uses of language, both his own and that of other people. In a wider sense, this all forms part of one's penetration into the different cultures of the world and their sympathetic appreciation. Linguistic stylistics, as such applications of linguistics may be called, is as yet little developed. It is to be hoped that singificant progress will reward the colloborative work of linguists and literary scholars, and that this will rank as not the least service of general linguistics to the world of learning.[34]

9.6 Outline of the history of linguistic studies in Western Europe

Every science and every branch of study is in part a development of what went on before, and in each age the workers in any field are in part determined in the directions they take by the work of their predecessors, if only, in extreme cases, in the terms and principles that they deliberately reject. Studies concerned with the nature, structure, and working of language, though on different lines, and with different ends in view, have been a feature of the intellectual activity of a number of civilizations, notably in ancient China, where particular attention was paid to lexicography, the construction of dictionaries, in Ancient India, in Greco-Roman world, and among the early Arabic scholars.

Of these, the linguistic work of Greece and of India is by far the most important in the history of linguistics in Europe and America today. In the study of language, as in so many other fields of the intellect, one can trace a continuous line of development, virtually from the beginnings in Greek thought in the sixth and subsequent centuries BC through its transmission by Rome, the Middle Ages, and the Renaissance, to the present day; and from the end of the eighteenth century, the quite remarkable work of the Ancient Indian linguistic scholars and their successors became known to the West, and this made a profound contribution to this branch of Western learning. By contrast, the impact of Chinese linguistic scholarship, except within the field of Sinology itself, has been relatively slight, and the linguistic work of the Arabs was partly a derivative of Western thinking, in particular of the philosophical writings of Aristotle.[35]

In Ancient Greece linguistics was not at first a separate branch of learning or enquiry, but it grew out of the wide fields of questioning that became known as φιλοσοφία /philosophía:/, a term that embraced numbers of topics that today would be assigned to separate disciplines, including the natural sciences, and cannot be simply equated with *philosophy* as this word is understood now. Early speculation on the nature of language turned largely on the degree to which it should be regarded as a 'natural' as opposed to a 'conventional' product of mankind.

This early debate conducted with almost exclusive reference to the Greek language, merged later in a more far-reaching controversy between the 'analogist' and 'anomalist' theories of language to some extent championed respectively by the Aristotelian and Stoic philosophical schools. The analogists emphasized the regularities of grammatical structures and word forms, and the parallels between grammatical forms and word meanings, as constituting the essence of language and the direction in which standards of correctness should be sought, and tended to take up a 'conventional' attitude towards language itself. The anomalists stressed the numerous irregular forms in grammatical paradigms, and 'anamalous' associations of plural number with singular entities, genders divorced from any sex reference, and the like, and leaned more to the 'naturalist' view of language, accepting its anomalies as they stood. This famous controversy would be of less historical importance, were it not for the fact that in the discussion which it aroused, the regular patterns of Greek grammar, the analogies, were first worked out and codified, subsequently to be taken over and applied to Latin by the Latin grammarians, and thence to form the basis of traditional grammatical theory and language teaching throughout Europe.

In the Alexandrian age, beginning towards the end of the fourth century BC, a second conditioning factor in the development of Greek linguistic studies began to take effect, the literary criticism and exposition of earlier recognized classical authors. With the spread of Greek over wide areas of the Near and Middle East after the Macedonian conquests, the growing differences between the Greek of the classical authors, not only Homer, but those whose language was Attic (Athenian) Greek as well, and the colloquial Greek spoken by the general public, gave rise to critical studies of the grammatical forms used by the great writers and to attempts to preserve, especially on the part of analogists, the 'correct' Greek of Attic literature for literary purposes. Throughout Greco-Roman antiquity and the Middle Ages, language studies were very much under the control of these two subjects, philosophy and literary criticism, one or the other being successively, or in different schools, the dominant consideration.

Greek grammarians dealt with many of the topics that fall within the linguistic study of languages today, though they concerned themselves almost exclusively with their own language, and within it, with the dialects used in literature, particularly Homeric and Attic Greek. Phonetics, grammar, and the analysis of meanings were all treated, but by far the greatest attention was paid to grammar. Phonetic observations were made on the pronunciation values of the letters of the Greek alphabet and on the accent signs, some theory of the syllable as a structural unit was developed, and it was realized that in different environments the same letter sign could have different phonetic values; but no very penetrating analysis was made at this level, and certain features of the phonetics of the language, notably the distinction between voiced and voiceless articulation escaped a correct description altogether.

Within grammar morphology held pride of place, and morphological description was built around the identification and definition of the word classes (parts of speech) of Greek. The first distinction recognized in this field was that of noun and verb, a distinction found in Plato, who based it on the logical distinction between subject and predicate. Subsequently Aristotle and the Stoics added further members of the system of word classes, and refined their defining criteria. The number was set at eight (noun, verb, pronoun, participle, adverb, preposition, conjunction, article) in the short Greek grammar attributed to Dionysius Thrax, which probably dates from the first century BC. This became recognized as a standard manual on the subject, and the system of eight word classes was accepted for most teaching and further research in Greek grammar. Thrax's definitions, largely the product of earlier work, were in the main formally grounded on the morphological categories of the variable words. Thrax had nothing specific to say on syntax, and later writings on this aspect of grammar, such as the Greek syntax of Appolonius Dyscolus do not show anything like the same degree of formal analysis or systematic description.

In linguistic studies, in this context specifically in grammar, the Romans were content largely to model themselves on Greek patterns. Throughout the classical period of Latin literature linguistic studies on the Latin language were undertaken, and among others Julius Caesar interested himself in some questions of grammar. But the great age of the codification of Latin grammar came later, during the period of imperial decline and disruption. Among several grammarians in this period known to us, the most famous are Donatus and Priscian, especially the latter, whose comprehensive Latin grammar, written about AD, 500, ran to eighteen volumes. Priscian models himself on Thrax and Appollonius. His word class system is the same as theirs except that the article, a class not represented in Latin, is omitted and the number of classes made up by the addition of the interjection, a class whose members had earlier been included among the adverbs.

Priscian's work, of which some hundreds of manuscripts survive, became the standard textbook of Latin in subsequent centuries. Mediaeval scholars worked over it in successive commentaries, and its influence is plainly seen in the standard grammars of Latin in use today.

Mediaeval European linguistic scholarship continued the study of Latin grammar through the works of Priscian and Donatus and the commentaries written on them. Knowledge of Greek, and of much of Greek thought and literature, was temporarily lost in the West after the breaking up of the Roman Empire. Latin continued to enjoy immense prestige as the language of the Church, the language of classical literature, and the common language of educated discourse and scholarly writing throughout Europe.

With the rediscovery of many of Aristotle's philosophical writings in the later Middle Ages, a particular flowering of mediaeval linguistics is seen in the production by several authors in the thirteenth and fourteenth centuries of what are called speculative grammars. In these writings the Priscianic framework of Latin grammar was integrated into a comprehensive scholastic theory of language, itself forming part of a scholastic philosophical system. These grammars represent the culmination of one line of scholastic thought. Now that they are better understood, their importance both in mediaeval history and in the history of linguistics is being increasingly appreciated.

The effects of the Renaissance on linguistic studies in Europe were firstly the rediscovery of Ancient Greek by the West and its incorporation into Western education and scholarship. The renewed study of the Greek language was accompanied by more grammatical study of Hebrew and Arabic, the first two non-I-E languages to be the objects of systematic European scholarship. Progressively thereafter, trade, exploration, colonization, and missionary work brought Europeans into contact with the languages of different parts of their expanding world and with cultures very far removed from the traditions of Greco-Roman and Christian civilization. This continuous widening of European linguistic horizons was accompanied by a growth in linguistic interest in the vernacular, spoken, languages of Europe itself, as the hold of Latin on the world of scholarship relaxed and printing presses produced books in more and more European tongues.

At the end of the eighteenth century a new and highly important stream entered European linguistic scholarship. This came from the European colonization of India, and took two forms, the discovery by European scholars of Sanskrit, the classical language of India, and of its indisputable relationship with the major language groups of Europe, and the transmission to the west of the Indian linguistic tradition itself, and in particular the work of Pāṇini on the Sanskrit language, the first translation of which appeared in Europe early in the nineteenth century. One effect of the discovery of Sanskrit was the remarkable interest shown in historical linguistics, in particular with regard to the I-E family, by European scholarship, especially in Germany. The nineteenth century saw comparative-historical linguistics established in much of its present form, and in this century linguistics was primarily envisaged as a historical discipline.

The Indian tradition of linguistic scholarship, devoted to the Sanskrit language, was of a very high order, and its influence on Western linguistics was profound, and is by no means over. Unlike the Greek and Latin grammarians and their mediaeval successors, Indian linguists exhibited great interest and masterly competence in the phonetic analysis and description of their speech; and the development of the phonetic and phonological levels of linguistic analysis in the last hundred years or so owes a great deal to their work.

Pāṇini is the best known of the Indian linguists. His date in uncertain, but around 600 BC or later has been suggested in the light of the evidence available. His Sanskrit grammar has been described by Bloomfield as 'one of the greatest monuments of human intelligence'.[36] Unfortunately its very perfection of method renders it extremely obscure to the reader even with a knowledge of Sanskrit, and its elucidation to the general linguist as a standard model of description, despite numerous commentaries and translations, remains to be done. Its main characteristic is the startling economy with which the details of Sanskrit morphology are expressed in statements of rules, often of great brevity, in which no avoidable repetition of a previous statement is made by any subsequent point, though this compression has always been recognized as a source of difficulty to the students. The similarity in format between Pāṇini's Sanskrit grammar and some current generative grammars has been pointed out by linguists today.[37] Pāṇini's work clearly constitutes the culmination of much previous scholarship, and it was afterwards the subject of extensive commentaries. Its origin lay in the need felt to understand and preserve intact the language of the Vedic scriptures, but the world of linguists is fortunate that the interest of this line of Indian scholars went far beyond these immediate requirements.

The work of the Indian linguistic scholars is distinguished historically by two features, the excellence of their phonetic description of Sanskrit, as regards both its accuracy and the systematic terms in which they stated it, and their ability to carry formal analysis below the word in terms corresponding to the modern *morpheme*. Greco-Roman morphological analysis was set out in terms of paradigms of whole words grouped together by similarities of morphological composition, but the actual concept of the morpheme as a formal component of such words was never clearly explicated by scholars in Western antiquity.

In Europe general linguistics of the modern period largely grew out of nineteenth-century comparative and historical studies, as scholars began to widen the scope of their interests. In America there was the additional influence of anthropological studies, especially those dealing with American-Indian peoples, whose languages at once presented a field of great difficulty and great interest. In Britain, both these sources contributed, and were supplemented by the strong British interest in phonetics, that can be traced back for some centuries and was reinforced by the Indian tradition. At the end of the nineteenth and in the first half of the twentieth centuries Sweet and Jones were among the pioneers of modern phonetics, and the latter contributed to a considerable extent to the development of the phoneme theory.[38]

Among others whose influence on the course of general linguistics in various parts of the world in this century has been profound, one must mention de Saussure, Trubetzkoy, Hjelmslev, Martinet, and Meillet on the continent of Europe, Sapir, Bloomfield, and latterly Chomsky in America, and Daniel Jones and Firth in Britain. Jakobson's work spans Europe and America and makes him truly a representative of the world of linguistic scholarship.[39]

During these men's lifetimes and through their work we have witnessed striking and encouraging growth, both in the subject itself and in the scholarly interest taken in it. Much remains to be accomplished; new lines of thought open up, and new methods must be devised to follow them; and general linguistic theory must be always keeping pace with methodological progress. The languages of mankind in all their fascinating detail and with all their immense power among the human faculties still present a potentially limitless field for disciplined investigation and systematic study. It is altogether right that they should be the object of scholarly enthusiasm, controlled imagination, and great reverence.

Bibliography for Chapter 9

1 J. AITCHISON, *The articulate mammal: an introduction to psycholinguistics*, London, 1976.

2 W. S. ALLEN, *Phonetics in ancient India*, London, 1953.

3 J. ALLWOOD, L.-G. ANDERSSON, and O. DAHL, *Logic in linguistics*, Cambridge, 1977.

4 W. P. ALSTON, *Philosophy of language*, Englewood Cliffs, 1964.

5 T. A. AMIROVA, B. A. OL'CHOVIKOV, and J. V. ROŽDESTVENSKIJ, *Abriss der Geschichte der Linguistik*, trans B. Meier, Leipzig, 1980.

6 E. ARDNER (ed), *Social anthropology and linguistics*, London, 1971.

7 D. ARMSTRONG and C. H. van Schooneveld (eds), *Romance Jakobson: echoes of his scholarship*, Lisse, 1977.

8 J. L. AUSTIN, *How to do things with words*, Oxford, 1962.

9 S. K. BELVALKAR, *An account of the different existing systems of Sanskrit grammar*, Poona, 1915.

10 B. BERNSTEIN, 'Elaborated and restricted codes: an outline', *IJAL*, 33.4, part 2 (1967), 126–33.

11 'Language and socialization', N. MINNIS (ed), *Linguistics at large*, London, 1971, Chapter 11.

12 L. BLOOMFIELD, *Language*, London, 1935.

13 'Language or ideas?', *Lang* 12 (1936), 89–95.

14 *An outline guide for the practical study of foreign languages*, Baltimore, 1942.

15 A. D. BOOTH, L. BRANDWOOD, and J. P CLEAVE, *Mechanical resolution of linguistic problems*, London, 1958.

16 C. BROCKELMANN, *Geschicte der arabischen Literatur*, Weimar and Berlin, 1898–1902.

17 R. BROWN, *A first language: the early stages*, Cambridge, Mass, 1973.

18 C. J. BRUMFIT and J. T. ROBERTS, *A short introduction to language and language teaching*, London, 1983.

19 C. D. BUCK, *Comparative grammar of Greek and Latin*, Chicago, 1933.

20 J. B. CARROLL, *The study of language*, Cambridge, Mass, 1953.

21 R. CHAPMAN, *Linguistics and literature*, London, 1973.

22 A. G. CHEJNE, *The Arabic language: its role in history*, Minneapolis, 1969.

23 M. K. L. CHING, M. C. HALEY, and R. F. LUNSFORD (eds), *Linguistic perspectives on literature*, London, 1980.

24 D. E. COOPER, *Philosophy and the nature of language*, London, 1973.
25 S. P. CORDER, *Introducing applied linguistics*, Harmondsworth, 1973.
26 D. CRYSTAL and D. DAVY, *Investigating English style*, London, 1969.
27 E. DELAVENAY, *An introduction to machine translation*, London, 1960.
28 T. A. VAN DIJK, *Some aspects of text grammars*, The Hague, 1972.
29 *Text and context*, London, 1977.
30 K. N. DODD, *Computer programming and languages*, London, 1969.
31 N. C. DORIAN, *Language death: the life cycle of a Scottish Gaelic dialect*, Philadelphia, 1981.
32 W. DOWNES, *Language and society*, London, 1984.
33 D. R. DOWTY, R. E. WALL, and S. PETERS, *Introduction to Montague semantics*, Dordrecht, 1981.
34 C. A. FERGUSON, 'Diglossia', *Word* 5 (1959), 325–40.
35 J. R. FIRTH, 'The English school of phonetics', *TPS* 1946, 92–132.
36 J. A. FISHMAN, *Sociolinguistics: a brief introduction*, Rowley, Mass, 1971.
37 D. C. FREEMAN (ed), *Linguistics and literary style*, New York, 1970.
38 A. V. GLADKIJ and I. A. MEL'ČUK, *Elements of mathematical linguistics*, Berlin, 1983.
39 A. C. GRAHAM, ' "Being" in Western philosophy compared with *shih/fei* and *yu/wu* in Chinese philosophy', *Asia major*, 7 (1959), 79–112.
40 R. GRISHMAN, *Computational linguistics: an introduction*, Cambridge, 1986.
41 M. R. HAAS, 'The linguist as a teacher of languages', *Lang* 19 (1943), 203–8.
42 M. A. K. HALLIDAY, A. MCINTOSH, and P. STREVENS, *The linguistic sciences and language teaching*, London, 1964.
43 M. A. K. HALLIDAY and R. HASAN, *Cohesion in English*, London, 1976.
44 B. HARRISON, *An introduction to the philosophy of language*, London, 1979.
45 R. A. HUDSON, *Sociolinguistics*, Cambridge, 1980.
46 D. HYMES (ed), *Language in culture and society: a reader in linguistics and anthropology*, New York, 1964.
47 M. IVIC, *Trends in linguistics*, The Hague, 1965.
48 H. KAHANE, 'A typology of the prestige language', *Lang* 62 (1986), 495–508.
49 J. J. KATZ, *The philosophy of language*, New York, 1966.
50 L. G. KELLY, *Twenty-five centuries of language teaching*, Rowley, Mass, 1976.
51 A. L. KROEBER (ed), *Anthropology today*, Chicago, 1953.
52 G. N. LEECH, *A linguistic guide to English poetry*, London, 1969.
53 W. P. LEHMANN, 'On the earlier stages of the Indo-European nominal inflection', *Lang* 34 (1958), 179–202.
54 E. H. LENNEBERG, *Biological foundations of language*, New York, 1967.
55 M. LEROY, *Les grands courants de la linguistique moderne*, Brussels and Paris 1963 (English translation, *The main trends in modern linguistics*, Oxford, 1967).

56 W. N. LOCKE and A. D. BOOTH (eds), *Machine translation of languages*, New York, 1955.

57 R. E. LONGACRE, *Grammar discovery procedures: a field manual*, The Hague, 1964.

58 J. LYONS (ed), *New horizons in linguistics*, Harmondsworth, 1970.

59 J. LYONS and R. J. WALES (ed), *Psycholinguistic papers*, Edinburgh, 1966.

60 B. MALMBERG, *New trends in linguistics*, trans E. Carney, Stockholm, 1964.

61 F. MAUTHNER, *Beiträge zu einer Kritik der Sprache*, Leipzig, 1923.

62 P. MENYUK, *The acquisition and development of language*, Englewood Cliffs, 1971.

63 V. N. MISRA, *The descriptive technique of Pāṇini: an introduction*, The Hague, 1966.

64 C. MOHRMANN, A. SOMMERFELT, and J. WHATMOUGH (eds), *Trends in European and American linguistics 1930–1960*, Utrecht, 1961.

65 C. MOHRMANN, F. NORMAN and A. SOMMERFELT (eds), *Trends in modern linguistics*, Utrecht, 1963.

66 G. MOUNIN, *Histoire de la linguistique*, Paris, 1970.

67 E. A. NIDA, 'Field techniques', *IJAL* 13 (1947), 138–46.

68 S. NIRENBURG (ed), *Machine translation*, Cambridge, 1987.

69 C. K. OGDEN and I A. RICHARDS, *The meaning of meaning*, London, 1946.

70 D. Y. PANOV, *Automatic translation*, London, 1960.

71 B. PARTEE, A. TER MEULEN, and R. WALL (eds), *Mathematical methods in linguistics*, Dordrecht, 1987.

72 J. S. PETÖFI and H. RIESER (ed), *Studies in text grammar*, Dordrecht, 1973.

73 R. K. POTTER, G. A. KOPP, and H. C. GREEN, *Visible speech*, New York, 1947.

74 V. PROPP, 'Morphology of the folktale', *IJAL* 24.4, part 3 (1958).

75 E. PULGRAM, *An introduction to the spectrography of speech*, The Hague, 1959.

76 K. K. RAJA, *Indian theories of meaning*, Madras, 1963.

77 R. H. ROBINS, *A short history of linguistics*, London, 1979.

78 S. ROMAINE, *Pidgin and creole languages*, London, 1988.

79 W. J. SAMARIN, *Field linguistics: a guide to linguistic field work*, New York, 1967.

80 E. SAPIR, *Language*, New York, 1921.

81 J. R. SEARLE, *Speech acts*, Cambridge, 1969.

82 T. A. SEBEOK (ed), *Style in language*, London, 1960.

83 (ed), *Portraits of linguists*, Bloomington, 1966.

84 C. SHANNON and W. WEAVER, *The mathematical theory of communication*, Urbana, 1949.

85 D. I SLOBIN, *Psycholinguistics*, Glenview, 1971.

86 J. B. SPENCER (ed), *Linguistics and styles*, London, 1964.

87 H. SWEET, *Handbook of phonetics*, Oxford, 1877.

88 *Primer of phonetics*, Oxford, 1890.
89 P. TRUDGILL, *Sociolinguistics: an introduction*, Harmondsworth, 1974.
90 S. ULLMANN, *Language and style*, Oxford, 1964.
91 Z. VENDLER, *Linguistics in philosophy*, Ithaca, 1967.
92 I. C. WARD, *Practical suggestions for the learning of an African language in the field*, London, 1937.
93 R. WARDLAUGH, *An introduction to sociolinguistics*, Oxford, 1986.
94 U. WEINREICH, *Languages in contact*, Publications of the Linguistic Circle of New York 1, 1953.
95 L. WITTGENSTEIN, *Tractatus logico-philosophicus*, London, 1922.
96 *Philosophical investigations*, trans G. E. M. Anscombe, Oxford, 1953.

Sebeok, 83, contains biographies of some of the more important linguistic scholars of the nineteenth and twentieth centuries. *Current trends in linguistics*, volume 13, The Hague, 1975, 'The historiography of linguistics', also edited by Sebeok, contains many chapters, with full documentation, covering the history and the historiography of linguistic scholarship in various parts of the world, from antiquity up to the present day.

The periodical *Historiographia linguistica* is devoted to articles and reviews on the history of linguistics.

Notes to Chapter 9

1 Ethnolinguistics, Carroll, 20, Chapter 4; Hymes, 46; Ardner, 6.
2 Anthropological linguistics, Hoijer, in Mohrmann *et al*, 64, 110–27.
3 As an example of what can be done when the linguist is of necessity limited to a single surviving speaker of a language, see M. R. Haas, *Tunica*, New York, 1941.
4 On field work, Ward, 92; Bloomfield, 14; Nida, 67; F. G. Lounsbury, 'Field methods and techniques in linguistics', in Kroeber, 51, 401–16; Longacre, 57; Samarin, 79; *cp* P. L. Garvin, 'American-Indian languages – a laboratory for linguistic methodology', *Foundations of language* 3 (1967), 257–60; and W. L. Chafe (ed), *American-Indian languages and American linguistics*, Lisse, 1976.
5 On the distinction between social anthropology and sociology, Carroll, 20, 117.
6 *Cp* Bernstein, 10; 11. More generally, on linguistic standards as norms, R. Bartsch, *Norms of language*, London, 1987.
7 Dorian, 31.
8 Ferguson, 34. The different ways in which one language may acquire and extend its prestige are examined in Kahane, 48.
9 On pidgin and creole, Romaine, 78. The whole subject of language contacts is dealt with by Weinreich, 94, with reference to both their synchronic and diachronic aspects.
10 On sociolinguistics, Trudgill, 89; Fishman, 36; Downes, 32; Hudson, 45; Wardlaugh, 93.

11 A brief account of this is to be seen in R. M. Eaton, *General logic*, New York, 1931, 462–7.

12 Allwood, 3; Gladkij and Mel'čuk, 38; Partee *et al*, 71.

13 Wittgenstein, 95; 96. On the influence of language on philosophy, Ogden and Richards, 69, 96–7; Mauthner, 61, volume 3, 4; with reference to Chinese, Graham, 39. *Cp* Wittgenstein, 96, §109: 'Philosophy is a battle against the bewitchment of our intelligence by means of language.'

14 G. Ryle, *The concept of mind*, London, 1949; J. L. Austin, 'Other minds', *Proc Aristotelian Society*, 20 (1946), 148–96.

15 Austin, 8; Searle, 81; Malinowski, in Ogden and Richards, 69, Supplement 1.

16 Attention is drawn to the following books, each of which contains further bibliographical references: Alston, 4; Katz, 49; Vendler, 91; Cooper, 24 ; Harrison, 44. Katz, 49, sets out a criticism of the logical positivists and of the ordinary language philosophers, together with a theory of language broadly on the lines of Chomsky's *Aspects of the theory of syntax*, Cambridge, Mass (1965). A particular development of formal semantics within generative theory is known, after its first proponent, as Montague semantics; see Dowty *et al*, 33.

17 Some grammarians have been too ready to use terms like *subject* and *predicate* without clearly distinguishing the grammatical and the logical meanings of these words. And it is hardly good enough to explain sentences like 'Redness is a concept' by the substitution of sentences like '*Redness* is a noun', as if *noun* designated some readily observable class of words irrespective of any theory of linguistic analysis (*cp* Bloomfield, 13).

18 Bloomfield 12, 28; *cp* Carroll, 20, 74.

19 On the early history of some grammatical categories, Buck, 19, 170; Lehmann, 53.

20 Psycholinguistics: Slobin, 85; Lyons and Wales, 59; Aitchison, 1; D. D. Steinberg. *Psycholinguistics: Language, mind, and world*, London, 1982.

21 D. B. Fry, 'Speech reception and perception', in Lyons, 58, 29–52; P. N. Johnson-Laird, 'The perception and memory of sentences', *ibid*, 261–70.

22 *Cp* Sapir, 'The psychological reality of phonemes', in D. G. Mandelbaum (ed), *Selected writings of Edward Sapir*, Berkeley, 1949, 46–60.

23 Lenneberg, 54, Chapter 4; see also Aitchison, 1, Chapters 3 and 4; D. B. Fry, *Homo loquens*, Cambridge, 1977, Chapter 9.

24 See further Menyuk, 62; Brown, 17; *The journal of child language*, 1974–.

25 On linguistics and the teaching of languages, Haas, 41; Moulton in Mohrmann *et al*, 64, 82–109; Halliday, 42; Corder 25; Brumfit and Roberts, 18; Kelley, 50

26 The extension of *communicative competence* to cover more than one language seems entirely legitimate; *cp* Chapter 1, note 26.

27 On communications engineering and linguistics, Carroll, 20, Chapter 7; 'Visible speech', Potter *et al*, 73; Pulgram, 75; communication theory, Shannon and Weaver, 84.

28 As is to be expected in such a fast developing field, there is a considerable body of literature now available, including a number of specialist periodicals. The following books may be mentioned here: M. F. Bott, 'Computational linguistics', in Lyons, 58, 215–28; Dodd, 30; Grishman, 40; R. Garside and G. N. Leech (eds), *The computational analysis of English*, London, 1987; P. Whitelock, *et al*, (eds), *Linguistic theory and computer applications*, Cambridge, 1987; G. E. Barton, R. Berwick, and E. Ristad, *Computational complexity and natural language*, Cambridge, Mass, 1987. Readers with this subject as a specialist interest may consult the relevant sections in the annual *Bibliographie linguistique*.

29 Machine translation, Locke and Booth, 56; Booth *et al*, 15; Panov, 70. Delavenay, 27; Nirenburg, 68; Halliday, 'Linguistics and machine translation', in A. McIntosh and M. A. K. Halliday, *Patterns of language*, London, 1966, 134–50.

30 Sapir, 80, 241.

31 Halliday and Hasan, 43. See also in this context Halliday's *Introduction to functional grammar*, London, 1985.

32 Propp, 74.

33 Two articles by Z. S. Harris, 'Discourse analysis', *Lang* 28 (1952), 1–30; and 'Co-occurrence and transformation in linguistic structure', *Lang* 33 (1957), 283–340, may be seen as a move towards text grammar. See further van Dijk, 28; 29; Petöfi and Rieser, 72; J. M. Sinclair and R. M. Coulthard, *Towards an analysis of discourse*, Oxford, 1975.

34 Linguistics and literature, Sebeok, 82, Ullmann, 90; Spencer, 86; Crystal and Davy, 26; Leech 52; Chapman, 21; Freeman, 37; Ching, 23. Sapir, 80, Chapter 11, remains one of the best short treatments of this subject. On classical Chinese versification in relation to the phonological and grammatical structure of the language, see M. Y. Chen, 'Metrical structure: evidence from Chinese poetry', *Linguistic inquiry* 10 (1979), 371–420. Some very interesting observations on the relations between the stress and length patterns of Greek and Latin words and the practice of the Greek and Latin poets are to be found in W. S. Allen, *Accent and rhythm: prosodic features of Greek and Latin*, Cambridge, 1973. A number of essays dealing with the linguistic analysis of different aspects of Shakespeare's dramatic styles are collected in V. Salmon and E. Burness (eds), *A reader in the language of Shakespearean drama*, Amsterdam, 1987.

35 On the history of linguistics in Europe, Robins, 77; Mounin, 66, Amirova *et al*, 5; Chinese linguistic scholarship, Robins, 77, 104–7; Arabic linguistic scholarship, Brockelmann 16; Chejne, 22, Chapter 3.

36 Bloomfield, 12, 11; on Pāṇini and ancient Indian linguistic studies, Belvalkar, 9; Allen, 2; Misra, 63; Raja, 76.

37 *Cp* J. F. Staal, *Word order in Sanskrit and universal grammar*, Dordrecht, 1967, and further references.
38 Phonetics in England, Sweet, 87; 88; Firth, 35.
39 On the recent history of linguistics, Mohrmann *et al*, 64; 65; Leroy, 55; Ivić, 47; Malmberg, 60; Robins, 77, Chapter 8. On Jakobson, see Armstrong and van Schooneveld, 7.

Index